Scientific Studies in Mental Retardation

Scientific Studies in Mental Retardation

Edited by

JOHN DOBBING
The Department of Child Health,
University of Manchester

with

A.D.B. CLARKE
The Department of Psychology,
The University, Hull

J.A. CORBETT
The Bethlem Royal Hospital, London

J. HOGG
The Hester Adrian Research Centre,
University of Manchester

and

R.O. ROBINSON
The Newcomen Centre, Guy's Hospital, London

Published jointly by
The Royal Society of Medicine
and
The Macmillan Press Ltd

First published jointly in 1984 by

THE ROYAL SOCIETY OF MEDICINE
1 Wimpole St., London W1M 8AE

and

Scientific and Medical Division
THE MACMILLAN PRESS LTD
London and Basingstoke
Companies and representatives throughout the world

ISBN 0 333 35454 0

Printed in Great Britain by
The Pitman Press, Bath

Contents

III. COGNITIVE AND LINGUISTIC RESEARCH

IV. RESEARCH INTO PSYCHOSOCIAL AND SERVICE ASPECTS

Contributors

ÅKESSON, H.O.
Psychiatric Department III,
Lillhagens Hospital,
S-42203 Hisings Backa 3,
Sweden

ALBERMAN, Eva D.
Department of Clinical Epidemiology,
The London Hospital Medical College,
Turner Street,
London E1 2AD,
UK

BAERT, A.E.
Commission of the European Communities,
200 Rue de la Loi,
Brussels 1049,
Belgium

BAKKE, J.
Health Services for the Mentally Retarded,
H.N. Havges Gardens,
44 Oslo 4,
Norway

BALAZS, R.
MRC Developmental Neurobiology Unit,
Institute of Neurology,
33 Johns Mews,
London WC1N 2NS,
UK

BARAITSER, M.
Clinical Genetics Department,
The Hospital for Sick Children,
Great Ormond Street,
London WC1N 3JH,
UK

BERG, J.M.
Ministry of Community and Social Services,
2 Surrey Place Centre,
Toronto,
Ontario M55 2C2,
Canada

BERRY, A. Caroline
Department of Genetics,
Prince Philip Research Laboratories,
Guy's Hospital,
London SE1 9RT,
UK

BEVERIDGE, M.C.
Department of Education,
The University,
Manchester M13 9PL,
UK

BICKEL, H.
Department of Paediatrics,
Ruprecht-Karls University,
6900 Heidelberg,
Grabengassel,
West Germany

BLAIR, J.A.
Department of Chemistry,
University of Aston in Birmingham,
Gosta Green,
Birmingham B4 7ET,
UK

BLEEKER-WAGEMAKERS, Elisabeth M.
The Netherlands Ophthalmic Research Institute,
Ophthalmogenetic Department,
PO Box 12141,
1100 AC Amsterdam,
The Netherlands

BRIMBLECOMBE, F.S.W.
Consultant Psychiatrist,
Royal Devon and Exeter Hospital (Heavitree),
Gladstone Road,
Exeter EX1 2ED,
UK

BRYANT, P.E.
Department of Experimental Psychology,
The University,
South Parks Road,
Oxford OX1 3UD,
UK

CARR, Janet
Department of Psychology,
St George's Hospital,
Jenner Wing,
Cranmer Terrace,
London SW17 0RE,
UK

CLARKE, A.D.B.
Department of Psychology,
The University,
Hull HU6 7RX,
UK

CLARKE, Ann M.
Department of Educational Studies,
The University,
Hull HU6 7RX,
UK

COHEN, B.E.
Chairman,
Department of Paediatrics 'B',
Tel-Hashomer Hospital,
Tel Aviv University,
Tel-Hashomer,
Israel

CORBETT, J.A.
Consultant Psychiatrist,
The Bethlem Royal Hospital,
579 Wickham Road,
Shirley,
Croydon CR0 8DR,
UK

CRASKE, J.
South Manchester Regional Virus Laboratory,
Withington Hospital,
Manchester M13 9PL,
UK

CROMER, R.F.
Developmental Psychology Project,
2 Taviton Street,
London WC1H 0BT,
UK

DAUNT, P.E.
Head of the Bureau for Action in Favour of Disabled People,
Commission of the European Communities,
200 Rue de la Loi,
Brussels 1049,
Belgium

DAVISON, A.N.
Department of Neurochemistry,
The National Hospital,
Queen Square,
London WC1N 3BG,
UK

DOBBING, J.
Department of Child Health,
The University of Manchester Medical School,
Oxford Road,
Manchester M13 9PT,
UK

DUDGEON, J.A.
Formerly:
Professor of Microbiology,
Institute of Child Health,
30 Guilford Street,
London WC1N 1EH,
UK

Present address:
Cherry Orchard Cottage,
Bonnington,
Ashford,
Kent TN25 7AZ,
UK

DUPONT, Annalise
Institute of Psychiatric Demography,
Aarhus Psychiatric Hospital,
DK-8240 Risskov,
Denmark

FRASER, W.I.
Consultant Psychiatrist,
Gogarburn Hospital,
Corstophine,
Edinburgh EH12 9BJ,
UK

GALJAARD, H.
Department of Cell Biology and Genetics,
Erasmus University,
PO Box 1738,
3000 DR Rotterdam,
The Netherlands

GRAHAM, Sara
Principal Research Officer,
Office of the Chief Scientist,
Department of Health and Social Security,
Alexander Fleming House,
Elephant and Castle,
London SE1,
UK

GREEN, S.H.
Institute of Child Health,
The Nuffield Building,
Francis Road,
Birmingham B16 8ET,
UK

HAGBERG, B.
University of Göteborg,
Department of Pediatrics II,
East Hospital,
S-416 85 Göteborg,
Sweden

HAGBERG, Gudrun
University of Göteborg,
Department of Pediatrics II,
East Hospital,
S-416 85 Göteborg,
Sweden

HERMANNS, J.M.A.
Institute for Educational and Human Sciences,
Heidelberglaan 1,
PB 80104,
3508 TC Utrecht,
The Netherlands

HERON, A.
Formerly:
Professor Emeritus of Psychology,
University of Melbourne,
Australia

Present address:
19 King Ecgbert Road,
Sheffield S17 3QQ,
UK

HOGG, J.
Developmental Psychologist,
Hester Adrian Research Centre,
The University,
Manchester M13 9PL,
UK

HOLLAND, Mary
MENCAP National Centre,
123 Golden Lane,
London EC1Y 0RT,
UK

JANCAR, J.
Consultant Psychiatrist,
Stoke Park Hospital,
Stapleton,
Bristol BS16 1QU,
UK

JANOTA, I.
Institute of Psychiatry,
Denmark Hill,
London SE5 8AF,
UK

KIERNAN, C.C.
Thomas Coram Research Centre,
Institute of Education,
41 Brunswick Square,
London WC1N 1AZ,
UK

KUSHLICK, A.
HCERT (Research in Mental Handicap and Care of the Elderly),
Dawn House,
Sleepers Hill,
Winchester SO22 4NG,
UK

*LANCIONI, G.E.
The University of Nijmegen,
The Netherlands

*LEEMING, R.J.
Department of Bacteriology,
General Hospital,
Steelhouse Lane,
Birmingham B4 6HN,
UK

LE QUESNE, Pamela M.
Department of Neurology,
The Middlesex Hospital,
London W1N 8AA,
UK

LEWIS, P.D.
Department of Histopathology,
Royal Postgraduate Medical School,
Hammersmith Hospital,
London W12 0HS,
UK

MEAZZINI, P.
Research and Training Centre on Handicap and Learning Disabilities,
Via Diaz 60,
3310 Udine,
Italy

McKINLAY, I.A.
Consultant Paediatric Neurologist,
Booth Hall Children's Hospital,
Charlestown Road,
Blackley,
Manchester M9 2AA,
UK

MITTLER, P.
Department of Education,
The University,
Manchester M13 9PL,
UK

MORRIS, D.
Consultant Paediatrician,
Flat 5,
1 Bryanston Square,
London W1,
UK

MULCAHY, M.D.
Supervisor,
Mental Health Section,
Medico-Social Research Board,
73 Lower Baggot Street,
Dublin 2,
Eire

NEVILLE, B.G.R.
Consultant Paediatric Neurologist,
Newcomen Centre,
Guy's Hospital,
St Thomas Street,
London SE1 9RT,
UK

O'CONNOR, N.
MRC Developmental Psychology Project,
2 Taviton Street,
London WC1H OBT,
UK

OUNSTED, C.
The Park Hospital for Children,
Old Road,
Headington,
Oxford OX3 7LO,
UK

PECKHAM, Catherine S.
Department of Community Medicine,
Charing Cross Hospital,
London W6 8RP,
UK

PILKINGTON, T.L.
Consultant Psychiatrist,
Whixley Hospital,
Whixley,
York YO5 8DR,
UK

POND, D.A.
Formerly:
Professor of Psychiatry,
University of London

Present address:
Chief Scientist,
Department of Health and Social Security,
Alexander Fleming House,
Elephant & Castle,
London SE1 6BY,
UK

PRATT, O.E.
Department of Neuropathology,
Institute of Psychiatry,
De Crespigny Park,
Denmark Hill,
London SE5 8AF,
UK

PRECHTL, H.F.R.
Department of Developmental Neurology,
University Hospital,
Oostersingel 59,
9713 EZ Groningen,
The Netherlands

PRIMROSE, D.A.A.
Consultant Psychiatrist,
The Royal Scottish National Hospital,
Larbert,
Stirlingshire FK5 4EJ,
UK

RAWNSLEY, K.
Department of Psychological Medicine,
Welsh National School of Medicine,
Heath Park,
Cardiff CF4 4XN,
UK

RICHARDSON, S.A.
Department of Paediatrics,
Albert Einstein School of Medicine,
Yeshiva University,
1300 Morris Park Avenue,
New York, NY 10461,
USA

RICKS, D.M.
Consultant Psychiatrist,
The Children's Department,
Harperbury Hospital,
Shenley,
Radlett,
Herts WD7 9HQ,
UK

ROBINSON, R.J.
Department of Paediatrics,
Guy's Hospital Medical School,
St Thomas Street,
London SE1 9RT,
UK

ROBINSON, R.O.
Consultant Paediatric Neurologist,
Newcomen Centre,
Guy's Hospital,
St Thomas Street,
London SE1 9RT,
UK

ROEHER, G.A.
IASSMD Secretariat,
Kinsman Building,
York University Campus,
4700 Keele Street,
Downsview,
Ontario N3J 2R2,
Canada

RONDAL, J.A.
Department of Psycholinguistics,
University of Liege,
Sart Tilman B-18,
Liege 1 4000,
Belgium

SARTORIUS, N.
Division of Mental Health,
World Health Organization,
1211 Geneva 27,
Switzerland

SHAPIRO, A.
Consultant Psychiatrist,
Forest Hospital,
78 Crawley Road,
Horsham,
West Sussex RH12 4HN,
UK

SMEETS, P.M.
Department of Developmental Psychology,
University of Leiden,
Hooigracht 15,
2312 KM Leiden,
The Netherlands

STALLWORTHY, J.A.
Formerly:
Emeritus Nuffield Professor of Obstetrics and Gynaecology,
Oxford University,
UK

Present address:
Shotover Edge,
Headington,
Oxford OX3 8TA,
UK

STEPHENSON, J.B.P.
Consultant Paediatric Neurologist,
Royal Hospital for Sick Children,
Yorkhill,
Glasgow G3 8SJ,
UK

SYLVESTER, P.E.
Formerly:
Consultant Psychiatrist,
St Lawrence's Hospital,
Caterham,
Surrey CR3 5YA,
UK

Present address:
Daleswood,
School Lane,
Llandinam,
Powys SY17 5BU,
UK

TAYLOR, D.C.
Department of Child and Adolescent Psychiatry,
Jesson House,
Manchester Road,
Pendlebury,
Manchester M27 1FG,
UK

TIZARD, J.P.M.
Formerly:
Professor of Paediatrics,
University of Oxford,
UK

Present address:
Ickenham Manor,
Ickenham,
Uxbridge UB10 8GT,
UK

WALD, I.
Psychoneurological Institute,
al Sobjieskiego 1/9,
02-957 Warsaw,
Poland

WALDRON, H.A.
Department of Occupational Health,
London School of Hygiene and Tropical Medicine,
Keppel Street,
London WC1E 7HT,
UK

WOOD, D.J.
Department of Psychology,
The University,
Nottingham NG7 2RD,
UK

YODER, D.E.
Department of Communicative Disorders,
University of Wisconsin,
1975 Willow Drive,
Madison,
WI 53706,
USA

YULE, W.
Department of Psychology,
Institute of Psychiatry,
Denmark Hill,
London SE5 8AF,
UK

---

*Co-authors not present at the meeting

Preface

Serious subjects of great importance to family and society happiness and wellbeing deserve serious and critical attention. Such are the complexities of modern medicine and its increasing tendency to specialization that a multidisciplinary approach is often necessary to define a problem in true perspective. Just as correct diagnosis is an essential preliminary to rational treatment, so an authoritative review of major areas such as mental retardation is necessary to help define avenues for further research and to make important advances in preventive medicine.

This book is the product of a three-day workshop, organized by The Royal Society of Medicine, and held at Lincoln College, Oxford, 22–26 March 1983. Seventy-nine specialists from fifteen countries were invited to discuss their research in many of the disciplines concerned. Since it was not possible to cover the whole field, this book is not a comprehensive account of current research in mental retardation. It demonstrates, however, that the boundaries of specialization that make for difficulties of communication between workers in different fields are not always insurmountable.

The meeting was designed on an idea previously devised by John Dobbing as an experiment in professional education. There were those who, from the outset, did not believe it possible for people from a variety of disciplines to describe their work to each other without prejudicing scientific standards. It did prove successful in that there was wide acknowledgement among the participants that they learned a great deal from those in other fields which led them to question basic ideas and long-cherished attitudes.

Authors were invited to submit their papers six months before the meeting. Others to be invited to the symposium were then asked to write commentaries on the papers, and all these were sent to all the participants before the meeting. At the workshop itself, the sessions therefore consisted entirely of further discussion, allowing a more-than-usual amount of time for free, spontaneous exchange of ideas. During the sessions, people were identified who made especially important comments and asked to write additional discussion statements. Several authors and commentary writers revised their work in the light of the ideas generated during the session.

By using the Dobbing method, modified for a larger multidisciplinary subject, we have a book of twenty-six chapters accompanied by more than a hundred attributed written commentaries. All parts of the book have thus been subjected to far more detailed critical peer review than is usual when such a composite work is put together. We hope that it will also convey something of the stimulation and excitement experienced by those who were fortunate enough to be there.

John Stallworthy (President)
David Morris (Chairman)
Graham Bennette (Coordinator)

Acknowledgements

The Royal Society of Medicine extends its warmest thanks to the following major sponsors, without whose financial help the symposium could not have been organized:

The Associated Octel Company Limited
Ciba-Geigy Pharmaceuticals
Commission of the European Communities
The Craigmyle Trust
Fidia Research Laboratories (Italy)
The Ford Motor Company, Product Development
Labaz Sanofi UK Limited
Ortho Pharmaceutical Limited
The Reabilities Trust
Rybar Laboratories Limited
SmithKline Beckman Corporation
Wyeth Laboratories

The Society also gratefully acknowledges donations from:

British Petroleum Company Limited – Council of Europe – Esso Petroleum Company Limited – Imperial Chemical Industries – John Lewis Partnership – Mencap – Merck & Company (USA) – Pfizer Limited – Roche Products Limited (Basle) – Sandoz Products Limited – Searle Pharmaceuticals – Syntex Pharmaceuticals Limited – Warner Lambert Limited – Winthrop Laboratories Limited

SECTION I

EPIDEMIOLOGY AND PREVENTIVE ASPECTS

Chapter 1

Epidemiological aspects of severe mental retardation

Eva D. Alberman

INTRODUCTION

> ... there is a continuity of natural ability reaching from one knows not what height, and descending to one can hardly say what depth. I propose ... to range men according to their natural abilities, putting them into classes represented by equal degrees of merit, and to show the relative number of individuals included in the several classes ... The method I shall employ for discovering all this is an application of the very curious theoretical law of "deviation from an average".
>
> Galton, 1892 (quoted by Clarke and Clarke, 1975)

Galton's work first suggested that one way of defining severe mental retardation rested on our ability to measure and rank mental ability, and then to decide on an arbitrary point below which an individual might be so classified. In practice the cut-off point generally chosen is one which segregates out individuals unable to live an independent existence in an unsheltered environment, primarily because of their mental incapacity. These comprise those individuals formerly known as imbecile and idiot.

In this paper I will examine more closely the problems of definition, how these may affect our scientific studies of this heterogeneous group of individuals, and outline some of the knowledge we already have about the epidemiology of the group as a whole, and of its constituent parts. The intention is to set a framework for the following accounts, which will take up in detail most of the points raised here.

DEFINITION

For the purpose of this account I will make the assumptions that "intelligence" as measured by standard tests is a valid concept, and that the tests have been standardized on large enough numbers of individuals to be meaningful. These assumptions have been questioned frequently, but even so it is a useful exercise to look again at the theoretical concepts involved in using such tests for defining severe retardation.

The attempts to define severe mental retardation as the lower tail of a hypothetical Gaussian description of human intelligence levels have raised many problems. These have been discussed in detail by numerous authors, notably Penrose (1972) and Tizard (1974). One fundamental issue is whether there is really only one normal curve for a given population, or whether individuals with severe retardation should be treated as a separate population altogether.

The implications of assuming that there is only one normal distribution of intelligence are that one can use multiples of the standard deviation to define "exceptional" individuals. Theoretically, commonly used age-adjusted intelligence scores have a mean of 100 and a standard deviation of 15, and a score of 70 or below will comprise individuals two standard deviations below the mean, i.e. 2.3% of the hypothetical population. A score of 55 or less will comprise individuals with a score of three standard deviations or less below the mean, i.e. 0.1% of the hypothetical population.

In practice it has frequently been shown (Penrose, 1972) that a cut-off point of a score of 70 or less selects more than the 2.3% expected. Likely explanations are that the hypothetical single curve is skewed towards the left, or that there is a separate distribution of scores in individuals who appear at the lower end of the intelligence range. Since a large proportion of these can be shown to have specific and multiple impairments the latter explanation may more nearly approach the reality of the situation.

These considerations become important in deciding the best cut-off point to discriminate between severely retarded and other individuals. If this is a given number of standard deviations below the mean, and populations with a different mean intelligence are studied, such a cut-off point will discriminate at different IQ levels depending on the position of the mean. It will however always select out the same proportion of individuals. If a fixed IQ level is accepted as a cut-off point, different proportions will be selected out in populations of different means, a higher proportion where the mean is low, and a lower proportion where the mean is high. In practice it is accepted that a fixed level of 50 segregates those who are severely handicapped by their IQ level from the remainder. Unfortunately in the latest revision of the International Classification of Diseases (WHO) the nomenclature departs from this definition somewhat, an IQ of 35-49 being defined as moderate mental retardation; of 20-34 as severe; and under 20 as profound. Mild mental retardation is defined as IQ of 50-70.

Although, as this definition suggests, lesser degrees of mental retardation are also commonly defined by fixed IQ levels, mild mental retardation is seen as largely representing the lower end of a normal distribution of intelligence, and it is readily accepted that their proportion varies with the mean IQ level in the population under study.

My own approach to these questions is to accept that there is a "pathological" subgroup with its own distinctive IQ distribution corresponding approximately to the lower end of a "normal" IQ distribution and that this probably occurs with a similar frequency in populations of similar genetic constitution. Within such populations testing may reveal deprived subgroups whose distribution of intelligence is shifted to the left. Where this occurs the "pathological" group, if defined by a fixed IQ level, may be enhanced in number by those in the deprived group at the lower end of the "normal" distribution. If privileged subgroups are tested (using the same standard) very few, if any, under the "normal" curve will fall below the fixed "pathological" level.

SEX DIFFERENCES

Other issues are raised by the use of IQ level as the means of defining severe mental subnormality. One of these is the comparison between the normal curves as constructed when testing males, and those constructed when testing females. There is general agreement that males have a larger variance of IQ scores and again this raises the question of whether this reflects a single normal distribution or whether there are distinct subgroups at either tail, particularly the lower tails where the excess in males is much more marked than in females.

An examination of individual pathological subgroups comprising severe mental deficiency suggests that some are indeed more common in males, and this question has been further illuminated by the recent interest in families with X-linked mental retardation, which is proving to be an important cause in males (Turner and Opitz, 1980).

REPEATABILITY OF IQ MEASUREMENT

A crucial element in the use of the definition of severe mental retardation is the question of its intra-subject repeatability when measured at different ages. Certainly in the milder degrees of mental retardation there have been reports of marked changes of IQ level over time, and this may be true, albeit to a lesser extent, in the more severe forms. It follows that the classification can only relate to the status as it was at the time of testing. The direction of the change will depend on the quality of care and stimulation given, so that individuals may either improve or regress according to their current circumstances.

Similarly, particularly since IQ testing has become so common, we need to be sure that inter- and intra-observer repeatability are established, and that overall the observer variability is considerably less than subject variability.

"ADMINISTRATIVE" DEFINITION

Even if the theoretical basis of IQ measurements were sounder, it would not be feasible to base the definition of severe mental retardation only on the results of IQ screening in whole populations. In practice the ascertainment is made administratively, that is in those who come to the attention of the relevant authorities as in need of care by reason of their mental capacity. IQ testing is usually carried out after, and not before, such ascertainment and as some validation of the administrative assessment.

As one might expect, administrative definitions, even more than those based on IQ measures, do not meet any rigorous tests of validity. Again the definition depends in part on the environment of the affected individual. The mental capacity required to achieve an independent existence depends on the availability of social and family support, and on the complexity, e.g. industrialization, of the environment. Moreover from time to time society itself varies the threshold at which it will wish to provide full support and shelter to retarded individuals. The method of offering such support may also vary. Thus in the UK it has become very unusual to take even a severely retarded child into institutional care, whereas some years ago it was relatively common. Instead, parents are encouraged to keep the affected children at home, or foster-homes or adoption is arranged. The number of young children in long-stay hospitals has therefore fallen sharply, although this does not reflect a real change in prevalence.

ASCERTAINMENT

The ascertainment of cases is the necessary basis for any epidemiological study. Any bias will bring into question the validity of studies based on that ascertainment, but it is extremely difficult to ensure that it is full and unbiased.

The method of ascertainment will depend on the definition used, and on the age of the population to be surveyed. To base the ascertainment on a full screening of a population is virtually impossible unless the age group chosen is of school age and effectively captive. Even then it is difficult to ensure that the most retarded children are fully ascertained, for they are most likely to be outside the educational system, even where, in theory, they are considered to be within it, as in the UK. The most severely retarded are likely to be in hospital or, often, to be cared for away from their district of residence.

Attempts to screen a defined population have been made. In this country Roberts and his colleagues (1935) administered an intelligence test to all children in one city in the 1930s, and Birch and his colleagues (1970) described a screening system in use in Aberdeen which formed the basis of ascertainment of mental defects in children resident in that city.

In practice such cases come to the notice of health, educational or social services in many different ways, usually early in childhood, and usually because the parents become aware that the children are not behaving normally. Some of the biases found in administrative ascertainment, notably those due to social class differences, were described in the Aberdeen study (Birch et al., 1970) which showed the deficit of administrative ascertainment of the mildly educationally subnormal in the higher social classes, and the excess in the lower classes. The nearest to complete ascertainment on an administrative definition that can be achieved is when multiple sources are approached for information about such individuals.

INCIDENCE AND PREVALENCE

In order to establish incidence and prevalence the number of ascertained cases needs to be related to the population from which they were derived. In practice it can be as difficult to define and enumerate this population as to ascertain cases, although it is less important to be precise about the denominator than the numerator of these very low rates.

The difference between incidence rate and prevalence rate in defined populations is between the occurrence of new cases in a given time period and the number of cases existing at a specified time. Incidence is usually measured during the course of a longitudinal study of a defined cohort of births, for although the cause may be congenital, its effects may not be detected for many months. Prevalence depends on incidence and the length of life of the affected individual (if we assume that changes in status are unusual). In recent years, with improvements in medical care, the prolongation of life of affected individuals, and the maintenance of life in the neonatal period of damaged infants, has tended to increase prevalence. We know less about trends in incidence because it is so difficult to ascertain cases very early in life, and there has been considerable discussion recently whether overall incidence has risen, fallen or remained the same (Alberman et al., 1982).

Certainly the levels of both rates depend crucially on both the definition and the full ascertainment of cases. In particular the use of the administrative definition has been shown to create apparent differences between age groups, for full administrative ascertainment is highest at school age, and lowest in pre-school children and adults (Kushlick and Blunden, 1974).

With this exception the use of "administrative" prevalence has proved to be a surprisingly robust measure, between and within countries and over time (Table 1). In contrast to mild mental subnormality, the prevalence of the severe form, administratively defined, does not vary very much with social or cultural factors, although it may vary with the incidence due to important specific causes, such as Down's syndrome (Hagberg, 1978).

Table 1

Comparison of the prevalence rates of IQ under 50 in age groups where all subjects are likely to be known (adapted from Birch *et al*., 1970)

	Year	Age of children	Total rate per 1000 with IQ<50
England and Wales, urban (Lewis, 1929)	1925/1927	7-14	3.76
Middlesex (Goodman and Tizard, 1962)	1960	7-14 10-14	3.45 3.61
Salford Susser and Kushlick, 1961)	1961	15-19	3.64
Wessex (Kushlick, 1964)	1964* 1964**	15-19 15-19	3.54 3.84
Baltimore, MD, USA (Lemkau *et al*., 1943)	1936	10-14	3.3
Aberdeen, Scotland (Birch *et al*., 1970)	1962	8-10	3.7
Edinburgh, Scotland (Drillien *et al*., 1966)	1962-64	7-14	4.9
Quebec, Canada (McDonald, 1973)	1966-1969	10	3.8
England, Wales and Scotland (Frew and Peckham, 1972)	1969	11	3.6
Uppsala County (Hagberg, 1978)	1975	11-16	2.8

* county boroughs
** counties
Derived from Alberman (1978)

SPECIFIC CAUSES

It has already been stated that severe mental retardation is a heterogeneous group of conditions of widely varying aetiology, and the relatively constant prevalence rate of the group as a whole must reflect a surprising constancy with which the constituent conditions occur. The proportion to which a specific cause can be assigned varies with the assiduity with which each is sought, but even in the most carefully studied groups no cause can yet be found for many of the cases. However new causes, often of rare conditions, are constantly being identified. Laxova and her colleagues (1977) studied the causes of a group of administratively defined cases ascertained in a geographical area (Table 2). A similar study has been reported by Hagberg (1978).

Table 2

Distribution of different types of condition in severely retarded children in Hertfordshire, 1965-1967 (adapted from Laxova *et al*., 1977)

	Distribution (%)	(*n* = 146)
Genetically determined		
Down's syndrome	32.2	
Trisomy-21		30.1
Translocation		2.1
Other	16.5	
Epilepsy - idiopathic	1.4	
Neural tube defect	4.8	
Cerebral palsy	6.8	
Postnatal brain damage (including one case of rubella syndrome)	4.1	
Other	34.2	
All	100	

As in Alberman (1978)

Using the former series, in a previous account I have suggested how one might expect the incidence to change over time (Alberman, 1978). Thus the birth prevalence of Down's syndrome will change both with changes in maternal age distribution and with the introduction of diagnostic amniocentesis and selective termination in older mothers. Similarly there is evidence of a decreasing birth prevalence of spina bifida, in part because of general diagnosis and termination (Weatherall, 1982), in part possibly because of improved nutrition. The latter question is currently the subject of large-scale trials (Smithells et al., 1981). Genetic counselling is probably also reducing the occurrence of some of the rarer genetically determined metabolic disorders.

MULTIPLE IMPAIRMENTS

Because severe mental retardation so often occurs as part of a more generalized disorder one of its most important aspects is the common association with other serious impairments. Hagberg (1978) reported on 122 children with severe mental retardation in Uppsala in Sweden, including all such children born in the country between 1959 and 1970 and alive at the age of 1 year. Of these, 42% had multiple impairments of the central nervous system, 30% epilepsy, 18% cerebral palsy, 8% epilepsy and cerebral palsy, 6% hydrocephalus, and 12% were blind, deaf or both. Physical defects are also common in this group. Congenital heart disease is frequently present in children with Down's syndrome, severe orthopaedic and renal defects may be present in children with spina bifida, and a large variety of metabolic and other defects may be present in children with severe mental defect due to other genetically determined causes.

MULTIPLE HANDICAPS (OR INCAPACITIES)

Kushlick and Blunden (1974) further subdivided the clinical subgroups of those with mental retardation by their capacity to undertake daily tasks, and showed that physical and behavioural incapacities were common. Overall 27% of such individuals were severely incapacitated, 8% being non-ambulant and 19% having a behaviour disorder and/or incontinence. A further 10% were mildly incapacitated in some way.

The significance of multiple impairment and handicap is two-fold. Firstly their very presence may have contributed substantially to the low IQ, as with blindness and deafness, if these are not particularly sought for and allowed for in the teaching of the child. Secondly such additional impairments further decrease the chance of maximizing a child's potential by offering a stimulating environment without the disadvantages of hospital admission or medical intervention.

CONCLUSION

It is evident that different definitions need to be used for different purposes. Definitions based on IQ levels make possible comparisons between different places and different times, if allowance is made for possible changes in distribution. Definitions based on the individuals' need for care are essential for planning and evaluating services. Aetiologically based definitions or classifications are essential for planning and evaluating preventive action.

Ideally one should use as many parameters as possible, with a view to segregating out homogeneous groups. It is suggested that such parameters include a simple measure of impairment, including IQ levels, a measure of disability (or incapacity), and an aetiological classification where this is known. Although this makes the classification of severe (or other) mental defect more complex it will be very much more useful in the long term, and will make possible epidemiological studies of homogeneous groups, no matter how defined.

REFERENCES

Alberman, E. (1978). Main causes of major mental handicap: prevalence and epidemiology. In **Major Mental Handicap: Methods and Costs of Prevention.** Ciba Foundation Symposium 59 (new series)

Alberman, E., McDonald, A. and Benson J. (1982). Cerebral palsy and severe education subnormality in low-birthweight children: a comparision of births in 1951-53 and 1970. **Lancet, i**, 606-608

Birch, H.G., Richardson, S.A., Baird, D., Horobin, G., and Illsley R. (1970). **Mental Subnormality in the Community.** Baltimore: Williams and Wilkins

Clarke, A.D.B. and Clarke, A.M. (1975). The changing outlook. In **Mental Deficiency,** pp 142-163. London: Methuen

Drillien, C.M., Jameson, S. and Wilkinson, E.M. (1966). Studies in mental handicap. **Archives of Disease in Childhood, 41**, 528-538

Frèw, R. and Peckham, C. (1972). Mental retardation: a national study. **British Hospital Journal Social Services Review, 82**, 2070-2072.

Goodman, J. and Tizard, J. (1962). Prevalence of imbecility and idiocy among children. **British Medical Journal, 1**, 216-222.

Hagberg, B. (1978). Severe mental retardation in Swedish children born 1959-1970: epidemiological paranormal and causative factors. In **Major Mental Handicap: Methods and Cost of Prevention.** Ciba Foundation Symposium 59 (new series)

Kushlick, A. (1964). The prevalence of recognised mental subnormality of IQ under 50 among children in the South of England with reference to the demand for places for residential care. In **Int. Copenhagen Congr. Scientific Study of Mental Retardation**, Ed. Oster, J. and Stetved, H.V., pp 550-556

Kushlick, A. and Blunden, A. (1974). The epidemiology of mental subnormality. In **Mental Deficiency**, Ed. Clarke, A.M. and Clarke, A.D.B. pp 31-81. London: Methuen

Laxova, R., Ridler, M.A.C. and Bowen-Bravery, M. (1977). An aetiological survey of the severely retarded Hertfordshire children who were born between 1 January 1965 and 31

December 1967. **American Journal of Medical Genetics, 1,** 75-86

Lemkau, P.V., Tietze, C. and Cooper, M. (1943). Mental hygiene problems in an urban district. **Mental Hygiene, 27,** 279-295

Lewis, E.O. (1929). **The Report of the Mental Deficiency Committee,** Part IV, An investigation into the incidence of mental deficiency. Joint Committee of Board of Education and Board of Control. London: HMSO

McDonald, A.D. (1973). Severely retarded children in Quebec: prevalence, causes and care. **American Journal of Mental Deficiency, 78,** 205-215

Penrose, L. (1972). **The Biology of Mental Defect,** London: Sidgwick and Jackson

Roberts, J.A.F., Norman, R.M., and Griffiths, R. (1935). Studies on a child population: definition of sample, method of ascertainments and analysis of results of a group of intelligence tests. **Annals of Eugenics, 6,** 319-338

Smithells, R.W., Sheppard, S., Schorah, C.J., Seller, M.J., Nevin, N.C., Harris, R., Read, A.P., and Fielding, D.W. (1981). Apparent prevention of neural tube defects by periconceptional vitamin supplementation. **Archives of Disease in Childhood, 56,** 911-918

Susser, M.W. and Kushlick, A. (Eds) (1961). **A Report on the Mental Health Services in the City of Salford for the Year 1960.** Salford Health Department

Tizard, J. (1974). Longitudinal studies. In **Mental Deficiency,** Ed Clarke, A.M. and Clarke, A.D.B. pp 223-256. London: Methuen

Turner, G. and Opitz, J.M. (1980). X-linked mental retardation. **American Journal of Medical Genetics, 7,** 407-415

Weatherall, J.A. (1982). Review of some effects of recent medical practices in reducing the number of children born with congenital abnormalities. **Health Trends, 14,** 85-88

COMMENTARY

H. O. Åkesson

I do agree with most of the statements made by Alberman in her paper. However I would like to stress even further a few of the problems related to the diagnostic criteria used.

Like other mental disorders, mental retardation presents great problems in diagnosis. These problems derive from the well known fact that an aetiological diagnosis can only be made in some cases. Naturally, mental retardation is not a disease in itself, but only a symptom which may be found in a number of different conditions. It is true that there are a great number of oligophrenia syndromes of known aetiology, but together they represent a numerically minor group. When one considers in addition that no clear distinction can be made between the normally intelligent and the mentally retarded, since the difference is merely quantitative, the difficulties of diagnosis become manifest.

Another aspect is, of course, that the diagnosis one employs must be adapted to the purpose of the investigation. If a population study is undertaken for scientific purposes only, for example to throw light on variations of rate, an operational definition of mental retardation must be employed. Only by this means will a comparison of one study with another be possible and meaningful. If, on the other hand, a field study is undertaken with a view to using the results to render the care of patients with impaired psychic development more effective, an operational definition cannot be employed; in every investigation of this sort the diagnosis must be based on a clinical and socio-medical judgement. Thus, for example, when studying the need for care one can never define one's criteria in advance. For practical reasons one cannot go farther than a subjective judgement. It is clear from this that one cannot compare different studies of this kind, nor is this the intention. One must simply bear in mind that the figure for mental retardation one has obtained can only serve the original purpose of the investigation, for instance to form a basis for the treatment planning. The diagnosis "mental retardation" will thus vary with the aim of the investigation.

B. Hagberg and G. Hagberg

This paper is divided into two main parts: (A) aspects of definition and ascertainment, including the consequences which follow with regard to prevalence; (B) distribution and changes in the aetiologies of mental retardation.

The author rightly underlines the two basic prerequisites for all epidemiological research, i.e. a clear and objective definition, and full ascertainment. The discussion of ways to achieve this and of the associated difficulties is valuable. The author has not restricted herself to an analysis of severe mental retardation (SMR) but repeatedly comments on mild mental retardation (MMR) as well. It is often difficult to sort out to which IQ range she refers. In fact, except for giving the definition of SMR (= IQ < 50) and acceptance of a pathological population at the lower end of the general IQ distribution, this discussion much more concerns MMR than SMR. The following three points will particularly be commented upon.

A: I. The IQ distribution

The author accepts the IQ distribution as normally distributed, with a mean of 100 and a SD of 15. She shows quite clearly the difference in prevalence of "low IQs" if a fixed value as opposed to fixed SDs from the IQ means are taken as limits for the diagnosis of MR. She does not discuss how to handle IQ fluctuation over time. Continuous changes in the mean IQ as well as in the SD have been demonstrated (Terman and Merrill, 1973; Flynn, 1982). White Americans have made a gain of almost a full SD over 42 years and Japanese over 24 years (Flynn, 1982). The problem of definition is, should a measured IQ be referred to earlier norms or later ones? This must be up to each author to decide, and will be independent of the aims of each study. It is essential, however, always to state the test used, when and where it was normed, and the year the testing was performed - so that comparisons of time and place can be made.

A: II. Distinction between SMR and MMR

It is important to underline that the problems of definitions and ascertainment differ between SMR and MMR. SMR is generally taken to refer to IQ < 50. Its recognition, delineation and ascertainment should not, in the large majority of cases, give any great problems. SMR is also taken to comprise mainly a pathological population, to have little relevance for the general IQ distribution and to be independent of social class. MMR is traditionally considered mainly to be of socio-cultural origin and to be highly dependent on social class or vice versa. The definition of MMR is contradictory. Should the definition be built on a fixed IQ range - where small changes in the general IQ distribution make a large difference in the prevalence - or based on fixed SDs with a static prevalence (23 per 1000)? Should earlier or later norms be used? The answers to these questions cannot be given at present. A complete ascertainment also raises large practical and theoretical problems. It is important that all investigators of MMR are aware of these problems.

B: Aetiologies - specific causes

Useful systems for classification of causes/risks with defined criteria are not discussed, which is a pity. The aetiological survey of SMR children referred to, that from Hertfordshire (Laxova *et al.*, 1977), could certainly be considered representative with regard to ascertainment. Unfortunately, however, no consequent pathogenic grouping according to known/likely pre-, peri- or postnatal origin to the SMR is given. Opitz, working with Laxova in Madison, has tried to apply the same aetological/pathogenic grouping system as was used in Sweden (Gustavson *et al.*, 1977a) to the Laxova series and to his own Wisconsin Central Colony series (institution-based). As shown in Table C1 the data from these series (Opitz, personal communication 1977) and two population-based Swedish series agree largely in spite of the differences in population and the original grouping.

It would be profitable to work out refined alternatives for aetiological groupings for such systematic analyses of comparable series from different geographic areas, populations and periods.

IQ testing as a method for defining populations of mentally retarded in scientific work

It is generally agreed that IQ testing, for various reasons, is not an ideal tool for defining populations of MR in scientific studies. Experts invited by the planning group of the Swedish Medical Research Council to suggest alternatives have, however, been unable to present any. For this reason IQ is still considered to be the least bad index available for epidemiological investigations.

Multidimensional scoring systems

One approach for better categorization of MR populations would possibly be to use multidimensional scoring profiles in relation to IQ groups in matrix systems. Dimensions that it may be possible to add for purposes of categorization would then, for example, be: degrees of functional disability (ADL, motor, communication, etc.) and aetiological grouping.

Example 1: Motor disability

	Score groups	I	II	III	IV
IQ < 50 --->					
IQ 50-70 --->					

Example 2: Aetiological grouping

	Prenatal				Perinatal		Postnatal	
	A	B	C	D	A	B	A	B
IQ < 50 --->								
IQ 50-70 --->								

Pilot study using scoring systems for measuring load of daily nursing care in a group of severely mentally retarded children with pronounced and multiple handicaps

An unselected series of 53 profoundly MR children born in 1966-76 were studied. They represented the most disabled one-third of those with IQ less than 50. Progressive biochemical disorders and cases of postnatal trauma ?missed drownings? were heavily overrepresented. The burden of nursing care and the need for medical assistance were evaluated with a specially designed scoring system. It was found that among MR children with IQ less than 50, 15-20% were sufficiently disabled to need long-term care or periodic short-term care with considerable medical, nursing and paediatric support (Hagberg *et al*., 1981).

References

Flynn, J.R. (1982). Lynn, the Japanese, and environmentalism. **Bulletin of The British Psychologistical Society, 35,** 409-413

Gustavson, K.-H., Hagberg, B., Hagberg, G. and Sars, K. (1977a). Severe mental retardation in a Swedish county. II. Etiologic and pathogenetic aspects of children born 1959-1970. **Neuropadiatrie, 8,** 293-304

Gustavson, K.-H., Holmgren, G., Jonsell, R. and Blomquist, H. K:son (1977b). Severe mental retardation in children in a northern Swedish county. **Journal of Mental Deficiency Research, 21**, 161-179

Hagberg, B., Edström, B. and Oskarsson, M. (1981). Pediatric long term/short term care service for profoundly mentally retarded children with severe multi-handicap syndrome. **Läkartidningen (Sw.), 78**, 3808-15

Laxova, R., Ridler, M.A.C. and Bowen-Bravery, M. (1977). An aetiological survey of the severely retarded Hertfordshire children who were born between January 1, 1965 and December 31, 1967. **American Journal of Medical Genetics, 1,** 75-86.

Terman, L.M. and Merrill M.A. (1973). **Stanford-Binet Intelligence Scale: 1972 Norms Edition** p 359. Boston: Houghton-Mifflin

Table C1

Origin		Wisconsin (Opitz, pers. commun. 1977)*		Hertfordshire (Laxova *et al.*, 1977)**		Uppsala, Sweden (Gustavson, *et al.*, 1977a)**		Umea, Sweden (Gustavson, *et al.*, 1977b)**	
Prenatal	Genetic	26		47		43		52	
	Unknown	41	72	31	79	20	73	7	68
	Acquired	5		1		10		8	
Perinatal			13		5		10		8
Postnatal			10		3		3		1.2
Psychotic			1		-		2		1.2
Untraceable			5		12		12		21.7

* institution-based series
** population-based series

S. A. Richardson

In considering epidemiological aspects of severe mental retardation the classification of severity needs to be considered in relation to the purposes for which the classification is to be used. One purpose is to provide estimates which may be used for planning services and this is the purpose I will adhere to in my comments. There is a considerable body of knowledge available for planning services for children who are mentally retarded, but much less is known about the post-school years of young adulthood. For this reason I will focus on the epidemiology in young adulthood.

To provide illustration and substance to the points that will be raised I will draw upon findings from the study referred to in the review (Birch *et al.*, 1970) and to a study of these and additional children from the same city we have followed to age 22 (Richardson, 1980). The time period of the results is ages 16-22, the first six years after leaving school. Clearly the findings represent a single study and their use here is primarily to raise questions.

The title of the paper must have been selected in the belief that it is important to dichotomize the mentally retarded population into two subsets. Alberman has not questioned this belief but I will do so. Further, I will question the assumption accepted by Alberman that IQ tests alone are adequate for distinguishing severe and non-severe mental retardation.

Alberman gives an excellent summary of various theoretical issues which have been prominent in the literature dealing with the definition of severe retardation as measured by standard tests of IQ. She has not considered the component of adaptive behaviour which is now incorporated into the definition of mental retardation (AAMD classification). By adaptive behaviour is meant the effectiveness with which the individual meets the standards of personal independence and social responsibility expected of his or her age and cultural group. If consideration is only given to those with IQ of under 50, it is reasonable to expect that their level of adaptive behaviour would not meet the standard of adaptive behaviour just given. There may, however, be some whose IQ may be 50 and over, but whose level of adaptive behaviour makes it important for them to receive services after school leaving age.

Alberman reviews the administrative prevalence of severe mental retardation during the school years. For the 12 studies the range is from 2.8 to 4.9 per 1000, with a median prevalence of 3.63 per 1000. For the population we have followed to the age of 22 the prevalence of those who have been steadily in services since leaving school at age 16 up to age 22 is 5 per 1000. An alternative way then of dividing mentally retarded persons in the post-school years is to consider those who need continuous service as less able than those who do without, or only occasionally use mental retardation services in the same period. By defining epidemiologically a population of children who are mentally retarded and following the population into early adulthood it is possible to identify those who continue to need services in young adulthood and then examine what factors in childhood best predict the subgroup. Such information would help in selecting those children who are most likely to need continuous care after leaving school and for whom services in childhood may need to be different from those of children who will disappear from further mental retardation services after leaving school. A danger of using only IQ and a cutting point of below 50 is that it may deflect attention from some young people who need some form of mental retardation service which to some extent stems from their mental incapacity.

Breaking down the overall prevalence of mental retardation by IQ cutting points is of very little use for planning services. In the past when less was known about evaluation of those who were mentally retarded and when institutionalization in mental retardation hospitals was the primary or only form of adult care, an IQ cut-off point of 50 was often given considerable weight in making admission decisions. With the move towards the development of a variety of community services - residential, day and home support services - decisions on the most appropriate service for an individual should be based on a broader functional assessment with intellectual functioning being only one of several functional modalities considered.

Mittler (1979) gives another reason for not using IQ alone and for not establishing some cutting point to distinguish severe from not severe.

> Most psychologists are now well aware of the limitations of placing too much emphasis on an IQ score in judging the presence or extent of mental handicap.
>
> It is important to stress that the IQ is in no sense a "magic" number. Unfortunately it has been credited with a degree of psychological significance out of all proportion either to its scientific status or its relevance to the practical problems of normal or handicapped persons. (p 23)

Alberman reviews the few epidemiological studies of multiple impairments and handicaps. Most of these studies give the distribution of particular disabilities for the population as a whole, but do not show how these disabilities combine for each individual in the population. To illustrate how patterns of disabilities add information helpful in planning services, Table C2 shows the distribution of moderate to severe disabilities for those in the follow-up study who were in day or residential services throughout the age period of 16-22. Of those with IQ under 50, half had two or more disabilities in the post-school years. The disabilities considered are epilepsy, behaviour disturbance, communication disorders of speech, hearing and vision, limb disabilities and incontinence. The most frequent disability was communication. The limitations of the IQ as a measure pointed out by Mittler need to be an even greater source of concern when evaluating a person with multiple disabilities. An IQ cutting point of 50 would exclude 31 young people with IQ of 50 and above who have been in mental retardation services throughout young adulthood (16-22 years). They constitute 45% of all those young adults in services at this time. Given the limitations of the IQ test, some of the below 50 IQ group shown in Table C2 may actually have IQs above 50. It is also possible that some of those shown with IQs above 50 may have lower IQs. From the broader perspective of patterns of disabilities, the two subsets of < 50 and 50-59 IQ show no significant difference in the number of their moderate to severe disabilities.

Alberman raises the question of sex differences and whether at the lower end of the IQ distribution there is an excess of males over females. In our follow-up study, within the subset with IQ of under 50, there is little difference in the IQ range of 20-49 (14 males and 11 females), but for the subset with IQ of less than 20 there are more males (9 males and 2 females).

Table C2

Patterns of disability for those in day or residential services throughout the age period of 16-22 (Aberdeen follow-up study ages)

	IQ		
	<50	50-59	60-69
No disabilities	5(14%)	4(21%)	1(08%)
E		1(05%)	
B	4(11%)	5(26%)	4(33%)
C	9(25%)	3(16%)	2(17%)
L			
I			
EB	1(03%)		
E C	1(03%)		
E L	1(03%)		
E I	1(03%)		1(08%)
BC	1(03%)	3(01%)	1(08%)
B L			1(08%)
B I			
CL	4(11%)		2(17%)
E CL	1(03%)	1(05%)	
EBC	2(06%)	1(05%)	
BCL	2(06%)		
BC I	1(03%)		
CLI	1(03%)		
EB LI		1(05%)	
EBCL	1(03%)		
E CLI	1(03%)		
Total *n*	36	19	12

E = Epilepsy
B = Behaviour disturbance
C = Communication (speech, hearing, vision)
L = Upper and lower limb disabilities
I = Incontinence

(Moderate and severe levels only included on above disabilities)

Adapted from Richardson *et al*. (1983)

It is necessary to be cautious in accounting for the excess of males by attributing the difference primarily to biological and genetic factors. Alberman has pointed out that a person's level of intelligence may be influenced by social environmental factors. In our follow-up study significantly more severely retarded males have been placed in residential care in institutions than females (Table C3). Further, many of those in institutional care were placed in childhood. It may be that the initial placement was made because the males were more severely mentally retarded. It also may be possible that placement in institutions was not primarily based on severity of retardation, but also on other disabilities and that long-term residence in an institution has hindered their intellectual development because of an unstimulating environment. The females largely avoided such environmental experiences.

Table C3

Numbers of males and females with IQ 50-69 who have been in mental retardation services throughout the age period of 16-22

	Full-time mental retardation services	
	Yes	No
Male	11	48
Female	20	35

$\chi^2 = 4.51$, d.f. = 1, $p < 0.05$

Data taken from follow-up study of Birch *et al*. (1970)

Our study suggests that young adult males and females may be different in their ability to live an independent existence in an unsheltered environment. Table C3 shows that for the population we have followed significantly more females than males with IQ of 50-69 are in full-time mental retardation services. If the same criteria for admission and keeping in full-time services were used for males and females we would expect no difference in the multiplicity of associated disabilities. The follow-up study shows that the males had significantly more disabilities than the females in the IQ 50-69 range (Table C4). The higher proportion of females than males in services and the greater multiplicity of disabilities in the males suggests that different criteria are used in admissions to service for females and males. This may be related to a greater concern for a given level of retardation for young women than men in their ability to manage independently in an unsheltered environment.

Table C4

Number of moderate to severe disabilities of males and females with IQ 50-69 aged 16-22

Number of disabilities other than mental retardation	Male	Female
0	0	5
1	4	11
3	4	4
4	3	0

$\chi^2 = 9.45$, d.f.= 1, $p < 0.025$.

Disabilities examined are: epilepsy, behaviour disturbance, communication disorders, limb disabilities and incontinence

I would question whether for a medically organized conference an epidemiological review should be limited to "severe" mental retardation. Traditionally medical interest has been primarily focused on severe retardation. This in part was related to the notion that severe retardation is of organic origin whereas mild mental retardation is based on cultural familial factors. It may also reflect doctors having much of their experience with mental retardation hospital inmates. The patterns of disabilities shown for the follow-up study show that those with IQ over 50 frequently have disabilities that require medical attention and for some suggest some organic factors in aetiology. In the Birch et al. (1970) study 39% of the 8-10 year old children with IQs of 50 and above showed positive evidence of central nervous system damage as evidenced by a paediatric neurological examination. This also suggests organic factors contributing to the aetiology of mild mental retardation in some cases.

In conclusion, there are two further minor points about Alberman's review.

In the Aberdeen study, Alberman makes reference to some evidence of social class bias found in administrative ascertainment of mentally retarded children. This bias was found only for mildly retarded children and not for children with IQ below 50.

Alberman quotes Kushlick and Blunden on age-specific prevalence rates with full administrative ascertainment being highest at school age, and lowest in pre-school children and adults. This point was made for mild mental retardation, but not for severe mental retardation.

References

Birch, H.G., Richardson, S.A., Baird, D., Horobin, G. and Illsley, R. (1970) **Mental Subnormality in the Community.** Baltimore: Williams and Wilkins

Mittler, P. (1979). **People Not Patients.** London and New York: Methuen

Richardson, S.A. (1980). Growing up as a mentally subnormal young person. A follow-up study. In **An Empirical Basis for Primary Prevention: Prospective Longitudinal Research in Europe.** Eds Mednick, S.A. and Baert, A.E., Oxford University Press

Richardson, S.A., Koller, H., Katz, M. and McLaren, J. (1983) Patterns of disability in a mentally retarded population between ages 16 and 22 years. In **Proceedings of the Sixth Congress of the International Association for the Scientific Study of Mental Deficiency**, Eds Berg, J.M. and de Jong, J.

Chapter 2

Social influences in the aetiology and prevention of mild retardation

Ann M. Clarke and A.D.B. Clarke

This chapter is concerned only with mild retardation, which does not imply that the more severe grades are immune to social influences. In terms of prevention, the take-up of services seems to exhibit the usual social class gradient. For example, late reporting of pregnancy makes prenatal diagnosis inappropriate; failure to seek genetic counselling may result in further births of retarded children. Moreover, the degree of severe retardation may be exacerbated or diminished by the child's social context.

There are three headlines in the aetiology of mild retardation: pathological, including rare genetic factors and the many environmental agents which promote CNS damage before, during or after birth; normal polygenic variation implied by the average 0.5 parent-child correlation; and subcultural factors, assumed to involve an interaction of both genetic and environmental influences. These are by no means mutually exclusive, and in individual cases which come to society's notice, aetiology is often complex. To have an IQ of 60 or 70 and to be well adjusted often enables the person to escape detection. But to have additional problems and to lack both the capacity or opportunity to solve them at once identifies the individual.

ADMINISTRATIVE VERSUS TRUE PREVALENCE

For mild retardation, as for some other conditions, there is a clear relationship between the provision of facilities and administrative prevalence. A survey we undertook for the year 1966 indicated that only about a third of those with IQs below 70 were specially identified at any one time; most of these were severely subnormal. A comparable very recent survey by one of our students yields a similar picture. The conclusion is therefore inescapable that, if one takes an IQ upper limit of 70 to 75, the majority are only specially provided for during the school years. Studies of administrative prevalence have been unanimous in showing a steep decline in numbers during adolescence and early adult life. Such a reduction is attributable to social camouflage in undemanding work, or to prolonged social learning and in many cases delayed maturation (Clarke and Clarke, 1959). For a proportion, then, mild mental retardation is a self-ameliorating condition.

True prevalence is difficult to establish, but Richardson (1981) gives an account of the methods and findings of a careful epidemiological survey in one city. All children in Aberdeen were routinely given group intelligence tests in middle childhood. Any child scoring below IQ 75 was then assessed individually on the WISC, as well as undergoing a paediatric examination and assessment of parental social class. The usual social class gradient was evident; prevalence of mild retardation was 28 times higher in social class V than in I to IIIa. Those without evidence of CNS damage were strongly over-represented in families where there were five or more children, living in the least desirable areas, in more crowded homes and when the mother's occupation before marriage was semi-skilled or unskilled manual work. The overall prevalence, based on both administratively defined criteria and also a record of children in ordinary classes with IQs below 75, was 2.7%.

Richardson summarizes this and other work by stating that in mildly retarded children without evidence of CNS damage, social background factors do make a contribution to this retardation. Its size and what other factors contribute remain open questions. His cautious statement reflects the growing sophistication of research workers. The pendulum swung from the older belief that subcultural retardation was entirely genetic in origin, to the 1960s view that it was entirely environmental. Neither extreme is now tenable.

Taking only administrative prevalence, Richardson's findings of 0.88% for the IQ band 50-69 have been broadly confirmed by other very low prevalence figures in Hagberg *et al.*'s (1981) study using the Terman-Merrill and WISC tests in approximately the same age groups. The estimate of 0.51% is also very low. The authors account for this by suggesting a general rise in children's IQs in Gothenburg with a possible mean of 110-112. There are a number of problems here; first, there is no clear historical trend, and other earlier studies in Edinburgh (Drillien *et al.*, 1966) and Stockholm (Borjeson and Klackenburg, 1960) also suggest a low prevalence. Further, Jensen (1981) draws attention to possible secular trends in item difficulty within tests. It may be difficult to discover whether there is a real secular trend, representing "genuine, important and highly relevant shifts in performance characteristics of children" (Terman and Merrill, 1973) or whether it is a matter of children's greater familiarity with test items with which their equivalent age group was less familiar 30 or 40 years earlier. Thus we do not really know whether general social progress has diminished mild retardation. But if it has, and if it continues to do so, individual differences will not disappear. The dullard of today might become the mildly retarded of tomorrow.

HERITABILITY OF INTELLECTUAL DIFFERENCES

There is a growing consensus that within a broad range of humane environments the heritability of intellectual differences is fairly high. Genes are implicated "as the major systematic force influencing the development of individual differences in IQ. In fact, we know of no specific environmental influences nor combination of them that account for as much as 10 per cent of the variance in IQ" (Plomin and DeFries, 1980). Scarr (1981) has indicated that "most evidence points to a 'heritability' of about .4 to .7 in the U.S. white population and .2 to .5 in the black, given that 'heritability' here means the proportion of genetic variance among individuals sampled in twin and family studies, which as I have repeatedly noted are not representative of bad environments". A similar point has been made by Clarke (1982) in arguing that a broad range of normal environments may be sufficient to potentiate individual differences with substantial genetic components. Inhumane environments, however, may profoundly depress intellectual development, and these are characteristic of an unknown but probably substantial minority of our population.

It is commonly believed that the high heritability of a trait implies its unmodifiability. Jensen (1981), however, indicates that "even with a heritability in the range of .70 to .80, the magnitude of environmental effects can be considerable". Intervention producing changes within a range of 45 IQ points, he writes, is not in the least incompatible with present estimates of the broad heritability of IQ.

There seems, in summary, to be a threshold above which humane environments of a wide range do not exercise a differential effect on measured intelligence, and below which differences in adversity do produce differentially retarding effects. There may be some reasonable analogy here with the dietary and other factors leading to rickets.

THE ECOLOGY OF DISADVANTAGE

Begab (1981), reviewing studies of the socially disadvantaged, indicates that hygiene and housing are poor, nutrition and medical care inadequate, and infectious diseases common. "Such factors characterize poor families in general, however, and they do not discriminate between the approximately 10% of this segment of the population who are retarded and the 90% who are not. The primary discriminants are maternal intelligence and level of education" (p 7). Interpretations of these facts can be genetic or environmental, according to one's choice! However, Begab goes on to point out that children born in such circumstances may suffer from subclinical deficits which may affect intellectual performance, but which are undetectable by existing technology.

> These women are particularly vulnerable to noxious agents such as infections, trauma, toxins and alcoholism, and they have a high incidence of prematurity and low birth weight. In extreme form, these agents cause demonstrable brain damage. In milder form, when considered in combination with the depressing psychological and social forces with which they commonly interact, adverse effects on intelligence are probable ... Neglect and abuse are not uncommon ... but most frequently the limited parent lacks the communication skills to stimulate the child's acquisition of language and cognitive development ... Descriptions of disorganized homes present a vivid picture of family pathology, inept parenting, and chaotic living conditions ... Adults live from crisis to crisis: separation, desertion and child abandonment are common ... (however) ... it is still not possible to assign etiological significance to any of these parameters. Taken singly, their effects on cognitive performance may be negligible. In their totality, however, the interactive influence of these elements may be geometric, not additive. (pp 9-10)

This is a very cautious and careful statement. It leads us to the most crucial test of the role of psychosocial factors in causation. If the deficits of many of the mildly retarded are indeed to some extent social in origin, then one would expect cumulative deficit as age increases. Let us turn to the evidence.

Cumulative Deficit

This concept seems to have had its roots in a cross-sectional study by Gordon (1923) who found that canal-boat children averaged an IQ of 87 at age six and 60 at age twelve. Jensen (1974, 1977) has published two studies using older with younger sibling comparisons. The first, in California, found a significant age decrement in verbal although not in non-verbal IQ among negro, but not white, elementary school children. This difference averaged only 2 IQ points for an average sibling age discrepancy between about 19 and 31 months in the age range 5-12. Jensen raises the possibility that this small decrement may reflect reading differences in the verbal test.

The second study took place in rural Georgia, and again used older with younger sibling comparisons. Significant and substantial linear IQ decrements, both verbal and this time non-verbal, between five and sixteen occurred in blacks but not whites. There was an average decrement of 1.62 verbal IQ points per year and 1.19 non-verbal IQ points, over the age range 6-16. Jensen believes that an environmental explanation seems reasonable in this case.

Heber *et al.*'s (1968) cross-sectional study in Milwaukee seems also to offer impressive additional evidence for cumulative deficit. Among the important factors to which he and his colleagues drew attention was that socio-economic status is a rather poor guide to the familial processes which result in cumulative deficit. He was able to differentiate between families living in the same slum, showing a considerable deficit across age groups in children whose mothers' IQs lay below 80 but no deficit among the children whose mothers' IQs lay above 80.

It seems obvious, then, that severe adversity is reflected in decelerating growth rates. Indeed, the slope of the curves over time is strikingly similar. Cumulative deficit thus implicates a clear psychosocial component in some forms of mild retardation, and it also seems likely that social disadvantage may lead to below average functioning without necessarily being cumulative. The possibility of social intervention to prevent or reverse this process is discussed next.

Intervention

For humane reasons, early intervention has been seen as necessary, although the further rationale that the early years represent a "magic period" in which later development is preformed is in need of very substantial revision (Clarke and Clarke, 1976). Yet mild retardation is seldom identified very early in the child's life, although it is often possible to specify ecological and familial factors which may be predictive of increased risk of mild retardation later.

The possiblity of preventing mild retardation was first raised by the strongly environmentalist Iowa Group in the 1930s. This early work was rather naive and methodologically very weak (McNemar, 1940; Clarke and Clarke, 1958; Clarke, 1982). The reports of Skeels and Dye (1939) and Skeels (1966) are so well known that they require no recapitulation here. The work of Kirk (1958) is extremely important for its carefully controlled findings anticipated later research in a remarkable way. He was the first to show the "wash-out" of pre-school intervention effects.

By the 1960s the belief that total ecological change could sometimes prevent the continuation of some forms of mild retardation had optimistically been generalized to the notion that anything called intervention could do the same. This was one of the origins of Head Start, a costly series of social and educational programmes which by relatively brief periods of intervention aimed to overcome the disadvantages of poverty, backwardness or mild retardation. No doubt these did, and still do, much concurrent good, but the hope that they would prove to be a one-shot inoculation against future troubles soon proved to be illusory (Zigler and Valentine, 1979). A series of reports, of which Jensen's (1969) is perhaps the most widely known, underlined the "wash-out" effect on IQ which gradually superseded the positive influences of early intervention. "Compensatory education has been tried", wrote Jensen, "and it apparently has failed".

Bronfenbrenner (1974) reviewed some 21 of the better studies, suggesting that intervention in the home is likely to be more successful than in pre-school alone, but those most likely to respond come from the "upper crust" of poor families whose children anyway are probably not at risk for mild mental retardation. As we have put it, those most in need of help fail to seek it or, if offered, to accept it or benefit from it. Someone aptly termed this notion the "inverse care law".

In 1972, the President's Committee stated optimistically that "Using present knowledge and techniques from the biomedical and behavioural sciences, it is possible to reduce the occurrence of mental retardation by 50 per cent before the end of the century". In 1976 in Washington one of us indicated that, while this might be correct for the more severe grades, the prospects of halving the incidence of the 75% comprising the mildly retarded were very, very slight. Thus the overall forecast must be highly inaccurate (Clarke, 1977). The point was rather quietly conceded (though not in so many words) in the same year by the President's Committee (1976).

Nevertheless, a number of studies involving long-term environmental change had shown that young people rescued from exceptionally adverse circumstances made substantial increases in IQ and social adjustment (e.g. Clarke et al., 1958; Dennis, 1973; Koluchova, 1976). Feuerstein's work with very disadvantaged immigrant adolescents in Israel makes similar claims (Feuerstein et al., 1980) but is weak methodologically and is currently under critical review.

In the last few years the long-term outcome of pre-school intervention has been investigated. The members of twelve research groups thus came together as a Consortium (Lazar et al., 1977; Lazar and Darlington, 1978). The authors made valiant attempts to obtain and analyse data on the long-term outcome from these unusually well designed and therefore atypical programmes, and to show that while significant IQ differences between experimental and control children failed to persist, nevertheless on such factors as allocation to special education or grade retention, very significant differences were evident. One of the several problems in interpreting these findings is the lack of knowledge on what happened to the families between programme termination and later follow-up. The second and longer (1978) report is commendably and rightly cautious, although sticking to the main conclusions. (See also Darlington et al., 1980.)

Perhaps the most impressive and well controlled study included in Consortium data is by Schweinhart and Weikart (1980). Their interpretation of their findings is well put. They write: "As data accumulate, it is clear that we are viewing a complex network of causes and effects. The pre-school intervention has been succcessful over the years because its effects became the causes of other effects as well". Table 1 indicates the main results of the adolescent status of 123 black children randomly allocated to experimental or control conditions in their fourth year, when the average IQ was 79. Their relatively brief intervention included both the home and the pre-school (see also Schweinhart and Weikart, 1981). It will be noted that in this large sample of socially disadvantaged children there was no cumulative deficit across time.

Table 1

The adolescent outcome for children from the Perry Preschool Program

	Age 15 results		
	Experimental group	Control group	Difference
Mean IQ	81	81	N.S.
Special education	19%	39%	Very sign.
Chronic delinquency	36%	52%	Very sign.
Standardized attainment tests	8% higher		Very sign.

Data extracted from Schweinhart and Weikart (1980)

The overall findings of the pooled Consortium data suggested that factors such as type or duration of programme, the presence or absence of language goals, the training or not of teachers, were all irrelevant to outcome. It appears that we are not dealing with early intervention alone, but transactional processes continuing within the family and the school, the details of which are not fully understood, but which may require a general systems model of development. Moreover, the differences between experimental and control children's later school achievement are concordant with those reported for the famous Milwaukee experiment (Garber and Heber, 1982).

DISCUSSION AND CONCLUSIONS

It seems clear that social factors can be substantially involved in the aetiology of some forms of mild mental retardation. This in turn suggests that <u>major</u> and <u>continuous</u> ecological improvement is likely to diminish or even prevent the handicap. More modest interventions, especially if they affect the parents, can sometimes trigger familial changes which in effect continue these modest interventions, increasing aspirations and achievements, but these improvements remain somewhat limited.

Moreover, even if society had the resources to transform the material situation for the disadvantaged, there would remain for many years a perseveration of familial attributes and attitudes which would at best delay individual change or at worst prevent it. The recent Warsaw study (Czarkowski et al., 1977), where for 30 years there has been substantial equality in housing and educational provision but where occupational class gradients in IQ and achievement still remain, is quite sobering.

In individual cases, it may be possible to offer major life changes and hence life chances by, for example, adoption. In more modest endeavours, intervention should be primarily directed towards the parents whose children seem likely to be at risk by virtue of large families, poor housing and low educational, occupational and intellectual levels. The most hopeful and consistent evidence of the past is that the long-term prognosis for many of the mild cases is much better than might be expected from their record in early childhood and the school years; life permits and promotes a degree of self-betterment even if such persons have received little positive help (Cobb, 1972; Tizard, 1974). This is perhaps an example of Waddington's (1957, 1966) "self-righting tendency". But the social movements now occurring in developed countries, characterized by massive unemployment, may now damage this hitherto more hopeful picture.

Primary prevention of mild retardation may well be occurring as a result of the gradual dissemination of knowledge about birth control. It is significant that in some countries, the decrease in births is most marked in the lowest occupational classes. This is a sensitive area, but clearly the disadvantaged should have the same rights of access to family planning information as their more privileged peers. The inverse care law may, however, again operate because the disadvantaged are often unwilling to seek advice. Large families in poor circumstances, as we have seen, are often unable to provide reasonable contexts for rearing their children. Unwanted and unplanned children reduce the life chances of the whole family.

To summarize:

(1) There is no doubt that social factors are implicated in the aetiology of subcultural mild retardation, the majority group for which administrative prevalence estimates are available. This view springs from (a) the fact of cumulative deficit, and (b) responsiveness to intervention which, if prolonged, can shift the level of retardation towards and sometimes into normality. There is, however, little doubt that polygenic factors are also involved, as well as some possibility of co-existing subclinical organic damage in a minority. It is as yet difficult to put a precise figure on either factor.

(2) Age may be no barrier to effective intervention at least within the range from infancy to puberty, provided there is substantial and permanent ecological change. Where this is not possible the evidence suggests that pre-school intervention combined with parental involvement followed by support during the years of schooling can reduce the handicap.

(3) With the advancement of society there will still be those who are intellectually at the bottom of the population hierarchy, but in a humane society efforts can be made to enable them to lead fulfilled lives.

(4) While there is a considerable individual escape from conditions of disadvantage, there continues to be recruitment. The familial attitudes which are associated with subcultural retardation, like familial attitudes at other and different levels, tend to persist both intra- and inter-generationally. To some extent there is a cycle of disadvantage (Brown and Madge, 1982).

(5) The most hopeful findings are that through social camouflage, prolonged social learning and delayed maturation, a large proportion of the mildly retarded ultimately succeed in making more or less adequate social adjustments. The implication is that with more help, such adjustments would be achieved earlier and at a better level.

Acknowledgement

This chapter is partly based on our lecture delivered on November 12th, 1981, at the conference on _The Prevention of Mental Retardation_, Queen's University, Ontario. Permission to use some of this material has been kindly granted by Dr Bruce D. McCreary.

REFERENCES

Begab, M. J. (1981). Issues in the prevention of psychosocial retardation. In Begab, M.J., Haywood, H.C. and Garber, H.L. (Eds.), **Psychosocial Influences in Retarded Development. I**, University Park Press, Baltimore

Börjeson, M. and Klackenburg, G. (1960). Studies in frequency and prognosis of mentally retarded in Stockholm. **Socialmedicinsk Tidskrift, 37**, 243

Bronfenbrenner, U. (1974). **A Report on Longitudinal Evaluations of Pre-school Programs.** Vol.2. **Is Early Intervention Effective?** DHEW Publication No. (OHD) 74-25, Washington, DC

Brown, M. and Madge, N. (1982). **Despite the Welfare State,** Heinemann Educational, London

Clarke, A.D.B. (1977). Presidential address: From research to practice. In Mittler, . (Ed.), **Research to Practice in Mental Retardation. I**, University Park Press, Baltimore, A7-A19

Clarke, A.D.B. and Clarke, A.M. (1959). Recovery from the effects of deprivation. **Acta Psychologica, 16**, 137-144

Clarke, A.D.B., Clarke, A.M. and Reiman, S. (1958). Cognitive and social changes in the feebleminded - three further studies. **British Journal of Psychology, 49**, 144-157

Clarke, A.M. (1982). Developmental discontinuities: An approach to assessing their nature. In Bond, L.A. and Joffe, J.M. (Eds.), **Facilitating Infant and Early Child Development**, University Press of New England, Hanover, NH

Clarke, A.M. and Clarke, A.D.B. (1958) (Eds.), **Mental Deficiency: the Changing Outlook**, Methuen, London; Free Press, New York

Clarke, A.M. and Clarke, A.D.B. (1976) (Eds.), **Early Experience: Myth and Evidence**, Open Books, London; Free Press, New York

Cobb, H.V. (1972). **The Forecast of Fulfilment**, Teachers' College Press, Columbia University, New York

Czarkowski, M., Firkowska-Mankiewicz, A., Ostrowska, A., Sokotowska, M., Stein, Z., Susser, M. and Wald, I. (1977). Some ecological, school, and family factors in the intellectual performance of children. In Mittler, P. (Ed.), **Research to Practice in Mental Retardation I**, University Park Press, Baltimore, pp 89-95

Darlington, R.B., Royce, J.M., Snipper, A.S., Murray, H.W. and Lazar, I. (1980). Preschool programs and later school competence of children from low-income families. **Science, 208**, 202-204

Dennis, W. (1973). **Children of the Creche**, Appleton-Century-Crofts, New York

Drillien, C.M., Jameson, S. and Wilkinson, E.M. (1966). Studies in mental handicaps. Part I. Prevalence and distribution by clinical type and severity of defect. **Archives of Diseases in Childhood, 41**, 528-538

Feuerstein, R., Rand, Y., Hoffman, M.B. and Miller, R. (1980). **Instrumental Enrichment: An Intervention Program for Cognitive Modifiability**, University Park Press, Baltimore

Garber, H. and Heber, R. (1982). Modification of predicted cognitive development in high-risk children through early intervention. In Detterman, D.K. and Sternberg, R. (Eds.), **How and How Much Can Intelligence be Increased?** Ablex, Norwood, NJ

Gordon, H. (1923). **Mental and Scholastic Tests among Retarded Children**. (Education Pamphlet 44. London: Board of Education), HMSO, London

Hagberg, B., Hagberg, G., Lewerth, A. and Lindberg, U. (1981). Mild mental retardation in Swedish school children, I. Prevalence. **Acta Paediatrica Scandinavica, 70**, 441-444

Heber, R., Dever, R. and Conry, J. (1968). The influence of environmental and genetic variables on intellectual development. In Prehm. J., Hamerlynck, L.A. and Crosson, J.E. (Eds.), **Behavioural Research in Mental Retardation**. University of Oregon School of Education, Eugene

Jensen, A.R. (1969). How much can we boost IQ and scholastic achievement? **Harvard Educational Review, 39**, 1-123

Jensen, A.R. (1974). Cumulative deficit: A testable hypothesis? **Developmental Psychology, 10**, 996-1019

Jensen, A.R. (1977). Cumulative deficit in IQ of blacks in the rural South. **Developmental Psychology, 13**, 184-191

Jensen, A.R. (1981). Raising the IQ: The Ramey and Haskins study. **Intelligence, 5**, 29-40

Kirk, S. (1958). **Early Education of the Mentally Retarded**, University of Illinois Press, Urbana

Koluchova, J. (1976). A report on the further development of twins after severe and prolonged deprivation. In Clarke, A.M. and Clarke, A.D.B. (Eds.), **Early Experience: Myth and Evidence**. Open Books, London; Free Press, New York, pp 45-66

Lazar, I. and Darlington, R. (1978). **Lasting Effects After Preschool**, DHEW Publication No. (OHDS) 79-30178, Washington, DC

Lazar, I., Hubbell, V.R., Murray, H., Rosche, M. and Royce, J. (1977). **The Persistence of Preschool Effects: A Long-term Follow-up of Fourteen Experiments**, The Consortium on Developmental Continuity. Education Commission of the States. DHEW Publication No. (OHDS) 78-30130, Washington, DC

McNemar, Q. (1940). A critical examination of the University of Iowa studies of environmental influence upon the IQ. **Psychological Bulletin, 37**, 63-92

Plomin, R. and DeFries, J.C. (1980). Genetics and intelligence: recent data. **Intelligence, 4**, 5-24

President's Committee on Mental Retardation (1972). **Entering the Era of Human Ecology**, Department of Health, Education and Welfare Publication No. (OS) 72-77, Washington, DC

President's Committee on Mental Retardation (1976). **Mental Retardation: Century of Decision**, Govt. Printing Office Stock No. 040-000-00343-6, Washington, DC

Richardson, S.A. (1981). Family characteristics associated with mild mental retardation. In Begab, M.J., Haywood, H.C. and Garber, H.L. (Eds.), **Psychosocial Influences in Retarded Performance. II**, University Park Press, Baltimore

Scarr, S. (1981). **Race, Social Class and Differences in IQ.** Lawrence Erlbaum Associates, Hillsdale, NJ

Schweinhart, L.J. and Weikart, D.P. (1980). **Young Children Grow Up: The Effects of the Perry Preschool Program on Youths Through Age 15**, High/Scope Press, Ypsilanti, MI

Schweinhart, L.J. and Weikart, D.P. (1981). Perry preschool effects nine years later: What do they mean? In Begab, M.J., Haywood, H.C. and Garber, H.L. (Eds.), **Psychosocial Influences in Retarded Performance, II**, University Park Press, Baltimore

Skeels, H.M. (1966). Adult status of children with contrasting early life histories. **Monograph of the Society for Research in Child Development, 31**(3), Serial No. 105

Skeels, H.M. and Dye, H.B. (1939). A study of the effects of differential stimulation on mentally retarded children. **Proceedings of the American Association on Mental Deficiency, 44**, 114-136

Terman, L.M. and Merrill, M.A. (1973). **Stanford-Binet Intelligence Scale: 1972 Norms Edition**, Houghton-Mifflin, Boston

Tizard, J. (1974). Longitudinal studies: problems and findings. In Clarke, A.M. and Clarke, A.D.B. (Eds.), **Mental Deficiency: the Changing Outlook**, 3rd edn., Methuen, London; Free Press, New York

Waddington, C.H. (1957). **The Strategy of Genes**, Allen and Unwin, London

Waddington, C.H. (1966). **Principles of Development and Differentiation**, Macmillan, New York

Zigler, E. and Valentine, J. (Eds.) (1979). **Project Head Start: A Legacy of the War on Poverty**, Free Press, New York

COMMENTARY

J. M. A. Hermanns

Clarke and Clarke present an overview of a number of relations that exist between mild retardation and the society in which it is found. Lucidly they discuss hereditary, psychological, interpersonal and social influences on the aetiology, the development and the prevention.

On one of the points they make, some digression seems worth while. In discussing the effects of intervention Clarke and Clarke conclude that "major and ongoing ecological improvement is likely to diminish or even prevent the handicap".

In addition to the studies they cite as support for their conclusion a number of clinical studies described by Kagan (1980) can be named: children who grow up in very stressful environments in the first two or three years of life (e.g. locked up in one room since birth) recovered after being transformed to a more benevolent environment, to the extent that one could speak of a normal development. Changing the ecology can cause dramatic changes in the course of development. By no means does this imply that hereditary factors are absent in the aetiology of mild mental retardation. We are talking here only about absolute changes, e.g. increase in IQ, that can be found when transforming the environment to a more optimal status. No doubt, the individual differences in the absolute changes will show hereditary influences.

In contrast to the dramatic reactions to a major ecological improvement, the effects of attempts to intervene in or remediate in the early development of the child who is at risk for, or actually shows, mild retardation, have been of only limited success.

A number of explanations can be thought of. They can be categorized in two groups. The first group contains reasoning about the quality of the intervention: the intervention is directed at the wrong aspects of development, is not adapted to the affective and motivational characteristics of the child, should be carried out earlier in the development, etc.

The second group of arguments is that there is not a limited number of key processes (such as language or disembedded thinking) that should be influenced to improve the academic and intellectual achievements of the individual.

Just for the sake of discussion, let us take the position of the devil's advocate and argue that development is a complex, dynamic process in which countless variables, in themselves rather meaningless, play a role. Only the cumulation and especially the interactions of all these variables constitute the organic and fertile soil on which a human being can come to a realization of its potentialities. These variables are not only those that are directly related to intellectual retardation, such as cognitive and motivational aspects of development, but have also to do with affective and social aspects.

Sroufe and co-workers (e.g. Sroufe, 1979) show how complex development is. They demonstrate a relation between the quality of attachment in the second year of life and cognitive development - the pre-school years. Socio-emotional factors are related to cognitive development. In addition their studies make clear that these kinds of relations are not mono-causal, but embedded in a transactional process in which child and environment both have their contribution.

If this point of view is correct, a rather pessimistic attitude to the limits of intervention seems defendable. To prevent mild retardation more is needed than a social technology that tries to defeat the adverse life circumstances of the child by a few well aimed shots. Whatever is needed in this respect can be left to the imagination of the reader. In each case one can state that in a time of economic recession a fundamental improvement will be hard to accomplish. There is, however, also a positive side. There are continuously spontaneous changes in the ecology of the individual in the course of the life-span. New opportunities are met. After school age, demands are made to a different area of the personality. Adequate social adjustments are no longer dependent on academic, intellectual achievements. Being a nice person with a number of manual skills is a good start for a lot of jobs. In this respect mild retardation is then not only camouflaged as Clarke and Clarke express it, but may even become non-existent.

References

Kagan, J. (1980). Four questions in psychological development, **International Journal of Behavioural Development, 3,** 231-241

Sroufe, L. (1979). The coherence of individual development, **American Psychologist, 34,** 834-841

P. Meazzini

Although I do agree with the overall conclusions of their paper, there are some issues which are worth discussing.

1. A propos of cumulative deficit

The evidence is that there is an approximately linear IQ decrement in children from socially disadvantaged families as a function of their chronological age. The interpretation is that this IQ decrement may be the result of verbal and reading disabilities. The interpretation is very plausible, although limited to some extent. As a matter of fact, data have been found showing that there is a cause and effect connection between test failure (owing to social and cultural disadvantage) and test anxiety (Meazzini, in press). In other words, failing a test results in bringing about anxiety and failure expectations. In situations such as this, children may have learned to avoid the test or to disengage from it as soon as the first difficult items are faced. This means that difficult items are cues that anticipate failure, hence accounting at least for part of the IQ decrement mentioned by Clarke and Clarke.

2. Has compensatory education really failed?

I have received the impression that Clarke and Clarke agree with Jensen's conclusion, according to which compensatory education has been more or less a failure.

Becker and Carnine (1980) seem to hold quite a different opinion. They summarized the major findings from a national evaluation (USA) of Project Follow Through, in which the outcomes brought about by different educational approaches were compared. The results showed:

(a) a marked superiority of behaviourally oriented instructional projects over the others;
(b) an undeniable efficacy of compensatory education, provided it is properly planned and implemented.

In spite of these positive results, however, I agree with Clarke and Clarke that a deep ecological change is to be effected in the families of socially disadvantaged children if these results are to be maintained.

References

Becker, W.C. and Carnine, D. (1980). Direct instruction: an effective approach to educational intervention with the disadvantaged and low performers. In Lahey, B.B. and Kazdin, A.E., **Advances in Clinical Psychology, 3**, Plenum Press, New York

Meazzini, P. (in press). Test anxiety: a survey

D. Morris

The social influences and their role in causation and prevention are well demonstrated and can obviously no longer be ignored by responsible authorities such as Health and Social Services.

The challenge of their basic argument is the conflict between the use of IQ to categorize the mentally retarded and their categorization by social behaviour. The IQ as such does not correlate with social behaviour and has a bearing on identification, prevalence and provision of facilities. How significant and of what practical relevance is the IQ of those with identical IQs who can function at widely different social levels? What is relevant is that the prevalence of mild retardation as identified by IQ is 28 times more prevalent in class V than in class I to IIIA.

It is salutary that the Clarkes point out some possible deficiencies in the reliability of IQ tests and the possible influence of social progress which could account for the lower prevalence of child mental retardation.

As for the heritability factor it is important that "inhumane environments may profoundly depress intellectual development" constitutes yet another challenge to our responsibilities.

The evidence for the "cumulative deficit" is controversial and they cite Heber's observations that maternal IQ is more important than socio-economic status.

Perhaps the most significant part of this paper is the role of intervention and the "grande illusion" of Head Start and its extension to mild mental retardation.

Future research workers will need to look at the "transactional processes continuing within the family", family attributes and attitudes since material and educational environmental factors do not obliterate occupational class gradients in IQ and achievement.

The final challenge is how the authors see changes being brought about realistically for the prevention and amelioration of the mildly mentally retarded.

S. A. Richardson

The concept of cumulative deficit is based on studies of IQ of children. On conceptual grounds an additional concept may be postulated in the opposite direction. From the viewpoint of socialization theory, a child who is brought up in a family where social environmental influences are disadvantageous for social and intellectual development will be maximally influenced in the early years when the family environmental influence is most encompassing. The process of socialization with increased age is a broadening of the social environment, e.g. the school, neighbourhood, and a wider range of adults and peers than the family. The transition from childhood to adult for most young people is a period of increased emancipation and independence from the parental home. Unless the young person is brought up in ghetto-like conditions where his entire socialization continues to be experiences which are highly disadvantageous for cognitive development, the young person has a good likelihood of experiencing some more advantageous conditions for cognitive development which may mitigate or counteract the early environment. If an unfavourable early social environment is the primary cause of MMR, the widening environmental influences are likely to enable the young person to make advances in intellectual development. In some cases where the later environment is favourable, the later experiences may raise the level of intellectual functioning substantially. There is anecdotal evidence from developmental histories of young adults in our Aberdeen study (in Clarke and Clarke, 1976). The Clarkes also give case studies in support of the postulate.

Reference

Clarke, A.M. and Clarke, A.D.B. (Eds.) (1976). **Early Experience: Myth and Evidence**, Open Books, London; Free Press, New York

W. Yule

Comments on IQ tests

It has become widespread, if not fashionable, for both psychologists and others to question the value of IQ tests both in diagnosis and description. This, perhaps, reached its zenith (or nadir, depending on your viewpoint) in the attempts by AAMD to dispense with the use of IQ tests altogether. It is clear from publications over recent years that this attempt was not successful. We have to ask ourselves why - and there is one simple answer - critics have yet to find a more useful index of functioning.

Psychologists are rightly aware of the limitations in the construction and use of IQ tests. Different tests such as Raven's Matrices and WISC measure different cognitive functions and do not therefore relate highly to each other. In part, this explains the poor predictive validity of "baby" tests which largely measure sensori-motor development with later childhood tests, especially those like the Binet which largely measure verbal functioning. Formal operations can never by predicted very well from pre-school tests, nor will they be. In contrast, when similar tests are used - as in the Yule et al. (1982) eleven year follow up of normal children from five and a half to six and a half years - very high correlations are obtained. In that instance, r = +0.86, testifying to considerable stability in the measures. However, it must be noted that this still leaves

24% of the variance unaccounted for and some children's measured IQ change radically over that time period.

A further important point is that whereas psychologists are cautious about interpreting one IQ score for an individual child and will draw attention to the range in which the "true IQ" will lie, studies of groups of children, as in the literature on the correlates of lead, may well produce evidence of small differences between the means, and these differences between groups are both meaningful and socially important. A difference of, say, 5 points in an individual child's IQ estimate at two points in time is well within the measurement of the tests. A difference of 5 points between the means of two groups of children implies that in one group compared with another there is an increase of twice the number of children with IQs below 70. Such a difference has important social policy implications.

An understanding of the classical theory of test measurement makes one aware of the errors inherent in all measurement. For example, the test-retest correlation of blood lead estimates approximates to +0.6 (or 36% of the variance in common) when the bloods are carefully obtained and analysed. A recent WHO-sponsored inter-laboratory calibration study demonstrated that experienced laboratories took two years to develop adequate comparability. Compared to that, IQ test results are highly reliable and stable.

Reference

Yule, W., Gold, R.D. and Busch, C. (1982). Long-term predictive validity of the WPSSI: an 11-year follow-up study. **Personality and Individual Differences, 3,** 65-71

Chapter 3

Aspects of prevention of pre-, peri- and postnatal brain pathology in severe and mild mental retardation An analysis from recent Swedish epidemiology research

B. Hagberg and Gudrun Hagberg

The Swedish Medical Research Council constituted in the middle of the 1970s a planning group to structure scientific studies on mental retardation (MR). It was thought that if the causes, mechanisms and distributions of MR could be better delineated, it might be possible to devise and apply preventive measures. Population-based investigations on aetiologies and their distribution were thus initiated, initially studying severe MR (SMR; IQ < 50), then proceeding to milder forms (MMR; IQ 50-70).

EPIDEMIOLOGIC STUDIES

Five recent epidemiologic studies covering various areas of Sweden have been tabulated in Table 1. The Uppsala series (Gustavson *et al.*, 1977a, b) concern SMR children born 1959-70 in a central Swedish county (population 210 000); the two Vasterbotten series (Gustavson *et al.*, 1977c; Blomquist *et al.*, 1981) SMR and MMR children born the same years but in a vast northern county (population 240 000); the Gothenburg series (Hagberg *et al.*, 1981a, b) SMR and MMR children born 1966-70 and living in a Swedish harbour town (population 450 000) (Figure 1). Very similar definitions, criteria and research methods were used in these studies. The Kopparberg series (Gostason, 1982) represents an adult population in a middle-western Swedish county (population 320 000) and is somewhat differently designed.

Clinical diagnosis and pathogenic grouping was mainly based on standard clinical examinations and routine laboratory tests. Refined techniques have since been applied particularly in the Vasterbotten studies (Blomquist *et al.*, 1982), but these data are not yet complete.

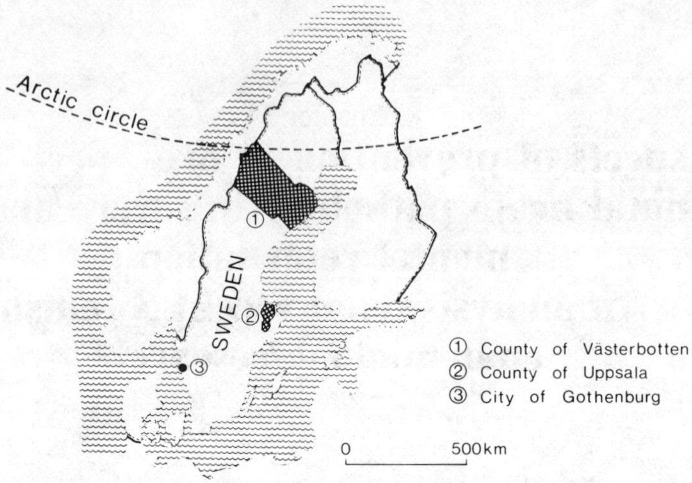

Figure 1 Various areas covered by the studies

Table 1

Recent Swedish epidemiology research. Prevalence per 1000 of severe (SMR) and mild (MMR) mental retardation in five population-based series

	Prev. Year	Ages	SMR	MMR
Gustavson *et al*. (Uppsala county, 1977a, b)	1975	11-16	2.8	--
Gustavson *et al*. (Vasterbotten county, 1977c)	1976	5-16	3.5	--
Hagberg *et al*. (Gothenburg, 1981a, b)	1978	8-12	3.0	3.7
Blomquist *et al*. (Vasterbotten county, 1981)	1979	8-19	--	3.8
Gostason (Kopparberg county, 1982)	1977	20-60	3.8	5.1

The prevalences (Table 1) of SMR were around 3 per thousand - that is the expected rate - while figures for MMR were surprisingly low - only 4-5 per thousand contrasting with the expected 23. The rates were, however, considered to be true and reflected a low proportion of polygenic subnormality within the investigated IQ range (IQ 50-70), when compared to many other countries.

The importance of pre-, peri- and postnatal pathology behind MR in Sweden is emphasized by the high proportion of additional neurological handicaps both in SMR and MMR children (Table 2). It was confirmed by the pathogenic/aetiologic groups from the Gothenburg series in Table 3, 81% of the SMR cases and 43% of the MMR cases having either a definite or a highly probable biologic cause for their MR. The main causes/risk factors will be commented on.

Table 2

Frequency and distribution of other handicaps associated with severe (SMR) and mild (MMR) mental retardation. Figures in per cent from the Gothenburg (1981) and the Vasterbotten (1977, 1981) studies

	SMR Gothenburg 1981	SMR AC-County 1977	MMR Gothenburg 1981	MMR AC-County 1981
Cerebral palsy	21	19	9	7
Epilepsy	37	36	12	18
Hydrocephalus	5	?	2	?
Severe impairment of hearing	8	6	7	2
Severe impairment of vision	15	10	1	9
One or more associated neurological handicap	40	52	24	30
Clumsy child syndrome	?	?	23	?
Psychiatric abnormalities	?	?	31	?

Table 3

Origin of mental retardation found in the Gothenburg series (Hagberg *et al*., 1981a, b). Figures are given in per cent

		SMR *n* =73		MMR *n* =91
Prenatal		55		23
A. Genetic				
Chromosomal	29		4	
Mutant genes	5		1	
B. Unknown				
Syndromes (specific)	0		2	
MCA/MR[a] (unspecific)	12		8	
C. Acquired				
Alcohol	0		8	
Infection	7		0	
Other	1		0	
Perinatal		15		18
A. FDS[b]/asphyxia/ hypoxia	12		17	
B. Infection, central nervous system	3		1	
Postnatal		11		2
Psychosis		1		2
Untraceable		18		55
A. Familial	4		29	
B. Non-familial	14		26	

a) MCA/MR: multiple congenital anomalies with mental retardation
b) FDS: fetal deprivation of supply (Hagberg *et al* ., 1976)

SPECIFIC CAUSES AND THEIR PREVENTION

Chromosomal Errors

With routine techniques (banding was not always performed), chromosomal aberrations were detected in 29% of SMR children and in 4% of MMR children. If all the refined techniques available today had been applied the figures would certainly have been considerably higher.

Down's syndrome was the largest single cause of SMR: 32%, 33% and 27% in the Uppsala, Vasterbotten and Gothenburg series respectively. Two per cent of MMR children in the Gothenburg study had Down's syndrome.

Fragile-X, an X-linked recessive error, has lately been revealed as an important cause of MR in boys. The Umea group has shown that "Fragile-X" accounts for 10% of MMR and 6% of SMR in boys (Blomquist *et al.*, 1981, 1982). Preliminary data indicate its occurrence in a small proportion of MMR girls (Blomquist, personal communication). This is in accordance with recent data from the USA (Webb *et al.*, 1982).

Minor deletions and other structural chromosomal abnormalities could - supported by literature reports (Coco and Penchaszadeh, 1976; Gripenberg *et al.*, 1980) and qualified guesses from repeated anecdotal experiences - be considered responsible for an additional proportion of both SMR and MMR of unknown so-called Multiple Congenital Anomalies/Mental Retardation (MCA/MR) type (Kaveggia *et al.*, 1973; Opitz, 1979). Altogether, chromosomal errors with present knowledge might be suspected of causing at least 40% of SMR and about 10% of MMR in Sweden.

Prevention can be approached in various ways. (1) All MR cases with prenatal stigmata, MCA/MR syndromes, should be regarded as potential index cases for further family investigations. When errors are found, prenatal examination can then be offered for prevention in further pregnancies. (2) Any finding of familial MR, especially in the absence of dysmorphologic features, should lead to the suspicion of a "Fragile-X syndrome". (3) Screening with amniocentesis of selected groups of pregnant women, particularly older ones, should be offered. (4) Recently, evidence for an additional influence of paternal age has been presented. Men 55 years or older may have a significantly increased risk that their newborn children will have trisomy-21 (Stene *et al.*, 1977) and this might therefore be an indication for prenatal examination. (5) Research should be directed to solve the causes of non-disjunction in trisomy-21 and to elaborate less invasive and more easily applied cytogenetic screening methods for diagnosing Down's syndrome. (6) Screening for this condition, ideally through simple blood testing of all pregnant mothers before the end of the first trimester, would be an important prevention measure. Isolation and analysis of fetal cells from the maternal circulation might be possible. Several technical and ethical problems here remain to be solved, however.

Fetal Alcohol Syndrome (FAS)

Most children of alcoholic mothers display some form of central nervous system injury, and the risk that these mothers will give birth to children with the FAS is estimated to be 20-50%. The complete FAS was found in Gothenburg in 1:600 liveborn (Olegard et al., 1979). They constituted 8% of MMR children (Hagberg et al., 1981b). The prevalence of incomplete FAS is less certain but it was concluded that at least 10% of Swedish MMR city children have the FAS, complete or incomplete. On the county level the prevalence so far has been found to be considerably lower (Blomquist et al., 1981).

The pattern for alcohol abuse has shown an alarming tendency to spread to ever younger ages and now to be as common among girls as boys. In city schools (year 1975) 7% of the girls and 12% of the boys at age 16 (ninth grade) were high consumers, i.e. drank more than 10 litres of 100% alcohol per year (cf Olegard et al., 1979).

For prevention society has tried particularly to change the attitudes and habits of the younger generation. Active anti-alcohol drives have been initiated by the school health, the child health and the maternal health authorities. The establishment of special maternal health teams to trace and actively support women at risk already very early in pregnancy - or before - has shown to be a promising approach (Rydberg et al., 1981; Larsson, 1983).

Inborn Errors of Metabolism

The proportion is modest (SMR 4-5%, MMR < 1%). The number of relevant neurometabolic disorders is, however, confusingly large. The panorama of diseases may vary substantially between the Scandinavian countries and even between different regions of Sweden. Local accumulation to certain geographic areas is characteristic for the "Swedish diseases": Norrbottnian (type III) Gaucher's disease (Dreborg et al., 1980), Sjogren-Larsson's ichthyosis-spastic diplegia-oligophrenia (Jagell et al., 1981), late infantile metachromatic leukodystrophy (Gustavsson and Hagberg, 1971) and a non-Jewish form of GM2-gangliosidosis (Hagberg and Svennerholm, 1982). An even distribution over the country is found for Krabbe's disease - globoid cell leukodystrophy (Hagberg et al., 1969), PKU (Larsson, 1979), the mucopolysaccharidoses, and probably also homocystinuria, glutaric aciduria and methyl-malonic aciduria.

A recent analysis of the Swedish neonatal metabolism screening programme for the period 1965-79 showed that screening for PKU, galactosaemia and congenital hypothyroidism is preventive and indeed justifiable (Alm and Larsson, 1981). Screening for histidinaemia, homocystinuria and tyrosinaemia was, however, shown not to be worth while, either from medical or from cost-benefit aspects. It is reasonable to expect that in the future more conditions will prove suitable for neonatal screening. Before such procedures are introduced as routines in a country, it is essential to know the incidence, the natural course and the possibility of treatment of the disease in question.

Accurate prenatal diagnosis of the deficient enzyme in inherited biochemical defects is now possible for about 80 different diseases. Such a diagnosis - followed by preventive abortion of affected fetuses - has in our country been invaluable for the individual family. Such programmes cannot, however, be expected to influence the general incidence of MR more than marginally until screening for heterozygotes is practised among selected populations in whom such recessive disorders occur with sufficiently high frequency. Nevertheless, a careful diagnostic work-up of the index case is always essential as the background for advice on future family planning, i.e. prevention for the individual family.

Biochemically derived conditions associated with MR are in general in a better position than others as regards availability to some sort of preventive therapy. The dietary treatment of PKU cases from early infancy to the middle of school age and the very early institution of hormones to hypothyroid babies are classic examples. There are, however, other possible methods. Early diagnosed cases of certain lysosomal diseases should be considered for possible enzyme substitution through bone marrow transplantation from a matching sibling. Advances from research on the usefulness of amnion transplants in such diseases are eagerly awaited.

Intrauterine Infections

Our data on the magnitude of this group of causes of MR are unfortunately fragmentary. The so-called ToRCH group (toxoplasma, rubella, cytomegalovirus, herpes) of infections are the most pertinent from the point of view of prevention. Congenital cytomegalovirus (CMV) infections hold a quantitatively leading position and have been suggested to be responsible for about 10% of SMR populations (for references, see Gustavson _et al._, 1977b). Corresponding figures for MMR are lacking. Recent investigations by Ahlfors (1982) indicate a proportionally low frequency of MR but a larger one of hearing deficits as sequelae in Sweden.

Congenital rubella infections are successively decreasing. General vaccination of schoolgirls (age 12 - grade 6) was introduced in 1975. After 20 years - with 90% vaccinated and 1% loss of immunity/year - this programme was calculated to reduce rubella embryopathies by two-thirds but not, however, eradicating them. Recently, therefore, a more effective programme was started comprising both sexes and with a combined vaccine (measles-mumps-rubella), a first shot at 18 months and a second one at 12 years of age (Jonsell _et al._, 1981). That would be expected to eradicate rubella embryopathies in Swedish society within ten years. A successful introduction with 91.2% covering has been achieved in Gothenburg (Taranger et al., 1982).

Congenital cytomegalovirus infections (CMV). Some 60 Swedish infants yearly (among around 100 000 newborn/year) could be expected to develop more or less severe neurologic sequelae (Ahlfors, 1982). As yet routine serological CMV screening would be premature. Vaccination is considered questionable in effect. Among other things, it cannot be expected to prevent secondary infections. Furthermore, we cannot be sure that available vaccines do not have certain negative, particularly oncogenic, properties and may also give latent maternal infections (Ahlfors, 1982).

Dr Baert, Commission of the European Communities, Brussels, pleaded for a less negative formulation: "It might be that with advances in genetic engineering more pure vaccines could be developed to avoid the disadvantages and give a better chance for preventive programs".

Congenital toxoplasmosis is hardly easier to prevent today than is CMV. The size of the problem in terms of number of affected children is, however, probably less.

Perinatal Brain Damage

The importance of perinatal causes to MR has often been overemphasized and preventive aspects have been a subject of lively debate, particularly among neonatologists (Roberton, 1978). From the Gothenburg series it was concluded that perinatal risk factors, even when defined in a broad sense (from 28 weeks gestational age until 4 weeks postpartal age) had been causative in 15% of SMR and 18% of MMR. A restriction of the perinatal concept to include just the delivery and the first postpartal week gave a corresponding figure of 10% for SMR as well as for MMR. In uncomplicated low-birthweight/appropriate-gestational-age (LBW/AGA) babies the risk for mental retardation today seems to be gratifyingly low with modern Swedish neonatal care. MR of perinatal origin is in the majority associated with cerebral palsy (CP). The incidence of CP has not decreased through the 1970s in spite of ongoing reduced perinatal mortality. Further advances in the intensive care of neonates probably cannot be expected to decrease the prevalence of mental retardation in Sweden more than marginally. This does not, however, exclude preventive expectations. Gains can be counted in an increasing number of surviving non-damaged babies, especially among our LBW/AGA population (Hagberg et al., 1982).

Postnatal Causes

Postnatal causes in terms of CNS infections or skull traumata were, in the Gothenburg series, found in two of 91 MMR and eight of 73 SMR children. The postnatal proportion of 11% in the SMR group in Gothenburg is four times larger than in the Uppsala and Vasterbotten county series with their combination of an average urban and rural population. As might be expected, accidents, suspected battered baby syndrome (subdural haematomata) and severe infections tend to be relatively more frequent in city populations. Preventive efforts should be approached accordingly.

Polygenic Mental Retardation - Interacting Brain Pathology

Polygenic MR has little relevance for SMR. Among MMR children, indications of familial subnormality in first degree relatives were present in 29%. It was estimated that about one-third of the Swedish MMR cases could be accounted for by polygenic constitutional factors. Furthermore, it was assumed, and also supported by clinical evidence, that minor pre- or

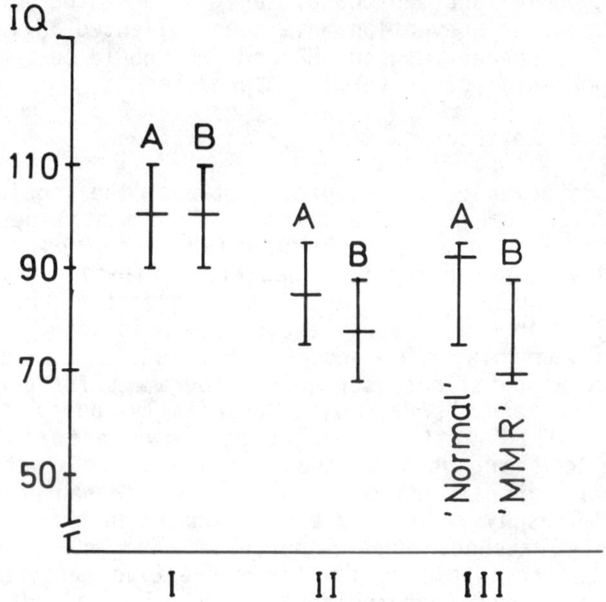

Figure 2 Hypothetical example of difference in outcome from interactions of genetic, biologic and socio-cultural influences

- I Genetic IQ potential.
- II Constitutional IQ potential after negative pre/perinatal influences.
- III Actual IQ secondary to positive (A) and negative (B) socio-cultural influences.
- A Child with average genetic IQ potential, negative effects of minor pre/perinatal brain damage factors but compensation by an optimal socio-cultural environment.
- B Child with corresponding IQ potential, moderate pre/perinatal brain damage, and further deprived by understimulation in a poor social environment.

perinatal prejudicial events could decrease the potential of an individual's intellectual capacity. It would then follow that moderate brain damage in genetically less well endowed individuals would be associated with an IQ in the range of 50-70; on the other hand, a slight decrease in intellectual capacity would never be noticed in those primarily more gifted and with a far greater margin from MMR. The probable effects of interactions between genetic potential, biologic brain pathology, socio-economic circumstances and developmental stimulation have been illustrated in two hypothetical cases in Figure 2.

GENERAL OUTLINES FOR PREVENTION

From indications of recent Swedish data, the main MR groups of pre-, peri- and postnatal origin and the corresponding aids/measures for prevention have been collected in Table 4. Some biologic differences between SMR and MMR should be remembered and are of importance for preventive approaches.

Severe Mental Retardation

SMR is evenly distributed between the social classes. Changes in its prevalence will not affect mental performance of the general population. Preventive projects have to be individually designed for the specific origin of SMR. In this IQ category the greatest potential for prevention lies within the cytogenetic, inborn error, exogenous-toxic and intrauterine-infectious aetiological groups. Vaccination programmes for rubella and neonatal mass screening programmes for certain inborn errors have already borne fruit. Perinatally caused SMR is nearly always combined with CP and preventive efforts should be connected to the causes of that condition. Interactions of the risk factors "fetal growth retardation", intrauterine asphyxia and neonatal asphyxia in term babies should in this connection be particularly watched. SMR of postnatal origin, a small group, ought to be accessible to further preventive measures. The role of accidental and non-accidental injuries of city children deserve particular attention.

Mild Mental Retardation

The situation for prevention of MMR is somewhat different to that for SMR. Corresponding specific biologic brain pathology is represented to a minor extent only. More non-specific pre- and perinatal prejudicial factors might play a more important role than previously imagined. It is reasonable to believe that biologic mechanisms for brain damage are of all grades of severity and operate throughout the whole scale of the genetic IQ potential. Each decrease in their severity or frequency will therefore cause a shift towards better mental performance in the general population. Non-biologic factors are also contributing to the same shift. Terman and Merrill (1973) have shown an

Table 4

Pathology behind mental retardation, estimated proportions and suggested preventive efforts

Origin	Preventive aids/measures
Prenatal (-28 weeks gestation)	
A. Genetic	Index case diagnosis
chromosomal errors	Prenatal diagnosis
(SMR~40%; MMR~10%)	Prenatal cytogenetic screening
biochemical inborn errors	Neonatal screening
(SMR 3-5%; MMR < 1%)	Substitution therapy
	Dietary elimination
	Index case diagnosis } affected family
	Prenatal diagnosis } affected family
B. Unknown "syndrome" (SMR~10%; MMR~10%)	(Research)
C. Exogenous - toxic	
alcohol fetopathy	Education - school programme
(SMR~1%; MMR 8-10%)	Preconceptional information
drug/chemical fetopathies	Tracing programs
(SMR <1%; MMR <1%)	Supporting programs
	Pregnancy supervision
D. Intrauterine infections	Vaccination programmes
ToRCH group	Counselling
(SMR 5%; MMR~1%)	
E. Maternal abnormalities	Pregnancy supervision
placental dysfunction	
(SMR ?%; MMR ?%)	
Perinatal (28 weeks gestation - 1 month of age)	
brain damage	Preterm birth prevention
(SMR~15%; MMR~15%)	Fetal growth supervision
	Optimal delivery for actual state
	Optimal neonatal care
Postnatal (1 month of age +)	
(SMR~10%; MMR~2%)	Child health supervision
	Child abuse prevention
	Child accident prevention

increasing mental performance over a time period especially in pre-schoolers, and attribute this increase to the impact of cultural changes and increased parental literacy and education. Thompson (1977) has shown that this improvement is found throughout the whole IQ range with the exception of the lowest levels (IQ < 50). MMR is known to be strongly associated with low social class. Our very low Swedish prevalence figures for MMR (0.4%) could partly be due to the fact that the Terman-Merrill and WISC tests used were standardized for Sweden 40 and 10 years ago, respectively. A true low prevalence is likely to remain. This is probably explained by a combination of factors which include good maternal preconceptional health, family planning, pregnancy supervision, well organized obstetric and neonatal care throughout the country, early stimulation programmes and a general high socio-economic level. All these factors together are likely to interact to contribute to the above mentioned shift and thereby to a decreasing prevalence of MMR (measured on unchanged norms). The most effective preventive factors are thought to be non-specific co-working programmes for good family health, and social and economic progress.

REFERENCES

Ahlfors, K. (1982). **Epidemiologic Studies of Congenital Cytomegalovirus Infection.** Thesis, Malmo

Alm, J. and Larsson, A. (1981). Evaluation of a nation-wide neonatal metabolic screening program in Sweden 1965-1979. **Acta Paediatrica Scandinavica, 70,** 601-607

Blomquist, H. K:son (1982). **Mental Retardation in Children. An epidemiolgical and etiological study of mentally retarded children born in 1959-1980 in a northern Swedish county.** Thesis, Umea

Blomquist, H. K:son, Gustavson, K.-H. and Holmgren, G. (1981). Mild mental retardation in children in a northern Swedish County. **Journal of Mental Deficiency Research, 25,** 169-186

Blomquist, H. K:son, Gustavson, K.-H., Holmgren, G., Nordenson, I. and Sweins, A. (1982). Fragile site X chromosomes and X-linked mental retardation in severely retarded boys in a northern Swedish county. A prevalence study. **Clinical Genetics, 21,** 209-214

Coco, R. and Penchaszadeh, V.B. (1976). Frequency of chromosomal aberrations in 131 patients with multiple congenital malformations and mental retardation, **Journal of Pediatrics, 80,** 325-335

Dreborg, S., Erikson, A. and Hagberg, B. (1980). Gaucher disease-Norrbottnian Type. I. General clinical description. **European Journal of Pediatrics, 133,** 107-118

Gostason, R. (1982). Mental retardation and its psychiatric complications. Preliminary report of an epidemiological study in an adult population in Sweden. Paper presented at the **Int. Congr. Scientific Study of of Mental Deficiency,** Toronto, Aug. 25

Gripenberg, U., Hongell, K., Knuutila, S., Kahkonen M. and Leisti, J. (1980). A chromosome survey of 1062 mentally retarded patients. Evaluation of a long-term study at the Rinnekoti Institution, Finland. **Hereditas, 92,** 223-228

Gustavson, K.-H. and Hagberg, B. (1971). The incidence and genetics of metachromatic leucodystrophy in northern Sweden. **Acta Paediatrica Scandinavica, 60,** 585-590

Gustavson, K.-H., Hagberg, B., Hagberg, G. and Sars, K. (1977a). Severe mental retardation in a Swedish county. I. Epidemiology, gestational age, birth weight and associated CNS handicap in children born 1959-70. **Acta Paediatrica Scandinavica, 66,** 373-379

Gustavson, K.-H., Hagberg, B., Hagberg, G. and Sars, K. (1977b). Severe mental retardation in Swedish school children. II. Etiologic and pathogenetic aspects. **Neuropadiatrie, 8,** 293-304

Gustavson, K.-H., Holmgren, G., Jonsell, R. and Blomquist, H. K:son (1977c). Severe mental retardation in children in a northern Swedish county. **Journal of Mental Deficiency Research, 21,** 161-181

Hagberg, B., Hagberg, G., Lewerth, A. and Lindberg, U. (1981a). Mild mental retardation in Swedish school children. I. Prevalence. **Acta Paediatrica Scandinavica, 70,** 441-444

Hagberg, B., Hagberg, G., Lewerth, A. and Lindberg, U. (1981b). Mild mental retardation in Swedish school children. II. Etiologic and pathogenetic aspects. **Acta Paediatrica Scandinavica, 70,** 445-452

Hagberg, G., Hagberg, B. and Olow, I. (1976). The changing panorama of cerebral palsy in Sweden 1954-1970. III. The importance of foetal deprivation of supply. **Acta Paediatrica Scandinavica, 65,** 403-408

Hagberg, B., Hagberg, G. and Olow, I. (1982). Gains and hazards of intensive neonatal care: an analysis from Swedish cerebral palsy epidemiology. **Developmental Medicine and Child Neurology, 24,** 13-19

Hagberg, B., Kollberg, H., Sourander, P. and Akesson, H.O. (1969). Infantile globoid cell leucodystrophy (Krabbe's disease). **Neuropadiatrie, 1,** 74-88

Hagberg, B. and Svennerholm, L. (1982) Swedish forms of G_{M1} and G_{M2} gangliosidoses. Unpublished data

Jagell, S., Gustavson, K.H. and Holmgren, G. (1981). Sjogren-Larsson syndrome in Sweden. A clinical, genetic and epidemiological study. **Clinical Genetics, 19,** 233-256

Jonsell, R., Broberger, O., Brzokoupil, K., Noren, C.E. and Rabo, E. (1981). Vaccination against measles, mumps and rubella. **Lakartidningen (Sw), 78,** 767-769

Kaveggia, E.G., Durkin, M.V., Pendleton, E. and Opitz, J.M. (1973). Diagnostic/genetic studies on 1224 patients with severe mental retardation. **Proceedings of the Third Congress of the International Association for the Scientific**

Study of Mental Deficiency, The Hague, The Netherlands, 4-12 September

Larsson, A. (1979). Screening of newborn infants in Sweden for congenital metabolic diseases. **Skandia International Symposium on Congenital Diseases in Childhood. Medical and Socio-Medical Aspects**, Stockholm, October 2-4

Larsson, G. (1983). Prevention of fetal alcohol effects - an antenatal program for early detection for pregnancies at risk. **Acta Obstetrica et Gynecologica Scandinavica**, (in press)

Olegard, R., Sabel, K.G., Aronson, M., Sandin, B., Johansson, P.R., Carlsson, C., Kyllerman, M., Iversen, K. and Hrbek, A. (1979). Effects on the child of alcohol abuse during pregnancy. Retrospective and prospective studies. **Acta Paediatrica Scandinavica**, suppl. **275**, 112-121

Opitz, J.M. (1979). Diagnostic/genetic studies in severe mental retardation. In **Genetic Counselling**, Eds H.A. Lubs and F. de la Cruz. New York: Raven Press

Roberton, N.R.C. (1978). Discussion. In: **Major Mental Handicap: Methods and Costs of Prevention**. Ciba Foundation Symposium **59**, Amsterdam: Elsevier/Excerpta Medica, pp 42-43

Ryberg, U., Larsson, G., Ottenblad, Ch., Rane, A. and Tunell, R. (1981). Early detection of alcohol and drug abuse in pregnancy. **Biological Psychiatry**. Proceedings of the IIIrd Congress of Biological Psychiatry, Stockholm, 1981, Elsevier/North-Holland Biomedical Press

Stene, J., Fischer, G., Stene, E., Mikkelsen, M. and Petersen, E. (1977). Paternal age effect in Down's syndrome. **Annals of Human Genetics, 40**, 299-308

Taranger, J., Sedvall, A., Kyllerman, M. and Garton, M. (1982). Experiences of combined vaccinations against measles, mumps and rubella in the 6th grade of school. **Lakartidningen (Sw), 79**, 3430-3431

Terman, L.M. and Merrill, M.A. (1973). **Stanford-Binet Intelligence Scale: 1972 Norms Edition**, p. 359. Boston, Houghton-Mifflin

Thompson, R.J. (1977). Consequences of using the 1972 Stanford-Binet Intelligence Scale norms. **Psychology in the Schools, 14**, 444-448

Webb, G.C., Halliday, J.L., Pitt, D.B., Judge, C.G. and Leversha, M. (1982). Fragile (X) (q27) sites in a pedigree with female carriers showing mild to severe mental retardation. **Journal of Medical Genetics, 19**, 44-48

COMMENTARY

E. A. Alberman

First amongst many interesting points raised by this paper was the statement that the Swedish Medical Research Council initiated a planning group to "structure scientific studies on mental retardation". In this, as in many other fields of research on rare conditions, we are beginning to see the benefits of collaborative research with common protocols and definitions, and such initiatives from national or indeed international research councils should be warmly encouraged.

It would therefore be of interest to other workers planning collaborative surveys of mental retardation to learn exactly how the cases described in this paper were ascertained, whether by population screening, or by their use of appropriate services - "administrative" prevalence. It has been demonstrated frequently particularly in regard to MMR that the latter varies with the facilities available and with age. However the Gostason study of adults of 20-60 revealed unexpectedly high rates, when from previous reports one would have expected to find them lower than in school-age children.

The most striking finding in this paper is the very low rate of MMR, and the authors discuss possible reasons for this. As they point out where rates are this low one does expect to find an unduly high proportion associated with evidence of pathological impairment, compared to the situation where a high rate of MMR is found, usually in very deprived populations. The important part played by the fetal alcohol syndrome in these studies is notable, but from these data one cannot say whether this is accounted for by the admittedly high rate of alcoholism in Sweden, or the proportionately low rate of other environmental causes.

What is becoming increasingly clear is that with advances in laboratory investigations, particularly of SMR, the proportion with unknown cause is falling all the time. Therefore, in theory at least, the possibility of preventive action should be increased, but so is the proportion which is known to be genetically determined. The recent identification of the "Fragile-X" syndrome has contributed substantially to our knowledge of the causes of MR and I would have been glad to have seen more discussion about the possibility of its prenatal diagnosis. As far as Down's syndrome is concerned it is worth stressing that the limitation of diagnostic amniocentesis for Down's syndrome to mothers or fathers designated by reason of high maternal age means that only a minority of cases can be identified. In most Western populations about half of children with Down's syndrome are born to mothers under 35, and only about one-eighth to mothers of 40 or more. The authors are to be supported in calling for more research into the possibility of detecting fetal cells in maternal blood, or other means of population screening for this condition.

Finally the authors show that in Sweden as in other countries, accidental and non-accidental injuries still play a not insignificant role in the causation of MR. In a situation of limited funds perhaps one would do well to remember to direct resources towards the prevention of such causes as well as into research into some of the excessively rare metabolic diseases mentioned in this paper.

R. O. Robinson

This account of epidemiology of mental handicap in Sweden is extremely valuable. There are two points I would like to pick up.

(1) Disorders of spinal dysraphism which generally contributes substantially to mental handicap are not specifically mentioned. I wondered under which group they would have been included and to what degree they contribute to the total. Clearly this is worth discussion even if the prevalence in Sweden is low because of the preventive aspects. It is probable from Smithells work (Smithells et al., 1981) that a component or components of a multi-vitamin preparation can, if taken before, during and after conception, reduce the risk of bearing a child with spina bifida in a woman already at high risk (having had one or more previous children with spina bifida). Careful surveillance of all pregnancies with serum alpha fetoprotein screening, confirmatory amniocentesis with high-quality real-time ultrasound can, with a high degree of accuracy, detect an affected fetus sufficiently early for a pregnancy to be terminated if the parents so wish.

(2) The assumption behind the statements "the incidence of cerebral palsy has not decreased in the 1970s in spite of ongoing reduced perinatal mortality" and "further advances in the intensive care of neonates probably cannot be expected to decrease the prevalence of mental retardation in Sweden more than marginally" can be challenged. There is little doubt that introduction of neonatal intensive care causes a fall in perinatal mortality rates particularly among the low birthweight group (less than 2500 g). Clearly this may and probably does influence the rate of handicap in graduates from neonatal intensive care units in two ways. It may procure the survival of handicapped children who would otherwise have died (raising the handicap rate) or it may prevent or treat effectively potentially brain-damaging events (lowering the handicap rate). Increasing deployment of resources to neonatal intensive care units is not only followed by improving the care of those who would have anyway survived. It is also followed by a fall in mortality

among very low birthweight babies who are most exposed to prejudicial episodes such as intraventricular haemorrhage. That this exercise has been achieved without a convincing rise in the handicap rate is a testimonial to the expertise of the perinatal staff. Small wonder that trends in both directions have been observed in a number of series (for review, see Keily et al., 1981). In the author's own work (Hagberg, 1979) the prevalence of cerebral palsy rose slightly in the early 1970s. The neonatologists now address themselves to the care of infants who two weeks earlier in gestation are regarded legally as abortuses. This ethical paradox has yet to be resolved. Nonetheless, it seems natural to assume that there is a length of gestation below which intact extrauterine survival is not possible with the principles of neonatal intensive care as we now know them. Generating a great expense, a higher proportion of significantly handicapped survivors is clearly not a worthwhile exercise. It is the responsibility of neonatologists to ensure that they simultaneously deploy their resources towards the assessment and maintenance of the integrity of the central nervous system.

References

Hagberg, B. (1979). Epidemiological and preventive aspects of cerebral palsy in severe mental retardation in Sweden. **European Journal of Paediatrics, 130**, 71-78

Keily, J.L., Paneth, N., Stein, Z. and Susser, M. (1981). Cerebral palsy and newborn care. 1. Secular trends in cerebral palsy. **Developmental Medicine and Child Neurology, 23**, 533

Smithells, R.W., Sheppard, S., Schorah, C.J., Sellar, M.J., Nevin, N.C., Harris, R., Reid, A.P., Fielding, D.W. and Walker, S. (1981). Vitamin supplementation and neural tube defects. **Lancet, ii**, 1425-1426

J. A. Stallworthy

Based on many years of experience and research in Sweden and supported by the results of other workers, as reported chiefly within the last five years and summarized in a valuable list of references, the authors have provided a comprehensive review of this tragic, exciting and difficult subject. Precise definitions are needed. What is an "alcoholic mother" and what is the "complete fetal alcohol syndrome". The authors have identified several avenues which need more detailed exploration.

Other participants, better equipped than I am, will doubtless make personal contributions of new and important knowledge on various aspects raised in this paper. It is perhaps surprising that, as an old obstetrician who really loved obstetrics and preserved an active and practical interest in it for 50 years, I still do not know with scientific accuracy the extent of the contribution made by obstetricians themselves, and by those trainee specialists for whom they are responsible, to the incidence of mental retardation, with or without associated neurological disasters following avoidable fetal cerebral hypoxia during labour and delivery.

Swedish published work referred to in this paper indicates that "perinatal brain damage occurring between the 28th week of gestation and the end of the first week postpartum" was the causative factor in 10-15% of severe retardation and in 10% of mild retardation. Moreover, perinatally caused SMR "is nearly always combined with cerebral palsy" which may be associated with other neurological manifestations. Table 2 emphazizes the importance of these observations.

Practising obstetricians, and particularly those responsible for establishing and maintaining standards of department care, need to know to what extent this 10-15% of severe mental retardation with its associated palsy is of iatrogenic origin. It is perhaps natural, though regrettable, that this is a subject which both obstetricians and neonatal paediatricians seem too often to be reluctant to discuss. Historically traditional comments such as "the cord was round the neck" or "no cause could be found" are made to distressed parents (when any explanation at all is offered) by doctors who must often themselves doubt the validity of the statements they make. In recent years new attitudes have developed in this field influenced by fears of litigation or belief in no fault compensation. In the search for scientific truth, neither fears nor beliefs are relevant if they prove obstacles to progress.

The best scientific evidence available of which I am aware comes from research in the animal field using the rhesus monkey. A number of models are available which inflict fetal asphyxia. A variety of patterns of brain pathology have been produced which differ according to the maturity of the fetus and the duration and severity of the asphyxia. There can be errors in interpreting results of animal research into equivalent human tissue responses to similar traumatic stimuli but there certainly are dangers in failing to explore their potential significance more than has been apparent in the teaching and practice of modern obstetrics. With the mass of peri- and postnatal data available in large obstetric units, if properly organized and controlled, there is ample scope for high-quality research of major potential practical application. It could effect a revolution in much currently accepted obstetric thought, teaching and practice, and the complacency often associated with it.

As one of those relatively few surviving ancient mariner obstetricians whose early training was in the days when puerperal fever was the dreaded complication of childbirth, and with no specific remedy; when caesarean section was a more dangerous operation, even in skilled hands, than the destruction and removal of a dead fetus per vaginam; when the dangers to both mother and baby of both intervention and non-intervention were carefully assessed in relation to an individual patient by senior experienced members of the midwifery or medical staff, with subsequent close personal supervision; when such neonatal paediatrics as was practised was the responsibility of the obstetrician and the exciting paediatric advances of recent years were only dreams in the minds of visionaries; I learned from dedicated wise and patient masters of the art of midwifery. They taught by example as well as by word the need for skilled personal supervision of labour and the value of regular frequent recording of the fetal heart rate and its behaviour, using the simplist of stethoscopes or, if one was not available, by listening with the ear on the mother's abdomen. A useful subject of debate would be "Has the advent of science in modern technology improved the fetal and infant prognosis?" Of course it can, but that is not the question. Has it done so and, if not, why not? It is to be hoped that we can contribute to an answer to this question by establishing fundamental facts.

J. P. M. Tizard

In their introduction, Hagberg and Hagberg write "It was thought that if the causes, mechanisms and distributions of mental retardation (MR) could be better delineated, it might be possible to devise and apply preventive measures". It is obvious that the causes and mechanisms of disease processes or defects have to be known before prevention becomes even a possibility. Equally obviously the distributions of the various types of MR must be known before one can make a realistic estimate of the extent to which MR as a whole might be reduced.

In the UK analyses of the various types of severe mental retardation (SMR) have in the past usually been based on hospital populations, unlikely to be representative of SMR children as a whole. Population-based studies can only be carried out in countries in which populations are relatively stable and in which socio-economic standards are high. The Hagbergs have played a leading role in the prosecution of these studies in Sweden.

Recent advances and developments, e.g. antenatal diagnosis and selective abortion, better perinatal care, detection and treatment of metabolic defects, general improvement in living standards, etc., have led to the belief that the prevalence of mental retardation might be greatly reduced in the near future. This optimism might be shown to be unfounded if the readily preventable causes of MR were a relatively small, and the non-preventable a relatively large, proportion of the whole. And this seems likely to be the case where SMR is under consideration.

Three years ago, Richard Lindenbaum and the author carried out a "paper exercise" to investigate the extent to which mental retardation might possibly be reduced in the light of present knowledge. We came to the conclusion that the maximum possible reduction in the prevalence of SMR at the age of five years was 18% and this estimate was based partly on guesswork and was greatly influenced by optimism.

In making the estimate we assumed that the distribution of the various types of SMR in the UK was the same as that reported by Gustavson et al. (1977). For example, nearly one-third of all cases were those of Down's syndrome. In Oxford in 1978 49% of mothers aged 40+ underwent amniocentesis and 17% of those aged 35-39. T is would have been expected to reduce the incidence of Down's syndrome by only 10%. If the rate of amniocentesis had been raised to 70% (probable maximum) for mothers aged 40+, 50% for those aged 35-39 and 25% for those 30-34, this would have resulted in:

(1) a five-fold increase in amniocentesis for this purpose;
(2) a reduction in incidence of Down's syndrome by a total of 23%; and
(3) the death of four times as many normal fetuses as of Down's syndrome fetuses.

In their paper Hagberg and Hagberg refer to the Fragile-X syndrome as an important cause of MMR and SMR in boys. It will be important to determine the biological fitness of affected males as a preliminary to determining mutation rates and thus the extent to which the condition might be prevented on the basis of family history of detection of the karyotype in parents.

Lindenbaum and I suggested that SMR due to single gene defects might be reduced by 10% due to treatment and by 5% as a result of counselling and selective abortion; thus reducing prevalence at five years from say 21 to 18 per hundred thousand. Known prenatal environmental defects (infection, alcohol, etc.) seem to be rare in Oxford. Congenital athyroidism is susceptible to screening and early treatment but only about 13% of those not treated early will be cases of SMR.

The prevention of SMR originating in the perinatal period seems to offer greater hope. For example it is now possible routinely to detect intraventricular haemorrhage in babies born very early and, while this condition seldom causes MR let alone SMR, it does so occasionally and the circumstances under which IVH takes place should now be easier to determine. A reduction in the prevalence of many types of postnatally acquired brain damage leading to SMR is certainly a possibility but the total numbers are very small in relation to SMR as a whole.

Of great interest in the Hagbergs' paper is the very surprising finding that whereas the numbers of cases of SMR are approximately 3/1000 (as expected) the incidence of MMR is only

4/1000 compared with an expected 23. From a study of their papers it seems improbable that this very low figure can be explained by non-ascertainment. It seems more likely that present "norms" in the distribution of intelligence quotients in the Swedish population are no longer valid. Of some philosophical interest is the question of the extent to which expectations of society have altered in respect of their less gifted citizens. Is an IQ of more than two standard deviations below a modal figure of > 100 more acceptable than an IQ of < 70 used to be?!

As suggested by Hagberg and Hagberg, it is arguable that few children with mental subnormality determined in part by poor genetic endowment would be ineducable in ordinary classes of ordinary schools if they had enjoyed the best possible environment from the standpoints of physical and emotional health and intellectual stimulus. But the parents of MMR children (unlike parents of the SMR) will usually provide them with an inferior environment.

The importance of early "discovery" of a handicapping condition is emphasized in the Warnock Report. However, the practical problems involved in the early detection of children without physical handicaps but who will later be categorized as MMR is not fully discussed. Health Visitors might be trained to recognize the likelihood of this arising not only by their judgement of the quality of the home environment, but also by an enquiry into the parents' and siblings' educational record. Priority for admission to "nurture groups", play groups or opportunity groups should be given to children thus identified and at a much younger age than is now the case.

S. A. Richardson

The prevalence rates for MMR children published by the Hagbergs and other colleagues in Sweden range from 3.7 (Hagberg et al.) to 5.1 (Gostason). These rates are so much lower than other rates that have been reported that they have excited great interest.

The difference between the rates in Sweden and elsewhere may be largely the consequence of terminology and method. If a psychometric definition of MMR is used defining MMR as between 50 and 69, the theoretical expectation from the normal curve gives 23/100. In US studies a psychometric approach was long used to classify children as MMR and resulted in prevalences around 23/100.

In Europe an administrative definition of MR is often used based on the children classified as MR by local authorities and placed in ESN schools and all other forms of childrens' MR services. Studies using this definition give an overall prevalence rate of approx. 12/1000. It is well known that some children administratively classsifed as MR have IQ scores of above 75, and there are also children in ordinary classrooms with IQs of under 75. In the Aberdeen study based on an administrative definition the overall prevalence was 12.5/1000. In addition 15/1000 children were in ordinary classes with IQs of under 75.

The Hagbergs' study defines MMR as children with IQs between 50 and 70. The majority of these children were administratively classified as MMR, but further search in the ordinary classes uncovered a few additional children with IQs below 70. No testing of all children in the population was carried out.

If the prevalence in Aberdeen is restricted to those administratively defined as MR with IQs between 50 and 70, the prevalence is 5.4/1000, a figure slightly higher than the Hagberg prevalence of 3.35/1000 after the children from regular classes are removed from the 3.7/1000 figure. The Swedish prevalence is still lower than Aberdeen, but the order of difference is far smaller than has generally been understood between Sweden and other countries.

SECTION II

RESEARCH INTO BIOMEDICAL ASPECTS

Chapter 4

Chromosomal aspects of mental retardation

M. Baraitser

INTRODUCTION

Chromosomal disorders contribute significantly to the load of severe mental retardation. Where whole communities as opposed to institutionalized populations have been studied, at least one-third of severe retardation is due to an alteration in chromosome number or structure. This was found in two Swedish studies (Gustavson _et al._, 1977a, b) and one from England (North Hertfordshire region) where almost full ascertainment was achieved (Laxova _et al._, 1977). If only an institutional population is studied (this excludes patients cared for in the community) the proportion due to a detectable chromosomal anomaly is 10% (Opitz _et al._, 1978). All studies show that the vast majority of patients in this category have Down's syndrome and in those groups where children under the age of two years are excluded (because of early death) the non-Down's contribution is very small. If, however, the burden of mental retardation as borne by the family is considered as opposed to the burden on the community, who might have to provide education and custodial care after the age of six years, then the retarded infant must be taken into account and one-third would be an underestimate.

In a study based on referrals to a genetic unit, in which the index patients included infants, and were chosen because of developmental delay plus three or more congenital abnormalities (Coco and Penchaszadeh, 1982), 21% had a chromosomal abnormality (Down's syndrome was excluded). Of these, just under half had a structural defect of a chromosome (mostly deletions). Other studies have shown figures varying between 2% and 20%, and even if an average figure of 10% is chosen, then this still remains an important category. The variation (2% to 20%) is mainly due to sampling of different populations and the diligence with which the abnormalities are sought. It should be noted that the chromosomal changes were visible in ordinary non-banded preparations and special techniques might not routinely be necessary. It is not certain that in all cases the observed chromosomal abnormalities were sufficient to account for the mental retardation but the correlation is probably good for the autosomal chromosomes (non sex chromosomes) but unproven for the sex chromosomes. In the Coco and Penchaszadeh study (1982) there were a small number of XYY and XXY karyotypes which might not totally have accounted for the mental retardation.

DOWN'S SYNDROME

There have been few recent advances in elucidating the aetiology of the non-disjunction responsible for trisomy 21 - the finding in 90% of Down's syndrome children. Nevertheless, this remains by far the most important single category responsible for mental retardation. Three aspects have been chosen for comment.

(a) It is an important part of prevention that each couple should be given an accurate age-related risk. In this context it has been noted that the calculated risks have been different if livebirth figures are compared with those calculated from amniocentesis data. Various reasons have been considered including fetal wastage after 16 weeks. Alternatively, the higher amniocentesis figures might result because high-risk couples are referred, or because livebirths have been incompletely ascertained. It might be that there is an increasing incidence of Down's syndrome which is reflected in the more recent amniocentesis figures as compared to the livebirth figures. A recent study from South Glamorgan (Young _et al_., 1980) suggests that the amniocentesis figures might not be too far in excess of the livebirth incidence. The total livebirth figure was 1 in 658. If single year figures are compared the difference no longer seems considerable for those less than 40 years old (Table 1).

Table 1

Maternal age	Livebirth figures/1000 (South Glamorgan)	Amniocentesis (European figures)
35	4.91	4.5
36	5.84	4.9
37	6.93	7.7
38	8.24	9.1
39	9.78	13.2
40	11.62	12.0
41	13.80	23.4
42	16.39	33.3
43	19.47	17.8
44	23.13	55.9

(b) If a reduction of one-third of cases of mental retardation caused by Down's syndrome is to be achieved then the screening programme needs to work. How far has success been achieved? Preventive strategies differ. Most centres in the UK recommend that amniocentesis be offered to all women over the age of 37 (the test is probably cost effective above the age of 35). The uptake has been remarkably poor and in some rural areas in the United States only 5-6% of all age-eligible women have their pregnancy monitored. In a survey performed in New York in 1979 (Bernard and Bannerman, 1982), only 28.7% of women who were eligible were screened. In England, 48% of women over 40 had an amniocentesis (Alberman *et al*., 1979). The reason for the poor compliance is unclear. Fewer than 10% of women decline to have the test so that this is unlikely to be the major factor and there did not seem to be evidence implicating late booking. There was, however, some suggestion that the attitude of the obstetricians played a role (professional under-referral). There were between 40 and 50% of obstetricians who had never referred a patient for amniocentesis. Women expect that the physician would offer the test if it were available or indicated. Clearly the way the programme is brought to the notice of families needs improvement. The rewards would be high. Chromosomal contribution to mental retardation is substantial and can be reduced by about one-third if all women over the age of 35 agreed to have the test.

(c) To what extent does father contribute to the load of Down's syndrome? Where the origin of the extra chromosome could be established, this was found to be paternal in 30% of cases (Hansson and Mikkelson, 1978). In general, non-disjunction occurs more frequently in meiosis I than in meiosis II especially when the female parent is implicated. The difference between maternal and paternal contribution is less marked if the non-disjunction takes place in meiosis II. The figures for paternal non-disjunction vary between 4.3 and 35.5%. There is also some evidence to suggest that there might be differences between areas as the figures from Funnen were 11% and from Zealand 26%.

It had been thought that there is a modest increase in the frequency of Down's syndrome only when fathers are over the age of 55. More recent data (Stene *et al*., 1981) suggest that the risks might begin to increase at an earlier age, i.e. above 41 years. It would appear that the risk of trisomy 21 increases more with advanced paternal age when mother is in the 41-46 age range than for the years 35-40. To account for this observation it is postulated that fetuses with trisomies might abort less frequently as mother gets older.

X-LINKED MENTAL RETARDATION DUE TO A FRAGILE SITE ON THE X CHROMOSOMES

There is a preponderance of males with severe mental retardation. Some of the sex difference was considered to be due to X-linked syndromes but these could only be identified by pedigree analysis. More recently, the whole field of X-linked mental retardation has been revolutionized by the discovery that one form, now called Martin-Bell or Gillian Turner syndrome, is due to a detectable chromosomal abnormality. First reported by Lubs (1969) many males have now been shown to have what appears to be a fragile site on the X chromosome.

Fragile Sites

Fragile sites are areas on a chromosome where breaks occur frequently and non-randomly. They occur at sites on chromosomes other than the X chromosome - 2, 9, 12, 16, 17, 20, are all vulnerable. They are especially visible when cells are cultured in a medium deficient in folic acid and some of these sites can be further induced by BUdR (bromodeoxyuridine). They are not frequent in the general population (non-X-chromosome fragile sites occur in only 1 in 1000 neonates (Sutherland, 1981). In contrast, using the same technique, they are present in 1 in 100 mentally retarded persons. The chromosomes involved were 2, 10, 11 and 20. The true significance of the non-X-chromosome fragile site is not yet known. Only the X-linked type has emerged as having profound clinical importance.

Frequency

It seems likely that the fragile site X-linked mental retardation will account for between one-third and one-half of families with non-specific X-linked mental retardation. In an unselected series of 96 severely mentally retarded boys (Blomquist _et al_., 1982) 6% were found to have the fragile sites. Thus the chance that any severely mentally retarded boy will be found to have this type of chromosomal abnormality is 1 in 16. On a general population basis it might be so common that 0.5 per 1000 males will have X-linked fragile site mental retardation, making it second only to Down's syndrome in importance. The fragile site has been localized to the long arm of the X, involving the q27 and q28 bands. These are near the end of the long arm.

Clinical Features in Males

The degree of retardation varies and IQs of 30-60 have been recorded. The males are of normal stature, have a long face, prominent ears and a broad forehead. Microcephaly is not present. Verbal skills are especially affected. Most males have macro-orchidism but this is now known not to be a constant feature. Postpubertally it is usually obvious but this is not always the case before puberty. Originally, all X-linked mental retardation was called Renpenning's syndrome. In the family originally described by Renpenning, males were short, had abnormal ears, prominent jaws and moderate microcephaly. The family was re-examined by Fox _et al_. (1980). Nine males had a mean IQ of 30, but one had an IQ of 70. Fragile sites were looked for but not found.

There is some correlation between the degree of retardation and the proportion of fragile sites. Most workers require a count of more than 4% for the finding to be significant.

Laboratory Techniques for Detection

Fragile sites are expressed in media deficient in folic acid and thymidine. They can be seen in lymphocytes grown in folic acid by adding 5-fluorodeoxyuridine (FUdR), which inhibits thymidylate synthesis. It should be emphasized that no-one yet knows whether the fragile site in males accounts for the mental retardation or whether it is linked to a gene which does. By prolonging the culture time to four hours and raising the pH to 7.2 the fragile sites are more easily visualized. Some workers suggest that altering the colcemid concentration, and air drying as opposed to flame drying, are also beneficial. The adding of methotrexate (10 mg/l) for the last 24 hours, to lymphocytes cultured for 96 hours in TC 199, has been advocated.

Female Carriers

In the study of Turner and Opitz (1980), only one-third of obligatory female carriers possessed fragile sites. There is good evidence that the likelihood of finding fragile sites in carrier females recedes with age. It might be that the reduction starts as early as the mid-twenties. A proportion of the carriers are retarded but the reason for this is not clear. Theoretically, as in Duchenne muscular dystrophy, the normal X should be sufficient to protect the carrier female. It is, however, possible that random inactivation of one X chromosome might not take place. In one study (Uchida and Joyce, 1982), two retarded females had 70% of cells in which the X with the fragile site was the active X chromosome.

Prenatal Diagnosis

The identification of female carriers is difficult. Fetal sex determination, followed by the termination of all males, has been adopted and follows the strategy used in the X-linked conditions such as Duchenne muscular dystrophy. Fetal blood sampling has been used in order to obtain a sample for the detection of fragile sites in the male fetus, but the test has a 5% risk of setting up a miscarriage. Detection in fibroblasts from amniotic fluid has now been achieved by using FUdR (5-fluorodeoxyuridine). In this way it is possible that affected males can be detected *in utero* and this would obviate the difficulty in detecting obligate carrier women.

Caution

The finding of a fragile X in an apparently normal male and his normal brother - the investigation was performed because the wife of the index patient had a poor obstetric history - (Daker et al., 1981) has introduced a further problem. It is as yet uncertain whether the males have a risk of having obligate carrier daughters with mentally handicapped males in their offspring or whether there is an overlap with normal.

NEW TECHNIQUES

Extended Banding

Most laboratories now use G-banding (Giemsa staining) as a routine, and this should be a part of the investigation of all mentally handicapped persons. Greater resolution can be obtained using prophase and prometaphase banding (high resolution banding) but the procedure is time consuming. It uses an amethopterin-synchronized technique, followed by brief exposure to colcemid. This procedure is not widely available but might in the future be utilized in those mental retardation syndromes where a small deletion is suspected in order to locate the specific site. Thereafter, G-banding might then be sufficient for diagnostic purposes as the cytogeneticist would know where to look.

If, as it seems likely, the approach to reducing chromosomal problems causing mental retardation will remain vested in prevention, techniques must become available to replace amniocentesis which carries an abortion rate of 1% and can only be performed at or after 16 weeks. A method is needed whereby fetal cells can be extracted from the mother's circulation by means of a simple venepuncture. Fetal cells can already be recognized in the maternal bloodstream as early as 15 weeks, but the method of extraction makes it impossible to culture the cells and chromosomal analysis relies on the ability to grow cells.

Chorion Biopsy

One of the problems of late diagnosis (i.e. 16 weeks) might be circumvented by chorion biopsy followed by the identification of trophoblasts in the sample. This can be performed at 8-9 weeks and in one series where more than 100 pregnancies were examined in this way, the results seem promising. Both endocervical aspiration and biopsy by means of an ultrasound-guided forceps have been tried. Sampling is successful in more than 80% of attempts but long term follow-up is needed.

Fluorescence-Activated Cell Sorters

A magnetic light beam, coupled with the use of antibodies to paternal cell surface markers (HLA), can detect antigen not present in mother and thereby isolate fetal cells from the maternal circulation. One Y chromatin bearing cell is present per 1000-5000 maternal lymphocytes. To date the fetal cells have not been successfully cultured.

WELL RECOGNIZED SYNDROMES NOW THOUGHT TO BE CAUSED BY DELETIONS

It has long been thought that some of the syndromes of mental retardation are associated with small deletions that might be difficult to detect by conventional cytogenetic techniques. With the advent of extended prometaphase banding, a small number of syndromes not previously known to be chromosomal have been recognized.

(a) Prader Willi syndrome

More than 200 cases of Prader Willi syndrome have been documented in the literature. In 70 a chromosome analysis has been performed and in 15 of these an abnormality of chromosome 15 has been detected. Some of these were initially thought to be balanced rearrangements without loss of chromosome material but where high-resolution techniques have been specifically applied, about a half will be found to have a small deletion (Ledbetter et al., 1982).

(b) Aniridia, Wilm's tumour and mental retardation

This triad has now been shown to be associated with a deleted band, p13, of chromosome 11. This is especially well shown with high-resolution banding techniques.

(c) Retinoblastoma and mental retardation

Bilateral retinoblastoma is sometimes associated with mental retardation. When this occurs, chromosome analysis has shown an interstitial deletion in the long arm of a number 13. Where the mental retardation is severe, the loss of bands q14 to q21 is found whereas children with mild mental retardation and retinoblastoma show loss of half of band q14. This not only locates the origin of the syndrome more precisely, but there seems to be a correlation between the amount of material lost and the degree of mental retardation. Using a similar phenotype/genotype correlation it has been shown that for chromosome 13, a loss of bands q33 and q34 results in a mental retardation syndrome quite different from loss of q32 and q31 where, for instance, hypoplasia of the thumb is found. Eventually more of the syndromes involving mental retardation will become clinically recognizable and found to be caused by small deletions.

(d) HbH and mental retardation

That a proportion of hitherto undiagnosed mental retardation might be associated with small deletions is evident from recent experience of the occasional occurrence of mental retardation in HbH disease (Weatherall et al., 1981). These authors report three families of North European origin in which a child was born with HbH disease and mental retardation. One parent was a carrier for mild alpha thalassemia whereas the other parent was normal. It could be argued that during the formation of the sperm or ovum, a small deletion occurred involving the globin gene but extending far enough along the chromosome, in addition, to cause mental retardation. The deletions are likely to be small as neither prometaphase nor Giemsa banding has to date shown the defect.

STRUCTURAL CHANGES AND SEX CHROMOSOME ANEUPLOIDIES

There are groups of chromosomal rearrangements which were originally thought to be harmless. Some of these now seem to be associated more frequently than expected with mental retardation.

(a) De novo balanced translocation

The term "balanced translocation" implies that no material has been lost or gained. There has been a suggestion (Breg et al., 1972) that mental retardation occurs more frequently than expected in those patients with a de novo balanced translocation - that is a rearrangement not inherited from either parent but present for the first time in the patient. They occur in about 0.15% of livebirths whereas in a population of mentally handicapped, (Tharapel et al., 1977) the figure is much higher. The pathogenesis of the retardation is obscure. It is possible that a small deletion or a gene mutation at the site of the break or even the detrimental effect of the rearrangement on a gene (a positional effect) might be responsible. All that can be concluded at present is that there is a marked increase in non-Robertsonian translocations in the retarded - five times greater than in the newborn surveys (Robertsonian translocations which involve the fusion of the short arms of two acrocentric chromosomes are more benign, possibly because there are few genes on the short arms).

(b) Inversions

Chromosomes may break and rejoin many times but especially during meiosis when crossing over occurs. Inversions describe those situations in which the reconstituted chromosome has a segment which has inadvertently been reinserted in an inverted position. In a pericentric inversion the inverted portion includes the centromere and a portion of both long and short arms. The frequency of inversions in the general population might be as high as 1% and some chromosomes (especially 9, 10 and 8) are more commonly involved. The inversions in this group are benign with no suggestion of a risk of further chromosomal rearrangement with mental retardation in the offspring. This might not be true for all inversions. In the report of Stine et al. (1982) there were 18 cases of inv.3. The carriers had 83 pregnancies and 9 abortions resulting in 25 liveborn infants with multiple congenital abnormality syndromes and 48 normal infants. The risk of a liveborn abnormal child was 30% - a substantial risk. It is speculated that the length of the inverted segment might be crucial. If crossover takes place within the loop and the pregnancy survives, abnormality might result. If inversions are divided into those that involve more than one-third of the total length and those that are smaller, then it is the first category that shows significant abnormalities at birth. At present a risk of 5-10% is appropriate in those where a recombinant has already occurred and 1% in the absence of one affected parent (Sutherland et al., 1976).

(c) Sex chromosome anomalies

The contribution of the sex chromosome aneuploidies to mental retardation is only small. Recent prospective studies from Edinburgh (Ratcliffe, 1982) show that delayed speech development rather than mild retardation results. In XXY males 62.5% needed remedial speech, they had IQs lower than their siblings but the mean IQ of the group was 100.9 which is not in the retarded category. (In the Edinburgh study 45% of the 47, XYY males needed remedial teaching in reading.) The average IQ for this group was 107. In this series the mean IQ for matched controls was 117. The triple X females (47, XXX) had more severe cognitive defects. 25% had IQ scores of less than 70.

(d) Inherited translocations

The proportion of mental retardation that results because a parent carries a translocation is not numerically important, but it is of great relevance for individual families. If a parent is a balanced translocation carrier then there is a risk that more than one child could be affected. Some translocations carry a higher risk than others (see Table 2) and the expected 1 in 3 risk to offspring is not seen in practice. A summary of empiric risks is shown in Table 2.

Structural rearrangements occur in 1 in 250 couples. It is unfortunate that in general the couples at risk are only identified after the birth of an affected child.

Table 2

Recurrence risks for various translocations
(after the birth of one affected child)

		Carrier mother	Carrier father
Robertsonian	13/14	1.6%	(Small numbers)
	14/21	11.9%	0
	21/22	21.4%	0
Reciprocal	(any chromosome)	13.8%	12.1%

(Based on Hamerton et al., 1980)

CONCLUSION

It is likely that progress will be made by the identification of yet smaller chromosomal deletions. In this way the categories of non-specific mental retardation and the group of multiple congenital anomalies with mental retardation could be further reduced. In addition the development of DNA probes linked to specific sites on the X chromosome will improve prenatal diagnosis and the prevention strategy for this important category of mental retardation. There also remains a real possibility of preventing Down's syndrome if screening can be extended to include a much wider proportion of the population. This can only be achieved by the development of relatively safe techniques for obtaining fetal cells and progress has been made in this direction.

Finally, there is a tentative suggestion that treatment of chromosomal syndromes might eventually be possible. A folic acid derivative has been tried in the fragile site mental retardation with unconfirmed evidence of at least an improvement in the autistic phenomena known to be a significant part of the syndrome (Lejeune, 1982). However, in the end prevention is likely to be more cost effective than treatment and it is a salutary lesson to find how relatively simple manipulations can alter incidence figures. If, for instance, all women had their offspring on average two years earlier, the frequency of Down's syndrome could be significantly reduced.

REFERENCES

Alberman, E., Berry, A.C., and Polani, P.E. (1979). Planning an amniocentesis service for Down syndrome, **Lancet, i**, 50

Bernard, B.A. and Bannerman, R.M. (1982). The influence of obstetricians on the utilization of amniocentesis. **Prenatal Diagnosis, 2**, 115-121

Blomquist, H.K:son, Gustavson, K-H., Holmgren, G., et al. (1982). Fragile site X chromosomes and X-linked mental retardation in severely retarded boys in a Northern Swedish county. A prevalence study. **Clin. Genet. 21**(3), 209

Breg, W.R., Miller, D.A., Allerdice, P.W. and Miller, O.J. (1972). Identification of translocation chromosomes by quinacrine fluorescence. **Am. J. Dis. Child. 123** 561-564

Coco, R. and Penchaszadeh, V.B. (1982). Cytogenetic findings in 200 children with mental retardation and multiple congenital anomalies of unknown cause. **Am. J. Med. Genet. 12**(2), 155-173

Daker, M.G., Chidiac, P., Fear, C.N. and Berry, A.C. (1981). Fragile X in a normal male: a cautionary tale. **Lancet, i**, 780

Fox, P., Fox, D. and Gerrard, J.W. (1980). X-linked mental retardation: Renpenning revisited. **Am. J. Med. Genet. 7** 491-495

Gustavson, K.-H, Hagberg B., Hagberg, G., and Sars, K. (1977a). Severe mental retardation in a Swedish county: I. Epidemiology, gestational age, birth weight and associated CNS handicaps in children born 1959-1970. **Acta Paediatr. Scand. 66** 373-379

Gustavson, K.-H., Hagberg, B., Hagberg, G. and Sars, K., (1977b). Severe mental retardation in a Swedish county: II. Etiological and patho-genetic aspects of children born 1959-1970. **Neuropadiatrie 8**(3), 293-304

Hamerton, J.L., Boue, A., Cohen, M.M., et al. (1980). Section 2. Chromosome disease. **Prenatal Diagnosis, 1** 11-21

Hansson, M. and Mikkelson, M. (1978). The origin of the extra chromosome 21 in Down syndrome. **Cytogenet. Cell Genet. 20** 194-203

Laxova, R., Ridler, M.A.C. and Bowen-Bravery, M. (1977). An etiological survey of the severely retarded Hertfordshire children who were born between January 1, 1965 and December 31, 1967. **Am. J. Med. Genet. 1** 75-86

Ledbetter, D.H., Mascarello, J.T., Riccard, et al. (1982). Chromosome 15 abnormalities and the Prader-Willi syndrome: A follow-up report of 40 cases. **Am. J. Hum. Genet. 34**(2), 278-285

Lejeune, J. (1982). Is the fragile X syndrome amenable to treatment? **Lancet, i**, 273-274

Lubs, H.A. (1969). A marker X chromosome. **Am. J. Hum. Genet. 21** 231-244

Opitz, J.M., Kaveggia, E.G., Durkin-Stamm, M.V. and Pendleton, E. (1978). Diagnostic/genetic studies in mental severe retardation. **Birth Defects: Original Article Series, XIV**(6B), 1-38

Ratcliffe, S.B. (1982). Speech and learning disorders in children with sex chromosome abnormalities. **Dev. Med. Child Neurol. 24** 80-84

Stene, J., Stene, E., Stengel-Rutkowski, S. and Murken, J-D. (1981). Paternal age and Down's syndrome. Data from prenatal diagnoses (DFG). **Hum. Genet. 59** 119-124

Stine, S.B., Clark, C.E., Telfer, M.A. et al., (1982). Ullrich-Turner syndrome (45, X, i(Xq)) in a child with a familial inversion of chromosome 3. **Am. J. Med. Genet. 12**(1) 57-62

Sutherland, G.R., (1981). The population cytogenetics of fragile sites. (Abstract). **The 6th International Congress of Human Genetics**, 12-19th Sept. 1981, Jerusalem, Israel, p.44

Sutherland, G.R., Gardiner, A.J. and Carter, R.F. (1976). Familial pericentric inversion of chromosome 19, inv.(19) (p13q13) with a note on genetic counselling of pericentric inversion carriers. **Clin. Genet. 1**, 54-59

Tharapel, A.T., Summitt, R.L., Wilroy, R.S. et al. (1977). Apparently balanced de novo translocations in patients with abnormal phenotypes: Report of 6 cases. **Clin. Genet. 11** 255-269

Turner, G., and Opitz, J.M. (1980). Editorial Comment: X-linked mental retardation. **Am. J. Med. Genet. 7** 407-415

Uchida, I.A., and Joyce, E.M. (1982). Activity of the fragile X in heterozygous carriers. **Am. J. Hum. Genet. 34**(2), 286-293

Weatherall, D.J., Higgs, D.R., Bunch, C. et al. (1981) Hemoglobin H disease and mental retardation. **New Engl. J. Med. 305**(11) 607-612

Young, I.D., Williams, E.M. and Newcombe, R.G. (1980). Down syndrome and maternal age in South Glamorgan. **J. Med. Genet. 17** 433-436

COMMENTARY

J. M. Berg

Baraitser's lucid presentation on this subject deals with many important facets, including innovative recent developments with significant potential practical implications. This commentary expands on some points raised in that paper and touches on related considerations.

Contrasting mental consequences of chromosomal aberrations

There is a striking difference between the mental effects of autosomal and sex chromosomal aberrations. In general, autosomal abnormalities result in more severe degrees of intellectual deficit (and often of physical anomalies), whereas sex chromosome disorders tend to be associated, when mental deficit is present, with relatively mild effects and, in some of these disorders, with an apparently greater likelihood of emotional and behavioural disturbance.

Some autosomal aberrations are lethal *in utero* or in early infancy. Among those that are not, whether involving excess or deficiency of chromosomal material, the mental level often approximates to the range found in Down's syndrome. On the other hand, the presence of a supernumerary X or Y chromosome, for example, usually is not associated with severe mental defect and can be found even in persons with above average mentality. An XO sex chromosome constitution (Turner's syndrome) also differs in its mental effects from those in autosomal deletions or duplications, in that intellectual level is generally at, or close to, that in the normal general population but with a curious discrepancy in verbal and performance skills - affected individuals usually score less well on tests in the latter area, in contrast to those with an extra X or Y in whom the reverse tends to occur (Nielson *et al*., 1981). Interestingly, although the mental effects in Turner's syndrome are relatively minor, the karyotype concerned is often the most frequently found one in spontaneous abortions (Carr and Gedeon, 1977). The reasons for the substantial and significant intellectual and behavioural differences between individuals with autosomal and those with sex chromosomal aberrations are essentially obscure.

Chromosomal mosaicism

Mosaicism can alter the mental effects of a chromosomal error but exact correlation of the two circumstances is difficult largely because the degree of mosaicism itself is difficult to establish accurately. In practice it is convenient generally to examine only one tissue (peripheral blood leucocytes) and rarely feasible to study more than one other (skin fibroblasts). As the proportions of chromosomally different cells may differ from tissue to tissue and even, over time, in the same tissue, the correlation referred to is imprecise. Nevertheless, mosaics, as a group, tend to have higher mental levels than a suitable control group without evident mosaicism (Penrose, 1967). This tendency, however, does not provide a definite indication of the mental level in individual instances - a mosaic Down's syndrome individual, for example, may be more severely retarded than is usually the case with standard (regular) trisomy 21, and occasionally an apparently non-mosaic person with Down's syndrome will show mental ability considerably above that generally found in the syndrome.

Mental deterioration

Mental deficit in association with chromosomal aberrations usually does not seem to be progressive with the passage of time. One finding related to possible mental deterioration in adult life is of special interest. This is the well established comparatively early development of the neuropathology of Alzheimer's disease in Down's syndrome. Malamud (1972), for instance, reported such neuropathological changes in all of 35 Down's syndrome individuals over 40 years examined at autopsy, compared to an incidence of 14% (31 out of 225) in similarly aged mentally retarded controls. The precise consequences of this brain pathology in Down's syndrome have not been widely studied to date, but memory deterioration has been observed in such persons at an earlier age than in control groups (Dalton and McLachlan, 1983).

Preventive aspects

Baraitser quite correctly indicates that there would be a substantial reduction of Down's syndrome among live births if more widespread use was made of the prenatal capacity to detect the syndrome. This is very likely to happen if fetal cells from the mother's circulation could be cultured, as he mentions, and thus become a reliable means of detecting fetal chromosomal abnormalities as an alternative to the present more invasive and hazardous undertaking of amniocentesis. However, it seems worth while stressing that general encouragement of child bearing at relatively young maternal ages could have an even more dramatic preventive effect without the emotional and monetary costs of technical prenatal identification procedures. Stein *et al.* (1977), for example, have calculated that the frequency of Down's syndrome among live births in New York City in 1973 would have been reduced by at least one-third if women over 34 years had not borne children and by one-fifth if those over 39 years had stopped childbearing.

Concluding remark

Continued study of the precise relationship of different chromosomal abnormalities with mental characteristics is important, both as a guide to prognosis in affected persons and as a means of investigating the role of individual chromosomes (or portions of them) in determining mental function.

References

Carr, D.H. and Gedeon, M. (1977). Population cytogenetics of human abortuses. In E.B. Hook and I.H. Porter (Eds.) **Population Cytogenetics - Studies in Humans.** Academic Press: New York.

Dalton, A.J. and McLachlan, D.R.C. (1983). Incidence of memory deterioration in aging persons with Down's syndrome. In J.M.Berg (Ed.) **Perspectives and Progress in Mental Retardation 2**, University Park Press: Baltimore.

Malamud, N. (1972). Neuropathology of organic brain syndromes associated with aging. In C.M. Gaits (Ed.) **Aging and the Brain.** Plenum Press: New York.

Nielson, J., Sorensen, A.M. and Sorensen, K. (1981). Mental development of unselected children with sex chromosome abnormalities. **Hum. Genet., 59**, 324-332.

Penrose, L.S. (1967). Studies of mosaicism in Down's anomaly. In G.A. Jervis (Ed.) **Mental Retardation.** Charles C. Thomas: Springfield.

Stein, Z.A., Susser, M., Kline, J. and Warburton, D. (1977). Amniocentesis and selective abortion for trisomy 21 in the light of the natural history of pregnancy and fetal survival. In E.B. Hook and I.H. Porter (Eds.) **Population Cytogenetics - Studies in Humans.** Academic Press: New York.

A. C. Berry

The paper covers this extensive topic in an informed and workman-like manner, though for a Symposium on the Scientific Aspects of Mental Retardation there is perhaps too great an emphasis on recurrence risks and prenatal diagnosis. The initial epidemiological review is good, but it would also be interesting to discuss reasons for the fact that mental retardation is universally found in those with autosomal chromosome abnormalities. The cerebral pathology found in chromosome abnormalities has been reviewed by Hsu and Hirschhorn (1973). Gross structural defects are found in the brains of a high proportion of infants with trisomy 13 and microscopic examination of those with macroscopically normal brains shows hypocellularity of both glial cells and neurones (Marin-Padilla, 1974). Similarly in trisomy 18, a wide range of structural anomalies are found, ranging from holoprosencephaly to absence of the corpus callosum and heteropia of the cerebellum. In Down's syndrome, the brain is usually small and round, but again structural anomalies may be present, and the early onset of Alzheimer's like disease suggests that these brains may have "reduced neuronal redundancy". Similar findings are reported in other autosomal anomalies, so that any chromosome abnormality seems to result in a non-specific disorganization of cerebral development at both the macroscopic and microscopic levels.

Down's syndrome

This is clearly the most important chromosome abnormality, and the choice of topics to discuss is difficult. However, Baraitser has devoted both sections (a) and (b) basically to a discussion of age-related risks and prenatal detection. These could be pooled, to allow the inclusion of a section discussing the origin of non-disjunction, as a deeper understanding of this could perhaps lead to true primary prevention. At present, two-thirds of Down's infants are born to young mothers, and the searches for predisposing factors have given conflicting results. Suggested factors are reviewed briefly by Mikkelson (1977), and range from raised grandmaternal age, through timing of coitus to antitrypsin genotype. The majority of studies were done without taking into account the fact that non-disjunction can occur in either the first or second meiotic division of sperm or ovum production. Mikkelson's recent (1982) review shows paternal non-disjunction to be responsible for about 20% of cases, while the first meiotic division is responsible for 75% of the maternal failures. The ova enter this cell division while the mother herself is *in utero*, so that the time during which noxious influences could act is very long indeed, and these are likely to be quite different from those affecting sperm. Of some concern is the finding of regional variation in the contribution of paternal non-disjunction (Mikkelson *et al.*, 1980), which raises the possibility of environmental influences.

Inversions

This section is unsatisfactory, as no distinction is made between inversions involving only inactive heterochromatin, which are benign, and those involving active euchromatin, where there is a real risk of chromosomally unbalanced offspring, though the magnitude of the risk will vary depending on the size of the site of the inversion. The final line of this section should read "1%, where there has been no reported abnormal offspring". Similarly, in Table 2, it should be stressed that for reciprocal translocations the risk varies considerably from one translocation to another. The figure quoted is probably too high to apply to translocations found by chance or in those presenting with a history of miscarriages.

Sex chromosome abnormalities

This fascinating group deserves fuller treatment. Children with these abnormalities are not usually retarded, but those with XXX and XXY make-up have a five-fold increased risk of mild or severe subnormality and of mental illness (Polani, 1977). Those with normal IQs frequently have demonstrable deficits in certain specific skills and learning areas.

Robinson *et al.* (1979) show that XXX girls and XXY boys both have head circumferences which, though normal, are definitely skewed to the left when compared with the normal distribution. XXY boys with normal intelligence tend to have better performance than verbal skills, poor speech development, easy distractibility, badly organized body image, and lack of verbal precision (Nielsen *et al.*, 1969). 45,X girls are known to have poor visual memory, word fluency and motor coordination (Waber, 1979). Ratcliffe *et al.* (1982) were able to identify small but definite defects in fine coordination and balance in children with an additional sex chromosome. A hint as to the mechanisms of these deficits comes from the work of Price *et al.* (1974), who demonstrated ECG abnormalities in XYY males and 45,X females, and of Wright and Lauder (1974), who found differences in motor nerve conduction in those with sex chromosome trisomies.

Thus these children perhaps span the spectrum from true global retardation through minimal brain dysfunction to normal variation. From the children's viewpoint, early recognition of their potential speech and learning disorders allows remedial treatment, while on the scientific side, they provide a real opportunity for increasing our understanding of cerebral organization and function.

References

Daker, M.G., Chidiac, P., Fear, C.N. and Berry, A.C. (1981). Fragile X in a normal male : a cautionary tale. **Lancet 1**, 8223, 780

Hsu, L.Y.F. and Hirschhorn, K. (1973). Cytogenetic aspects of brain dysfunction. In **Biology of Brain Dysfunction** (Gaull, G.E. Ed.) **1**, 89-142

Marin-Padilla, M. (1974). Structural organization of the cerebral cortex (motor area) in human chromosomal aberrations. A Golgi study. 1. D1 (13-15) trisomy, Patau syndrome. **Brain Research 66**, 375-391

Mikkelson, M. (1977). Down's syndrome. Current stage of cytogenetical research. In **Medical Genetics**, (Szabo, G. and Papp, Z. Eds.) 89-105. Amsterdam, Oxford: Excerpta Medica; Budapest: Akademiai Kiado

Mikkelson, M. (1982). Parental origin of the extra chromosome in Down's syndrome. **J. Ment. Defic. Res. 26**, 3, 143-151

Mikkelson, M., Poulsen, H., Grinsted, J. and Lange, A. (1980). Non-disjunction in trisomy 21: study of chromosomal heteromorphisms in 110 families. **Ann. Hum. Genet. 44**, 1, 17-28

Nielsen, J., Sorensen, A., Theilgard, A., Froland, A. and Johensen, S.G. (1969). A psychiatric-psychological study of 50 severely hypogonadal male patients, including 34 with Klinefelter's syndrome, 47,XXy. **Acta Jutlandica XLI**, 3

Polani, P.E. (1977). Abnormal sex chromosomes, behaviour and mental disorder. In **Developments in Psychiatric Research** (Tanner, J.M. Ed) 89-128. London, Sydney, Auckland: Hodder and Stoughton

Price, W.H., Lauder, I.J. and Wilson, J. (1974). The electrocardiogram and sex chromosome aneuploidy. **Clin. Genet. 6**, 1, 1-14

Ratcliffe, S.G., Therney, I. and Nshaho, J. (1982). The influence of additional sex chromosomes on cerebral function. **J. Med. Genet. 19**, 5, 373.

Robinson, A., Lubs, H.A., Neilsen, J. and Sorensen, K. (1979). Summary of clinical findings: profiles of children with 47,XXY, 47,XXX and 47,XYY karyotypes. In **Birth Defects: Original Article series** XV, 1 (Robinson, A., Lubs, H.A. and Bergsma, D. Eds.) **Sex Chromosome Aneuploidy: prospective studies on children**, 261-266. New York: Alan R. Liss

Waber, D.P. (1979). Neuropsychological aspects of Turner's syndrome. **Dev. Med. Child Neurol. 21**, 1, 58-70

Wright, M.O. and Lauder, I.J. (1974). Motor nerve conduction in 47,XXY and 48,XXYY males, and 47,XXX and 45,X females. **Clin. Genet. 6**, 3, 205-215

H. Galjaard

The most important points on chromosomal aspects of mental retardation are covered by the excellent review of Baraitser. A few additional comments may be appropriate.

The methodology of chromosome analysis is now well established and there is also agreement about the indications. Postnatal karyotyping will be carried out in the case of recurrent (>2) abortion or stillbirth, the presence of multiple congenital anomalies, unexplained mental retardation, abnormal sexual development, suspicion of carriership for a balanced translocation and syndromes associated with chromosomal instability. Most Western European countries have regional centres for chromosome analysis and the percentage of chromosome aberrations detected varies from 10% to 30%.

Using normal "banding techniques" some 300 transverse bands can be observed during metaphase (ISCN, 1978) and with special techniques it is even possible to distinguish 1000-2000 bands in the human genome (Yunis, 1981). Yet the total number of genes coding for a polypeptide is in the order of 50 000 and hence the microscopic resolution at present allows us to diagnose deletions, translocations and other chromosomal aberrations involving parts of chromosomes which on average contain from several dozens to a hundred genes. Taking into account that a deletion or mutation of one single gene often results in physical or mental handicap (McKusick, 1978) it can be expected that chromosome aberrations involving from several to a few dozen genes may also be associated with severe clinical manifestations; still these will remain undetected with the present methodology of light microscopy after staining (pro)metaphase cells. In the near future radioactively labelled or fluorescent probes specific for (very) small segments of the various chromosomes will be available (for review, see Evans, 1982). By *in situ* hybridization (Bauman *et al.*, 1980; Harper *et al.*, 1981; Barton *et al.*, 1982; Malcolm *et al.*, 1982; Kirsch *et al.*, 1982) it may well become possible to discover hitherto undetected small chromosome aberrations and hopefully this will also lead to a diagnosis in patients with unexplained mental retardation.

Such new techniques may also contribute to the explanation of the higher frequency of mental retardation among carriers of a balanced chromosome translocation (see review by Baraitser) and among individuals with chromosome heteromorphism (Bardhan *et al.*, 1981).

The two main approaches towards prevention of the birth of patients with a chromosomal aberration are early diagnosis of patients and carriers followed by genetic counselling and prenatal monitoring of pregnancies at higher risk. The main factors limiting an optimal use of the available facilities are insufficient knowledge of clinical genetics both among physicians and the general public, and inadequate referral to centres for prenatal diagnosis by general practitioners, midwives and obstetricians. Investigations among mothers of 38 years and older in Rotterdam who had not undergone amniocentesis (Thomassen-Brepols, personal communication, 1983) indicate that 20% declined prenatal monitoring and selective abortion because of religious or ethical considerations. In 40% of the cases the pregnant woman was not aware of the possibility of prenatal diagnosis nor had it been discussed by the doctor or midwife who was responsible for the prenatal care. In the remaining 40% of the cases the possibility of prenatal monitoring had been brought up by the pregnant woman but the general practitioner, midwife or obstetrician had not approved of referral, mostly because they did not see the necessity or because they overestimated the risks of the procedure. These results indicate that we are still far away from the ideal situation that couples who consider procreation are aware of the risks and of the possibilities of prevention and that they are able to take their own decision without being influenced by the personal opinion of their doctors.

Studies in various centres (Duncan, 1978; Taben and Nitowski, 1978; Marion *et al.*, 1979; Adams *et al.*, 1981; Thomassen-Brepols *et al.*, 1982; Mikkelsen, personal communication, 1983) show that if pregnant women of 35 years and older are properly informed, 60-80% of them want prenatal monitoring.

In order to realize optimal prevention of chromosomal aberrations the most important aspects of human genetics, reproduction and early recognition of an increased risk must be included in general school education. Also, new developments in early diagnosis of index patients and carriers must be brought to the attention of those working in the care of mother and child. Finally, it must be stressed that experts should not put too much emphasis on their personal judgement of a genetic risk, the severity of a handicap or the acceptability of certain methods of diagnosis and prevention. The ultimate aim in clinical genetics is to provide good information and to help couples at risk to take a decision which fits best to their religion, feeling and specific living conditions.

References

Adams, M.M., Finley, S. and Hansen, H. (1981). **Am. J. Obstet. Gynecol., 139**, 673-677

Bardhan, S., Singh, D.N. and Davis, K. (1981). **Clin. Genet., 20**, 44-47

Barton, P., Malcolm, S., Murphy, C. and Ferguson-Smith, M.A. (1982). **J. Mol. Biol., 156**, 269-278

Bauman, J.G.J., Wiegant, J., Borst, P. and van Duyn, P. (1980), **Exptl. Cell Res., 128**, 485-490

Duncan, S.L.B. (1978). **J. Biosoc. Sci., 10**, 141-146

Evans, H.J. (1982). Conventional and molecular cytogenetics for detecting chromosome anomalies: current reality and future prospects, **The Future of Prenatal Diagnosis**, H. Galjaard (ed), Churchill Livingstone, Edinburgh

Harper, M.E., Ullrich, A. and Saunders, G.T. (1981). **Proc. Natl. Acad. Sci., 78**, 4458-4460

ISCHN (1978). International System for Human Cytogenetic Nomenclature, **Cytogenet. Cell Genet., 21**, No. 6

Kirsch, I.R., Morton, C.C., Nakamara, K. and Leder, Ph. (1982) **Science, 216**, 301

McKusick, V.A. (1978). **Mendelian Inheritance in Man**, 6th ed., The Johns Hopkins University Press, Baltimore

Malcolm, S., Barton, P., Murphy, C., Ferguson-Smith, M.A., Bentley, D.L. and Rabbits, T.H. (1982). **Proc. Natl. Acad. Sci., 79**, 4957-4961

Marion, J.P., Fernhoff, P.M. and Priest, J.H. (1979). **Am. J. Hum. Genet., 31**, 138A

Taben, E. and Nitowski, H.M. (1978). **Am. J. Hum. Genet., 30**, 69A

Thomassen-Brepols, L.J., Jahoda, M.G.J., Drogendijk, A.C. and Galjaard H. (1982). **Ned. Tijdschr. Geneesk, 126**, 2262-2266

Yunis, J.J. (1981). **Human Genetics, 56**, 293-298

P. Mittler

An important challenge for the future is to come to a better understanding of the very substantial range of individual differences within a group of Down's syndrome individuals. The IQ range varies from below 20 to 100 (in a few cases) even though most fall within a narrower band.

Furthermore, some children continue to function at very low levels despite heroic multidisciplinary intervention (including parental involvement), while other children come to function at a high level without special measures.

M. D. Mulcahy

Regarding Blair's question on the metabolic pathways in Down's syndrome, we may get some clues to these from studies on older patients. The increased survival rate of Down's patients in recent years is producing new clinical situations. It has been suggested that hypothyroidism was a common complication in elderly Down's patients. Our study did not confirm this.

However, more recently there is the suggestion that early liver failure may be a feature of the elderly Down's patient.

What I am trying to say is that we may have to work backwards, so to speak, to elucidate the abnormal metabolic pathways in Down's syndrome.

Chapter 5

Pathology and vulnerability of the developing brain

J. Dobbing

Of the very great variety of things which can go wrong with the developing brain this paper will necessarily be confined to a general statement about a few of them. Those bizarre pathologies which are well described in standard texts, comparatively rare and often completely without explanation, will be excluded, as will those associated with chromosomal anomalies and the later injuries caused by physical trauma, hypoxia and hypoglycaemia in the perinatal period. We shall mainly be concerned with environmentally determined disorders of growth at various stages of development, some of which result in severe distortion and significant handicap, and others with relatively minor but probably important structural and functional change. In general in this group, the earlier the disturbance the more severe the effects, albeit in fewer surviving children. The later, less severe pathologies nevertheless afflict very much larger numbers, sometimes approaching whole populations. Each has its own position on the scale of importance. Degrees of handicap from these causes occur through a continuous range from the most severe and relatively rare to the very large numbers whose achievement is only a little short of their individual potential, while still falling well within the "normal" range. Perhaps everyone comes, at least theoretically, within this latter, extreme end of the continuum.

GENERAL PRINCIPLES AND DEFINITIONS

These "growth" pathologies of the brain often depend at least as much on the stage of brain development at which they are inflicted as on the inflicting agent. In this respect they resemble classical teratology, except that they occur well beyond the ordinary teratological period of embryogenesis during the first trimester of human gestation, into the remainder of fetal life and, postnatally, at least until the second or third birthday.

The second general principle is that such alterations of brain growth, although not destructive of structures already in place, tend to produce permanent deficits and distortions in brain architecture, failure to recover being due to an incapacity of the developing brain for rehabilitation after the normal period for the accomplishment of a particular developmental stage. We are not sure how absolute such a failure is in all cases. For example it is likely that a deficit in neuronal number cannot be made good after the ordained time of differentiation of the affected neuroblasts. On the other hand we can suspect a considerable plasticity of neural connections, perhaps even later than the normal period of dendritic growth and synaptogenesis, which continues at least to the end of the time we are discussing. We should probably be very cautious, however, in assuming such plasticity, much of which has only been demonstrated in creatures such as newts who can also regenerate whole limbs, even as adults, and which has in no case been shown to be of functional significance in higher mammalian species. Equally, functional compensation or "recovery" by no means implies structural reconstruction. The candour of the amphibian experimenter as well as of the clinical observer in these matters is often less than may be desired, even though the one is often led erroneously by the other along important, main channels of thought.

The term _mental retardation_ is, of course, imprecise, and this has led to important misunderstanding. For some it carries the necessary connotation of severe, functional, mental handicap; for others any demonstrable reduction of achievement, however small, compared with an assumed potential, can be fairly described as mental retardation. (In neither case is the word "retardation", meaning a slowing down, accurately used. A better word might be deficiency.) This confusion is importantly counterproductive. For example early malnutrition can never cause mental retardation in the first sense, although it can certainly participate in causing it in the second (Dobbing, 1981a) and to tell our lay fellow-citizens (including politicians and research-funding bodies) that early malnutrition causes mental retardation has frequently led to the erroneous assumption that one may only have to feed poor children to prevent Down's syndrome and the other severe deficiencies mentioned above. The term "mental handicap" is a little more useful, but it will still be important to define the degree of severity of the functional consequences.

The term _microcephaly_ promises to be capable of more exact definition. Unfortunately it is also variously and confusingly used. Some confine its use to an extremely small head indeed, less than 4SD below the mean for the population at a given age. At this level there is, of course, no diagnostic problem, nor any doubt about severely impaired function. Others use the term "microcephaly" for heads less than 2SD below the mean, or below the 3rd, 5th or 10th centile, amongst which will be found (by definition) a significant proportion of the normal population. Still others think of microcephaly as including any reduced head size, however slightly smaller than would be that individual's normal potential for growth. Unfortunately, important as it is to identify this later group, because they are by far the most numerous, most of them will fall within the normal range for the age, while still being abnormal (often seriously so) for the individual. Head size, like that of other parts of the body, is closely related to body size, and this should help us to overcome the difficulty of definition by taking body size into account as well as age in identifying a deficit. In short, a head which is smaller than it should be for that individual's body size at a given age may be as close as we can get to the identification of a mild or moderate deficit. If the centile for head circumference is below that for other anthropometric measures such as height, or even weight, this theoretically could be regarded as a head "smaller than it should be". However serious errors can arise where the centile standards for the various anthropometric parameters are derived from different populations. Almost unbelievably this still occurs in much clinical practice and leads to systematic error.

It is most likely that environmentally imposed, abnormal smallness of the head occurs in a continuous gradation from the fairly common minor degree to the much less common severe microcephaly. For this reason the term microcephaly has been used, perhaps also confusingly, by the present author amongst many others, to include all degrees of head-size deficit.

The parallels between classical teratology and later vulnerability of the developing brain have already been referred to. Teratological malformations are specific for the time of exposure to an agent during the first human gestational trimester, the period of embryogenesis. In the case of brain development, however, the principle also holds for much later, post-embryogenic developmental stages, throughout the second and third trimesters of human gestation and well into the first years of postnatal life. Another difference is that the brain's later vulnerability is related to quite prolonged periods of vulnerability, rather than to sharp, critical points in time, especially in species which, like humans, grow slowly. Major examples of such periods can be predicted from the crude, general sequence (Dobbing, 1981b) outlined in Figure 1.

After embryogenesis there is a period of cell multiplication (10-18 human gestational weeks) which predominantly concerns the neuronal precursors or neuroblasts. This is followed by a second, numerically much larger and much longer period of multiplication (20 weeks of gestation to about the second birthday in man) of glial precursors or spongioblasts, with very little overlap between the two cell-multiplicative periods. A relatively small number of microneurons (which are nevertheless very important functionally) multiply outside this sequence in the cerebellum and hippocampus, in the perinatal period in humans. Since one important glial cell type is responsible for myelination, this latter phase follows that of glial multiplication. The great sensitivity of the brain growth spurt (mid-gestation to the

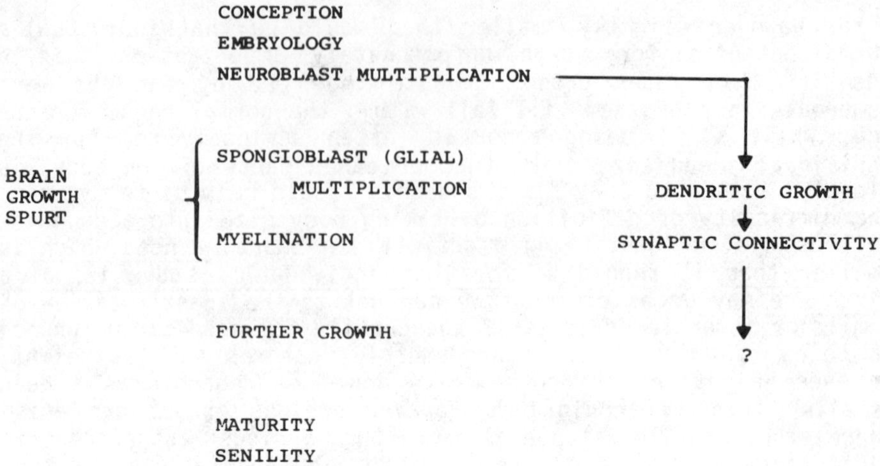

Figure 1 A greatly simplified scheme to describe the common mammalian pattern of brain growth (Dobbing, 1981b)

second human birthday) to environmental restriction is presumably related to the enormous number of component developmental events during this time. Amongst these the development of dendritic trees and of synaptic connectivity are major identifiable processes. The need to understand the different timing of this common sequence in different animal species before findings can be extrapolated from one another will not be repeated here. The general sequence is indeed common to all mammalian species. The major hindrance to meaningful cross-species extrapolation has been a failure to take into account the different timing of birth relative to the sequence of brain developmental events, as well as the related question of different developmental time scales (Dobbing and Sands, 1979). Thus in the rat, the period of neuroblast multiplication occurs in the last one-third of gestation and lasts less than a week, compared with the human equivalent in the early second trimester lasting about eight weeks (Dobbing, 1973). The effects of interference with brain development in both cases are therefore related to stages of development, not to prenatal or postnatal ages.

THE FIRST HUMAN TRIMESTER OF GESTATION

Neural tube defects are numerically the main teratological malformation in human babies occurring during the first gestational trimester at about four weeks after conception. A recent development, suggesting a means of preventing them in certain circumstances (Dobbing, 1983), arises from the finding that mothers at increased risk of giving birth to a second or third such infant can be prevented from doing so by taking a mixture of certain vitamins including folic acid in the periconceptional period. In a first study by Smithells (Smithells et al., 1981) of 177 babies born to fully supplemented mothers who had had one previously affected child, only one was affected, compared with nine recurrences among 264 born to unsupplemented mothers. Of 18 babies born to fully supplemented mothers who had had two previously affected children none were affected, compared with four recurrences among 31 born to unsupplemented mothers. A further 51 babies born to mothers who had taken vitamin supplements but had failed to complete the full programme (for example, by forgetting to take the tablets for more than one day) were unaffected. There was no evidence of any harm done by the vitamins in about half the sample examined later. In a second study there was a similar result. At the most pessimistic estimate, vitamin supplementation has prevented 75% of recurrences. So far, combining other, smaller studies, there have been three recurrences among about 450 babies, or 1 in 150. The usual recurrence rate is 1 in 20 to 1 in 25. A suggestion that the effective ingredient of the intervention mixture is folate comes from equally striking results from Laurence's team in Cardiff using only folate supplementation (Laurence et al., 1981). There is, of course, no clear suggestion that neural tube defects are caused by vitamin deficiency. The pathogenesis is likely to be much more complex, but the problem is so pressing, and the results to date so dramatic, that this may well be amongst the most important preventive work so far accomplished. Its interpretation is fully discussed in a recent monograph (Dobbing, 1983).

THE SECOND HUMAN TRIMESTER AND MICROCEPHALY

Virtually all brain cells of whatever type are diploid, and therefore their total number is related to the total amount of DNA in the brain. Since, in general, one cell type (neurons) multiplies at a different time from another (glia), it follows that to plot total brain DNA against time will reveal the timing of both these periods. This is illustrated in Figure 2 (a and b) for the human forebrain, where the earlier of the two periods of brain cell multiplication from 10 to 18 weeks of gestation must be assumed to be that of neuroblast multiplication (Dobbing and Sands, 1973).

The first indication that the pathogenesis of microcephaly may be temporally related to the first half of the second gestational trimester came from the concurrent and independent observation (Miller and Blot, 1972) that microcephaly in the survivors of the atomic attacks on Japan occurred mainly in those whose fetal age corresponded to the same period of gestation (Figure 3). It seemed possible that the curtailment of neuroblast multiplication which might be expected in such circumstances could be a fore-runner of microcephaly, although it is still by no means clear how this could so disturb the sequence of brain development as to reduce the ultimate mass of brain tissue so severely. More recently Otake and Schull (1980) cited by Mole

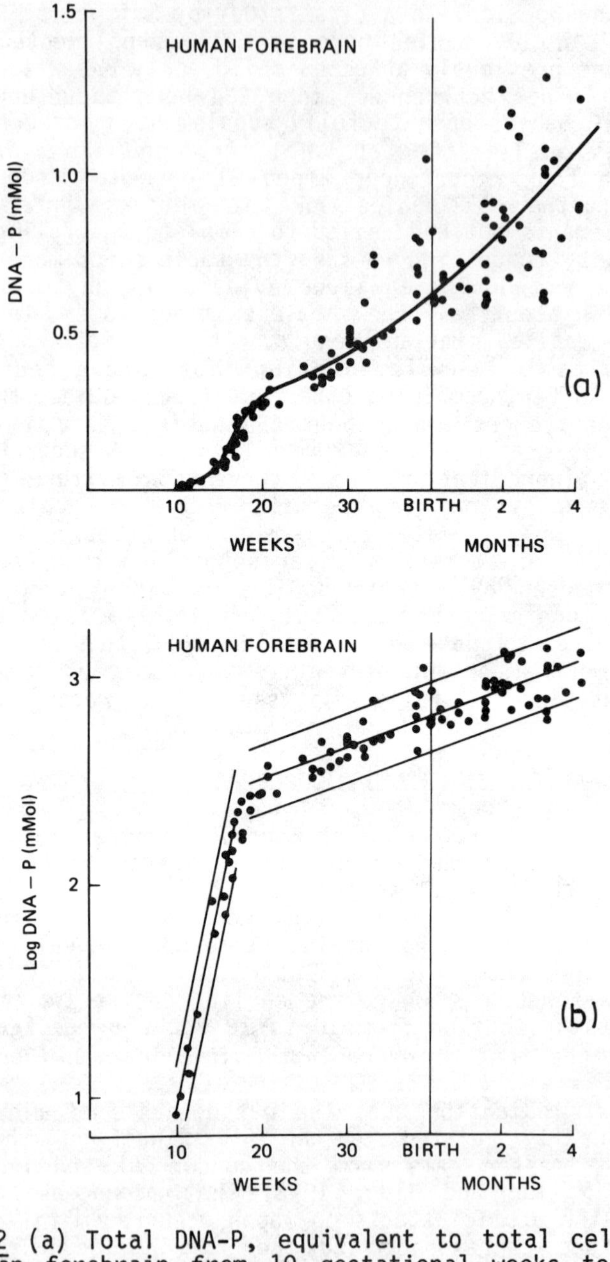

Figure 2 (a) Total DNA-P, equivalent to total cell number, in the human forebrain from 10 gestational weeks to 4 postnatal months, showing the two-phase characteristics of prenatal cell multiplication. (b) A semi-logarithmic plot of the same data as appear in (a) to show the sharp separation of the two phases at 18 gestational weeks. Regression lines with 95% confidence limits are added (Dobbing, 1981b)

(1980) have re-examined the records of the Japanese survivors and have divided those with small heads according to the presence or not of severe mental retardation (Figure 4). Those without retardation numbered 21 and were exposed between 4 and 16 weeks gestational age, 14 of them before 10 weeks and therefore before the onset of the main period of neuroblast multiplication. Clearly a "small head" can be produced by even earlier exposure. However, of the 18 whose small head was associated with severe mental retardation, all but three were fetuses between 10 and 18 weeks old when they were exposed. Mole (1980) discusses many of the implications of this finding.

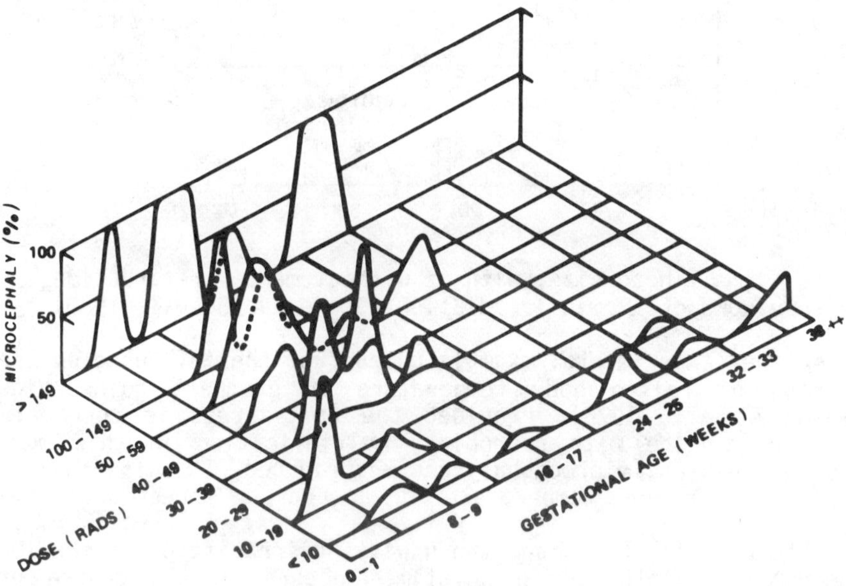

Figure 3 Distribution of small head size by fetal age and dose in survivors of atomic irradiation (Miller and Blot, 1972)

In the experimental rat it is quite difficult to produce microcephaly except by inhibiting cell division during the same period of neuroblast multiplication. This had been done using inhibitors of DNA synthesis (Adlard and Dobbing, 1975; Adlard et al., 1975), and a head disproportionately small for the body size is routinely produced, together with severe deficits in behaviour. Most other restrictions on growth, such as undernutrition (Dobbing, 1981a, b) result in heads which are too large for the body size (due to an effect on the body which is greater than that on the head). It seems to be necessary to interfere with neuroblast multiplication to produce specifically smaller heads with behavioural concomitants.

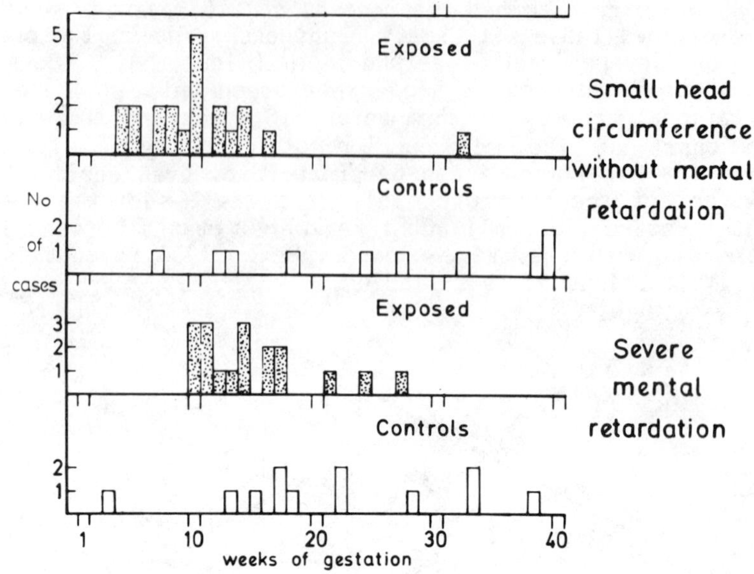

Figure 4 Small head size, with or without mental retardation, in survivors of atomic irradiation (Otake and Schull, 1980)

Another experimental example comes from the influence on the offspring of raised body temperature in pregnant guinea-pigs (Edwards et al., 1976). Provided the heat-stress is correctly timed to coincide with neuroblast multiplication in this more precocial species, microcephaly can be produced. It only requires a 2-3°C rise in core temperature for an hour on three successive days.

Returning to the human, the unwitting irradiation of the 10-18 week human fetus which sometimes occurs in the course of inducing an artificial menopause, characteristically results in a multitude of disasters for the surviving fetus, amongst which is said to be microcephaly. This is an example which is difficult to document, since such cases are often the subject of litigation and are probably rarely published.

More recently it has been shown that some newborn babies of mothers treated for hypertension during pregnancy using methyldopa have slightly smaller head circumferences than normally expected. Such cases are confined to those exposed to the drug during this same period of neuroblast multiplication (Moar et al., 1978). It must be emphasized that such babies appear to suffer no subsequent disadvantage. The degree of "microcephaly" is very slight, and no functional disability has been detected in them (Redman and Ounsted, 1982). However it is at least possible that the phenomenon is the same as the one being discussed, although to an extremely mild degree. If so, the Japanese populations in whom a few very severe effects have been retrospectively chronicled may well have contained very many more, much less severe cases, only some of whom might have been of functional significance. Head circumference is an insensitive measure of head volume or of brain weight (Dobbing and Sands, 1978). It is unlikely as well as highly undesirable that any direct proof, involving a prospective design and very careful measurement, will ever be available.

Two other examples of conditions in which there is unexplained microcephaly are certain viral infections of the fetus (rubella, cytomegaly) and certain inborn errors of metabolism (maternal phenylketonuria, etc.), in both of which the causative agent (virus or abnormal level of metabolite) surrounds and permeates the brain at this critical time.

THE THIRD HUMAN TRIMESTER AND THE FIRST FEW POSTNATAL YEARS

The brain as a whole does not grow along a straight line in any species, but passes through a transient period of rapid growth known as the brain growth spurt. During this time an especially large number of brain structures as well as new biochemical and other functions are developing (Dobbing, 1981a, b). Since growth pathology of the developing brain depends on the events occurring at the time of the infliction of insult or restriction, it follows that this period of a multitude of growth processes will be especially vulnerable. However, in humans it is a long drawn-out period lasting from about 30 gestational weeks to at least the second birthday (Dobbing and Sands, 1973). It has to be assumed (since all the evidence necessarily comes from animal experiments (Dobbing and Sands, 1979)) that a major proportion of the whole 30-month period has to be affected. In a slowly growing species like ours a few days would not be enough.

With these caveats in mind the following are some of the physical consequences of growth restriction during the comparable period in experimental animals. These effects are permanent, having resisted long periods of subsequent energetic attempts to induce catch-up growth.

(1) Firstly, and associated with the permanent stunting of bodily growth, the brain is found to be small. However it is not very much smaller than would be appropriate for the smaller body weight.

(2) All parts of the brain are not reduced to the same extent. For example the cerebellum is much more reduced in weight than is the rest of the brain (Dobbing *et al.*, 1971). This is almost certainly attributable to the cerebellum's peculiar growth characteristics. In humans as well as in animals it grows much faster, although at the same time as the rest of the brain (Dobbing and Sands, 1973). Thus, on the assumption that long-term vulnerability is related to speed of early growth, restriction of the whole growing brain would be expected to affect the part which grows fastest: and so it does. This differential effect on the cerebellum is also associated in animals with a detectable clumsiness (Lynch *et al.*, 1975). It is therefore possible that some human clumsiness may be of similar aetiology. The cerebellar

growth disorder does not include any focal lesions nor any easily detectable alteration of shape and would therefore easily escape the pathologist's notice if examined by conventional post-mortem techniques. It can only be shown whether it occurs in human brains when pathologists begin to weigh the cerebellum separately and express it as a proportion of the whole brain, or by laborious quantitative histology, as will be mentioned next.

(3) Histologically it is possible to detect a differential absence of granular neurons in the cerebellum by appropriate quantitative techniques (Dobbing et al., 1971). Also there appears to be a loss of cerebral cortical neurons in certain layers. These are further examples of the fact that distortion (in this case of the histological architecture) accompanies mere quantitative deficit.

(4) The deficit in brain lipids is greater than that expected from the reduction in brain size (Dobbing, 1968). The lipid picture is further distorted by there being a differential reduction specifically in myelin lipids.

(5) It has been suggested that the number of synapses per cortical neuron is substantially reduced (Cragg, 1972). This potentially important finding has recently been substantiated using modern techniques of quantitative histology (Thomas et al., 1979). In rats moderately undernourished for a period corresponding in human terms from mid-gestation until about the third birthday there was a deficit of 38% in the number of synapses per neuron in the frontal cortex at the end of the period of undernutrition. This is an area where the normal number is about 22 000 for each neuron at this age. Restoration of a highly nutritious diet until adulthood resulted in an apparent recovery, illustrating that some features of restricted brain growth can be recovered, at least to some extent, by vigorous rehabilitation of a kind which is frequently not available to human populations. More study of the conditions for recovery is urgently needed.

(6) This is not the place to discuss the behavioural consequences in animals of early growth restriction. There are formidable difficulties in interpretation of animal behavioural experiments, some of which are discussed elsewhere (Smart, 1977). In the human field a large literature presents even more complex interpretive problems which are probably best discussed in relation to a recent study of Jamaican children (Hertzig et al., 1972; Pan American Health Organisation, 1972). However, there are some striking alterations of higher mental function in both human and other animal species, which seem to persist, following early growth restriction correctly timed.

It is by no means clear at the time of writing whether the effects on higher mental function are mediated through such physical brain deficits and distortions as have been mentioned above, whether they result from altered endocrine settings including those known to produce permanent alterations of sexuality and aggression at this same early period, whether they are related to differences induced in the "stress" response as measured by alterations in circulating steroid, or whether by a combination of several of these things (Dobbing, 1981a, b). The important concept of early influences on later achievement is still a nebulous one in nearly all branches of paediatric research, but it is likely to be one of the most rewarding in the next half century, and nowhere more so than in the field of developing intellect and personality.

CONCLUSIONS

A series of growth pathologies of the developing brain have been discussed in relation to the developmental stage at which they occur. These range from serious malformation during the first human gestational trimester, through severe microcephaly thought to occur mainly in the early second trimester, to the relatively less severe effects produced during the prolonged brain growth spurt from then until at least the second birthday. Although less severe, it is likely that these latter affect a very much larger number of children, most of them in the normal or para-normal population.

REFERENCES

Adlard, B.P.F. and Dobbing, J. (1975). Maze learning by adult rats after inhibition of neuronal multiplication in utero. **Ped. Res. 9** 139-142

Adlard, B.P.F., Dobbing, J. and Sands, J. (1975). A comparison of the effects of cytosine arabinoside and adenine arabinoside on some aspects of brain growth and development in the rat. **Brit. J. Pharmacol. 54** 33-39

Cragg, B.G. (1972). The development of cortical synapses during starvation in the rat. **Brain 95** 143-150

Dobbing, J. (1968). Vulnerable periods in developing brain. In **Applied Neurochemistry**, Eds. A.N. Davison and J. Dobbing. Blackwell, Oxford. 287-316

Dobbing, J. (1973). The developing brain: a plea for more critical interspecies extrapolation. **Nutr. Rep. Int. 7** 401-406

Dobbing, J. (1981a). Nutritional growth restriction of the nervous system. In **The Molecular Basis of Neuropathology.** Eds. A.N. Davison and R.H.S. Thompson. Edward Arnold, London. 221-233

Dobbing, J. (1981b). The later development of the brain and its vulnerability. In **Scientific Foundations of Paediatrics,** 2nd Edition. Eds. J.A. David and J. Dobbing. Heinemann, London. 744-759

Dobbing, J. (Ed) (1983). **The Prevention of Neural Tube Defects.** Academic Press.

Dobbing, J., Hopewell, J.W. and Lynch, A. (1971). Vulnerability of developing brain: VII. Permanent deficit of neurons in cerebral and cerebellar cortex following early mild undernutrition. **Exp. Neurol. 32** 439-447

Dobbing, J. and Sands, J. (1973). The quantitative growth and development of the human brain. **Arch. Dis. Childh. 48** 757-767

Dobbing, J. and Sands, J. (1978). Head circumference, biparietal diameter and brain growth in fetal and postnatal life. **Early Hum. Dev. 2** 81-87

Dobbing, J. and Sands, J. (1979). Comparative aspects of the brain growth spurt. **Early Hum. Dev. 3** 79-83

Edwards, M.J., Wanner, R.A. and Mulley, R.C. (1976). Growth and development of the brain in normal and heat-retarded guinea pigs. **Neuropath. Appl. Neurol. 2** 439-450

Hertzig, M.E., Birch, H.G., Richardson, S.A. and Tizard, J. (1972). Intellectual levels of school children severely malnourished during the first two years of life. **Paediatrics 49** 814-824

Laurence, K.M., James, N., Miller, M.H., Tennant, G.B. and Campbell, H. (1981). Double-blind randomised controlled trial of folate treatment before conception to prevent recurrence of neural tube defects. **Brit. Med.** J. (i) 1509-1511

Lynch, A., Smart, J.L. and Dobbing, J. (1975). Motor coordination and cerebellar size in adult rats undernourished in early life. **Brain Res. 83** 249-259

Miller, R.W. and Blot, W.J. (1972). Small head size after _in utero_ exposure to atomic radiation. **Lancet** (ii), 784-787

Moar, V.A., Jefferies, M.A., Mutch, L.M.M., Ounsted, M.K. and Redman, C.W.G. (1978). Neonatal head circumference and the treatment of maternal hypertension. **Brit. J. Obstet. Gynaecol. 85** 933-937

Mole, R.J. (1980). Personal communication. International Symposium on Developmental Effects of Pre-natal Irradiation, Neuherberg, Munich

Otake, M. and Schull, W.J. (1980). Relationship of gamma rays and neutrons to mental retardation in children exposed _in utero_ to the atomic bombs, Hiroshima and Nagasaki. **Radiation Effects Research Foundation Report**, cited by Mole (1980)

Pan American Health Organisation (1972). **Nutrition, the Nervous System and Behaviour.** Pan American Health Organization Scientific Publication No. 251

Redman, C.W.G. and Ounsted, M.K. (1982). Safety for the child of drug treatment for hypertension in pregnancy. **Lancet** (i) 1237

Smart, J.L. (1977). Early life malnutrition and later learning ability. A critical analysis. In **Genetics, Environment and Intelligence**. Ed. A. Oliverio. Elsevier, Amsterdam. 215-235

Smithells, R.W., Sheppard, S., Schorah, C.J., Seller, M.J., Nevin, N.C., Harris, R., Read, A.P., and Fielding, D.W. (1981). Apparent prevention of neural tube defects by periconceptional vitamin supplementation. **Arch. Dis. Child. 56** 911-918

Thomas, Y.M., Bedi, K.S., Davies, C.A. and Dobbing, J. (1979). A stereological analysis of the neuronal and synaptic content of the frontal and cerebellar cortex of weanling rats undernourished from birth. **Early Hum. Dev. 3** 109-126

COMMENTARY

R. Balazs

Although I completely agree with Dobbing that the clinical application of repair mechanisms and transplantation is not yet a practicable proposition, I feel it is worth mentioning here some of the relevant, exciting new developments in neurobiology. It has been shown that in experimental animals fetal brain tissue can be successfully transplanted into the adult brain. The fetal grafts placed into a corresponding lesioned region in the adult are able to innervate the proper targets in a cell type specific manner and are innervated by the normal afferents. It seems that the structural integration of the graft into the host tissue is paralleled by a partial restoration of normal functional connections, as monitored by electrophysiological responses and by performance in behavioural tests. Furthermore, grafts comprising the whole organized tissue can be successfully replaced by perikarya suspensions, which after injection into the proper site are able to rectify the defects caused by the brain lesion. It is especially important that the fetal grafts are not rejected even though, in comparison with the host, they are derived from a different species (e.g. mouse to rat) or if from the same species from strains with different histocompatibility antigens (e.g. Sprague-Dawley and Wistar). Finally, certain neural crest derivatives, such as the adrenal medullary cells, exhibit a potential of changing their phenotypic expression under proper conditions, when in culture they can be induced to emit fibres and can innervate a target. These experimental observations raise the possibility that transplantation may be used in treatment, e.g. of neurodegenerative disorders, in the not so distant future.

I. Janota

This is excellent; thoughtful, critical but highly selective: "bizarre pathologies" such as those associated with chromosomal abnormalities and what can go wrong in the perinatal period are excluded. In the section on general principles and definitions, in connection with "mental retardation" or "mental handicap" it should be remembered that the neuropathological principles are the same in children and in adults where the terminology includes another unsatisfactory term: dementia. Dobbing's discussion, via small head (with a small brain in it), centres on neural tube defects that arise in the first human trimester of gestation, numbers of nerve cells determined largely in the second trimester, and pathologies of later growth. Rubella and cytomegaly are mentioned; they perhaps better belong to the "bizarre pathologies" that are dismissed at the beginning. The disproportionately (to the total bulk of the brain) small cerebellum makes one wonder whether Down's subjects are more clumsy. The differential reduction specifically in myelin lipids does among other things relate to myelination - a component of growth. There are references to another growth phenomenon: the development and number of synapses. Dobbing's stated criteria may exclude the consideration of some of the following: animal models of gangliosidosis in dogs, cats and cattle (for references see Purpura, 1979), or the work on fetal alcohol syndrome in the rat (as presented, for example, by Stoltenburg-Didinger, 1982). Attention to the development and abnormalities of the dendrites and their spines would fit before the mention of the synapses. A critical review of what a variety of specialists make of fetal alcohol syndrome would be welcome.

To a neuropathologist who is drawn by his clinical colleagues to look at or for the more obvious in "bad" children, there is a hiatus between the so-called bizarre pathologies, etc., and the "populations" that may suffer deficiencies of growth. In that hiatus are most "children" in our society who die early, or who graduate via paediatricians, paediatric neurologists, paediatric psychiatrists, psychologists, teachers and many others to sheltered existence in their families or in institutions. Often enough admission to institutions comes when the family can no longer cope or is no longer there to cope. Such instances, by no means rare in our society, are reflected in a load on social services and on the society in general. It may be too optimistic to imagine that Dobbing's message and suggested research approaches will make much difference to all that.

References

Purpura, D.P. (1979). Pathobiology of cortical neurons in metabolic and unclassified amentias. In Katzman, R. (Ed.) **Congenital and Acquired Cognitive Disorders**, Raven Press, New York

Stoltenburg-Didinger, G., et al. (1982). Paper presented at **IXth International Congress of Neuropathology**, Vienna, September 5-10, 1982

I. A. McKinlay

The major mysteries of developmental medicine are the pathological explanations for neurological and neuropsychiatric disorders in children without the physical stigmata of specific syndromes, genetic or acquired. No doubt species adapting to a changing environment will experiment with brain architecture and individuals will show individual accelerated or decelerated learning ability in relation to family characteristics. Clinicians still have much to do in the delineation of the limits of normality. (Educational systems with a narrow curriculum directed towards the average child create problems for exceptional children. Children have only recently been expected to read, write and master mathematics in developed countries. Those who fail to do this within the average range are seen as unsuccessful though their capacity to appreciate music, look after animals or find their way about the world may be ignored or underdeveloped.)

Contemporary neurophysiological and neuroradiological investigation of children with unexplained mental handicap, disabling epilepsies, severe learning difficulties, clumsiness, infantile and childhood psychosis and adolescent schizophrenia has been disappointing. The brain disorders must be more subtle. Conversely there are children whose brains show severe focal structural pathology (porencephaly) or diffuse pathology (hydrocephalus) who show average or above average intellectual ability. Again compensatory mechanisms must be at a cellular level.

This is where the new developmental neurobiology has so much to offer. The level of organization of the brain in terms of the modular arrangement of neurons in the cerebral cortex and the vast interconnection network of dendritic interconnections is as awe-inspiring to contemplate as the astronomy of the universe. Techniques for studying this biology and its pathologies require very exceptional expertise and the application to human clinical material has been slight. In only a few score human brains has there been adequate study of cell numbers and dendritic organization but the results have sometimes been spectacular.

In addition the unravelling of the sequences and timescale of brain organization has added a fascinating perspective. If the most rapidly evolving parts of the nervous system are the most vulnerable to insult at a particular time it can be predicted that the same insult may have widely varying effects at different times according to the state of development of individual brains. Lesions may constitute loss of neurons, poverty of dendritic connections or delayed maturational processes with different prospects for recovery depending on environmental factors.

It is becoming conceivable that aspects of brain structure and function relevant to this theme will be studied *in vivo* relatively non-invasively. For example it will be possible to study the cross-sectional area of the corpus callosum (pure interconnection tissue) and the volume of the cerebellum using brain scans. Emission tomography, neuromagnetic resonance, very sophisticated electroencephalography and brain metabolic studies will enable better understanding of the parts of the brain in cognitive processes.

Such intense bioscientific investigation is clearly possible in very few centres in wealthy developed countries but the knowledge gained has world-wide implications. Large populations are undernourished and exposed to debilitating infectious illnesses. The children born to hungry, sick parents may lose the cerebral capacity to cope with a stressful and difficult environment. It may be that thorough study of brain DNA and dendritic pathology will have extensive implications for the world's economic and political thinking. It will also help clinicians to explain individual children's handicaps to their families.

H. F. R. Prechtl

In his chapter, Dobbing expresses a pessimistic view on the plasticity of the developing nervous system. No mention is given to the rapidly expanding field of descriptive and experimental studies on cell death and on reinnervation and rewiring occurring in damaged brains of higher mammals, including infra-human primates.

There is substantial evidence for an overgrowth in the number of neurons during early development, not only in tadpoles and chick embryos but also in mammals (for reviews see Cowan, 1973; Oppenheim, 1981). When neuroblasts have migrated to the place of destination (e.g. in the spinal cord or visual cortex) a varying percentage of them are subjected to cell death, often reducing the original neuronal population by a half, even though many of them have made functional connections. Proliferation of neurons is thus followed by a matching process between central areas and other central or peripheral projection areas. Function seems to be of importance in this process as experimental blocking of functions reduces cell death (Pittman and Oppenheim, 1979). Enlargement of the periphery also reduces cell death of motor neurons (Hollyday and Hamburger, 1976).

In the lumbar cord of the fetal mouse, 65% of motor neurons die between 13 and 19 days gestation (Lance-Jones, 1982). In the macaque's visual cortex neuron numbers decrease from birth to 3 months by 20-34% (O'Kusky and Colonnier, 1982) depending on the cortical layer. Similar data have been found in other areas of the brain. Overproduction of neurons followed by regression seems to be a universal phenomenon in developing higher vertebrates. It is quite conceivable that the regulating mechanisms, which obviously exist, may compensate if neuronal cell proliferation is reduced by adverse conditions, such as intrauterine undernutrition in the human.

As far as the results on the timing of neuronal proliferation between 10 and 18 weeks gestation are concerned, one should keep in mind that these values may differ for different areas of the nervous system. In the human spinal cord differentiation of neurons and synapse formation have reached functional maturity at 8 weeks (Okado, 1981), an age at which movement patterns emerge for the first time (de Vries *et al.*, 1982). Moreover, not all glial cells are proliferated after neuronal proliferation.

A certain kind of glia - the radial glial cells - is produced very early and the migrating neuroblasts use them as a guiding structure, as has been shown for the cerebellum and the cortex (Rakic, 1971, 1972).

As a final point, I want to raise the problem of reconstruction of the nervous system after lesions. Such reconstructions do take place in the injured developing nervous system of higher vertebrates. Although the damaged neuronal population is never replaced, the undamaged tissue reacts by reinnervating neurons which have lost their synaptic input. Injured axon bundles can sprout collaterals which may then reinnervate those neurons deprived of their input due to the lesion. Although these discoveries were enthusiastically welcomed as mechanisms of structural and functional repair, it has turned out to be a process which may produce adverse effects (Schneider, 1979; Gramsbergen, 1982; Gramsbergen and IJkema-Paassen, 1982). On the other hand, a unilateral lesion of the cortico-spinal system may be functionally compensated for by a hypertrophy of the ipsilateral cortico-spinal tract, even in man. At present we must consider the powerful plasticity of the developing nervous system in response to damage which leads to brains biologically different from those normally occurring (Prechtl, 1978).

References

Cowan, W.M. (1973). Neuronal death as a regulative mechanism in the control of cell number in the nervous system. In: **Development and Aging in the Nervous System.** Rockstein, M. (Ed.). Academic Press, New York

Gramsbergen, A. (1982). The effects of cerebellar hemispherectomy in the young rat. I. **Behavioural Brain Research, 6,** 85-92

Gramsbergen, A. and IJkema-Paassen, J. (1982). CNS plasticity after hemicerebellectomy in the young rat. Quantitative relations between aberrant and normal cerebellorubal projections. **Neuroscience Letters, 3,** 129-134

Hollyday, M. and Hamburger, V. (1976). Reduction of the naturally occurring motor neuron loss by enlargement of the periphery. **Journal of Comp. Neurology, 170,** 311-320

Lance-Jones, C., (1982). Motoneuron cell death in the developing lumbar spinal cord of the mouse. **Developmental Brain Research, 4**, 473-480

Okado, N. (1981). Onset of synapse formation in the human spinal cord. **Journal of Comp. Neurology, 201**, 211-219

O'Kusky, J. and Colonnier, M. (1982). Postnatal changes in the number of neurons and synapses in visual cortex (area 17) of the macaque monkey: a stereological analysis in normal and monocularly deprived animals. **Journal of Comp. Neurology, 210**, 3, 291-306

Oppenheim, R.W. (1981). Neuronal cell death and some related regressive phenomena during neurogenesis: a selective historical review and progress report. In: **Studies in Developmental Neurobiology: Essays in Honor of Viktor Hamburger**, Cowan, W.M. (Ed.). Oxford University Press, New York - Oxford, 74-133

Pittman, R. and Oppenheim, R.W. (1979). Cell death of motoneurons in the chick embryo spinal cord. IV. Evidence that a functional neuromuscular interaction is involved in the regulation of naturally occurring cell death and the stabilization of synapses. **Journal of Comp. Neurology 187**, 425-446

Prechtl, H.F.R. (1978). Minimal brain dysfunction syndrome and the plasticity of the nervous system. **Advances in Biological Psychiatry, 1**, 96-105

Rakic, P. (1971). Neuron-glia relationship during granule cell migration in developing cerebellar cortex. A Golgi and electronmicroscopic study in Macacus rhesus. **Journal of Comp. Neurology, 141**, 283-312

Rakic, P. (1972). Mode of cell migration to the superficial layers of fetal monkey neocortex. **Journal of Comp. Neurology, 145**, 61-84

Schneider, G.E. (1979). Is it really better to have your brain lesion early - revision of the Kennard principle. **Neuropsychol., 17**, 557-594

Vries, de J.I.P., Visser, G.H.A. and Prechtl, H.F.R. (1982). The emergence of fetal behaviour I. Qualitative aspects. **Early Human Development, 7**, 301-322

D. A. A. Primrose

In connection with the statement in Dobbing's paper that undernourishment in rats reduces synaptic development, I wish to suggest that synaptic development is dependent on neurotransmitter substances, and that it is a lack of specific neurotransmitter substances in the period of synaptic development which leads to mental handicap in some of those cases in which it occurs. A human experimental situation may occur in certain cases with tumours; for example in ocular malignant melanoma a severe restriction of dietary phenylalanine (as in phenylketonuria) will cause regression of the tumour with cell death and eventual fibrosis.

Chapter 6

Neurobiology and neurochemistry of the developing brain

A.N. Davison

INTRODUCTION

Little is still understood about the nature of the anatomical structures or interrelationships associated with higher mental activity. For the most part, the aetiology of mental retardation is also unknown. Apart from genetic abnormality (e.g. 21 trisomy), inborn errors (e.g. galactosaemia) and infections (viral and bacterial), there are environmental factors which may permanently affect the brain during critical stages of its development. A study of the neuropathology of these diverse conditions may provide some clues to structures affected and possible mechanisms leading to mental impairment (Davison, 1977). In order to appreciate these possibilities, it is first necessary to consider the series of events which lead to the ordered development of the central nervous system.

After early embryological development, the central nervous system undergoes a series of interrelated and exceedingly complex morphological and biochemical changes. Initial formation of neuroblasts leads to an early achievement of adult numbers of neurons (Dobbing, this volume). Neurogenesis first occurs in the phylogenetically older regions of the brain. Formation of glia overlaps and continues for a longer period. After neurogenesis, there is increase in the size of the nerve cell body, with formation of dendrites, axons and synaptic connections. Changes occur in the architectural organization of the brain due to cell migration and the loss of redundant cells (which fail to form synapses).

ORGANOGENESIS

In the embryo the nervous system originates from the neural plate which subsequently folds into the hollow neural tube. How this happens through gene induction and other control mechanisms is still poorly understood. It appears that some of the cells in the neural crest are multi-potential. When single crest cells are grown in tissue culture, they can give rise to colonies of mixed phenotypes. For example, three major cell types are known to originate from the primitive sympathoadrenal lineage. Some experiments indicate that balance between nerve growth factor (a protein necessary for survival and growth of sympathetic neurons) and glucocorticoids influences the choice between development into either neuronal or adrenal medullary phenotypes (Landis and Patterson, 1981). However, even when neurons begin to express noradrenergic properties, other factors (e.g. neuronal activity) can induce change of neurotransmitter. If newborn rat superior cervical ganglion cells are dissociated and grown in culture, the neurons would initially express noradrenergic properties. However, if conditioned medium - from heart myocytes or fibroblasts - is added, the cultured neurons can develop cholinergic properties.

The Cell Cycle

Knowledge of the timing of neurogenesis relies on experimental use of tritiated thymidine labelling of cells. The thymidine is incorporated into the DNA of dividing cells and subsequently the labelled cells are traced by autoradiography. As a result, rigid time-tables for neurogenesis can be identified. There is a short period of mitosis and a longer period during which synthesis of DNA occurs. Studies by Balazs, Patel and Lewis (Patel and Lewis, 1982) have shown that various drugs as well as hormonal insufficiency and undernutrition can interfere with cell proliferation. This provides one explanation for the structural and behavioural deficits induced by such conditions.

Selective Neurotoxicity

Another possibility is that toxic substances (e.g. environmental poisons, bacterial or viral toxins) may kill certain classes of cells when they are exposed at critical times during neurogenesis. An experimental example is the use of a natural poison, methylazoxymethanol acetate. If the drug is given at birth, cerebellar development is disrupted but not neocortical development. When a single dose of this carcinogen is given to fetal rats (15th day of gestation) it can produce microcephaly and reduction in cortical cell number (Johnston and Coyle, 1982). Affected adult animals show learning deficits. Biochemical studies on the brain show a resultant imbalance in neurotransmitters. The GABA-ergic interneurons of the cortex are relatively reduced in number, whereas the concentration of noradrenergic markers (representing the cortical afferent system) are not so affected. Johnston and Coyle (1982) make the interesting suggestion that relative hyper-innervation by aminergic or other projections to the cortex is a common outcome from naturally occurring fetal or perinatal brain injury or developmental dysgenesis. Lesion experiments in developing primates suggest that this may well be the case. In monkey fetuses with surgical cortical lesions, callosal inputs to the resected cortex are re-routed to adjacent undamaged cortex. It is also known that developing cortical connections in the brain display considerable plasticity by expanding their territories of termination in response to injury. For example, monkey thalamocortical fibres representing one eye in the lateral geniculate expand into areas deprived of afferents from the other eye during fetal life. Johnston and Coyle (1982) conclude that the persistence of unusual interneuronal relationships after injury may thus be important as a substrate of abnormal brain function.

Migration and Aggregation of Neurons

Since most neurons arise from the neuroepithelium of the ventricular lining, the cells have to undergo migration to reach their final destiny (e.g. in the cortical plate or in the marginal zone of the cortex). Their passage, by amoeboid movement, frequently over considerable distances, is sometimes directed by long glial processes which radiate from the ventricular zone to the outer surface (Rakic, 1981). Migration is further facilitated by the secretion of a proteolytic enzyme, plasminogen activator (Seeds *et al.*, 1980). When the neurons reach their destination, they tend to aggregate and orientate to form recognizable layers or nuclear masses.

Aggregation

When developing nervous tissue is dissociated by gentle disruption or by agents such as trypsin, the mixed cells can be shown to be capable of controlled reaggregation. Distinctive patterns occur for each region, and the ability to do so is critically age-dependent. Aggregation patterns are closely correlated with proliferative activity, migration schedules, and states of differentiation of the cells (Garber and Moscona, 1973). For example, dissociated fetal mouse hippocampal cells can form a curved lamina of pyramidal cells with oriented apical processes, but the pattern only occurs in cells dissociated from 17.5-18.5 day old fetuses. When aggregates are prepared of the isocortex of an autosomal recessive mutant reeler mouse, very distinct abnormalities are found in the organization (Seeds *et al.*, 1980). These correlate with the histological changes found in the reeler mice. Microscopic examination shows defects in cellular architecture. The general shape of the reorganized hippocampus in the reeler is still intact, but the pattern is fuzzy. The cells are present, but not in their proper locations.

Aggregating fetal brain cells when supplemented by insulin or insulin-like growth factor-I show increased synthesis of DNA during the first week in tissue culture, and there is an increase in glutamate decarboxylase and choline acetyltransferase activities (these enzymes synthesize the putative neurotransmitter GABA and acetylcholine respectively). There is a whole range of growth-promoting peptides (molecular weights 7000-8000), including somatomedin A and C, known to be present in human plasma. Insulin-like growth factor has a high binding affinity with fetal brain membranes, and less so with increasing age (Sara and Hall, 1979).

Experiments on re-aggregation of nervous tissue *in vitro* have been extended to studies *in vivo*. An example is the injection of brain cell suspensions into the peritoneal cavity and into the anterior chamber of the eye. Dissociated embryonic hippocampus will grow and differentiate in the eye. The possibility of transplantation has been raised by demonstrations that suspensions or explants of substantia nigral tissue will re-innervate the striatum when the cells are placed close to this area in animals in which the substantia nigra was destroyed (for review see Marx, 1982). There is evidence that re-innervation of the hippocampal formation from cholinergic-rich embryonic septal transplants is functional in terms of the physiology of neural connectivity, and that the newly formed connections can interact with the perforant path - an intrinsic afferent system (Low *et al.*, 1982). Adult rats with neural transplants following septohippocampal lesions show partial recovery as tested by maze performance. It suggests that functional synaptic connections are responsible for the partial physiological recovery. Cross-species neural grafting has also been demonstrated (Bjorklund *et al.*, 1982), supporting the possibility of clinical application of transplantation in the treatment of neurodegenerative disorders (e.g. Parkinson's disease).

Neuronal Loss

Nerve cell populations are significantly reduced during the later stages of development. Possibly, loss of redundant neurons is an adaptive mechanism to remove errors in connectivity to their targets, but the loss in many neural units is larger than can be accounted for by such a process (Hamburger and Oppenheim, 1982). It seems that all neurons differentiate normally and send processes to their target areas, but that they then compete for life-maintaining substances (trophic agents) produced by other cells. Experimental removal of target (e.g. limb-bud extirpation) increases neural death, and those procedures extending the target area (e.g. transplanted limbs) allow more nerve cells to survive. In addition, neuromuscular blockade to decrease muscular activity increases survival of nerve cells, whereas chronic electrical stimulation of a hind limb increases the number of dying motor neurons in the lateral motor column.

Neuronal Specificity and Synaptogenesis

The work of Sperry and others on the optic system suggests that chemical cues present on receiving neurons of the tectum, serving to guide pioneer axons from the retina to their final site. Retinal ganglion cell axons project to and synapse with the tectal region of the brain in topographic order, thus translating the ordered map of retinal neuronal fields onto very limited regions of the tectum (Trisler, 1982). The remarkable specificity of interaction in the developing or regenerating nervous system is illustrated by the example of fibres which travel relatively large distances discarding many other sites before synapsing at their final destination. The path-finding mechanisms for axons include guidance by physical (e.g. glial) channels as well as by the presence of diffusable substances, stimulating forward movement of the growth cone.

Growth cones from different neurons have different surface carbohydrates on them - identified by lectin labelling. The membrane is distinctive from the cell wall of the nerve cell perikarya and contains small intramembranous particles derived from axon flow. Thus, sodium channels (identifiable with saxitoxin) are absent from the growing axon tip. Upon target cell contact ultrastructural and labelling properties alter, making it likely that transformation of the growth cone membrane into a presynaptic nerve terminal requires insertion of new membrane components or modification of existing ones. The glycoconjugates (protein synaptin, D_2-adhesion protein and lipid) are important on the presynaptic and postsynaptic side.

Trisler (1982) suggests that several categories of molecule may act for coding for neuronal position or synapse formation. The molecules must signal selectively for the major areas of the nervous system, they may be cell-type specific, or even be restricted to single neurons or neural networks. There is now evidence of molecular gradients on cell surfaces (such as the chick neural retina), which may code for the positional information for establishment or maintenance of appropriate synaptic connection. This important concept would provide an explanation for mechanisms which can conceivably control the organization of the brain.

Synapse formation occurs prior to and following functional development. For example, in the rat, before the eyes open, junctions are formed in the lateral geniculate nucleus. Since tubulin is localized in axonal microtubules, this protein has been studied as a measure of innervation (Cronly-Dillon and Perry, 1976). The peak in tubulin synthesis in the visual cortex coincides with opening of the eyes and the concentration of tubulin can be modified by deprivation (restricted sensory experience) affecting functional connectivity within the brain. In conditions leading to mental retardation, such as hypothyroidism or undernutrition, synapse formation is significantly inhibited.

Neurotransmitters

During growth of nerve cells and their processes, changes occur in brain biochemistry. Oxidative metabolism of glucose assumes a predominant role in providing energy and in supplying intermediates (e.g. α-ketoglutarate) for synthesis of non-essential amino acids by transamination. Thus, as the concentration of taurine drops, that of glutamate and aspartate (both putative excitatory transmitters) rises in the developing brain. As electrical activity appears and synapses form, there is an increase in enzymes involved in neurotransmitter synthesis. An example is the enzyme glutamate decarboxylase which in the nerve terminals is responsible for the synthesis of the inhibitory transmitter GABA.

There are interesting data (Reis *et al*., 1982) on inborn strains of mice which show that genetic control can affect the final number of nerve cells utilizing a specific neurotransmitter. During development, divergence of transmitter synthesizing activity can be shown in different brain regions. Thus, from about 10 days onwards in the basal ganglia, tyrosine hydroxylase (the enzyme synthesizing catecholamines) activity increases in the BALB mouse, so that eventually this region contains 30% more enzyme than is found in the CBA strain. There is also a physiological difference between the mice. The BALB mouse is more curious and the enhanced activity correlates with increased dopaminergic capacity.

Table 1

Biochemical changes in the putamen in Lesch-Nyhan syndrome

	Control	Lesch-Nyhan syndrome
Hypoxanthine-guanidine phosphoribosyl transferase	1075.0	3.0 nmol/h/mg protein
Dopamine	4.6	1.5 μg/g
Serotonin	0.34	0.42 μg/g
DOPA decarboxylase	2.61	0.28 nmol CO_2/mg protein/h
Glutamate decarboxylase	35.2	23.2 nmol CO_2/mg protein/h
Choline acetyltransferase	117.0	39.0 AcCh/mg protein/h

(After Lloyd *et al*., 1981)

It may be relevant that in Lesch-Nyhan syndrome (a disease in which there is self-mutilation and movement disorder) there are biochemical changes in the brain indicating involvement of cholinergic and especially dopaminergic neurons (Table 1). Lloyd *et al*. (1981) reasonably infer that these interesting findings are most compatible with a marked deficit in the terminal arborizations of dopaminergic neurons, and that this is probably responsible for the extrapyramidal dysfunctions characteristic of the Lesch-Nyhan syndrome. However, the primary genetic defect in the Lesch-Nyhan syndrome is the virtual absence of activity of a single enzyme, hypoxanthine-guanidine phosphoribosyl transferase (Table 1).

PATHOLOGICAL AND BIOCHEMICAL CHANGES IN HUMAN MENTAL RETARDATION

In the mentally retarded in whom the developmental process is impaired, no distinctive neuropathology is found (Crome and Stern, 1972). Microencephaly is the commonest finding and the cerebellum seems to be particularly affected. The relationship between mental retardation and cortical synaptic adult density is controversial. In a morphological study of brains from subjects with mental retardation (some with Down's syndrome), Cragg (1975) found no difference in density of nerve endings, although the overall number was probably reduced, as the brain weights were lower compared to controls from another series.

Phenylketonuria

A recent study by Bauman and Kemper (1982) on the morphology of the brain in untreated human phenylketonuria emphasizes the type of change found in this form of mental retardation. Delay was found in cytoarchitectonic development of the cortical plate (there was increased cell packing density), and there was also reduced nerve cell size. Paucity of dendrite development, especially in the terminal branches of apical dendrites, and reduction in synaptic spines is apparent. Alterations in the development of Nissl granulation in cortical neurons provided additional evidence of maturational delay. The Nissl substance and cell size of the giant Betz cells and Meynert pyramids which have a long developmental schedule extending over the sixth postnatal year of life were reduced. In contrast, neurons of the oculomotor nucleus and the nucleus basalis of Meynert, which are all fully developed at birth, failed to demonstrate any recognizable abnormality of Nissl granules when compared with age-matched controls. Thus, it seems likely that the paucity of Nissl granules of the cortical pyramidal cells and their reduced cell size represent a retardation or an impairment of normal development rather than a regressive change. Lack of Nissl substance (rough endoplasmic reticulum) would lead to impaired protein synthesis. Although cell size was unaffected in the oculomotor nucleus, it was reduced in the nucleus basalis of Meynert. The latter is of particular interest inasmuch as the nucleus basalis of Meynert has been found to contain cholinergic neurons which project to the neocortex. Thus, the reduction in cell size in these phenylketonuric brains may reflect a deficiency of this neurotransmitter, a deficiency which has also been demonstrated in experimental animal models of phenylketonuria (Loo *et al*., 1980).

Table 2

Comparison of the activities of enzymes involved in acetylcholine synthesis and hydrolysis in Down's syndrome and Alzheimer's disease

Area of brain	Choline acetyltransferase (mol/h/g wet wt.)			Acetylcholinesterase (mmol/h/g wet wt.)		
	Down	Alzh.	Contr.	Down	Alzh.	Contr.
Caudate nucleus	1.84	3.89	7.78	1.30	1.24	1.75
Amygdala	0.05	0.36	2.09	0.05	0.10	0.29
Frontal cortex	0.07	0.10	0.20	0.02	0.02	0.04
Parahippocampal gyrus	0.03	0.09	0.30	0.03	0.02	0.05
Mid-temporal gyrus	0.04	0.06	0.24	0.2	0.2	0.04

(After Yates *et al.*, 1980)

Down's Syndrome

In Down's syndrome there is also evidence of a defect in brain development. About half the expected amounts of myelin (compared to age-matched controls) have been found in cortical white matter and a decrease in total synaptic protein isolated from the cortical grey matter (Banik *et al.*, 1975). There are data which indicate changes in size of nucleoli (Mann *et al.*, 1982) within the nerve cell nucleus (comparable to similar alterations found in Alzheimer's disease). These changes indicate altered protein metabolism and interference with RNA synthesis. Using fetal brain material, Lim and his colleagues in my department have isolated messenger RNA and found expression of proteins to be different from that of controls. Similarly, in phenylketonuria there are data suggesting that increased concentration of phenylalanine in the circulation competes for entry of essential amino acids into the brain and interferes with protein synthesis at a critical time. Some of the biochemical features and possibilities are discussed by Blair and Leeming (this volume).

Synapses depleted of vesicles and others full of a primitive form of coated vesicles have been found by Ohara (1972), suggesting a defect in the formation of transmitter-containing vesicles. Microscopic lesions in the cerebral cortex of adult patients with Down's syndrome have been described as identical with those of Alzheimer's disease. A loss of nerve cells from the cholinergic neurons of the nucleus basalis (Price et al., 1983) and marked depletion of noradrenergic neurons from the locus coeruleus (Mann et al., 1982) have been described in Down's syndrome and in Alzheimer's disease. Thus, in both there are comparable changes in the indices of cholinergic neuronal activity (Bowen, 1981) in some - but not all - areas of the brain (Table 2).

CONCLUSIONS

Although the aetiology of most examples of brain growth pathology remains obscure, there are indications from neurobiological studies of mechanisms which may be initially affected. Defective formation, migration and aggregation of nerve cells may occur. Pathological studies indicate that abnormal nerve terminals or reduction in synaptic networks seems to be a common finding in the brain of the mentally retarded. Changes in markers of neurotransmitter activity are also evident, and these may be related to lack of afferent fibres from depleted subcortical neurons.

REFERENCES

Ball, M.J. and Nuttall, K. (1980). Neurofibrillary tangles, granulovacuolar degeneration and neuron loss in Down syndrome: quantitative comparison with Alzheimer dementia, **Ann. Neurol., 7**, 462-466

Banik, N.L., Davison, A.N., Palo, J. and Savolainen, H. (1975). Biochemical studies on myelin isolated from the brains of patients with Down's syndrome, **Brain, 98**, 213-218

Bauman, M.L. and Kemper, T.L. (1982). Morphologic and histoanatomic observations of the brain in the untreated human phenylketonuria, **Acta Neuropath. (Berl.), 58**, 55-63

Bjorklund, A., Stenevi, U., Dunnett, S.B. and Gage, F.H. (1982). Cross-species neural grafting in a rat model of Parkinson's disease, **Nature, 298**, 652-654

Bowen, D.M. (1981). Alzheimer's disease. In: **The Molecular Basis of Neuropathology** (A.N. Davison and R.H.S. Thompson, eds.) pp. 649-665. Edward Arnold, London

Cragg, B.G. (1975). The density of synapses and neurons in normal, mentally defective and ageing human brains, **Brain, 98**, 81-90

Crome, L. and Stern, J. (1972). **Pathology of Mental Retardation**, 2nd edition. Churchill-Livingston, Edinburgh and London

Cronly-Dillon, J.R. and Perry, G.W. (1976). Tubulin synthesis in developing rat visual cortex, **Nature, 261**, 581-583

Davison, A.N. (1977). The biochemistry of brain development and mental retardation, **Royal College of Psychiatrists: The Eleventh Blake Marsh Lecture**, (February, 1977)

Garber, B.B. and Moscona, A.A. (1973). Neural patterning: aggregate patterns of regionally differentiated brain cells, **Neurosci. Res. Symposium Summaries, 10**, 331-335

Hamburger, V. and Oppenheim, R.W. (1982). Naturally occurring neuronal death in vertebrates, **Neurosci. Commentaries, 1**, 39-55

Johnston, M.V. and Coyle, J.T. (1982). Cytotoxic lesions and the development of transmitter systems, **Trends in Neurosci., 5**, 153-156

Landis, S.C. and Patterson, P.H. (1981). Neural crest cell lineages, **Trends in Neurosci., 4**, 172-175

Lloyd, K.G., Hornykiewicz, O., Davidson, L., Shannak, K., Farley, I., Goldstein, M., Shibuya, M., Kelley, W.N. and Fox, I.H. (1981). Biochemical evidence of dysfunction of brain neurotransmitters in the Lesch-Nyhan syndrome, **New Engl. J. Med., 305**, 1106-1111

Loo, Y.H., Fulton, T., Miller, K. and Wisniewski, H. (1980). Phenylacetate and brain dysfunction in experimental phenylketonuria: synaptic development, **Life Sci., 27**, 1283-1290

Low, W.C., Lewis, P.R., Bunch, S.T., Dunnett, S.B., Thomas, S.R., Iversen, S.D., Bjorklund, A. and Stenevi, U. (1982). Function recovery following neural transplantation of embryonic septal nuclei in adult rats with septohippocampal lesions, **Nature, 300**, 260-262

Mann, D.M.A., Yates, P.O. and Hawkes, J. (1982). Plaques and tangles and transmitter deficiencies in dementia, **J. Neurol. Neurosurg. Psychiat., 45**, 563-564

Marx, J.L. (1982). Transplants as guides to brain development, **Science, 217**, 340-342

Ohara, P.T. (1972). Electron microscopical study of the brain in Down's syndrome, **Brain, 95**, 681-684

Patel, A.J. and Lewis, P.D. (1982). Effects on cell proliferation of pharmacological agents acting on the central nervous system. In: **Mechanisms of Actions of Neurotoxic Substances** (K.N. Prasad and A. Vernadakis, eds) pp. 181-218. Raven Press, New York

Price, D.L., Whitehouse, P.J., Struble, R.G., Coyle, J.T., Clark, A.W., DeLong, M.R., Cork, L.C. and Hedreen, J.C. (1983). Alzheimer's disease and Down's syndrome, **Ann. N.Y. Acad. Sci., 396**, 145-164

Rakic, P. (1981). Neuronal-glial interaction during brain development, **Trends in Neurosci., 4**, 184-187

Reis, D.J., Fink, J.S. and Baker, H. (1982). A genetic control of numbers of dopamine neurons in brain: relationship to behavior and responses to psychoactive drugs. In **Genetics of Neurological and Psychiatric Disorders** (S.S. Kety, L.P. Rowland, R.L. Sidman, and S.W. Matthysse, (eds) pp. 55-75. Raven Press, New York

Sara, V.R. and Hall, K. (1979). Growth hormone, growth factors, and the brain, **Trends in Neurosci., 2**, 263-265

Seeds, N.W., Haffke, S.C. and Krystosek, A. (1980). Cell migration and recognition in cerebellar reaggregate cultures. In: **Tissue Culture in Neurobiology** (E. Giacobini, et al., eds) pp. 145-154. Raven Press, New York

Trisler, D. (1982). Are molecular markers of cell position involved in the formation of neural circuits?, **Trends in Neurosci., 5**, 306-310

Yates, C.M., Simpson, J., Maloney, A.F.J., Gordon, A. and Reid, A.H. (1980). Alzheimer-like cholinergic deficiency in Down syndrome, **Lancet, ii**, 979

COMMENTARY

R. Balazs

It is evident that in order to understand better the disorders in mental retardation we have to learn much more about the factors underlying brain development and the neurological mechanisms involved in higher mental functions. My comments will mainly relate to the first of these large questions and I will rely to a great extent on information obtained in our laboratory.

The development of the nervous system is determined primarily by genetic factors, but it is also influenced by the external and the internal environment. We have attempted to approach the better understanding of the neurobiological mechanisms underlying behavioural disorders, which result from insults of various kinds inflicted during ontogenesis, by studying the effects of metabolic imbalance on the structural and biochemical development of the brain.

Developing neuronal circuits in the CNS seem to depend on the proliferation and differentiation of nerve cells being closely coordinated in time and space. Normal development also depends on the formation and differentiation of both glial and nerve cells occurring in an inter-related fashion. Observations in experimental animals have indicated that changes in the metabolic balance can disturb these developmental features.

Cell acquisition in the CNS is significantly influenced by metabolic factors. Thus in undernutrition there is a lasting reduction in brain cell numbers that is one of the few irreversible effects observed in this condition. It is important to note that alterations in cellular composition in certain brain parts have been detected and that glia seems to be especially sensitive to nutritional deficiencies (for review see e.g. Balazs *et al.*, 1979). Studies on cell proliferation kinetics showed distortions in the cell generation cycle (Lewis *et al.*, 1975) and these were found to be specific to tissues such as the brain where extensive cell replication occurs during a restricted period.

Psychotropic drugs which affect transmitter balance in the CNS also interfere with cell replication in the brain (for review see e.g. Patel and Lewis, 1982). These effects may reflect a role of transmitter substances, apart from their conventional function, in influencing the growth and differentiation of cells in developing nervous tissues as neurohumoral agents (for references see Balazs *et al.*, 1977). It should be mentioned in this context that the functional consequences of transient interference with cell formation in the CNS depends, in part, on the timing, which - because of the chronological order in nerve cell generation - determines the cell types affected. For example, it was found that temporary exposure to chlorpromazine during gestation or in the neonatal period resulted in a selective reduction of the prenatally formed Purkinje cells or the postnatally generated granule cells (Patel et al., 1983).

Cell acquisition in the brain is also affected by experimental thyroid disorders. Thyroid functions commence in the rat near to term, and in man towards the end of the first trimester. Thus, in order to gain relevant information on the human disorder, we paid particular attention to brain regions where neurogenesis is extensive in the rat during the period when thyroid functions are already expressed. These include the cerebellum, the hippocampus and the olfactory bulbs, and it was observed that thyroid deficiency affects cell acquisition primarily in these brain parts (Balazs, 1977). In the cerebellum, which was studied in most detail, the rate of cell acquisition was transiently depressed but, as a result of the prolonged persistence of the germinal site, cell numbers were ultimately restored to normal (Lewis et al., 1976). The effects of hyperthyroidism were just the opposite involving an initial increase in the germinal pool and a premature termination of cell proliferation (Patel et al., 1979). In both conditions cell cycle parameters remained essentially unaltered. The analysis of the results indicated that the thyroid status affects cell acquisition primarily through influencing the differentiation rather than the replication of cells. In fact in the cerebellum effects on the differentiation of the Purkinje cells, rather than the newly formed interneurons, seem to account for most of the observed changes. The most dramatic effect of thyroid hormone is on the development of the dendritic arborization of the Purkinje cells (Legrand, 1977) that plays a vital role in the growth of the cortex and consequently in the size of the surface which can be populated by the expanding cohort of neuronal progenitor cells, thus resulting in a temporary increase or decrease in the germinal pool in hyperthyroidism or thyroid deficiency. Furthermore, the hypoplasia of Purkinje cells in thyroid deficiency seems to be responsible for the transient increase in the degeneration of postmitotic granule cells (Lewis et al., 1976). The survival of nerve cells in certain stages of their differentiation depends on a successful innervation of their targets (Hamburger and Levi-Montalcini, 1949). We have proposed that, because of the reduced Purkinje dendritic area, a fraction of the granule cells fail to make synaptic contact and dies.

It seems that in the developing brain thyroid hormone affects primarily neuronal maturation which, in general, is retarded in thyroid deficiency and advanced in hyperthyroidism. It is, however, more important that the development of the different transmitter and peptidergic systems is apparently dissynchronized (Smith et al., 1980; Patel et al., 1980; Woodhams et al., 1983). Distortions in the development of neuronal circuits have also been observed in electron microscopic and neurophysiological studies (Hajos et al., 1973; Crepel, 1974). Such distortions in the "wiring" of the brain during development may be involved in the impaired performance of the hyperthyroid animal in tests of adaptive behaviour, and in man in mental retardation associated with cretinism.

Brain maturation is retarded in undernutrition. However, many of the physical alterations can be corrected by nutritional rehabilitation even after weaning (for review, Balazs *et al.*, 1979). Concerning the functional consequences it is, therefore, important that temporary imbalance is detectable in the coordinated development of certain transmitter systems (Patel *et al.*, 1978).

Descriptive knowledge concerning the consequences of metabolic insults in the developing brain are quite extensive. However, the elucidation of the mechanisms at the molecular level has been hampered by the complexity *in vivo* of secondary reactions and by the heterogeneity of brain tissue. Advances in the separation of cell types (Garthwaite and Balazs, 1981) and especially in tissue culture techniques (e.g. Giacobini *et al.*, 1980) offer distinct advantages in these respects. Thus neural cells from different parts of the nervous system can now be reproducibly cultivated, and selection can be achieved for particular classes of cells, whose development and the mechanisms involved in their interaction can be studied under well controlled conditions. Recognition of cell-type specific markers have significantly contributed to the progress of these studies (e.g. Raff *et al.*, 1979; Schachner, 1982) and this is already paying dividends in neuropathology. It is particularly important that many observations are consistent with the view that development *in vitro* parallels, by and large, *in vivo* ontogenesis (e.g. Abney *et al.*, 1981; Balazs *et al.*, 1980, 1982).

An important new development in tissue culture technology is the introduction of chemically defined media, including some which permit the survival and differentiation of neural cells (Bottenstein and Sato, 1979). This has stimulated studies aimed at the identification of trophic factors and the elucidation of the effects of humoral agents including hormones on the development of neural cells.

Before I describe some of the effects of thyroid hormone *in vitro* I want to mention briefly that in comparison with cultures grown in the presence of serum the survival of nerve cells is similar, but their behaviour is different in the serum-free medium (Gallo *et al.*, 1983). Significantly, whereas nerve cells in the presence of serum migrate and form aggregates and big fibre bundles, in the serum-free medium they are "antisocial", cell migration and adhesion among cells and neurites being very limited. These cultures may, therefore, permit the study of factors involved in these basic developmental functions. The changes in the behaviour of cells was associated with alterations in the organization of the plasma membrane, including the expression of a protein, D_2, which seems to be involved in neuronal adhesion (Jorgensen *et al.*, 1980). The "social" behaviour of nerve cells was not much affected by thyroid hormone in these monolayer cultures. However, in forebrain aggregating cultures, which have a more complex three-dimensional organization, the hormone markedly advanced biochemical development (Atterwill et al., 1983). Furthermore, a stimulation of the maturation of neuronal fibres was indicated by the increased staining of the neurites with anti-neurofilament serum (unpublished observation by P.D. Woodhams from our laboratory). Other recent studies have also shown that thyroid hormone affects neuronal differentiation in vitro. Romijn et al. (1982) have observed that fibre growth and synaptogenesis are advanced, especially when forebrain cultures are exposed to both thyroid hormone and corticosteroids. Tixier-Vidal et al. (1982) have noted that in hypothalamic cultures the hormone promotes the differentiation of dopaminergic neurons and synaptic maturation, in terms of the stimulation-coupled release of TRH. However, thyroid hormone does not influence neuronal differentiation indiscriminately. Muscarinic receptor binding was unaltered by the hormone in the cerebellar cultures, which do not contain cholinergic cells (Atterwill et al., 1983), but it was increased in the forebrain cultures where choline acetyltransferase activity is enhanced, implying a stimulation of cholinergic fibre proliferation (Honegger and Lenoir, 1980). In contrast to the marked effects on cholinergic fibres and receptors, thyroid hormone has little influence on the GABA-ergic system in the forebrain cultures (Honegger and Lenoir, 1980). Studies on cell lines from a pituitary tumour have contributed significantly to the current knowledge on thyroid hormone action at the molecular level (e.g. Baxter et al., 1979). The results obtained hitherto on neural cultures are promising in terms of leading to information which may significantly further the better understanding of thyroid hormone action on neuronal differentiation. It is also worth mentioning here that, besides studying animal models of human disorders and basic neurobiological mechanisms in cultured cells, recent observations are encouraging in terms of the biochemical examination of the post-mortem human brain (as exemplified by the mapping of biochemical defects in certain diseases of CNS, such as Parkinsonism, Huntington's chorea and Alzheimer's disease). Post-mortem studies have also been conducted on the developing human brain, with the aim of providing baseline information against which abnormal development may eventually be assessed (for review Brooksbank and Balazs, 1981).

References

Abney E., Bartlett P.P. and Raff M. (1981). Astrocyte, ependymal cell and oligodendrocyte develop on schedule in dissociated cell cultures of 10-day old embryonic rat brain. **Dev. Biol., 30,** 301-310

Atterwill C.K., Balazs R., Bermudez I. and Kingsbury A. (1983). Effect of thyroid hormone on certain membrane properties of developing neuron tissue in vitro. **Proc. 4th ESN Meet. (Catania),** 454

Balazs R. (1977). Effect of thyroid hormone and undernutrition on cell acquisition in the rat brain. In: **Thyroid Hormone and Brain Development,** (G.D. Graves, Ed.), Raven Press, New York, 288-298

Balazs R., Lewis P.D. and Patel A.J. (1979). Nutritional deficiencies and brain development. In: **Human Growth, 3,** (F. Falkner and J.M. Tanner, Eds.), Plenum Press, New York, 415-480

Balazs R., Patel A.J. and Lewis P.D. (1977). Metabolic influences on cell proliferation in the brain. In: **Biochemical Correlates of Brain Structure and Function,** (A.N. Davison, Ed.), Academic Press, New York, 43-83

Balazs R., Regan C., Gordon R.D., Annunziata P., Kingsbury A.E. and Meier E. (1982). Certain surface properties of isolated and cultured cerebellar cells. In: **Neurotransmitter Interaction and Compartmentation,** (H.F. Bradford, Ed.), Plenum Press, New York, 515-534

Balazs R., Regan C., Meier E., Woodhams P.L., Wilkin G.O., Patel N.J. and Gordon R.D. (1980). Biochemical properties of cell types from rat cerebellum. In: **Tissue Culture in Neurobiology,** (E. Giacobini, A. Vernadakis and A. Shahar, Eds.), Raven Press, New York, 155-168

Baxter J.D., Eberhardt N.L., Apriletti J.W., Johnson L.K., Ivarie R.D., Schachter B.S., Morris J.A., Seeburg P.H., Goodman H.M., Lathem K.R., Polansky J.R. and Martial J.A. (1979). Thyroid hormone receptors and responses. In: **Recent Progress in Hormone Research, 35,** (R.O. Green, Ed.), Academic Press, New York, 97-144

Bottenstein J. and Sato G. (1979). Growth of a rat neuroblastoma cell line in serum-free supplemented media. **Proc. Natl. Acad. Sci. U.S.A., 76,** 514-517

Brooksbank B.W.L. and Balazs R. (1981). Aspects of biochemical development of the brain. In: **Maturation and Development: Biological and Psychological Perspectives,** (K.J. Connolly and H.F.R. Prechtl, Eds.), Heinemann Medical Books, London, 131-161

Crepel F. (1974). Excitatory and inhibitory processes acting upon the cerebellar Purkinje cells during maturation in the rat: influence of hypothyroidism. **Exp. Brain Res., 230,** 403-420

Gallo V., Kingsbury A., Woodhams P.D. and Balazs R. (1983). Development of nerve cells in cerebellar cultures in the presence of foetal calf serum or in chemically defined media: differences in cell adhesion and the organisation of the plasma membrane. **Biochem. Soc. Trans.,** (in press)

Garthwaite J. and Balazs R. (1981). Separation of cell types from the cerebellum and their properties. **Adv. Cell Neurobiol., 2,** (S. Federoff and L. Hertz, Eds.), Academic Press, New York, 461-489

Giacobini E., Vernadakis A. and Shahar A. (eds.) (1980). **Tissue Culture in Neurobiology,** Raven Press, New York

Hajos F., Patel A.J. and Balazs R. (1973). Effect of thyroid deficiency on the synaptic organisation of the rat cerebellar cortex. **Brain Res., 50**, 387-401

Hamburger V. and Levi-Montalcini R. (1949). Proliferation, differentiation and degeneration in the spinal ganglia of the chick embryo under normal and experimental conditions. **J. Exp. Zool., 111**, 457-500

Honegger P. and Lenoir D. (1980). Triiodothyronine enhancements of neuronal differentiation in aggregating fetal rat brain cells cultured in a chemically defined medium. **Brain Res., 199**, 425-434

Jorgensen O.S., Delouvee A., Thiery J.-P. and Edelman G. (1980). The nervous system specific protein D2 is involved in adhesion among neurites from cultured rat ganglia. **FEBS Lett., 111**, 39-42

Legrand J. (1977). Morphological and biochemical effects of hormones on the developing nervous system in mammals. In: **Brain, Fetal and Infant. Current Research on Normal and Abnormal Development**, (S.R. Berenberg, Ed.), Martinus Nijhoff Medical Div., The Hague, 137-164

Lewis P.D., Balazs R., Patel A.J. and Johnson A.L. (1975). The effect of undernutrition on all generation in the rat brain. **Brain Res., 83**, 235-247

Lewis P.D., Patel A.J., Johnson A.L. and Balazs R. (1976). Effect of thyroid deficiency on cell acquisition in the postnatal brain: a quantitative histological study. **Brain Res., 104**, 49-62

Patel A.J., Barochovsky O., Borges S. and Lewis P.D. (1983). Effects of neurotropic drugs on brain cell replication _in vivo_ and _in vitro_. In: **Drugs and Hormones in Brain Development**, (M. Schlumpf and W. Lichtensteiger, Eds.), Karger, Basel (in press)

Patel A.J., Del Vecchio M. and Atkinson D.J. (1978). Effect of undernutrition on the regional development of transmitter enzymes: glutamate decarboxylase and choline acetyltransferase. **Dev. Neurosci., 1**, 41-53

Patel A.J. and Lewis P.D. (1982). Effects on cell proliferation of pharmacological agents acting on the central nervous system. In: **Mechanism of Actions of Neurotoxic Substances** (K.N. Prasad and A. Vernadakis, Ed.), Raven Press, New York, 181-218

Patel A.J., Lewis P.D., Balazs R., Bailey P. and Lai M. (1979). Effects of thyroxine on postnatal cell acquisition in the rat brain. **Brain Res., 172**, 57-72

Patel A.J., Smith R.M., Kingsbury A.E., Hunt A. and Balazs R. (1980). Effects of thyroid state on brain development: muscarinic acetylcholine and GABA receptors. **Brain Res., 198**, 389-402

Raff M.C., Fields K.L., Hakomori S.-I., Mirsky R., Pruss R.M. and Winter J. (1979). Cell specific markers for distinguishing and studying neurones and the major classes of glial cells in culture. **Brain Res., 174**, 283-308

Romijn H.J., Habets A.M.M.C., Mud M.T. and Walters P.S. (1982). Nerve outgrowth, synaptogenesis and bioelectric activity in fetal rat cerebral cortex tissue cultured in serum-free chemically defined medium. **Dev. Brain Res., 2**, 583-585

Schachner M. (1982). Immunological analysis of cellular heterogeneity in the cerebellum. In: **Neuroimmunology**, (J. Brooks, Ed.), Plenum Press, New York, 215-250

Smith R.M., Patel S.J., Kingsbury A.E., Hunt A. and Balazs R. (1980). Effects of thyroid state on brain development: beta-adrenergic receptors and 5'-nucleotidase activity. **Brain Res., 198**, 375-387

Tixier-Vidal A., Faivre-Bauman A., Loudes C. and Purymirat J. (1982). Effect of hormones on neuron survival and development in culture. **Proc. 3rd Int. Meet. Int. Soc. Dev. Neurosci.**, (Patras), 215

Woodhams P.L., McGovern J., McGregor G.P., O'Shaughnessey D.J., Ghatei M.A., Blank M.A., Adrian T.H., Lee Y., Polak J.M., Bloom S.R. and Balazs R. (1983). Effects of changes in neonatal thyroid status on the development of neuropeptide systems in the rat brain. **Int. J. Dev. Neurobiol.**, (in press)

P. D. Lewis

Amongst the mechanisms involved in structural brain development, derangement of which may produce disturbance of integrated brain function, cell acquisition merits further discussion. So inflexible is the chronological programme for neurogenesis that perturbation of cell generation during the limited period in which any nerve cell type is normally produced will inevitably lead to numerical alterations and changes in neural network formation. Many powerful influences on cell generation in the developing brain have already been identified, chiefly from quantitative studies on postnatally developing secondary germinal zones. These include severe undernutrition, which retards cell acquisition while producing gross changes in the cell cycle, notably a greatly prolonged DNA synthesis phase; neonatal hypothyroidism, which both reduces and prolongs cell acquisition in the cerebellum, thereby inducing alterations in the ratios of different neuronal types; neonatal hyperthyroidism, which prematurely expands the germinal pool in the cerebellar external granular layer at the expense of cell migration, and then produces premature germinal zone maturation; and a variety of pharmacological agents which affect monoaminergic activity, some of which impair cell acquisition and alter the cell cycle. As well as influencing cell proliferation, some of these factors also affect the survival of either germinal cells or newly formed neurons. This is seen in neonatal hypothyroidism, where survival of granule cells is jeopardized in the second week by a deficiency of Purkinje cell sites for synaptogenesis, and with chlorpromazine or reserpine treatment, where massive external granule cell death is induced. The relationship of such changes to subsequent performance dependent on integrated brain function deserves close attention.

O. E. Pratt

The detailed consideration of the neurobiology of brain development provides a basis for useful indications of possible mechanisms of brain damage in early life. The development of the brain after early embryogenesis through the processes of neurogenesis, cell migration and synapse formation differs in timing in different parts of the CNS (Shimada et al., 1982). A problem in identifying mechanisms causing abnormal development is to separate the effects of such regional or local variation from possible differences in vulnerability to interference of processes like cell division and migration.

The association between mental retardation and micrencephaly, or abnormally small brain, especially affecting the cerebellum, may well reflect the adverse effects of metabolic disorders upon postnatal maturation of this region. It is of interest to note the difference between the lesions seen in an infant with untreated PKU and those seen in the metabolically normal child of a phenylketonuric mother not treated during the pregnancy. In the PKU infant there are defects in myelination and sponginess and gliosis in the white matter (Crome and Pare, 1960; Crome and Stern, 1972) and various defects in nerve cell maturation (Bauman and Kemper, 1982), all of which seem to be the result of interference with the nutrition of brain cells during the first months of postnatal life, probably from competitive inhibition of amino acid transport across the blood-brain and other barriers (Pratt, 1980a). In contrast, the brain of the metabolically normal child of a phenylketonuric mother will have suffered from nutritional problems during intrauterine development, which will have interfered with the maturation of brain cells, leading to a generalized micrencephaly and an IQ usually below 80, as well as severe congenital abnormalities, commonly affecting the heart (Hsia, 1970; Angeli et al., 1974; Komrower et al., 1979; Smith et al., 1979).

There is some evidence that the timing of any insult is at least as important as its nature for it seems that a somewhat similar pattern of damage, with generalized micrencephaly as the main feature, can be caused by various adverse factors operating during embryogenesis, about 3 to 6 weeks after conception in the human (Pratt, 1980b; Lipson et al., 1981). This micrencephaly pattern is commonly associated with gross anomalies of brain development. These affect not only the heart and other organs but the CNS also usually with ectopic neurons, or other sequelae of disrupted migration, and often also anomalies in the development of the face. The cause of such a condition is only rarely maternal PKU, more commonly the mother has drank heavily (Clarren et al., 1978; Peiffer et al., 1979) or taken multi-anti-epileptic drugs, especially hydantoins (Hanson and Smith, 1975) during pregnancy. Other possible causes include folate antagonists (Hsia, 1970; Jones and Chernoff, 1978) and cytotoxic drugs (Dambska et al., 1982). In personal experience it is sometimes possible to recognize a pattern of pathology, of micrencephaly with ectopic nerve cells, for example in the middle of a cerebellar peduncle, without being able to identify with certainty the specific cause. Experimental work with X-irradiation or cytotoxic drugs has shown that reduced brain cell numbers and heterotopia can be explained by interference with neuronal migration and subsequent disorder of synaptogenesis (Altman, 1976; Shimada et al., 1982). It seems likely that the earlier the damage occurs the more severe the effects. Nutritional factors also seem to have a complex role, as B-vitamins in reducing the incidence of neural tube defects (Smithells et al., 1980).

Two further points which emerge from the survey are the need for a better understanding of synapse formation and the possible role of neurotransmitter imbalance. This may be the cause not only of the behavioural abnormalities of untreated phenylketonurics, which are usually reversible when dietary treatment is given (Knox, 1972), but also of mental defect associated with the adverse effects upon brain development of various drugs and chemicals during pregnancy (Jones and Chernoff, 1978). Not only does alcohol have such an adverse effect but there is also a slowing of antenatal brain growth in children born to mothers who drink heavily (Little, 1977; Olegard et al., 1979). One possible cause of the latter effect appears to be interference with the hypothalamo-pituitary axis leading to a reduction in growth hormone (Tze and Lee, 1975; Tze et al., 1976; van Thiel et al., 1978; Thadani and Schanberg, 1979), probably produced by a direct effect upon the hypothalamus and associated neurotransmitters (Redmond, 1981).

Disturbance of neurotransmitter metabolism may arise in different ways. In PKU the brain cells may suffer a deficiency of one or more of the amino acid precursors of neurotransmitters (tryptophan or tyrosine, or methionine, the major source of methyl groups) due to transport inhibition (Pratt, 1982). In alcoholism disturbance of neurotransmitter metabolism and possible formation of false transmitters are well known effects of the metabolic load of ethanol oxidation (Littleton, 1978).

References

Altman J. (1976). Experimental reorganisation of the cerebellar cortex. V. Effects of early X-irradiation schedules that allow or prevent the acquisition of basket cells. **J. Comp. Neurol., 165**, 31-48

Angeli E., Denman A.R., Harris R.F., Kirman B.H. and Stern J. (1974). Maternal phenylketonuria: a family with seven mentally retarded siblings. **Dev.Med.Child.Neurol., 16,** 800-807

Bauman M.L. and Kemper T.L. (1982). Morphologic and histoanatomic observations of the brain in untreated human phenylketonuria. **Acta Neuropath.(Berl.), 58,** 55-63

Clarren S.K., Alford E.C., Sumi S.M., Streissguth A.P. and Smith D.W. (1978). Brain malformations related to prenatal exposure to ethanol. **J.Pediat., 92,** 64-67

Clarren S.K. and Smith D.W. (1978). The fetal alcohol syndrome. **New Engl.J.Med., 298,** 1063-1067

Crome L. and Pare C.M.B. (1960). Phenylketonuria: a review and a report of the pathological findings in four cases. **J. Ment. Sci., 106,** 862-883

Crome L. and Stern J. (1972). **Pathology of Mental Retardation.** 2nd Edn, Churchill-Livingstone, Edinburgh and London

Dambska M., Haddad, R., Kozlowski P.B., Lee M.H. and Shek J. (1982). Telencephalic cytoarchitectonics in the brains of rats with graded degrees of micrencephaly. **Acta Neuropathol. (Berlin), 58,** 203-209

Hanson J.W. and Smith D.W. (1975). The fetal hydantoin syndrome. **Pediatr., 87,** 285-290

Hsia, D. Y.-Y. (1970). Phenylketonuria and its variants. **Prog.Med.Genet., 7,** 29-68

Jones K.L. and Chernoff G.F. (1978). Drugs and chemicals associated with intrauterine growth deficiency. **J. Reprod. Med., 21,** 365-370

Knox W.E. (1972). Phenylketonuria. In **The Metabolic Basis of Inherited Disease,** Eds. Stanbury J.B., Wyngaarden J.B. and Fredrickson D.S., 3rd Edn, McGraw-Hill, New York

Komrower G.M., Sardharwalla I.B., Coutts J.M.J. and Ingham D. (1979). Management of maternal phenylketonuria: an emerging clinical problem. **Br.Med.J., 1,** 1383-1387

Lipson A.H., Yu J.S., O'Halloran M.T. and Williams R. (1981). Alcohol and phenylketonuria. **Lancet, 1,** 717-718

Little R.E. (1977). Moderate alcohol use during pregnancy and decreased infant birth weight. **Am.J.Publ.Health, 67,** 1154-1156

Littleton J. (1978). Alcohol and neurotransmitters. **Clin.Endocrinol.Metab., 7,** 369-384

Olegard R., Sabel K.G., Aronsson M. et al (1979). Effects on thc child of alcohol abuse during pregnancy: retrospective and prospective studies. **Acta Pediatr.Scand.,** Suppl. **275,** 112-121

Peiffer J., Majewski F., Fischbach H., Bierich J.R. and Volk B. (1979). Alcohol embryo- and fetopathy. **J.Neurol.Sci., 41,** 125-137

Pratt O.E. (1980a). A new approach to the treatment of phenylketonuria. **J.Ment.Defic.Res., 24,** 203-217

Pratt O.E. (1980b). The fetal alcohol syndrome: transport of nutrients and transfer of alcohol and acetaldehyde from mother to fetus. In **Psychopharmacology of Alcohol**, Ed. Sandler, M., Raven Press, New York, 229-256

Pratt O.E. (1982). Transport inhibition in the pathology of phenylketonuria and other inherited metabolic diseases. **J. Inher. Metab. Dis., 5,** Suppl. 2, 75-81

Redmond G.P. (1981). Effect of ethanol on spontaneous and stimulated growth hormone secretion. **Progr. Biochem. Pharmacol., 18,** 58-74

Shimada M., Abe Y., Yamano T., Ohta S., Yamazaki S. and Ohya N. (1982). The pathogenesis of abnormal cytoarchitecture in the cerebral cortex and hippocampus of the mouse treated transplacentally with cytosine arabinoside. **Acta Neuropathol. (Berlin), 58,** 159-167

Smith I., Erdohazi M. et al (1979). Fetal damage despite low-phenylalanine diet after conception in a phenylketonuric woman. **Lancet, i,** 17-19

Smithells R.W., Sheppard S., Schorah C.J., Seller M.J., Nevin N.C., Harris R., Read A.P. and Fielding D.W. (1980). Possible prevention of neural tube defects by periconceptual vitamin supplementation. **Lancet, i,** 339-340

Thadani P.V. and Schanberg S.N. (1979). Effects of maternal ethanol ingestion on serum growth hormone in the developing rat. **Neuropharm., 18,** 821-826

Tze W.J., Friesen H.G. and MacLeod P.M. (1976). Growth hormone response in fetal alcohol syndrome. **Arch.Dis.Childh., 51,** 703-706

Tze W.J. and Lee M. (1975). Adverse effects of maternal alcohol consumption on pregnancy and fetal growth in rats. **Nature, 257,** 479-480

Van Thiel G.H., Gavaler J.S., Lester R. and Sherrins R.J. (1978). Alcohol-induced ovarian failure in the rat. **J. Clin. Inv., 61,** 624-632

R. O. Robinson

Volpe (1981) has classified a number of syndromes presenting in the neonatal period by the process of neuronal proliferation migration or organization which has gone awry. It is from the clinical point of view quite helpful to think of mental handicap syndromes in these terms.

Disorders of neuronal proliferation

Numbers of neurons may be either:

(a) Insufficient. Although it is difficult to obtain direct evidence for technical reasons, it is probable that primary microcephaly is associated with depletion of neuronal number. Primary microcephaly may be either sporadic or familial. Since the recurrence risk for microcephaly is about 1 in 8, approximately half the cases are inherited as an autosomal recessive condition. An X linked recessive condition has been described as has a familial type with ocular abnormalities.

(b) Excessive. Familial isolated macrocephaly is most frequently inherited as an autosomal dominant in which case mental handicap does not appear to be associated. However, an autosomally recessive type has been described in which mental handicap is common. Sotos syndrome is a strange disorder characterized by an overall excessive rate of growth in the first year or two of life associated with some degree of mental handicap which may appear exaggerated by the clumsiness and language difficulty of these children. Beckwith's syndrome, another growth disorder, has as its most consistent features general macrosomia, macroglossia, omphalocoele and nesidioblastosis. Mental handicap is an inconsistent feature and may in part be caused by neonatal hypoglycaemia or hypoxia secondary to upper airways obstruction. An over growth of both neurons and glia is found in tuberose sclerosis and excessive growth of the glia only is associated with neurofibromatosis. An interesting condition called unilateral macrencephaly is an over growth of one side of the brain only with a disordered thick cortex, large bizarre neurons, heterotopic neurons and increased size in the number of astrocytes. Focal cortical dysplasia may represent a more localized expression of this growth anomaly and is associated with a sometimes intractable seizure disorder.

Disorders of migration

A number of mental retardation syndromes appear to be caused by failure of neurons to migrate properly from the periventricular layers to the cortex. Schizencephaly is the most severe example of this when a cleft in the cerebral cortex is caused by a genesis of a portion of the cortical wall. The sides of the cleft contain disorganized and frequently heterotopic neurons. This disorder is caused by a failure no later than the second month. Lissencephaly is a term given to a brain in which no gyri have formed because of a failure of neurons to arrive in sufficient numbers at the cortex. This occurs no later than the third month. Pachygyria describes a brain with a few thick broad gyri due to a disorder of neuronal layering. This is determined by a failure around the fourth month of fetal life. Polymicrogyria, excessive numbers of small thin gyri, sometimes coexists with pachygyria. It is caused by condensation of the molecular layers of the cortex. It may be caused either by a disorder of migration as in Zellweger's syndrome or from laminar cortical necrosis due to solitary events such as cytomegalovirus infection, or carbon monoxide poisoning around the 20th-24th week.

Disorders of organization

Because of the daunting complexity of neuronal interconnections in the cerebral complex, study of this important group is still in its infancy. Huttenlocher (1974) made a careful study of eleven individuals with severe undifferentiated mental handicap. In six he found the dendrites were few in number and abnormally arranged. Purpura (1975) has also described dendritic disorganization in Down's syndrome. A number of widely differing causes of mental handicap have dendritic disorganization as a feature associated with other developmental and central nervous system anomalies. Examples include congenital rubella, phenylketonuria, Rubenstein-Taybi and trisomy 13,15.

Disorders of myelination

The final phase of neuronal development involves laying down of the myelin sheaths. This does not begin in the cerebral hemispheres until after birth. Mental handicap conditions due to this cause therefore are not manifest at birth. The earliest to become evident is cerebral white matter hypoplasia which generally becomes apparent during the first few weeks. Others which occur during the first year are Alexander's disease and Krabbe's disease. Thereafter other examples include metachromatic leukodystrophy, adrenoleukodystrophy and Pelizeus-Merzbacher's disease.

Thus whilst neurobiology has improved the clinician's understanding of the timing and mechanisms of a variety of conditions of mental handicap, the clinician can furnish examples of relatively circumscribed disorders, the further study of which should give us a deeper insight into the mechanisms of neuronal maturation.

References

Huttenlocher P.R. (1974). Dendritic development in neocortex of children with mental defects and infantile spasms. **Neurology, 24,** 203

Purpura G.P. (1975). Dendritic differentiation in human cerebral cortex: Normal and aberrant patterns. Kreutzberg G.W. (Ed.), **Advances in Neurology, 12,** New York, Raven Press, 91-116

Volpe J.J. (1981). Neurology of the newborn. Schaffer A.J. and Markowitz M. (Eds.), **Major Problems in Clinical Paediatrics, 22,** Philadelphia, W. B. Saunders

P. E. Sylvester

This exciting chapter offers hope for the future. The laboratory based scientist has given new avenues for exploration by the clinician. Unfortunately, the clinician's tests in the field of developmental medicine and geriatrics are thus far limited. Reid and Aungle (1974) have shown that in the field of mental retardation senile dementia can be diagnosed accurately. However, there is a discrepancy in Down's syndrome that the neuropathological features (plaques, tangles and granulovacuolar degeneration) antedate the clinical features probably by several years. Thus, by the time overt clinical features are present it is too late to intercede prophylactically. Davison's nimble dissertation has thrown down new challenges. In Down's syndrome there is the problem of a small brain with important territories of underdevelopment. One of these affects the temporal lobe and the adjacent parts of the limbic system, notably the hippocampus. This territory is fundamental to the processing of memory and expression of emotional attitudes. It is also a target territory for the neuropathological features of ageing. It would be correct, if possible, to stimulate neurogenic growth in intrauterine life but there is a conflict with present treatment of recommending termination of pregnancy following the discovery of chromosomal abnormality in amniotic fluid. This means that help is needed for those Down's babies who escape the antenatal care net and young individuals already growing up in the community, too late for them to receive stimulation of neurogenic growth. This then leaves open the problems of how to prevent or curb premature ageing. Davison has given us some guidelines about this, and he has told us that various drugs, hormonal insufficiency and undernutrition can interfere with cell proliferation; other possibilities are that environmental poisons, either bacterial or viral, may kill certain classes of cells.

Neuronal degeneration leading to senile changes is commonly judged to begin in the seventh decade in non-Down's patients. However, in Down's syndrome the pathological senile changes can occur as early as the middle of the fourth decade in 2% of patients and in 100% past that age (Mann *et al.*, 1980). The human brain continues to increase in weight till the end of the third decade, and thereafter there is a slow decline in weight throughout life. The decrements follow a statistically significant line. However, in Down's syndrome a similar plotting of brain weights does not follow the same pattern, and there is no statistical significance in the line of decline in brain weight. This observation suggests that growth maturity in Down's syndrome, on a weight basis, is achieved at around 18 years of age; if that is the case then the conclusion must be that prevention of the ageing process needs to start before that age (Rundle, 1983). This provides a clue that therapeutic attempts to prevent ageing must start earlier than the third decade. Recent work by Harrell and colleagues (1981) has claimed that megavitamin doses and trace elements given to mentally retarded children have improved the intelligence by as much as 20 IQ points. Physical features in Down's syndrome are also claimed to have been improved. Many workers over several years have shown deficiencies of vitamins in Down's syndrome, including vitamins A, B1, nicotinamide, C and E. Other workers have demonstrated shortages of trace elements (manganese, copper and calcium). The evidence points to the fact that these are life-long deficiencies. Who can tell then what effect the deficiencies may have on neuronal health? Nutritional studies are one way that clinicians can contribute and furnish answers, either to confirm or refute, to the important matter of preventing premature ageing in Down's syndrome.

Davison draws attention to paucity of dendrite development especially in the terminal branches of apical dendrites and reduction in synaptic spines in phenylketonuria. Takashima and colleagues (1981) draw attention to a change in dendritic spines from normal in the Down's fetus when compared to the non-Down's fetus, to the appearance of abnormal forms and reduced numbers in newborn infants. This suggests that the newborn Down's infant is probably in the same position as the newborn PKU and that treatment to prevent mental deterioration should start early. The problem is finding the treatment.

References

Harrell R.F., Capp R.H., Davis D.R., Peerless J. and Ravitz L.R. (1981). Can nutritional supplements help mentally retarded children? An exploratory study. **Proc. Natl. Acad. Sci. U.S.A., 78,** 574-578

Mann D.M.A., Lincoln J., Yates P.O. and Brennan C.M. (1980). Monoamine metabolism in Down's syndrome. **Lancet, ii,** 1366-1367

Reid A.H. and Aungle P.G. (1974). Dementia in ageing mental defectives. A clinical psychiatric study. **J.Ment.Defic.Res., 18,** 15

Rundle (1983). Personal communication

Takashima, S., Berker, L.E., Armstrong, D.L. and Chan, F.N. (1981). Abnormal development in the visual cortex of the human foetus and infant with Down's syndrome. A quantitative and qualitative Golgi study. **Brain Research, 225,** 1-21

Chapter 7

Metabolic disorders in the aetiology of mental retardation

H. Bickel

INTRODUCTION

In infancy and childhood the rapidly growing brain is particularly vulnerable to metabolic disorders. In this chapter only inborn (hereditary) errors of metabolism will be discussed. Many different metabolic pathways may be involved such as those of the amino acids, carbohydrates and lipids, plasma proteins, mucopolysaccharides, vitamins, pterins, hormones, electrolytes, trace elements, bilirubin, etc. (Table 1). In a catalogue of 170 inborn metabolic errors (McKusick, 1978), in which altered activity of a specific enzyme has been demonstrated, 70 were associated with more or less severe brain damage. Of 89 well defined disorders with oligophrenia (Eggers and Bickel, 1974), 41 were due to various inborn errors of metabolism, 48 to other causes such as chromosomopathies (12), inherited syndromes affecting the brain, eyes, ears and skin (12), heredodegenerative disorders (11), embryofetopathies (4), multiple malformations (7) and psychotic disturbances with dementia (2). Table 2 lists 50 metabolic disorders, with 70 subtypes, which are usually associated with brain damage. In some instances the number of cases recorded so far is too small for a definite statement that oligophrenia and heredity are essential features of the condition.

The practical importance of these disorders - besides their fundamental interest for the physiology and pathology of brain development and function - lies in the possibility of early detection by neonatal screening and even by prenatal diagnosis, in treatment or prevention, and in genetic counselling. The best known example is phenylketonuria, which was detected in 1934 by Folling and has since been described in many hundreds of publications.

Table 1

Examples of brain damage due to inborn errors of different metabolic pathways

Disturbed metabolic pathways	Clinical example
Amino acids	Phenylketonuria
Carbohydrates	Galactosaemia
Lipids	M. Tay-Sachs
Mucopolysaccharides	M. Hurler
Water-electrolytes	Renal diabetes insipidus
Phosphate	Pseudohypoparathyroidism
Bilirubin	Crigler-Najjar syndrome
Vitamins	Pyridoxine dependency
Hormones	Familial goitre
Trace elements	M. Wilson
Plasma proteins	Abetalipoproteinaemia

Frequency

Most of the inborn metabolic disorders with or without mental retardation are rare or very rare. This statement is largely empirical and is generally not based on hard data. These can best be provided by non-selective screening for metabolites or enzymes in blood or urine of all newborns in the population (Bickel et al., 1981; Bickel, 1983). By this procedure the frequency of phenylketonuria in 57 million newborns in Europe and overseas has been found to be 1:10 500, that of histidinaemia in 6.5 million newborns 1:30 000, that of galactosaemia in 17 million newborns 1:57 700, and that of maple syrup urine disease in 22 million newborns only 1:245 000. These frequency figures can vary widely in different ethnic groups and populations. Thus phenylketonuria is more than 6 times rarer in Japan than in Western Europe, histidinaemia 3 times more frequent. Tay-Sachs disease has a frequency in Ashkenazi Jews of 1:3300, whilst it is extremely rare in non-jewish populations. It would be of great help for any statements on the frequency of these disorders if more large-scale screening programmes were carried out, ideally non-selective in the neonatal age group, but also selective in neonatal intensive care units (e.g. for organic acidurias), and in schools and institutions for the mentally retarded (survey by Bickel, Guthrie and Hammersen in 1980).

Inheritance

The mode of inheritance is in most of the disorders autosomal recessive, in only a few sex-linked (Table 2). The inheritance of pseudohypoparathyroidism is mostly considered to be sex-linked dominant but needs further clarification by specific biochemical analysis, detailed studies of X chromosome morphology and observations of bone and kidney cell cultures *in vitro* (Potts, 1978).

For some of the disorders in Table 2 biochemical *heterozygote tests* have been developed, either by measuring the metabolites quantitatively before and after the enzyme block, with or without additional metabolite loading, or by determining the activity of the defective enzyme in various cells and organs, e.g. in erythrocytes in galactosaemia or in needle biopsy specimens of the liver in homocystinuria or phenylketonuria. In the latter condition Folling and coworkers (1938) performed historically the first heterozygote test by offering an oral load of phenylalanine to the parents of their patients, unfortunately in its racemic DL form which gives false-positive results also in

Table 2

Inborn metabolic errors usually associated with brain damage

Phenylketonuria and variant forms
Tetrahydrobiopterin deficiencies I,II,III
Tyrosinaemia II Richner-Hanhart
Histidinaemia
Homocystinuria I,II,III,IV
Maple syrup urine disease
Hypervalinaemia
Isovaleric acidaemia
Beta-ketothiolase deficiency
Propionic acidaemia
Methylmalonic acidaemia I,II,III
Hyperprolinaemia I,II
Hydroxyprolinaemia
Hyperammonaemia I,II
*I Carbamylphosphate synthetase defic.
II Ornithine carbamyl transferase defic.
Citrullinaemia
Argininosuccinic aciduria
Hyperargininaemia
Hyperornithinaemia I,II
Hyperlysinaemia, persistent
Hypersarcosinaemia
Nonketotic hyperglycaemia
Hyper-beta-alaninaemia
Serum carnosinase deficiency

Galactosaemia
Abetalipoproteinaemia
GM2-Gangliosidoses I,II,III
GM1-Gangliosidoses I,II
Metachrom. leukodystrophy (sulphatidosis)
M. Gaucher (acute, subacute)
M. Nieman-Pick types A,B,C,D
Globoid cell leukodystrophy: M. Krabbe
Leigh's necrotizing encephalopathy
Cerebrotendinous xanthomatosis
*Lesch-Nyhan syndrome
M. Wilson
*Menkes' kinky-hair disease
Criggler-Najjar syndrome
Mucopolysaccharidoses IH,II*,III,VII
Mucolipidosis II (I-cell disease)
Fucosidosis
Mannosidosis
Thyroid hormonogenesis defects
*?Pseudohypoparathyroidism
*Nephrogenic diabetes insipidus
Hartnup's disease
*Oculo-cerebro-renal syndrome Lowe
Idiopathic severe hypercalcaemia
Pyridoxine dependency

---

*Sex-linked, all others autosomal recessive inheritance

homozygote normal subjects. Probably the best and least invasive heterozygote test for phenylketonuria is by oral or intravenous application of deuterated phenylalanine, measuring the transformation of deuterated phenylalanine to deuterated tyrosine in vivo.

Even the most sensitive heterozygote tests permit a clearcut discrimination between heterozygotes and genetically normal subjects in only 80 to 90% of cases. The overlap of 10 to 20% with normal subjects renders the result of a negative heterozygote test doubtful. A better discrimination would be an important future research goal, as would the question why heterozygotes usually show a residual enzyme activity of 30 to 40%, not 50% as expected (Bartholome, 1980). Still more puzzling and quite unexplained are data showing that heterozygote parents of patients with atypical phenylketonuria, also called "hyperphenylalaninaemia", may have still lower enzyme activity than heterozygotes of typical phenylketonuria, namely 7 to 10% (Kaufmann et al., 1975). These observations deserve further exploration.

There have been suggestions by Penrose (1935), and others, that heterozygotes for phenylketonuria and other metabolic disorders with mental retardation may exhibit milder or minimal symptoms of CNS involvement in their phenotypes. Though such claims have been repeatedly made for several of these disorders, they could usually not be confirmed by later investigators (Cowie, 1971).

EXAMPLES OF METABOLIC DISORDERS CAUSING MENTAL RETARDATION

A great number and variety of these disorders have been listed in Table 2. In the frame of this chapter only four out of seventy diseases can briefly be discussed. They have been chosen because they are not too rare, have been studied thoroughly, show different clinical and biochemical manifestations, and they are well known to the author by personal experience.

Phenylketonuria (PKU) and Variant Forms (Hyperphenylalaninaemias, HPHE)

Neonatal screening programmes have discovered various forms of "hyperphenylalaninaemia" (Bickel et al., 1971; Bickel, 1980). The severest form, usually called classical or typical phenylketonuria, shows no or very small residual activity of phenylalanine hydroxylase, less than 5% of the norm. This enzyme deficiency leads to a reduction of the gene products tyrosine, melanine and serotonin, as well as to accumulation of phenylalanine, phenylpyruvic acid and other phenolic acids, resulting in severe, but sometimes also milder, mental retardation, uncontrolled hyperkinetic behaviour, poor motor coordination and various psychotic reactions such as autism (Cowie, 1971). Convulsions are present mainly in childhood in 25-50%, presenting in young infants as infantile spasms. The exact pathogenesis of the brain damage is still largely obscure except for the fact that it can be completely prevented by a phenylalanine-restricted diet.

Milder forms of HPHE are believed not to damage the brain though this has not been proven over a longer period of time. They show residual enzyme activities of over 5% normal except for a rare form of HPHE, also called "malignant PKU", which has a normal activity of phenylalanine hydroxylase but exhibits a deficiency of the coenzyme tetrahydrobiopterin. With the exception of this condition the other forms of HPHE cannot always be separated into well defined disturbances with or without development of brain damage, even if phenylalanine loading tests or measurements of enzyme activity *in vitro* or *in vivo* with deuterated phenylalanine are used for this differentiation. Nor do genetic explorations of the families segregate the various forms of HPHE clearly from each other (see also under "inheritance").

Compared with these uncertainties, the HPHE of tetrahydrobiopterin deficiency is well defined and of special interest. Since its discovery in 1974 by Bartholome and by Smith it has been observed in many centres, its frequency being estimated to be 1 to 2% of PKU. During the first months of life these patients show little or no differences from classical PKU. Because of their raised phenylalanine blood level they are detected by newborn screening and normalize this level under a phenylalanine-restricted diet. Despite this diet and in contrast to PKU after some months progressive brain damage and a severe extrapyramidal syndrome develop which lead to death within the first years of life. Substitutional therapy with synthetic tetrahydrobiopterin and with the neurotransmitters 5-OH-tryptophan (a precursor of serotonin) and DOPA is very effective in preventing brain damage and death.

Neurotransmitter substitution is necessary because tetrahydrobiopterin acts also as coenzyme in tryptophan and tyrosine metabolism, its deficiency interfering with neurotransmitter production. More details on this topic will be given in the following chapter by Blair and Leeming and in surveys of Curtius *et al.* (1979) and of Niederweiser *et al.* (1980).

The malformation syndrome of maternal PKU and HPHE is another recent discovery in this field. Owing to world-wide screening more than 2000 girls with PKU have up to now been detected early and treated successfully, many of them now reaching the reproductive age, being phenotypically quite healthy. After termination of the strict diet around puberty their brain does not seem to be further damaged, probably because myelination of the brain is largely complete. But their rising phenylalanine blood level intoxicates the fetus and embryo *in utero*, leading to microcephaly, oligophrenia, neonatal dystrophy and cardiac malformations, as reported by Lenke and Levy (1980) from a survey of 524 pregnancies. Even milder forms of maternal HPHE can cause this severe fetoembryopathy. As damage starts already a few weeks after conception the hope of preventing this malformation syndrome lies in reinstituting the phenylalanine-restricted diet in the woman before conception. The exact mechanism of fetal damage in this disease is open to further research, as is the still unresolved question whether similar events can occur in other inborn errors, such as in homocystinuria, and the best way to manage these pregnancies in order to prevent fetal damage.

Maple Syrup Urine Disease (MSUD)

The enzymatic defect of this disease is not yet known exactly, but it interferes with the oxidative decarboxylation of

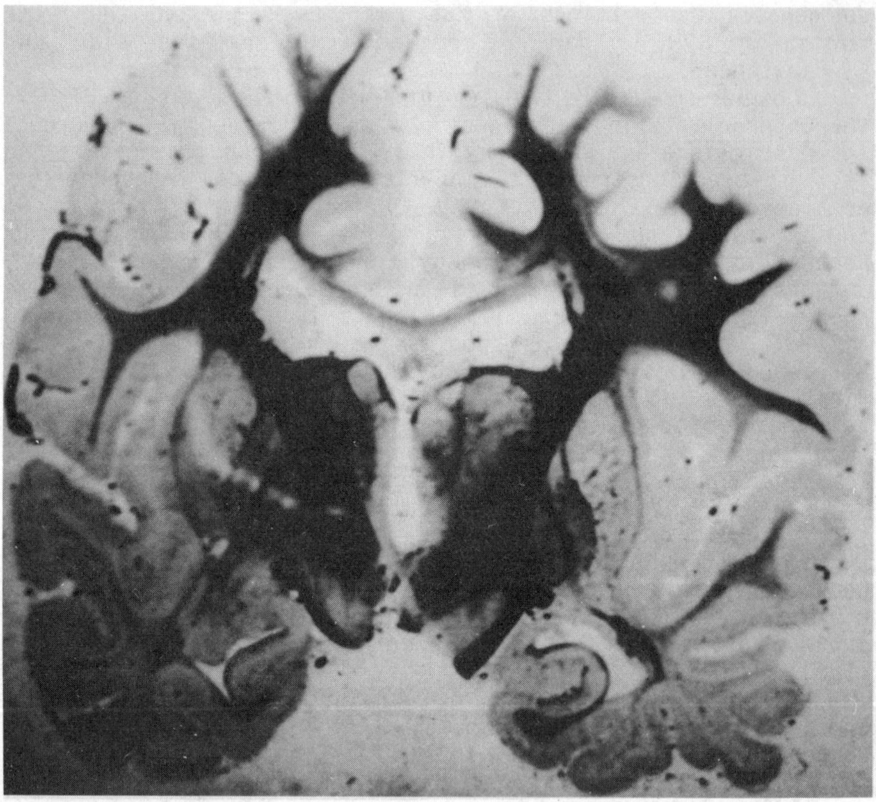

(a)

Figure 1

(a) Brain section of a treated patient with maple syrup urine disease aged 4 months. Staining of the myelin sheets shows normal myelogenesis. (b) In an untreated patient of the same age staining fails to show practically any myelogenesis. (After Bickel, 1967.)

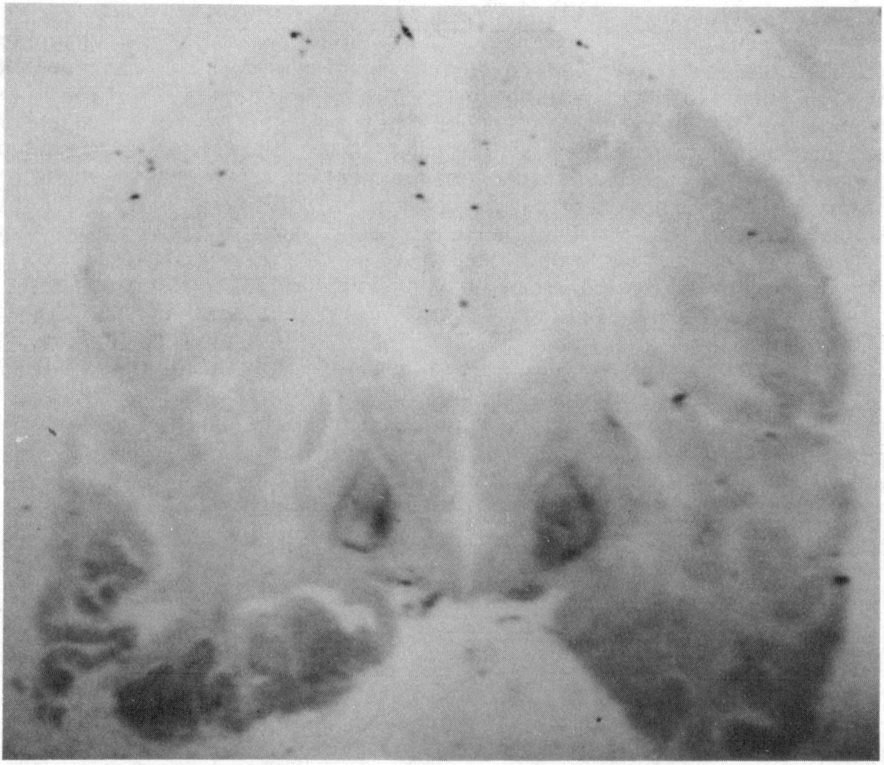

(b)

the keto acids of leucine, isoleucine and valine (Dancis and Levitz, 1978). These branched-chain amino acids and their keto acids accumulate before the enzyme block, being easily detected in blood, urine and other biological fluids in high concentrations. The increase in leucine is used in a newborn screening test similar to that for PKU showing that the disease is much rarer. The enzyme defect is, in contrast to PKU, also detectable in amniotic cell cultures in the 16th week of pregnancy, which allows an interruption of pregnancy if the fetus is suffering from the same disorder. The peculiar name of the disease is derived from the urine odour of the children resembling that of maple syrup. The biochemical correlate for this odour is not known.

Acute MSUD leads to quickly progressive brain damage within the first week of life (Hammersen et al., 1978). Already at the end of the first week the infant may show opisthotonos and attacks of asphyxia, loss of the Moro reflex and convulsions. Cerebral demyelination continues and death usually ensues in the first weeks or months of life. The severely defective myelination is well demonstrated in brain sections of an untreated patient aged four months as compared to a treated infant of the same age (Figure 1).

The mild intermittent form of the disease is very rarely observed (Muller et al., 1971). For many years these children may appear healthy, their mental development being borderline normal or slightly subnormal. During minor infections or triggered off by travel sickness they may suffer from prolonged attacks of ketonaemic vomiting and coma. They have a somewhat higher activity of oxidative decarboxylation of the keto acids in their skin fibroblasts than the typical disease with 0 to 2% normal activity. Whilst patients with intermittent MSUD can generally be kept in good health on a protein-restricted diet, children with acute MSUD can only be kept alive and serious brain damage can only be avoided if very early treatment with a highly synthetic diet restricted in leucine, isoleucine and valine is instituted, well monitored and maintained probably for a lifetime. Acute metabolic crises need peritoneal dialysis as an emergency measure. Despite all these efforts mild to moderate mental retardation can often not be avoided. The cause of the brain damage is not yet known though it must be due to a metabolic anomaly, as treatment can largely prevent it.

The Homocystinurias (HCY)

The classical form of HCY (Carson, 1982) is caused by a defect of cystathionine synthase. Clinical manifestations are a Marfan-like syndrome with skeletal changes, arachnodactyly, dislocation of the lenses, mental retardation in about 50% of the cases, and thromboembolic insults which can lead to further neurological complications such as paraplegia, spasticity and seizures, and finally to death. Microemboli in the brain may contribute to the cause of mental retardation, though this is probably not the whole explanation for the non-obligatory oligophrenia. The metabolic disturbance concerns the transformation of homocystine to cystine, resulting in an accumulation of methionine, homocystine and the mixed disulphide in blood and urine. The detection of hypermethioninaemia is used as a screening test in newborns, but this test is not as reliable as the screening tests for PKU and MSUD. Frequency figures have therefore a broad range from 1:100 000 to 1:330 000.

Pyridoxine-dependent HCY. The coenzyme of cystathionine synthase is pyridoxine. A third to a half of the cases of HCY can be normalized biochemically by treating them with pharmacological doses of pyridoxine. These patients show similar clinical manifestations but have a small residual enzyme activity whilst the pyridoxine-resistant cases exhibit no detectable enzyme activity and have to be treated with a methionine-restricted diet. It is not yet clear how far mental retardation can be influenced by this therapy, whilst a positive effect on the eye changes and on the prevention of thromboembolic insults has been observed with some certainty. The evaluation of therapy is complicated by the prolonged course of the disease.

Homocystinuria can also be due to defective remethylization. One of these defects concerns the methylenetetrahydrofolate reductase (Mudd et al., 1972). Its deficiency causes severe illness which so far has been reported in at least 9 families with 15 patients, two of them by my coworkers (Michalk et al., 1980). Such patients show a disordered reduction from methylenetetrahydrofolate to methyltetrahydrofolate, the lack of which leads to homocystine accumulation and methionine reduction. The disease is characterized by severe, progressive oligophrenia and spastic paraparesis, and by myoclonic seizures. Death occurs in childhood or adolescence and is generally due to thromboembolic insults. Rational treatment would be substitution of methyltetrahydrofolate. As this is commercially not available, we used leucovorine, formyltetrahydrofolate, for the first time in our two patients with advanced mental and neurological damage. There was a definite biochemical change towards normalization of homocystine and methionine levels in the plasma. More importantly, marked improvement was observed in mental retardation and in upper motor neuron dysfunction. Though the exact metabolism of formyltetrahydrofolate in these patients is unknown, we conclude that because of the beneficial effect at least part of the formyltetrahydrofolate must be converted to methyltetrahydrofolate.

Wilson's Disease (Hepato-lenticular Degeneration, HLD)

This is another rare inborn metabolic error, which is characterized by progressive degeneration of the brain, especially of the basal ganglia, by liver cirrhosis and by the Kayser-Fleischer corneal ring (Sass-Kortsak and Bearn, 1978). These manifestations are caused by copper deposition, which also takes place in the kidneys, the skin and other organs. The basic enzyme defect concerns the synthesis of the copper transporting plasma protein caeruloplasmin which is formed in insufficient amounts in the liver. Though a low caeruloplasmin blood level is one of the most constant changes in HLD, the decrease can be very variable, and in exceptional cases (4%) even normal. As healthy newborns also exhibit a reduced caeruloplasmin level in their first months of life, newborn screening for HLD by caeruloplasmin measurement is not possible.

The pathognomonic copper storage is due to the fact that any surplus of ingested copper cannot be sufficiently excreted in the bile, the reason for this needing further research. The retained copper, not being firmly bound in the blood to caeruloplasmin, is either deposited in the organs or excreted in the urine, so hypocupraemia and hypercupruria are other biochemical signs of the disease.

The clinical symptoms are very variable. They do not appear before the sixth year of life when the storage capacity of the liver cells for copper is exhausted. Only when free copper is overflowing into the CNS will neurological symptoms be noticed. They may at first be quite nonspecific, consisting of sudden bursts of temper, violence, kleptomania, sexual maladjustment and other behavioural problems (Bickel and Cleve, 1967). Typical neurological symptoms are to be expected when copper storage leads to degeneration of some especially sensitive areas of the brain. Extrapyramidal, choreoathetotic and cerebellar symptoms will then appear, such as tremor, ataxia, an empty facial expression with drooling of saliva, dysarthria, dysphagia, spasticity and rigidity. Schizophrenia, comatose states, seizures and an increasing dementia are other features, the disease ending after months or years in decerebration or liver coma.

Hepatic manifestations of the increasingly severe liver involvement are usually more discrete. They may be absent for many years, after which hepatosplenomegaly, abdominal pain, bouts of jaundice, ascites and raised transaminases without changes of the cholostatic enzymes will be noted. Occasionally the hepatic symptoms are much more predominant than the neurological ones, and may even be isolated ("abdominal Wilson").

A rational base for treatment would be the substitution of caeruloplasmin gained from human plasma by fractionation, but a therapeutic trial had to be abandoned because of toxic side effects (Bickel, 1961). D-Penicillamine treatment introduced in 1956 by Walshe improved the prognosis greatly, especially if started early and continued subsequently for a lifetime. Mental and other neurological dysfunctions can only be influenced successfully if ganglion cell degeneration has not progressed too far. The extent of cerebral damage in HLD can now be shown rather well by computed tomography (Harik and Donovan, 1981).

DIFFERENT PATTERNS OF BRAIN DAMAGE IN INBORN METABOLIC DISORDERS

Considering the four examples of inborn errors described above in some detail, but also those given in Table 2, it is obvious that the metabolic disturbances involved in these diseases are of great variety. So it is not surprising that the response of the brain is also very different from disease to disease, and even in the same disease in the various subtypes. Some diseases, like phenylketonuria, homocystinuria and Wilson's disease, lead to slowly progressive brain damage, the exact mechanism of which is usually not known, though disturbed myelination, thromboembolic insults and copper intoxication, respectively, seem to play a role in their pathogenesis. Others, like galactosaemia, maple syrup urine disease, propionic acidaemia, methylmalonic acidaemia and hyperammonaemia types I and II have very acute courses already in the newborn period with quickly progressive neurological dysfunction, lethargy, coma, muscular hypotonia, but also spasticity, seizures and death in asphyxia (survey by Rosenberg, 1974).

Not only are the age at presentation and the speed of progression so different in the various diseases, but also the pattern of the nervous dysfunction and changes in other organs contributing to the final clinical picture. A relatively even, generally severe reduction of all intellectual capacities is observed in phenylketonuria, with little or no involvement of the extrapyramidal system, the sensory, spinal or peripheral nervous systems. Seizures in the form of infantile spasms or grand mal epilepsy are frequent as in other inborn metabolic errors, but with a frequency of 30-50% and not as essential a symptom as e.g. in pyridoxine dependency. Autistic or schizoid behaviour patterns are exceptional. In complete contrast the cerebral manifestations of Wilson's disease often start with extrapyramidal or psychotic symptoms, whilst mental retardation develops later, if at all. Cerebellar ataxia and comatose states, generally without permanent oligophrenia, have been observed repeatedly in more than 40 patients with Hartnup's disease and resemble similar clinical behaviour in classical pellagra. In the urea cycle disorders, all of which are characterized by more or less pronounced hyperammonaemia, it is rather difficult to decide whether the brain damage presenting with screaming, headache, vomiting, confusion, lethargy, stupor and intellectual retardation is caused by attacks of hyperammonaemia or by the primary metabolic defect.

Differences in the severity of the brain damage are exemplified in the relatively benign course of histidinaemia and of the intermittent type of maple syrup urine disease which may or may not exhibit mild cerebral symptoms, and in the rapidly progressive decerebration of acute maple syrup urine disease and some lipidoses, e.g. Tay-Sachs' disease with attacks of asphyxia, spasticity, startle reaction and blindness. There are also remarkable contrasts in mood and behaviour in the various disorders. Whilst in some diseases a placid, quiet and even friendly behaviour is the rule, such as in familial goitre, in Hurler's disease and in most Wilson's patients, other metabolic errors tend to induce restlessness, aggressiveness and even self-mutilation, such as in Lowe's syndrome and in the Lesch-Nyhan syndrome.

For the specialist in this field the individual differences of the cerebral involvement from patient to patient suffering from seemingly identical diseases are even more striking. These differences may often be due to genetic heterogeneity, which is probably true for classical phenylketonuria with generally severe oligophrenia and atypical phenylketonuria with little or no oligophrenia, or for the acute as contrasted to the relatively benign intermittent maple syrup urine disease. Similar differences have also, however, been observed among siblings in histidinaemia and even in identical phenylketonuric twins. There are in fact very few instances among the 50 metabolic errors with brain damage listed in Table 2 that, despite a complete pattern of the biochemical abnormalities, produce brain damage in every single patient suffering from this disease. In homocystinuria, pseudohypoparathyroidism, Hartnup's disease and cerebrotendinous xanthomatosis, only 50% of the patients or less show permanent brain damage, but sometimes well marked involvement of other organs, such as ectopy of the ocular lens in homocystinuria or brachydactyly in pseudohypoparathyroidism. The reasons for this variable expression of the clinical features of these and other metabolic errors are not clear and can probably not all be traced to differences in the primary genetic defect. Some environmental factors may occasionally play a role, such as different dietary habits, e.g. in galactosaemia, or the age at which the biochemical "noxa" begins to work, e.g. pre- or postnatally, in infancy, later childhood or adult life, or the availability of cofactors, such as vitamins B6, B12 and C. The detection of the true reasons for this striking variability, and the finer mechanism which from disease to disease, but also in the same disease causes the damage to the brain and to other organs, should have priority in future research in this field.

REFERENCES

Bartholome, K., (1980), Die molekulare Basis der Heterogenitat der Phenylketonurie. **Naturwissenschaften, 67**, 495

Bickel, H., (1961), Attempts at caeruloplasmin substitution in Wilson's disease. In: **Wilson's Disease. Some Current Concepts**. Eds. J.M. Walshe and J.N. Cumings. Blackwell, Oxford, 273

Bickel, H., (1967), Hirnatrophie und Störungen des Aminosäurenstoffwechsels. **Mschr. f. Kinderheilk., 115**, 254-258

Bickel, H., (1980), Phenylketonuria: Past, present, future. F.P. Hudson Memorial Lecture, **J. Inher. Metab. Dis., 3**, 123

Bickel, H., (1983), Screening auf angeborene Stoffwechselkrankheiten: Indikation und Ergebnisse. **Dtsch. Ges. f. Kinderheilk. 78. Tagung, Mschr. f. Kinderheilk.** In press

Bickel, H., Bachmann, C., Beckers, R., Brandt, N.J., Clayton, B.E., Corrado, B., Feingold, H.J., Giardini, D., Hammersen, G. and Schonberg, D., (1981), Neonatal mass screening for metabolic disorders. Summary of recent sessions of the committee of experts to study inborn metabolic diseases. Public Health Committee, Council of Europe. **Eur. J. Pediatr., 137**, 133

Bickel, H. and Cleve, H., (1967), Metabolische Schwachsinnsformen. In: **Humangenetik. Ein kurzes Handbuch in funf Banden**. Ed. P.E. Becker. Thieme Verlag, Stuttgart, 263

Bickel, H., Hudson, F.P. and Woolf, L.I., (1971), **Phenylketonuria and Some Other Inborn Errors of Amino Acid Metabolism**. Thieme Verlag, Stuttgart

Carson, N.A.J., (1982), Homocystinuria: clinical and biochemical heterogeneity. In: **Inborn Errors of Metabolism in Humans**. Eds. Cockburn, F., and Gitzelmann, R. MTP Press, Lancaster, 53

Cowie, V.A., (1971), Neurological and psychiatric aspects of phenylketonuria. In: **Phenylketonuria and Some Other Inborn Errors of Amino Acid Metabolism**. Eds. H. Bickel, F.P. Hudson and L.I. Woolf. Thieme Verlag, Stuttgart, 29

Curtius, H.-Ch., Niederweiser, A., Viscontini, M., et al., (1979), Atypical phenylketonuria due to tetrahydrobiopterin deficiency. Diagnosis and treatment with tetrahydrobiopterin, dihydrobiopterin and sepiapterin. **Clin. Chim. Acta.**, **93**, 251-262

Dancis, J. and Levitz, M., (1978), Abnormalities of branched chain amino acid metabolism. In: **The Metabolic Basis of Inherited Disease**, 4th Edn, Eds. Stanbury, J.B., Wyngaarden, J.B. and Fredrickson, D.S. McGraw-Hill, New York, 397

Eggers, C. and Bickel, H., (1974), Prä-, peri- und post-natal bedingte Schwachsinnsformen: eine Synopse in Tabellenform. **Ergeb. Inn. Med. Kinderheilk.**, **34**, 155-205

Folling, A., (1934), Uber Ausscheidung von Phenylbrenztraubensaure in den Harn als Stoffwechselanomalie in Verbindung mit Imbezillitat. **Hoppe-Seylers Z. Physiol. Chem.**, **227**, 169

Folling, A., Closs, K. and Gamnes, T., (1938), Vorlaufige Schlussfolgerungen aus Belastungsversuchen mit Phenylalanin an Menschen und Tieren. **Hoppe-Seylers Z. Physiol. Chem.**, **256**, 1

Hammersen, G., Wille, L., Schmidt, H., Lutz, P. and Bickel, H., (1978), Maple syrup urine disease: Treatment of the acutely ill newborn. **Eur. J. Pediatr.**, **129**, 157

Harik, S.I. and Donovan, M.J., (1981), Computed tomography in Wilson disease. **Neurology (NY)**, **31**, 107

Kaufmann, S., Max, E.E. and Kang, E.S., (1975), Phenylalanine hydroxylase activity in liver biopsies from hyperphenylalaninemia heterozygotes: Deviation from proportionality with gene dosage. **Pediat. Res.**, **9**, 632

Lenke, R.R. and Levy, H.L., (1980), Maternal phenylketonuria and hyperphenylalaninemia: An international survey of the outcome of untreated and treated pregnancies. **New Engl. J. Med.**, **303**, 1202-1208

McKusick, V.A., (1978), **Mendelian Inheritance in Man.** Catalogs of autosomal dominant, autosomal recessive and X-linked phenotypes. The John Hopkins University Press, Baltimore

Michalk, D., Schmidt, H., Mittermaier, G., Wong, P. and Lutz, P., (1980), Homocystinuria due to 5,10-methylenetetrahydrofolate reductase deficiency: Clinical presentation and treatment. **Pediatr. Res**, **14**, 175

Mudd, S.H., Uhlendorf, B.W., Freeman, J.M., Finkelstein, J.D. and Shih, V.E., (1976), Homocystinuria associated with decreased methylenetetrahydrofolate reductase activity. **Biochem. Biophys. Res. Commun.**, **46**, 905-912

Muller, H., Bickel, H., Feist, D. and Putz, P., (1971), Ahornsirupkrankheit mit intermitierendem, relativ gutartigem Verlauf. **Dtsch. Med. Wschr.**, **96**, 1552

Niederweiser, A., Curtius, H.C., Gitzelmann, R., Otten, A., Baerlocher, K., Blehova, B., Berlow, S., Grobe, H., Rey, F., Schaub, J., Scheibenreiter, S., Schmidt, H. and Viscontini, M., (1980), Excretion of pterins in phenylketonuria and phenylketonuria variants. **Helv. Paediat. Acta**, **35**, 335

Penrose, L.S., (1935), Inheritance of phenylpyruvic amentia. **Lancet, II**, 192

Potts, J.T.Jr., (1978), Pseudohypoparathyroidism. In: **The Metabolic Basis of Inherited Disease**, 4th Edn, Eds. Stanbury, J.B., Wyngaarden, J.B. and Fredrickson, D.S. McGraw-Hill, New York, 1362

Rosenberg, L.E., (1974), Diagnosis and management of inherited aminoacidopathies in the newborn and unborn. In: **Congenital and acquired diseases of amino acid metabolism.** Ed. H. Bickel. **Clinics in Endocrinology and Metabolism, 3,** W.B. Saunders, London, Philadelphia, Toronto, 145

Sass-Kortsak, A. and Bearn, A.G., (1978), Hereditary disorders of copper metabolism. In: **The Metabolic Basis of Inherited Disease**, 4th Edn, Eds. Stanbury, J.B., Wyngaarden, J.B. and Fredrickson, D.S. McGraw-Hill, New York, 1098

Smith, I., (1974), Atypical phenylketonuria accompanied by a severe progressive neurological illness unresponsive to dietary treatment. **Arch. Dis. Childh., 49**, 245

Walshe, J.M., (1956), Wilson's disease: New oral therapy. **Lancet, I,** 25

Wesch, H., Przuntek, H. and Feist, D., (1980), Morbus Wilson. Rasche Diagnose und Differenzierung hetero- und homozygoter Anlagetrager mit $CuCl_2$. **Dtsch. Med. Wschr., 105**, 483

COMMENTARY

B. E. Cohen

With regard to the frequency figures in various ethnic groups of hyperphenylalanaemia, one must beware of possible errors from inadequate numbers of specimens. Thus in Israel our original cases led us to believe that the condition was confined to Yemenite Jews but later results showed it to exist amongst all the non-Ashkenazic Jewish ethnic groups and with a relatively high incidence also amongst the Israeli Arab population. Now, after screening over a million newborns, we have only found one Ashkenazi-Jewish family with a variant or atypical PKU (the diet being modified at one year after a negative result to a standardized milk tolerance test) and one family with a mixed Ashkenazi-North African Jewish parentage. On the other hand we have found a proportionate number of Ashkenazi-Jewish families amongst the mild persistent hyperphenylalaninaemias (with serum phenylalanine levels up to 16 mg % on normal diet). If this milder form of hyperphenylalaninaemia was due to an allele of the PKU gene it is possible that this last family was due to mixed heterozygotes for the PKU gene and its allele. Unfortunately neither enzyme studies nor heterozygote testing are sufficiently sensitive to decide this question. Once again the initial impression of the sex difference from the early screening studies were later proven incorrect (Holzman et al., 1974).

One of the problems about early neonatal screening is whether we might not miss cases by taking the samples too early especially with the recent tendency to early discharge from maternity hospitals. We have studied this point and our results suggest that in classical PKU even on the second postnatal day very few if any cases will be missed but in variant cases there may be some justification for recommending a second blood specimen (Szeinberg and Cohen, 1982).

Bickel writes "Milder forms of HPHE are believed not to damage the brain though this has not been proven over a longer period of time". Berry and co-workers (Berry et al., 1979) have brought some disturbing evidence to suggest that the group of children with high variant or atypical PKU (blood phenylalanine levels of 14-20 mg %, or even up to 30 mg %) do better when treated with dietary restriction, and have a significantly higher IQ, suggesting the need for this treatment in all children with persistent phenylalanine levels above 15 mg %/dl. There has been no support for this view from other teams. Our own experience has been equivocal and insufficiently documented to allow conclusions.

The question of when, if ever, to stop the diet has not been mentioned in Bickel's paper. Murphy (1969) was the first to warn about this danger and subsequently Cabalska from Poland (Cabalska et al., 1977) and Smith (Smith et al., 1978) supported this finding. Koch (Koch et al., 1982) in his preliminary report of the collaborative study in June 1982 suggests caution as subtle changes may occur if the diet is discontinued at 4-6 years without any obvious reduction of the IQ. Our group have tried to continue diet until 8-10 years of age but usually the child or their parents have given up before we legalize their decisions on receipt of repeated high blood phenylalanine levels, in spite of all efforts to prevent this.

The malformation syndrome of maternal PKU and HPHE still needs much clarification. Are the milder HPHEs dangerous? At what blood phenylalanine level should we start dietary restriction? What blood level should we aim at during the pregnancy? What about the tyrosine levels? How much tyrosine should we add and what serum tyrosine levels should we aim at? Evidence suggests that the mental retardation and other embryopathies occur at different stages of pregnancy - the latter being decided in the early weeks. Will this artificial diet started prior to the onset of pregnancy and continued throughout produce other untoward effects that have not yet been reported - perhaps other rare congenital abnormalities. All these and other details still have to be answered when further controlled pregnancies have been studied. In an editorial in the *Canadian Medical Association Journal* Hanley and Bell (1982) pointed out the need for identifying mothers with PKU or HPHE who had been lost to follow-up or were unknown to their obstetricians. Obviously antenatal examinations are too late and they suggest using the genetic counselling units and premarital examinations. Ideally there should be a register of all PKU and HPHE patients for pregnancy control.

In maple syrup urine disease, the disease is so rare that smaller countries may have to go for years without discovering any cases and where the postal service is slow or there are undue delays in getting specimens to the laboratory the results might be better from an alert neonatologist rather than routine screening.

Wilson's disease is ubiquitous but the clinical manifestations are not always identical. In Israel (Passwell *et al*., 1977) the hepatic picture appears to be far more common *in* Arab children and appears earlier and the nervous symptoms are rarer. There are no particular explanations for this phenomenon as it is biochemically identical.

Different patterns of brain damage: even in the same disease it is not clear why some patients are relatively spared and thus in classical PKU we occasionally get normal or near normal IQ whereas in other comparable cases there is severe retardation even in the same families.

References

Berry H.K., O'Grady D.J., Perimutter L.J. and Bofinger M.K. (1979). Intellectual development and academic achievement of children treated early for phenylketonuria. **Dev. Med. and Child Neurol. 21**, 3, 311

Cabalska B., Duszynska N., Borzymowska J., Zorska K., Kosiacz-Folga A. and Bozkowa K. (1977). Termination of dietary treatment in phenylketonuria. **Eur. J. Pediatr. 126,** 253

Hanley W.B. and Bell L. (1982). Maternal phenylketonuria: finding and treating women before conception. **Can. Med. Assoc. J., 126** 1259

Holzman N., Meek A., Mellits S. and Callman C. (1974). Neonatal screening for phenylketonuria. III. Altered sex ratio, extent and possible causes. **J. Pediatr., 85,** 175

Koch R., Azen C.G., Friedman E.G. and Williamson M.L. (1982). Preliminary report on the effects of diet discontinuation in PKU. **J. Pediatr. 100,** 4, 870

Murphy D. (1969). Termination of dietary treatment of phenylketonuria. **J. Med. Sci., 2,** 177

Passwell J., Adam A., Garfinkel D., Streiffler M. and Cohen B.E. (1977). Heterogeneity of Wilson's disease in Israel. **Israel J. Med. Sci., 13** 15

Smith I., Lobascher M., Stevenson J., Wolff O.H., Schmidt H., Grubel-Kaiser S. and Bickel H. (1978). Effect of stopping low-phenylalanine diet on intellectual progress of children with phenylketonuria. **Br. Med. J., 2,** 723

Szeinberg A. and Cohen B.E. (1982). Early blood sampling in neonatal programs for the detection of phenylketonuria. **Padiatrie and Padologie, 17,** 267

H. Galjaard

In the industrialized countries congenital disorders have become the major cause of infant mortality and morbidity. At least 4-6% of all liveborns have a congenital abnormality and 0.5-1% are genetic diseases due to a single gene mutation (Trimble and Doughty, 1974; Edwards, 1974; Carter, 1976; Trimble and Smith, 1977). At present more than 3300 abnormalities of Mendelian inheritance are known in man, and in about 10% of these the responsible molecular defect is known (McKusick, 1982). The clinical manifestations vary widely among this large number of genetic diseases, but also within each individual metabolic disease there may be considerable clinical heterogeneity (for reviews, see Galjaard, 1980; Stanbury _et al_., 1982).

The early diagnosis of genetic diseases is complicated by the enormous variability of symptoms and signs, the differences in time of onset and course, the low incidence of most diseases, and the fact that a proper diagnosis usually requires the collaboration of different experts and institutions.

Initially the diagnosis of genetic diseases was exclusively based on clinical and pathological examination of the patient, and the pattern of inheritance was usually established by pedigree studies. During the last two decades our insight into the genetic, molecular and metabolic background of an increasing number of diseases has greatly improved, and as a result in many instances the early diagnosis of patients and the identification of carriers, and hence the pattern of inheritance, are based on laboratory tests more or less independent of clinical manifestations.

Analysis of metabolites in blood and urine using aminoacid analysis, gas chromatography, mass spectrometry, high pressure liquid chromatography and electrophoresis has become an indispensable tool in the diagnosis of newborns and other patients with unexplained metabolic disturbances, psychomotor retardation or clinical manifestations which might be associated with a genetic metabolic disease (Goodman and Markey, 1981; Bremer et al., 1981).

If possible, the ultimate diagnosis of a genetic metabolic disease must, however, be based on the demonstration of the responsible (enzyme) protein defect. Sometimes the necessary biochemical assays have to be performed on tissue biopsies but in many instances erythrocytes or white blood cells can be used and about 100 genetic metabolic defects are also demonstrable in cultured skin fibroblasts (for reviews, see Galjaard, 1980; Stanbury et al., 1982). The latter is important both for research purposes and as a basis for prenatal diagnosis in subsequent pregnancies of parents or other relatives at risk (for reviews, see Murken et al., 1979; Milunsky, 1979; Galjaard, 1980).

During the last few years the recombinant DNA technology has permitted yet another step forward, i.e. the diagnosis of a genetic disease at the level of the mutation in the DNA itself (for reviews, see Williamson, 1981-1983; Humphries and Williamson, 1982).

Early diagnosis by neonatal mass screening seems to be justified only if a disease can be successfully treated, if a reliable, simple and inexpensive diagnostic test is available, and if the incidence is high enough to convince parents, experts and authorities. Thus far these criteria seem to be met by two diseases only: phenylketonuria and congenital hypothyroidism, and in nearly all countries neonatal mass screening at a national level is restricted to these two diseases (for review, see Bickel et al., 1980).

Since many genetic metabolic diseases are associated with severe physical and mental handicaps and no treatment is available, increasing attention is being paid to their prevention. One approach is of course to avoid as much as possible exposure of large populations to harmful environmental factors which might result in an increase in the mutation rate, such as ionizing radiation (see U.N. report 1977). A second approach towards prevention is to identify couples at risk for an affected child and to give them genetic counselling. Several studies have shown that 50-90% of the couples who have been informed that they have a relatively high genetic risk (1 in 10 or more) will not reproduce (Carter et al., 1971; Emery et al., 1972; Clow et al., 1973; Briard et al., 1977; Klein and Wyss, 1977; Emery, personal communication, 1980).

In most instances couples at risk for offspring with a genetic metabolic disease will be identified on the basis of the diagnosis of their first affected child. Preventive measures on this basis will have a limited effect on the reduction of the incidence of the particular disease. Depending on the family size this reduction will amount to 12.5% in families with a total of two children, up to about 33% in families who will reproduce until they have two normal children (Motulsky et al., 1971).

A more effective way of prevention is the detection of carriers before their first pregnancy. This is often possible in the case of X-linked metabolic diseases where the diagnosis of an affected male and a heterozygous mother will initiate further carrier studies in healthy female relatives often before reproduction. Another possibility is large-scale carrier detection for autosomal recessive mutations which occur relatively frequently in certain populations. An example of such a disease associated with severe mental retardation is GM2-gangliosidosis type 1 (Tay-Sachs disease), which occurs among Ashkenazy Jews with an incidence of 1 in 2500 liveborns (Kaback, 1977). Simple, reliable and automated assays for the responsible hexosaminidase A deficiency are available and, up to 1981, 310 000 young adults had been screened; more than 10 000 carriers had been identified, among whom were 300 couples at risk who had not yet reproduced. By informing these couples about their high (25%) risk the birth of affected children can be prevented (Kaback, 1981). Similar carrier screening programmes are carried out for sickle-cell anaemia, which occurs very frequently among the black populations in the USA and Africa, and for thalassaemia, which has a high incidence in Mediterranean, Middle-East and Asian countries (Weatherall and Clegg, 1981; Modell, 1982; WHO report, 1981). With further advancement and simplification of the DNA technology it may well be that in the future carrier screening will become feasible for many other diseases (Humphries and Williamson, 1982).

Although the preventive value of early diagnosis of index patients and of carrier detection and genetic counselling is important, it is difficult for couples at risk to take the decision of no (further) pregnancies, especially when they have not yet given birth to one or more healthy children. During the last decade there has been an important alternative for many of these parents because of the possibility of prenatal monitoring for fetal abnormalities. In all Western countries facilities have become available for ultrasound control, amniocentesis in the 15-16th week of pregnancy, followed by chromosomal analysis or biochemical tests of fetal cells. The methods have greatly improved during the last decade and the risk of fetal loss as a result of amniocentesis has decreased to less than 0.5% (for reviews, see Murken et al., 1979; Milunsky, 1979; Galjaard, 1980). At present nearly 100 different genetic metabolic diseases can be detected in the fetus and the scope will further increase by the use of recombinant-DNA technology and fetal blood analysis (for recent reviews, see Galjaard, 1982; Proc. Cold Spring Harbor Symposium, 1982).

In the near future parents at risk for a child with phenylketonuria will have to decide whether they want their baby to be born and treated (see contribution by Bickel in this volume) or whether they want prenatal monitoring (using a DNA probe for phenylalanine hydroxylase) and abortion in the case of an affected fetus. Many experts, especially paediatricians, will object against this latter option in the case of diseases that can be treated. Others will point to the uncertainties which still exist about the long-term development of PKU children who have been on a diet for many years; also adult females with PKU are at great risk to give birth to a child with congenital anomalies.

Choices like those mentioned above will not only depend on the opinion of the experts consulted, but also on the socio-economic and cultural development in a society. In my opinion there is the danger of increasing confrontations between doctors and psychosocial workers who want to treat severely handicapped children at any price, even when the results are limited, and parents or close relatives who do not want this. At the same time we must be very careful that an overemphasis of the importance of preventing the birth of an affected child does not lead to a decreased motivation to provide optimal medical and psychosocial care to our handicapped.

Open discussions between experts in various disciplines related to the care and study of mental retardation and a dialogue between experts and patient and parent organizations are important means to discover which ways we have to go. From what we know already, the complexity of the genetic, molecular and biochemical basis of mental retardation is enormous and so are the problems of optimal psychosocial care. We must therefore convince the authorities that they should not expect short-term results and that they must have the courage to invest in basic research.

References

Bickel, H., Guthrie, R. and Hammersen, G (eds.) (1980). Neonatal **Screening for Inborn Errors of Metabolism.** Springer, Berlin and New York

Bremer, H.J., Duran, M., Kamerling, J.P., Przyrembel, H. and Wadman, S.K. (eds.) (1981). **Disturbances of Amino Acid Metabolism: Clinical Chemistry and Diagnosis.** Urban and Schwarzenberg, Baltimore and Munich

Briard, M.L., Frezal, J. and Kaplan, J. (1977). Le conseil genetique. **J. Genet. Hum. 25**, no 3, 157-176

Carter, C.O. (1976). Genetics of common single malformation. **Brit. Med. Bull. 32**, 21-26

Carter, C.O., Fraser Roberts, J.A., Evans, K.A. and Buck, A.R. (1971) Genetic clinic; a follow-up. **Lancet i**, 281-285

Clow, C.L., Fraser, F.C., Laberge, C. and Scriver, C.R. (1973). On the application of knowledge to the patient with genetic disease. In **Progress in Medical Genetics 9**, 159-213. Grune and Stratton, New York

Edwards, J.H. (1974). The mutation rate in man. In A.G. Steinberg and A.G. Bearn (eds.) **Progress in Medical Genetics**, 1-16. Grune and Stratton, New York

Emery, A.E.H., Watt, M.S. and Clark, E.R. (1972). The effect of genetic counselling in Duchenne muscular dystrophy. **Clin. Genet. 3**, 147-150

Galjaard, H. (1980). **Genetic Metabolic Diseases; Early Diagnosis and Prenatal Analysis.** Elsevier/North Holland, Amsterdam and New York

Galjaard, H. (ed.) (1982). **The Future of Prenatal Diagnosis.** Churchill Livingstone, Edinburgh

Goodman, S.I. and Markey, S.P. (1981). Diagnosis of organic acidemias by gas chromatography - mass spectrometry. **Laboratory and Research Methods in Biology and Medicine 6.** Alan R. Liss, New York

Humphries, S.E. and Williamson, R. (1982). Recombinant DNA and the study of the inheritance of human hereditary disease. In **The Future of Prenatal Diagnosis**, H. Galjaard (ed.) 62-68. Churchill Livingstone, Edinburgh

Kaback, M.M. (ed.) (1977). **Tay-Sachs Disease: Screening and Prevention.** Alan R. Liss, New York

Kaback, M.M. (1981). Heterozygote screening and prenatal diagnosis in Tay-Sachs disease; a world wide update. In **Lysosomes and Lysosomal Storage Diseases**, J.W. Callahan and A.J. Lowden (eds.) 331-342. Raven Press, New York

Klein, D. and Wyss, D. (1977). Retrospective and follow-up study of approximately 1000 genetic consultations. **J. Genet. Hum. 25**, no. 1, 47-57

McKusick, V.A. (1982). The human genome through the eyes of a clinical geneticist. **Cytogenet. Cell Genet. 32**, 7-23

Milunsky, A. (ed.) (1979). **Genetic Disorders and the Fetus.** Plenum, New York

Modell, B. (1982). Social aspects of prenatal monitoring of genetic disease. In H. Galjaard (ed.) **The Future of Prenatal Diagnosis**, 146-160. Churchill Livingstone, Edinburgh

Motulsky, A.G., Fraser, G.R. and Felsenstein, J. (1971). Public health and long-term implications of intrauterine diagnosis and selective abortion. **Birth Defects Original Article Series, 7**, no. 5, 22-33. Natl. Found. March of Dimes

Murken, J.D., Stengel-Rutkowski, S. and Schwinger, E. (eds.) (1979). **Prenatal Diagnosis. Proceedings of the Third European Conference.** Enke, Stuttgart

Proceedings Cold Spring Harbor Symposium on Prospects of Gene Treatment, Banbury Centre, 1982

Stanbury, J.B., Wyngaarden, J.B., Frederickson, D.S., Goldstein, J.L. and Brown, M.S. (eds.) (1982). **The Metabolic Basis of Inherited Disease**, 5th edn. McGraw-Hill, New York

Trimble, B.K. and Doughty, J.H. (1974). The amount of hereditary disease in human populations. **Ann. Hum. Genet. (London), 38,** 199-223

Trimble, B.K. and Smith, M.E. (1977). The incidence of genetic disease and the impact on man of an altered mutation rate. **Can. J. Genet. Cytol. 19,** 375-385

United Nations Scientific Commmittee on the Effects of Atomic Radiation. Report to the General Assembly. U.N., New York, 1977

Weatherall, D.J. and Clegg, J.G. (1981). **Thalassemia Syndromes,** 3rd edn. Blackwell, Oxford

Williamson, R. (ed.) 1981-1983. **Genetic Engineering 1-3.** Academic Press, New York

World Health Organization Report on the Community Control of Hereditary Anemias. Geneva, 1981

S. H. Green

Prenatal diagnosis is mentioned by Bickel as one practical aspect of the diagnosis of metabolic disease. Abortion of the affected fetus is at the moment the only method we have of preventing the effects of the majority of the known inborn areas of metabolism. Although the total number of mentally retarded children which could be prevented by this method is small, nevertheless it is important to the individual family where there has been a previously affected child or where there is a known high risk of the disease occurring. The successful implementation of such a programme requires not only sophisticated laboratory services but highly effective organization, because:

(a) usually the clinical diagnosis has to be made in a previous sibling, and confirmed by enzyme analysis; and

(b) the parents have to be counselled, amniocentesis performed, cells cultured and the enzyme analysis performed preferably by the same laboratory as performed the diagnosis on the previous sibling.

Bickel points out the different incidences of metabolic diseases in different races. Further epidemiological data are needed on this, particularly on immigrant groups in Western countries. We need to know whether or not there is a higher incidence of certain diseases because of increased gene frequency or whether consanguineous marriages contribute significantly.

Bickel touches on the subject of heterozygote screening. The only reasonably successful programme of this nature, i.e. to determine heterozygote carriers of serious disease and counsel them, has been for Tay-Sachs screening on Ashkenazi Jews in parts of North America. Further epidemiological studies and pilot surveys need to be done to see whether in certain racial groups this form of preventive medicine is a viable proposition. It is particularly justified to consider it where the disease concerned is not amenable to any form of treatment whatsoever and inexorably leads to chronic deterioration and death. But there are problems in defining the overlap between heterozygote and normal as Bickel points out.

With regard to treatment of inborn areas of metabolism causing mental retardation Bickel has clearly pointed out that some of these diseases may be responsive to dietary manipulation and others to supplementation with vitamins. It is still not known in many of these conditions for how long the diet has to be continued and it is imperative that regionalized specialist services are available for such children.

Serious consideration must be given to the possibility (although at the moment experimental) that some of the inborn areas of metabolism, e.g. the mucopolysaccharidoses, may be arrested in their progress or even possibly somewhat reversed by the use of marrow transplantation or placental implant. It is very important that this is critically evaluated by one or two centres before embarking on what would be an enormously costly programme for all such children with this group of conditions. Even if this form of therapy were proved to be successful it is only likely to be possible in a limited number of lysosomal disorders. In the hexosaminidase group of disorders the brain may already be significantly damaged at the time of birth, because of intraneuronal accumulation of storage material. It is doubtful that this could be reversed.

It has recently been shown that among the group of disorders with deficiency of hexosaminidase A or B or combinations thereof the clinical picture may deviate from that of the classical Tay-Sachs or Sanahofs disease. Johnson has recently reported from the United States a number of children with progressive conditions including anterior horn cell disease, spinocerebellar degenerations, neuromuscular problems and dementias who have turned out to have hexosaminidase deficiencies of one type or another. Further research needs to be done in this area, and there may be parallels with other enzyme systems. The clinician must be aware that two clinically similar diseases may be genetically different and vice versa two apparently clinically different diseases may at least in the first instance appear to have the same deficiency. This is why it is absolutly mandatory as discussed above to have an enzyme diagnosis before any attempt is made at amniocentesis and prenatal counselling.

The clinician is usually aware that a child who has a progressive degenerative disease of the central nervous system may have an inborn error of metabolism and should search for this appropriately. There are, however, other groups of conditions where he may not be aware that he is dealing with a metabolic disorder. For example, there are some infants with inborn errors of metabolism who die in early infancy following an infection and it is wrongly presumed that this was an infective cause whereas in fact an infective process had triggered off a metabolic disease. Secondly, in some inborn errors the picture is one of an intermittent downhill course with plateaux (as in some of the intermittent metabolic acidoses). Thirdly, the possibility should be considered, and this is more speculative, that some children with non-progressive mental retardation may in fact have underlying metabolic disorder.

O. E. Pratt

Mechanisms of brain damage in inherited metabolic defects

Bickel's paper illustrates the wide variety of metabolic pathways affected by inherited metabolic defects and it is now timely to move the emphasis from descriptive work to elucidations of mechanisms of damage. There are three main ways in which the brain may be damaged as a result of an inherited metabolic disorder:

1. Failure to make an essential metabolite. Brain cells may need to synthesize an essential metabolite which is normally made as a result of metabolism in the pathway beyond the block. For example, in homocystinuria due to deficiency of cystathionine synthase the brain cells will lack not only cystathionine but also probably many other sulphur-containing compounds, and cystine (or cysteine), which would normally be made from methionine, becomes an essential amino acid for many of these patients (Mudd and Levy, 1978). That this is so is confirmed by the value of dietary L-cystine supplements in treatment. In this condition damage is also caused by toxic metabolites and it is often possible to overcome the block by high doses of pyridoxin, a cofactor for the defective enzyme (Mudd *et al.*, 1970).

2. Deprivation of a nutrient by transport inhibition. This mechanism will most likely be important when:

(a) the metabolic block is outside the central nervous system (as in PKU where the defective phenylalanine hydroxylase is mainly a liver enzyme); and

(b) carrier-mediated transport across the blood-brain (or other) barrier is critical.

Since the original suggestion of Christensen (1953), evidence has steadily accumulated that damage may be caused in PKU by competitive inhibition at various transport sites, especially the blood-brain barrier (BBB) at the level of the cerebral blood capillaries. Thus a high level of phenylalanine alters the levels of other amino acids in the body fluids (McKean and Boggs, 1966; Efron *et al.*, 1969). The severity of competition between amino acids for transport across the BBB shows that inhibition is highly likely (Banos *et al.*, 1971, 1974a, b; Pardridge and Oldendorf, 1975; Pratt, 1976). Direct measurement in phenylketonurics of amino acid transport across the BBB (the only achievement of such measurements in the human) has provided evidence of saturation of the carrier by the high concentration of phenylalanine (Oldendorf et al., 1971). By kinetic study of transport across the BBB (Pratt, 1979) those amino acids which are most likely not to reach the brain in adequate amounts in untreated PKU have been identified and the rationale of treatment is to restore as normal a balance as possible between different amino acids (Pratt, 1980, 1982). Perhaps the most telling evidence that the high blood phenylalanine causes brain damage largely through transport inhibition is the lack of effectiveness of treatment with a diet in which protein is restricted to body needs without adding any preparation of amino acids excluding phenylalanine. Consistent with the transport inhibition hypothesis are the findings of an international survey of 524 pregnancies in 155 phenylketonuric women that the severity of the mental damage to the baby correlated with the level of phenylalanine in the mother's blood (Lenke and Levy, 1980). The need to start treatment before conception is emphasized by the lack of consistent effects of treatment started only during early pregnancy contrasted with the success of preconceptual dietary treatment in a recently reported case (Tenbrinck and Stroud, 1982).

A reduction in the flux of an amino acid into the brain does not necessarily interfere with brain development. Interference with brain development is most likely to occur when any reduction in the influx of an amino acid which is needed by the brain cells is both severe and prolonged, reducing the net flux. This will happen when there is not only a high concentration of an inhibitor (e.g. phenylalanine) but also a reduction below normal in the concentration of the nutrient (e.g. tryptophan). There is evidence that the early morning is likely to be the danger period: in phenylketonurics on similar low phenylalanine diets, below-normal blood tyrosine concentrations seem to occur more often in fasting samples (Brouwer et al., 1977) than in those taken at noon (Koepp and Held, 1977). Another important general consideration is that for the brain to continue making protein all of the amino acids which are needed must be supplied.

3. Toxic abnormal metabolites. Not only will metabolites which come before the block in a metabolic pathway accumulate but also alternative pathways round the block may cause other metabolites to build up in abnormal concentrations. Any of these accumulating metabolites may be directly toxic. In extreme cases a metabolite may accumulate in gross amounts in tissue cells over a long period because of a failure to remove it, as in Tay-Sachs' or other storage diseases (O'Brien, 1978). The rational treatment is some form of enzyme replacement although for most disorders practicable ways of doing this have not so far been found.

The relative importance of different mechanisms of brain damage is a matter of some practical importance for in PKU and many similar inherited metabolic defects in which transport inhibition is a major factor, the brain is normal at birth and damage can be prevented by suitable dietary treatment.

References

Banos, G., Daniel, P.M., Moorhouse, S.R. and Pratt, O.E. (1971) The entry of amino acids into the brain of the rat in the postnatal period. **J. Physiol. 213**, 45P

Banos, G., Daniel, P.M., Moorhouse, S.R. and Pratt, O.E. (1974a) Inhibition of entry of some amino acids into the brain, with observations on mental retardation in the aminoacidurias. **Psychol. Med. 4**, 262-269

Banos, G., Daniel, P.M. and Pratt, O.E. (1974b) Saturation of a shared mechanism which transports L-arginine and L-lysine into the brain of the living rat. **J. Physiol. 236**, 29-41

Brouwer, M., De Bree, P.K., Van Sprang, F.J. and Wadman, S.K. (1977) Low serum-tyrosine in patients with phenylketonuria on dietary treatment, **Lancet, i**, 1162

Christensen, H.N. (1953) Metabolism of amino acids and proteins. **Ann. Rev. Biochem. 22**, vide 235

Efron, M.L., Kang, E.S., Visakorpi, J. and Fellers, F.X. (1969) Effect of elevated plasma phenylalanine levels on other amino acids in phenylketonuric and normal subjects. **J. Ped., 74**, 399-405

Koepp, P. and Held, K.R. (1977) Serum-tyrosine in patients with hyperphenylalaninaemia. **Lancet, ii**, 92-3

Lenke, R.R. and Levy, H.L. (1980) Maternal phenylketonuria and hyperphenylalaninemia: An international survey of the outcome of untreated and treated pregnancies. **New Engl. J. Med., 303**, 1202-1208

McKean, C.M. and Boggs, D.E. (1966) Influence of high concentrations of phenylalanine on the amino acids of cerebrospinal fluid and blood, **Proc. Soc. Exp. Biol. Med., 122**, 987-991

Mudd, S.H., Edwards, W.A., Loeb, P.M., Brown, M.S. and Laster, L. (1970) Homocystinuria due to cystathionine synthase deficiency: the effect of pyridoxine, **J. Clin. Invest., 49**, 1762-1771

Mudd, S.H. and Levy, H.L. (1978) Disorders of transsulfuration, In **The Metabolic Basis of Inherited Disease**, 4th edn, Eds. Stanbury, J.B., Wyngaarden, J.B. and Fredrickson, D.S. McGraw-Hill, New York, 458-503

O'Brien, (1978) The gangliosidoses, In **The Metabolic Basis of Inherited Disease**, 4th edn, Eds. Stanbury, J.B., Wyngaarden, J.B. and Fredrickson, D.S. McGraw-Hill, New York, 841-865

Oldendorf, W.H., Sisson, W.B. and Silverstein, A. (1971) Brain uptake of selenomethionine Se75 in phenylketonuria, **Arch. Neurol., 24**, 524-528

Pardridge, W.M. and Oldendorf, W.H. (1975) Kinetic analysis of blood-brain barrier transport of amino acids, **Biochem. Biophys. Acta, 401**, 128-136

Pratt, O.E. (1976) Transport of metabolizable substances into the living brain, In **Transport Phenomena in the Nervous System: Physiological and Pathological Aspects** Eds. Levi, G., Battistin, L. and Lajtha, A., Plenum Press, New York and London, 55-75

Pratt, O.E. (1979) The kinetics of tryptophan transport across the blood-brain barrier, **J. Neural Transm. Suppl. 15,** 29-42

Pratt, O.E. (1980) A new approach to the treatment of phenylketonuria. **J. Ment. Defic. Res., 24,** 203-217

Pratt, O.E. (1982) Transport inhibition in the pathology of phenylketonuria and other inherited metabolic diseases, **J. Inher. Metab. Dis. 5, Suppl. 2,** 75-81

Tenbrinck, M.S. and Stroud, H.W. (1982) Normal infant born to a mother with phenylketonuria, **J. Am. Med. Assoc., 247,** 2139-2140

Chapter 8

Tetrahydrobiopterin metabolism, neurological disease and mental retardation

J.A. Blair and R.J. Leeming

BIOCHEMISTRY OF TETRAHYDROBIOPTERIN

Tetrahydrobiopterin (THB) is widely distributed in human body fluids and tissues in concentrations from 2 μg/ml to 1 ng/ml being found in urine, plasma, cerebrospinal fluid, breast milk, liver, kidney, brain, gut, breast, erythrocytes, carcinoid tumours, colonic and rectal tumours and breast tumours. It is the coenzyme in the conversion of phenylalanine to tyrosine, tyrosine to dopa and tryptophan to 5-hydroxytryptophan. It therefore has a key role in the formation of the CNS neurotransmitters, dopamine, noradrenaline and serotonin (Leeming _et al_., 1981).

THB crosses cell membranes with great difficulty. The level of THB within the cell is maintained by synthesis from guanosine triphosphate and by its salvage after functioning as a coenzyme, in which it is converted to quinonoid-dihydrobiopterin, by the enzyme dihydropteridine reductase (DHPR). Reduction in either THB synthesis or salvage will lower its cell concentration, reduce the formation of dopamine, noradrenaline and serotonin and cause hyperphenylalaninaemia (Leeming _et al_., 1981). q-DHB may leave the cell and be reduced to THB by ascorbate or glutathione in the extracellular fluid. Alternatively it may rearrange to 7,8-dihydrobiopterin (DHB). DHB is reduced to THB by dihydrofolate reductase (DHFR) or hydroxylated and oxidized to dihydroxanthopterin.

DEFICIENCY OF TETRAHYDROBIOPTERIN

Gross THB Deficiency (Malignant Hyperphenylalaninaemia)

In two rare genetic metabolic disorders occurring about one in every million births there is gross THB deficiency (malignant hyperphenylalaninaemia) (Danks _et al_., 1978). Affected infants fail to progress through normal developmental milestones, have hyperphenylalaninaemia and commonly die within a few years of birth. Several cases are now known in which patients have survived untreated to adolescence in good physical health but with severe mental retardation. An effective therapy consists of a low phenylalanine diet and the neurotransmitter precursors dopa and 5-hydroxytryptophan (Danks *et al*., 1978). Tetrahydrobiopterin is now available and has been claimed to have been successfully used (Niederweiser *et al*., 1982). This gross THB deficiency is due either to failure of *de novo* biosynthesis of THB or to absence of active DHPR.

Quantitative Estimation of THB, Related Compounds and Enzymic Activity

Precise quantitative measurements of THB, its derivatives and related enzymes are required for the diagnosis of the two variants of gross THB deficiency and the study of the health effects of partial THB deficiency. Direct analysis of the appropriate CNS tissue would be ideal but is ethically unacceptable. Analyses are therefore carried out on urine, serum, cerebrospinal fluid, liver and erythrocytes and the results, extended by animal experimentation, extrapolated to events in the CNS.

THB and its related compounds 7,8-dihydrobiopterin (DHB) and biopterin (B) have been measured in urine, plasma and cerebrospinal fluid by (a) an enzymic assay using phenylalanine hydroxylase, (b) a microbiological assay using the protozoon *Crithidia fasciculata*, (c) a chemical assay using high performance liquid chromatography (HPLC) and (d) a radioimmunoassay (Leeming *et al*., 1981). Although the greatest amount of data have been obtained using the very sensitive *Crithidia* assay because of its lesser specificity and underestimation of THB it should now be replaced by the much more informative, specific and accurate HPLC technique except for mass screening (Blair *et al*., 1983). The enzymic assay measures THB only and the radioimmunoassay B only. Both techniques are thus more limited than HPLC which will measure THB, DHB and B.

DHPR activity has been measured in liver (Rey *et al*., 1977) and erythrocytes (Barford *et al*., 1983). THB synthesis has been measured in liver (Rey *et al*., 1977).

Total biopterin and DHPR activity have been measured using dried blood spots on Guthrie cards and the results obtained correlated well with those using liquid blood samples (Blair *et al*., 1983; Barford *et al*., 1983). This technique now provides an easy and cheap method for the mass screening of neonates for gross tetrahydrobiopterin deficiency.

Where total biopterin levels have been measured in normal human tissues and body fluids the major portion has been shown to be THB.

Diagnosis of Gross THB Deficiency

In THB synthesis deficiency urine and serum levels of total biopterins are significantly lower than normal, and the urine level of neopterin (a precursor of THB) is much elevated above normal (Leeming *et al*., 1981). THB synthesis is absent from liver (Rey *et al*., 1977).

With *total* DHPR lack serum levels of total biopterins are always much higher than normal; urine concentrations are often increased but may be within the normal range (Leeming *et al*., 1981) and DHPR activity is zero in liver (Rey *et al*., 1977) and erythrocytes (Barford *et al*., 1983). The *increased* serum level of total biopterins is *due to* increased cell efflux of biopterins caused by the lack of the salvage enzyme.

In both deficiency states cell THB concentrations are much reduced, dopamine, noradrenaline and serotonin concentrations substantially lowered, blood phenylalanine levels significantly increased and there is gross neurological disorder.

Gross THB Deficiency as a Model for Other Defects in THB Metabolism

The two genetic disorders of tetrahydrobiopterin deficiency provide suggestive models for other disorders of tetrahydrobiopterin metabolism.

By analogy with THB synthesis deficiency, lower serum and urine levels of total biopterins than normal accompanied by increased urinary neopterin concentrations above normal are, after exclusion of malignant disease, thought to be due to decreased THB synthesis. This could lead to reduced cell concentrations of THB.

By comparison with DHPR deficiency, increased serum concentrations of total biopterins above normal are considered to be caused by increased cell efflux of biopterins. Again this is thought to reduce cell THB concentrations.

Lowering of cell THB levels may produce neurological disease.

DHPR Deficiency Heterozygotes

A number of DHPR deficiency heterozygotes (parents of DHPR deficiency homozygotes) are known and are apparently normal. Examination of DHPR deficiency homozygotes show the homozygotes to have zero DHPR in whole blood and the DHPR deficiency heterozygotes to have DHPR activity about half that of a group of normals (Barford *et al*., 1983). Serum biopterins in DHPR deficiency heterozygotes are within normal values.

Reduced THB Synthesis

A small number of children have reduced THB synthesis (Rey *et al*., 1977). Some are mentally retarded (Rey *et al*., 1983).

OTHER DEFECTS OF TETRAHYDROBIOPTERIN METABOLISM

THB Metabolism in Classical Phenylketonuria

Untreated classical phenylketonuria, in which because of an almost total lack of phenylalanine hydroxylase activity the patient is unable to metabolize phenylalanine to tyrosine, is accompanied by elevated levels of blood phenylalanine, significantly increased serum biopterins and severe mental retardation (Leeming _et al_., 1976a, 1981). Analogy with DHPR deficiency suggests that the increase in serum biopterins arises from DHPR inhibition and that cell THB levels are lowered. Rats given large oral doses of phenylalanine show similar increases in serum and urine biopterins and have reduced cell THB concentrations (Dhondt _et al_., 1981). Thus classical phenylketonuria is accompanied by partial THB deficiency. DHPR activity in whole blood in adult untreated phenylketonurics is similar to normals (Barford _et al_., 1983).

The contribution of _this_ THB deficiency to the mental retardation of classical phenylketonuria is unclear but it may have a major role. Serum biopterins levels in adult untreated phenylketonurics are similar to those of severely mentally retarded DHPR deficient homozygotes (Blair _et al_., 1982d) in whom the mental retardation is wholly attributable to THB deficiency. Thus the mental retardation of untreated classical phenylketonuria may be wholly due to THB deficiency.

Serum biopterins levels correlate significantly with blood phenylalanine levels (Leeming _et al_., 1976a; Leeming, 1982). Blood phenylalanine levels are significantly inversely correlated with IQ score (MRC/DHSS, 1982). Thus reduced cell THB levels may produce reductions in IQ score, an effect apparent even with small changes in cell THB levels. Increased time of exposure to THB deficiency may also reduce IQ scores (MRC/DHSS, 1982).

Phenylpyruvate from the excess phenylalanine in phenylketonuria inhibits DHPR with a maximum of about 50% inhibition at a phenylpyruvate concentration of about 10^{-4} M and about 20% inhibition at 5×10^{-5} M (Purdy and Blair, 1980) at saturating substrate concentrations. With lower substrate concentrations inhibition would be greater. Phenylalanine also inhibits DHPR but less so than phenylpyruvate (Purdy and Blair, 1980). These inhibitory effects may explain the efflux of THB from the cell. The lesser inhibition of DHPR in phenylketonuria may explain the clinical differences between phenylketonuria and DHPR reductase deficiency.

THB Metabolism in Down's Syndrome

A large group of adult patients with Down's syndrome had serum biopterins concentrations significantly higher than normal controls and a group of non-specific mentally retarded patients from the same hospital, suggesting a lowered cell THB due to an increased rate of loss from the cells (Aziz _et al_., 1982a). It was proposed that this increased loss was caused by the more rapid oxidation of THB in the enhanced oxidation conditions of Down's syndrome. DHPR activity in whole blood was similar to normals (Barford _et al_., 1983).

THB Metabolism in Tuberose Sclerosis with Mental Retardation

Mentally retarded adults with tuberose sclerosis had serum biopterins levels similar to normal controls and significantly higher than non-specific mentally retarded patients from the same hospital (Aziz _et al_., 1982b). DHPR activity in whole blood was similar to normal (Barford _et al_., 1983). Thus in mental retardation associated with tuberose sclerosis there appears to be no effect on THB metabolism.

THB Metabolism in Non-Specific Mental Retardation and Mental Retardation Associated with Fragile-X Syndrome

Non-specific mental retardation patients had total serum biopterins significantly lower than normal controls (Aziz _et al_., 1982a). DHPR activity measured in erythrocytes was similar to normals (Barford _et al_., 1983).

Mentally retarded adults with fragile-X syndrome had erythrocyte DHPR activity similar to normals (Barford _et al_., 1983).

THB Metabolism in Parkinson's Disease

THB concentrations in the cerebrospinal fluid of patients with Parkinson's disease are significantly lower than age-matched controls (Lovenberg _et al_., 1979). An earlier report that serum biopterins levels in Parkinson's disease were similar to normals (Leeming _et al_., 1976b) was probably due to the patients receiving L-dopa medication. Oral administration of L-dopa to controls significantly raised the total serum biopterins level (Leeming _et al_., 1982) due to inhibition of DHPR by dopamine (Purdy _et al_., 1981a) and could have obscured a fall due to reduced THB synthesis. Recent reports have claimed that oral administration of large doses of THB produces a considerable improvement in early Parkinson's disease (Curtius _et al_., 1982).

THB Metabolism in Dystonia

THB concentrations in the cerebrospinal fluid of patients with inherited dystonia are lower than normals (Williams _et al_., 1979). Oral administration of THB in large doses has been reported as alleviating the symptoms (Le Witt _et al_., 1983).

THB Metabolism and Oestrogen Levels

In normal female subjects aged 20-40 not taking oral contraceptives serum biopterins levels are significantly less than age-matched men. Levels are further reduced if the subjects are taking oral contraceptives. During the menstrual cycle serum biopterins are lowest at mid-cycle, highest at end of cycle and are the mirror image of oestrogen levels. This fluctuation is absent in women taking oral contraceptives (Leeming and Blair, 1980a). Serum biopterins levels are significantly lower in pregnant women (Leeming, 1979), again when oestrogen levels are elevated. Serum biopterins levels in women correlate significantly with FSH levels and thus inversely correlate with oestrogen levels (Blair *et al.*, 1982c). Blood DHPR activity is significantly increased in pregnancy (Barford *et al.*, 1983). Rat liver DHPR activity is significantly increased after oral administration of stilboestrol (Eggar *et al.*, 1983). Oestrogens thus have a considerable effect on THB metabolism, raising the cell levels of THB by increased activity of DHPR, presumably by increasing its synthesis.

The small changes in human performance which commonly occur towards the end of the menstrual cycle (d'Orban and Dalton, 1980), when DHPR activity and cell THB levels may be lowered, suggest that small changes in THB levels can produce minor changes in intellectual performance.

THB Metabolism and Lead

Lead is known as a potent neurotoxin and it now seems likely that low body lead concentrations can produce small but significant reductions in the intellectual performance of children (Ruttle, 1982). Lead significantly inhibits THB synthesis in rat brain extracts at concentrations as low as 10^{-8} M (Purdy *et al.*, 1981b). DHPR activity is significantly inhibited at 10^{-6} M in rat liver extracts (Purdy *et al.*, 1981b) and in human blood (Barford *et al.*, 1983). At low blood lead levels in man serum biopterins correlate significantly with lead levels indicating inhibition of DHPR (Blair *et al.*, 1982b). At high blood lead levels serum biopterins levels in man are significantly lower than normal suggesting that after saturation of DHPR inhibition there is continuing reduction in THB synthesis (Hilburn, 1979; Leeming *et al.*, 1981). Similar results have been shown in the rat (McIntosh *et al.*, 1982). Small increases (10^{-7} moles per 1000 g) in the lead content of the rat brain significantly lower the THB concentration (Blair *et al.*, 1982a).

Thus lead apparently reduces THB concentration in the brain by inhibiting both THB synthesis and salvage and this may play a major role in the neurotoxic action of lead. The observations that low levels of lead effect a small reduction in THB metabolism and produce slight reductions in intellectual performance again suggest that small changes in THB metabolism will produce minor changes in intellectual performance.

THB Metabolism, Aluminium and Dialysis Dementia

Epidemiological studies suggest that dialysis dementia is caused by accumulation of aluminium within the brain (McDermott et al., 1978; Davison et al., 1982). Aluminium inhibits DHPR at 10^{-4} M, a concentration found in the brains of those dying with dialysis dementia (Leeming and Blair, 1979). Studies in man have shown that patients receiving aluminium hydroxide gel have increased levels of serum biopterins indicating in vivo inhibition of DHPR (Dhondt et al., 1982). Thus it seems likely that at least some of the neurotoxic effect of aluminium is caused by loss of cell THB by inhibition of DHPR and that this loss of cell THB could be a factor in dialysis dementia.

THB Metabolism, Ageing and Confusional States

Although serum biopterins levels in man are constant in health and show no diurnal variation, analysis of a large group shows that levels increase significantly with age suggesting depletion of cell THB by loss of DHPR activity (Leeming and Blair, 1980a). CSF levels of THB fall significantly with age as do dopamine metabolite concentrations (Lovenberg et al., 1979). Thus dopamine synthesis and THB levels are closely correlated supporting the contention that THB levels control the formation of the CNS neurotransmitter dopamine. The reduction in CNS levels of THB due to loss of DHPR activity may be the cause of the age-related decline in intellectual functioning known as benign senescence (Leeming and Blair, 1980a).

Patients with reversible intellectual confusion due to ill health had higher serum biopterins levels than normal suggesting cell THB loss due to DHPR inactivity (Aziz et al., 1983).

THB Metabolism and Senile Dementia of the Alzheimer Type (SDAT)

Early reports showed that total serum biopterins levels were significantly lowered in SDAT and that such patients had mild hyperphenylalaninaemia (Leeming et al., 1979; Leeming and Blair, 1980a,b). Examination of a larger and better defined group of SDAT patients confirmed the lowered serum biopterins (Aziz et al., 1983). Total biopterin in cerebrospinal fluid from autopsy in SDAT (confirmed by histopathology) as measured by HPLC was significantly reduced to 40% of normal concentrations confirming the same picture while neopterin was not significantly lowered (Blair et al., 1983; Morar et al., 1983). Other studies have confirmed that serum biopterins in SDAT are significantly lower than normal while serum neopterin concentrations were similar to normals (Young et al., 1982). In addition lymphocyte DHPR activity was significantly reduced in SDAT (Young et al., 1982). Thus from examination of about 70 patients with SDAT there seems no doubt that SDAT is associated with a gross tissue depletion of THB arising from a reduction in the synthesis of THB. The lowered biopterin levels cannot be due to tissue loss because the levels of neopterin, a precursor of biopterin, are not significantly reduced. That this tissue depletion of THB, possibly steadily increasing over years, is a possible cause of SDAT is supported by (1) the severe neurological disease caused in infants by gross THB deficiency; (2) aluminium, a neurotoxin causing dementia, may do so by depletion of cell THB by inhibiting DHPR and (3) in Down's syndrome, a disorder in which cell THB levels are probably lowered by oxidative loss, all patients dying at 40+ years have the brain histopathology characteristic of SDAT and may display dementia. A neurotoxin or group of neurotoxins which could inhibit DHPR and reduce THB synthesis, such as has been shown to be possible with lead, would produce the biochemical picture of reduced THB metabolism found in SDAT. DHPR activity is significantly increased and THB synthesis reduced in the temporal lobe of subjects with SDAT compared to normals (Barford et al., 1983).

CONCLUSIONS

Tetrahydrobiopterin metabolism has a crucial role in proper intellectual functioning in man. Gross tetrahydrobiopterin deficiency in the infant causes amentia. Lesser degrees of tetrahydrobiopterin deficiency are found in untreated phenylketonuria and Down's syndrome where it may have a major role in the mental retardation of these disorders. Tetrahydrobiopterin metabolism is probably reduced in Parkinson's disease and dystonia. Senile dementia of the Alzheimer type is associated with a substantial reduction of tetrahydrobiopterin metabolism and this metabolic deficiency may be the cause of Alzheimer's dementia. Oestrogens affect tetrahydrobiopterin metabolism by increasing the activity of dihydropteridine reductase. Lead, aluminium and dopamine inhibit dihydropteridine reductase. Lead also inhibits tetrahydrobiopterin synthesis.

Slight reductions in tetrahydrobiopterin concentrations can cause minor changes in intellectual performance.

Acknowledgement

The authors thank the many workers who have contributed to the theme of this chapter. Financial assistance from Billiton Ltd and Shell (UK) Ltd is gratefully acknowledged.

REFERENCES

Aziz, A., Blair, J.A., Leeming, R.J., and Sylvester, P.E. (1982a). Tetrahydrobiopterin metabolism in Down's syndrome and in non-Down's syndrome mental retardation. **J. Ment. Defic. Res. 26**, 67-71

Aziz, A.Z., Blair, J.A., Leeming, R.J. and Sylvester, P.E. (1982b). unpublished

Aziz, A., Leeming, R.J. and Blair, J.A. (1983). Tetrahydrobiopterin metabolism in senile dementia of Alzheimer type (SDAT). **J. Neurology, Neurosurgery and Psychiatry, 46**, 410-413

Barford, P.A., Blair, J.A. and Leeming, R.J. (1983). Dihydropteridine activity in normal and diseased man. **Second Winter Symposium on the Chemistry and Biology of Pterins**. (in press)

Blair, J.A., Hilburn, M.E. and Leeming, R.J. (1982a). unpublished

Blair, J.A., Hilburn, M.E., Leeming, R.J., McIntosh, M.J. and Moore, M.R. (1982b). Lead and tetrahydrobiopterin metabolism: possible effects on IQ. **Lancet, i**, 964

Blair, J.A., Leeming, R.J. and Parsons, A. (1982c). unpublished

Blair, J.A., Leeming, R.J., Primrose, D.A. and Sylvester, P.E. (1982d). unpublished

Blair, J.A., Whitburn, S.B., Pheasant, A.E., Leeming, R.J., Morar, C. and Al-Beir, A. (1983). **Proc. Seventh Int. Symp. Chem. Pteridines**. W. de Gruyter, Berlin and New York. 165-169

Curtius, H.-Ch., Muldner, H. and Niederweiser, A. (1982). Tetrehydrobiopterin: efficacy in endogenous depression and Parkinson's disease. **J. Neural Transmission, 55**, 301-318

Danks, D.M., Bartholome, K., Clayton, B.E., Curtius, H., Grobe, H., Kaufman, S., Leeming, R.J., Pfleiderer, W., Rembold, H. and Rey, F. (1978). Malignant hyperphenylalaninaemia. Current status (June 1977). **J. Inher. Metab. Dis. 1**, 49-53

Davison, A.M., Oil, H., Walker, G.S. and Levins, A.M. (1982). Water supply aluminium concentration, dialysis dementia and effect of reverse osmosis water treatment. **Lancet, iii**, 785-787

Dhondt, J.L., Ardouin, P., Hayte, J.M. and Farriaux, J.P. (1981). Developmental aspects of pteridine metabolism and relationships with phenylalanine metabolism. **Clin. Chim. Acta 110**, 143-152

Dhondt, J.L., Bellahsene, Z., Vanhille, Ph. and Noel, C. (1982). Tetrahydrobiopterin metabolism in chronic uraemia: possible explanation of dialysis encephalopathy. **Lancet, iii** 491

d'Orban, P. T. and Dalton, J. (1980). Violent crime and the menstrual cycle. **Psychol. Med. 10**, 353-359

Eggar, C., Barford, P.A., Blair, J.A., Pheasant, A.E. and Oates, D.G. (1983). Dihydropteridine reductase levels in human normal and neoplastic tissues. **Proc. Seventh. Int. Symp. Chem. Biol. Pteridines**, 869-874

Hilburn, M.E. (1979). Environmental lead in perspective. **Chem. Soc. Rev., 8**, 63-64

Leeming, R.J. (1979). Metabolism of biopterin and its derivatives in man and the rat. Ph.D. Thesis, Chemistry Department, University of Aston in Birmingham

Leeming, R.J. (1982). personal communication

Leeming, R.J. and Blair, J.A. (1979). Dialysis dementia, aluminium and tetrahydrobiopterin metabolism. **Lancet i**, 556

Leeming, R.J. and Blair, J.A. (1980a). The effects of pathological and normal physiological processes on biopterin derivative levels in man. **Clin. Chim. Acta 108**, 103-111

Leeming, R.J. and Blair, J.A. (1980b). Serum Crithidia levels in disease, **Biochem. Med., 23**, 122-125

Leeming, R.J., Blair, J.A., Aziz, A. and Brown, S.E. (1982). unpublished

Leeming, R.J., Blair, J.A., Green, A. and Raine, D.N. (1976a). Biopterin derivatives in normal and phenylketonuric patients after oral loads of L-phenylalanine, L-tyrosine and L-tryptophan. **Arch. Dis. Childhood 51**, 771-777

Leeming, R.J., Blair, J.A. and Melikian, V. (1979). Biopterin derivatives in senile dementia. **Lancet i**, 215

Leeming, R.J., Blair, J.A., Melikian, V. and O'Gorman, D.J. (1976b). Biopterin derivatives in human body fluids and tissues. **J. Clin. Path. 29**, 444-451

Leeming, R.J., Pheasant, A.E. and Blair, J.A. (1981). The role of tetrahydrobiopterin in neurological disease: a review. **J. Ment. Defic. Res., 25**, 231-241

LeWitt, R.A., Newman, R.P., Miller, L.P., Lovenberg, W. and Eldridge, R. (1983). Treatment of dystonia with tetrahydrobiopterin. **New Engl. J. Med., 308**, 157-158

Lovenberg, W., Levine, R.A., Robinson, D.S., Ebert, M., Williams, A.C. and Calne, D.B. (1979). Hydroxylase cofactor activity in cerebrospinal fluid of normal subjects and subjects with Parkinson's disease. **Science, 204**, 624-627

McDermott, J.R., Smith, A.I., Ward, M.K., Parkinson, I.S. and Ken, D.N.S. (1978). Brain aluminium concentration in dialysis encephalopathy. **Lancet i**, 901-903

McIntosh, M., Moore, M.E., Blair, J.A., Hilburn, M.E., and Leeming, R.J. (1982). Lead and tetrahydrobiopterin metabolism in man and animals. **Clin. Sci. Mol. Med.** 44P

Morar, C., Whitburn, S.B., Blair, J.A., Leeming, R.J. and Wilcock, G.K. (1983). Tetrahydrobiopterin metabolism in senile dementia of the Alzheimer type. **J. Neurol. Neurosurg. Psychiat. 46**, 582

MRC/DHSS (1982). Phenylketonuria news letter no. 8.

Niederweiser, A., Curtius, H-Ch., Wang, M. and Leupold, D. (1982). Atypical phenylketonuria with defective biopterin metabolism. Monotherapy with tetrahydrobiopterin. **Eur. J. Pediatrics, 138**, 110-112

Purdy, S.E. and Blair, J.A. (1980). Rat liver dihydropteridine reductase inhibition. **Biochem. Soc. Trans. 8**, 565

Purdy, S.E., Blair, J.A. and Barford, P.A. (1981a). Inhibition of dihydropteridine reductase by dopamine. **Biochem. J. 195**, 769-771

Purdy, S.E., Blair, J.A., Leeming, R.J. and Hilburn, M.E. (1981b). Effect of lead on tetrahydrobiopterin synthesis and salvage: A cause of neurological dysfunction. **Int. J. Environmental Studies 17**, 141-145

Rey, F., Harpey, J.P., Leeming, R.J., Blair, J.A., Aicardi, J. and Rey, J. (1977). Les hyperphenylalaninemies avec activite normale de la phenylalanine-hydroxylase: Le deficit en tetrahydrobiopterine et la deficit en dihydropteridine reductase. **Arch. Franc. Ped. 34**, CIX-CXX

Rey, J., Saudubray, J.M., Leeming, R.J., Niederweiser, A., Curtius, H-Ch., and Rey, J. (1983). Les deficits partiels en tetrahydrobiopterin. **Arch. Franc. Ped., 40**, 237-241

Ruttle, M. (1982). Proc. CLEAR Int. Symp. on Lead. London. in press

Williams, A., Eldrige, R., Levine, R., Lovenberg, W. and Paulson, G. (1979). Low CSF hydroxylase co-factor (tetrahydrobiopterin) levels in inherited dystonia. **Lancet ii**, 410

Young, J.H., Kelly, B. and Clayton, B.E. (1982). Reduced levels of biopterin and dihydropteridine reductase in Alzheimer type dementia. **J. Clin. Exp. Gerontol.** in press

COMMENTARY

R. Balazs

Several electrophysiological abnormalities have been described recently in peripheral nerve cells cultured from fetal autopsy specimens of trisomy 21 Down's syndrome (Scott *et al.*, 1982). These seem to be consistent with alterations in the properties of the cell membrane. Brooksbank in our laboratory has investigated whether changes in the plasma membrane may take place in these disorders as a consequence of increased lipoperoxidation related to an imbalance between the enzyme systems which catalyse the removal of the superoxide radicals and the resultant H_2O_2 (Brooksbank and Balazs, 1983). We have found that the activity of superoxide dismutase I (SOD-I) coded for on chromosone 21 is indeed increased in Down's syndrome in the brain to the same degree as has previously been found in other tissues. The elevated enzyme activity results in an increase in the production of H_2O_2, the products of which - rather than superoxide itself - seem to be the primary initiator of lipoperoxidation (Fridovich, 1979). It has been shown previously that in peripheral cells, such as erythrocytes or fibroblasts, the extra dosage of SOD-I is compensated by a reduction in the activity of SOD-II and by an increase in the activity of glutathione peroxidase (Sinet *et al.*, 1975). We observed no such adaptation in the brain, where the abnormally high H_2O_2 production thus presents a threat of free radical damage to lipids. It was also found that such damage can indeed occur, since *in vitro* lipoperoxidation (especially the non-enzymic component) was markedly increased. Since the non-enzymic component of lipoperoxidation depends to a large extent on the concentration in the tissue of available polyunsaturated fatty acyl groups in membrane lipids and of vitamin E (McCay and King, 1980) these factors deserve special attention in further studies on the brain in Down's syndrome.

References

Brooksbank, B.W.L. and Balazs, R. (1983). Superoxide dismutase and lipoperoxidation with Down's syndrome foetal brain. **Lancet**, (in press)

Fridovich, I. (1979). Superoxide dismutases: defence against endogenous superoxide radical. In: **Oxygen Free Radicals and Tissue Damage**; CIBA Found. Symp. No. 65, pp 77-93

McCay, P.B. and King, M.M. (1980). Vitamin E: its role as a biological free radical scavenger and its relationship to the microsomal mixed function oxidase system. In: **Vitamin E: a Comprehensive Treatise**, Dekker, New York, pp 289-317

Scott, B.S., Petit, T.L., Becker, L.E. and Edwards, B.A.V. (1982). Abnormal electric membrane properties of Down's syndrome dorsal root ganglion neurons in cell culture. **Dev. Brain. Res. 2**, 257-270

Sinet, P.M., Michelson, A.M., Bagin, A., Lejeune, J.K. and Jerome, H. (1975). Increase in glutathione peroxidase activity in erythrocytes from trisomy 21 subjects. **Biochem. Biophys. Res. Commun. 67**, 910-915

H. Bickel

Variability in the effects of any one metabolic disorder upon brain development

There are a number of reasons why the effects of any particular metabolic disorder can be expected to vary from patient to patient. For example, in hyperphenylalaninaemia (HPLA), blood phenylalanine concentrations above 240 nmole$_{litre}$ in a neonate, if the condition is untreated (or in the gap from birth to diagnosis and treatment), the details of diet will determine how high the blood phenylalanine rises and how much brain damage there is likely to be. A still more important cause of variability in the effects of the disorder arises from differences in the causation of the HPLA which may be due to:

1. Total or near-total lack of phenylalanine hydroxylase (PAH) (ca 98% of cases).
2. Gross deficiency of tetrahydrobiopterin (THB) due to failure to convert dihydroneopterin triphosphate (DHNP) to THB or failure to make DHNP from guanosine triphosphate.
3. Partial synthesis of THB.
4. Gross deficiency of THB caused by lack of dihydropteridine reductase (DHPR) or the presence of a catalytically incompetent enzyme.

In untreated phenylalanine hydroxylase deficiency, the majority are severely mentally retarded, a minority have low normal IQ; physical health and life span are generally normal. Successful treatment is to lower blood phenylalanine by maintaining the patient on a low phenylalanine diet. The degree of permanent mental defect increases as the length of time during which the patient is exposed to raised blood phenylalanine increases and as the level of blood phenylalanine increases. Phenylalanine hydroxylase deficiency manifests itself only when substantial amounts of phenylalanine are present in the diet. In the unusual circumstances where dietary phenylalanine is low the common clinical manifestations may be reduced or absent.

In untreated, gross THB deficiency due to lack of DHPR or the presence of the catalytically incompetent enzyme there is amentia, gross hypotonia and early death. Rarely subjects have good physical health, survive to adolescence and are severely mentally retarded.

In untreated complete THB synthesis deficiency there is amentia, gross hypotonia and early death.

In untreated partial THB synthesis deficiency some have normal IQ while others are severely mentally retarded.

Reduced dietary phenylalanine alone has no effect on the clinical symptoms of patients with partial or gross THB deficiency. Present successful therapy is to maintain a patient on a low phenylalanine diet plus neurotransmitter precursors and in some cases tetrahydrobiopterin.

These causes of variability in hyperphenylalaninaemia apply in principle to other disorders.

A. N. Davison

Trace amounts of biopterin are widely distributed in nature. The pteridine ring together with *para*-aminobenzoic acid and glutamic acid are present in the cofactor - folic acid (important in active C_1 metabolism). Folate probably gains access to the brain through the choroid plexus and there appears to be energy-dependent uptake against a concentration gradient (Ordonez, 1977). Tetrahydrofolate also only diffuses slowly into the central nervous system. It seems likely (Kettler *et al.*, 1974) that similar systems lead to only restricted accumulation of tetrahydrobiopterin (THB) - the rate-limiting (Mandell and Russo, 1981) cofactor of aromatic amino acid mixed function oxidases (phenylalanine, tyrosine and tryptophan hydroxylases).

There is some evidence that low CSF concentrations of THB are paralleled by reduction in cofactor concentration in the brain tissue. This is associated with reduced dihydropteridine reductase (DHPR) activity (Brewster *et al.*, 1979; Blair and Leeming, this volume). Reductase (DHPR) deficiency in atypical phenylketonuria is associated with low brain dopamine and serotonin levels (Butler *et al.*, 1978). In Parkinson's disease low concentrations of THB in the CSF (Williams *et al.*, 1980) but not blood (Leeming *et al.*, 1976) are accompanied by significant reduction in tyrosine hydroxylase activity in the substantia nigra (Javoy-Agid *et al.*, 1981). One possibility therefore is that there is a reduction in either THB synthesis or salvage (Blair and Leeming, this volume), and perhaps this could be measured in post-mortem tissue. However, in a wide group of degenerative diseases affecting the mature brain, localized cell loss is the probable reason for loss of neurotransmitter and associated synthetic enzyme activity. Thus, tyrosine hydroxylase present in the noradrenergic neurons is lost from cells originating in the substantia nigra in Parkinson's disease and from the locus coeruleus in Alzheimer's disease. Depletion of catecholaminergic cell bodies would therefore be expected to be reflected secondarily in the CSF concentration of THB.

Apart from atypical phenylketonuria (Blair and Leeming, this volume), the role of the biopterins in mental retardation is controversial. Despite a deficiency in hepatic phenylalanine hydroxylase in classical phenylketonuria, there are higher than normal biopterin levels in the blood (Leeming et al., 1976). It is more probable that high levels of circulating phenylalanine block entry of other essential amino acids utilizing a common transport system, and so inhibit protein synthesis during the postnatal growth spurt. Possibly within the brain raised phenylalanine concentration inhibits tyrosine hydroxylase activity and interferes with tryptophan metabolism (Hsia and Wolf, 1981). As suggested by Blair, accumulation of lead in the brain may act by inhibiting DHRB activity and thereby reducing catecholamine concentrations. However, in our experiments in developing animals exposed to chronic lead intoxication (20-80 μg lead/100 ml blood and 0.3 μg lead/g brain), we have been unable to demonstrate inhibition of lead-sensitive cerebral enzymes (Davison, 1977). It is therefore important to show that comparable levels of lead in the brain affect THB concentration, and thereby reduce cerebral catecholamine concentrations. In examples of mental retardation of unknown aetiology and in Down's syndrome, there seems little basis for the concept of THB deficiency.

References

Brewster T.G., Moskowitz M.A., Kaufman S., Breslow J.L., Milstien S. and Abroms I.F. (1979). Dihydropteridine reductase deficiency associated with severe neurologic disease and mild hyperphenylalaninemia. **Pediatrics, 63**, 94-99

Butler I.J., Koslow S.H., Krumholz A., Holtzman N.A. and Kaufman S. (1978). A disorder of biogenic amines in dihydropteridine reductase deficiency. **Ann. Neurol., 3**, 224-230

Davison A.N. (1977). The biochemistry of brain development and mental retardation. **The Eleventh Blake Marsh Lecture**, delivered to the Roy. Coll. Psych., February

Hsia Y.E. and Wolf B. (1981). Disorders of amino acid metabolism. In: **Basic Neurochemistry** (3rd ed.), (Siegel G.J., Albers R.W., Agranoff B.W. and Katzman R., eds.). Little, Brown α Co., Boston, 563-600

Javoy-Agid F., Ploska A. and Agid Y. (1981). Microtopography of tyrosine hydroxylase, glutamic acid decarboxylase, and choline acetyltransferase in the substantia nigra and ventral tegmental area of control and Parkinsonian brains. **J. Neurochem., 37**, 1218-1227

Kettler R., Bartholini G. and Pletscher A. (1974). In vivo enhancement of tyrosine hydroxylation in rat striatum by tetrahydrobiopterin. **Nature (London), 249**, 476-478

Leeming R.J., Blair J.A., Melikian V. and O'Gorman D.J. (1976). Biopterin derivatives in human body fluids and tissues. **J. Clin. Path., 29**, 444-451

Mandell A.J. and Russo P.V. (1981). Short-term regulation of hydroxylase cofactor activity in rat brain. **J. Neurochem., 37**, 1573-1578

Ordonez L.A. (1977). Control of the availability of the brain of folic acid, vitamin B_{12}, and choline. In: **Nutrition and the Brain, 1**, (Wurtman R.J. and Wurtman J.J., eds.), New York, Raven Press, 205-248

Williams A.C., Levine R.A., Chase T.N., Lovenberg W. and Calne D.B. (1980). CSF hydroxylase cofactor levels in some neurological diseases. **J. Neurol. Neurosurg. Psych., 43**, 735-738

D. A. A. Primrose

In the pretreatment era of phenylketonuria, patients were found whose intelligence was within the normal range and phenylalanine levels and IQ were not always closely related.

The suggestion by Blair that retardation in phenylketonuria is the result of tetrahydrobiopterin deficiency is supported by our finding of a family in which there are two children with untreated phenylketonuria. One is severely retarded and the other has an IQ within the normal range. The normal sibling has a higher than average level of serum biopterins. The fact that the metabolism in the two cases is different is supported by the difference in hair colour. The retarded male sibling has typical fair hair while his sister's is dark brown.

R. O. Robinson

Until more direct tetrahydrobiopterin (THB) estimations are available, the evidence that THB plays an important role in mental handicap states is indirect and at times contradictory. Thus elevated DHPR levels in phenylketonuria would not appear to support this suggestion. Changes in urinary biopterin levels can be (and are) interpreted in various ways. In particular we need to know what level of THB is critical for neurotransmitter synthesis.

Whilst the suggestion that THB plays a central role in the pathogenesis of neurological disease is arguable, without question is the evidence which has been accumulating for the role of neurotransmitter deficiency in mental handicap and dementia. The clinical situations which have fuelled speculation about this association have been the occurrences of dementia in two conditions closely identified with neurotransmitter deficiency - Parkinson's disease and Huntington's chorea.

More recently dopaminergic activity has been found to be deficient in boys with the Lesch-Nyhan syndrome (Lloyd et al., 1981). This unusual syndrome causes choreoathetosis, compulsive self-mutilation and intellectual deterioration. Dopamine synthesizing enzymes dopa-decarboxylase and tyrosine hydroxylase together with end products dopamine and its degradation product homovanillic acid were found to be reduced in the caudate nucleus, putamen and nucleus accumbens. These basal ganglion structures are those implicated in choreoathetosis. The result indicated a loss of 65-90% of the nigrostriatal and mesolimbic dopamine terminals in these structures. Interestingly the area in which the cell bodies for these terminals lie, the substantia nigra, had normal dopamine levels. This is in direct contrast to Parkinson's disease in which these cell bodies are primarily affected. The Lesch-Nyhan syndrome is caused however by an enzyme concerned with purine synthesis - hypoxanthine guanine phosphoribosyl transferase. How a failure of purine synthesis preferentially affects dopaminergic terminals is unknown. It is unlikely to be due to a purine deficiency as alternative routes for synthesis exist. More feasible is some intervention in the function of purines which in the past ten years have found an alternative role themselves as neurotransmitters (Pull and McIlwain, 1977; Burnstock, 1975; Fredholm and Hedqvist, 1980; Rodbell, 1980). High and low affinity adenine receptors have been identified. AMP which depresses the firing rate of cortical neurons in rats is potentiated by diazepam (Phillis, 1979). This drug which is singularly well tolerated in boys with Lesch-Nyhan syndrome is the most effective in ameliorating their behaviour. Diazepam has its own specific binding sites and this binding is inhibited by hypoxanthine (Skolnick et al., 1980), which is markedly elevated in the CSF in this syndrome. Similarly caffeine which can elicit self-mutilation in animals also interferes with diazepam binding. It is possible therefore that oxypurines, by-products of HGPRT deficiency, interfere with diazepam receptor function to cause the distressing neurological effects of this condition.

Whilst investigation of neurotransmitter function in this rare syndrome appears to be disclosing new areas of brain biochemistry, this group of substances also appears to be involved in the much commoner Alzheimer's disease. This form of dementia affects 10% of people aged more than 65 and 20% of those aged more than 80. Six years ago choline acetyltransferase (Ch AT) the enzyme responsible for acetylcholine synthesis was found to be reduced by 40-70% in cerebral cortex of individuals with Alzheimer's disease (Bowen et al., 1976; Davies and Maloney, 1976; Perry et al., 1977). The most marked changes were found in the temporal neocortex, the hippocampus and amygdala. These first two structures may be particularly involved with memory storage. Short-term memory is preferentially affected in Alzheimer's disease. Other areas of the cortex such as the frontal lobes may be little affected. Cholinergic terminals in the cortex arise from an input system. Few are intrinsic to the cortex itself. Thus the cell bodies for the hippocampus lie within the medial septal nucleus. A substantial contribution to neocortical cholinergic terminals derives from the nucleus basalis of Meynert (Mesulam and Van Hoesen, 1976). In Alzheimer's disease the Ch AT activity is found deficient in both these nuclei (Whitehouse *et al.*, 1982). By contrast Ch AT activity in the putamen and globus pallidus adjacent to the basal nucleus is normal.

Most individuals with Down's syndrome aged more than 40 acquire an Alzheimer's-like dementia. A similar reduction in Down's cortical Ch AT has been demonstrated (Yates *et al.*, 1981). Neurotransmitter activity in younger Down's people has not yet been described.

Other ascending neurotransmitter systems also affect general cortical activity - noradrenergic systems being one example. Noradrenaline and its marker enzyme dopamine beta hydroxylase are reduced in Alzheimer's cerebral cortex (Adolfsson *et al.*, 1979; Cross, *et al.*, 1981). The cell bodies for much of the noradrenergic projection lie in the locus coeruleus - which is frequently depleted in Alzheimer's disease (Bondareff *et al.*, 1981). Similarly serotonin (5HT) is reduced in Alzheimer's hippocampus (Winblad *et al.*, 1982) and 5HT uptake is reduced in temporal cortical biopsy samples (Benton *et al.*, 1982). However, neither the noradrenergic nor the serotonergic defects appear to be as consistent as those for the cholinergic pathways.

These pathways probably form part of the ascending activating system which originating in the diffuse mid brain and the brain stem reticular formation "switches on" the cerebral cortex. Additionally the cholinergic synapse in animals may be particularly important in memory function (Deutsch, 1971). Scopolamine, an acetylcholine blocker causes amnesia in rats. Scopolamine dementia in man can be improved by physostigmine which increases acetylcholine levels (Drachman, 1977).

Other neurotransmitters intrinsic to the cerebral cortex such as GABA, cholecystokinin, vasoactive intestinal peptide and somatostatin, do not appear to be affected in Alzheimer's disease.

A biochemical profile of the most common form of dementia begins to emerge therefore. Neurotransmitters involved with point to point circuitry within the cerebral cortex are, perhaps fortunately for therapeutic purposes, not primarily involved. Modulatory neurotransmitters involved in pathways responsible for "tuning" the cerebral cortex are affected.

Attempts to improve the cholinergic function of the brain by giving acetylcholine precursors choline or lecithin have been disappointing. Almost certainly this is because these substrates rely on adequate Ch AT levels. This enzyme is however confined to cholinergic neurons. Thus a residual population of neurons must be available for this strategy to work. The use of direct acetylcholine agonists such as oxotremorine and arecholine has been limited by unwanted side effects. This is particularly frustrating as the population of acetylcholine receptors in Alzheimer's disease appears to be unaffected. More detailed characteristics of cortical cholinergic receptors and development of tailor-made artificial transmitters may provide an answer to some of these problems.

References

Adolfsson R., Gottfries C.G., Roos B.E. and Winblad B. (1979). Changes in brain catecholamines in patients with dementia of Alzheimer type. **J. Psychiatry, 135**, 216-23

Benton J.S., Bowen D.M., Allen S.J., Haan E.A., Davison A.N., Neary D., Murphy R.P. and Smurden J.S. (1982). Alzheimer's Disease as a disorder of isodendritic core. **Lancet, I**

Bondareff W., Mountjoy C.Q. and Roth M. (1981). Selective loss of neurons of origin of projection to cerebral cortex (nucleus locus coeruleus). Senile dementia. **Lancet, 1**, 783-84

Bowen D.M., Smith C.B., White P. and Davison A.N. (1976). Neurotransmitter related enzymes and indices of hypoxia in senile dementia and other abiotrophies. **Brain, 99**, 459-96

Burnstock G. (1975). Purinergic transmission. In: Iversen L.L., Iversen S.D and Snyder S.H. Eds. **Handbook of Psychopharmacology, 5**, New York, Plenum Press, 131-94

Cross A.J., Crow T.J., Perry E.K., Perry R.H., Blessed G. and Tomlinson B.E. (1981). Reduced dopamine beta hydroxylase activity in Alzheimer's Disease. **Brit. Med. J., 282**, 93-94

Davies P. and Maloney A.J. (1976). Selective loss of central loss of central cholinergic neurons in Alzheimer's Disease. **Lancet, II**, 1403

Deutsch J.A. (1971). The cholinergic synapse and the site of memory. **Science, 174**, 788-94

Drachman D.A. (1977). Memory and cognitive function in man: does the cholinergic system have a specific role? **Neurology, 27**, 783-90

Fredholm B.B. and Hedqvist P. (1980). The modulation in neuron transmission by purine nucleotides and nucleosides. **Biochem. Pharmacol., 29**, 1635-43

Lloyd K.G., Hornykiewicz O., Davidson L., Shannak K., Farley I., Goldstein M., Shibuya M., Kelly W.N. and Fox I.H. (1981). Biochemical evidence of dysfunction of brain neurotransmitters in the Lesch-Nyhan syndrome. **New Engl. J. Med., 305**, 1106-11

Mesulam M-M and Van Hoesen T.W. (1976). Acetylcholinesterase-rich projections from the basal forebrain of the rhesus monkey to neocortex. **Brain Res., 109**, 152-57

Perry E.K., Perry R.H., Blessed G. and Tomlinson B.E. (1977). Necropsy evidence of central cholinergic deficits in senile dementia. **Lancet, 1**, 189

Phillis J.W. (1979). Diazepam potentiation of purinergic depression of central neurons. **Can. J. Physiol. Pharmacol., 57**, 432-5

Pull I. and McIlwain H. (1977). Adenine mononucleotides and their metabolites liberated from and applied to isolated tissues of the mammalian brain. **Neuro. Chem. Res., 2**, 203-16

Rodbell M. (1980). The role of hormone receptors and GTP - regulatory proteins in membrane transduction. **Nature, 284**, 17-22

Skolnick P., Paul S.M. and Marangos P.J. (1980). Purines as endogenous ligands of the benzodiazepine receptor. **Fed. Proc., 39**, 305-5

Whitehouse P.J., Price D.L., Struble R.G., Clark A.W., Colye J.T. and De Long M.R. (1982). Alzheimer's Disease in senile dementia: loss of neurons in the basal forebrain. **Science, 215**, 1237-39

Winblad B., Adolfsson R., Carlsson A. and Gottfries C-G. (1982). Biogenic amines in brains of patients with Alzheimer's Disease. In: Corkin S., Davies K.L., Crowdon J.H., Usdin E. and Wurtman R.J. Eds. **Alzheimer's Disease: a Report of Progress and Research** (Ageing volume XIX). Raven Press, New York, 25-33

Yates C.M., Ritchie I.M., Simpson J., Maloney A.F.J. and Gordon A.(1981). Noradrenaline in Alzheimer-type dementia in Down's syndrome. **Lancet, II**, 39-40

P. E. Sylvester

Blair has introduced a new agent into the field of neurotransmission. He has summarized the role of tetrahydrobiopterin explaining that it is the keynote in the formation of neurotransmitters dopamine and serotonin. He believes it makes an important contribution to intellectual functioning and supports his claim using lead neurotoxicity as his model: even low lead levels effect a small reduction in tetrahydrobiopterin (THB) metabolism and produce a slight reduction in intellectual performance.

The critical point in the story of tetrahydrobiopterin is the level within the nerve cell where it is synthesized. If the level falls cell metabolism is impaired. During the course of intracellular metabolism it may be produced either in excess, reduced amounts or reduced by failure in salvage by the enzyme dihydropteridine reductase (DHPR). Down's syndrome has a special problem since there is an excess of intracellular superoxide dismutase caused by a dosage effect within the cell: the gene responsible has been located on chromosome 21 and therefore is present in triplicate (Sinet _et al._, 1976). The level of tetrahydrobiopterin is reduced by excessive oxidation.

Clearly, Blair's message is to remind us that in tetrahydrobiopterin there is a potent stimulant of intellectual functioning. He believes that a high IQ occasionally seen in untreated phenylketonuria may be explained by the fact that such patients retain a high level of intracellular tetrahydrobiopterin. The reduced levels found in Down's syndrome prompt consideration of tetrahydrobiopterin replacement therapy in young subjects to improve intellectual functioning. He has told us that tetrahydrobiopterin is now available and explained that it has been successfully used in malignant phenylalaninaemia. So why not in other conditions?

A reduction in tetrahydrobiopterin in the ageing process and presenile dementia of the Alzheimer kind has brought it into line with other neurotransmitters in these conditions. Senile dementia is essentially a degenerative phenomenon. The pathology of the dementing process explains the deficiencies since there is severe cell and neuritic pathology. It does not seem conceivable that replacement therapy will be helpful once the disease is established; however, further studies of the natural histories of the dementias may easily reveal an optimum time to introduce replacement treatment and maintain the vitality of nerve cells to forestall the devastating features that follow. However, there is a snag since tetrahydrobiopterin crosses cell membranes with difficulty, so there is a practical problem of getting it to its target area. Blair has not yet had a chance to test tetrahydrobiopterin and its role in general psychiatry. He has given an illuminating report and guidance to a better understanding of intellectual functioning in mental handicap and offered hope that something therapeutic can be done. Soon, no doubt, he will tell us about its significance in depression.

Reference

Sinet P.M., Couturier J., Dutrillaux B., Poissonnier M., Raoul O., Rethore M.O., Allard D., Lejeune J. and Jerome H. (1976). Exp. Cell Res., **97**, 47-55

Chapter 9

Exposure to lead as an environmental factor in mental retardation

H.A. Waldron

In discussing the role of exposure to lead as an aetiological factor in mental retardation it is important to separate clearly the effects which may follow from an attack of clinical lead poisoning in childhood and the effects of lead in doses which are insufficient to cause the signs and symptoms normally attributed to plumbism.

Here I shall confine myself to those degrees of mental retardation which are severely disabling; the possibility that exposure to lead may cause less severe behavioural changes or small deficits in IQ is important but beyond the scope of present discussion.

THE EFFECTS OF CLINICAL LEAD POISONING

There is no doubt that children who have suffered from clinical lead poisoning, particularly if they have had lead encephalopathy, are liable to be left with severe and permanent mental and neurological sequelae. The reported estimates of the proportion of cases in whom permanent sequelae may be found varies widely from about 25% to over 90% but inclines towards the lower figure in the more recent studies (see Waldron, 1978 for references). The sequelae which have been reported include not only mental retardation but also convulsions, cerebral palsy, optic atrophy and behavioural and learning disorders, the last of which may resolve with time. With prompt recognition of the symptoms of lead poisoning and the institution of treatment, few children should nowadays be left with serious residual effects.

In a much quoted paper, Byers and Lord (1943) reported that children who had developed lead poisoning without encephalopathy might also be permanently affected. Between 1931 and 1939, they found that 128 children had been admitted to their hospital in Boston with lead poisoning. Of these, 71 were still living close enough to Boston to be available for follow-up. Twelve of this group had severe cerebral damage at the time of discharge but the remainder had been discharged as cured; twenty had entered the school system. The twenty at school were contacted and all were found to be handicapped in some way, although they had been thought to be normal children by the medical staff on admission. Common features were low IQ, poor performance at school, short attention span, learning difficulties, impulsive behaviour and neurological impairment (Table 1). The child found to have the lowest IQ was one of those who had not had encephalopathy although this was also the child in whom exposure to lead was least well documented.

At least five of the children had been re-exposed to lead following their discharge from hospital and had developed symptoms of lead poisoning again. This undoubtedly contributed to the difficulties they were experiencing at school.

It is unfortunate that it was not possible to make estimates of the blood lead concentrations of the children at the time of their admission as it would have been of considerable interest to know if there was any relationship between outcome and tissue lead levels.

MENTAL RETARDATION IN THE ABSENCE OF LEAD POISONING

Whether exposure to lead, in the absence of the symptoms of lead poisoning, can cause mental retardation is a matter about which there is great concern but no general agreement. In examining the evidence which relates to this topic I shall refer to the paper by Bradford Hill (1965) in which he showed the circumstances under which epidemiologists might reasonably pass from an observed association between a disease and some environmental feature to a verdict of causation.

Bradford Hill set out nine criteria which he considered should be satisfied in order to establish causality. I shall deal with five of his criteria, plausibility, analogy, consistency, temporality and biological gradient.

Plausibility and Analogy

If exposure to some environmental agent is to be considered as causing an observed effect then the relationship must be biologically plausible in the light of what is already known in man, or by analogy with evidence derived from animal experiments.

The proposition that exposure to lead at some time in life may result in mental retardation seems plausible given that lead is neurotoxic and that it has this effect in high doses. The matter is one of deciding the minimum dose required and of whether there is an optimum time at which exposure to lead is most damaging. Under experimental conditions lead is found to induce teratogenic effects in the central nervous system of chick embryos (but not those of other species). This effect is not unique to lead, however, and many other metals (both in excess and deficiency) may impair the normal development of the brains of experimental animals (see Ferm, 1972 for further details). By analogy with animal studies, then, there are grounds for supposing that lead may affect the developing CNS in the human fetus.

When interpreting the results of animal experiments, however, two things should be borne in mind. The first is that

Table 1

Summary of results of follow-up study of twenty children with lead poisoning**

	Sex	Age at admission yr	Age at admission mo	Age at follow-up yr	Age at follow-up mo	IQ
Group 1						
No neurological involvement						
	M		10	12	6	103
	M	1	5	6	10	100
	M*	1	6	8		82
	M	1	6	9	2	67
	M	1	7	9		96
	M	2	4	9		87
	F	2	6	6	6	94
	M	3	1	6	10	87
	F	6	9	6	9	100
				12	6	82
Group 2						
Peripheral neuropathy						
	F*	2	5	5	8	106
				10	10	92
	M	2	6	9		105
	F	12		15		75
Group 3						
Encephalopathy						
	M		10	7		103
	M		11	6	1	109
	M	1	6	6		90
	F*	1	11	6		94
	M*	2		12		***
	F*	3		9	6	79
	F	3	4	6	7	102
				7	7	91
	F	4	7	7	2	90
				12	4	69

* Child re-exposed to lead after discharge
** Data from Byers and Lord (1943)
*** IQ not determined at follow-up

the CNS is most vulnerable to damage during the period of maximum growth which varies from species to species. In assessing its likely effects on the developing human brain, therefore, it is important to ensure that lead is given to the animal model at the age at which the growth of the CNS is maximal; in the rat, for example, this would be during the first weeks after birth and not *in utero* (Dobbing, 1973).

The second aspect of metal toxicity of which it is important to be aware is the complex interaction which may occur between different metals. Some metals act to protect against the harmful effects of another whilst others may potentiate them. For example, zinc will protect against the teratogenic effects of cadmium; selenium protects against the toxic effects of arsenic and cadmium; but cadmium and lead potentiate each other. It is probable that some of the inconsistent results in the literature are due to the unforeseen interactions of metals other than lead in the test system.

Consistency

If there is a true causal relationship between exposure to relatively low levels of lead, either pre- or postnatally, and mental retardation, then this association is likely to have been observed repeatedly by different persons, in different places, circumstances and times. That is, the effect is consistent. This, however, is not the case although lead has been known for many years to have some effects on the human fetus.

In his Goulstonian lectures of 1891, Thomas Oliver drew attention to the high rate of abortion in female lead workers and noted that as many as three-quarters of pregnancies in some groups ended in miscarriage. At the time that Oliver was making these observations lead was commonly taken to procure abortions. This practice came into prominence particularly at the turn of the century (Hall, 1905). Lead probably causes abortion through its effect on the placenta but it is also able to cross the placenta and fetal tissue levels are related to those in the maternal circulation.

Thus, deliberate or occupational exposure would have resulted in a range of effects related to fetal tissue levels in children born to mothers whose blood leads were high, but not high enough to cause abortion. Amongst those effects, mental retardation might have been noted given the large at-risk population, but this is not the case. Infants born to mothers with lead poisoning were reported to be undersized, to have delayed growth, to have convulsions and neurological disorders, effects which were all due to fetal lead poisoning. The fact that many of the children in whom these effects were noted were brought up in conditions in which continuous postnatal exposure was probable makes it likely that they had chronic lead poisoning. If lead poisoning during pregnancy is treated, then the fetus may be spared and develop normally. Angle and McIntyre (1964) reported the case of a woman who was treated with chelating agents in the eighth month of pregnancy; her blood lead was 11.6 μmol/ℓ (240 μg/dℓ) when treatment was begun but she was delivered of a normal boy whose developmental assessment at the age of 4.5 years was normal.

Thus, exposure to inorganic lead during pregnancy, although it may have severe effects on the fetus, does not invariably cause mental retardation, or at least, not often enough to have been commented upon by authors who were writing at a time when lead poisoning in women was common.

Exposure to organic lead during pregnancy has been reported to be associated with profound retardation (and other congenital abnormalities) by Hunter and his colleagues (1979). They described two cases of children born in a small community to mothers who sniffed leaded petrol during their pregnancy; one of the mothers also drank alcohol heavily. The authors were able to discount the effects as being simply due to chance and were inclined to the view that the organic lead compounds in the petrol were the causal agents, although some other volatile constituents of the petrol might also have produced the effects. Neither blood nor urine lead concentrations were estimated in the mothers or in the fetuses.

One study, undertaken in Glasgow, has attempted to assess the role of lead exposure in the aetiology of mental retardation in children born to mothers who did not have lead poisoning. In the first part of the study (Beattie et al., 1975), mentally retarded children were matched for age, sex, social class and geographical location with a normal child. Lead concentrations in the water taken from the house in which the mother had lived during pregnancy were determined. The water lead content was found to be significantly higher in the houses of the mothers with retarded children and the probability that a child would be defective was significantly increased if water lead levels were in excess of 3.86 μmol/ℓ (800 μg/ℓ). The authors concluded that if all that was known about exposure to lead in the water was that it exceeded 3.86 μmol/ℓ, then the child would be at least 1.7 times as likely to be defective as a child whose exposure to lead in the water was unknown.

The authors were able to measure the blood lead concentration in only thirty of the retarded children (not selected at random) and these were compared with those of twenty children in the same age range who were inpatients in a paediatric ward. The means were significantly different in the two groups, 1.22 ± 0.58 and 0.85 ± 0.24 μmol/ℓ respectively. Rightly, the authors attached little weight to this difference in blood lead concentrations and were careful to state that their findings did not point to a causal relationship between lead in drinking water and mental retardation but that they indicated the need for a more detailed investigation.

In the second part of this Glasgow study (Moore et al., 1977), the blood lead concentrations of some of the children were estimated retrospectively by making use of stored PKU cards. Cards were traced for 80 of the 154 children in the original study but only 77 could be used, 41 from retarded children and 36 from the controls. The blood lead concentrations were 1.23 ± 0.43 and 1.01 ± 0.38 μmol/ℓ respectively, a difference which was highly significant. Since it had already been shown (Addis and Moore, 1974) that water lead and blood lead concentrations are highly correlated in Glasgow, a city which had exceedingly plumbosolvent water and a wealth of lead pipes and cisterns in the water supply, this result was entirely to be expected. Knowing (from the original study) that the mothers of the retarded children had lived in houses where the water lead levels were high, their offspring would have certainly had higher blood lead levels than the offspring of mothers who drank water less rich in lead since maternal and fetal blood leads are highly correlated.

The authors of this study considered that they had demonstrated a probable relationship between exposure to lead and mental retardation. Their results have to be set against those of Elwood and his colleagues (1976) who were able to find no difference in the water lead levels in the houses of educationally subnormal and normal children, however, and thus consistency is lacking here also.

Temporality and Biological Gradient

When determining that exposure to a toxic substance is the cause of an observed effect, it is essential to show that the exposure always precedes the effect and an attempt should also be made to show that there is a dose-response relationship. I shall now discuss how far these criteria have been satisfied in relation to lead exposure and mental retardation, dealing with them in the reverse order to that shown in the heading of this section.

Children who develop lead encephalopathy and who thus have a greatly enhanced risk of residual brain damage commonly have blood lead concentrations in excess of 5.8 μmol/ℓ. Is there any evidence to suggest the concentration at which retardation might be produced in children who have not had lead poisoning?

Three recent studies have attempted to answer this question (David _et al._, 1976, 1982; Youroukos _et al._, 1978), the study design being the same in each. Mentally retarded children in a wide age range were placed into one of two groups depending on whether or not a probable cause was known for their condition. A control was also selected, either from a paediatric outpatient clinic (in the David studies) or from children living at home; none of the subjects was selected at random. Blood lead concentrations were found to be significantly higher in the children for whom there was no known cause for their retardation (Table 2). On this account, the authors concluded that lead exposure was a factor in the aetiology of mental retardation in the "cause unknown" group and that relatively modest levels of lead were able to produce severe retardation.

Table 2

Mean blood lead concentrations (µmol/ℓ) in mentally retarded children

	n	Mean age (years)	Blood lead*	Range
Study 1				
Unknown cause	31	7.4 (4-11)	1.23 (0.44)	0.24-2.63
Probable cause	33	7.3 (4-12)	0.90 (0.31)	0.24-2.15
Controls	30	7.9 (5-11)	0.91 (0.35)	0.24-2.15
Study 2				
Unknown cause	35	7.6 (3.8-12)	1.21 (0.44)	0.24-2.63
Probable cause	48	7.2 (3.8-12)	0.91 (0.34)	0.24-2.15
Controls	40	7.4 (4-11)	0.91 (0.29)	0.24-2.15
Study 3				
Unknown cause	60	8.4 (2-15)	1.45 (0.55)	0.48-2.90
Probable cause	30	8.5 (2-15)	1.00 (0.33)	0.58-1.84
Controls	30	8.4 (2-15)	1.01 (0.33)	0.58-1.93

Study 1 David *et al*., 1976; Study 2 David *et al*., 1982; Study 3 Youroukos *et al*., 1978. It is not clear whether any of the children in David's first study were also included in the second.

* Standard deviation shown in parentheses.

This conclusion, however, is subject to criticism on several grounds, the first of which relates to the allocation of the mentally retarded children into subgroups. This was done on a retrospective basis and there is no reason to suppose that discrimination was total. Children might appear to have an unknown cause for their retardation for many reasons. For example, information about a probable cause might be missing from clinical notes or from the memory of the person questioned. Moreover, there may well be a cause that awaits discovery. The authors commit errors of logic in assuming that because they have not elicited a probable cause one does not exist or that it must be related to lead exposure; and they cannot conclude that because they have elicited a cause this necessarily excludes lead exposure as an aetiological factor. One result of the incomplete discrimination in the allocation of children into "unknown cause" and "probable cause" groups is to enhance the difference in the mean blood lead concentrations. A more complete knowledge of the cause of the retardation will result in children being transferred from the group which has the highest blood lead into the group with the lowest blood lead; the difference in the means will thus tend to diminish.

Another feature of the studies which calls into question the view that exposure to lead might contribute to mental retardation is the age of the children who were examined. They were all aged between two and fifteen years and, although we are not told, they were all presumably retarded from birth. The crucial time for exposure would thus have been *in utero*, but blood lead concentrations measured several years after birth give no information about prenatal exposure since they are a reflection only of recent exposure.

The last observation calls into question the temporality of the lead exposure in the children with mental retardation. Studies of mentally retarded children have shown that their blood lead levels are likely to be elevated, especially if they are known to have pica. Bicknell and her colleagues (1968) demonstrated this clearly in a study of mentally retarded children with and without pica. From a group of 330 severely subnormal children two subgroups were chosen; those who were frequent scavengers (27) and those who never scavenged (12). In addition, a subgroup who were also severely physically handicapped, most being unable to put hand to mouth, were also studied. Blood was taken for lead analysis and, on the following day, a random urine sample was also taken. The children were then given a three day course of calcium EDTA to mobilize lead from tissue stores. On the third day following the end of treatment, further blood and urine samples were taken for lead analysis. The children with pica had much higher blood and urine lead levels than the children in the two other groups and excreted much more lead in response to the EDTA, indicating greater body stores of lead (Table 3).

The effect of pica in elevating blood lead levels has been noted by other authors (Gibson *et al*., 1968; Cohen *et al*., 1976) and the importance of this observation is that lead exposure may further impair the functioning of retarded children (Moncrieff *et al*., 1964) and should thus be avoided as far as possible.

Thus, so far as temporality is concerned, a much more probable explanation for the raised blood lead levels found in some mentally retarded children is that it is a *post hoc* rather than a *propter hoc* phenomenon.

CONCLUSIONS

There is little evidence to support unequivocally the view that, in the absence of clinical lead poisoning, exposure to lead is causally related to mental retardation. The results from the

Table 3

Blood and urine lead concentrations (μmol/ℓ) in mentally retarded children*

	Pica	No Pica	Physically Handicapped
Pre-chelation			
Blood lead	2.32 (0.93)	0.92 (0.45)	0.58 (0.25)
Urine lead	0.58 (0.50)	0.17 (0.04)	0.17 (0.10)
Post-chelation			
Blood lead	2.17 (0.96)	0.92 (0.36)	0.58 (0.23)
Urine lead	3.63 (5.22)	0.53 (0.33)	0.20 (0.11)

* Data from Bicknell *et al*., 1968

Glasgow study, however, indicate the need for a carefully designed study relating prenatal exposure to the incidence of mental retardation.

In the presence of lead encephalopathy (when the blood lead is likely to be in excess of 5.8 μmol/ℓ) the probability of permanent damage is high unless the condition is recognized early and treatment begun promptly.

Children who are mentally retarded are at risk of having elevated blood lead levels and, since this may impair them still further, all practical steps should be taken to reduce their exposure to the minimum. When their blood lead concentration is in excess of about 3.0 μmol/ℓ, it may be desirable to reduce the level by treatment with chelating agents, at the same time as eliminating the source of the lead in their environment so far as is practicable.

REFERENCES

Addis, G., and Moore, M.R., (1974), Lead levels in the water of suburban Glasgow. **Nature, 252**, 120-121

Angle, C.R. and McIntyre, M.S., (1964), Lead poisoning during pregnancy. **American Journal of Diseases of Children, 108**, 436-439

Beattie, A.D., Moore, M.R., Goldberg, A., Finlayson, M.J., Graham, J.F., Mackie, E.M., Main, J.C., McLaren, D.A.,

Murdoch, R.M., and Stewart, G.T., (1975), Role of chronic low-level lead exposure in the aetiology of mental retardation. **Lancet, i**, 589-592

Bicknell, J., Clayton, B.E., and Delves, H.T., (1968), Lead in mentally retarded children. **Journal of Mental Deficiency Research, 12**, 282-293

Bradford Hill, A., (1965), The environment and disease: association or causation. **Proceedings of the Royal Society of Medicine**, 295-300

Byers, R.K., and Lord, E.E., (1943), Late effects of lead poisoning on mental development. **American Journal of Diseases of Children, 66**, 471-494

Cohen, D.J., Johnson, W.T., and Caparulo, B.K., (1976), Pica and elevated blood lead level in autistic and atypical children. **American Journal of Diseases in Children, 130**, 47-48

David, O., Grad, G., McGann, B., and Koltun, A., (1982), Mental retardation and "nontoxic" lead levels. **American Journal of Psychiatry, 139**, 806-809

David, O., Joffman, S., McGann, B., Sverd, J., and Clark, J., (1976), Low lead levels and mental retardation. **Lancet, ii**, 1376-1379

Dobbing, J., (1973), The developing brain: a plea for more critical interspecies extrapolation. **Nutr. Rep. Int., 7**, 401-406

Elwood, P.C., Morton, M., and St Leger, A.S., (1976), Lead in water and mental retardation. **Lancet, i**, 590-591

Ferm, V.H., (1972), The teratogenic effects of metals on mammalian embryos. In **Advances in Teratology, 5**, (ed. D.H.M. Woolam), Logos Press, London, 51-75

Gibson, S.L.M., Lam, C.M., McCrae, W.M. and Goldberg, A., (1968), Blood lead levels in normal and mentally retarded children. **Archives of Diseases in Childhood, 42**, 573-581

Hall, A., (1905), The increasing use of lead as an abortifacient. **British Medical Journal, 1**, 584-587

Hunter, A.G.W., Thompson, D., and Evans, J.A., (1979), Is there a fetal gasoline syndrome? **Teratology, 20**, 75-80

Moncrieff, A.A., Koumides, O.P., Clayton, B.E., Patrick, A.D., Renwick, A.G.C., and Roberts, G.E., (1964), Lead poisoning in children. **Archives of Diseases in Childhood, 39**, 1-13

Moore, M.R., Meredith, P.A., and Goldberg, A., (1977), A retrospective analysis of blood-lead in mentally retarded children. **Lancet, i**, 712-719

Oliver, T., (1891), Lead poisoning in its acute and chronic manifestations. **Lancet, i**, 530-531; 588-589; 644-646

Waldron, H.A., (1978), Lead and human behaviour. **Journal of Mental Deficiency Research, 22**, 69-78

Youroukos, S., Lyberatos, C., and Philippidou, A., (1978), Increased blood lead levels in mentally retarded children in Greece. **Archives of Environmental Health, 33** 297-300

COMMENTARY

P. D. Lewis

In this paper the author examines on the one hand the immediate and delayed effects of human clinical lead poisoning and on the other the question of functional brain involvement in "subclinical" lead intoxication. High-dose lead neurotoxicity has dramatic, readily recognizable and sometimes permanent manifestations. Low-level exposure, according to several recent studies not cited here, may be associated with intellectual and behavioural changes in children. There has been some argument about the nature of such changes and their relationship to lead, and the weight of the author's opinion is against the concept of chronic low-level lead neurotoxicity as a cause of mental retardation. Nevertheless, since we know that lead at high doses is unequivocally toxic to the developing brain any suggestion of a low-dose effect must be evaluated very seriously.

One of Bradford Hill's (1965) criteria of causality that was not dealt with in this paper was experiment. Laboratory studies demonstrate the overall correspondence of pathological findings in lead-poisoned man and rats. Data in man relate to relatively high exposure levels. In human childhood lead encephalopathy, which occurs with blood lead levels in the range 100-800 μg/100 ml, such changes as brain oedema, vacuolation, haemorrhage and gliosis appear to be secondary to microvascular lesions. No primary neuronal lesions have as yet been clearly identified. Neurological signs and a pathological picture closely resembling that seen in human lead encephalopathy are obtained in young lead-exposed rats with blood lead levels above 500 μg/100 ml. Oedema and haemorrhage, cyst formation, reactive glial changes and nerve cell alterations are observed consequent to effects on capillary endothelial cells and basement membranes. High-level lead exposure in rats also produces disturbances in myelinated axons and may affect neural network formation in the central nervous system. With intermediate blood lead levels (200-500 μg/100 ml), vascular changes and their sequelae are not seen in the brain of exposed rats, but nutritional effects, themselves capable of producing neuropathology, may be prominent. Data from recent studies on developing rats with low blood levels corresponding to those seen in urban children without lead encephalopathy but believed by some to show neuropsychiatric changes (40-80 μg/100 ml) appear to demonstrate effects of lead on maturing and differentiated neuronal populations (for review see Winder et al., 1983). Such findings, together with studies showing changes in hippocampal function in low-level lead-exposed rats (Winder, Garten and Lewis, in preparation) suggest that continued investigation of behaviour and intelligence in children with moderate blood lead levels is obligatory.

Reference

Winder C., Garten L.L. and Lewis P.D. (1983). The morphological effects of lead on the developing central nervous system. A review. **Neuropathology and Applied Neurobiology, 9,** in press

P. M. Le Quesne

Although the role of fetal exposure to lead as a factor in producing mental retardation is controversial, exposure to certain other agents *in utero* has been more clearly associated with this disorder. Some examples will be briefly discussed.

The occurrence of psychomotor retardation following prenatal exposure to methyl mercury was recognized during the investigation of families exposed to this substance in Minamata Bay in the late 1950s (Harada, 1968), but the degree of exposure could not be assessed in affected individuals. The syndrome is quite different from the focal neurological disorder which occurs in adults and consists of paraesthesia, cerebellar ataxia and concentric constriction of the visual fields.

More detailed quantitative evaluation was possible following the brief epidemic of methyl mercury intoxication which occurred in Iraq in late 1971 and early 1972. By analysis of hair samples of mothers two to three years after the episode, the degree of exposure could be correlated with neurological abnormalities in children that had been *in utero* during the epidemic. Marsh *et al*. (1981) analysed 84 infant-mother pairs and found a dose-related incidence of symptoms in the mothers. These had usually been mild, consisting of transient paraesthesia; some of the children had severe psychomotor retardation. Greatest damage occurred following exposure during the second trimester. Abnormalities appeared in the group in which maternal peak hair concentrations were in the range 68-180 ppm.

The effects of alcohol on the fetus have been extensively studied since the recognition of the fetal alcohol syndrome a few years ago. The level of maternal alcohol intake necessary for production of the syndrome has not been clearly established, but there is a dose-response effect of incidence and severity of abnormalities. The full syndrome consists of growth retardation and facial abnormalities affecting the eyes, nose, maxilla and mouth in addition to mental retardation (Clarren and Smith, 1978). A variety of other congenital malformations have been occasionally associated.

The fetal hydantoin syndrome is in many ways similar and occurs amongst epileptic mothers receiving this treatment during pregnancy. Retardation of mental function and of growth also occur. Affected children have a characteristic facial appearance (different from that in the fetal alcohol syndrome), hypoplasia of the nails or distal phalanges and may have an abnormal thumb (Hanson et al., 1976). Other developmental abnormalities are common.

In the fetal alcohol and hydantoin syndromes characteristic development abnormalities are features of the full syndrome and were important in their delineation originally. However, mental retardation, usually with associated growth retardation, may occur without any other abnormality. Only following delineation of the full syndrome has it been possible to establish an aetiological relation in individuals with only some of the features.

In the instances discussed the fetus is more vulnerable to the toxic agent than the mother, but the fetal effects do not occur at a substantially lower level of exposure than those which produce some manifestations of intoxication in the mother. Thus in seeking possible toxic causes of mental deficiency it seems that some clue is likely to be found in a study of abnormalities in the mother.

References

Clarren S.K. and Smith D.W. (1978). The fetal alcohol syndrome. **New England Journal of Medicine, 298,** 1063-1067

Hanson J.W., Myrianthopoulos N.C., Harvey M.A.S. and Smith D.W. (1976). Risks to the offspring of women treated with hydantoin anticonvulsants, with emphasis on the fetal hydantoin syndrome. **Journal of Pediatrics, 89,** 662-668

Harada Y. (1968). Congenital (or fetal) Minamata disease. In Kutsuna M., (Ed.), **Minamata Disease,** Study group of Minamata disease, Kunamo-to University, Japan, 93-117

Marsh D.O., Myers G.J., Clarkson T.W., Amin-Zaki L., Tikriti S. and Majeed M.A. (1981). Dose-response relationship for human fetal exposure to methyl mercury. **Clinical Toxicology, 18,** 1311-1318

N. Sartorius

The paper is an elegant demonstration of a serious deficiency in current disease and health theories: there is at present no appropriate universally accepted paradigm by which noncommunicable diseases and health states such as mental retardation can be studied, understood, managed or prevented. Waldron classified the findings of his review by reference to the outstanding paper by Bradford Hill. This way of presentation serves well to illustrate this difficulty. The inconsistency (or consistency) of results, for example, quoted in the paper can be considered and understood only if there is sufficient information about all the other relevant factors. Speaking of effects of lead exposure without specific reference to other factors that could have been present at the time that a child or fetus was exposed to lead is useful but not sufficient: a multifactorial consideration, perhaps using concepts current in systems theory, would be needed and any progress in this direction would be valuable. A recent study by Smith _et al_. provides support to this way of proceeding, demonstrating once more that the likelihood of lasting damage to mental functioning in children exposed to lead must be considered in the context of other social, environmental and perhaps hereditary factors.

The criterion of temporality mentioned illustrates another difficulty in studies of chronic and noncommunicable diseases and conditions which somehow escape the normal epidemiological rules and the paradigm of communicable diseases (on which these rules have been constructed). It is of course true that exposure to lead must _precede_ the effect but the meaning of the word _precede_ is not discussed and in the literature it is only rarely specified with sufficient clarity and precision. In the instance of slow viruses causing degenerative disorders of the brain, the distance between the point of exposure, the point of infection and the point of occurrence of disease is enormous. Two or three decades and perhaps more in the instance of certain types of dementia may pass before the effects of exposure are noticeable. In the instance of exposure to environmental hazards, the situation may be similarly complicated, particularly in instances in which an environmental factor's action prepares the ground for a harmful influence of another agent. The temporality, therefore, becomes a point of particular importance which could be given more emphasis. Only very special conditions will in these instances allow the temporal proof - as for geographical isolation of tribes without much contact with other sources of contamination.

The author has come to the conclusion that it is impossible to prove at the moment that exposure to lead in the absence of clinical lead poisoning is causally linked to mental retardation. In my opinion neither this conclusion nor an affirmation of causal relation can be supported at the present moment, not only because of lacking evidence but also because of the difficulties that arise in the instance of mental retardation, and in other chronic noncommunicable conditions for which we have no appropriate paradigm of causality.

•

W. Yule

Waldron is correct to point out that in considering any possible role of lead in the aetiology of mental handicap, one must differentiate between those children who suffer acute lead poisoning - these days usually from the accidental ingestion of leaded paint, cosmetic or the like - and those children who are chronically exposed to low levels of environmental lead. It seems clear that blood lead levels which are persistently above 60-80 μg/dl are associated in many instances with clear evidence of encephalopathy. However, even at these levels, some children survive without apparent sequelae, testifying both to the probability of individual differences in reaction to lead and to the human child's remarkable resilience. Such cases cannot be used, as Waldron tries to do, to argue for there being no causal effect of lead on the CNS. Rather than argue through all the other weaknesses and fallacious arguments in the paper as presented, I will summarize the main studies which have been published since 1979 and which address the second question relating to the possible role of lead at low, chronic levels to the aetiology of mental retardation.

The evidence up to 1979 was summarized by the DHSS Working Party (DHSS, 1980) and by Rutter (1980), and the studies published since then are discussed in two other recent publications (Rutter and Russell Jones, 1983; Yule and Rutter, 1983).

A variety of studies of clinic populations tended to indicate that where blood lead levels were persistently raised above 60 μg/dl, this was associated, on average, with a 3 to 4 point reduction in IQ. Findings were even less secure in the 40-60 μg/dl range, and scarcely any studies had systematically examined children below 40 μg/dl. As Waldron notes, there have been a number of studies of mentally retarded children's body lead burdens. There are so many methodological weaknesses in these studies that no firm conclusions are permissible (Rutter, 1980). It is true that deviant groups tended to have higher lead levels, but the methodologies make it impossible to ascertain whether the higher lead levels represented a cause, or an effect, or a mixture of the two. I will return to this crucial question later.

Chelation studies provide a potentially powerful way of examining causality if reductions in body lead are followed by improvements in intelligence. However, none of the early studies had adequate controls to show that the improvements claimed were specifically related to the fall in lead levels, or that the gains in IQ exceeded those expected on test-retest and maturational effects.

Studies up to the late 1970s drew attention to a number of methodological weaknesses - sampling biases, problems in the assessment of the body burden of lead, difficulties involved in the assessment of psychological and behavioural impairment, inadequate statistical analyses to control for the effects of possible confounding variables, and small sample sizes. Studies over the past four to five years have greatly improved.

Animal studies (reviewed in Silbergeld, 1983) have also improved and now one of the best documented effects of lead concerns inhibition of the haem biosynthetic pathway - an effect that is present below 30 μg/dl and possibly below 20 μg/dl. Lead also interferes with neuronal systems utilizing acetylcholine, catecholamines and GABA as neurotransmitters. There is, therefore, a case that there are important biological consequences in animals of lead exposure at levels well below those associated with clinical signs and symptoms of lead poisoning. The functional significance of these changes, especially the implications for humans, remains uncertain, but biological effects do occur at low levels of lead and are not the same as those at high levels.

Recent neurophysiological studies of children also suggest that changes in EEG and in peripheral nerve conduction velocities may occur at blood lead levels below 30 μg/dl. Burchfiel _et al._ (1980) compared 22 children with "low" lead levels with 19 with "high" lead levels using power spectrum analyses. The high lead levels were associated with an increased amount of low-frequency delta activity. These findings suggest a possible neurophysiological mechanism for some of the reported psychological changes, but the numbers are too small and the validity of the EEG changes are too uncertain to make stronger claims. Otto and his colleagues (summarized in Otto _et al._, 1983) studied 1 to 6 year old children using a passive conditioning paradigm to study evoked potentials. They found effects varied with lead levels, and found effect below 30 μg/dl without evidence of any threshold. Alas, the EEG paradigm is novel and its validity is unclear, but the findings suggest some measurable effects at low lead levels. The only other EEG study (Guerit _et al._, 1981) reported substantially negative findings but they did not use the EEG data quantitatively and the study had other weaknesses.

The other methodological difficulties mentioned above have been discussed in detail elsewhere (Yule and Rutter, 1983) and will not be repeated here. Instead, I will try to summarize the recent studies which have particularly tried to sort out the extent to which lead is a cause, a consequence or merely a correlate of differences in children's development. Children from working class homes are consistently found to have higher lead levels. Is it the lead or the social environment which influences the dependent variables - be they IQ or behavioural problems. It is important to control for social factors without overcorrecting for their influence.

Needleman _et al._'s (1979) tooth lead study was a landmark in improving on previous ones. It does have a number of methodological weaknesses, but essentially they found that, after controlling for social factors, the children in their "high" lead group scored, on average, some 4 IQ points lower than those in their "low" lead group. Teachers were asked to rate the children's behaviour, and a proportion of deviant ratings on items relating to attention span rose with increasing tooth lead level, although social factors could not be controlled for in that part of the study. Our own pilot study (Yule _et al._, 1981; Lansdown _et al._, 1983) tended to parallel Needleman's results.

Winneke and his colleagues also report on two studies in Germany in which tooth lead was used as the index of body lead burden (see Winneke, 1983 for a summary). In the main study, three groups of children - low, middle and high tooth lead - were intensively studied. Before correction for confounding variable, the high lead group had a verbal IQ score 7.6 points below that of the low lead group. After correction, the difference was reduced to 4.6 points which was statistically non-significant.

A very similar result was reported in the recently completed London Institute of Child Health/University of Southampton study (Smith, 1983) in which tooth lead was the index of body lead burden and considerable attention was paid to getting good measures of social factors. The mean full scale IQ of their groups were: High lead 103.7; Medium 104.9; Low 108.7 - before various social factors were controlled. These differences reduced after controlling for social factors, but the trend of the differences between the groups remained. The difference between the high and low lead groups reduced from 5 to 2.7 IQ points after statistical correction.

Where the data are reported, it is generally noted that the relationship between lead and IQ is stronger in working class than in middle class groups. Indeed, in one of our own most recent studies in a predominantly middle class area, no relationship could be found with either IQ or teachers' behaviour ratings.

What then can be concluded from these recent studies? Firstly, it is increasingly clear that the neuropsychological effects of lead within the range usually encountered in European countries today is quite small. Lead accounts, at most, for only 2 to 3% of the variance in intelligence and is a minor contributor compared to genetic and other social factors. But some children may be more susceptible to the effects of lead than others. Secondly, and more importantly, for the theme of this conference, an overall difference of only 2 to 5 IQ points has considerable implications for the prevalence of mild mental handicap. If one assumes that lead results in no change in the distribution of IQ (but that the whole bell-shaped distribution shifts down to the left), a difference of 5 points means a doubling in the number of children with an IQ below 70. This statistical prediction receives empirical backing in Needleman _et al._'s (1979) re-examination of their data.

Finally, I must say that I disagree with Waldron's assessment of the likelihood of lead acting as a causal agent. I have spelled this out in detail elsewhere (Lansdown _et al._, 1983; Yule and Rutter, 1983), but suffice it to say that in considering Bradford Hill's suggestions, I would conclude that the recent findings are consistent with a causal inference, but I agree that they do not unambiguously prove it.

The recent epidemiological studies have probably taken us as far as we can go, within the limits of our current technologies, and other research strategies are needed to attempt to understand the biological mechanisms that mediate the apparent lead effect on neuropsychological functioning. We need to develop more sensitive, reliable and valid measures of neuropsychological functioning in children, particularly measures of attention and vigilance, before such studies can yield more informative results. Longitudinal studies of larger numbers are already planned or under way, and by assessing the effective social environments contemporaneously with the children's body lead burden and their intellectual and behavioural development, some of these relationships will be better understood.

References

Burchfiel J., Duffy F., Bartels P.H. and Needleman H.L. (1980). Combined discriminating power of quantitative encephalography and neuropsychologic measures in evaluating CNS effects of lead at low levels. In H.L. Needleman (Ed.), **Low Level Lead Exposure: The Clinical Implications of Current Research,** New York, Raven Press

Department of Health and Social Security (1980). **Lead and Health: The Report of the DHSS Working Party on Lead in the Environment,** (The Lawther Report), London, HMSO

Guerit J.M. et al. (1981). Lead neurotoxicity in clinically asymptomatic children living in the vicinity of an ore smelter. **Clinical Toxicology, 18,** 1257-1267

Lansdown R., Yule W., Urbanowicz M.A. and Millar I.B. (1983). Blood lead, intelligence, attainment and behaviour in school children: Overview of a pilot study. In M. Rutter and B. Russell Jones, (Eds.), (op cit)

Needleman H., Gunnoe C., Leviton A. et al. (1979). Deficits in psychological and classroom performance of children with elevated dentine lead levels. **New Engl. J. Med., 300,** 689-695

Otto D. et al. (1983). Evidence of changes in CNS functions at low-to-moderate blood lead levels in children. In M. Rutter and R. Russell Jones, (Eds.), (op cit)

Rutter M. (1980). Raised lead levels and impaired cognitive/behavioural functioning: a review of the evidence. **Develop. Med. Child Neurol., 22,** Suppl. 42

Rutter M. and Russell Jones R. (Eds.) (1983). **Lead versus Health: Sources and Effects of Low Level Lead Exposure,** Chichester, Wiley

Silbergeld E.K. (1983). Experimental studies of lead neurotoxicity: implications for mechanisms, dose-response and reversibility. In M. Rutter and R. Russell Jones, (Eds.), (op cit)

Smith M. (1983). Lead, intelligence and social factors. Paper presented to Association for Child Psychology and Psychiatry. London, January

Winneke G. (1983). Neurobehavioural and neuropsychological effects of lead. In M. Rutter and R. Russell Jones, (Eds.), (op cit)

Yule W., Lansdown R., Millar I.B. and Urbanowicz M.A. (1981). The relationship between blood lead concentrations, intelligence and attainment in a school population: A pilot study. **Develop. Med. Child Neurol, 23,** 567-76

Yule W. and Rutter M. (1983). Effect of lead on children's intellectual development: a critical review. In K.R. Mahaffey (Ed.) **Health Implications of Typical Levels of Lead Exposure: Dietary and Environmental Sources.** Amsterdam, Elsevier

Chapter 10

Infectious agents in the aetiology of mental retardation

J.A. Dudgeon

INTRODUCTION

It has long been recognized that recovery from any of the bacterial meningitides, treated or untreated, could result in mental retardation. Even if allowance is made for the great differences in the incidence of infectious disease throughout the world we do not know today the impact of infectious disease as a whole as a cause of mental retardation, however that term is defined, even in countries where sound epidemiological and statistical data are available. Nor can we at present determine the aetiology of the great majority of cases of mental retardation (Eichenwald, 1962). Those that appear to be related to acquired and environmental, as opposed to non-genetic, causes may be attributed to "infection" contracted before or soon after birth. But it is important to establish with certainty that a particular case of mental retardation is the direct result of an infectious disease rather than to label it as such on insufficient evidence. We need more precise information on the aetiological role of infectious disease and mental retardation, both mild and severe.

In collating this information we must be aware of the factors that determine the frequency and outcome of infectious disease. Host factors such as age and socio-economic conditions are of special importance in this connection when looked at from the international scene. And we must remember too that many infections, in particular viruses, occur in a mild or asymptomatic form and that a mild infection can also lead to the same devastating illness as a severe one. This is particularly important in infections acquired before birth.

The importance of identifying individual infectious diseases as causes of mental retardation and arriving at an estimate of their impact on the total problem cannot be too strongly emphasized. Many infectious diseases are amenable to preventive measures, to specific treatment, or both. If a cause can be identified then a remedy may be found. The need for continued research and application of new techniques to this problem is of paramount importance.

CLASSIFICATION OF AETIOLOGICAL AGENTS

For the purpose of this review the term mental retardation will be used to include both severe and mild forms without any attempt at further subdivision or precise definitions. The classification is based on the stage in life when the initial insult, i.e. the infection, is deemed to have caused or triggered off a process which ultimately has led to mental retardation. It is important to stress that mental retardation resulting from an infection does not necessarily occur as a sudden event such as after an accident or cerebrovascular accident. It is more often an on-going process, often with deterioration, and in some cases may develop a long time after the initial exposure to the infection.

The principal stages in life when infection can lead to mental retardation are:

1. prenatal, i.e. preconception to parturition;
2. perinatal;
3. postnatal: from the perinatal period to childhood (in the context of this article).

Table 1

Infective causes of mental retardation

Prenatal	Perinatal	Postnatal
Cytomegalovirus (CMV)	Group B streptococci	Bacterial meningitides
Rubella	*Esch. coli*	Pneumococcal
Varicella zoster	Enteroviral infections	Meningococcal
Herpes simplex	Herpes simplex	*H. influenzae*
Listeriosis	Cytomegalovirus	*B. pertussis*
Syphilis	Other Gram-negative organisms	Herpes simplex
Toxoplasmosis		Enteroviruses
Malaria		Echo
Trypanosomiasis		Coxsackie A and B
Cysticercosis		Aseptic meningitis syndrome
Cryptococcosis		Post-infectious encephalitides
		Viral encephalitides
		Viral and bacterial vaccines

Into this broad classification can be grouped a wide variety of infectious agents, ranging from protozoa to viruses, which by virtue of their pathogenesis may infect or affect the central nervous system and thereby lead to mental retardation. It is also important to emphasize that involvement of the CNS may be secondary to a generalized systemic infection and that the brain and its appendages are not necessarily the main target organs of the infectious process. The agents listed in Table 1 have been incriminated to a greater or lesser degree as causes of mental retardation, but not as already stressed as their sole or even primary pathological effect.

The agents have been grouped in a broad order of priority per group as causative factors of mental retardation rather than on their size (e.g. the large protozoa and the small viruses) or on their biological properties. The list is not comprehensive as there are a number of microbial agents where doubt still exists as to their causative role. In this context it is important to stress the need for hard facts in order to establish a cause and effect relationship. In establishing a causal relationship between a maternal infection and congenital defects or fetal damage various criteria have been proposed (Hanshaw and Dudgeon, 1978). These can be readily adapted to the study of infective causes of mental retardation. These are listed in Table 2.

Table 2

Criteria for establishing a causal relationship between an infectious disease and mental retardation

1. Clinical:	For each infection there showed a consistency of clinical features of retardation and the infective agent. A consistency of clinical pattern is less easy to discern in mental retardation without defects such as CMV, but is fairly consistent in congenital rubella and varicella zoster.
2. Epidemiological:	The relationship between agent and retardation should be established in different countries.
3. Microbiological:	Identification of the causative agent from the CNS, spinal fluid or other specimens in sufficient cases.
4. Immunological:	Specific immune response in the newborn in cases of prenatal infection and in the blood and/or CSF in cases of postnatal infection.

The criteria shown in Table 2 are only intended as guidelines for investigators into the causes of mental retardation particularly where a prenatal infection is thought to be the cause, or in the case of bacterial meningitis acquired postnatally.

CLINICAL MANIFESTATIONS

Prenatal Infections

(a) Cytomegalovirus

This virus usually known as CMV (cytos, cell, megalo large) is one of the most common viral infections of human beings. It has been estimated that between 1 and 2% of pregnant women in London contract primary CMV infection. The figure in North America may be in the region of 3 to 5% (Hanshaw and Dudgeon, 1978). Maternal infection is invariably asymptomatic so that the mother does not know if and when infection has been acquired, but there is clear evidence that if maternal infection is acquired at any stage in pregnancy the risk that the fetus may be infected is high. Probably about half of those maternal infections would result in the birth of an infected infant and about 90% of these would be "normal" at birth, but the remainder carry a high risk of showing some evidence of mental retardation. Many are mentally retarded without associated defects other than deafness. This effect is different from that which is encountered in congenital rubella. It has been calculated that on the basis of 0.5 to 2% of pregnant women being infected with CMV the end-result might be as follows:

(i) 50% not infected therefore normal;
(ii) 50% infected with 60% normal neonates; 38% damaged neonates and 2% stillbirths.

The figures for the Manchester area with a rather low CMV excretion rate of 0.24% would yield the following figures for the United Kingdom with the current birth-rate:

(i) number of CMV excretors at birth: 1500;
(ii) number of normal infants and those remaining normal: 825;
(iii) number of deaths 5%: 75;
(iv) number with serious mental handicap and deafness 15%: 225;
(v) number with less severe handicap: 375;

As these figures almost certainly represent an underestimation, some idea of the size of the problem can be gauged. A conservative estimate would put the incidence of mental retardation due to primary CMV in pregnancy at about 500-750 new cases per annum, and this does not take into account the possibility of later onset retardation, slow development and deafness. It is known that latency and reactivation occur quite regularly with CMV infection. When this occurs in the mother, the fetus may be infected, but there is little or no evidence that the fetus has been damaged from reactivation infection.

(b) Rubella

Intrauterine rubella is a less serious cause of mental retardation than CMV although it is an important cause of congenital defects. In the original series of congenital rubella cases encountered in Australia in 1940-41 Swan and his colleagues (Swan _et al._, 1946) observed that 5% of 101 documented cases had signs of mental deficiency as a predominant sign. Subsequent studies have shown that central nervous system defects with microcephaly and mental retardation may occur more frequently in congenital rubella than was originally thought to be the case. The majority, however, exhibit other symptoms of congenital rubella or have had a history of CNS involvement in the neonatal period (Dudgeon, 1967; Cooper, 1975; Hanshaw and Dudgeon, 1978). A few cases of chronic progressive and degenerative panencephalitis have been reported in patients with congenital rubella in adolescence. Signs of severe psychomotor retardation were common in the few fatal cases reported (Townsend _et al._, 1975; Weil _et al._, 1975). Chess and her colleagues in New York City found a surprisingly high incidence of mental retardation ranging from mild to moderate to severe and profound in a group of 54 retarded congenital rubella children.

As far as numbers are concerned it has been estimated that in the United Kingdom in a non-epidemic year before rubella immunization was introduced in 1970 approximately 250-300 children with congenital rubella would be born each year (Ciba Symposium, 1973). Since the introduction of immunization the number has declined, but not as fast as one would hope.

The decline in the United States appears to be more rapid (CDC, 1980). It should be emphasized that congenital rubella is a more important cause of physical rather than mental handicaps in contrast to CMV where the reverse is the case. Nevertheless congenital rubella is a preventable disease.

(c) Syphilis

Congenital syphilis is a well known cause of fetal damage and mental retardation which can occur in successive pregnancies unless treated. The danger is that cases can be missed either because of lack of recognition or failure to think of the possibility in the differential diagnosis. The average number of cases reported per annum in the UK in the past decade is 10-20.

(d) Listeria monocytogenes (Listeriosis)

This is a rare infection which if contracted in pregnancy or if it persists untreated may lead to abortion, repeated abortions, stillbirths and in surviving infants encephalitis with mental retardation. Listeriosis appears to be more common in Europe and particularly in East Germany. The number of cases occurring annually and causing mental retardation appears in the UK to be very small.

(e) Congenital toxoplasmosis

The incidence in the UK is about one case per 20 000 live births (Fleck, 1973). Congenital cases may develop mental retardation as a result of infection of the brain with _Toxoplasma gondii_. Infection can be acquired by infection of the parasite in raw or undercooked meat or by infection of the oocyst from the faeces of young cats. Congenital toxoplasmosis may occur in successive pregnancies but it is rare for clinical disease to be present in the newborn of a second pregnancy (Desmonts _et al_., 1965).

(f) _Varicella zoster (VZ)_

Varicella zoster infections are not uncommon in pregnancy, but only rarely is the fetus apparently either infected or affected. However despite this a number of cases of a congenital varicella syndrome have been described in recent years in which brain involvement, rudimentary digits, cutaneous scars and limb hypoplasia have been evident (Dudgeon, 1976; Hanshaw and Dudgeon, 1978). Eighteen cases have now been fully documented and four more are known to exist. The mortality rate is extremely high and the known survivors suffered from severe physical and mental handicap. Sixteen cases result from primary maternal varicella between the 12th and 22nd week of pregnancy. Two have resulted from maternal zoster. Of the six survivors a spectrum of damage has been observed with slow psychomotor development in some and severe retardation in others. Neonatal varicella is less rare than is generally envisaged. The risk is much greater if maternal varicella is contracted within 5 days of parturition than 5-10 days. Infected infants may show evidence of meningo-encephalitis and if they survive are likely to be brain damaged.

(g) _Herpes simplex (HSV) infection_

Only a few cases of intrauterine HSV infection (about 12 in all) have been reported, but all had signs of extensive brain involvement (Hanshaw and Dudgeon, 1978).

2. Perinatal Infections

(a) _Lancefield group B haemolytic streptococci_

This has become a major paediatric problem in the newborn period in many countries especially the United States. Attack rates of 4 per 1000 live births have been reported (Yow, 1975; Baker, 1979; McCracken, 1981). At present it appears to be less common in the UK, but as the natural history of infectious disease is constantly changing there should be a general awareness of this extremely severe infectious disease. Group B streptococcal infections may be present in two forms. First, the early or acute onset type which presents within the first 5 days of life with signs of generalized septicaemia, respiratory distress, and concomitant meningitis in about 30% of cases. The case fatality ratio is over 50%. The early onset cases are closely related to obstetric complications in the mother, whereas in the second group of cases presenting as late onset type between 7 and 28 days no such association has been observed. A significant number of these late onset cases have meningeal rather than pulmonary involvement and about 30 to 50% can be expected to have permanent neurological sequelae.

There is a close relationship between the presence of these bacteria in the maternal genital tract and infection of the newborn, pointing to a perinatal vertical transmission. Also a major determining factor of either early or late onset illness is the deficiency of type specific antibody in the capsular polysaccharide antigen of the group B streptococcus in the mothers' serum (Baker, 1979).

(b) Esch. coli septicaemia

This is an extremely severe disease contracted in the perinatal-neonatal period with an incidence of approximately 0.5 to 2.0 per 1000 live births (McCracken, 1981). Septicaemia with meningitis is common. The mortality even with prompt antibiotic treatment is high as is the incidence of neurological sequelae in those who recover.

(c) Other bacterial causes

The other main bacterial causes of perinatal bacterial infections are listed in Table 1. Together they present an important but heterogeneous group which are responsible for at least 10 times as many clinically recognized cases as congenital rubella and CMV together (Gamsu, 1973). Although pneumonia is the more frequent complication of these infections, this is frequently associated with meningitis and CNS involvement with neurological sequelae is common.

(d) Herpes simplex (HSV) infection

HSV infection may be transmitted to the newborn at the time of birth. Infection with type 2 strains of HSV are more common than with type 1 strains. A higher incidence of premature deliveries occur in women who have genital herpes (Nahmias *et al.*, 1971) and it is possible that the HSV infection *per se* may be the cause of the prematurity (Whitley *et al.*, 1980a, b). The morbidity and mortality are high with at least 80% of newborns showing signs of lethargy and seizures. Recovery is frequently associated with severe psychomotor retardation.

(e) Enteroviral infections

Infections with Coxsackie B viruses or the echo viruses if contracted in the early newborn period may lead to a fatal disseminated infection in which the CNS is usually extensively damaged. Recovery is often associated with neurological deficits. Outbreaks have occurred in maternity and special care units where the risk to the newborn is high (Hanshaw and Dudgeon, 1978).

Postnatal Infections

(a) Bacterial meningitis

Bacterial meningitis is the most important single cause of mental retardation in infants and children. The principal bacterial causes are shown in Table 1 but it must also be remembered that bacterial meningitis is also common in the perinatal period. The mortality from these infections is high but lower since the advent of chemotherapy. The morbidity particularly from CNS damage is high and is influenced by the following factors:

(i) late recognition or late diagnosis;
(ii) late institution of appropriate chemotherapy or an insufficient dosage;
(iii) length of treatment too short;
(iv) failure to correlate laboratory results on sensitivity with antibiotic therapy;
(v) emergence of drug resistant strains of bacteria and in particular of *N. meningitidis* and *H. influenzae*.

(b) Herpes simplex infection

Herpes simplex is now recognized as the most common cause of sporadic and usually fatal encephalitis. Neurological sequelae in those who recover with or without antiviral chemotherapy are common and invariably associated with severe mental retardation. It is probable that many cases of herpes encephalitis in the past may have been incorrectly diagnosed, as the disease is not invariably fatal and may account for a proportion of mentally retarded patients in institutions. The extent of the problem cannot at present be assessed, but the diagnosis is being made with increased frequency.

(c) Post-infectious encephalitides

Encephalitides, usually of the perivenous demyelinating type, may occur after measles (incidence between 1 in 1000 and 5000 cases), varicella (incidence 1 in 10 000 cases), smallpox vaccine (1 in 15 000 to 1 in 70 000), mumps and rubella (very rare). Gibbs (1962) has reviewed these common infections as a cause of mental retardation, but fortunately the principal causes measles and smallpox vaccine are now preventable by immunization.

(d) The group A and B arboviruses

This vast group of insect-borne encephalitides can cause mental retardation in a varying proportion of those who recover. The subject is too vast to cover in this communication and as these agents have only a limited geographical distribution readers are referred to comprehensive reviews on the subject (Casals and Clarke, 1965; Clarke and Casals, 1965).

(e) Enteroviral and mumps infection as causes of the aseptic meningitis syndrome

The Coxsackie A and B viruses and mumps viruses are all common causes of the aseptic meningitis syndrome. Fortunately, the prognosis in all such cases in the postnatal period is extremely good and the incidence of permanent neurological sequelae is extremely rare.

(f) Bacterial and viral vaccines

(i) Smallpox vaccine. This has resulted in post-vaccinal encephalitis in approximately 1 in 50 000 cases following primary vaccination. The incidence was much higher in some countries, notably the Netherlands (1 in 15 000), than in others. Now that smallpox has been eradicated the risk no longer exists.

(ii) Live attenuated measles vaccine. Encephalitis following measles vaccine has been reported rarely, but initially appeared to be associated with earlier batches of vaccine which have now been discontinued. A conservative estimate of the incidence would be as low as 1 in 300 000 doses of vaccine administered compared with 1 in 4000 cases from the natural disease. Convulsions occur not infrequently after measles vaccine but they do not appear to have any more lasting ill-effect than often uncomplicated convulsions in chidren.

(iii) Pertussis vaccine. Vaccines containing pertussis antigen, i.e. monovalent pertussis or triple vaccine, have been reported to be a cause of brain damage on several occasions in the past 20 years (DHSS, 1981). The data supporting the association between this vaccine and brain damage have been critically reviewed and furthermore carefully investigated as the result of a prospective study, the National Childhood Encephalopathy Study (NCES). Miller and his colleagues (Miller et al., 1981) estimate that there was a statistically increased risk of acute neurological illness following triple vaccine compared with diphtheria-tetanus vaccine. Thirty-five cases of triple vaccine associated cases were encountered in 32 previously neurologically normal children; 21 children made a complete recovery; 9 children had neurological deficits. The estimated attributable risk was assessed at 1 in 110 000 immunizations or 1 in 310 000 injections. The risk of encephalopathy with permanent brain damage from the natural disease, pertussis, is almost certainly much higher, but there are no reliable data on incidence from which to quote.

(iv) Prevention, treatment and management. Where there is evidence that an infectious disease can result in mental retardation every attempt should be made to prevent the event from occurring, or by appropriate treatment to modify that effect. Examples of this approach are listed in Table 3.

Table 3

Infective causes of mental retardation.
Examples of control by prevention or treatment

Prevention	Treatment
1. By vaccination	1. Chemotherapy
a) Rubella to prevent congenital rubella	a) Bacterial meningitides emphasis on correct antibiotic in adequate dosage for correct time
b) Measles to prevent measles encephalitis	b) Neonatal infections as above
c) CMV if a safe vaccine can be developed	c) Syphilis and Listeriosis
d) H. influenzae and meningococcal vaccines in special cases only	2. Antiviral chemotherapy
e) Pertussis vaccine	a) Use of Ara-A in treatment of herpes simplex
2. By immunoprophylaxis Neonatal varicella with zoster immune globulin (ZIG)	b) Acyclovir in herpes virus infections in children and neonatal varicella
3. General measures Obstetric care to reduce effect of bacterial infections in newborn Adequate cooking of meat to prevent toxoplasmosis	

Table 4 lists postulated mechanisms whereby mental retardation might be induced by infectious agents. It is an expanded version of a table due to Stephenson (see comment by Stepnenson that follows).

Table 4

Postulated mechanisms* whereby infectious agents induce mental retardation

Main effect	Specific effect	Examples
A. Direct effect of agent on CNS	1. toxic neuronal damage	neuraminidase production, by pneumococcus **
	2. neuronal invasion	herpes simplex encephalitis
	3. barrier disruption (?)	ventriculitis (neonatal meningitis/ spina bifida)
	4. dysfunction	rabies

Table 4 continued

Main effect	Specific effect	Examples
	5. cytolytic changes: vasculitis and endothelial necrosis in small blood vessels	rubella
	probably vascular damage	CMV
	6. virus persistence	rubella panencephalitis late onset deafness in rubella and CMV
B. Metabolic consequences	1. hyperpyrexial cell damage	miscellaneous virus infections of infancy
	2. cerebral swelling from febrile status epilepticus	miscellaneous infectious agents
	3. hypernatraemic	gastroenteritis
C. Indirect CNS damage	1. asphyxic-hypoxic	respiratory arrest in haemophilus epiglottitis; pertussis (?)
	2. ischaemic	hypotension in viral gastroenteritis
	3. CSF obstruction	infected shunt in hydrocephalus (spina bifida etc)
	4. placentitis vasculitis	rubella? CMV CNS lesions in rubella and CMV
	5. reduced mitotic activity	rubella? CMV retardation of growth microcephaly
	6. immunopathological immune complexes	late onset disease in rubella deafness meningo-encephalitis in congenital rubella
D. Sensory deprivation	1. deafness and blindness	congenital rubella
	(1a deafness and receptive dysphasia (?)	congenital rubella and CMV (?))

* more than one may co-exist

O'Toole R.D., Goods, L. and Howe, C.V. (1971). Neuraminidase activity in bacterial meningitis. **J. Clin. Invest., 50, 979

This table is included here but is due to Stephenson - see his comments later

CONCLUSIONS

In numerical terms the impact of infectious diseases as a cause of mental retardation is not very great, but a significant reduction can be made by appropriate preventive measures or by treatment, both general and specific. The importance of bacterial meningitis and CMV infections in this connection should be stressed.

The main emphasis, however, is to concentrate on research into the large category of mental retardation of "unknown aetiology" and into the development of safe vaccine or some alternative procedure to reduce the incidence of mental retardation due to primary CMV infection.

REFERENCES

Baker, C.J. (1979). **Pediatrics in Review, 1**, 5-15

Casals, J. and Clarke, D. (1965). In **Rickettsial Diseases of Man.** 4th Edition. J. B. Lippincott, Philadelphia, 580-582

CDC (1980). **Rubella Surveillance** Jan 1976 - Dec 1978. Centre for Disease Control, Issued May 1980

Ciba Symposium (1973). **Intrauterine Infections, Ciba Foundation Symposium, 10.** Elsevier, Excerpta Medica, North-Holland, Amsterdam

Clark, J. and Casals, J. (1965). In **Rickettsial Diseases of Man.** 4th Edition. J. B. Lippincott, Philadelphia, 583-605

Cooper, L.Z. (1975). In **Infections of the Fetus and Newborn Infant**, Alan R. Liss, New York, 1-21

Desmonts, G., Courvreur, J., Alison, F., Baudelot, J., Gerblause, J. and Lelong, M. (1965). **Rev. Fr. Etud. Clin. Biol. 10**, 952-958

DHSS (1981). **Reports from the Committee on Safety of Medicines and the Joint Committee on Vaccination and Immunisation**, HMSO, London

Dudgeon, J.A. (1967). **Arch. Dis. Child, 42**, 110-125

Dudgeon, J.A. (1976). **Brit. Med. Bull. 32**, 77-83

Eichenwald, H.E. (1962). In **The Prevention of Mental Retardation through the Control of Infectious Disease**, Public Health Service Publication (USA) No. 1692, 1-2

Fleck, D.G. (1973). In **Intrauterine Infections, Ciba Foundation Symposium, 10**, 45-49. Elsevier, Excerpta Medica, North-Holland, Amsterdam

Gamsu, H. (1973). In **Intrauterine Infections, Ciba Foundation Symposium, 10**, 135-146. Elsevier, Excerpta Medica, North-Holland, Amsterdam

Gibbs, F.A. (1962). In **The Prevention of Mental Retardation through Control of Infectious Disease.** Public Health Service Publication (USA) No. 1692, 143-165

Hanshaw, J.B., and Dudgeon, J.A. (1978). **Viral Infections of the Fetus and Newborn.** First edition. W.B. Saunders, Philadelphia

McCracken, G.H. (1981). **Pediatric Infectious Disease.** Fegin and Cherry (Eds.). W.B. Saunders, Philadelphia, 747-756

Miller, D.L., Ross, E.M., Alderslade, R., Bellman, M.H. and Rawson, N.S.B. (1981). **Brit. Med. J., 282**, 195

Nahmias, A.J., Josey, W.E., Naib, Z.M., Freeman, M.G., Fernandez, R.J. and Wheeler, J.H. (1971). **Am. J. Obstet. Gynecol. 110**, 825-837

Swan, C., Tostevin, A.L. and Black, G.H.B. (1946). **Med. J. Aust., 2**, 889

Townsend, J.J., Baringer, J.R., Walinsky, J.A., Oshiro, A.L.A. and Cremer, N.E. (1975) **New Engl. J. Med., 292**, 990-993

Weil, M.L., Habastim, H.H., Cremer, N.E., Oshiro, L.S., Lennette, E.H. and Carney, L. (1975). **New Engl. J. Med. 292**, 994-998

Whitley, R.A., Nahmias, A.J., Visintine, A.M., Fleming, C.L. and Alfard, C.A. (1980a). **Pediatrics, 66**, 489-494

Whitley, R.A., Nahmias, A.J., Soong, S.J., Galasso, G.S., Fleming, C.L. and Alfard, C.A. (1980b). **Pediatrics, 66**, 495-501

Yow, M.D. (1975). In **Infections of Fetus and Newborn Infant**, Alan R. Liss, New York. 159-166

COMMENTARY

B. E. Cohen

Prenatal cytomegalovirus infection

One of the problems here is that these infants are usually asymptomatic at birth (Saigal *et al*., 1982) and as the maternal infection is also asymptomatic there is no way of knowing the infant is infected unless routine examination of the urine is carried out to look for the virus. The first clue might be the developmental retardation or hearing defect and at that time we would hopefully find complement-fixing antibodies in the serum (if sought). The urine might or might not still be excreting the virus. Thus in the absence of a routine screening programme we should maintain a high index of suspicion in all cases of developmental delay especially with a concomitant hearing defect. This has even been reported in twins infected prenatally.

As Dudgeon states he could not possibly mention all the possible virus prenatal infections that have been suspected. There is however an interesting relation to prenatal infection with hepatitis virus and Down's syndrome mentioned by Stoller and his colleagues as early as 1966 (Collman *et al*., 1966). Thus an epidemic of Down's syndrome was reported following contact with infectious hepatitis in the three months prior to conception. Chromosome and chromatid breakages have been found in the peripheral leucocytes in acute hepatitis. Epidemiological studies in Australia have shown a correlation between the incidence of Down's syndrome in certain specific geographical locations clustering in poor socio-economic areas with a high incidence of infectious hepatitis, together with a high incidence of reported cases of Down's syndrome 9-12 months later, i.e. contact in the three months prior to conception. Attempts to duplicate these findings have not been very successful. These studies were reported before virus isolation was possible and have not been repeated since. With modern techniques these studies might bear repetition.

Postnatal infections

Bacterial meningitis - In addition to the factors already mentioned stress should also be laid on the route of administration of antibiotics. We must assure an adequate cover with intravenous administration taking into account possible resistant strains from the onset so that a wider cover is used originally until suitable bacteriology is available and then the cover tailored according to bacterial sensitivity. In the newborn, those with ventriculitis particularly may fail to respond to standard intravenous therapy and especially where previous intraventricular shunts have been placed only the intraventricular route will suffice.

One of the problems with bacterial meningitis especially with *H. influenzae* and meningococcal meningitis is what to do about contacts to prevent secondary spread (Committee on Infectious Diseases, 1982). The Committee on Infectious Diseases of the American Pediatric Association state that the risk in children under 4 years is some 500 times that of the general population in household and day-care settings. Considering the various drugs available for prophylaxis in spite of its cost the committee advises the use of Rifampicin for contacts especially where at least two cases of invasive disease were found in the same day-care setting. It is said to reduce the carriage by approximately 95% and thus minimizes the risk of disease.

Herpes simplex - Both neonatal and postnatal, as disseminated infection or encephalitis, has been increasingly recognized as a serious and potentially crippling disease with serious sequelae (Arvin *et al.*, 1982). In view of the availability of effective treatment with Ara-A or Acyclovir where treatment is started early in the course of the disease early diagnosis becomes critical. This is particularly important where there is no mucocutaneous lesion to suggest the aetiology. Lethargy and signs suggestive of sepsis with progressive signs of hepatitis, pneumonia, seizures generalized or unilateral and resistant to anticonvulsant therapy and thrombocytopenia may suggest the diagnosis. Attempts at establishing the diagnosis include lumbar puncture, EEG, CT scan of brain, oropharyngeal blood and CSF cultures for virus serological demonstration of neutralizing antibodies and even brain biopsy for virus identification and culture have been suggested. Maternal examination and genital cultures may help the diagnosis.

References

Arvin, A.M., Yeager, A.S., Bruhn, F.W. and Grossman, M. (1982). Neonatal herpes simplex infection in the absence of mucocutaneous lesions, **Journal of Pediatrics, 100(5)**, 715-721

Collman, R.D., Krupinski, J. and Stoller, D. (1966). Incidence of infectious hepatitis compared with the incidence of children with Down's syndrome born nine months later to younger and older mothers, **Journal Mental Deficiency Research, 10** 266

Committee on Infectious Diseases (1982). Red Book Update. **Pediatrics, 70(5)**, 819-822

Saigal, S., Eisele, W.A. and Cherneskey, M.A. (1982). Congenital cytomegalovirus infection in a pair of dizygotic twins. **American Journal Dis. Child., 136(12)**, 1094-1095

J. Craske

Dudgeon has given his review the right emphasis in pointing out that the importance of infectious agents as causes of mental retardation is that the techniques for the diagnosis, treatment and prevention of infectious disease are more readily available than similar methods for other causes of mental handicap. This makes it essential to establish causal relationships between infectious agents and the subsequent development of mental handicap in an affected patient on a sound scientific basis. In Table 2 of his article, a fifth criterion of establishing such a causal relationship would be: The demonstration that preventive measures, such as the immunization of young women with rubella vaccine, are effective in reducing the associated mental retardation.

Classification of the infective causes of mental retardation

This should also reflect the different mechanisms by which infectious agents establish themselves in their human host. Table 1 should be reclassified under the headings:

Congenital (intrauterine) infection. The causes in this category are the same as those listed under perinatal in Table 1.

Perinatal infections. This includes infections acquired by the infant from the onset of parturition until 7 days postnatal. Agents included under this heading are those given under the same heading in Table 1, with the addition of cytomegalovirus (CMV).

Postnatal. The criteria and causes are the same as in Table 1.

The use of the term prenatal for infections acquired up to the 28th week of gestation in my view makes an artificial division between periods in pregnancy where intrauterine infection can occur. Although developmental abnormalities in the infant due to congenital rubella are usually associated with a primary maternal infection in the first trimester of pregnancy, Cradock-Watson *et al.* (1980) have recently shown that intrauterine infection with rubella virus can occur at any stage of pregnancy associated with a primary infection in the mother, whereas developmental abnormalities were only observed after infections up to 18 weeks' gestation. Intrauterine infection with CMV can also occur as a result of maternal infection at any stage of pregnancy (Griffiths, 1981). The precise period of maximum risk for developmental abnormalities is not known, as most maternal infections in pregnancy with CMV are symptomless. The evidence from prospective studies suggests that the first trimester is the period of most risk, but that developmental abnormalities can occur as a result of a primary CMV infection in the mother at any stage of pregnancy. Further information on this question is urgently needed.

Developmental abnormalities associated with recurrent CMV infection in pregnancy

The statement that the fetus can contract an infection with CMV due to reactivation of latent infection in the mother but no fetal damage has resulted as a result of pregnancy is no longer true. Prospective studies under way in the UK (see commentary by Peckham on Dudgeon's paper) have already identified children with developmental abnormalities due to congenital CMV infection whose mothers had CMV antibodies in their serum before conception. It is important to establish the relative risk of abnormalities occurring as a result of recurrent CMV infection in pregnancy compared with that in primary infections, as attempts to develop a vaccine for CMV will be jeopardized if the risk after recurrent CMV infection in pregnancy is significant.

Perinatal infection due to CMV

The distinction between intrauterine and perinatal infection with CMV is important when considering the risk of developmental abnormalities from the two modes of infection. Perinatal infection of the infant usually occurs as the result of contamination from the cervix during passage of the child down the birth canal. This is usually due to reactivation of latent CMV infection in the cervix associated with pregnancy. The child acquires a symptomless infection, but no developmental abnormalities have been associated with this mode of infection, in contrast to congenital infection. Perinatal CMV infection can also be acquired from breast milk.

Congenital and perinatal infection due to herpes simplex virus (HSV)

The evidence concerning the risk of mental retardation due to both modes of infection with HSV has come mainly from the USA and is mainly associated with the increased prevalence of genital infection. While there has undoubtedly been an increase in genital HSV infections in the last few years in the UK, I only know one child who was identified as suffering from neonatal HSV infection with a serious outcome in the South Manchester area in the past six years. Prospective studies are therefore needed to establish the incidence of this infection.

References

Cradock-Watson, J.E., Ridehalgh, M.K.S., Anderson, M.J., Pattison, J.R. and Kangro, H.O. (1980), **J. Hyg.**, Camb., **85**, 381-91

Griffiths, P. (1981). **Hospital Update**, January, 35-42

C. S. Peckham

I agree with Dudgeon's overall conclusion that in numerical terms the contribution that infections make to the cause of mental retardation is not great but they are of particular importance because a significant reduction can be made by appropriate preventive measures and treatment.

I should like to make a few suggestions and to expand some of the ideas presented. As Dudgeon states, "it is important to establish with certainty that a particular case of mental retardation is the direct result of an infectious disease rather than to label it as such on insufficient evidence". In view of this it is important to define the term "mental retardation" and to separate the severe and milder forms. Mild mental retardation and educational backwardness are frequently associated with social and environmental disadvantage and it is often difficult to establish whether the environmental disadvantage or the infection is the cause of mental retardation. This highlights the need for comparing children with congenital infections (such as CMV) with carefully selected controls. Only then is it possible to establish whether the infection is the likely cause of backwardness rather than the type of child who is more at risk of contracting infection.

The phenomenon of deterioration or delayed manifestation of physical or mental impairment following initial exposure to infection is an important one which could have been expanded.

Cytomegalovirus

I shall concentrate on the congenital CMV section and expand it because the paper's overall conclusion is that this is a major cause of mental retardation. Although earlier studies suggested that 1-2% of all pregnant women in London, only half of whom would be seronegative, contract primary CMV infection, more recently lower rates have been reported (Griffiths *et al.*, 1980; Grant *et al.*, 1981). Rates in the UK are lower than those reported in the United States and this emphasizes the importance of not extrapolating from one population to another. There are also marked differences in the incidence of congenital infection in different parts of the world.

With regard to the statement that there is "clear evidence that if maternal infection is acquired early in pregnancy the risk that the fetus may be infected is high", I am unaware of data to support this. In fact recent studies suggest that maternal infection in late pregnancy may result in higher congenital infection rates.

Dudgeon has used the data from a study carried out in Manchester to calculate the amount of handicap in the population which is due to congenital CMV. The prospective study did not include a representative sample of births in that 48% of the babies screened were in Special Care Baby Units (SCBUs). 9233 babies were screened and the overall rate of congenital infection was four per 1000 births. However, the rate of infection was 1.7 per 1000 in "normal" babies and 5.5 per 1000 among SCBU babies. As 9% of total births in Manchester receive special care the overall expected rate of congenital CMV in Manchester would be 2.4 per 1000. It is not surprising therefore that only 60% of the infected babies followed up in this prospective study were asymptomatic neonates. This might well reflect the high proportion already receiving special care.

The proportion of babies with congenital CMV who are normal at birth is certainly higher than 60% and I would agree with Dudgeon's quoted rate of 90%. In the remaining 10% of infants who have clinical manifestations of congenital CMV at birth there is a high risk of death or subsequent handicap. However, in congenitally infected infants who are asymptomatic at birth or who show no neurological problems, mental retardation is not common. I will be the devil's advocate and challenge the statement that "many are mentally retarded without associated defects other than deafness".

The risk of handicap quoted by Dudgeon is too high because it is again based on the Manchester study. In this study the 37 babies identified in the prospective study are included together with the 43 referred on clinical grounds and the combined group cannot be used for calculating risk.

There have been four major prospective studies following up congenitally infected CMV infants. Kumar _et al._ (1973) in a follow-up study of 15 congenitally infected infants found that when a seriously handicapped child was excluded the mean IQ of cases and controls was not significantly different.

Reynolds _et al._ (1974) found that the mean IQ score of 18 children with congenital CMV tested at an average of 38 months was not significantly different from the controls although there was a trend towards lower intelligence in infants with CMV infection compared with matched controls. Hanshaw _et al._ (1976) studied 44 congenitally infected children and found significantly lower IQ scores and a higher percentage of school failures in children with CMV infection than in matched controls or random controls. School failure was predicted in 16 of the 44 infected children and this was based on an IQ of <90 in 13. Of the remaining four children, one had a profound hearing loss but normal IQ and two with normal IQs were hyperactive and distractable. There were no school failures among congenitally infected infants from social classes I, II and III. This highlights the need for carefully matched controls when looking for subtle differences in intellectual development. Mental retardation is not synonymous with educational failure.

Recently Saigal _et al._ (1982) tested 47 children with congenital CMV infection and matched control subjects at three and five years of age. They found no significant differences in mean IQ scores, nor was there any tendency for either group to be in the lower or higher range of IQ scores. In this study the majority of infants were asymptomatic.

The screening method used to identify congenitally infected infants in these various studies may have influenced the frequency of neurological and perceptual problems. Recent evidence suggests that when asymptomatic newborns are identified by elevated cord blood IgM they may have a more severe form of congenital CMV and some milder cases may be missed. For example, this method was used by Reynolds et al. (1974) and by Hanshaw et al. (1976) to identify children with congenital CMV. Another factor to consider is the type of population screened. In these two studies the populations screened were compiled largely of low income groups which may have contributed to the poorer outcome.

In conclusion, symptomatic neonates have a high risk of subsequent handicap but when the infection is asymptomatic the risk of mental handicap is likely to be low. Apart from the paper by Hanshaw and his colleagues (1976), it has not been demonstrated conclusively that congenital CMV causes depression of IQ without other evidence of CNS disease such as microcephaly or cerebral palsy. This point is important when establishing the overall numerical importance of congenital CMV as a cause of mental handicap.

The issue of reactivation of latent infection or reinfection with a new strain during pregnancy must be discussed more fully. Recurrent maternal infection can result in congenital infection and cases of damage in these children have been reported (Ahlfors et al., 1981). Stagno et al. (1982) reported that five of 33 congenitally infected infants born after primary maternal infection had apparent disease in the newborn period whereas none of the 27 congenitally infected infants born to mothers with secondary infection had symptoms. The follow-up was too short, however, to determine whether there were also differences in the risk of delayed sequelae in the two groups. This requires further study.

Finally, the risk to the pregnant woman of coming into contact with an infant with congenital CMV should be considered. CMV can be transmitted by person-to-person spread and it is known that infants who acquire infection from their mother either in utero or in the first month of life may shed the virus for years and infect susceptible adults. Because of this, people working with young children are thought to be potentially at greater risk from CMVs than other individuals. Few data exist to confirm or refute this concern, but there appears to be little difference in the proportion of nurses with evidence of previous CMV infection compared with women of similar backgrounds in the community. In addition several studies have failed to show any differences in sero-conversion rates between nurses and controls. Unlike rubella, available data suggest that relatively close contact is necessary for transmission and studies in progress should help to provide information on the degree of risk.

Rubella

250-300 born per year but the majority would not be mentally retarded. As Dudgeon stressed, mental retardation alone does not appear to be a complication of congenital rubella.

Toxoplasmosis

Early maternal infection results in a lower rate of congenital infection than does late infection, but if early infection occurs the risk of damage is far greater. Again, the problems of asymptomatic infection may be important.

Herpes simplex

The exact risk of perinatal HSV infection has not been determined accurately and in its clinically recognizable form it appears to be an extremely rare disease in the United Kingdom. In a current enquiry, only eight cases have been observed by neonatologists in England during the past two years (Dinwiddie, 1982) and 66 cases were reported by the PHLS to the Communicable Disease Surveillance Centre in the seven years prior to 1980. More research is required in order to determine whether infection is being missed. How important is asymptomatic infection? How often does it occur and what are the long-term sequelae? We have very little epidemiological data and no information about risk. With the development of antiviral drugs and treatment, this would be a fruitful area to research.

References

Ahlfors, K., Harris, S., Ivarsson, S. and Svanberg, L. (1981). Secondary maternal cytomegalovirus infection causing symptomatic congenital infection. **The New England Journal of Medicine, 305**, 284

Dinwiddie, R. (1982). Personal communication

Grant, S., Eomond, E. and Syme, J. (1981). A prospective study of cytomegalovirus infection in pregnancy I: Laboratory evidence of congenital infection following maternal primary and reactivated infection. **Journal of Infection, 3**, 24-31

Griffiths, P.D., Campell-Benzie, A. and Meath, R.B. (1980). A prospective study of primary cytomegalovirus infection in pregnant women. **British Journal of Obstetrics and Gynaecology, 87**, 308-314

Hanshaw, J.B., Scheiner, A.P., Moxley, A.W., Gaev, L., Abel, V. and Scheiner, B. (1976). School failure and deafness after "silent" congenital cytomegalovirus infection. **The New England Journal of Medicine, 295**, 468-470

Kumar, M.L., Nankervis, G.A. and Gold, E. (1973). Inapparent congenital cytomegalovirus infection. A follow-up study. **The New England Journal of Medicine, 228**, 1370-1372

Reynolds, D.W., Stagno, S., Stubbs, K.G., et al. (1974). Inapparent congenital cytomegalovirus infection with elevated cord IgM levels. Causal relation with auditory and mental deficiency. **The New England Journal of Medicine, 290**, 291-396

Saigal, S., Lunyk, O., Larke, R.P.B. and Chernesky, M.A. (1982). The outcome in children with congenital cytomegalovirus infection. **American Journal Dis. Child., 136**, 896-901

Stagno, S., Pass, R.F., Oworsky, M.E., et al. (1982). Congenital cytomegalovirus infection. The relative importance of primary and recurrent maternal infection. **New England Journal of Medicine, 306**, 945-949

R. O. Robinson

I would first like to pick up some specific points in the text and then go on to suggest ways in which this contribution can be developed.

1. The aetiology of many cases of mental retardation as presented to the paediatric neurologist cannot be determined. However, of cases presenting in the community an aetiology can be assigned with confidence to the great majority (Fryers and Mackay, 1979).

2. Tuberculous meningitis must be included under postnatal infections, and under viruses rubella, measles and JC virus should all be included. In terms of worldwide infectious causes of mental handicaps, malaria, trypanosomiasis, cysticercosis and cryptococcosis are all very high contenders.

3. There is evidence that morbidity and mortality in meningitis are, in addition to the variables mentioned, also related to the dose of the organism.

4. It may be true that in this country herpes simplex is the commonest known cause of necrotizing encephalitis. In the majority of cases of acute necrotizing encephalitis, of course the cause is unknown.

5. Measles virus can cause encephalitis in four ways. Acute post-infectious encephalomyelitis and acute non-inflammatory encephalopathy occur at the time of the eruption. Acute primary encephalitis of the delayed type occurs 2-3 months after an attack of measles in those who are immuno-suppressed. SSPE, which appears to relate to a lack of M protein in the virus, can occur up to several years later.

6. Immunosuppression is associated with viral infection causing mental handicap. Echo virus and agammaglobulinaemia and progressive multifocal leucoencephalopathy due to the JC virus are two such examples.

Ways in which this topic can be developed include the following:

1. <u>What is the mechanism of handicap in acute infections?</u>

(a) Direct neuronal invasion.
(b) Arterial occlusion (rare) and venous thrombosis (more commonly).
(c) Hydrocephalus due to interference with CSF circulation or absorption.
(d) Raised intracranial pressure due to either acute swelling of the infected brain or venous thrombosis or subdural collections.
(e) Seizure disorders which may be damaging in themselves.
(f) Effects of treatment causing handicap: ototoxicity due to aminoglycosides or cerebral oedema following over-enthusiastic fluid therapy which can of course be exacerbated by failure to recognize inappropriate ADH secretion.

2. <u>What is the relationship between mental handicap and infection?</u>

Infection may cause bilateral hemisphere damage as described above. It may also interfere with perceptual processes either centrally or peripherally, particularly those concerned with vision and hearing. The relationship may be less direct. Thus, for example, there is a complex and two-way relationship between infection and malnutrition leading to a diminished IQ which will be commented on in more detail elsewhere in this volume. Infection elsewhere indirectly affecting the central nervous system may, of course, secondarily cause central nervous system damage; thus, dehydration secondary to gastroenteritis is associated with cerebral venous thrombosis. Hypernatraemic dehydration (the variety of electrolyte imbalance found in about 10% of cases of gastroenteritis in developing countries) is closely associated with brain damage. Sickling crises frequently precipitated by infection causing cerebral venous thrombosis is yet another example.

3. <u>What is the relationship between infection and sporadic handicapping events in childhood?</u>

The relationship between febrile convulsions and subsequent handicap is complex but needs to be discussed. The contribution of virus infections to Reye's syndrome, West's syndrome, Lennox-Gastaut syndrome and acute necrotizing encephalitis is unknown but may play a part. Speculatively, infections may determine whether individuals predisposed to mental handicap actually suffer from it or not. Thus of monozygous twins with tuberous sclerosis one may be mentally handicapped with seizures and the other may be mentally normal and seizure free. Another extremely important relationship which needs exploring under this heading is the contribution of infections which cause irritability either in the child or in the parent, leading to the handicapping sequelae of non-accidental injury.

4. What are the mechanisms of handicap in delayed infection?

What are the immunological mechanisms underlying post-infectious encephalitis? The mechanism for SSPE is becoming clearer and has been mentioned. Slow virus infections of which Creutzfeldt-Jacob disease and kuru are the most notorious examples may yet be only the tip of the iceberg. The author mentioned progressive rubella panencephalitis. Persistent cytomegalovirus infections may account for the progressive sensori-neural deafness of this condition. Recrudescence of congenital toxoplasmosis is well documented. Spongy degenerations in childhood which in some respects resemble these conditions are in a proportion of cases associated with metabolic disorders but in a large majority the cause is quite unknown.

Reference

Fryers, T. and Mackay, R.I. (1979). The epidemiology of severe mental handicap. **Early Human Development, 3**, 277

J. B. P. Stephenson

Dudgeon has put this topic well into perspective. The varied nature of the infections implicated prompts me to highlight only selected aspects. To do this I have introduced a further table listing postulated mechanisms whereby mental retardation might be induced, which is now included in Dudgeon's paper in an expanded form as Table 4. Dudgeon has concentrated on the first mechanism, but others are likely to be numerically important and preventable. For example, the mechanism of prolonged convulsions with fever (febrile status epilepticus) induced by various viruses and bacteria including shigella and the pneumococcus without meningitis (pneumococcal bacteraemia). The pneumococcus is an example of an agent which can retard by multiple mechanisms, and I would emphasize the severity of the handicapping sequelae of pneumococcal meningitis (Laxter and Marks, 1977) (confirmed by an unpublished study in Glasgow, paper read at BPNA 1982). How much retardation is produced by infection in the spina bifida/hydrocephalus complex deserves investigation: in Table 4, mechanisms include CSF-brain barrier disruption by ventriculitis and acutely increased intracranial pressure when a ventricular drainage system becomes infected.

I am not happy about the first criterion in Table 2, the "consistency of clinical features of retardation and the infective agent". It may be that to implicate an agent as aetiologically important a characteristic clinical illness should be demonstrable (such as is not the case with pertussis immunization, hence my disbelief in it as a cause of mental retardation), but one cannot go on from this to say that the mental retardation should have consistent features. Postnatal causes, at any rate, tend to induce focal or multifocal CNS lesions, whose retarding effect on development will vary with age at insult, sex, site and location.

Dudgeon rightly emphasizes the importance of CMV. He might profitably expand further. How precisely should we be diagnosing congenital CMV? How clear is the prognostic optimism for non-recurrence? How should the congenitally infected and still excreting infant be handled by the home teachers, teachers of the deaf and other helpers who tend to be both female and liable to become pregnant? And for the neurologists rather than the virologists, how does one evaluate precisely the degree of receptive dysphasia in the young child with severe deafness? And what is the significance of the microcephaly - what intellectual functions are most at risk in the usual CMV baby?

Prevention is of course our prime concern. To Table 3 I would add pneumococcus and pertussis immunization as likely to reduce mental handicap. Measles immunization will prevent most SSPE as well as the more common encephalitis. Possibly more important, better paediatric neurological intensive care organization might reduce some of the effects of the postnatal acute encephalopathies in which infectious agents play a direct or indirect role.

I am concerned that the contra-indications to pertussis immunization recommended by the DHSS in this country are depriving a high proportion of the neurologically handicapped from protection against this unpleasant and seizure-provoking disease. Prensky (1974) has pointed out the lack of evidence that such children are at increased risk for complications from such immunization, and recent studies (Butler and Goulding, 1983) support this. It is unfortunate that legal implications make it difficult to implement this policy, but I do not see why parents who beg for pertussis immunization for their handicapped baby should be denied it. Evidence derived from the National Childhood Encephalopathy Study (Bellman, 1983) even justifies the selective immunization of babies identified as having tuberose sclerosis.

References

Bellman, M.H., Ross, E.McD. and Miller, D. (1983). Infantile spasms and pertussis immunisation. **Lancet** (in press)

Butler, N. and Goulding, J. (1983). Personal communication

Laxter, R.M. and Marks, M.I. (1977). Pneumococcal meningitis in children. **Am. J. Dis. Child., 131**, 850-853

Prensky, A.L. (1974). Pertussis vaccination. **Developmental Medicine in Child Neurology, 16**, 539-543

R. J. Robinson

There are two possible reasons for observing the official contraindications to pertussis immunization. The first is a genuine medical reason - that children in whom these contraindications are present may be at higher risk for developing neurological complications of immunization (Robinson, 1981). However, there is disagreement as to whether this is actually so, and some have strongly disputed it. The Dudgeon and Meade reports (Goldberg and Badenoch, 1981) appeared to provide circumstantial evidence that children with contraindications were at increased risk - thus among the children with serious neurological disorders thought likely by the Meade panel to be caused by pertussis immunization, 49% had at least one contraindication to vaccination. However, this was in no sense a controlled trial, and the incidence of contraindications in the population at large was not examined. The National Childhood Encephalopathy Study (Goldberg and Badenoch, 1981) did not study the influence of contraindications on the risk of neurological disorder following immunization.

The second possible reason for observing the contra-indications is a medico-legal or defensive one - the fear that the child with these contraindications must be at somewhat more than average risk of developing a neurological disorder irrespective of immunization, and that if such a disorder by chance becomes apparent soon after immunization, the immunization (and in turn the doctor) will be blamed. This kind of defensive attitude can be regarded as abandoning our proper responsibilities to children. However, those who adopt it may not just be defending their own skins - they may be defending the immunization programme. We do not want it to fall into public disrepute again because a group of children <u>appear</u> to have been damaged by immunization - even if this is really just coincidence.

The whole unhappy saga of the whooping cough immunization controversy has been at least in part the result of extreme and polarized attitudes being taken by the defenders and the opponents of pertussis immunization. We do not want to see the same happen now in relation to the contraindications. I believe we should work towards a closer definition of how the present contraindications should be interpreted, so that children are not unnecessarily excluded from protection, and a continuing review of the contraindications to see if any parts of them can be dropped. We should aim for a consensus among all doctors concerned with paediatrics and child health, so that parents do not receive widely conflicting advice. Individual doctors will not help the cause of immunization by throwing all the contraindications overboard in an excess of scientific rationalism.

If we keep the contraindications, or some of them, how should we protect the children who have them against pertussis? We should do it by establishing as high a level of herd immunity as we can, by achieving very high rates of immunization among the children for whom it is safe. This requires public as well as medical confidence in the immunization programme and the way it is administered - and this will not be achieved if the doctors themselves are putting polarized views in public debate, nor if they are giving conflicting advice to individual parents.

References

Goldberg, A. and Badenoch, J. (1981). **Whooping Cough.** Reports from the Committee on Safety of Medicines and the Joint Committee on Vaccination and Immunization. HMSO, London

Robinson, R.J. (1981). The whooping cough immunization controversy. **Archives of Disease in Childhood, 56,** 577-580

E.D. Alberman, J. Carr and M. Holland

Effectiveness of immunization programmes in prevention of rubella damage to infants

Take-up of rubella immunization amongst schoolgirls varies widely. Some areas report a 95% take-up, others fall as low as 50%. Reasons for failure in the school programmes may be due to the following.

1. Administrative factors. For example, immunization may be offered only once in a term and some girls will miss out. Of even greater concern is the poor implementation of the post-partum programme. There is evidence that 10-12% of women are found to be sero-negative at antenatal testing and yet are not immunized following delivery. Some women have gone through subsequent pregnancies without protection and have subsequently given birth to infants with the congenital rubella syndrome.

2. Parents. Parents may believe that their daughters have acquired natural immunity but this will not be true of 15-20% of girls.

3. Inappropriate presentation of the programme. As currently implemented, it relies on a punishment paradigm and furthermore one which it is intended to control: "Accept immunization as you may, in several years time, have a deaf, retarded autistic child". This may have the counter-effect of poor take-up by the girls themselves. If instead a suitable positive consequence was offered to be given immediately following immunization, take-up might increase immediately.

The responsibility for failure of this programme must be borne both by the professionals and the public. Measures such as those suggested above can and should be taken to reduce this state of affairs.

J. A. Dudgeon

I have stressed the need for establishing causal relationships as a prerequisite for introducing preventive measures. As an example, I have quoted the difficulties in proving a causal relationship between pertussis or triple vaccine and brain damage. Additional criteria for Table 2 proposed by Craske would be useful in showing that specific preventive measures were effective (i.e. rubella vaccine). They would not provide proof of causation.

Table 1 should be suitably amended as suggested by Craske and Robinson. The term prenatal or intrauterine is preferred to congenital, as in some cases of late onset disease in congenital rubella occurring late in childhood, the damage to the fetus occurred as the result of a prenatal insult at a much earlier stage before birth.

Cytomegalovirus

Peckham correctly pointed out that the risk to the fetus in CMV occurred as the result of infection at any stage in pregnancy. The original paper was suitably amended. As far as symptomatic infection in the newborn is concerned, the risk of damage and subsequent handicap is high, whereas more recent studies than those of Hanshaw *et al.* (1976) and Saigal *et al.* (1982) would suggest that asymptomatic CMV infection does not constitute a hazard in the form of mental retardation although there was an increased risk of late onset development of sensorineural deafness. As a crude estimate of 4 cases per 1000 births in the UK, the number of infants born with congenital infection would be about 2600 per annum and if between 10 and 15% were damaged, this would mean about 260-320 handicapped infants born per annum. These figures are very similar to those quoted by Hagberg from Sweden.

What are the prospects of prevention of congenital CMV by immunization? There are a number of difficulties and imponderables here which I will endeavour to unravel. When one compares the theoretical problems between prevention of congenital CMV with congenital rubella some of these "difficulties" become more apparent. With rubella the main risk to the fetus is primary maternal infection - i.e. fetal damage from reinfection is a very remote risk indeed. Reactivation with rubella does not occur and there is no problem of antigenic heterogeneity. Although the proof of rubella vaccine effectiveness has still to be established, and here I would accept the comment made by Craske in his critique in which he refers to the criteria in my Table 2, the signs are encouraging that congenital rubella defects can be prevented by the use of the live attenuated vaccines.

CMV presents different problems. CMV is a DNA virus of the herpes virus group, and latency of infection is a constant feature after primary exposure. We have heard that the main risk of fetal or perinatal damage is due to primary CMV infections, but we have yet to learn how important are reactivation infections. It could be argued that a CMV vaccine either attenuated or killed inactivated would stimulate an immunoresponse, both humoral or cellular, and thereby reduce the risk of primary infection. Would such an immune response, acquired as a result of a CMV vaccine, prevent reactivation as opposed to primary infection? The analogy with herpes simplex infections, where reinfection commonly occurs in the presence of high levels of herpes antibody, suggests that vaccination would only be of benefit in preventing primary infections.

Probably the most important single factor which is holding back research into the prevention of CMV infections is that of safety. The herpes viruses are DNA viruses and under certain circumstances can produce tumours in animals. There is no evidence that they can produce, or have produced, tumours in human beings, but the possibility that the viruses have an oncogenic potential makes vaccine development extremely difficult as there are no tests which one can use to determine this crucial point. Proof of a negative is the most difficult thing to achieve. Faced with the standard procedures of development of either an attenuated vaccine or a killed inactivated CMV vaccine one is again dealing with practical problems (see reviews by Hanshaw and Dudgeon, 1978; Dudgeon, 1973).

As far as the long term is concerned, I think that a solution may be found by the use of genetic engineering recombination techniques whereby part of the CMV viral genome is incorporated into an organism such as *Esch. coli* and a potentially "safer" product results. This has already been done with other viruses and is a prospect for the future.

Rubella

As far as congenital rubella is concerned, it was generally agreed that mental retardation was not a common sole manifestation as in CMV, although a number of such cases had been reported from the New York study. It was emphasized that congenital rubella was a preventable disease and the current problems concerned with the vaccination programme were largely administrative in the UK.

Herpes simplex

No obvious explanation for the difference in the incidence of perinatal infection with herpes simplex infections (HSV) between the USA and UK could be found, but the number of severe disseminated HSV infections in the newborn and young infant was appreciable. The diagnosis of herpes encephalitis is now much easier as a result of new procedures such as EMI scanning, brain biopsy and tests such as culture, immunofluorescence and electron microscopy.

HAV infection in Down's syndrome

The suggestion proposed by Cohen that Down's syndrome might be related to infectious type A (HAV) infection in pregnancy, or even in preconception, was difficult to accept. If studies to settle this issue were considered necessary, then the criteria set out in Table 2 might well be utilized, bearing in mind the inability at present to culture this virus (HAV).

Measles vaccine and SSPE

There is evidence from the USA that the incidence of SSPE is declining as the uptake of measles vaccine increases throughout that country. There is a strong probability that SSPE can be prevented by measles immunization although chance association of SSPE and measles vaccination must be expected for the next few years.

Hepatitis B (HSV) virus infection in hospital staff

There has been a tendency to overreact to the risk of contracting hepatitis B from carriers. Many screening programmes and precautionary measures have been totally unnecessary. The guidelines prepared by hospital Control of Infection Officers should be based on common sense, bearing in mind that the risks of acquiring infection can now be identified.

References

Dudgeon, J.A. (1973). Future developments in intrauterine infections. In **Intrauterine Infections, Ciba Foundation Symposium, 10**, Elsevier, Excerpta Medica, North-Holland, Amsterdam

Hanshaw, J.B. and Dudgeon, J.A. (1978). **Viral Infections of the Fetus and Newborn**, 1st Edn. W.B. Saunders, Philadelphia

Hanshaw, J.B., Scheiner, A.P., Moxley, A.W., Gaev, L., Abel, V. and Scheiner, B. (1976). School failure and deafness after "silent" congenital cytomegalovirus infection. **New Engl. J. Med., 295**, 468-470

Saigal, S., Lunyk, O., Larke, R.P.B. and Chernesky, M.A. (1982). The outcome in children with congenital cytomegalovirus infection. **Am. J. Dis. Child., 136**, 896-901

Chapter 11

The consequences of malnutrition for intellectual development

S.A. Richardson

INTRODUCTION

In the 1960s concern became widespread that malnutrition in infancy caused permanent intellectual impairment or mental retardation. The first major international conference on the subject was held in 1967 (Scrimshaw and Gordon, 1968). Numerous studies have been carried out in the past two decades and there has been a plethora of reviews and conference proceedings (for example, Pan American Health Organization, 1972; Kallen, 1973; Manocha, 1972; Serban, 1975; Brozek, 1979; Winick, 1976; Galler, 1983; Levitsky, 1979; Cravioto *et al.*, 1974; Stein and Kassab, 1970; Greene, 1977). While the reviews largely dealt with the same studies, a remarkable diversity of interpretation of the results was given by the reviewers. For example:

> There is overwhelming evidence that severe malnutrition during the early years of life, especially the first two years, leads to retarded brain growth, permanent reduction in brain size and defective intellectual development. Malnutrition has, therefore, been rightly blamed as one of the main causes of mental retardation. (Manocha, 1972, p. 123)

> Our review of knowledge about the effects of post-natal nutrition on later mental development suggests to us that such effects do exist but that they are not large or easily detected. There are many areas of ambiguity. There is as yet no evidence to support the hypothesis that nutritional deprivation not only retards development but that its effects persist into adulthood and prevents the full realization of potential mental competence. (Stein *et al.*, 1975, p. 32)

In this review the primary focus will be an examination of the conceptual models used, the design of the studies, the results, how they have been interpreted and how warranted are the interpretations. Most of the paper will deal with studies of children. Animal studies and studies of the brain will be dealt with only briefly.

The early studies of the consequences of malnutrition for intellectual development tested children for whom there was evidence of malnutrition in infancy, finding their scores to be lower than the means of national standards for the test (Cabak and Najdanvic, 1965; Monckeberg, 1968). It was pointed out that malnourished children came from low income, socially deprived families and that their social backgrounds could account for their lower scores. A number of studies were then undertaken with the aim of overcoming this objection. The children with evidence of malnutrition in infancy were compared with children who had not been malnourished. These controls were selected by matching with one or more of the characteristics of the malnourished children. Matching variables included age, sex, socio-economic status and attending the same class at schol (Champakam et al., 1968; Stoch and Smythe, 1963, 1976; Chase and Martin, 1970). In some studies siblings who were not malnourished were used for comparisons (Birch et al., 1971; Hansen et al., 1971; Moodie et al., 1980). While this controls for membership in the family, the siblings differ in ordinal position, may differ by sex and many have very different experiences in their upbringing. It is difficult to believe that if one child is malnourished but the sibling is not then nothing else in their background histories was different. If so, why should malnutrition have occurred? The terms "experimental" and "control" were then used for the malnourished and non-malnourished children. Once the two sets of subjects were labelled, it was then tempting to believe that the requirements of an experimental model had been fulfilled: namely, that all factors that might contribute to intellectual development had been held constant by the matching process, the two groups differing only in their history of nutrition. That matching with one or a few general background factors could achieve this requirement seemed a vain hope. These studies generally showed that malnourished children had lower intelligence test scores than their "controls", and the authors used varying degrees of caution in interpreting their results to mean only an association, or to mean that malnutrition was a causal factor.

The conceptual model underlying most of the research was that malnutrition caused damage to the central nervous system which was then reflected in intellectual impairment, and further, that the brain's vulnerability was related to the speed of growth of the brain. In the 1960s, it was suggested that the brain growth spurt in humans extended from the last trimester of pregnancy and through the first nine months of age (Chase et al., 1967; Davison and Dobbing, 1966; Dobbing, 1964). This model, which only takes into account the development of the body, may have led to scant attention being paid to social environmental experiences and their influence on intellectual development. This was despite a growing interest in and separate research into cultural deprivation together with the effects of different levels of stimulation on children.

The focus on early life suggested by the brain growth spurt theory was reinforced by the long-held belief of laymen and scientists, recently challenged by Clarke and Clarke (1976), that "the environment in the early years exerts a disproportionate and irreversible effect on a rapidly growing organism, compared with the potential for later environmental influences". In spite of such challenges, the belief is still strong and contributes to the fear of consequences of malnutrition in early infancy.

Because of the inadequacies of the controls in the studies that have been described, there is an alternative explanation of the results obtained, i.e. that malnutrition is an indicator of a general set of biological and social factors in the history of the children which was disadvantageous for their social and intellectual development. The association between malnutrition and intellectual development could be spurious with malnutrition being unrelated. Alternatively malnutrition could be one of many factors which in combination cause intellectual impairment.

MALNUTRITION AS THE CONSEQUENCE OF DISEASE

In order to disentangle malnutrition from the context in which it is usually found, of poverty, disease and a generally disadvantageous set of conditions for social and intellectual development, some investigators have studied children who have suffered diseases which involve a period of starvation in infancy. This occurs in hypertrophic pyloric stenosis and cystic fibrosis. The diseases are not associated with poverty and social deprivation and the subjects come from Western industrial countries. Children with histories of these diseases were compared with those without. Selection of comparisons included siblings or non-siblings matched on variables such as age, sex and father's level of education. In one study (Ellis and Hill, 1975) comparison was made between a sample of children with cystic fibrosis who were designated malnourished because of poor weight gain in their first year of life and controls who did not show weight loss. Ages at which children were followed up for testing range from two years to adulthood. Results varied from finding no differences between experimental and control subjects to finding differences in auditory memory (Klein et al., 1975), differences only in intelligence test scores for those under five, or non-significant trends in the expected direction (Ellis and Hill, 1975). These studies were imaginative in finding a form of malnutrition separated from extreme poverty and deprivation, but can be criticized for not comparing the type and degree of malnutrition with other studies and for not being able to separate malnutrition from the possible consequences of other aspects of the disease, hospitalization and separation from the family. The various studies suggest that lower performance on some components of intelligence is most apparent the younger the age at which the child is tested.

In the studies reported thus far, scant attention was given to the social and biological histories of the children because it was assumed that this range of factors was controlled by the study design. There are a number of studies, however, which have used a natural history or ecological approach, and these have shed light on the environmental histories of children with malnutrition. This approach does not use nutritional intervention but examines the variability of a wide range of biological and social factors and their interaction during a child's development. Cravioto and his colleagues used this approach. They selected a Mexican village which would have approximately 250 births a year, a considerable range of social conditions and nutritional status, and where the population was stable and willing to co-operate in a longitudinal study. The cohort studied comprised all children born over a twelve-month period in 1966-67. The 300 children in the cohort were followed for over seven years. A record of all children was maintained from birth. Variation in weight gain was related to a series of biosocial factors. Cravioto et al. (1967, p. 81) used the following diagram to illustrate hypothetical interrelations among biosocial factors and low weight gain:

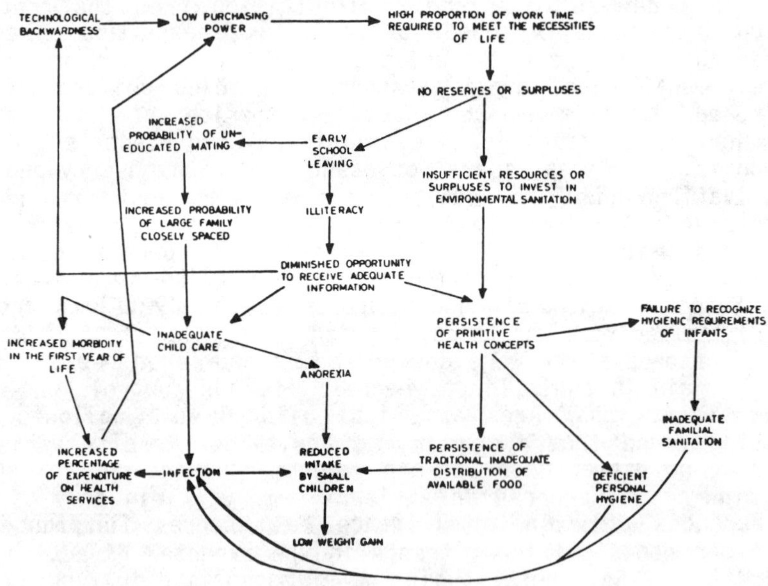

Their longitudinal study has pointed to the importance of the microenvironment surrounding the child, particularly the behaviour of the child's mother and major caretakers in influencing the intellectual development of the child. These conditions in families with a malnourished child were less favourable than in the families where children were not malnourished (Cravioto, 1981). Despite medical efforts at prevention, twenty-two children developed severe clinical malnutrition during the first five years of the study. The study was the first to examine some of the conditions of the children's environments prior to the onset of severe malnutrition. For example, they found the mothers of these children exhibited more passive behaviour towards their children. This included less verbal communication (Cravioto and DeLicardie, 1974). This suggests less favourable conditions for the child's intellectual development prior to the malnutrition.

A somewhat different approach to the examination of biosocial factors associated with malnutrition was used by Richardson and his colleagues. The study was designed to examine the following questions: (1) At school age, are boys malnourished during infancy functioning less well than boys not malnourished during infancy? (2) In addition to experiencing malnutrition, do the index boys experience more disadvantageous environmental conditions for the development of their social and intellectual skills? Seventy-one school aged boys in Jamaica were studied who had been admitted to hospitals with a primary diagnosis of marasmus, kwashiorkor, or marasmic-kwashiorkor. For each malnourished boy a boy was selected who had no history of malnutrition, and who was the classmate nearest in age. For index boys not attending school, the nearest neighbouring boy of the same age was selected. No assumption was made that the "comparison" cases were controls in the experimental sense. The index children had lower IQ and poorer school performance than their comparisons. Having obtained the same association between malnutrition and lower intelligence found in other studies, the environments of the index and comparison children were studied by means of home interviews and observations. From these the following variables were developed (Richardson, 1974):

<u>Caretaker variable</u>

a) upbringing and education
b) reproductive history
c) level of capability
d) contact with media
e) human resources
f) child rearing practices

<u>Economic and housing variables</u>

a) structure and condition of the house
b) home furnishings and appliances
c) crowding

<u>Social and educational experience of the children</u>

a) extent and diversity of social relations
b) intellectual stimulation
c) amount of schooling

Mortality

a) mortality among siblings of study child

For all variables except child rearing practices and extent and diversity of social relations, the index child had less advantageous conditions than comparisons.

A composite measure of social background, malnutrition and height up to the time of follow-up was used in a multiple regression to predict IQ. By far the largest contributor to the prediction was social background. Social background and height were then held constant for index and comparison cases. Under the most favourable conditions of tall stature and advantageous social background there was only a two point difference in WISC IQ between index and comparisons. Under the most unfavourable conditions of short stature and disadvantageous social conditions, the difference was nine points in the WISC (Richardson, 1976). This suggests that the effects of malnutrition may vary depending on the overall social and biological context in which it occurs. Waterlow and Rutishauser (1974) proposed that children who have had marasmus are more likely to show later impairment of intellect than those who had kwashiorkor. Using measures of these two forms of malnutrition suggested by Waterlow and Rutishauser, no support was found in the Richardson et al. study that marasmus and kwashiorkor caused different degrees of intellectual impairment (Richardson et al., 1978).

Graves (1978, 1979) in South East Asia studied the potential impact of malnutrition on infants' capacity to explore their environment, and to form trusting secure ties with others, especially the mothers. Graves also studied the maternal readiness to initiate interaction with or respond to the child's signals, or to interact with the child through looking, smiling, talking and giving toys. She examined the mother-infant interactions of well and undernourished children. She characterized an undernourished infant as rather inactive, seldom leaving his or her mother's lap to explore.

Chavez and Martinez (1982) also conducted longitudinal observational studies of malnourished infants in a village in Mexico. They summarize their experience in the following hypothetical model:

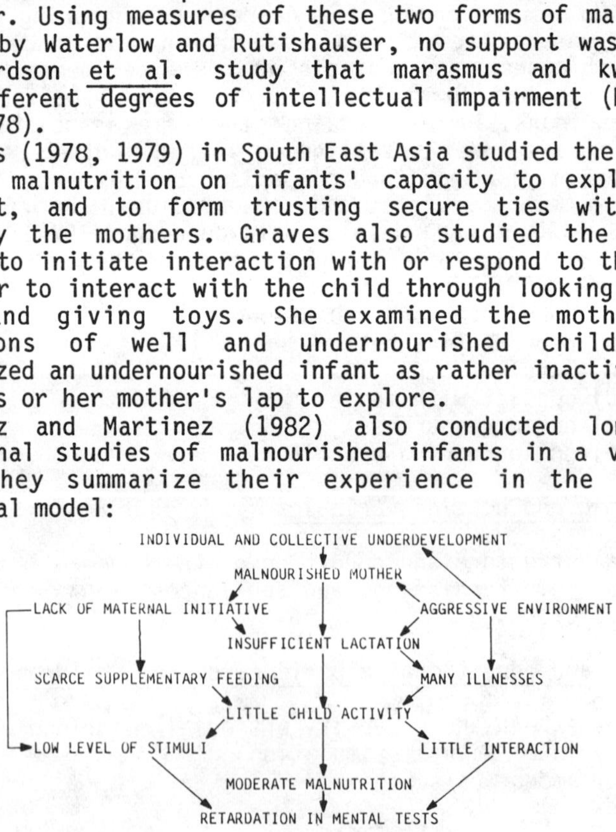

In this scheme, nutrition is the axis of the problem. It acts through poor maternal nutrition, first through the placenta and then through the breast; this does not favour infant development and results in a passive, undemanding, child. If in addition mother does not give the child other foods and that the child suffers many illnesses, then malnutrition becomes even more serious. This directly affects brain capacity, which indirectly leads to poor relations to the environment and deficient stimuli. These latter factors are the most important; they are the consequence of malnutrition and not directly of poverty. The environment near the child is very limited: the mother and what she gives the child - her breast, other foods, stimuli, contamination. This small environment is neither static nor unidirectional; the child and its condition are very much involved in the dynamics of malnutrition.

Characteristic of the behaviour of the undernourished child is his timidness when confronting different environmental stimuli, his passive attitude, and his markedly slow responses (p. 137).

The work of Chavez and Martinez suggests that malnourished children may be intellectually impaired not only by central nervous system damage and being raised in an environment that is disadvantageous for intellectual development, but also by the direct consequences of malnutrition causing alterations in behaviour which further limit the child's opportunity for intellectual development.

INTERVENTION STUDIES

There are studies on the effects of providing supplementary feeding of pregnant women and children and some of these studies have also provided programmes of intellectual stimulation of the children (Brozek *et al.*, 1977; Chavez and Martinez, 1982; Hicks *et al.*, 1982; Vuori *et al.*, 1979; Waber *et al.*, 1981; Klein *et al.*, 1975; Klein, 1979). The use of a nutritional supplement is the alternative approach to inducing malnutrition in children, which, while the method of choice in animal studies, is clearly unacceptable on ethical and moral grounds for children. There are many serious practical and ethical problems in designing and executing food intervention studies which meet the requirements of a controlled scientific study and which seek to use a food supplement to produce a study group who are not malnourished and a control group who are. These problems include the following:

1. The population for study should have a high incidence of malnutrition and this must be predicted before the study begins. If it turns out that severe marasmus and kwashiorkor become widespread, the investigators face a serious ethical dilemma if they do not treat or obtain treatment for the control group. In fact no intervention studies report this situation in the control group. More often it is presumed, without giving evidence, that

subclinical malnutrition, protein calorie malnutrition, or protein energy malnutrition is present. These forms of malnutrition are generally defined by anthropometric measures of weight for age. It is a lesser ethical dilemma not to intervene in the control group if the children are not sick, the only evidence being that the children are somewhat smaller than middle class US children. If the experimental group of children who receive food supplementation are to be considered not malnourished, evidence of this should be presented to show they are significantly different on anthropometric measures from the control group and that this difference is not a consequence of other variables which differentiate the two groups. The measures of nutrition would be more direct evidence than the inferences made about nutrition from supplementation of food.

2. In a clinical trial, the experimental and control groups should be randomly selected from those who volunteer to participate in the trial and who give informed consent. Such an arrangement is not practicable if malnutrition is widespread. Alternative procedures have been used such as providing food supplements for all mothers who wish to cooperate, or comparing two communities where a supplement is provided in one of the communities. In the former case, the study group is formed of volunteer mothers who are likely to be more generally capable mothers and may provide more favourable conditions for the intellectual development of their children. In the latter case it is difficult to find two communities that are similar in all respects.

3. Distribution of a food supplement is no guarantee that the food will be given to the study child in the family or that it will be used as a supplement and not a substitute food. The amount of supervision necessary to ensure the food is used as a supplement requires an encroachment on the daily life of the family by the investigators that may result in changes in the family and study child over and above the food alone.

4. Food is so intimately tied to customs, practices, habits and beliefs that a change in food is likely to lead to chains of reaction that affect other aspects of living.

5. If some random procedure of food supplementation is used within a community, how can the passing on of some of the supplement from study to control population be avoided?

6. Intervention studies are necessarily longitudinal, and as the children get older and increase their initiative in seeking and finding food, it becomes increasingly difficult to monitor the food supplementation.

7. If a food supplement is provided in a community, it may, over time, change the ecology of food in the community. The community may become dependent on the supplement and difficulties may arise when the food supplement terminates with the end of the study.

With these kinds of difficulties it is questionable whether intervention studies can determine the effects of malnutrition on intellectual development any more effectively than the other kinds of studies that have been described.

The results of the intervention studies are difficult to evaluate because they rarely give the kind of information needed to examine the kinds of problems and questions that have been raised.

THE CONSEQUENCES OF MALNUTRITION DURING THE MOTHER'S PREGNANCY ON HER CHILD'S INTELLECTUAL DEVELOPMENT

To single out the effects of malnutrition of the pregnant mother on the intellectual development of her child after it is born is extremely difficult because conditions which cause malnutrition prenatally are likely also to cause malnutrition postnatally. Stein *et al.* (1975) took advantage of a natural experiment in which there was a severe famine in part of Holland during the winter of 1944-45 caused by the Germans cutting off food supplies. The famine was at its worst during the winter and ended in the spring of 1945 with the liberation of the Western Netherlands by the Allied Forces. In post-war Holland all males were examined at 18 years of age at the time of entering military service. These examinations included intelligence tests. Stein and her colleagues obtained these intelligence test scores for all males who were in different stages of fetal development, or in the first month of life, at the time of the famine. From the test scores they were unable to find any detectable effects of early exposure to the famine. For reasons of confidentiality there was no linkage given between the data on each male at age 18 and his mother's obstetrical history. While there was good evidence of the general severity of the famine, there were no individual data on the mothers of the males in the study. It is possible that these women who were pregnant had better access to food or were given extra food informally because of their pregnancy. This study was different from others in that there were more favourable biological and social conditions important for intellectual development that existed in Holland in the decades before and after the famine compared to the conditions where the majority of malnutrition studies have been carried out.

REHABILITATION THROUGH INTELLECTUAL STIMULATION

Studies which have shown that malnourished children are intellectually impaired because of a disadvantageous social environment for intellectual development have led some investigators to ask whether providing intellectual stimulation for malnourished children will improve their level of functioning. This question was also raised because of concern about the effects of hospitalization and separation from the family that occurred for children with marasmus and kwashiorkor who were in some cases kept in hospitals for considerable periods of time. In the hospitals the primary focus of attention was the child's bodily needs and relatively little attention was given to the child's social and intellectual needs. McKay and his colleagues (1973) in Colombia focussed their research on identifying the kinds of social interventions necessary to overcome the damaging effects of early malnutrition. To do this they set three objectives: (1) to identify the specific aspects of psychological development retarded by nutritional, health and environmental deficits; (2) to determine what deficits were modifiable; (3) to identify the relevance of the modifiable and non-modifiable behaviour for the children's future lives. Initial studies examined the effects of different combinations of cognitive, physical and nutritional intervention. The studies showed that there were many psychological characteristics that were retarded for malnourished children in the first years of life and that some of these characteristics were remediable through treatment beginning in the pre-school years.

Researchers in Jamaica (Grantham-MacGregor, 1975; Grantham-MacGregor *et al*., 1979) provided stimulation to children hospitalized with malnutrition through giving them an hour of play each day. After discharging the child, they visited the mother and child weekly to encourage the mother to play with her child. The children were compared on the Griffith Mental Developmental Scale with control children hospitalized for reasons other than malnutrition and children who were hospitalized for malnutrition and had not been in the play programme. A year after leaving the hospital the malnourished children with play experience had similar intelligence measures to the hospital controls who were not malnourished and higher scores than the malnourished children who had not been played with.

Studies along the same lines were done by Cravioto and Arrieta (1979) in Mexico and by Yatkin and McLaren (1970) in Lebanon.

ANIMAL BEHAVIOUR AND MALNUTRITION

Many studies have also been done on the effects of early malnutrition in animals (Fleischer and Turkewitz, 1983). A variety of methods were used to cause severe malnutrition in early infancy. The young animals were then fed *ad libitum* and their behaviour was assessed and compared to controls who were not malnourished. These studies showed disturbance in behaviour of the experimental animals compared to the controls. These findings were used to support the findings of human studies of an association between malnutrition and lower intelligence that were interpreted as showing that malnutrition causes intellectual impairment.

The belief that animal experiments were rigorously controlled was called into question as investigators with more experience with animal behaviour became interested in the malnutrition issue. They showed that every procedure used experimentally to produce malnutrition altered the behaviour of the mother towards her pups, e.g. malnutrition was caused by doubling the litter size of the nursing mother. The mother's behaviour in caring for small and large litters differed in many respects such as the amount of attention given to each pup, and the size of the litter varied the relationships between the pups. Animal behaviourists argued that because of the inadequacies of the controls, the differences seen in the later behaviour of the experimental and control animals could be a function of uncontrolled differences in maternal behaviour, and these differences alone or in conjunction with the nutritional differences, could account for the findings of altered behaviour and learning in the experimental animals (Levin and Weiner, 1976). There is a clear parallel between human and animal studies in premature assumption of adequate control of all variables other than malnutrition in the design of the studies.

STUDIES OF THE BRAIN

A third stream of research which has influenced thinking about the causative role of malnutrition in intellectual impairment are direct studies of the brain (Winick, 1976). It was proposed "that there are periods of heightened vulnerability in the physical development of the brain, during which growth retardation results on long-lasting and detectable distortions and deficits in adult brain structure" (Dobbing, 1972, p. 15). The period of heightened vulnerability was during the brain growth spurt which begins in mid-gestation and lasts until at least the second birthday (Dobbing and Sands, 1973). Using rats, Dobbing (1976) showed that "undernutrition need not be severe, but it has to be prolonged, lasting throughout the major part of the brain growth spurt, if it is to have detectable effects on the human brain". There is now a body of research which supports these statements. What is still largely missing is research which shows what behavioural changes are brought about by biochemical and molecular changes in the brain. The inference that the changes in the brain caused by malnutrition in turn cause permanent intellectual impairment is not warranted. Unfortunately, speculation on the connection between changes in the brain and intellectual impairment or retardation was accepted by many as fact.

IMPLICATION OF RESEARCH RESULTS

The early studies gave support to the belief that malnutrition caused brain damage which leads to irreversible intellectual impairment, or mental retardation. This gave little hope for the future of malnourished children. The only action was prevention by providing additional food to pregnant women, nursing mothers and infants. Programmes of sending large quantities of dried milk to areas of poverty were intended as a preventive measure. The programmes had administrative appeal because of their simplicity. An unintended consequence of the programmes only became apparent later when it was found that the dried milk was sometimes mixed with dirty water and caused illness and death for some of the infants being fed.

The more recent research shows that malnutrition must be considered among an array of social and biological variables over time that influences intellectual development and that there is evidence that the effects of malnutrition can be overcome by later favourable experiences. This position provides a much more hopeful prognosis for children who have been malnourished and points to the provision of learning experiences for the child to develop his social and intellectual capacities. Some programmes of social and intellectual stimulation carried out in conjunction with better feeding have already been shown to be promising, although what their long-range consequences will be is not yet known. It is now clear that primary prevention of malnutrition cannot be achieved by shipments of food but must attend to the social and economic needs of those who are impoverished.

WHY WAS THE BELIEF SO WIDESPREAD THAT MALNUTRITION CAUSED MENTAL RETARDATION?

By the late 1960s and early 1970s the conventional wisdom at an international level was that malnutrition caused mental retardation. This view was expressed in newspapers and magazines and by professionals and governmental officials. It is of interest to speculate on some of the reasons why this conventional wisdom developed so quickly and widely.

1) International relief agencies involved in feeding infants in areas where there was famine publicized the plight of starving people and there was widespread dissemination of pictures of infants with severe marasmus and kwashiorkor. This aroused strong emotions and there was widespread support for feeding programmes. Epidemiological studies of the prevalence of severe malnutrition were not available. It was generally thought that severe malnutrition was widespread in developing countries and that malnutrition took the form of severe marasmus and kwashiorkor.

2) In developing countries a large proportion of hospital beds for children were occupied because the patients had severe malnutrition. In the first half of this century most of these children died, but with the introduction of antibiotics and increased knowledge about the control of fluid loss and electrolyte balance an increasing number of young children with severe malnutrition survived. In the acute stage they were very sick children and doctors became concerned that the illness might produce permanent damage to the brain with impaired intellect. Many assumed the high proportion of beds occupied by malnourished children was a reflection of a high rate of malnutrition in a large area surrounding the hospital.

3) From the early famine model of malnutrition there developed a broader conception of malnutrition. This was well stated by Birch (1972). "We have visions of famines in India, of

victims of typhoons and of young Biafrans starved by war. The images reflect only a highly visible tip of an iceberg. Intermittent and marginal incomes as well as a technology which is inadequate to support a population result less often in the symptoms characteristic of starvation than in subclinical malnutrition or what Brock (1961) has called 'dietary subnutrition' defined as any impairment of functional efficiency of body systems which can be corrected by better feeding" (p. 174).

The broadening of the concept of malnutrition increased concern about malnutrition in Western industrial countries. This occurred at a time of growing awareness of the problems of poverty and planning to deal with the problems of poverty. Feeding programmes were a part of these plans. Nixon, in his 1969 message to Congress said, "Severe malnutrition during pregnancy and infancy can impair normal physical and mental development in children. Special efforts must be made to protect this vulnerable group from malnutrition". The broader conception of protein calorie or protein energy malnutrition defined by anthropometric measures was adopted in studies in developing countries when it was found that the frequency of severe clinical marasmus and kwashiorkor was far less common than earlier had been expected from the famine model. It vastly increased the numbers of children for whom mental retardation was feared.

4) If malnutrition causes mental retardation, then the implications for social policy throughout the world are enormous at a time when developing countries need a large number of citizens with intellectual competence for industrial development.

5) The early human and animal studies provided support for the conventional wisdom until it was realized that the so-called "controls" were inadequate and no more than an association between malnutrition and mental impairment had been demonstrated. In brain research the findings which were commonly spoken of as "brain damage" led to widespread interpretation that the "brain damage" caused mental retardation.

6) Once malnutrition as a causal factor in mental retardation became part of the conventional wisdom and with the strong emotions engendered by the feeding of children and mental retardation it became difficult to disengage the issue for scientific study because findings contrary to the conventional wisdom might be used to suggest the authors of the study were endangering the programmes to deal with malnutrition. The grounds of equity, humanity and ethics alone should be sufficient reason to try to end hunger in children without having to depend on scientific support that malnutrition causes mental retardation. It was difficult to separate research from personal values and emotions.

7) There may be some parallel between the early finding of a causal role of genetics in mental retardation and malnutrition. When the causal role of genetics became recognized the whole eugenics movement developed and in the conventional wisdom of the

day the role of genetics as a causal factor was given more prominence than was supported by later studies. The same appears to be true for malnutrition.

CONCLUSION

There has been the lack of a clear agreement upon a classification of malnutrition, in terms of types and severity. Some studies have used clinical judgements of marasmus, kwashiorkor and their combination. There is no standardization of clinical judgement and no way of knowing how much variation there is between children in the different studies. It would also be valuable to have a longitudinal record of the course of the marasmus and/or kwashiorkor.

In many studies malnutrition is inferred from anthropometric measures of the child. The most usual measure is the weight for age of a child compared with standards obtained from well fed children. Degrees of malnutrition are inferred from the extent the child's weight falls below the 50 percentile of the weights of the children who form the standard. An additional measure less used is weight for height. There is continuing controversy over the use of anthropometric measures and there are no clear unequivocal measures of what should and should not be included in the term. It is not difficult to agree on severe cases. It is the mild and borderline that are in question. It is difficult to compare studies which use different measures of malnutrition and where often the description of the status of the study children is vague.

With the advantage of hindsight, the question which guided the research, "Does malnutrition cause intellectual impairment?", has overly constricted the focus of the research. Had the question been, "What role does malnutrition play in the range of factors which influence intellectual and social development of children?", then the research might have developed in less isolation and moved more quickly to the wider concerns more evident in current work.

At the beginning of the review two very different conclusions were quoted. This review suggests that the position of Stein et al. (1975) is the more warranted by the evidence. It is still an open question of what forms of malnutrition under what conditions have long-term effects on impairing intellect, and at present there is no clear evidence that such effects exist.

REFERENCES AND BIBLIOGRAPHY

Ashley, D.V.M., Stewart, M.E. and Davison, A.N. (1979). Malnutrition and psychological development. In: **Handbook of Biological Psychiatry** (in press). Van Praag, H.M., Lader, M.H., Rafaelsen, D.J. and Sacher, E.J., (eds.). New York: Marcel Dekker

Balazs, R., Lewis, P.D. and Patel, A.J. (1979). **Nutritional Deficiencies and Brain Development.** Falkner, F. and Tanner, J.M. (eds.), Human Growth, 415-480, New York: Plenum

Birch, H., (1972), Malnutrition, learning and intelligence, **Am. J. Public Health, 62**, 6, 774-784

Birch, H.G., Pineiro, C., Alcade, E., Toca, T. and Cravioto, J., (1971), Relation of kwashiorkor in early childhood and intelligence at school age, **Pediatr. Res., 5**, 579

Brozek, J., (Ed.), (1979), **Behavioural Effects of Energy and Protein Deficits**, NIH Publication No. 79-1906, U.S. Government Printing Office

Brozek, J., Coursin, D.B. and Read, M.S., (1977), Longitudinal studies on the effects of malnutrition, nutritional supplementation, and behavioral stimulation, **Bulletin of the Pan American Health Organization, 11**, 3, 237-249

Cabak, V. and Najdanvic, R., (1965), Effect of undernutrition in early life on physical and mental development, **Arch. Dis. Childh., 40**, 532-534

Champakam, S., Srikantia, S.G. and Gopalan, C., (1968), Kwashiorkor and mental development, **Am. J. Clin. Nutr., 21**, 844

Chase, H.P., Dorsey, J. and McKhann, G.M., (1967), The effect of malnutrition on the synthesis of a myelin lipid, **Pediatrics, 40**, 551

Chase, H.P. and Martin, H.P., (1970), Undernutrition and child development, **New Engl. J. Med., 282**, 933

Chavez, A. and Martinez, C., (1982), **Growing Up in a Developing Community**, Instituto Nacional de la Nutricion, San Fernando y Viaducto Ilalpan, Mexico

Clarke, A.M. and Clarke, A.D.B., (1976), **Early Experience: Myth and Evidence**, London: Open Books

Cravioto, J., (1981), Nutrition, stimulation, mental development and learning/W.O. Atwater Memorial Lecture, presented at XII International Congress of Nutrition, San Diego, California, August 20

Cravioto, J. and Arrieta, R., (1979), Stimulation and mental development of malnourished infants, **Lancet, 2**, 899

Cravioto, J., Birch, H.G., DeLicardie, E.R. and Rosales, L., (1967), The ecology of infant weight gain in a pre-industrial society, **Acta Paed. Scand., 56**, 71-84

Cravioto, J. and DeLicardie, E.R., (1974), Mother-infant relationship prior to the development of clinical severe malnutrition in the child. In: P.L. White and N. Selvey (Eds.), **Proceedings IV-Western Hemisphere Nutrition Congress**, Acton, Mass: Publishing Science Group Inc

Cravioto, J., DeLicardie, E.R., and Birch, H.G., (1966), Nutrition, growth, and neurointegrative development: an experimental and ecologic study, **Pediatric Monograph Supplement, 35**, 319

Cravioto, J., Hambraeus, L. and Vahlquist, B. (Eds.), (1974), **Early Malnutrition and Mental Development**, Symposia of the Swedish Nutrition Foundation XII, Uppsala: Almquist and Wiksell

Davison, A.N. (1973). Nutrition and amino acid imbalance as factors influencing brain development. **Biochem. Soc. Spec. Publ.**, **1**, 27-37

Davison, A.N. and Dobbing, J., (1966), Myelination as a vulnerable period in brain development, **Brit. Med. Bull.**, **20**, 1, 40

Dobbing, J., (1964), The influence of early nutrition on the development and myelination of the brain, **Proc. Roy. Soc.**, **B159**, 503

Dobbing, J., (1972), Lasting deficits and distortions of the adult brain following infantile undernutrition. In: Pan American Health Organization Scientific Publication No. 251, **Nutrition, The Nervous System and Behavior**, Proceedings of the Seminar on Malnutrition in Early Life and Subsequent Mental Development

Dobbing, J., (1976), Food and human brain development. In: D.N. Walcher, N. Kretchmer and H.L. Barnett (Eds.), **Food, Man and Society**, New York: Plenum Press

Dobbing, J. (1981a). Nutritional growth restriction and the nervous system. In: A.N. Davison and R.H.S. Thompson (eds.), **The Molecular Basis of Neuropathology**, 221-233, London: Edward Arnold

Dobbing, J. (1981b). The later development of the brain and its vulnerability. In: J.A. Davis and J. Dobbing (eds.), **Scientific Foundations of Paediatrics** 2nd Edition, 744-759

Dobbing, J. and Sands, J., (1973), Quantitative growth and development of human brain, **Arch. Dis. Child.**, **48**, 757

Dodge, P.R., Prensky, A.L. and Feigin, R.D., (1975). **Nutrition and the Developing Nervous System**. St Louis: C. Mosby

Dyson, S.E. and Jones, D.G. (1976). Undernutrition and the developing nervous system. **Prog. Neurobiol.**, **7**, 171-196

Ellis, C.E. and Hill, D.E., (1975), Growth, intelligence, and school performance in children with cystic fibrosis who have had an episode of malnutrition during infancy, **J. Pediatrics**, **87**, 565-568

Fleischer, S.F. and Turkewitz, G., (1983), The use of animals for understanding the effects of malnutrition on human behavior. Models V. A comparative approach. In: J.R. Galler (Ed.), **Nutrition and Behavior**, Vol. V of Human Nutrition, A Comprehensive Treatise. New York: Plenum Publishing Corp.

Galler, J.R., (Ed.), (1983), **Nutrition and Behavior**, Vol V of Human Nutrition: A Comprehensive Treatise, New York: Plenum Publishing Corp.

Grantham-MacGregor, S., (1975), A home visiting intervention program with Jamaican mothers and children, **Dev. Med. Child Neurol.**, **17**, 605-613

Grantham-MacGregor, S., Stewart, M., Powell, C., and Schofield, W.N., (1979), Effect of stimulation on mental development of malnourished child, **Lancet**, **2**, 200-201

Graves, P.L., (1978), Nutrition and infant behaviour. A replication study in Nepal, **Am. J. Clin. Nutr.**, **31**, 541-551

Graves, P.L., (1979), Cross-cultural comparisons of mothers and their under-nourished infants in Asia. In: J. Brozek (Ed.), **Behavioral Effects of Energy and Protein Deficits**, NIH Publication No. 79-1906, U.S. Government Printing Office

Greene, L.S. (Ed.), (1977), **Malnutrition, Behavior and Social Organization**, New York: Academic Press

Hansen, J.D.L., Freesemann, C., Moodie, A.D. and Evans, D.E., (1971), What does nutritional growth retardation really imply?, **Pediatrics, 47**, 299

Hicks, L.E., Langham, R.A. and Takenaka, J., (1982), Cognitive and health measures following early nutritional supplementation: a sibling study, **Am. J. Public Health, 72**, 1110-1118

Kallen, D.J. (Ed.), (1973), **Nutrition, Development and Social Behavior**, Proceedings of the Conference on the Assessment of Tests of Behavior from Studies of Nutrition in the Western Hemisphere, U.S. Government Printing Office

Klein, P.S., Forbes, G.B. and Nader, P.R., (1975), Effects of starvation in infancy (pyloric stenosis) on subsequent learning abilities, **J. Pediatrics, 87**, 8-15

Klein, R.E., (1979), Malnutrition and human behavior: A backward glance at an ongoing longitudinal study. In: D.A. Levitzky (Ed.), **Malnutrition, Environment and Behavior: New Perspectives**, Ithaca: Cornell University Press

Levin, S. and Weiner, S., (1976), A critical analysis of data on malnutrition and behavioral deficits. In: I. Schulman (Ed.), **Advances in Pediatrics**, Vol 22

Levitsky, D.A., (Ed.), (1979), **Malnutrition, Environment and Behavior: New Perspectives**, Ithaca: Cornell University Press

Lloyd-Still, J.D. (1976). Clinical studies on the effects of malnutrition during infancy and subsequent physical and intellectual development. In: J.D. Lloyd-Still (ed.), **Malnutrition and Intellectual Development**, Lancaster: M.T.P. Press

McKay, H.E., McKay, A. and Sinisterra, L., (1973), Behavioral intervention studies with malnourished children: a review of experiences. In: D.J. Kallen (Ed.), **Nutrition, Development and Social Behavior**, Proceedings of the Conference on the Assessment of Tests of Nutrition in the Western Hemisphere, U.S. Government Printing Office

Manocha, S.L., (1972), **Malnutrition and Retarded Human Development**, Springfield, Ill: Charles C. Thomas

Monckeberg, F., (1968), Effect of early marasmic malnutrition on subsequent physical and psychological development. In: N.S. Scrimshaw and J.E. Gordon (Eds.), **Malnutrition, Learning and Behavior**, Cambridge, Mass: M.I.T. Press

Moodie, A.D., Bowie, M.D., Mann, M.D. and Hansen, J.D.L., (1980), A prospective 15-year follow-up study of kwashiorkor patients, **S. Afr. Med. J., 58**, 677-681

Nowak, T.S. and Munro, H.N. (1977). Effects of protein-calorie malnutrition on biochemical aspects of brain development.

In: R.J.Wurtman and J.J. Wurtman (eds), **Nutrition and the Brain, 2**, 193-260. New York: Raven Press

Pan American Health Organization (1972), **Nutrition, The Nervous System and Behavior**, Scientific Publication No. 251, Proceeding of the Seminar on Malnutrition in Early Life and Subsequent Mental Development

Richardson, S.A., (1974), The background histories of school children severely malnourished in infancy. In: I. Schulman (Ed.), **Advances in Pediatrics, 21**, 167-195

Richardson, S.A., (1976), The relation of severe malnutrition in infancy to the intelligence of school children having differing life histories, **Pediat. Res., 10**, 57-61

Richardson, S.A., Koller, H., Katz, M., and Albert, K., (1978), The contributions of differing degrees of acute and chronic malnutrition to the intellectual development of Jamaican boys, **Early Human Development, 2/2**, 163-170

Scrimshaw, N.S. and Gordon, J.D., (Eds.), (1968), **Malnutrition, Learning and Behavior**, Cambridge, Mass.: MIT Press

Serban, G., (Ed.), (1975), **Nutrition and Mental Functions**, New York: Plenum Press

Stein, Z. and Kassab, H., (1970), Nutrition. In: J. Wortis (Ed.), **Mental Retardation**, Vol. II, New York: Grune and Stratton

Stein, Z., Susser, M., Saenger, G. and Marolla, F., (1975), **Famine and Human Development**, New York: Oxford University Press

Stoch, M.B. and Smythe, P.M., (1963), Does undernutrition during infancy inhibit brain growth and subsequent intellectual development?, **Arch. Dis. Child, 38**, 546

Stoch, M.B. and Smythe, P.M., (1976), 15-year developmental study on effects of severe undernutrition during infancy on subsequent intellectual functioning, **Arch. Dis. Child, 51**, 5, 327-336

Vuori, L., Christiansen, N., Clement, J., Mora, J.O., Wagner, M. and Herrera, M.G., (1979), Nutritional supplementation and the outcome of pregnancy, II. Visual habituation at 15 days, **Am. J. Clin. Nutr., 32**, 463-469

Waber, D.P., Vuori-Christiansen, L., Ortiz, N., Clement, J.R., Christiansen, N.E., Mora, J.O., Reed, R.B. and Herrera, M.G., (1981), Nutritional supplementation, maternal education and cognitive development of infants at risk of malnutrition, **Am. J. Clin. Nutr., 34**, 807-813

Waterlow, J.C. and Rutishauser, I., (1974), Nutrition in man. Swedish Nutrition Foundation Symposium on Early Malnutrition and Mental Development, Stockholm, No. XII

Winick, M., (1976), **Malnutrition and Brain Development**, New York: Oxford University Press

Yatkin, U.S. and McLaren, D.S., (1970), The behavioral development of infants recovering from severe malnutrition, **J. Ment. Defic. Res., 14**, 25-32

COMMENTARY

R. Balazs

Whether or not undernutrition should be considered in connection with mental retardation, the belief of such an association has stimulated a lot of experimental work, and we are now probably in a position when the consequences of undernutrition on the structural and biochemical development of the brain in experimental animals can be evaluated.

It seems that irreversible effects are very few and they primarily involve cell numbers. In certain brain parts, such as the cerebellum, the reduction in cell number also results in a persistent change in the composition of the tissue in terms of nerve cell types. Most of the other alterations (involving synaptogenesis, dendritic arborization, the development of enzyme systems, etc.), even if they were rather severe, can be restored more or less to normal by nutritional rehabilitation instituted relatively late (e.g. after weaning) and, in certain cases, even without rehabilitation. Thus it would appear that brain development is only retarded by undernutrition, and these results are consistent with the evaluation by Richardson of the behavioural effects under these conditions. It is, however, important to note that the structural and biochemical development is not simply delayed, but it is also distorted. Thus a temporary imbalance is detectable in the coordinated development of certain transmitter systems and although the number of synapses per nerve cell is ultimately normal this has come about through an abnormal route without a transient overproduction of synapses. It is not yet known what are the functional consequences (e.g. in terms of "higher nervous" functions) of these distortions in brain development.

J. Dobbing

Richardson has summarized the enormous problems surrounding the belief that early malnutrition leads to later deficits in achievement and it is very helpful to have many of the difficulties set out so clearly, especially those confronting the epidemiologist.

I would like to make some changes in emphasis:

(1) The terms "mental retardation" and "brain damage" should be ruthlessly expunged in this context. In "English" English at least, mental retardation carries a connotation of severity which goes far beyond the "deficits in achievement" the more responsible participants in this field ever had in mind. It may be that Richardson's heavy bias towards the North American literature has led him to the need to attack more severely the extravagance of much North American terminology in this subject.

Similarly, and for the same reasons, "brain damage" should be reserved to describe what it says: that is "destruction of brain tissue". No-one has ever shown brain damage, either in humans or in the experimental animal, as a result of early malnutrition. Both expressions should therefore be reserved for politicians and lay research-funding agencies; or better still abandoned.

(2) It may well be that epidemiologists and statisticians can bring themselves to use a numerical expression for "social background", and feed it into the computer with "malnutrition" and "height" to determine their relative contribution to later performance. The rest of us, however, cherish the thought that only height in the three parameters quoted is a simple entity (although even that too consists of lower limb length plus spine length plus cranial depth, each responding differently to developmental malnutrition). For us, social background is a galaxy of positives and negatives whose algebraic sum may conceal more than it reveals about a child's environment. Similarly, malnutrition is beguiling in its pseudo-simplicity. Is it not possible that malnutrition may add to 99 other environmental disadvantages when they are present, but that its functional ill-effects can be compensated for by corresponding advantages when not enough of them are, even though the malnutrition may have produced the irreversible deficits and distortions we know about in the growing brain?

(3) Richardson need not have brought in the question of maternal pregnancy malnutrition. It was only asked in the old days when it was not understood how much the human brain developed postnatally, and was already obsolete two years at least before the Dutch Famine Study was published. Here again one sees an irresistible temptation for the epidemiologist to feed quantitative estimates of "intelligence" into the computer along with "social background" and "malnutrition". He who lives by epidemiology is in serious danger of dying from it!

(4) More complete, and considerably more critical, attitudes to studies of animal behaviour and to the general topic than most of these quoted can be found in the following references.

References

Dobbing J. (1981). Nutritional growth restriction of the nervous system. In: **The Molecular Basis of Neuropathology**, (Eds. R.H. Thomson and A.N. Davison), Edward Arnold, London, 221-233

Smart J.L. (1979). Undernutrition and the development of brain and behaviour. In: **Chemical Influences on Behaviour**, (K. Brown and S.J. Cooper, Eds.), Academic Press, London

Smart J.L. (1980). Behavioural correlates of brain development in the rat. In: **A Multidisciplinary Approach to Brain Development**, (Eds. C Di Benedetta et al), Elsevier/North Holland Biomedical Press, Amsterdam, 213-225

Smart J.L. (1981). Undernutrition during early life and its effects on animal development and behaviour. **Neuropharmacology, 20**, 1251-52

N. Sartorius

The paper deals with an important issue likely to affect hundreds of millions of children in developing countries: that of the causal relation between malnutrition and mental development.

As much as I admired the scholarly review of available evidence, I felt uneasy when reading this paper. This was because I am convinced that the examination of effects of malnutrition on mental development is unjustifiably in the centre of many research agendas. Malnutrition is a consequence of many factors and is thoroughly undesirable regardless of its effects on mental development.

The results of research could demonstrate that there is no effect of malnutrition on mental development or that the effects are variable; in both instances, our determination to remove malnutrition using all means at our disposal would remain the same. Furthermore, if results were to show that there is a fair chance that damage to mental development does occur and that therefore a large proportion of adults who were malnourished have a higher than average probability to be retarded, this would still not affect public health action in any way more than to aim at the elimination of malnutrition.

There are, however, other issues which deserved much more emphasis. They concern the effects of various kinds of psychotropic drugs (and other medicaments or substances) given to children suffering from malnutrition. The effects of medication in the malnourished is an underresearched issue deserving primary attention. Solid evidence of a dose-effect relationship in the malnourished could be invaluable and could significantly improve health care.

Another issue of similar importance is the <u>relative</u> contribution of malnutrition by damage to growth and development in the presence of other social, physical and psychological factors affecting the child. Good knowledge in this area could shape intervention strategies and a better use of resources. Currently, however, we lack a good model for handling the complex web of causality affecting non-communicable disease.

W. Yule

It was a pleasure to read Richardson's paper for a number of reasons. Not only does it challenge conventional received opinion, but it does so in a constructive way which indicates directions for future research which will inform both our understanding of development, and, hopefully, social policy. As I read the paper, I was struck by the parallels in conceptual and methodological problems facing research into supposed effects of malnutrition with that into the supposed effects of lead on development. Richardson addresses some of the issues in his contribution; Tizard (1974a) wrote eloquently on others nearly a decade ago; Rutter (1983) has more recently produced a masterly analysis of one of the key issues - that of the nature of "interaction" - which is central to the problems under consideration. My task is to synthesize these contributions.

We are all agreed that animal analogue studies can serve both to formulate and to test specific hypotheses, but they can never be conclusive in trying to understand human development. As with exposure to lead, acute malnutrition may have different mechanisms and effects from chronic low-level undernourishment. There are problems in identifying adequate indices of malnourishment - height provides an indication of past nutritional status (as tooth lead does of past exposure); whereas weight (as blood lead) is an indicator more influenced by current status. Tizard (1974b) points out that long-term follow-up studies may well help solve some of these technical problems but their results will be of more historical interest if social circumstances have changed in the meantime.

Chronic undernourishment is not randomly distributed across the population. It is intimately related to poverty and to deprived social stimulation. Even in the most affluent developed countries, social class differences in nutrition remain as the Black Report (DHSS, 1980) so graphically reminds us. How can one disentangle the direct effects (if any) of malnutrition from the equally direct and correlated effects of poor social stimulation? Tizard (1974b) points out that in far too many group contrast studies, the selection of matching factors is arbitrarily decided by the investigator and that the methodology focusses too much on an attempt to find thresholds below which no effects occur. It is all too easy to over-correct for the very effects one is seeking to study. It is also becoming increasingly clear that merely matching for "social class" does not equate groups for important social factors. This was brought out clearly in the Cravioto and De Licardie (1972) study, mentioned by Richardson. Because of the importance of the methodology for both lead and malnourishment, I want to spell it out in more detail.

The 22 children who developed severe clinical malnutrition before the age of 5 years were compared with "matched" families. As Tizard (1974b) summarizes it - the families did <u>not</u> differ on "...family structure, economic status, or socio-cultural characteristics as measured by personal cleanliness, literacy or educational level. Nor did they differ in the biological characteristics of the parents - height, weight, age, number of pregnancies, size of families. However, they did differ very significantly indeed in characteristics of the micro-environment as assessed by the Caldwell Inventory of Home Stimulation...". Even as early as 6 months of age, the control families were providing better home environments, correlated to better cognitive development, than were those families whose children later became malnourished.

There are two morals from this: (1) Social class or socio-economic status is a useful but crude <u>index</u> of social interactions. We must get better ways of measuring these interactions before we can understand the processes which mediate effective environment and development. (2) Longitudinal studies of small, but well documented, groups can clarify the questions posed in this symposium in ways that cross-sectional epidemiological studies cannot.

But another conclusion should not be drawn from the Cravioto study. No one is saying that only the social environment is important. Tizard (1974a) concluded that "...both home stimulation and good nutrition are important for intellectual growth and that both act synergistically to exert a powerful influence on the development of children throughout childhood". Most would agree that we must move away from simple single-cause-to-complex-effect models, but how?

Rutter (1983) argues that we should distinguish clearly between the conceptual issues involved in understanding the interaction between an individual and his/her environment and the statistical issues which are involved in partitioning variance and interpreting "interaction" terms. The two sets of issues are not the same, and failure to realize this has led to many apparently paradoxical findings. I belong to the old fashioned school which believes that statistics should be the tools of the investigators, not their masters. Rutter (1983) reinforces my belief by differentiating five types of person-environment interaction that affect outcome variables and a further five types of interaction in which the process of operating mechanisms are affected. Most of these types of interaction are not readily detectable by multivariate analyses which make fundamentally different assumptions about the nature of the world we live in. Rutter argues that a truly interactionist perspective will force us to formulate hypotheses about cause and effect much more specifically than hitherto.

Thus, both the malnutrition and the lead researches began with reasonable, if simple, hypotheses - a lot of it clearly is harmful; can a bit less also do (a bit less) harm? Both sets of researches began with a variety of case/control or group contrast studies of varying quality. Both had the underlying hypothesis that the environmental insult damaged the CNS and gave rise to intellectual impairment. This impairment was difficult to test because of inadequate psychometric tools. Social factors proved difficult to measure and to control. Sloppy concepts of "subclinical" effects obscured the issues. Pressure groups and politicians quickly took "sides", making rational discussion even more difficult.

So what has been learned after twenty years of research effort? Cynics might argue that the money spent on research should have been donated to famine relief agencies instead. This would be to misunderstand the advances. Some of the studies underline the basic resilience of human infants. Others underline the wide individual differences which are the essence of our humanness. All point to the complex reactive interactions between children and their effective social environments. As we gain better understanding of the mechanisms of development, so we can plan better prevention and intervention programmes. We must not expect simple solutions, nor short term ones, but we can predict that more effort into understanding early adult-child interactions within specified environments will pay rich dividends.

References

Cravioto J. and De Licardie E.R. (1972). In **Nutrition, the Nervous System and Behavior, 251,** Pan American Health Organization (World Health Organization) Scientific Publication, 73-94

Department of Health and Social Security (1980). Report of the Working Group on Inequalities in Health (Chairman, Sir Douglas Black), London, HMSO

Rutter M. (1983). Statistical and personal interactions: facets and perspectives. In D. Magnusson and V. Allen (Eds) **Human Development: An Interactional Perspective,** London, Academic Press

Tizard J. (1974a). Early malnutrition, growth and mental development in man. **Brit. Med. Bull., 30,** 169-174

Tizard J. (1974b). Ecological studies of malnutrition: Problems and methods. In J. Cravioto, L. Hambraeus and B. Vahlquist (Eds.). **Early Malnutrition and Mental Development,** (Symposium of the Swedish Nutrition Foundation No. XII), Stockholm: Almquist and Wicksell

S. A. Richardson

Comment on the use of social class as an adequate control

Many of the studies on the effects of lead and malnutrition have used control groups where social class is one of the controlled variables. I would like to make a comment about the shortcomings of this approach.

The concept of social class is a broad, rather crude, classification by which differences in lifestyles may be distinguished. It is based on the occupation of the head of the household and sometimes also includes income and the educational background of the head of the household. There is a certain middle class ethnocentrism in this measure, because it is based on the assumption that children live with two parents throughout their upbringing, and that there is a clearly defined head of household who has some form of steady employment. The concept avoids the reality that there are a sizeable number of children who have not had such an upbringing. One or more parents may have died, and the family may have broken up through divorce, separation, chronic illness or many other reasons. Children are brought up in foster homes (and often several), local authority hostels, institutions, or have a succession of caretakers. When both parents are alive the head of the household may be chronically unemployed, ill or disabled. Often the anomalous situations are overrepresented in populations of children who are mentally retarded, and for such children there is no way of obtaining a social class control.

With each social class there is a wide variation in lifestyle and the levels of social environment the children will experience. Again, especially for MMR children who are heavily overrepresented in social class IV and V the MMR may come from families at the lower end of the variation within each social class, whereas the controls if randomly selected will distribute across the social class.

The correlation between social class and the upbringing a child experiences is not one-to-one and some children in a lower class may have more favourable conditions of upbringing than a child in a higher social class family.

The purpose of control is to hold constant all variables except for the variable being investigated. It is ludicrous to believe that a single variable as broad and crude as social class can control the entire background history of two children, one chosen as the experimental and the other the control. The use of matching on social class is a useful way of reducing extreme differences between a study child, say, with MR and a comparison who is not MR. A question for investigation is how these two children matched on social class may differ in their social histories.

Chapter 12

Ageing in the mentally retarded

P.E. Sylvester

This chapter is about ageing and mental retardation. It does therefore confine itself to problems which are relevant to the mentally retarded individual. The approach is to present known causes of ageing. The classification of these is piecemeal and it is quickly apparent that several different factors may operate in any one individual.

MORTALITY TRENDS

Richards and Sylvester (1969) examined the mortality trends of the mentally retarded, over the age of five, in a long stay hospital over a period of 40 years. The most noteworthy factor to emerge was a large rise in the mean age at death of males and an absence of any appreciable difference between Down's syndrome and non-Down's syndrome of equivalent mental status up to the age of fifty years; thereafter there was a sharp increase in mortality of the Down's subjects.

Richards and Siddiqui (1980) followed the mortality age trends for a further ten year period in the same large institution and they found an ageing population and a sharp rise in mortality occurring in Down's syndrome at a considerably earlier age than for other mentally handicapped residents. Reduction in admissions of children, reduced turnover and earlier mean age of discharge probably influenced the findings. Carter and Jancar (1982) confirmed these findings in the Stoke Park group of hospitals in Bristol, and in particular were able to show that people with Down's syndrome live to 40-50 years. As in the studies of Richards and Siddiqui, pulmonary tuberculosis had (since the 1940/50 era) ceased to be a major cause of death. Instead causes found in the normal population, such as coronary disease and cancer, were important causes of death.

The studies of McCurley *et al*. (1972) and Richards and Siddiqui (1980) have shown a trend towards increasing life expectancy in the mentally retarded, reflecting a similar trend in the general population. Heaton-Ward (1968) found that a low IQ is associated with decreased life expectancy. Decreased life expectancy in Down's syndrome was associated for many years with a high incidence of respiratory tract infection, congenital heart disease and leukaemia. Several studies including those of Forssman and Akesson (1965), Richards and Sylvester (1969), Gallagher and Lowry (1975), Richards and Siddiqui (1980) and Carter and Jancar (1982) have shown an improving survival in patients with Down's syndrome. Fewer die during childhood and more live to the fourth and fifth decades. Relatively few live into their sixties with no published cases living beyond the age of 70 years; though one female with mosaicism at St Lawrence's Hospital did reach that age. Thus the future services for the mentally retarded will be faced more and more with an ageing population.

TRENDS IN MORBIDITY

This introduces several questions. One concerns the matter of a changing pattern of morbidity. In the 1940s and early 1950s pulmonary tuberculosis accounted for a large number of deaths. The introduction of anti-tuberculosis drugs dramatically changed the picture in favour of increased longevity. Correspondingly, heart disease and different forms of cancer appear more frequently as contributory causes to death. Jancar and Jancar (1977) in a forty year review found an eightfold increase in gastro-intestinal cancer in the Stoke Park Hospital group from 1936 to 1975 (see Table 1). These data and those for St Lawrence's are compared with those of the Registrar General for the general population in 1973.

Other patterns of morbidity can be considered. Richards and Enver (1979) measured the systolic and diastolic blood pressure of 468 patients with Down's syndrome and 807 other patients used as controls, all living in long stay care, and compared them with figures from a normal population. Subjects with Down's syndrome had the lowest pressures at all ages, the mean pressures of the mentally retarded without Down's syndrome fell between the Down's syndrome group and the controls. There is some difference of opinion about the incidence of atherosclerosis in Down's syndrome. Murdoch *et al.* (1977) examined the aortas of five institutionalized adults (aged 60-66 years) and found them to be free from atheroma whereas Moss and Austin (1980) found normal prevalence of preatherosclerotic lesions in seven non-institutionalized Down's subjects. Observations confined to macroscopic assessment of the aorta, basal cerebral and coronary vessels of 25 adults with Down's syndrome and 25 non-Down's syndrome subjects matched for age and sex, done at St Lawrence's Hospital, failed to reveal any difference between the two groups. Fenestrations of the aortic and pulmonary valves (11 subjects with Down's syndrome) were reported by Sylvester (1974) and their presence regarded as an index of ageing.

Renal pathology was demonstrated 94 times in 539 post-mortems (17.4%) over a 12 year period at St Lawrence's. The

Table 1

Comparison of morbidity data from three sources (see text)

	HMSO (1973)	Jancar and Jancar (1977)	St Lawrence's Hospital 1981
Gastro-intestinal			
Oesophagus		0.9%	0.4%
Stomach	2.1%	2.0%	1.1%
Pancreas		0.2%	0.7%
Colon	1.8%	0.5%	1.3%
Rectum		0.5%	0.2%
Genito-urinary			
Kidney	0.3%	0.2%	0.7%
Testes	0.09%	0.2%	0.4%
Bladder	0.7%	-	0.7%
Prostate	1.43%	-	0.8%
Respiratory tract			
Trachea, Bronchus, Lung	5.5%	0.3%	2.0%
Breast	3.9%	2.2%	2.2%

incidence of renal pathology increased as decades went by from 6% in the first decade to 25.3% in the fourth and 23.5% in the fifth decade and 43.5% in the seventh decade. The commonest disease was chronic pyelonephritis in the fourth to seventh decades occurring in 27.7% of deaths (72 instances in a population of 260 examined which included seven patients with Down's syndrome).

Liver disease is not as common as renal disease. Hepatitis and cirrhosis account for approximately half the cases occurring in the third, fourth and fifth decades. It is felt, though not proved, that this was due to infection with the Australian antigen. In older people liver disease is confined to metastatic invasion and cholecystitis with gallstones.

Lymphoid thyroiditis was found histologically at post-mortem in 30% of Down's adults over the age of 33 by Sylvester (1973a). Maternal age was studied in two groups with and without thyroiditis. A significant association between maternal age and the development of thyroiditis later in the life of the Down's child was established. This coincided with the findings of Fialkow (1964) that thyroid antibodies were more frequent in mothers of Down's children than in controls. Fialkow et al. (1971) also studied the relationship of Australian antigen and circulatory thyroid antibodies in Down's syndrome but there was no conclusive evidence to support the notion that the two diseases are linked. The liver was judged by Sylvester (1973a) to be free from hepatitis histologically in seven out of eight Down's patients with thyroiditis.

A post-mortem examination of the testes of 50 mentally handicapped adults (Down's syndrome and non-Down's subjects included) (Sylvester, 1973b) revealed that 68% had pathological features in either the interstitial cells, seminiferous tubules or both. There were variations in brain pathology and its location in relation to testicular pathology. The cerebellum appeared to be more consistently involved than the cerebral hemispheres in patients who had testicular disease. Unrelieved obstruction of the renal tract was a threat to spermatogenesis. Patients with testicular hypofunction lived 3.9 years longer than those with normal testicular function.

Cerebrovascular Disease

Pathological changes of senility in the temporal lobe were found in 27.9% of patients over the age of 60 years who had died at St Lawrence's Hospital. In the same population rarer forms of brain disease linked with senility, notably Pick's disease and Creutzfeldt-Jakob disease, were not encountered. A larger sample may have produced cases. Multi-infarct pathology was seen in 12 patients whose ages ranged from 50 to 90 years. Scheinberg (1978) described multi-infarct senility as a secondary consequence of hypertension and the formation of small brain infarcts or lacunae. Roth (1978) described it, clinically, as more frequent in men than women, the course being intermittent and fluctuating, punctuated by episodes of clouding. Emotional lability with depression was more pronounced than in senile dementia. Convulsions, mild Parkinsonism, and pseudo-bulbar palsy suggest that the associated intellectual deterioriation is of the multi-infarct type. These observations refer to the non-retarded but it is probable that similar clinical features occur in people with mental retardation. Another rare disease of the elderly was first described by Binswanger in 1894 and clinically associated with hypertension, bulbar symptoms, aphasia and mental deterioration. Pathologically there is demyelinization and diffuse gliosis of the white matter of the cerebral hemispheres. One patient, a female aged 84 years who had diabetes mellitus, was considered to have this disease in the sample studied at St Lawrence's Hospital.

Alzheimer's Disease

The intriguing topic in the field of mental retardation is that of Alzheimer's disease in Down's syndrome. Pathological changes were present in 88.9% of patients over the age of 30 years, 95% over 40 years and 100% over the age of 50 years, judged by the presence of neuropathological features of plaques, tangles and granulo-vacuolar degeneration in the temporal lobes from 27 patients with Down's syndrome who had died at St Lawrence's Hospital. However, it is not clear how these features tally with the clinical presentation of presenile dementia.

Reid and Aungle (1974), surveying the prevalence and clinical features of the psychosis of senescence in 155 mentally retarded patients over 55 years, found eleven suffering from dementia. Seven of these subsequently died. Neuropathological examinations (Reid et al., 1978) confirmed the diagnosis of cerebral arteriosclerotic dementia in three, senile dementia in one, senile dementia of early onset in one patient with Down's syndrome and diffuse sclerosis of the Pelizaeus-Merzbacher type in another. The study confirmed that dementia can be diagnosed in mental retardation with a reasonable degree of accuracy. It is possible that the pathological features can antedate the appearance of clinical signs by a considerable margin of time. Clearly, many Down's people remain in good physical and mental health during their forties and fifties, senile changes not being overtly present.

Epilepsy and Down's Syndrome in Relation to Ageing

Epilepsy may occur in Down's syndrome as a consequence of ageing. The incidence of epilepsy in Down's syndrome was reviewed by Smith and Berg (1976) who reported figures of between 1 and 10% according to the age under review.

Veall (1974) surveyed 1654 patients and found the prevalence of fits to vary according to age. Under 20 years it was 1.9%; between 22 and 25 years about 6%; 30-34 years - 12%; and over 55 years - 12.2%. Six patients in this study out of 27 studied post-mortem had had epilepsy, the ages ranging from 34 to 68 years. All had senile changes in the hippocampus. Fits started over the age of 45 years in four (i.e. 18% over the age of 40 years). Scarring of the Sommer sector typical of Ammon's horn sclerosis associated with temporal lobe epilepsy was present in one patient only, a male aged 68 years whose epilepsy started at the age of ten and lasted for 21 years. The sixth case started at the age of 17 years.

Anatomical and Physiological Considerations

The hippocampus or Ammon's horn is part of the limbic system. Brierley (1966) after studying memory disturbances in people with well defined and isolated cerebral lesions (Korsakoff's psychosis and temporal lobectomy for the relief of epilepsy) concluded that the hippocampal formations, mammillary bodies and possibly certain thalamic nuclei were structures essential for the process of memorizing. Sommerhoff (1974) believes that the storage of memory does not necessarily occur in the hippocampus but that it acts as a link in reverbatory circuits concerned with memory. These sustain patterns of excitations, which form neural representations of significant external events, until permanent, structual or chemical storage can be accomplished. Ganong (1979) refers to hippocampal neurons as being particularly prone to iterative discharge and hippocampal seizures presumably disrupt the normal function of this structure.

McDade and Adler (1980) compared short-term memory in eight children with Down's syndrome with two other groups of school-age children, one matched for chronological age, the other for mental age. The results indicated that the Down's children had deficits in both storage and retrieval abilities with storage of visually presented stimuli being particularly impaired. Miranda and Fantz (1973) studied 20 Down's infants using 13 pairs of visual targets. Their results suggested that the findings of early perceptual-cognitive development pointed to an early relationship between visual-attentional responses and intellectual potential.

The brain in most cases of Down's syndrome weighs less than normal (Crome and Stern, 1972), and its shape is roundish, largely due to the smallness of the frontal lobes. Other abnormalities of form are described. Of these, narrowness of the superior temporal gyrus is common and the brain stem and cerebellum are also small. Failure of the frontal lobe and the cerebellum to develop adequately in Down's syndrome infants was seen by Crome and Stern as a possible explanation of why many do not develop fine movements of the hands and fingers, as well as similar control over the lips, tongue and vocal cords, vital for the development of speech.

The hippocampus also appears not to develop adequately in Down's syndrome. This was tested by the author measuring its size in a coronal section. Images at a constant magnification from 20 patients who had had Down's syndrome and 13 from subjects without Down's syndrome, matched for age, were traced onto paper. The areas occupied by the pyramidal cell layer and the end folia were identified and measured with an Albrit planimeter. The hippocampi were significantly smaller in the Down's group. Probabilities derived from *t*-tests in the means for the end folia and pyramidal cell layers were highly significant ($p < 0.0001$) in both cases.

There was no significant correlation with age, suggesting that some other factor such as congenital deformity might account for this finding. This was further borne out by comparing cross-sections of the hippocampi from two fetuses, one from an 18 week fetus, chromosomally normal, and the other a 19 week fetus with trisomy 21. Incomplete folding of the hippocampus, smallness of the end folium and pyramidal cell layer and crenation of the ependymal surface of the dilated inferior horn were also seen.

Structural abnormalities of the dendritic spines (post-synaptic structures) of the pyramidal cells in the motor cortex of a child of 19 months with Down's syndrome were found by Marin-Padilla (1976). He reported reduced numbers of spines, unusually long spines and very short spines. These observations are important because axo-spinous synapses were considered to be altered by these abnormalities. Takashima et al. (1981) found similar dendritic changes in the visual cortices of 14 fetuses and infants with Down's syndrome. However, they observed that the dendritic structural defects were present in newborns and older infants but not in fetuses with trisomy 21, where the neuronal morphology and spine counts were the same as in matched non-Down's fetuses. This observation has fundamental implications because it implies some harmful influence causing pathological change at or shortly after birth.

O'Hara (1972) studied ultrastructurally five brains from Down's patients. He demonstrated that the ageing changes were the same as those occurring in Alzheimer's disease. Additionally, he found absence of synaptic vesicles and complex vesicles in some myelinated axons and considered that the latter were the inactive precursor of the ordinary vesicle.

The brain normally reaches a peak in weight between 25 and 35 years of life and thereafter decreases over the next decade. This is also true of the mentally handicapped (Sylvester, 1961), a fact which may have some importance when considering the timing of any therapeutic measures. However, Rundle (1983) pointed out that in Down's syndrome there is no statistical significance in the line of decline in brain weight in contrast to that of the non-Down's patients. On the contrary, growth maturity in Down's syndrome, on a weight basis, is achieved at 18 years of age; that being the case then preventive measures need to start before that age.

Genetic Factors in Down's Syndrome and Alzheimer's Disease

Apart from familial instances of Alzheimer's disease (Corsellis, 1976), it is not unusual to encounter psychiatric illness in the families of affected patients. Schenk (1955) found a history of dementia in a near relative in ten out of 35 cases, and of severe neurological disease in 15. Heston et al. (1981) studied relatives of 125 probands who had dementia of the Alzheimer type proved histologically after post-mortem. The relatives had an excess of dementing illness consistent with genetic transmission. Risks to relatives decreased sharply as severity of the probands' illness decreased. Comparison with a control group in the general population revealed increased evidence of Down's patients, lymphomas and auto-immune diseases, including thyroiditis, amongst relatives. Whalley et al. (1982) in a similar study were unable to confirm these observations. Sylvester (1973a) made an estimate of thyroiditis in adults with Down's syndrome of 30% and was able to show a significant association between young maternal age and a tendency to develop lymphocytic thyroiditis in the Down's child. Fialkow (1964) found that thyroid antibodies are commoner in mothers of Down's children than in controls; furthermore, that the age of mothers was considerably less than those of controls.

Harris (1982) states that dramatic pedigrees with multiple cases of presenile dementia do occur and should alert the genetic counsellor to the higher risk in these families. He bases this on the reports of Larsson et al. (1963), Constantidis et al. (1965) and Sjogren et al. (1952). Heston et al. (1981) reported that, in 60% of their cases, the index patients were isolated with no other cases in the family. Patients were younger and the disease had a more rapid course in families in which secondary causes occurred. Heston's findings seem to clinch the fact that symptoms of dementia first occurring after the age of 70 carry little genetic risk for close relatives. In contrast, when the disease occurs in patients below 65, and when another relative has had the disease, the risk is considerable. When the proband and a parent are affected, nearly half the siblings eventually become demented, the pattern closely resembling autosomal dominant inheritance in these unusual families.

Current epidemiological and clinical studies outlined by Harris (1982) promise to help identify subtypes of Alzheimer's disease. The patterns of familial occurrence, resembling autosomal dominant inheritance, may be mimicked by a transmissible agent, but the effect of genes in controlling response to a slow virus may explain why only some relatives develop the disease. Alzheimer's disease may prove a classic example of the relation between genes and viral disease.

Gene location on chromosome 21 has so far revealed one for an antiviral protein, one for superoxide dismutase-1 and one for phosphoribosyl glycinamide synthetase. Slater and Cowie (1971), in a detailed discussion of senile and presenile dementias (not related to Down's syndrome), state: "we are inclined to attribute the genetical basis of senile dementia to a major autosomal gene, dominant in the heterozygote. A number of other questions arise which will require further research. Perhaps the most obvious is the question whether one or many loci are involved, whether one should think of only a single autosomal gene or of many different ones. The general discussion of the evolutionary aspect of deteriorative disorders of later life leads one to think that there have probably been many independent mutations which have gradually accumulated in the species on an evolutionary time-scale. Senile dementia would then be a congeries of theoretically but not practically distinguishable disorders, each with its own specific genetic determinant." Whalley et al. (1982) inferred from evidence on 74 cases of non-Down's syndrome with Alzheimer's disease confirmed at autopsy that autosomal dominance with complete penetrance could only acount for a small proportion of cases. Their results were more compatible with a simple polygenic model. The fivefold increase in the incidence of Down's syndrome in families with established dementia of the Alzheimer type found by Heston et al. (1981) seems to point a way to start understanding the genetic basis for the disease. This is not easy to explain because of the difficulties in attempting to estimate risk for diseases at the extremes of life.

The frequently quoted increase of Alzheimer's disease in females compared with males and borne out by the Mortality Statistics for England and Wales (HMSO, 1980) of 2:1 is not found in Down's syndrome. The almost total universality of the disease, judged by the neuropathological evidence over the age of 40 years, affects males and females equally.

Infection

Henscke et al. (1978) studying HLA antigens have found that HLA/B7 and HLA/CW3 occur more frequently in patients with Alzheimer's disease than in normal controls. Harris (1982) claims that finding this rare combination of HLA antigens in population studies of unrelated patients should encourage the search for major histocompatibility of complex-linked genes controlling susceptibility to a putative slow virus in Alzheimer's disease.

Patients with Down's syndrome who possess the allele HLA/B8 were found to have a reduction of circulatory T cells by Gershwin et al. (1977). Additionally, the frequency of cardiac anomalies was increased in Down's syndrome with allele HLA/AZ. Serum IgA was significantly reduced whereas levels of IgG were elevated. The percentage of E rosette forming cells was lower in patients with Down's syndrome, whereas the percentage of EAC rosettes and monocytes was increased. It was concluded that patients with Down's syndrome have major quantitative abnormalities of immune function. Franceschi et al. (1978) examined the T and B lymphocyte populations in the peripheral blood of 24 non-institutionalized Down's syndrome patients and reported small but significant reductions of E and EAC rosette forming cells. Kadowaki et al. (1976) found a significant elevation of IgE in 39 patients with Down's syndrome compared with 40 miscellaneous non-Down's syndrome and 30 non-mentally retarded subjects without allergic disease. Their findings did not support the low IgE levels related to immunodeficiency states.

Immune dysfunction in ageing was further demonstrated by Tam and Walford (1980). They found the levels of cyclic adenosine 3'5'-monophosphate (cAMP) in resting peripheral blood T lymphocytes from normal elderly humans and young adults with Down's syndrome were similar in that they were markedly decreased compared with the levels found in young normal humans. The cyclic guanosine 3'5'-monophosphate (cGMP) in resting T cells from normal old and young adults with Down's syndrome were, by contrast, greatly increased. The unstimulated or resting cAMP/cGMP ratios for T cells therefore declined in normal aged and Down's syndrome. The specific activities of the appropriate enzymes were altered, adenylate cyclase was elevated and guanylate cyclase decreased in the T cells with age in Down's syndrome. Disturbance of surface membrane receptors on peripheral mononuclear cells of patients with Down's syndrome and aged individuals was found by Naeim and Walford (1980) when they studied the redistribution of immunoglobulins and concanavalin A receptors. A demonstrable disturbance of the mobility of such receptors indicated alterations in cell membrane receptors in aged persons. Similar findings in Down's syndrome supports the supposition that Down's syndrome individuals show features of accelerated ageing.

Jonker et al. (1982) found no indication that patients without Down's syndrome but with Alzheimer's disease were able to produce immunoglobulins within the central nervous system judged by studies on cerebrospinal fluid.

However, Katencamp et al. (1970) regarded the amyloid content of plaques as a reaction to the exudation of serum. It was concluded that a senile plaque is a particular form of senile amyloidosis due to insufficient regulatory mechanisms of glial cells. Glenner (1978) considered that there are two forms of amyloid involved. On the basis of its localization, the amyloid central core of the plaque is probably derived by proteolysis of locally secreted protein in contrast to that of congophilic angiopathy, which is probably of serum origin. Ishii et al. (1975) and Ishii and Haga (1976) have reported finding IgG within the fibrils of senile plaques.

Animals have been infected experimentally with virus-like agents from patients with either Creutzfeldt-Jakob disease (spongiform encephalopathy) or Alzheimer's disease. Will and Matthews (1982) reported three cases of probable iatrogenic transmission of Creutzfeldt-Jakob disease by neurosurgery together with a cluster of three patients possibly connected with dental procedures. Another patient developed Creutzfeldt-Jakob disease after being in contact with a familial case. Whalley et al. (1982) argue against an infective agent, such as a slow virus, causing Alzheimer's disease on the basis that it is likely that the excess genetic material on chromosome 21 is sufficient for the ageing changes to take place without involving the action of an unusual infective agent. Myoclonus and progressive intellectual deterioration in a 46 year old woman with trisomy 21 during the final stages of her illness was reported by Blumbergs et al. (1981) to have been diagnosed Creutzfeldt-Jakob disease but ultimately this was found at post-mortem to be Alzheimer's disease with cardiovascular amyloidosis in the meningeal vessels.

Chemical Factors

Acetylcholine metabolism is reduced in Down's syndrome. Yates and colleagues (1980) demonstrated cholinergic deficiency in several territories of the brain in Down's syndrome including the temporal lobe. Their findings were similar to those of non-Down's syndrome patients with senile changes. There were decreases in the activities of choline acetyl transferase and acetylcholinesterase. Bowen and Davison (1980) related the loss of choline acetyl transferase activity to loss of neurons especially in the hippocampus, this alteration paralleling the intensity of neuropathological damage. This must further be compounded by the fact that in Down's syndrome the hippocampus is poorly developed and starts with fewer neurons than usual. It is not certain how efficiently those cells that are present can metabolize acetylcholine without help from environmental factors such as nutrients. Leeming et al. (1981) described how 5,6,7,8-

tetrahydrobiopterin functions as a natural co-factor in the hydroxylation of phenylalanine to tyrosine, tyrosine to dopa and tryptophan to 5-hydroxytryptophan. These are all reactions of importance in neurotransmitter synthesis. Biopterin metabolism is reduced in various disease states such as Alzheimer's disease as well as in phenylketonuria. Aziz *et al*. (1982) studied tetrahydrobiopterin in Down's syndrome subjects in long stay care. They found reduced levels in the blood and an increase in the breakdown product dehydrobiopterin in the urine. Tetrahydrobiopterin is subject to breakdown by intracellular peroxidation and this is increased in Down's syndrome through the action of superoxide dismutase, the gene of which was localized by Sinet *et al*. (1976) to chromosome 21. There is thus an increase of 50% of dismutase in Down's syndrome as a result of gene dosage effect from the extra chromosome.

A defect in protein metabolism was studied by Crapper *et al*. (1979) in presenile and senile dementia of the Alzheimer type. Chromatin samples were prepared from 40 human brains. The chromatin was separated into heavy heterochromatin fractions and two euchromatin fractions. A reduction of DNA of 55% was found based on the estimation of euchromatin content in patients with advanced senile or presenile dementia of the Alzheimer type. This was compared with a reduction of only 75% of the total DNA demonstrated in brains from patients with dialysis dementia and elderly patients with or without dementia of a type other than Alzheimer's disease.

Reduced protein synthesis within nerve cells of the temporal cortex in Alzheimer's disease was also demonstrated by Mann *et al*. (1981). They found a reduction of 43% in nuclear volume, 86% in nucleolar volume and 26% in cytoplasmic RNA. Crapper and colleagues comment that deficits in hormones or metal ion metabolism within the brain can affect chromatin configuration. Facultative heterochromatin can be influenced by magnesium, calcium, manganese, sodium and potassium.

Nutritional Aspects

Vitamin studies in Down's syndrome have suggested on many occasions that such people have either difficulty in assimilating or difficulty in utilizing a variety of vitamins. Low serum vitamin A was found by Sobel *et al*. (1958). Auld *et al*. (1959) demonstrated impaired absorption of the vitamin following administration. Griffiths and Behrman (1967) tested dark adaptation in Down's syndrome and found it to be impaired. Palmer (1978) showed that children with Down's syndrome were short of vitamin A and this was associated with increased incidence of infections and an increase of serum IgG. Griffiths *et al*. (1969) found significantly higher levels of IgA globulin in male Down's syndrome when compared with female Down's syndrome and non-Down's syndrome control groups. They attributed this partly to the fact that males had a higher incidence of pyrexial illnesses over a five year period and partly to vitamin A dysmetabolism. A disturbance of vitamin B1 metabolism was found in three male trisomics by Reading _et al_. (1979) in spite of them being on a normal diet. Replacement therapy was successful.

Matin _et al_. (1981) investigated 12 patients with Down's syndrome and six non-Down's syndrome mentally retarded for vitamins A and E, thiamine, nicotinic acid and ascorbic acid. They found 30% of the subjects studied had low values for vitamin A and E and 70% had low values for thiamine, nicotinic acid and ascorbic acid.

Trace elements were assessed in the suboccipital hair by Barlow _et al_. (1981) using atomic absorption spectroscopy. The results from 69 male and 67 female patients with Down's syndrome were compared with 69 non-Down's syndrome mentally retarded patients, eight hospital staff and 86 people in Birmingham. There were striking reductions in manganese and copper between the sexes. Manganese levels in female Down's syndrome were significantly lower than in women without Down's syndrome ($p < 0.001$). Similar differences were found between males and females with Down's syndrome. The sex differences for copper were found in reverse, the level in males being significantly less than those in females ($p < 0.0001$). However, the caeruloplasmin levels in both sexes appeared not to be reduced. Multiple deficiencies occurred. Levels below -1 SD of the mean of the hospital control population revealed that three or more deficiencies were found in 13% of the male and 8% of the female Down's subjects; two deficiencies occurred in 41% males and 31% females and one deficiency in 29% males and 34% females. Deficiencies of trace elements were not found in 17% males and 24% females.

Experimentally, vitamin E deficiency has led to the accumulation of lipofuscin in spinal and cortical neurons (Adam 1965). The vitamin appears to have an antioxidant effect in protecting lipids in tissues against peroxidation and subsequent formation of lipofuscin. Adam felt that lipofuscin in neurons in adult man was not due to vitamin deficiency but is probably the result of normal ageing process manifested by lipid peroxidation. Einarson (1954) was able to cause posterior column damage in vitamin E deficient rats. These changes were irreversible. Rudra _et al_. (1975), also working with rats, although not able to influence the number of cells containing lipofuscin, was able to lower the amount present in each cell significantly after giving vitamin E. Harman (1961) was able to prolong the half-survival time of certain strains of mice by as much as 26% by giving them an antioxidant (2-mercapto-ethylamine hydrochloride).

Dementing conditions of nutritional origin include thiamine deficiency (Wernicke's encephalopathy), nicotinamide deficiency (pellagra) and tryptophan deficiency (Hartnup's disease). Nicotinamide deficiency was shown in the study of Matin and colleagues. Tryptophan absorption, according to O'Brien and Grosher (1962), is either delayed or diminished in Down's syndrome. Tryptophan is converted to nicotinamide. Therefore there is the possibility that nicotinamide deficiency may be secondary to poor tryptophan absorption.

Sinet _et al._ (1976) localized the gene of superoxide dismutase-1 (SOD-1) to a segment of chromosome 21 - represented by between 1/5 and 1/10 of the whole chromosome. There is an increase of SOD in Down's syndrome of approximately 50% regarded by Sinet and Lejeune (1979) as a gene dosage effect from the extra chromosome. Increased copper-zinc SOD activity has been observed in red cells, platelets, leucocytes and fibroblasts in Down's syndrome. SOD catalyses superoxide activity within cells, leading to the formation of peroxides which are controlled by glutathione peroxidase in preventing lipid peroxidation and cell ageing. Thus an increase in SOD activity as found in Down's syndrome should lead to an increase in peroxide formation. Unless the glutathione peroxidase activity matches that of the increased peroxidation then the ageing process is likely to be accelerated. Copper and possibly manganese in conjunction with thiamine and nicotinic acid influence superoxide activity or SOD catalysis, thereby tending to aggravate the equation towards hyperperoxidosis, whereas selenium and vitamin E tend to counter the formation of peroxides and prevent lipid peroxidation and protect cell ageing.

Trauma

Cerebral changes similar to those seen in ageing, but not necessarily linked with Down's syndrome, are seen in some mentally retarded individuals with repeated subconcussive head injury, following either pre-epileptic falls or episodes of head banging.

Neurofibrillary tangles are liable to occur as a later sequel to cerebral trauma either in association with senile plaques or on their own. Corsellis _et al._ (1973) found that neurofibrillary changes, usually with the absence of plaques, were a major pathological feature in the brains of 15 retired boxers whom they had examined. The substantia nigra, locus caeruleus, amygdala and hippocampus were affected.

A male subject reported by the present author died, aged 33 years. He suffered head banging in childhood severe enough to cause a soft tissue swelling 5.0 cm in circumference and 4.0 cm deep on the left side of his forehead. He was severely mentally retarded and also had epilepsy associated with the oculocerebrorenal syndrome of Lowe _et al._ (1952). He died of bilateral bronchopneumonia. The brain weighed 1127 g, and both hemispheres were symmetrical. Cerebellar sclerosis was present. There was dilatation of the cerebral aqueduct which was not due to a distal blockage. Histologically, there were numerous neurofibrillary tangles in the pyramidal cell layer of the hippocampus but plaques and granulovacuolar degeneration were not detected. The findings were regarded as conforming with presenile changes reported by others as the punch-drunk or boxer syndrome (Matin and Sylvester, 1980).

THE FUTURE

Roth (1982) points out prognostically that all the intensive investigations and studies into Alzheimer's disease provide a measure of support for the view that there are reversible as well as irreversible changes in the course of the disease. The studies in Down's syndrome contribute considerably to this view. One difficulty is sifting from the numerous studies, cause and effect, and concentrating on the cause. Certainly there are genetic implications and these could be supposed to stem entirely from the extra number 21 chromosome. It would appear, however, that the female sex chromosomes too may be involved, since in the non-Down's subjects there is a 2:1 bias towards females having the disease but this is not evident in Down's syndrome. There is the question of the environment of the nerve cells and whether or not congenital malformations of the brain and the temporal lobe, in particular, contribute to a predisposition to ageing. Lifelong shortages of important nutrients such as vitamins and trace elements may also be relevant. Deficiencies of neurotransmitters, such as acetylcholine and tetrahydrobiopterin, may indicate reduced amounts of nerve tissue but deficiencies could also arise from deficiencies of other substances, e.g. nutrients in the neuronal environment.

Whatever future biological mechanisms are judged to be at fault, it seems from past experiences in clinical and pathological appraisals of Down's syndrome that the pathological changes antedate, by a considerable margin of time, the clinical presentation of dementia, so that by the time a person is found to be demented irreversible changes are present. A better time to intervene in prevention is suggested by the fact that brain weight reaches a peak at about thirty years of age and thereafter declines in weight. Programmes of prevention, logically, need to be introduced during the pre-thirty period of age in the hope of preventing irreversible pathological changes which have been demonstrated in 88.9% of Down's subjects by their mid-thirties.

REFERENCES

Adam, C.W.M. (1965). **Neurohistochemistry.** Amsterdam, London, New York, Elsevier Publishing Co.

Auld, R.M., Pommer, A.M., Houck, J.C. and Burke, F.G. (1959). Vitamin A absorption in mongoloid children. **American Journal of Mental Deficiency, 63,** 1010-1015

Aziz, A.A., Leeming, R.J., Blair, J.A. and Sylvester, P.E. (1982). Tetrahydrobiopterin metabolism in Down syndrome and in non-Down syndrome mental retardation. **Journal Mental Deficiency Research, 26,** 67-71

Barlow, P.J., Sylvester, P.E. and Dickerson, J.W.T. (1981). Hair trace metal levels in Down syndrome patients. **Journal Mental Deficiency Research, 25,** 161-168

Blumbergs, P., Beran, R. and Hicks, P. (1981). Myoclonus in Down's syndrome. **Arch. Neurol., 38,** 453-454

Bowen, D.M. and Davison, A.N. (1980). Biochemical changes in cholinergic system of the aging brain in senile dementia. **Psychol. Med., 19**, 315-319

Brierley, J.B. (1966). The neuropathology of amnesic states. **Amnesia** Second Edition. Whitty, C.M. and Zangwill, O.L. (eds.). Edinburgh and London, Butterworth

Carter, G. and Jancar, J. (1982). **Mortality in the Mentally Handicapped: a Fifty-year Survey (1930-1980)**. Frenchay Health Authority

Constantidis, J., Garrone, G. and Tissot, R. (1965). L'incidence familiale des alterations neurofibrillaires corticales d'Alzheimer. **Psychiat. Neurol.** (Basel), **150**, 235-247

Corsellis, J.A.N. (1976). Ageing and the dementias. In: **Greenfield's Neuropathology 3**, Blackwood, W. and Corsellis, J.A.N. (eds.). London, E. Arnold

Corsellis, J.A.N., Bruton, C.J. and Freeman-Brown, D. (1973). The aftermath of boxing. **Psychol. Med., 3**, 270-303

Crapper, D.R., Quittkat, S. and De Boni, U. (1979). Altered chromatic confirmation in Alzheimer's disease. **Brain, 102**, 183-95

Crome, L. and Stern, J. (1972). **Pathology of Mental Retardation, 2**, Edinburgh and London, Churchill Livingstone

Einarson, L. (1954). Structural changes and functional disturbances in the nervous system. Neurovascular lesions in vitamin E deficient adult rats. **Anatomiske Skrifter, 1**, NR1, Universitetsforlaget, Aarhus

Fialkow, P.J. (1964). Autommunity: A predisposing factor in chromosomal aberrations. **Lancet, 1**, 74

Fialkow, P.J., Blumberg, B.S., London, W.T., Sutnick, A.I. and Thuline, H.C. (1971). Thyroid antibodies and Australia Antigen in Down's syndrome. **Journal Mental Deficiency Research, 15**, 177-185

Forssman, H. and Akesson, H.O. (1965). Mortality in patients with Down's syndrome, **Journal Mental Deficiency Research, 9**, 146-150

Francheschi, C., Licastro, F., Paolucci, P., Masi, M., Cavicchi, S. and Zannotti, M. (1978). T and B lymphocyte subpopulations in Down's syndrome. A study on non-institutionalised subjects. **Journal Mental Deficiency Research, 22**, 179-183

Gallagher, R.P. and Lowry, R.C. (1975). Longevity in Down's syndrome in British Columbia. **Journal Mental Deficiency Research, 19**, 157-162

Ganong, W.F. (1979). **Review of Medical Physiology, 9**, California, Lange

Gershwin, M.E., Crinella, F.M., Castles, J.J. and Trent, J.K.T. (1977). Immunologic characteristics of Down's syndrome. **Journal Mental Deficiency Research, 21**, 237-249

Glenner, G. (1978). Current knowledge of amyloid deposits as applied to senile plaques and congophilic angiopathy. In: **Alzheimer's Disease: Senile Dementia and Related**

Disorders, (**Ageing**, **10**), Katzman, R., Terry, R.D. and Bick, K.L. (eds.). New York, Raven Press

Griffiths, A.W. and Behrman, J. (1967). Dark adaptation in mongols. **Journal Mental Deficiency Research**, **11**, 23-30

Griffiths, A.W., Sylvester, P.E. and Bayliss, E.C. (1969). Serum globulins and infection in mongolism. **Journal Clin. Path.**, **22**, 76-78

Harman, D. (1961). Prolongation of the normal life span and inhibition of spontaneous cancer by antioxidant. **Journal Gerontology**, **16**, 247-254

Harris, R. (1982). Genetics of Alzheimer's disease. **British Medical Journal**, **284**, 1065-1066

Heaton-Ward, W.A. (1968). Life expectation of mentally subnormal patients in hospital. **British Journal Psychiat.**, **114**, 591-592

Henscke, P.J., Bell, D.A. and Cape, R.D. (1978). Alzheimer's disease and HLA, **Tissue Antigens**, **12**, 132-135

Heston, L.L., Mastri, A.R., Anderson, E. and White, J. (1981). Dementia of the Alzheimer type. **Arch. Gen. Psych.**, **38**, 1085-1090

HMSO, (1973). **The Registrar General Statistical Review of England and Wales (1973)** Part 1 (A), Tables Medical

HMSO, (1980). **Mortality Statistics (cause) for England and Wales (1980)**

Ishii, T. and Haga, S. (1976). Immuno-electron microscopic localisation of immunoglobulins in amyloid fibrils of senile plaques. **Acta Neuropathologica (Berl.)**, **36**, 243-50

Ishii, T., Haga, S. and Shimizu, F. (1975). Identification of components of imunoglobulins in senile plaques by means of fluorescent antibody technique. **Acta Neuropathologica Scandinavia**, **59**, 225-240

Jancar, M.P., and Jancar, J. (1977). Cancer and mental retardation. **Bristol Med-chir. J.**, **92**, 341-342

Jonker, C. Eikelenboom, P. and Tavenier, P. (1982). Immunolgical indices in the cerebrospinal fluid of patients with presenile dementia of the Alzheimer type. **British Journal Psychiat.**, **140**, 44-49

Kadowaki, J-I, Shiono, H., Umetsu, A., Ohnishi, M. and Nakao, T. (1976). Serum IgE concentration in Down's syndrome. **Journal Mental Deficiency Research**, **20**, 105

Katencamp, D., Stiller, D. and Thoss, K. (1970). Unterschungen zum immunohistochemischen Verhalten der senile placques des meuschlichen Gehirnes virchows, **Archiv. Abtellung A, Pathologische Anatomie**, **351**, 333-9

Larsson, T., Sjogren, T. and Jacobsen, G. (1963). Senile dementia: A clinical sociomedical and genetic study. **Acta Psychiatr. Scand.**, **39**, (suppl. 67)

Leeming, R.J., Pheasant, A.E. and Blair, J.A. (1981). The role of tetrahydrobiopterin in neurological disease: A review. **Journal Mental Deficiency Research**, **25**, 231

Lowe, C.U., Terrey, M. and MacLachlan, E.A. (1952). Organic-aciduria, decreased renal ammonia production, hydrophthalmos and mental retardation. **American Journal Dis. Child., 83**, 164-8

McCurley, R., Mackay, D.N. and Scally, B.G. (1972). The life expectation of the mentally subnormal under community and hospital care. **Journal Mental Deficiency Research, 16**, 57-66

McDade, H.L. and Adler, S. (1980). Down syndrome and short-term memory impairments: a storage or retrieval deficit? **American Journal Mental Deficiency, 84**, 561-565

Mann, D.M.A., Neary, D., Yates, P.O., Lincoln, J., Snowden, J.S. and Stanworth, P. (1981). Alterations in protein synthetic capability of nerve cells in Alzheimer's disease. **Journal Neurol. Neurosurgery, Psychiat., 44**, 97-102

Marin-Padilla, M. (1976). Pyramidal cell abnormalities in the motor cortex of a child with Down's syndrome. A Golgi study. **Journal Comp. Neurol., 167**, 63-5

Matin, M.A. and Sylvester, P.E. (1980). Clinicopathological studies of occulocerebrorenal syndrome of Lowe, Terrey and MacLachlan. **Journal Mental Deficiency Research, 24**, 1-16

Matin, M.A., Sylvester, P.E., Edwards, D. and Dickerson, J.W.T. (1981). Vitamin and zinc status in Down's syndrome. **Journal Mental Deficiency Research, 25**, 121-126

Miranda, S.B. and Fantz, R.L. (1973). Recognition and memory in Down's syndrome and normal infants. **Child. Develop., 44**, 555

Moss, L.T.J. and Austin, G.E. (1980). Pre-atherosclerotic lesions in Down's syndrome. **Journal Mental Deficiency Research, 24**, 137-141

Murdoch, J.C., Fodger, J.C., Rao, S.S, Fletcher, C.D. and Dunnigan, M.G. (1977). Down's syndrome - an atheroma-free model. **British Medical Journal, 2**, 226-228

Naeim, F. and Walford, R.L. (1980). Disturbance of redistribution of surface membrane receptors in peripheral mononuclear cells of patients with Down's syndrome and aged individuals. **Journal Geront., 35**, 650-655

O'Brien, D. and Grosher, A. (1962). The abnormality of tryptophan metabolism in children with mongolism. **Arch. Dis. Child., 37**, 17-20

O'Hara, P.T. (1972). Electron microscopical study of the brain in Down's syndrome. **Brain, 95**, 681-685

Palmer, S. (1978). Influence of vitamin A nutriture on the immune response. Findings in children with Down's syndrome. **International Journal of Vitamin Nutrition Research, 48**, 188-216

Reading, C.M., McLeary, A. and Nobile, S. (1979). Down's syndrome and thiamine deficiency. **Journal Orthomol. Psychiat., 8**, 4-12

Reid, A.H. and Aungle, P.G. (1974). Dementia in ageing mental defectives: A clinical psychiatric study. **Journal Mental Deficiency Research, 18**, 15

Reid, A.H., Maloney, A.F.J. and Aungle, P.G. (1978). Dementia in ageing mental defectives: a clinical and neuropathological study. **Journal Mental Deficiency Research, 22**, 233

Richards, B.W. and Enver, F. (1979). Blood pressure in Down's syndrome. **Journal Mental Deficiency Research, 23**, 123-135

Richards, B.W. and Siddiqui, A.Q. (1980). Age and mortality trends in residents of an institution for the mentally handicapped. **Journal Mental Deficiency Research, 24**, 99-105

Richards, B.W. and Sylvester, P.E. (1969). Mortality trends in mental deficiency institutions. **Journal Mental Deficiency Research, 13**, 276-292

Roth, M. (1978). Differentiation of senile and arteriosclerotic dementia in Alzheimer's disease, senile dementia and related disorders. In: **Ageing, 7**, Katzman, R., Terrey, R.D. and Black, K.L., (eds.). New York, Raven Press

Roth, M. (1982). Neural aging and its implications in human neurological pathology. In: **Ageing, 18**. Terrey, R.D., Blis, C.L. and Torrano, G. (eds.). New York, Raven Press

Rudra, D.N., Dickerson, J.W.T. and Walker, R. (1975). The effect of some antioxidants on lipofuscin accumulation in rat brain. **Proc. Nutrition Soc., 34**, 122A

Rundle, A.T. (1983). Personal communication

Scheinberg, P. (1978). Multi-infarct dementia in Alzheimer's disease, senile dementia and related disorders. In: **Ageing, 7**, Katzman, R., Terrey, R.D. and Black, K.L. (eds.). New York, Raven Press

Schenk, V.W.D. (1955). Syndrome d'Alzheimer: etude anatomoclinique de 35 cas. **Folia Psychiat. Nederl., 58**, 422-439

Sinet, P.M., Couturier, J., Dutrillax, B., Poissonier, M., Raoul, O., Rethore, M.O., Allard, D., Lejeune, J. and Jerome, H. (1976). Trisomie 21 et superoxide dismutase-1 (1PO-A). **Experimental Cell Research, 97**, 47-55

Sinet, P.M. and Lejeune, J. (1979). Trisomy 21 (Down's syndrome), glutathione peroxidase, hexose monophosphate shunt and IQ. **Life Science, 24**, 29-34, Pergamon Press

Sjogren, T., Sjogren, H. and Lundgren, A.G.H. (1952). Morbus Alzheimer and morbus Pick. A genetic, clinical and patho-anatomical study. **Acta Psychiatr. Neurol. Scand., 82**, 1-152

Slater, E. and Cowie, V. (1971). **The Genetics of Mental Disorders**. Oxford University Press

Smith, G.F. and Berg, J.M. (1976). **Down's Anomaly**, Edinburgh, Churchill

Sobel, A.E., Strazzalla, M., Sherman, B.S., Elkan, B., Morgenstern, S.W., Marius, N. and Meisel, A. (1958). Vitamin A absorption and other blood composition studies in mongolism. **American Journal Mental Deficiency, 62**, 642-656

Sommerhoff, G. (1974). **Logic of the Living Brain**. Chichester, J. Wiley & Sons

Sylvester, P.E. (1961). Brain weight in mental deficiency. **Journal Mental Deficiency Research, 5**, 98-107

Sylvester, P.E. (1973a). Autoimmune thyroiditis in mental handicap. Epidemiological study based on thyroid histology. **Journal Mental Deficiency Research, 17**, 18-22

Sylvester, P.E. (1973b). The testes in the mentally handicapped. **Journal Mental Deficiency Research, 17**, 52-57

Sylvester, P.E. (1974). Aortic and pulmonary valve fenestrations as ageing indices in Down's syndrome. **Journal Mental Deficiency Research, 18**, 367-376

Takashima, S., Berker, L.E., Armstrong, D.L. and Chan, F.W. (1981). Abnormal neuronal development in the visual cortex of the human fetus and infant with Down's syndrome. A quantitative and qualitative Golgi study. **Brain Res., 225**, 1-8

Tam, C.F. and Walford, R.L. (1980). Alterations in cyclic nucleotides and cyclase-specific activities in T-lymphocytes of ageing and normal humans and patients with Down's syndrome. **Journal Immunol., 125**, ii, 1665-1670

Veall, R.M. (1974). The prevalence of epilepsy among mongols related to age. **Journal Mental Deficiency Research, 18**, 99-106

Whalley, L.J., Carothers, A.D., De Mey, R., Collyers, S. and Frackiewicz, (1982). A study of familial factors in Alzheimer's disease. **British Journal Psychiat., 140**, 249-256

Will, R.G. and Matthews, W.B. (1982). Evidence for case-to-case transmission of Creutzfeldt-Jakob disease. **Journal Neurol. Neurosurg. Psychiat., 45**, 235-238

Yates, C.M., Simpson, J., Maloney, A.E.J., Gordon, A. and Reid, A.M. (1980). Alzheimer-like cholinergic deficiency in Down's syndrome. **Lancet, ii**, 979

COMMENTARY

J. Carr and J. Hogg

Sylvester has raised the question of the relation between biochemical change in Down's syndrome children and the possible measurement of developmental correlates. With respect to early infancy and childhood two related measures have been considered in developmental studies of Down's syndrome, mental age (MA) and developmental quotient (DQ). MA reflects the progressive development in competence that is seen in handicapped children as they advance in cognitive, communicative and motor competence. DQ is a measure of rate of development. The child whose MA progresses more slowly than is normative will accordingly have a DQ below average reflecting this slower rate of increasing competence.

Carr (1975) followed the development of a group of Down's syndrome infants from shortly after their birth to four years of age. She found that DQ was close to that of handicapped children in the early months but slowed between 6 and 9 months of age. Accordingly, MA increased relatively slightly during this period. After 10 months, the rate became more constant, showing only a slight but consistent fall thereafter. Thus MA also increased at a greater rate than during the first year.

It is not possible to say whether these changes parallel the course of the endogenous processes to which Sylvester refers. However, if a study on these lines were to be considered, we would suggest that finer measures of development should be used instead of or additional to DQ and MA. These are global estimates based on a heterogeneous sample of items selected primarily because they differentiate children's competence at various ages, not necessarily because of their intrinsic developmental significance. Instead, finer-grain experimental studies of early development are needed, perhaps complemented by recent tests of cognitive development derived from theory.

Within any such correlational study, however, it would have to be borne in mind that the developing Down's syndrome infant, like his or her non-handicapped peer, is influenced by environmental events and conditions and changes in both global and fine-grain measurements would also reflect such factors.

Reference

Carr, J. (1975). **Young Children with Down's Syndrome.** Butterworth, London

W. I. Fraser

I wish to make a plea for better clinical descriptions of the early stages, or the harbingers of dementia in the elderly. I am thinking most especially of Alzheimer's. In Down's one encounters quite often mischievousness, tantrums or antisocial conduct as the first stages, and we may have to wait two years for incontinence - the usual benchmark of dementia in the retarded. It is sad that the elderly parents must often wait for a diagnosis.

A. Heron

It is obvious from this valuable paper and from the critiques that the bulk of what knowledge we have about the concomitants of ageing in intellectually disabled adults comes from those whose lives have been spent in hospitals. With the trend towards "an ordinary life in the community", with varying degrees of support, it is becoming a matter of urgency to study the ageing process in an obviously different social and material environment, and to go beyond research on specific syndromes and conditions. Existing data and techniques of assessment, from the earlier (Heron and Chown, 1967) and recent work on "normal ageing", can and should be drawn upon. For example, there are methods available for assessing cognitive functioning which greatly improve on the "global IQ", derived from standardized tests which become increasingly inappropriate and uninformative with increase in age.

Reference

Heron, A. and Chown, S.M. (1967). **Age and Function.** London, Churchill

J. Jancar

This is a difficult topic about which to write, in the sense that very limited information is available about the elderly mentally retarded, and this should be mentioned at the outset.

There is, however, one major reservation about the research which needs to be stated, and that is its concentration on Down's syndrome. This is not, of course, the fault of the author, but it does require emphasis. The likelihood is that Down's syndrome individuals are atypical of the mentally handicapped as a whole in many respects; in fact their distinction as a group was rightly the reason for much of the research in the first place. However, one must be very cautious in generalizing from Down's syndrome individuals to the general population of the mentally handicapped, most especially when considering ageing which we know to be qualitatively and quantitatively distinct in those with Down's syndrome.

The final section of this contribution, "The Future", is somewhat limited in that it considers possible preventive measures which might reduce pathological changes in Down's syndrome subjects. Whilst this is obviously an important aspect of "Ageing in the Mentally Retarded", it does not really give the overview which one might expect to see. No mention is made of increasing longevity in the mentally handicapped and its implications - the increasing incidence of medical disorders and of the psychosyndromes of old age - nor of the urgent need for more research and planning in this increasingly important area.

I. Janota

The author must be complimented on his devotion to his subject over a clinical lifetime. My comments reflect a neuropathologist's experience, and that includes examining, amongst others, several brains of older Down's cases and many brains of other mentally retarded subjects.

The key to the relevance of this paper to scientific studies in mental retardation is in the section headed "The Future". In relation to the pathological changes of Alzheimer's disease in Down's syndrome the author writes "One difficulty is sifting from the numerous studies, cause and effect, and concentrating on the cause". Further in that section he says "it seems...in Down's syndrome that the pathological changes antedate, by a considerable margin of time, the clinical presentation of dementia...".

There is an emphasis on ageing Down's subjects with the pathological features of Alzheimer's disease. That, although not provoking new lines of research into Down's syndrome, a common enough form of mental retardation, could contribute to research into the very common organic dementing condition Alzheimer's disease. Sylvester refers to plaques, tangles and granulovacuolar degeneration in the temporal lobes from 27 patients with Down's syndrome who had died at St Lawrence's Hospital; in 88.9% of patients over the age of 30 years, 95% over 40 years and 100% over the age of 50 years. What were the numbers and other details of patients hidden in the percentages? For example, how big were their brains? What were the pathological changes elsewhere in the brain than in the temporal lobes?

It is interesting to read about the size of the hippocampus in coronal sections in 20 patients who had Down's syndrome. Were these patients 20 of the 27, or did they include some younger (than 30 or 34 years) subjects? It would be helpful to have the actual figures for this study, and not only the statement that "the hippocampi were significantly smaller in the Down's group". It would also help if the measurements of the hippocampus were related to the size of the brain and its components, and also to the senile or Alzheimer's and to any other changes.

Epilepsy is another vast subject. One reads that six of the 27 Down's cases had had epilepsy. In one of them fits started at the age of 17 years: he must be the one that died at the age of 34 years and had "senile changes" in the hippocampus; probably the youngest one of the 88.9%!

One is provoked to think of a host of points such as: the relation of the plaques and tangles, etc., to the function (in some at least of the Down's cases they appear to be there while the patients are not "dementing"), the size of the brain (in Down's), the changes in size as people grow older and or as they dement, or the justification for equating the pathology of ageing without dementia, Alzheimer's disease, Senile Dementia Alzheimer's Type, and Down's with plaques, tangles, etc. It would seem that in Down's syndrome the clinical course is very different from what is held for Alzheimer's disease. The paper also raises the spectre of "early" or "later" dementia, and whether the pathological changes, when measured (by weighing, counting, etc.) or seen under light or electron microscope, or estimated by chemists, are ever reversible.

It is important, especially if therapeutic trials from an early age are considered, to determine as far as possible the diagnosis. A sine qua non must be, for Down's syndrome, the karyotype. The imaging of the brain in life by non-invasive techniques like CT scanning, nuclear magnetic resonance and cerebral blood flow is constantly improving. The outcome of any therapeutic influences on the various aspects of Alzheimer's disease must also be kept in mind: unlikely as any beneficial effect may seem, it may in theory lead to increasing numbers of "better" Down's cases who live longer than in the past (or now). There are problems: I have found no senile changes in the brain of a 47 year old Down's case. Had that case been on a therapeutic trial for the last twenty years or longer - which was not the case - it may have been used as proof of successful treatment!

K. Rawnsley

Although the point is not made very explicit in Sylvester's paper, I believe it is important to distinguish between the ageing process generally and age-related diseases. A question easily posed and just as difficult to answer is whether certain categories of the mentally handicapped show evidence of premature ageing (perhaps demonstrated by tissue histology) irrespective of their liability to frank pathology. If this question was answered affirmatively then an important field of study could be opened up by examining the biochemical and biophysical correlates.

On the pathological front, some of the established findings are of the greatest interest, notably perhaps the universal liability of Down's syndrome subjects to Alzheimer's disease. Here again, as in so many ways, research in the field of mental handicap could illuminate wider issues. The state of the art is such that already the genetic basis of immune mechanisms can be tentatively mapped. Demonstrated anomalies in the immune enzyme profile in Down's cases may bear upon susceptibility to slow virus infection. The speed of development in molecular biology and immunology gives hope that a basis for the prevention of neuropsychiatric disorders of the presenium and senium may be acquired within the next decade or two.

The causation of age-related neurological change in the mentally handicapped will need much disentangling. Apart from the influence of "endogenous" factors such as the genetically based immune mechanisms mentioned above, there are also nutritional elements to be considered. Trace elements and vitamins may be low in the tissues of mentally handicapped subjects due to poor diet or impaired absorption. As mentioned in Sylvester's paper, vitamin E deficiency may cause accumulation of lipofuscin in spinal and cortical neurons. The effects of this phenomenon, normally associated with ageing, are conjectural in terms of producing neurological damage in humans, though this seems to happen in experimental rats.

Although the paper dwells at length on Down's syndrome which, understandably, provides a remarkable test bed for studying genetic influences on ageing and age-related diseases, the way seems to be wide open for the extension of these studies. In mental handicap there are many inborn errors of metabolism of a specific nature whose effect upon the ageing process in general and upon the age of the central nervous system in particular, could be fruitful.

P. E. Sylvester

Pathological changes of ageing can be demonstrated in the olfactory bulb of Down's patients and Alzheimer-type changes. This association with the rhinencephalon which is associated with the limbic in which Alzheimer changes are frequently located prompts the thought that changes in character or loss of the sense of smell may be a valuable asset to detecting early clinical effects of the ageing process.

SECTION III

COGNITIVE AND LINGUISTIC RESEARCH

Chapter 13

Social and educational adjustment of deaf children in relation to mental retardation

D.J. Wood

INCIDENCE OF PRELINGUAL HEARING IMPAIRMENT

In a recent survey of the incidence and effects of hearing impairment in EEC countries, it was estimated that 0.9/1000 children born in 1969 suffered hearing impairment of 50 dB or more in their better ear (CEC, 1979). In functional terms, only 12% of these children were able to hear a normal, conversational voice at 3 metres, when wearing their hearing-aids. In 33% of children, hearing losses were 100 dB or more. Even when attending a discotheque in full swing such children would only hear the faintest murmur. Perceptive (sensori-neural) hearing loss accounted for 92.0% of the population. There is no medical treatment for such cases. Only 2.6% were reported as suffering from conductive deafness. Such deafness was attributable to congenital deformities of both ears or to chronic middle-ear disease. Although the incidence of deafness fluctuates from time to time, this estimate is close to the 1 per 1000 which is most often cited for (developed) countries. It should be noted that only children with bilateral losses in excess of 50 dB were surveyed. The incidence of less severe and monaural loss is not documented. Nor do we have any extensive data on the incidence and effects of acute conductive losses.

Aetiology

Deafness has many causes, and somewhat different classifications are used in different countries. A distinction is always drawn, however, between people who are born deaf or become deaf in the first year or two of life (prelingual deafness) and those who become deaf having acquired speech (postlingual deafness). The CEC study, and the majority of other studies which I shall consider in this paper, are concerned with prelingual deafness. Another distinction which is usually made within the category of prelingual deafness, is one between congenital and acquired deafness. The major causes of congenital losses are maternal rubella (16% in the CEC survey and 17.6% in a survey of children born during 1962-68 in the USA by Jensema and Trybus (1975) and genetic (9% CEC; 8.5% USA). The major causes of acquired deafness include meningitis (about 6% in the CEC survey and 5% in the USA survey). Such estimates, however, are almost certainly on the low side, because there are a substantial proportion of children for whom the cause of deafness is not known (42% CEC; 45.6% in the USA survey). Since the cause of deafness has important prognostic implications (see below), this lack of information is a serious weakness in considering educational provision, etc. (see Recommendation 1(b) of CEC Report (1979)).

Recent analysis suggests that the large group of children reported as "cause unknown" in such surveys probably include a large congenital/genetic factor. This genetic analysis suggests that of the congenitally deaf population, 40% are recessive, 10% dominant and 2% X-linked. The estimate of 9% genetic causes in the CEC survey is almost certainly an underestimate. Furthermore, analyses of date-of-birth data from this survey reveal marked seasonal variations in incidence of rubella births. A similar pattern (much less marked) was found in the cause unknowns but not the congenital group. This suggests that another subgroup of the cause unknowns are rubella children.

The analyses point to the potential value of genetic counselling in prevention of deafness. The need for action to prevent rubella births is widely acknowledged but such children are still being diagnosed (see Taylor, 1981) and more should be done to reduce this population.

Dual Incidence of Mental Retardation and Hearing Impairment

Studies of non-verbal intelligence in hearing-impaired populations reveal a normal distribution of intelligence. This, coupled with evidence showing no correlation between degree of hearing loss and intelligence, demonstrates that deafness and intelligence are independent. Although the non-verbal IQ of deaf samples tends to average some 5-6 IQ points below that for hearing populations, the high incidence of children with other handicapping conditions amongst the deaf (see below) makes it unlikely that such a small difference indicates a lower overall intelligence.

The CEC survey identified 28.8% of the hearing-impaired population studied as suffering from one or more handicaps in addition to deafness (USA, 29%, from Ries et al. (1975)). Mental retardation was one of the three major additional handicaps (alone or in combination with others) accounting for 9% of the total population. The American study identified approximately 8% as mentally retarded and a further 3% suffering from brain damage. It should be noted, however, that the estimates of mental retardation were subjective ones and were not based on any formal test scores. In addition they include a number of children for whom relevant data were not reported

(14.4% in the USA survey). Nevertheless these figures suggest an estimate of about 1 child in every 10 000 suffering both hearing impairment and mental retardation. However, this is an extremely conservative estimate of the magnitude of the problem. Children with binaural losses less than 50 dB and those with monaural losses or suffering acute hearing loss are not included. It has been reported, for example, that a proportion of Down's syndrome children suffer from middle-ear infections which are extremely difficult to eradicate (e.g. Taylor, 1981). The magnitude of such problems is not established.

The relatively high proportion of hearing-impaired children suffering from multiple handicaps underlines the heterogeneity of this population.

EDUCATIONAL CONSEQUENCES OF DEAFNESS AND MENTAL HANDICAP

A large number of studies in several different countries testify to the serious and intractable educational consequences of prelingual deafness. Any language-based measures - speech intelligibility, speech comprehension, reading and writing - reveal marked deficits. For example, average reading ages are about 8-9 years at age 16 years chronological age. Spoken language ability and speech comprehension are similarly impaired. The CEC survey (again based on subjective estimates) found that only 47% of its sample were able to speak intelligibly to strangers at age 8 years and 6% had no speech or totally unintelligible speech. Only 32% were reported as reading at a normal reading age; 10% were unable to read at all.

Studies of academic achievement in non-language areas (e.g. mathematical computation) reveal less pronounced effects. Even in these areas, some retardation is found, however. A British study, for example (Wood _et al._, in press), established a maths age of 12.5 years at school leaving over the population of children in special schools and units. Even partially hearing children in ordinary schools with mean hearing losses of 48 dB leave school at 16 with average maths ages of 14 years.

Achievement, Severity of Hearing Loss and Intelligence

In most studies of language achievements, the degree of hearing loss emerges as a major correlate of performance (e.g. Jensema and Trybus, 1978; CEC survey, 1979). In non-verbal tasks, e.g. mathematical computation, the pattern is less clear cut. One US study (DiFrancesca, 1972) found a positive relationship between hearing loss and some aspects of mathematical abilities; the UK study found a significant but weak negative correlation.

Intelligence is also correlated with achievement in both language and non-language areas, though, in the case of language, the effect is less marked than that for hearing loss. An American survey of the relationships between hearing loss, additional handicapping conditions and academic achievement established that mental retardation exerted the greatest additional effects on performance in both linguistic and non-linguistic activities. Brain damage and epilepsy were next in their effects (Jensema, 1975).

Another major factor affecting achievement - which is partially confounded by the incidence of secondary handicaps - is aetiology. Here, prematurity was most negatively related to performance, but rubella and other causes also exerted some effect.

It seems clear, then, as might be supposed, that the dual handicaps of deafness and mental retardation interact in their effects on educational development to the detriment of the child. The possibility of the development of functional linguistic and academic skills in such children, on present evidence, seems remote.

Deafness, Mental Retardation and Behavioural/Emotional Adjustment

A recent survey of the prevalence of behavioural and emotional problems in hearing-impaired and deaf children (Meadow, 1980) compared the results of five different studies which indicate rates of disturbance ranging from 8 to 22%. These studies were undertaken in the USA, Canada and the Isle of Wight. Despite the marked variation in estimates of the magnitude of this problem, all studies conclude that behavioural problems are more frequent in the deaf than in the hearing populations. As in studies of academic achievement, there is clear evidence that aetiology is a powerful factor determining incidence (which, in part, explains some of the discrepancies between studies). One study reported by Meadow suggests that rubella children show more than 3 times the incidence of problems than children whose deafness is hereditary (31% to 10%). Deafness associated with prematurity (27%), Rh factor (15%) and meningitis (12%) were also associated with higher incidence.

One estimate of the frequency of serious behaviour problems in American hearing children estimated that 2% of children and adolescents required immediate psychiatric help and a further 8-10% needed some form of help. The Isle of Wight survey estimated psychiatric disorder in 6.6% of the general population. It seems clear, then, that deafness is associated with a higher incidence of serious behavioural disturbance. Given the subjective nature of many estimates, precise comparison is hazardous.

It appears that the cause of deafness relates to both academic achievement and the probability of behavioural and emotional disturbance in a similar fashion.

Another finding relevant to the present survey is that deaf children of low intelligence show higher rates of problems than the more intelligent deaf (Schlesinger and Meadow, 1972; Jensema and Trybus, 1975). Jensema and Trybus, for example, report an overall incidence of emotional/behavioural problems in 8.9% of their hearing-impaired sample. But the incidence was only 5.3% in deaf children with no additional handicaps, while 17% of children who were also mentally retarded and 26% of children suffering brain damage evinced such problems. Subsequent analyses (Goulder and Trybus, 1977) provided evidence for the validity of these estimates.

ORIGINS OF POOR ACHIEVEMENT AND PSYCHOLOGICAL DISTURBANCE

An analysis of the reasons for low educational attainment and the high incidence of psychological disturbance in hearing-impaired children and, in particular, those who are also mentally retarded, is both complex and controversial. The main issues involved together with the educational and research implications arising out of these are considered below.

Early Diagnosis and the Assessment of Needs

One general assumption which pervades work with hearing-impaired children holds that early diagnosis coupled with provision of good hearing aids and consistent family support will benefit future generations of deaf children and improve their linguistic, emotional and educational development. As yet, however, there is no compelling evidence to support this assumption. Although there is evidence to show that early provision of aids and their consistent use at home and school correlates with measures of academic achievement (and, by implication, with psychological wellbeing), this relationship is confounded with other variables (e.g. family income, ethnic background, degree of hearing loss and educational environment). Whilst it would be inexcusable to ignore the potential causal influence of early diagnosis and provision, there is, as the CEC report recommends, a need for "accurate studies of the relation of time of hearing aid issue to communication skills and patterns of educational provision" (Recommendation 2(a)). The results of a study of communication patterns and educational achievement of hearing-impaired children in the USA (Jensema and Trybus, 1978) also found correlations between use of aids and achievement, but they conclude, having partialled out the effects of other variables, that "relatively fixed and unchangeable factors presently have the greatest impact on the educational achievement of hearing-impaired children" (p.19). They recommend greater attention in future research to materials, teaching methods, attitudinal and cognitive factors. This work draws attention to the need to look in detail at the actual experiences of hearing-impaired children in different family and educational environments to identify new factors which might be causally involved in relative success and failure.

There is some basis for confidence that our ability to detect hearing impairment in infants is improving. New technology, like the Linco-Bennett cradle, is currently being evaluated, and some attempts to improve screening techniques by developing the skills of health visitors and by exploiting the diagnostic insights of parents are under way. Preliminary evidence suggests that this latter course of action can significantly improve the age of diagnosis.

However, early diagnosis is only likely to prove of benefit if infants can be provided with good-quality hearing aids and if their parents can be helped to improve their children's developmental environment. Current research shows quite clearly that the quality of family relationships is often seriously impaired by infant deafness, leading not only to dislocation of parents' natural capacities for helping their children develop communication and speech, but also to a good deal of emotional upset for both parent and child (e.g. Gregory, 1976; Schlesinger and Meadow, 1972). The success of any system of family support can now be measured against its ability to attenuate or ameliorate such effects. Thus, we need not wait for measures of long-term progress in children to make useful evaluations of the effectiveness of different systems of support.

Although there is a growing awareness amongst professionals of the importance of such factors there is, as yet, no evidence to show that such increased awareness results in improved support. Indeed, some research indicates that early support may have counter-productive consequences (e.g. Gregory and Mogford, 1980; Wood, 1982). In part, this may be a consequence of the training of those providing support. In the UK, this is usually in the hands of trained teachers. Whether such training is necessary or sufficient to meet the needs of families with very young children remains open to question.

When we turn our attention to the detection and support of children suffering multiple handicaps, and, more specifically, to children who are both hearing-impaired and mentally retarded, the picture is even more vague. Current evidence makes it clear that our capacity to detect and support such children is limited. A screening survey in the Midlands and North of England (Ives, 1974) revealed that detailed assessment of deaf children's intelligence, psychological adjustment and general progress is relatively rare. Furthermore, children's special needs were often decided in the absence of "indicated psychological and/or psychiatric investigation" (p 114). The CEC survey reported only 5-6% of multiply handicapped children being educated in schools designed for the multiply handicapped - in comparison with an estimated incidence of such handicaps in 22.8% of the population. It seems clear that detailed assessment of, and provision for, multiply handicapped children - including those who are mentally retarded - is the exception and not the rule.

Here too, however, careful assessment and special provision are only useful if they lead on to more skilled and appropriate support. Given our ignorance about the numbers and needs of such children, it is not surprising to find that we have no compelling evidence about how best they should be placed and educated.

Methods of Communication

The issues surrounding the question of which mode of communication is best suited to the needs of hearing-impaired children lead us to a conceptual and empirical quagmire. A variety of different techniques are currently in use, ranging from a "natural oral/aural" approach which relies on amplification and a "normal" speech environment, through techniques which supplement oral communication (e.g. cued speech and finger spelling) to "natural" sign languages. A detailed consideration of the nature and (professed) merits of these different systems is beyond the scope of the present exercise. To date, no compelling evidence favouring any one approach over another has been forthcoming (e.g. Jensema and Trybus, 1978). More seriously, perhaps, is the fact that widespread uncertainty and disagreement about the needs of children is accompanied by a lack of consistency in children's experiences. Jensema and Trybus found, for example, that a child who experienced the same mode of communication at home and school, with teachers, parents and peers, was exceptional. Usually, children are exposed to and use two or more different modes of communication. It seems highly likely that a child's ability to master different modes of communication without a systematic experience in the use of any one is severely limited - particularly if he is of less than average intelligence. This implies that children who do experience systematic use of one language or another are likely to do better than average.

Turning back to the specific needs of children who are also mentally retarded, we find ourselves, again, largely involved in speculation. Ideally, a consideration of the cognitive abilities of children of different levels of intelligence, coupled with a sound psychological analysis of the processes involved in the development of any system of communication should produce the design constraints for an effective system of provision. There has now been a good deal of research which has examined the general cognitive abilities of children who are mentally retarded. Problems such children face in the maintenance of attention, generalization of learning and specific problems involved in the acquisition of language have, for example, been explored at some length. There is also a growing body of knowledge about the processes of language and educational development in the hearing-impaired. This work provides, at minimum, some general insights into the role of intelligence and mental capacities in the linguistic and educational development of the deaf. Work into the processes involved in the development of sign language is also making progress and this indicates that early communication is "easier" or more "natural" (and which word one chooses betrays a fundamental stance in relation to the nature of hearing impairment) for many deaf children. This, coupled with the fact that sign vocabularies like "Makaton" are being used increasingly with normally hearing, severely mentally retarded children, points to the possible benefits of sign language use with the mentally retarded, deaf child.

In the final analysis, however, we are unable to provide a compelling basis for decisions about all forms of provision for a given child. As the 1981 Education Act comes into force, we may hope that the greater attention it demands to the assessment and evaluation of provision for every child with special needs will accelerate the process of gathering the evidence we demand. The kinds of evidence we need are becoming increasingly clear; the process of gathering it is still to be determined in any detail.

Educational Goals and Quality of Life

Processes of education have grown up, largely, to facilitate the transmission of knowledge, skills and culture from the mature to the immature. Although educational systems are not without their critics both in relation to the goals they serve and their competence in achieving them, there is still, one suspects, some measure of agreement about what basic skills and knowledge they should attempt to engender. However, when we come to consider the needs and likely levels of achievement of tiny populations - such as the mentally retarded, hearing-impaired - there is no guarantee that those abilities which schools are designed to foster are relevant or desirable. So small is the population, so rare are those who have had extended experience of both handicaps, that we lack, as a culture, any detailed intuitions about the needs and capacities of such children. The evidence we have been considering about the impact of deafness on the development of linguistic and educational achievements suggests strongly that we may have to pursue a different and more realistic set of goals for such children if their education and general quality of life is not to be one of constant frustration, emotional disturbance and failure. At the same time, we must not underestimate the capacities of any particular child nor impose additional constraints on his development or life-chances by denying him an opportunity to achieve any educational objectives of which he may, ultimately, prove capable. The dividing line between lack of opportunity and unrealistic demands is a difficult one to draw with any child. With the children we have been considering here, it is even more daunting. By integrating the knowledge of those who have a wide experience of mental handicap and others who have worked with the deaf, it is to be hoped that the process of finding the line might be facilitated. In the longer term, however, we must aim for much more detailed and objective information about the nature, needs and abilities of such children.

REFERENCES

Commission of the European Communities, (1979), **Childhood Deafness in the European Community.** ECSC-EEC-EAEC, Brussels and Luxembourg

DiFrancesca, S., (1972), **Academic Achievement Test Results of a National Testing Program for Hearing-Impaired Students.** Office of Demographic Studies, Gallaudet College, Washington, DC

Goulder, T.J. and Trybus, R.J., (1977), **The Classroom Behavior of Emotionally Disturbed Hearing Impaired Children.** Office of Demographic Studies, Gallaudet College, Washington, DC

Gregory, S., (1976), **The Deaf Child and His Family.** London, Allen & Unwin

Gregory, S., and Mogford, K., (1980), Early language development in young deaf children. In Woll, B., Kyle J., and Deuchar, M., (Eds). **Perspectives on British Sign Language and Deafness.** London, Croom Helm

Ives, L.A., (1974), **A Screening Survey of 2060 Hearing Impaired Children in the Midlands and North of England.** The Royal School for the Deaf (Manchester), England

Jensema, C., (1975), **The Relationship between Academic Achievement and the Demographic Characteristics of Hearing Impaired Children and Youths.** Office of Demographic Studies, Gallaudet College, Washington, DC

Jensema, C., and Trybus, R.J., (1975), **Reported Emotional/Behavioral Problems among Hearing Impaired Children in Special Educational Programs: United States, 1972-73.** Office of Demographic Studies, Gallaudet College, Washington, DC

Jensema, C., and Trybus, R.J., (1978), **Communication Patterns and Educational Achievement of Hearing Impaired Students.** Office of Demographic Studies, Gallaudet College, Washington, DC

Meadow, K.P., (1980), **Deafness and Child Development.** London, Edward Arnold

Ries, P.W., Bateman, D.L., and Schildroth, A., (1975), **Ethnic Background in Relation to Other Characteristics of Hearing Impaired Students in the United States.** Office of Demographic Studies, Gallaudet College, Washington, DC

Schlesinger, H.S., and Meadow, K.P., (1972), **Sound and Sign: Childhood Deafness and Mental Health.** Berkeley, University of California Press

Taylor, I.G., (1981), Medicine and education, **Teacher of the Deaf, 5**,5, 134-143

Wood, D., (1982), The linguistic experiences of the pre-lingually hearing-impaired child, **Teacher of the Deaf, 6**, 4, 86-93

Wood, D., Wood, H.A., and Howarth, S.P., (in press), Mathematical abilities in deaf school leavers, **British Journal of Developmental Psychology**

COMMENTARY

J. Hogg

Wood's paper amply highlights our considerable ignorance concerning the developmental consequences of hearing impairment, and our even greater ignorance regarding the impact of such impairment on mentally retarded children. He also points towards the context in which we might begin to seek clarification of such consequences - namely the ecology of the child as a determinant of cognitive, social and emotional development. While it may eventually prove possible to investigate in its own right the ecology of the severely or profoundly retarded deaf child, the starting point for such research will almost certainly be the work that has been undertaken with deaf children not at obvious risk for mental retardation.

Wood's response to this research and its relevance is at best one of extreme caution, and it might be helpful to invite some reaction to a more positive evaluation. Two areas merit particular attention, namely those of communication and behaviour disorders. Schlesinger and Meadow (1972) and Bellugi and Klima (1972) have both reported impressive development in the communication skills of deaf children raised by deaf or hearing parents committed to the use of a sign language (in these instances the American Sign Language, AMESLAN). With regard to a variety of developments these children showed most of the major psycholinguistic features of hearing children acquiring spoken language. In addition, Schlesinger and Meadow show that bilingual deaf children, i.e. those exposed to visual and spoken language, are not impaired in the acquisition of spoken language as a result of learning signing.

With depressing monotony discussions about the education of deaf children inevitably seem to founder on the oral/signing debate, and I would like to avoid leading us in that direction here. Indeed, this debate is much more of an issue in the field of deaf education than it is in the area of augmented communication systems (including signing) in the fields of mental and physical handicap. Nevertheless, I feel that whether, to use Wood's expression, this area is "a conceptual and empirical quagmire" or not, the above findings on the acquisition of non-oral language by deaf children are sufficiently impressive to direct our attention to the need for creating communicative environments for retarded children which parallel those of the deaf child communicating through signing. Both the form of non-oral communication system and the content of such a programme will depend on the nature and degree of the retarded child's handicap, and will of course take into account specific cognitive delays, deficits and additional handicaps.

Acquisition of a communicative system of any sort will not only depend on what might be described as the overall communicative context, but will be inextricably bound up with the overall emotional or affective quality of that context. Conner

(1976) reports work by Greenstein (1975) that suggests that the more balanced development of deaf children of deaf parents reflects more than the appropriateness of their communicative medium (i.e. signing). It is also an indication of the parents' greater acceptance of their child's hearing impairment than is sometimes the case with hearing parents of deaf children. Indeed, he reports that Greenstein's work suggests that when hearing parents of deaf children are also accepting of their child, then his or her emotional and behavioural development is closer to that of the deaf child of deaf parents.

Research on the relation between communication difficulties and behaviour disorders is, however, admittedly slight and future studies focussing on the genesis of the latter as a consequence of the former are required if we are to go beyond simple epidemiological information describing the relation. Certainly it must be anticipated that this relation is complex, and that a variety of other factors will also be involved. How far the elucidation of these factors will illuminate the nature of communicative and behavioural disorders in mentally retarded children will depend on several complicating factors. Two require special attention. First, it is clear that even in the absence of additional sensory and physical handicaps the ecology of the mentally retarded child differs substantially from that of the non-retarded child in both family and school settings (e.g. Berger and Cunningham, 1981; Beveridge and Evans, 1978). The additional impact of hearing impairment within these distinctive ecologies should provide a prime focus for research in this area with respect to communication and also behaviour disorders. Second, it will be necessary to distinguish behaviour disorders conditioned by hearing and other sensory impairment from those arising from other sources. Vernon (1969) has shown how the incidence of behaviour disorders in a hearing-impaired population are related to different aetiologies. Rubella-damaged children, for example, showed most profound maladjustment, followed by meningitic children. Children with hereditary deafness and Rh factor children showed significantly higher levels of adjustment. Vernon suggests that these distinctions reflect presence or absence of brain damage (e.g. rubella vs hereditary deafness) or site of damage (e.g. rubella vs Rh factor). Thus, on the basis of comparisons some attribution of behaviour disorders to degrees *per se* and to the nature of brain damage can be made.

To distinguish relative causes as we move into the extremely complex area of profound retardation with multiple handicap is a major problem. Though some practitioners may have documented individual cases for their own purposes, this complex situation is not to my knowledge one that has been reported on in the research literature. Since matching of groups in this area is probably inherently impossible, such studies will almost certainly have to explore the issues involved through single-case or small group designs (e.g. Hogg, 1983; Hogg *et al.*, 1979; Remington *et al.*, 1979). From this basis it is possible to envisage longitudinal studies of hearing-impaired severely and profoundly retarded individuals in which a combination of psychological and sensory assessment would be integrated with ecological analysis in order to account for a variety of aspects of behavioural development including maladjustment.

References

Bellugi U. and Klima E.S. (1972). The roots of language in the sign talk of the deaf. **Psychology Today, 76**, 61-64

Berger J. and Cunningham C.C. (1981). The development of eye contact between mothers and normal versus Down's syndrome infants. **Developmental Psychology, 17**, 678-689

Beveridge M. and Evans P. (1978). Classroom interaction: two studies of severely subnormal children. **Research in Education, 19**, 39-48

Conner L.E. (1976). New directions in infant programs for the deaf. **The Volta Review, 78**, 8-15

Greenstein J.M. (1975). **Methods of Fostering Language in Deaf Infants.** Final Report to HEW, Grant no. OEG-P-72-539, June

Hogg, J. (1983). Sensory and social reinforcement of head-turning in a profoundly retarded multiply handicapped child. **British Journal of Clinical Psychology**, (in press)

Hogg J., Remington R.E. and Foxen T.H. (1979). Classical conditioning of profoundly retarded, multiply handicapped children. **Developmental Medicine and Child Neurology, 21**, 779-786

Remington R.E., Foxen T. and Hogg J. (1977). Auditory reinforcement in profoundly retarded multiply handicapped children. **American Journal of Mental Deficiency, 82**, 299-304

Schlesinger H.S. and Meadow K.P. (1972). **Sound and Sign: Childhood Deafness and Mental Health**, University of California Press, Berkeley

Vernon M. (1969). **Multiply Handicapped Deaf Children: Medical, Educational and Psychological Considerations**, Council for Exceptional Children Research Monograph, Washington D.C.

J. Carr

One of the major questions discussed by Wood concerns the methods of communication that the deaf mentally handicapped child should be encouraged to use. Clearly a child who has some hearing will be fitted with a hearing aid, in the expectation that speech will develop. Hearing aids however are not always well accepted by mentally handicapped children, and sometimes a carefully planned programme will be required to teach the child to use it (Wilson and Moore, 1979).

What advice however should be given to the family of a young profoundly deaf mentally handicapped child? Not only is there still controversy as to whether only speech, or speech plus signing, should be used, but several different signing systems exist. Each has its ardent proponents and each is used and taught in different areas, even in different schools within the same area. Some (British Sign Language, Paget Gorman Sign System) rely on hand and finger signs. Others (Bliss, Rebus) make use of pictorial symbols. The former are more flexible and require no equipment, the latter are more practicable for those with manual co-ordination problems. Any of the systems may facilitate communication with those in his immediate circle for the mentally retarded deaf person (and for an increasing number of non-deaf mentally retarded people): all are usually incomprehensible to the general public. At present those who use signs, whether or not they are mentally retarded, cannot communicate outside their own environment, within which the system they know is used. Perhaps research is needed to discover what is the most widely used signing system, and then how this could be publicized and popularized amongst the general public so that those who rely on signing to communicate would meet at least some comprehension in the outside world.

Like many multiply handicapped children the deaf mentally handicapped child does not fit easily into the educational system, and the problems are compounded when the child is also emotionally disturbed. Aetiology of the deafness is important, and a far higher level of emotional disorder can be expected of children suffering from the effects of maternal rubella. Chess (1971) diagnosed autism in 6.8% of rubella children, compared with 7.8 per 10 000 in the general population (Lotter, 1966). Children who are both deaf and autistic pose some of the severest problems of management, even where they are not severely mentally handicapped, because of their inability to make sense of the world, coupled with the difficulty of communicating with them. Some of these children may be taught signing, which they will demonstrate when this is demanded of them; what remains extremely difficult is to convey to these children that the signs have a useful function for them and to arrive at a point where they will use signs spontaneously (Carr, 1976).

There is some suggestion that deafness does not severely disadvantage the working adult. Jackson (1975), reviewing the effect of secondary handicaps on employment for mildly mentally handicapped people, found deafness the least likely to be associated with poor work adjustment. This somewhat surprising result Jackson attributes to the fact that deafness is not visibly apparent, and is remediable by mechanical aids, and is "the subject of greater public understanding, sympathy and tolerance" (though some might dispute this latter viewpoint). Speech defects were related to a high level of adverse adjustment, and, especially in the congenitally deaf, the two are likely to be closely associated and hence might lead to more severe difficulties.

References

Carr J. (1976). The severely retarded autistic child. In: **Early Childhood Autism**, Wing, L. (Ed.), Pergamon, New York

Chess S. (1971). Autism in children with congenital rubella. **Journal of Autism and Childhood Schizophrenia, 1**, 33

Jackson R. (1975). The effect of secondary handicaps on the employment adjustment of educable mentally handicapped adolescents in Scotland. **British Journal of Mental Subnormality, 21**, 61-70

Lotter V. (1966). Epidemiology of autistic conditions in young children. I: Prevalence. **Social Psychiatry, 1**, 124

Wilson B.A. and Moore P. (1979). A chaining procedure to teach a retarded deaf girl to wear her hearing aid. **British Journal of Mental Subnormality, 25**, 88-90

For additional comments by D.M. Ricks, see Commentary following Chapter 14 [Editor]

Chapter 14

Visual impairment in the mentally retarded

Elisabeth M. Bleeker-Wagemakers

GENERAL ASPECTS

Visual Disorders

The close temporal, spatial and histological correlation between the development of the eyes and the brain explains the high frequency of disorders of the eye in the mentally retarded. Studies such as those by Bankes (1974a, b, c), Markovits (1975) and Henry (1980) yield abnormalities of refraction in about 50%, strabismus in 40% and nystagmus in 10% of mentally retarded children. The ocular disorders are often not recognized by caregivers and medical staff, or are thought to be a sign of mental deterioration. Strabismus may be an isolated symptom by itself and such as being a cause of amblyopia. It can also be an expression of primary ophthalmological or neurological disease. Early detection of abnormalities of refraction, followed by proper correction, may improve the social and intellectual performance of the child and prevent visual impairment caused by amblyopia. Nystagmus always indicates pathology. In childhood routine ophthalmological examination therefore should be done regularly in every case of mental retardation, followed by more extensive investigation if abnormalities are found.

Visual Impairment

Visual impairment is the term used if an individual is handicapped by blindness or partial sightedness. According to the International Association for the Prevention of Blindness (IAPB) (1964), blindness implies a visual acuity of less than 6/60, partial sightedness a visual acuity of more than 6/60 but less than 6/18. A serious restriction of the visual field may be an important factor determining visual impairment.

Mental retardation and visual handicap mutually amplify their disadvantageous effect on the intellectual and social functioning of the child. Thus a visual disturbance which in a mentally normal child would not be a reason for special care or attention, can be a disability to a mentally handicapped child; on the other hand, in a child of normal intelligence, a serious visual impairment can give the false impression that the child has low intelligence.

In Denmark, Warburg (1963, 1970, 1975) and Warburg et al. (1979) intensively studied the amount of visual impairment in the mentally retarded. In the populations of mentally retarded children she studied, about 5% were blind and 7-8% partially sighted. According to Hyvärinen and Lindstedt (1981) the prevalence of visual impairment in mentally retarded children is 11-15%; a hundred times more frequent than in normal children (around 1/1000). In the Netherlands more than 5% of institutionalized mentally retarded children are living in institutions for the visually handicapped mentally retarded. The actual percentage of visually handicapped mentally retarded in the overall population is higher since a fair number have been allocated to non-specific institutions for the mentally retarded.

Ophthalmological Examination in the Mentally Retarded

For effective ophthalmological examination it is most important to be familiar with the mentally retarded, to be patient and to take time for careful observation. The investigator should know whether the child can talk, if he can name objects and how he names them. The place of investigation preferably should be the child's own surroundings, i.e. the institution or school. Sometimes in the clinic room a conclusion about the social and visual function of the child cannot be reached; it can be useful then to observe the child in his play, outside, in school, or in his living-quarters.

Assessment of visual acuity may be hindered by the lack of concentration of the child, as well as by difficulties of interpretation. In order to remove the interfering effect of other dysfunctions, the test for measuring visual acuity in the retarded subject must be as simple as possible. With the increasing complexity of the visual test, the measured acuity diminishes. In the very young and seriously retarded child a fair impression of visual functioning can be obtained from the corneal light reflexes, the cover test, the amount of following, the appearance of the corneas, the ocular pupils and the pupillary reactions. This is a technically simple method of screening which in the Netherlands is applied in the primary medical care (Child Welfare Clinics) for infants of 9 months and older (Loewer-Sieger, 1976). In the seriously mentally retarded this procedure can be used at later ages as well. Depending on the age and extent of mental retardation other tests which can be used are: Snellen's optotypes, Landolt rings, Ffooks optotypes, the Stycar Vision Test and Candy Beads. If abnormalities are found with these screening tests an ophthalmologist must be consulted for further diagnosis and treatment. He has at his disposal methods of investigation that are less likely to be influenced by mental retardation.

Special Care for and Education of the Visually Handicapped Mentally Retarded

Before the foundation of specific institutions, the visually handicapped and mentally retarded were taken care of and educated in institutions either for the mentally retarded or for the visually handicapped. It is clear that for each of these handicaps a specific educational programme is required. An educational programme for the visually handicapped mentally retarded cannot be a simple combination of these; on the contrary they mutually exclude each other. On the one hand, for the development of the mentally retarded child concrete and practical situations are important, together with opportunities to learn by imitation. However, this cannot be realized for a child who has a visual handicap as well, who cannot see the concrete situation, nor whom or what has to be imitated. On the other hand, the mentally retarded child will have only a limited understanding of spoken language, which involves definitions and abstractions. Similarly the development of touch, which requires imagination to be useful is once again dependent upon intelligence. There is a clash between the abstract way in which the blind child contacts the world and the cognitive skills which the mentally retarded child needs. Thus, an educational programme for the visually handicapped mentally retarded cannot only consist of a combination of both methods. They need their own programme consisting of selected aspects of these programmes in addition to new elements developed to make optimal use of their restricted potential (de Jong, 1981).

EARLY DETECTION OF VISUAL DISORDERS AND VISUAL IMPAIRMENT

In the past it was usually thought that for a mentally retarded child the only thing that really mattered was good care. In particular, a detailed investigation into the possible causes of the handicap was held to be of little use, since knowing a cause would neither influence the handicap, nor have any therapeutic consequence. Even now many parents and those taking care of mentally retarded children do not realize the consequences of a correct diagnosis. This is especially true for visual functioning in respect of the overall diagnosis. The most important reasons why any child suspected to be mentally retarded should be seen, preferably in the first year of life, by an ophthalmologist experienced in child ophthalmology, are as follows:

To Make an Ocular and General Diagnosis

As stated above, ocular disorders and visual impairment are much more frequent in mentally retarded than in mentally normal children.

Some congenital morphological abnormalities are clinically manifest directly after birth (microphthalmos, aniridia, coloboma). Others are progressive and will not be noticed until the child is some months old (retinoblastoma, glaucoma, some types of cataract).

Of the disorders of function strabismus is by far the most frequent in the first year of life. Amblyopia (defined as loss of sight by lack of use of one or both eyes) may follow when the retina is deprived of light impulses (as in cataract), or when the image of one eye is suppressed centrally as in strabismus or refractory abnormalities. Nystagmus may have a cerebral cause, but may also be of ocular origin, i.e. when the central part of the retina is underdeveloped, morphologically or functionally. Erratic eye movements indicate very poor sight. If no ocular explanation if forthcoming, they indicate cerebral blindness. A definite diagnosis is made by electrophysiological investigation. Abnormalities of refraction usually have no practical consequences before the age of six in normal children. Sometimes high myopia may already be prominent in babies as may high hypermetropia and astigmatism. In the mentally retarded however abnormalities of refraction are far more frequent and attention should be paid to a good correction. As a rule most disorders of function point to an underlying pathology that should be detected.

Apart from its importance for the ocular diagnosis, the ophthalmological investigation may contribute considerably to or establish the general diagnosis.

To Improve the Quality of Life

One may wonder whether early detection of a visual disorder is of any use; why not wait until it is clinically manifest? At birth the development of the eyes and of sight is not yet complete. In the first months of life there is an acceleration of growth with development of functions that may disappear quickly and forever if perturbed. This is called a "critical period". For the optimal development of sight and the prevention of visual impairment, abnormalities should be detected and treated as early as possible in the critical period. Treatment of amblyopia, for instance, has less good results and takes more time if postponed to the age of 2-3 years. In some congenital abnormalities the results of treatment depend on the moment it is started (cataract, retinoblastoma). Other congenital abnormalities cannot themselves be treated (microphthalmos, aniridia). In these cases it may be worth while to find out if the ocular abnormality is part of a syndrome which is known to have therapeutic consequences for the child. In the case of sporadic aniridia, which is sometimes associated with a chromosomal abnormality (a deletion of the short arm of chromosome 11), the child has an increased chance of acquiring Wilms' tumour. This is a malignant growth of the kidney, which requires regular physical examination to be detected, and may be treated successfully.

Apart from its consequences for the visual handicap, early ophthalmological diagnosis is important for the prevention of secondary retardation (a lack of development as a consequence of the visual handicap), which is additive to the existing mental retardation.

In the third place early detection of visual impairment may initiate, at the earliest possible age, the specific approach to the doubly handicapped child. In the Netherlands the institutes for the blind and partially sighted run a home-teaching service for parents, assisting them in the education of the visually handicapped child, as well as planning with them the future care and education (home-care, day-school, institution) of their child.

To Help Parents Accept Their Handicapped Child

Most parents are quite unprepared when the handicap of their child becomes manifest. At that moment they see all their expectations blocked. They are preoccupied by questions about the cause of the child's handicap, whether it could have been prevented, and what to expect of the future. These questions can only be answered after careful investigation leading to a diagnosis. The results may help the parents work through their sorrow and eventually accept the handicapped child. Only under these conditions can the child find its place in the family and can realistic plans be made for the child and family.

To Initiate Counselling and Prevention

If, after accepting the handicapped child, the parents consider having another child, the question will arise "what are the chances that a new child will have the same handicap?" The answer to this question involves genetic counselling. A proper diagnosis is a prerequisite for genetic advice, but in addition data may have to be collected on the pregnancy, birth, neonatal period and the further development as well as on the other members of the family in order to determine the aetiological moment and the risk of recurrence. Genetic counselling should take place as early as possible. The effect of genetic counselling is twofold; on the one hand it provides information in the case of a hereditary disorder; on the other hand, if the disorder appears to be non-genetic, parents and other members of the family may be reassured. In this case any preventive measures that may be taken to prevent the non-genetic congenital disorder can be discussed as part of the counselling.

CAUSES OF VISUAL IMPAIRMENT IN THE MENTALLY RETARDED

Jaeger (1975) pointed out that the most important cause of blindness in the period 1885-1914 was infectious lesions of the cornea, whereas in the period 1960-1967 it was malformations of the eye. In the latter period infectious lesions of the cornea no longer appeared as a cause of blindness at all. A similar difference is seen if one compares the causes of blindness in Third World countries (eye affections arising as a result of infections or a deficient diet), with those of developed areas of the world (inherited eye abnormalities and eye lesions acquired during the perinatal period) (Newcomb, 1977). A working party of the International Association for the Prevention of Blindness (Schappert-Kimmijser et al., 1975) studied the causes of visual impairment in children in five Western-European countries. For the Netherlands the causes were considered to be genetic in 45% of the children; for Belgium, Norway and Sweden the figures were respectively 37%, 36% and 25%. However, it was not possible to subdivide these groups into mentally normal and mentally retarded children. In Denmark this distinction could be made: the cause was genetic in 41% of the mentally normal and in 20% of the mentally retarded. These Danish figures are remarkably comparable to those obtained in two earlier Dutch studies: genetic causes in 46% of mentally normal children (van Veelen et al., 1969) and in 22% of mentally handicapped (Copper and Schappert-Kimmijser, 1970).

After the opening in 1972 of Bartiméushage (Doorn, The Netherlands), a residential centre for the visually and mentally handicapped, it was evident that the relatives of the inmates had a growing need for genetic advice. In order to meet this need, an investigation was required to determine the frequency with which inherited visual disorders were found in the institution as well as to investigate the nature of such affections.

All inmates present in the institute between April 1975 and January 1979 were included in the investigation. Data were gathered on the pregnancy, birth, neonatal period and the development, as well as on the family and its members. Possible consanguinity was traced by genealogical investigation. All the inmates had an extensive physical and ophthalmological examination; a chromosome investigation was performed on each inmate. If necessary and possible, other members of the family were approached for complementary investigation.

353 inmates (207 males and 146 females) were included in the investigation. The majority were between 5 and 30 years of age; 9 were younger, 6 were older. In 51 inmates it was not possible to say whether they were blind or partially sighted; 187 were blind, 113 were partially sighted and 2 had a visual acuity better than 6/18. It was not possible to classify the inmates according to the degree of mental retardation because of the lack of exact figures. For the institute it is more important to know the extent of the need for care. This is expressed in the degree of social self-reliability measured according to the Vineland Social Maturity Scale and given as the Social Quotient (SQ) (Doll, 1965). If we take an SQ of 50 as an approximate division between those who have great need of care and those who have a moderate need of care, then in the population investigated there were 238

inmates who needed intensive care and 72 who needed less intensive care. The SQ of 43 inmates was unknown.

A survey of the aetiological factors of the visual handicap in 353 inmates of Bartiméushage is given in Table 1.

Genetic Causes

In 148 inmates (42%) there was a definite, probable or possible genetic aetiology for the visual handicap.

A chromosomal aberration was the cause in 16, 8 of whom had Down's syndrome. Two chromosomal aberrations were found related

Table 1

Survey of the aetological factors of the visual handicap in 353 inmates of Bartiméushage *

Genetic			148 (41.9%)
chromosomal	16		
autosomal dominant	17		
autosomal recessive	72		
X-chromosomal	10		
undefinable mode of inheritance	20		
possibly genetic cause	13		
Non-Genetic			188 (53.5%)
prenatal		40	
congenital rubella	25		
congenital toxoplasmosis	14		
other causes	1		
perinatal		129	
retrolental fibroplasia	32		
cataract	29		
optic nerve atrophy	29		
cerebral blindness	37		
other complications	2		
postnatal		19	
infection	12		
trauma	5		
tumour	2		
Unknown			17 (4.8%)
Total			353 (100 %)

* Bleeker-Wagemakers (1981, 1982)

to a specific eye abnormality: an 11p deletion with aniridia and a 13q deletion with retinoblastoma.

In 11 of 17 subjects with an autosomal dominant condition, one of the parents had the same abnormality (without the mental retardation). In the other 6 a new mutation might have been involved in the child or reduced penetrance might be responsible.

Autosomal recessive disorders (_n_=72) were involved in about half the cases with a certain or probable inherited condition. 22 had congenital retinal blindness (Leber's congenital amaurosis), 16 had Batten-Spielmeyer-Vogt disease, 8 Bardet-Biedl syndrome and 9 microphthalmos. Parental consanguinity was recorded for 22 inmates.

X-chromosomal conditions were responsible for the visual handicap in 10 inmates: 6 boys with Norrie's disease, 2 with Lowe's syndrome, 1 with ocular albinism and 1 girl with incontinentia pigmenti.

In 20 inmates a genetic cause of the visual handicap was thought to be very likely, but the actual mode of inheritance could not be established. In all these patients the nature of the disease was compatible with a genetic defect, known to occur with different modes of inheritance.

Inherited factors may have played a role in the visual handicap of 13 inmates. This includes 7 subjects with persistent hyperplasia of the primary vitreous (PHPV), a condition reported to be unilateral in 90% of the cases and to occur sporadically. Accompanying mental retardation is not common. Our PHPV patients were bilaterally affected and mentally retarded; in 4 boys the ophthalmic condition was not distinguishable from Norrie's disease, an X-linked condition.

For most of the inherited conditions diagnosed, the birth of the first handicapped child in a family could not have been prevented. Thus for the time being, the total prevention of most inherited abnormalities does not seem to be possible. However, proper and timely genetic counselling may in a number of cases prevent the birth of further children with the abnormality. Establishing an early diagnosis is of essential importance in this respect; investigation of at least the parents and siblings is a minimal requirement in most cases. Prenatal diagnosis by amniocentesis can play an important role in the prevention of chromosomal aberrations, of some conditions with a known biochemical defect, of neural tube defects, and of some X-linked conditions. In X-linked recessive disorders the ability to demonstrate the carrier status in heterozygous women is important. Up to the present time this is impossible in Norrie's disease, but may be possible in Lowe's syndrome. The finding of a specific type of cataract almost proves the carrier status, but one cannot exclude the carrier status if the cataract is absent (Delleman _et al_., 1977). The finding of a typical biochemical defect in patients with Lowe's syndrome by Akasaki _et al_. (1978) and Fukui _et al_. (1981) may allow new possibilities in the prevention of Lowe's syndrome by prenatal diagnosis. Further search for the biochemical basis of genetic diseases and for the linkage between abnormalities and biological characteristics will lead to an improvement of genetic counselling services.

Non-Genetic Causes

The inmates with a non-genetic cause of the visual handicap formed the larger group in our investigation (n=188). We classified these causes as prenatal, perinatal and postnatal.

A prenatal cause was defined as one which had afflicted the child by a non-genetic factor in the intra-uterine period. For 25 inmates a diagnosis of congenital rubella was established; 14 were diagnosed as having congenital toxoplasmosis.

Perinatal causes were considered to be associated with the process of birth and the adaptation to extra-uterine life, from the beginning of labour up to and including the 28th postnatal day. Because of the complicated interaction of various causative factors in this period, no classification was attempted on the basis of aetiology; instead, the group was subdivided according to the most obvious visual handicap: retrolental fibroplasia (n=32), cataract (n=29), optic nerve atrophy (n=29), cerebral blindness (n=37), and other complications (n=2). Perinatal causes form the second important group in our investigation and this together with the group with a genetic aetiology accounts for three quarters of the visual handicapped children in Bartiméushage. In this group the percentages of low-birthweight, premature and dysmature children are very high: 65% had a birthweight less than 2500 g, 46% were premature, 43% were dysmature (-2 SD birthweight for gestational age). Furthermore most of this group had in addition to the visual and mental handicaps one or more signs of perinatal brain damage, such as epilepsy and spasticity. A handicap finding its origin later than the 28th day after birth is classified as postnatal. In 12 cases an infection was involved, 5 experienced trauma (2 suspected battered child syndrome) and 2 had a tumour.

Since the group of non-genetic causes in the mentally retarded is more than twice that in the mentally normal visually handicapped (Table 2), the prevention of non-genetic conditions in the mentally retarded is very important. Prevention of congenital rubella is possible. About 90% of the 18 year olds in the Netherlands have a natural immunity to rubella because of an earlier (subclinical) infection. It would therefore be sufficient to vaccinate only those girls who have not developed antibodies. For practical reasons it appears preferable to vaccinate all 11 year old girls. Similarly for toxoplasmosis a great proportion of the population has had an (often unnoticed) infection. One might suggest that it would be sensible to test for antibodies before the beginning of a pregnancy; if negative, measures during the pregnancy should be taken to avoid contact with young cats and the handling and eating of raw meat.

The members of the population investigated were born before 1970. Because of the medical and technical developments in that period, more premature children survived. There were, however, also more with perinatal damage. Around 1970 there were important developments in perinatal care with a decrease of perinatal mortality. Optimalization of perinatal care (which means care of the pregnant woman as well as of the neonate) could be best attained by regionalization and centralization of health care, especially for high-risk pregnancies. Women could then be admitted to departments where intensive obstetric and neonatal care is available. If this was to result in a reduction of the number of severely handicapped children, it would also mean fewer children with perinatal causes for visual and mental handicap.

CONCLUSION

Early diagnosis, proper and timely genetic counselling, optimal perinatal care, vaccination against rubella and precautionary measures against toxoplasma infection during pregnancy are of importance for the prevention of visual handicap in the mentally retarded.

Table 2

Causes of the visual handicap (percentages)

	Bartiméushage - Doorn * mentally retarded	Bartiméus - Zeist ** mentally normal
Genetic	41.9	72.4
Non-genetic	53.3	24.1
Unknown	4.8	3.5

* Bleeker-Wagemakers (1981, 1982)
** Cozijnsen and Delleman (1981)

REFERENCES

Akasaki, M, Fukui, S., Sakano, T., Tanaka, T., Usui, T., and Yamashina, I. (1978). Urinary excretion of a large amount of bound sialic acid and of undersulfated chondroitin sulfate A by patients with the Lowe syndrome. **Clin. Chim. Acta**, **89**, 119-125

Bankes, J.L.K. (1974a). The assessment centre and ocular problems of mentally handicapped children. **Trans. Ophthal. Soc. UK**, **94**, 244

Bankes, J.L.K. (1974b). Ocular problems of mentally handicapped children. **Am. J. Ophthalmol. 2**, 71-74

Bankes, J.L.K. (1974c). Eye defects of mentally handicapped children. **Brit. Med. J., 2**, 533-535

Bleeker-Wagemakers, E.M. (1981). On the causes of blindness in the mentally retarded, with special reference to the genetic aspects. Thesis. Bartiméus Foundation Series No. 3, Bartiméushage, Doorn, The Netherlands

Bleeker-Wagemakers, E.M. (1982). On the causes of blindness in the mentally retarded, with special reference to the genetic aspects. **Ophthalmic Pediatrics and Genetics, 1**, 89-96

Copper, A.C. and Schappert-Kimmijser, J. (1970). The causes of blindness in 156 visually and mentally defective children. **Ophthalmologica, 160**, 292-302

Cozijnsen, M. and Delleman, J.W. (1981). The causes of the visual handicaps in Bartiméus-Zeist. In: **Ophthalmological Disorders Resulting from Perinatal Damage.** Bartiméus Foundation Series no. 4., Bartiméushage, Doorn, The Netherlands

Delleman, J.W., Bleeker-Wagemakers, E.M. and van Veelen, A.W.C. (1977). Opacities of the lens indicating carrier status in the oculo-cerebro-renal (Lowe) syndrome. **J. Pediatr. Ophthalmol. Strabismus, 14**, 205-212

Doll, E.A. (1965). **Vineland Social Maturity Scale, Condensed Manual of Directions.** American Guidance Service Inc. Minnesota

Fukui, S., Yoshida, H., Tanaka, T., Sakano, T., Usui, T., and Yamashina I. (1981). Glycosaminoglycan synthesis by cultured skin fibroblasts from a patient with Lowe's syndrome. **J. of Biological Chemistry, 256**, 10313-10318

Henry, J.G. (1980). The ophthalmological assessment of the severely retarded child. **Aust. J. Ophthal., 8**, 1-4

Hyvärinen, L. and Lindstedt, E. (1981). **Assessment of Vision of Children**, S.R.F. Tal and Punkt, Stockholm

International Association for the Prevention of Blindness. (1964). Standard classification of causes of blindness for international use. **J. of Soc. Ophthal. 35**

Jaeger, W. (1975). Changes in the causes of blindness in childhood over the last hundred years. **Child Care Health Dev., 1**, 299-307

Jong, C.G.A. de (1981). Director Bartiméushage, Doorn, The Netherlands. Multiply handicapped. Read to the **Third Asian Congress of the International Council for the Education of the Visually Handicapped.** Jakarta, Indonesia, 5 Nov. 1981

Loewer-Sieger, D.H. (1976). Screening of young children. **Ophthalmologica (Basel), 173**, 340-343

Markovits, A.S. (1975). Ophthalmic screening of the mentally defective. **Ann. Ophthal. 7**, 846-848

Newcomb, R.D. (1977). The causes of blindness in children: a review of the literature. **J. Am. Optom. Assoc., 48**, 499-503

Schappert-Kimmijser, J., Hansen, E., Haustrate-Gosset, M.F., Lindstedt, E., Skydsgaard, N. and Warburg, M. (1975). Causes of severe visual impairment in children and their prevention. **Doc. Ophthalmol., 39**, 213-342

Veelen, A.W.C., van, Delleman, J.W., and Heslinga, K. (1969). Een inleidende algemene beschouwing aangaande de aard der oogafwijkingen bij 211 visueel gehandicapten uit "Bartiméus", Chr.Instituut voor blinden en slechtzienden. **C.B.O. Orthopedagogisch en Sociaal Pedagogisch Tijdschrift, 31/12**, 251-255

Warburg, M. (1963). Diseases of the eye among mental defectives. **Acta Ophthal. 14**, 157-166

Warburg, M. (1970). Tracing and training of blind and partially sighted patients in institutions for the mentally retarded. **Danish Medical Bulletin, 17**, 148-152

Warburg, M. (1975). Blindness in mentally retarded children, a survey of the causes in blindness of 201 notified patients. **Doc. Ophthalmol. 39**, 343-349

Warburg, M., Frederiksen, P., and Rattleff, J. (1979). Blindness among 7700 mentally retarded children in Denmark. In: **Visual Handicap in Children. Clinics in Developmental Medicine**, no. 73. W. Heinemann, Medical Books, London

COMMENTARY

M. Baraitser

A good deal of this account concerns the genetic contribution to visual and mental handicap. This would be an ideal opportunity to consider a combined approach to the problem. The author states that there is a growing need for genetic advice and, although it is not clearly stated, the syndromes covered are individually rare and genetically complex. It must therefore benefit parents and patients to have both an ophthalmic and genetic opinion, ideally at combined clinics. In any event a multidisciplinary approach would seem necessary.

The author lists the modes of inheritance for the genetically determined conditions and gives a partial breakdown of the various types of recessive and X-linked syndromes. This is not done for the dominant disorders - where genetic counselling might be the most productive. It is stated, for instance, that there were 17 subjects with an autosomal dominant condition and in 11 a parent had the same ocular abnormality without mental retardation. This is a remarkable and worrying statistic. It would be interesting to know what these conditions are and whether such variable expression is recognized in them.

There were 22 cases of Leber's amaurosis with mental retardation. We are not sure whether Leber's amaurosis without mental retardation is the same condition. A family study would be useful. The high M:F ratio needs an explanation and the contention that persistent hyperplasia of the primary vitreous might be genetically determined needs a family study.

In her population, non-genetic perinatal causes are almost as prevalent as the genetic causes. However, disproportionately little space is given to this group. Improved obstetric and neonatal care with the aim of reducing the incidence of small-for-dates and low-birthweight babies needs greater emphasis.

J. Hogg

I would like to focus on two related issues that are only briefly touched upon in Bleeker-Wagemakers' paper, and a third which should figure prominently in any consideration of the consequences of visual impairment.

The first issue concerns the developmental consequences of visual impairment for early development in the areas of motor, cognitive and communicative development, while the second concerns the implications of such consequences for intervention with mentally retarded children. The third consideration is the effect of visual impairment on disordered behaviour.

Bleeker-Wagemakers notes that: "Mental retardation and visual handicap mutually amplify their disadvantageous effect on the intellectual and social functioning of the child." In reality there are few studies that demonstrate this outcome or the nature of the amplification. In the present state of knowledge the best way of making a start on understanding such a process is to review knowledge of the developmental impact, in its own right, of visual impairment on children not at risk for severe mental retardation. A recent review of this literature (Hogg and Sebba, 1983) suggests the following consequences:

1. Development is within the normal range with respect to early gross motor abilities (e.g. sitting) but there is a marked delay in mobility (whether crawling, hitching or walking) (Adelson and Fraiberg, 1974, 1976).
2. Mobility is dependent on the child learning to reach for an object on the basis of sound which occurs later than visually directed reaching (4-5 months) in the sighted child, not earlier than 7 months and as late as 12 months. Fraiberg (1968) notes: "We have no baby in our series who learnt to creep before he gave us a demonstration of reaching on sound cue alone."
3. Manipulative ability and tactile and haptic skills are not impaired markedly in blind children (Fraiberg, 1968).
4. Early cognitive development, so dependent upon action and interaction with the world, is delayed (Reynell, 1978; Warren, 1977). The internalization of thought attained by 2 years in sighted children is not fully achieved in the blind child until 3-5 years. Fraiberg (1968) suggests that this results from delays in achieving the full concept of an object.
5. Delays in the internalization of thought will result in language delays (Stephens, 1972). This is accentuated by the impoverishment of experience resulting from the sensory impairment.
6. Language, both comprehensive and expressive, is delayed, though, with one exception, vocabulary and syntax do "catch up".
7. This one exception is self-reference and this results from the major difficulty the blind child has in differentiating him/herself from the rest of the world in the absence of vision (McGuire and Mayers, 1971).
8. Parent-infant interaction is disrupted in the absence of sustained visual regard. "What we miss in the blind baby, apart from the eyes that do not see," writes Fraiberg (1979), "is the vocabulary of signs and signals that provides the most elementary and vital sense of discourse long before words have meaning." She goes on to document the means by which interaction between parent and child is evolved.
9. The failure by the parent to sustain such interactions can lead to further impoverishment of the blind child's

experience through reduction in tactile, kinaesthetic and auditory stimulation by the parent.

This summary is concerned essentially with early development, though the aspects dealt with obviously embrace most of our concerns with respect to the profoundly retarded person and many with respect to the severely retarded child. If we adopt a developmental view of retardation (see Kiernan and also Rondal in the present volume) then clearly delays and deviancies of the sort noted with non-mentally retarded children will manifest themselves in the retarded child at the appropriate point in development. (This assumes, of course, that there are no additional auditory or physical handicaps.) Our knowledge of development in blind children can therefore guide our programme planning and serve as a model for sequence objectives. In such cases, Bleeker-Wagemakers' conclusion that an educational programme for the visually impaired mentally retarded person cannot consist of a combination of methods adopted from the mental retardation field, on the one hand, and the visual impairment field, on the other, appears questionable. Teaching mobility to the neuromuscularly ready, visually impaired, retarded child would wait upon acquisition of reach-for-a-sounding-object. Encouragement and training of these successive objectives would employ the sort of procedures described by Fraiberg and refined by the technology of instruction employed in teaching mentally retarded individuals. Similarly, the disruption of parent-child interactions caused by visual impairment would also be anticipated in the blind retarded child and practices described by Burlingham (1961, 1965), Fraiberg (1979), Rowgow (1980) and others employed within the wider curriculum.

Such a view, however, is dependent upon adopting a developmental model of retardation with a single concomitant additional handicap. If the development of the retarded child is seen as not simply slow, but deviant, then such information would have to be reinterpreted against the implications of this state of affairs. Paradoxically, it might be argued that the non-mentally retarded blind child's development is already "different" in several respects to that of a sighted child, and that the development of the blind retarded child will reflect similar deviancies. In reality it may not prove possible to distinguish rigidly "delay" from "difference" in such children, and indeed both formulations may operate and interact. The nature and balance of this interaction may vary across distinct aspects of development and at different stages of development. Even within this more elaborate framework we would argue that "insights from the blind" and intervention with the blind can inform, and be integrated with, programmes for retarded individuals.

Over and above the handicapping consequences of blindness it is also necessary to consider the impact of such impairment on behaviour disorders. Many authors (e.g. Burlingham, 1965) have suggested that the void created through absence of vision in blind children is filled by self-directed activity. Such self-stimulatory activity takes many forms: hand waving in front of the face, eye rubbing and poking, body rocking, head turning and rolling, etc. These inappropriately named "blindisms" are strikingly similar to those observed in both sighted and blind retarded individuals. Berkson and Davenport (1962) note that the extent of such behaviour increases with increasing developmental delay.

Given these parallels, two questions need to be considered: Under what conditions do blind children exhibit such behaviour? Do the behaviours result directly from visual deprivation or other forms of attendant sensory deprivation such as touch? With respect to the former, a general, if provisional, answer is that such behaviours emerge to regulate the blind child's level of arousal, either increasing or reducing arousal. Stone (1974) has suggested that qualitative differences may be observed in the behaviour depending on which function they serve. Warren (1977) comments that these suggestions may "... be interpreted as attributing to the blind child a fairly active role in the manipulation of his level of consciousness in order to regulate the extent of his contact with reality".

With respect to the second question, it is clear that deprivation of vision _per se_ does not contribute to the self-stimulatory behaviour (Thurrell and Rice, 1970). Prescott (1976) has argued persuasively that much stereotyped and self-stimulatory behaviour reflects not visual deprivation, but what he calls somatosensory stimulation, a term embracing bodily sensation arising from feelings associated with movement and balance, as well as cutaneous stimulation. Thus, reduced mobility in the blind child and lack of parental handling is the ultimate cause of self-stimulation rather than lack of visual stimulation. There is considerable evidence from both animal and human studies to support this view and Berkson (1976) concludes that "... blindness does not appear to be a sufficient condition for the development of stereotyped movement".

The development of self-stimulation in blind children then serves a variety of functions and reflects a number of modalities. These insights can readily be applied to our analysis of stereotyping and other behaviour disorders in blind retarded and sighted retarded individuals and can guide learning-theory based intervention of the kind reviewed by Baumeister and Forehand (1973).

I have reported on the effect of specific sensory handicaps on children not at risk for severe mental handicap. The question of the relevance of these findings to work with severely mentally handicapped people has received some attention in the literature. My introduction of this material suggests that I do consider it has implications, and this is in contrast to a number of practitioners who suggest that the combination of sensory and mental handicap leads to what might be termed an "emergent" state of affairs in which the consequences of the sensory handicap are not predictable from our knowledge of their effects in non-mentally handicapped children. In contrast, the suggestion that such prediction <u>is</u> possible might be termed an "additive" model.

In reality there is little, if any, empirical information on either position, both of which are likely to be overstatements. In the first case the impact of the sensory handicap on the mentally retarded child will be determined in part by the level of the child's development and the extent to which his/her development is slow rather than deviant. In such cases, in the absence of other additional handicaps, an additive situation might hold. As development becomes increasingly deviant in a qualitative manner, so emergent properties could be noted. Complex though a longitudinal study of mentally handicapped children with sensory impairment might be, such an investigation is called for in its own right and in order to enable practitioners to draw on information concerning the development of non-mentally handicapped children with such impairments.

References

Adelson, E. and Fraiberg, S. (1974). Gross motor development in infants blind from birth. **Child Development 45,** 114-126

Adelson, E. and Fraiberg, S. (1976). Sensory deficit and motor development in infants blind from birth. In: Z.S. Jastrzembska (ed.). **The Effects of Blindness and Other Impairments on Early Development.** The American Foundation for the Blind, New York, pp 1-15

Baumeister, A.A. and Forehand R. (1973). Stereotyped acts. In: Ellis (ed.), **International Review of Research in Mental Retardation 6,** pp. 55-96. Academic Press, London.

Berkson, G. (1976). Stereotyped behaviours in humans. In: Z.S. Jastrzembska (ed.), **The Effects of Blindness and Other Impairments on Early Development.** The American Foundation for the Blind, New York, pp. 131-132

Berkson, G. and Davenport R.K. (1962). Stereotyped movement of mental defectives: 1. Initial survey, **American Journal of Mental Deficiency 66,** 849-852

Burlingham, D. (1961). Some notes on the development of the blind. **Psychoanalytic Study of the Child, 16,** 121-145

Burlingham, D. (1965). Some problems of ego development in blind children. **Psychoanalytic Study of the Child, 20,** 194-208

Fraiberg, S. (1968). Parallel and divergent patterns in blind and sighted infants, **Psychoanalytic Study of the Child, 23,** 264-300

Fraiberg, S. (1979). Blind infants and their mothers: An examination of the sign system. In: M. Bullova (ed.) **Before Speech: The Beginning of Interpersonal Communication,** pp. 149-169. Cambridge University Press, Cambridge

Hogg, J. and Sebba, J. (1983). **Working with Profoundly Retarded Mentally Handicapped Children**, London, Croom Helm (in press)

McGuire, L.L. and Mayers, C.E. (1971). Early personality in the congenitally blind child. **New Outlook for the Blind, 65**, 137-143

Prescott, J.W. (1976). Somatosensory deprivation and its relationship to the blind. In: Z.S. Jastrzembska (ed.), **The Effects of Blindness and Other Impairments on Early Development**, pp. 65-122. The American Foundation for the Blind, New York

Reynell, J. (1978). Developmental patterns of visually handicapped children, **Child: Care, Health and Development, 4**, 291-303

Rowgow, S.M. (1980). Language development in blind multi-handicapped children: A model of co-active intervention, **Child: Care, Health and Development 6** 306-308

Stephens, B. (1972). Cognitive processes in the visually impaired, **Education of the Visually Handicapped, 4**, 106-111.

Stone, A. (1974). Consciousness: altered levels in blind retarded children, **Psychosomatic Medicine, 26**, 1-19

Thurrell, R.J. and Rice, D.G. (1970). Eye rubbing in blind children: application of a sensory deprivation model, **Exceptional Children, 36**, 325-330

Warren, D.H. (1977). **Blindness and Early Childhood Development**, American Foundation for the Blind, New York

R. O. Robinson

This is an interesting account of the ophthalmological diagnostic process and its results when applied to a highly selected population of visually impaired mentally handicapped children.

In order for us to find common ground with other disciplines, we need to know more about the ways in which these children can best be helped. Hogg outlined the ways in which this problem might be approached.

An additional area of mutual interest lies in the possible responses to the question, "What is the interaction between visual handicap and mental handicap?" There are a number of possibilities:

(a) a pathological process involving both eyes and brain, for example toxoplasmosis;

(b) events in time affecting both the eye and the brain, for example prematurity being associated with both intraventricular haemorrhage (causing mental handicap) and retrolental fibroplasia (causing blindness);

(c) "central blindness", which is a blanket term used to cover underdeveloped visual behaviour secondary either to severe mental handicap or to post-chiasmatic and bilateral involvement of the optic pathways;

(d) lack of visual input giving rise to further mental handicap (see above);

(e) increased vulnerability of visually handicapped children to injury, accidental and non-accidental: hence the acquisition of secondary mental handicap.

We need to examine whether these relationships are similar to or different from the interaction between deafness and mental handicap. Can analogies in the one situation be used in the other, particularly the therapeutic and preventive aspects mentioned in (d) and (e) above.

Finally this discussion of aetiology is of course drawn from an institutionalized population. I wonder what the selection for institutional care is in the Netherlands and to what extent it affects the figures provided. A population-based study might well have different proportions of aetiologies. I would also anticipate that the severity and forms of mental handicap would be different. We should not be too hasty in assigning a perinatal cause for conditions such as optic atrophy and cataract. Evidence gleaned years later from medical records of others is highly fallible. The pattern and timing of the events seem very heterogeneous. With the possible exception of hypoglycaemia causing cataract, there are no clear causal pathological mechanisms. The viability of these children may be threatened before birth by the events which cause ocular abnormality and were thus secondarily associated with the subsequent stormy perinatal period.

D. M. Ricks

(Editor's note: These comments also concern Chapter 13.)

Many retarded children have multiple handicaps; some, for example, have seizures or potentially subluxating hips. When treating these conditions the neurologist or orthopaedic surgeon will take the child's retardation into account as complicating the indications for or likely response to treatment. Similarly with these informative papers: their authors, with their extensive experience of visual or auditory defect, will be involved with the diagnosis and treatment of these sensory defects in children with a wide spectrum of intelligence, a proportion of whom will be retarded. From such a viewpoint retardation will be seen as intensifying the difficulties imposed on any child by deafness or blindness and the manner in which it does so has been cogently emphasized by both authors. I would like to add another perspective to the discussion based on my own, rather different, clinical commitment. I am part of a team to which are referred problematic retarded children. All our patients are mentally handicapped, most of them profoundly so. They are problematic because the severity or combination of their handicaps, or the "level" of their retardation, is such as to obstruct or distort any developmental progress to an extent that the child seems set to become either totally dependent or unmanageable. Many of these children have visual or auditory defects or both, but from our viewpoint these defects are seen as one component of a variety of disabilities. For us, serious or suspected sensory defect is a complication of a basic problem - how to help unmotivated or inaccessible children. We ask ourselves how much does sensory defect further aggravate the problems of a child who in any case cannot initiate simple developmental skills or make sense out of his world. This in its turn compels us to look as closely as we can at the way in which intact vision and hearing contribute to the spontaneous development of basic developmental skills such as standing up, reaching or vocalizing needs, which our children lack. It would seem reasonable to assume that, thus equipped, we could better help blind or deaf retarded children compensate for these additional defects. For a number of reasons outlined below we have found that a very naive assumption.

Effective treatment of sensory defect relies on a level of motivation and social response understandably taken for granted in normally intelligent blind or deaf children in whom an assumed interest in becoming mobile, exploring and communicating is amenable to encouragement and reassurance. If the mentally retarded child could safely be assumed to have similar personal characteristics but was slower to develop them, then the tactics of his education and treatment would not differ greatly from accepted practices. In fact, apart from Down's syndrome children, very few retarded children are "just" slower than their more able peers. Their disabilities impose learning strategies which differ not in degree but in kind, so that, as emphasized in both papers, practices which help the normally intelligent deaf or blind are inappropriate. Many of the retarded children we see do not resort spontaneously to alternative sensory channels, nor benefit from regular or repetitive experiences, nor respond reliably to social reinforcement. Consequently, for example, it is extremely difficult to judge whether aids, if tolerated at all, should be persevered with in a disturbed child because they are not necessarily beneficial. We have found retarded rubella children, ferociously resistive to standing, to using their hands or to virtually any stimulus including solid food, when equipped with aids, who have mellowed without them to become mobile, exploratory and self-feeding when allowed, presumably, to build their world out of tactile and proprioceptive feedback. Conversely we have known blind children insist on spectacles which have no apparent connection with their visual performance, as confirmed to an ophthalmological colleague (Gardiner, 1982) and us all in the unit by one child's indifference whether the lens correction of 10 D was plus or minus! Presumably there is an even stronger case for trying aids at the earliest moment in retarded children since their bizarre idiosyncratic responses are even more difficult to remedy, once entrenched, than in the normal child. But the recognition of even severe sensory defect in the very young unresponsive retarded child is problematic (Ricks, 1981) - and emphasizes the value of diagnostic techniques that depend on physiological rather than behavioural responses (Tucker, 1982).

Recognizing the need for prescribing and persevering with aids must take into account not only the unpredictable responsiveness of the retarded child; his particular combination of defects may further complicate this issue, and indeed the whole pattern of his management. For example ataxia greatly intensifies the apprehension of the brain-damaged child with visual defect, a combination not uncommon following perinatal cerebral hypoxaemia. Frequent minor fits may disrupt the attention and hence the visual monitoring on which a deaf retarded child so depends. A lively but retarded 9 year old we knew, with a bilateral flat 40 dB hearing loss, also had tunnel vision in his one seeing eye. He was active and mischievous but virtually uncontrollable (hence his referral) until he lost his hearing aid. We then discovered how much he relied on visual cues of approval and disapproval to guide his behaviour, automatically reinforced by vocal inflection of staff he could hear well enough without his aid. He could not cope with language, so, it seems, was confused by variably intelligible signals because they distracted him, interfering with the active scanning he needed to appreciate behavioural or situational clues. Without his aid he became cooperative and greatly extended his self-help and domestic skills.

Our stumbling efforts as clinicians to help the blind or deaf retarded child in these comparatively simple practical ways become even more tentative when considering how their sensory defects _further_ obstruct their inability to acquire simple developmental skills. Yet this is the very arena we should be entering. In what particular ways do normal babies rely on vision and hearing to sit or stand up, reach, walk or vocalize their needs? We need to know much more about these strategies in looking, listening motivated children before we can assist the retarded to attempt them with such sensory defects _when they are young_ and our efforts most likely to bear fruit. Although this exciting field of study is expanding it has not as yet captured the interest of clinicians. Yet the fact that establishing a visual target may prompt the distinctive way children first get unaided to their feet (Ricks, 1982), or initiate grasping (Bower, 1974), or experiment with preliminary changes in posture to begin reaching (Bruner, 1973), or monitor mouth movements in learning to listen to speech (Dodd, 1979), are all vital indicators of how vision is "needed" to convert a baby into a talking toddler. How are these same tasks tackled in the intelligent blind who eventually achieve them? We need to know if we are to help their retarded peers. Similarly why are some motor acts in deaf children slower than normal (Wiegeresina and Van der Velde,

1983)? How much does listening monitor movement? How much is hearing needed to clarify (or even recognize) visual categories among diverse appearances (various tables, cars, etc.) which children must grasp to generate label words - and indeed, if they are deaf, to establish a conceptual order necessary for even simple signing? We have much to learn.

I am conscious of having raised many doubts and suggested many inadequacies in our understanding of the connection between mental retardation and severe sensory defect. In such company this is as it should be and is inevitable if discussion is focussed not only on the complications of sensory defect imposed by retardation but, conversely, on the manner in which such defects intensify the obstacles to development of the retarded child.

References

Bowen, T. (1974). Development of infant behaviour. **Br. Med. Bull.**, **30**, 175-178

Bruner, J.S. (1973). Organisation of early skilled action. **Child Develop.**, **44**, 1-11

Dodd,B. (1979). Lip reading in infants: attention to speech presented in and out of synchrony, **Cognitive Psychiatry**, **11**, 478-484

Gardiner, P.A. (1982). The development of vision: In: **Studies in Developmental Paediatrics**. Chap. 7, p.125, M.T.P. Press, Lancaster

Ricks, D.M. (1981). Sensory defect, impaired awareness and maladaptive parent-child interaction: their assessment and comparison as indicators of mental handicap in unresponsive motor intact infants. In: **Assessing the Handicaps and Needs of Mentally Retarded Children**, Ed. Cooper, B., Academic Press, London

Ricks, D.M. (1982). Early developmental skills in normal and retarded children. **Br. J. Hosp. Med.**, 667-669

Tucker, S.M. (1982). Testing for defects in the new-born using the Auditory Response Cradle. **Topics in Perinatal Medicine**. Ed. Warton, p.126

Wiegeresina, P.H. and Van der Velde, A. (1983). Motor development of deaf children. **J. Child. Psychol. Psychiat.**, **24**, 1, 103-112

J. B. P. Stephenson

Two disorders with visual impairment and actual or potential mental handicap may be recognized in the neonatal period by attention to their striking physical signs, but the infants may easily die without the fundamental lesion being diagnosed.

Congenital retinal blindness (Leber's congenital amaurosis) may present as Joubert's syndrome with extremely rapid panting respiration: ultrasound will confirm agenesis of the cerebellar vermis (Tomita et al., 1979; Stephenson and King, 1983).

Optic hypoplasia or septo-optic dysplasia with hypothalamic-hypopituitarism will present as prolonged "obstructive" jaundice and hypoglycaemia in the neonate as a result of cortisol deficiency secondary to failure of ACTH release. Cortisol replacement reverses these features and prevents consequent cerebral damage (Leblanc et al., 1981). It is of interest that such children tend to be the first-born offspring of young mothers (Elster and McAnarney, 1979) but the explanation is not known.

References

Elster, A.B. and McAnarney, E.R. (1979). Maternal age re: septo-optic dysplasia. **J. Paediatr.**, **94**, 162-163

Leblanc, A., Odieavre, M., Hadchoel, M., Gendrell, D., Chaussian, J. and Rappoport, R. (1981). Neonatal cholestasis and hypoglycaemia: possible role of cortisol deficiency. **J. Paediatr.**, **99**, 577-580

Stephenson, J.B.P. and King, M. (1983). How fast can babies breathe? **Arch. Dis. Child.**, **58**, 80

Tomita, H., Ohno, K. and Tamai, A. (1979). Joubert's syndrome associated with Leber's congenital amaurosis. **Brain and Development** (Domestic Edition), **11**, 459-465

Chapter 15

Linguistic and prelinguistic development in moderate and severe mental retardation

J.A. Rondal

Teaching a first language to the mentally handicapped child is perhaps the most exciting and demanding challenge facing teachers and parents. Exciting because it is rewarding to help a child to understand and produce his* first words, to develop his language abilities earlier, faster and more completely than he might have otherwise. Demanding because neither our professional training, the psycholinguistic theories, nor our knowledge of normal children fully equip us for such a task.

Faced with mentally retarded children, we have to ask ourselves basic questions about the nature of language, the way it develops in early childhood, about the processes and mechanisms involved, and the several functions that speech and language fulfil in social life and private mental functioning.

It is only comparatively recently that we have begun to think about the problems in a more systematic manner, and come to understand something of the complexity of the issues involved. I believe that important technical progress was achieved when the development of speech and language in retarded children began to be systematically compared with those in normal children. This comparative strategy was made possible by the significant increase in the studies on language development in the normal child from approximately 1960 on. It is now usual practice to relate the observations made with mentally handicapped subjects to data available in the literature on language acquisition in normal children or, better, to compare directly mentally handicapped and normal subjects.

The chapter is divided into three parts. The first problem addressed is the delay-difference issue in the language development of the retarded subjects. The second section reviews

---

*I will use the masculine pronoun to refer to the child in order to avoid repetition of the cumbersome "his or her", "he or she". It is acknowledged, however, that the semantic category "child" has two genders.

available data on the language behaviour of mentally retarded adults. The last section is devoted to the prelinguistic stage in retarded infants.

THE DELAY-DIFFERENCE ISSUE

The question is whether language development in retarded children is a delayed but basically similar version of normal development or whether it follows a different path. It has particular significance for language intervention. Suppose one can prove that retarded children acquire language in the same way as normal children but for rate (slower) and ultimate level (incomplete development). This is essentially the delay position, and has been defined by Lenneberg (1967). Suppose, on the contrary, that language development in the retarded proceeds in a different way from the development in normal subjects. In this case, any type of normative intervention may not be sufficient. It could even prove inappropriate. This position seems to be the one adopted by Cromer (1973, 1974), for example.

There are a number of caveats in the way the delay-difference issue is usually set out. I shall not attempt to discuss them in detail nor to be exhaustive here. (For a more complete treatment of this problem, see Rondal and Lambert, 1983.)

(1) No complete dichotomy exists between delay and difference. A simple answer to the question largely depends on whether one considers the whole language system or separate components. Imagine a mentally retarded child who is acquiring one aspect of language, say lexicon, in the normal sequence but moderately delayed, while another aspect of language, say productive syntax, is also being acquired in the normal sequence but markedly delayed. The answer to the delay-difference question is delay for the two aspects considered separately. However, it should be difference with respect to language as a whole. Indeed suppose our retarded child is a seven-year old and he is, say, at the five-year level for lexicon and at the three-year level for syntax. That does not make him equivalent to any younger normal child. Whenever there is delay in varying degrees for aspects of language, there is difference with respect to language as a whole. A meaningful search in this problem should try to cover various aspects of language in an attempt to establish whether for each aspect considered the development proceeds similarly for normal and for retarded children. "Similarly" means that the various stages passed by the normal and the retarded subjects are basically the same and succeed each other in the same order. If this is so, language development in the retarded can be said to be "... simply delayed ...".

(2) The delay position predicts that language development in the retarded will come to a stop before reaching the final stage. It is conceivable that one might distinguish between incomplete and different developments. However, no studies known to me at this time have addressed this issue. Therefore we are

unable to indicate whether some of the differences observed between normal and retarded children should be interpreted as evidence for a difference position or whether they can be explained in terms of an arrested development at an earlier but normal stage.

(3) The label "mental retardation" covers a number of aetiological categories (autosomal abnormalities, metabolic disorders, etc.). There is no guarantee that their linguistic problems are the same. The delay-difference issue should be raised separately for the various categories of mental handicap.

(4) Any definitive answer to the delay-difference question should be based on extensive longitudinal data. There is a marked lack of large-scale longitudinal studies in the communicative and linguistic development of retarded children. Moreover, we do not know at this time whether there is only one or several alternative ways to language acquisition. Longitudinal data on the language development of retarded childen will have to be interpreted according to indications as to the existence of one or several alternative but proper ways to language mastery in order to solve the delay-difference issue.

As the above section indicates, the delay-difference question cannot be answered in simple terms. As usually set, the issue is somewhat artificial. It is possible, however, to use a loose delay-difference framework to assess which aspects of language create specific problems in the retarded and should therefore be given maximum attention. I shall review data bearing on the delay-difference issue in this perspective.

Three types of matching procedures have been used in comparing speech and language in retarded and normal children.

The CA-match

Studies using a CA-match most often reveal large gaps between retarded and normal children. These studies are helpful with respect to the delay-difference question only insofar as the data obtained with the retarded can also be compared to corresponding data from younger normal children.

The MA-match

Matching children for MA should guarantee that they function cognitively at similar levels. If it can be shown that retarded children differ linguistically from MA-matched normal children, this is considered to be supportive for a difference hypothesis. If it is not the case, one considers that a delay hypothesis is supported.

The assumption that matching subjects on MA guarantees that they are equivalent in cognitive functioning has been questioned (e.g. Baumeister, 1967). There is no one-to-one correspondence between IQ scores (and MA) and the response patterns to the test items. The same IQ can be obtained in many different ways. One cannot be fully confident that MA-matched children function at corresponding cognitive levels. This makes the interpretation of linguistic comparison between such children difficult.

The LLD-match

Another strategy is to match normal and retarded children for linguistic level (e.g. Rondal, 1978a,b). One may use mean length of utterance - MLU - as the criterion variable and look at various characteristics of the language used by the subjects. If the language produced by the two groups of children matched for MLU can be characterized in the same way, this would have to be considered as supportive of the delay position.

With the LLD-matching both the criterion and the dependent variable(s) pertain to the linguistic domain. The rationale behind this type of matching procedure is the following: if normal and retarded children matched on linguistic aspect X (disregarding other parameters like CA or MA) can be shown to be basically similar with respect to aspects Y, Z, A, B,... of the language system, then it may be assumed that this system is structured in much the same way in the two groups of children, which is consistent with the delay position and antithetical to the difference position.

A search through the available literature has yielded the information summarized in Table 1. Owing to the extreme rarity of relevant studies on pragmatic and functional aspects of language in the retarded, no mention is made of these aspects in the following sections (see Greenwald and Leonard, 1979, however, for a study on the production of performative imperatives and declaratives by young retarded children).

The data were obtained using a chronological age (CA) matching procedure, a mental age (MA) matching procedure, or a matching on level of linguistic development (with mean length of utterance - MLU - as the criterion variable except on one occasion where it was the receptive vocabulary score obtained at the English Peabody Picture Vocabulary Test - EPPVT) with normal and moderately and severely mentally retarded children (either Down's syndrome children - DS - or retarded of other aetiologies - O). V means retarded children of various aetiologies including Down's syndrome, P means production, and C comprehension, + indicates that no difference was found between normal and retarded children and - means that one difference was found between normal and retarded children (to the advantage of the normal children unless the indication "MR>N" appears).

Babbling and Phonological Development

A large proportion of moderately and severely retarded children have articulation, voice and stuttering difficulties (Spradlin, 1963). There is some agreement that the incidence of speech disorders including stuttering is higher among Down's syndrome children than in the rest of the retarded population (Keane, 1972; Zisk and Bialer, 1967).

Table 1

Data on the delay-difference issue in moderately and severely mentally retarded children

Item	Linguistic aspect	Matching	Children's CA in years	Production/ Comprehension	Aetiology of retardation	Result
	1. Babbling and phonological development					
1.	Characteristic sounds of babbling (vowels, consonants, syllables). Phonetic patterns and sequences of development (Dodd, 1972; Smith, 1977)	CA	1 0-2	P	V	+
2.	Phonological aspects of meaningful speech (phoneme substitutions and approximations in the articulation of k, f, and *th*) (Smith, 1977)	CA	2-5	P	DS	+
3.	Frequency of phonological errors made spontaneously and in imitation (Dodd, 1975)	MA	6-15	P	DS&O	DS-O+
4.	Acoustical clarity and intelligibility of speech (Ryan, 1975; Rondal, 1978a)	MLU	5-19 3-12	P	DS	-
	2. Lexical development					
5.	Understanding common words (Lyle, 1961)	CA	6-14	C	DS&O	+
6.	Understanding the meaning of spatial terms (big, long, in, on, under) (Cook, 1977)	CA	3-6	C	DS	+
7.	Understanding the lexical items on the Carrow Test of Linguistic Comprehension (Bartell *et al.*, 1973)	MA	9-13	C	V	+
8.	Basic vocabulary of use (Mein and O'Connor, 1960; Beier *et al.*, 1969; Lozar *et al.*, 1972)	MA	9-13 11-24 5-15	P	V	+
9.	Responses on word association and word generalization tasks (Sersen *et al.*, 1970; O'Connor and Hermelin, 1959, 1963)	MA	2-14 9-16 10-20	P	V	+

Item	Linguistic aspect	Matching	Children's CA in years	Production/ Comprehension	Aetiology of retardation	Result
10.	Type-token ratio (an index of lexical diversity of speech) (Rondal, 1978a)	MLU	3-12	P	DS	(MR>N)
11.	Diversity of noun vocabulary (Ryan, 1975)	MLU	5-9	P	DS&O	(MR>N)
	3. Semantic structural development					
12.	Frequency and type of basic semantic relations (Buium et al., 1974; Rondal, 1978a; Coggins, 1976; Dooley, 1976; Layton and Sharifi, 1979)	MLU	4 3-12 1-6 2-5 7-12	P	DS	+
13.	Comprehension of basic semantic relations (Duchan and Erickson, 1976)	MLU	4-8	C	DS&O	+
	4. Grammatical morphological development					
14.	Use of familiar English inflections as assessed by the subtest Auditory-Vocal Automatic or Grammatical Closure of the Illinois Test of Psycholinguistic Abilities (Mueller and Weaver, 1964; Bateman and Wetherell, 1965; Bilovsky and Share, 1965; Glovsky, 1970)	CA;MA	10-16 6-12	P	V	-
15.	Omission, substitution and incorrect generalization of grammatical inflections in free speech (Ryan, 1975)	MLU	5-10	P	DS&O	+
	5. Syntactical development					
16.	Change in the relative proportions of nouns in the speech produced at the early stages of language development (Mein, 1961)	CA	3-7	P	V	+
17.	Progression through various "stages" of early language development ("mostly babble", "mostly words", "primitive phrases", and "sentences") with increasing CA. The progression proceeds much like in normal chidren if one disregards the delays (Lenneberg et al., 1964)	CA	3-22	P;C	DS	+

Item	Linguistic aspect	Matching	Children's CA in years	Production/ Comprehension	Aetiology of retardation	Result
18.	Progressive use of imperative, active affirmative, negative and interrogative sentences with increasing MA (Lackner, 1968; Gordon and Panagos, 1976)	MA	2-9 3-5	P	V DS	+ +
19.	Rank ordering of syntactical difficulties in a sentence comprehension task (Mittler, 1970; Wheldall, 1976)	MA EPPVT	8-12 9-15	C	V	+
20.	Comprehension of grammatical words, gender and number agreement and double object construction (Semmel and Dolley, 1970; Bartell et al., 1973; Lambert, 1978)	CA MA MA	6-14 9-13 6-12	C	DS V V	- - -
21.	Comprehension of active affirmative sentences (Semmel and Dolley, 1970)	CA	6-14	C	DS	+
22.	Comprehension of active negative, affirmative passive, and negative passive sentences (Semmel and Dolley, 1970; Dewart, 1979; Chipman, 1979)	CA MA MA	6-14 7-18 8-15	C	DS V V	- + +
23.	Comprehension of various active affirmative sentences including sentences with "ing forms" and possessive construction (e.g. "The boys' fishes are here") (Berry, 1972)	EPPVT	10-16	C	V	+
24.	Comprehension of temporal propositions and temporal relationship between propositions (Barblan and Chipman, 1978)	MA	6-10	C	V	I
25.	Upper-bound (i.e. length of utterance in a corpus of speech) (Rondal, 1978a)	MLU	3-12	P	DS	+
26.	Number of modifiers MLU per utterance (Rondal, 1978a)	MLU	3-12	P	DS	+
27.	Incidence of utterances without verb (Rondal, 1978a)	MLU	3-12	P	DS	+
28.	Productivity (number of words and utterances produced in a corpus of speech obtained in a given period of time) (Rondal, 1978a)	MLU	3-12	P	DS	+

Item	Linguistic aspect	Matching	Children's CA in years	Production/ Comprehension	Aetiology of retardation	Result
29.	Proportions of imperative, declarative, wh-interrogative, and yes-no interrogative utterances (Rondal, 1978c)	MLU	3-12	P	DS	+
30.	Proportion of complete and incomplete sentences (Ryan, 1975)	MLU	5-9	P	DS&O	+
31.	Proportion of so-called "cliches" and "ready-made" utterances (Ryan, 1975)	MLU	5-9	P	DS&O	+
32.	Range and variety of verb transformations (Ryan, 1975)	MLU	5-9	P	DS&O	+
33.	Word order (Ryan, 1975)	MLU	5-9	P	DS&O	+
34.	Word order in early combinatorial speech (Dale, 1977)	MLU	4-6	P	DS	+
35.	Strategies used to identify agents and objects in the basic strings received (chance performance first, semantic-lexical strategies second, and responses based on word order third) (Dale, 1977)	MLU	4-6	C	DS	+
36.	Reversal of order of subject and copula or auxiliary verb *be* in interrogative sentences (Developmental Sentence Scoring Procedure) (Rondal, 1978b)	MLU	5-12	P	DS	-
37.	Frequency of use of elementary main verbs (i.e. uninflected verbs like "I see you", copula "It's red", *is* + verb + *ing* "He is coming", *can*, *will*, *may* + verb "I can go") (Developmental Sentence Scoring Procedure) (Rondal, 1978b)	MLU	5-12	P	DS	(MR>N)
38.	Frequency of use of elementary secondary (i.e. infinitives "I wanna see", "I'm gonna see"), non-complementing infinitives "I stopped to play", present and past participles "I see a boy running", "I found the toy broken" (Developmental Sentence Scoring Procedure) (Rondal, 1978b)	MLU	5-12	P	DS	-

Item	Linguistic aspect	Matching	Children's CA in years	Production/ Comprehension	Aetiology of retardation	Result
39.	Proportion of sentences that are grammatically correct in every respect (Developmental Sentence Scoring Procedure) (Rondal, 1978b)	MLU	5-12	P	DS	(MR>N)
40.	Frequency and type of indefinite pronouns (Developmental Sentence Scoring Procedure) (Rondal, 1978b)	MLU	5-12	P	DS	-
41.	Developmental level of personal pronouns used (Developmental Sentence Scoring Procedure) (Dale, 1977)	MLU	4-6	P	DS	-
42.	Proportion of progressive but erroneous forms (e.g. "goed", "I want go") (Dale, 1977)	MLU	4-6	P	DS	-

As to phonetical development of babbling, Smith and Oller's (1981) and Dodd's (1972) studies clearly indicate that babbling proceeds in the same way in Down's syndrome and in normal infants.

Smith and Oller (1981) have extended their search into the phonological development of their Down's syndrome subjects. They have concentrated on the development on three phonemes <u>k</u>, <u>f</u>, and <u>th</u>. They report a marked delay in the onset of meaningful speech but the articulatory approximations and substitutions made by Down's syndrome children are of the same type as those made by younger normal subjects (i.e. the order of development was <u>k</u>, <u>f</u> and <u>th</u>, and the easier phonemes <u>k</u> and <u>f</u> tended to be substituted for the more difficult <u>th</u>). Dodd (1975) has compared the phonological errors made by normal, Down's syndrome, and other severely subnormal children matched for MA. She reports that the number and type of errors made by the non-Down's syndrome children (for example, consonant cluster reduction) are the same as those of their MA-matched normal pairs. But the Down's syndrome children made far more errors and were more inconsistent. A lower intelligibility of speech than expected on an MLU basis was also reported by Ryan (1975) and by Rondal (1978a) for Down's syndrome children between 3 and 12 years.

Dodd (1975) has suggested that the Down's syndrome children's articulatory deficit is due to a basic difficulty in programming the motor movements of speech. Such a hypothesis is consistent with the findings of Frith and Frith (1974) that the motor disability in Down's syndrome subjects is due to an inability to use short-term motor programmes for sequences of movements. The articulatory problem in Down's syndrome subjects, therefore, may be more a symptom of a type of general motor disability than the expression of a different phonological development.

Lexical Development

The retarded children are comparable to younger normal children in the way they acquire lexical knowledge. They understand, use and associate as many words and similar types of words as their MA-matched normal pairs. When matched for MLU with normal children, the retarded appear to use a more diversified set of vocabulary terms. Recent theorizing (e.g. Clark, 1973) has presented lexical development as proceeding through the addition of semantic features. Cook (1977) has found Down's syndrome children to acquire the meaning words like _big_, _long_, _in_, _on_, _under_, in the same order as the normal children (i.e. _big_ before _long_, and _in_ before _on_, and then _under_).

Semantic Structure Development

The semantic structure basic to multiword expression and understanding (i.e. the notions of agent, object, possessor, benefactor, instruments, presence, absence, attribution, location, etc.) seems to be organized along the same lines in the normal and retarded subjects. The explanation probably is that the sensory-motor cognitive knowledge on which the basic semantic structure of language appears to rest (Fillmore, 1967; Chafe, 1970; Piaget, 1954; Brown, 1973; Edwards, 1973) is a prerequisite for the onset of combinatorial speech.

However, it is possible, as some data collected by Willis (1978) with mildly retarded children indicate, that retarded people are limited in their ability to combine several semantic relations in order to set the semantic framework for more complex utterance.

This ability should be distinguished from the morphosyntactic organization of surface structure strings. Retarded children have a great deal of difficulty understanding and applying complex morphological and syntactical rules. It is also possible that they are deficient in the ability to embed two-term relations in order to realize complex semantic structures.

Grammatical Morphological Development

The data on this aspect mainly come from the Grammatical Closure subtest of the Illinois Test of Psycholinguistic Abilities (see Ryan, 1975, however). In this subtest, the child is presented with a set of pictures and has to complete statements like _Here is a bed, here are two - (beds)_. The test controls for the productive knowledge of the rules of plural, progressive, past tense, past participle, third person present tense, and comparative form inflections applied to real words located in final position in the sentence. The retarded children lag far behind the normal children in the use of grammatical morphemes. They may fail to acquire the complete morphological system and/or settle for some peculiar morphological organization yet to be defined.

Syntactical Development

Superficially, it looks like the retarded children develop syntactical knowledge in the same way as normal children. They advance through the early stages of language development with increasing mental age. When matched with normal children for MLU, the Down's syndrome children have identical upper-bounds, number of modifiers per utterance, and incidence of utterance without verb. They produce the various syntactical types of utterances in proportions similar to normal children. As to word order, the evidence collected by Dale (1977) suggests that the early combinatorial speech of Down's syndrome and normal children follow similar patterns. Identical strategies are used by the two groups of children in interpreting the relational structure of elementary sentences (i.e. identifying agent, action and object).

However, as more sophisticated aspects of syntactical knowledge are examined, MLU-matched normal and Down's syndrome children are no longer comparable. Lee's Developmental Sentence Scoring Procedure has been instrumental in revealing some finer differences between the two groups of subjects. Retarded subjects often fail to invert the order of subject and copula or auxiliary verb in interrogative sentences, except in stereotyped questions like what's that, who's that, or the like. They seem to have difficulties with the personal as well as with the indefinite pronouns (for example, some, all, a few, both, several, somebody, anybody, etc.), again except in simple constructions like all done which may possibly function as single lexical units (Dale, 1977). A difficulty with the indefinite pronouns has also been observed by Willis (1978) in his study of mildly retarded children.

The Down's syndrome children studied by Rondal (1978b) had higher proportions of sentences grammatically correct in every respect than their MLU-matched normal pairs. The Down's syndrome children also used more elementary main verbs whereas the normal children constructed more sentences with secondary verbs according to the Developmental Sentence Procedure. Dale (1977) reports that at comparable MLU levels the normal children use more grammatically progressive but erroneous forms. They seem to be taking more risks, henceforth committing more errors, in trying to construct more sophisticated syntactic structures. Willis (1978) has reported a markedly higher frequency of conjunctions as opposed to embedding one idea inside another in mildly retarded compared to younger normal subjects.

Whether these indications are suggestive of a freezing process taking place in the language development of the Down's syndrome and other retarded subjects or whether they signal a different organization of the advanced syntactical aspects of language is a matter for further investigation.

In summary, the findings are not fully in agreement either with the DELAY or with the DIFFERENCE positions. At a relatively superficial level and particularly for the phonological, lexical and semantic structural aspects of language, it is possible to compare the retarded to younger normal children. However, when finer-grained analyses are made, particularly as to the morphosyntactical aspect of language, the same comparison is far less satisfactory. Longitudinal studies should greatly help clarify the issue. This work will eventually prompt a more precise tailoring of the language training and remedial programmes to the specific needs of mentally retarded children.

LANGUAGE AND COMMUNICATION IN RETARDED ADOLESCENTS AND ADULTS

Research has focused recently on the communicative capabilities of mentally retarded adults and late adolescents. Evans (1977) has analysed individual samples of free speech as well as data from the Illinois Test of Psycholinguistic Abilities (ITPA) obtained with a large group of Down's syndrome subjects aged 12 to 31 years. A quarter of the subjects were living in specialized institutions. The others were being cared for at home and attended occupational centres during the day-time. Virtually none of the measures computed on the samples of speech (e.g. mean length of the longest ten utterances recorded, type-token ratio, verbal fluency, frequency distribution of various grammatical classes, etc.) plus the scores on the ITPA subtests showed significant differences between the subjects according to sex. As expected (for example, Mittler, 1974), the subjects in institutions obtained lower mean scores than those living at home (with the possible confounding of a lower average MA in the institutionalized group). When compared for CA, the adult subjects (17 to 31 years) proved significantly superior to the adolescents (12 to 16 years) on most speech indices, including the auditory-vocal subscores on the ITPA (no progress after 16 years was observed on the visual motor subtests).

Rondal and Lambert (1980) have recorded free dyadic conversations between 22 French-speaking retarded adults (aged 21 to 35 years) and a familiar normal adult at a day care centre. They were 12 subjects with Down's syndrome (DS group) - 8 men and 4 women - and 10 retarded subjects of other aetiologies (NDS group) - 3 men and 7 women. For the DS group the mean CA, IC and number of years spent in special schools were 26, 45 and 12 respectively. They were 29, 46 and 7 respectively for the NDS group. None of the subjects in the DS and NDS groups had been or were institutionalized at the time of the study. Ten measures of the retarded adults' speech in their lexical, syntactical and pragmatic aspects were computed (Table 2).

Table 2

Average scores and standard deviations for Down's syndrome (DS) and non-Down's syndrome (NDS) adults

Speech indices	DS adults		NDS adults	
	Mean	SD(1)	Mean	SD
1. Type-token ratio	0.575	0.075	0.568	0.045
2. Mean length of utterance (in morphemes)	5.980	2.620	6.950	2.520
3. Proportion of sentences	0.412	0.311	0.533	0.299
4. Sentence complexity (2)	0.217	0.173	0.327	0.241
5. Number and gender (3)	0.563	0.235	0.690	0.214
6. Proportion of articles	0.381	0.212	0.518	0.154
7. Verbal inflections (4)	0.547	0.365	0.781	0.379
8. Proportion of pronouns	0.624	0.504	0.876	0.501
9. Proportion of new information (5)	0.692	0.121	0.693	0.114
10. Conversational continuity (6)	0.833	0.077	0.824	0.117

1. Standard deviation.
2. Ratio of the number of compound verbs plus subordinate clauses to the number of utterances.
3. Ratio of the number of morphological markers for number and gender to the number of utterances.
4. Ratio of the number of correct verbal inflections to the number of utterances.
5. Ratio of the number of informations not previously stated in the conversation to the number of informations given verbally. By information, was meant a complete relational meaning (i.e. a verb with its obligatory argument(s) in the sense of Chafe, 1970), an elliptical statement to a question referring back to an immediately preceding utterance by the interlocutor. Echoic and onomatopoeic productions were not counted as instances of informative utterances.
6. Ratio of the number of times the retarded subjects correctly followed on the topic introduced or developed by the non-retarded adult to the number of topics introduced or developed.

As expected (Schlanger, 1953; Mein, 1961; Blanchard, 1964; McCarthy, 1965; Lambert *et al.*, 1980; Rondal *et al.*, 1980, 1981a, b; Rondal and Lambert, 1983), Down's syndrome subjects obtained lower mean scores than the other retarded subjects, on the indices concerned with the morphosyntactical aspects of speech. However, none of the differences proved significant due to the relatively large interindividual variability in the two groups. The DS and NDS groups did not differ as to the diversity of lexical use (type-token ratio), new information and conversational continuity. Also none of the comparisons according to sex with aetiological category confounded proved significant.

Mentally retarded adults use simple formal means to express meaning. The conversational MLUs average 6 to 7 with standard deviations around 2.5. Only about half of the utterances are grammatical sentences. Sentence grammatical complexity remains low. These subjects may never reach the stage where they would make a proper use of grammatical morphology in order to modulate basic meanings. Yet despite severe formal limitations, their language appears to have functional value: it is informative and shows conversational continuity in topics.

Similar conclusions have been presented in other studies of the retarded adult's communicative competence (Bedrosian and Prutting, 1978; Berry *et al*., 1978; Owings and McManus, 1980; Veit *et al*., 1976; Sabsay, 1975; Bedrosian, 1979). It is suggested, first, that mentally retarded adults are able to take part in conversation and to demonstrate similar types of conversational controls as non-retarded adults; and, second, that they use similar communicative functions (e.g. questions, commands, information giving) with similar frequency as non-retarded subjects.

It is interesting to relate Rondal and Lambert's (1980) data on MLU with previous data on younger Down's syndrome subjects (Table 3).

Table 3

Cross-sectional data on mean length of utterance in Down's syndrome children and adults

Studies	Chronological age Mean	SD(2)	MLU(1) Mean	SD
Rondal (1978a)	4.1	0.9	1.26	0.23
	6.6	2.1	1.94	0.19
	9.9	1.9	2.87	0.14
Rondal *et al*. (1980)	11.6	1.8	3.40	0.95
Rondal and Lambert (1980)	26.0	1.7	5.98	2.63

1. Computed in number of morphemes.
2. Standard deviation.

The figures in Table 3 are indicative of a possible continued language growth in the Down's syndrome subjects. This goes with an increase in interindividual variability. One has to be cautious, however. The above indication may be entirely or partially spurious for the following two reasons: (1) Rondal's study (1978a) was conducted with monolingual American Down's syndrome subjects whereas the other studies had French-speaking subjects. Common knowledge indicates that French uses more words than English to express similar meaning but no systematic test has ever been made on this point to my knowledge; (2) the data come from cross-sectional studies. It seems possible, however, to hypothesize a continued growth in MLU with chronological age after 10 or 11 years in Down's syndrome subjects and possibly in retarded individuals of other aetiologies (cf. Rondal *et al*., 1980, 1981b, for some preliminary data).

PRELINGUISTIC DEVELOPMENT

Turning now to the early side of the life continuum, it has been suggested (e.g. Bruner, 1975) that there exist a number of prelinguistic precursors of speech. Mother-infant interaction, long the province of researchers in social development and attachment, has more recently captured the interest of those hoping to explore and explain the roots of language. The early reciprocal exchanges between mothers and infants have been likened to and studied as preverbal conversation or proto-dialogue (Bruner, 1975; Bateson, 1975). Such component skills of the interaction sequences as joint attention on the mother and child's part, smiling, laughing, showing, pointing, giving and receiving are studied as early forms of social and communicative sharing (e.g. Rheingold *et al*., 1976). Dore (1973) has suggested that even crying expresses attitudes and contributes to later language acquisition. However, as Bretherton and Bates (1979) point out the search for precursors of verbal communication has its dangers. Psycholinguists searching for the roots of discourse in prelinguistic mother-infant interaction are clearly postulating something conceptually similar to Piaget's notion of "vertical decalage" (i.e. structural similarity across cognitive level). But if a child is able to interact meaningfully before knowing a language, it does not necessarily follow that the structure of language is derived from or homologous to the structure of prelinguistic communication.

Despite the agreement concerning their possible importance for further development, the early signalling and interacting behaviours of *retarded infants* have received only minimal attention.

Jones (1977) has reported that the average rate per minute of interactional exchanges for mother-child pairs is about the same for normal and Down's syndrome infants between 8 and 18 months. However, unlike normal infants, Down's syndrome children tend to vocalize either in continuous strings or repeat vocalizations on top of each other with less than 1/2 second left for dialogue. Those patterns of vocalizations reveal lapses of interactive turn-taking skills. They make up for the high frequency of "vocal clashes" between Down's syndrome children and their mothers as opposed to normal children of corresponding ages. Buckhalt *et al*. (1978) and Berger and Cunningham (1981) confirm Jones' observations.

Several studies (Berger and Cunningham, 1981; Cicchetti and Sroufe, 1976; Cytryn, 1975) have reported delayed smiling and laughing in Down's syndrome babies. The onset of smiling comes later for the Down's syndrome babies (between 5 and 9 weeks). Also the percentage of time infants spend smiling at different ages is lower in Down's syndrome infants.

Berger and Cunningham (1983) and Gunn et al . (1982) have investigated eye contact between mothers and normal as well as Down's syndrome infants over the first nine months of life. The Down's syndrome infants show chronological delays in the onset of eye contact (onset of sustained eye contact with mother around 7 weeks in DS infants versus 1 month in normal babies) and in the establishment of high levels of this behaviour (DS infants exhibit around six months of age similar levels of eye contact as observed in normal infants around four months). High levels of eye contact are attained during the third month. They are maintained in the following months and occur in long episodes (ten seconds and over) whereas the gazing behaviour of the normal infants directed to the mother shows a marked decrease in frequency and duration of episodes after four months.

Frequent and longer episodes of eye contact with the mother in Down's syndrome babies extending over several months would appear to be beneficial for the formation of the mother-infant bond. Interpersonal looking behaviour may also be regarded as a first step in learning communication skills. However, the delays and deviations in these children in the relational patterns of mother-child communication as well as in the timing and referential uses of eye contact deserve careful attention.

These problems imply impairments in both maturational and psychological processes. The age of onset of eye contact and first increase in normal infants seems to correspond with the reported age of maturation of the macular area of the retina which is considered necessary for sustained focusing on relatively small objects (Bronson, 1974). It could be the case that the low levels of eye contact and the short gaze duration found in Down's syndrome infants during the early months are related to some impairments or slower maturation of the macular retina or corresponding areas in the nervous system. The short gazes might also result from the hypotonia in the muscles of the eyes. There may also be a relationship between Down's sydrome infants' delays in smiling and laughing and their degree of muscular hypotonia (Cicchetti and Sroufe, 1976).

The handicapped infants' greatly prolonged period of frequent and long-lasting eye contact (while indicating that the visual system has matured sufficiently by 3 or 4 months to allow frequent and prolonged eye contact) suggests new types of difficulties: a possible slower maturation of the peripheral visual field (Salapatek, 1975), of the inhibitory mechanisms (Parmelle and Stern, 1972), a slow development of competing responses, and a low distractibility (Miranda and Fantz, 1974). Alternatively, or complementarily, the impairment(s) may be limited in the learning processes and information processing capacity particularly with respect to acquisition of the face schema (Miranda, 1976). The problem reported by Jones (1977) regarding lapses of interactive turn-taking skills in Down's syndrome infants may also be cognitive in nature (failure to take the conversational partner into account) or indicate a lack of inhibitory capacity in the auditory-vocal channel. Further research is required to test these hypotheses and suggest ways for remediation.

An explanation of the difference between handicapped and normal infants in looking behaviour does not seem to be obviously related to maternal behaviour. In Gunn et al . (1982) study, looking by the Down's syndrome children was not associated with the amount of mother vocalization at 6 months in contrast to the normal group where a positive correlation was found. Also, vocalization, looking and holding behaviours as well as loudness were not more successful in holding their child's attention than mothers of first born children. Berger and Cunningham (1983), however, warn parents against overstimulating their handicapped infant in order to avoid inhibiting the infant's signalling activities. They suggest to the parents who have a tendency to overstimulate, reducing the intensity of maternal stimulation and making it more contingent on the infant's own behaviour.

There is no need to stress further the importance of this current research on the early communicative behaviours of handicapped infants. If one assumes at least partial sequential dependency between prelinguistic and linguistic developments, learning more about the early relational problems of the handicapped child gives the best hope of being able to specify the content and method of an efficient early intervention procedure.

REFERENCES

Barblan, L. and Chipman, H.H. (1978). Temporal relationships in language: a comparison between normal and language retarded children. In Drachman, G. (ed.), **Salzburger Beitrage zur Linguistik**, W. Neugebaner, Salzburg, 46-65

Bartell, N., Bryen and Keehn, S. (1973). Language comprehension in the moderately retarded child. **Exceptional Children, 39**, 375-382

Bateman, B. and Wetherell, J. (1965). Psycholinguistic aspects of mental retardation. **Mental Retardation, 3**, 8-13

Bateson, M. (1975). Mother-infant exchanges: the epigenesis of conversational interaction. In Aaronson, D. and Rieber, R. (eds.), **Developmental Psycholinguistics and Communication Disorders**, New York Academy of Sciences, New York, 101-113

Baumeister, A. (1967). Problems in comparative studies of mental retardates and normals. **American Journal of Mental Deficiency, 71**, 869-875

Bedrosian, J.L. (1979). Communicative performance of mentally retarded adults: A topic analysis. Paper presented at the Symposium of the American Association on Mental Deficiency:

The Linguistic Environment of the Mentally Retarded Child. Miami Beach, Florida

Bedrosian, J.L. and Prutting, C.A. (1978). Communicative performance of mentally retarded adults in four conversational settings. **Journal of Speech and Hearing Research, 21**, 79-95

Beier, E., Starkweather, J. and Lambert, M. (1969). Vocabulary usage of mentally retarded children. **American Journal of Mental Deficiency, 73**, 927-934

Berger, J. and Cunningham, C.C. (1981). The development of eye contact between mothers and normal and Down's syndrome infants. **Developmental Psychology, 17**, 678-689

Berger, J. and Cunningham, C.C. (1983). The development of early vocal behaviour and interaction in Down's syndrome and non-handicapped infants. **Developmental Psychology**, (in press)

Berry, P. (1972). Comprehension of possessive and present continuous sentences by non-retarded, mildly retarded, and severely retarded children. **American Journal of Mental Deficiency, 76**, 540-544

Berry, P., Pountney, C. and Powell, I. (1978). Meal-time communication in moderately and severely retarded adults: An ethological study. **Australian Journal of Mental Retardation, 5**, 105-108

Bilovsky, D. and Share, J. (1965). The ITPA and Down's syndrome: an exploratory study. **American Journal of Mental Deficiency, 70**, 78-83

Blanchard, I. (1964). Speech pattern and etiology in mental retardation. **American Journal of Mental Deficiency, 68**, 612-617

Bretherton, I. and Bates, E. (1979). The emergence of intentional communication. In Uzgiris, I. (ed.), **Social Interaction and Communication During Infancy**, Jossey-Bass, San Francisco, 81-101

Bronson, G. (1974). The postnatal growth of visual capacity. **Child Development, 45**, 873-890

Brown, R. (1973). **A First Language**, Harvard University Press, Cambridge, MA

Bruner, J.S. (1975). From communication to language - a psychological perspective. **Cognition, 3**, 256-287

Buckhalt, J.A., Rutherford, R.B. and Golberg, I. (1978). Verbal and non-verbal interaction of mothers with their Down's syndrome and non-retarded infants. **American Journal of Mental Deficiency, 82**, 337-343

Buium, N., Rynders, J. and Turnure, J. (1974). **A Semantic Relational Concepts Based Theory of Language Acquisition as Applied to Down's Syndrome Children**. Research report No. 62, Reseach, Development, and Demonstration Center in Education of Handicapped Children, University of Minnesota, Minneapolis, Minnesota

Chafe, W. (1970). **Meaning of the Structure of Language**, University of Chicago Press, Chicago

Chipman, H.H. (1979). Understanding language retardation: a developmental perspective. Paper presented at the 5th I.A.S.S.M.D. Conference, Jerusalem

Cicchetti, D. and Sroufe, L.A. (1976). The relationship between effective and cognitive development in Down's syndrome infants. **Child Development, 47**, 920-929

Clark, E. (1973). What's in a word? On the child's acquisition of semantics in his first language. In Moore, T. (ed.), **Cognitive Development and the Acquisition of Language.** Academic Press, New York

Coggins, J. (1976). Cited by de Villiers, P. and de Villiers, J., 1978

Cook, N. (1977). Semantic development in children with Down's syndrome. Communication presented at the 85th Annual Convention of the American Psychological Association, San Francisco

Cromer, R. (1973). **Are Subnormals Linguistic Adults?** Paper No. 10, M.R.C. Developmental Psychology Unit, London

Cromer, R. (1974). Receptive language in the mentally retarded: Processes and diagnosis distinctions. In Schiefelbusch, R.L. and Lloyd, L. (eds.), **Language Perspective - Acquisition, Retardation and Intervention.** University Park Press, Baltimore, 237-268

Cytryn, L. (1975). Studies of behavior in children with Down's syndrome. In Anthony, E.J. (ed.), **Explorations in Child Psychiatry**, Plenum Press, New York

Dale, P. (1977). Syntactic development in Down's syndrome children. Communication presented at the 85th Annual Convention of the American Psychological Association, San Francisco

de Villiers, P. and de Villiers, J. (1978). **Language Acquisition**, Harvard University Press, Cambridge, MA

Dewart, H.H. (1979). Language comprehension processes of mentally retarded children. **American Journal of Mental Deficiency, 84**, 177-183

Dodd, B. (1972). Comparison of babbling patterns in normal and Down-syndrome infants. **Journal of Mental Deficiency Research, 16**, 35-40

Dodd, B. (1975). A comparison of the phonological systems of mental age matched normal, severely subnormal and Down's syndrome children. **British Journal of Communicative Disorders, 11**, 27-42

Dooley, B. (1976). Cited in de Villiers, P., and de Villiers, J., 1978.

Dore, J. (1973). **On the Development of Speech Acts**, Doctoral dissertation, City University of New York

Duchan, J.F. and Erickson, J.G. (1976). Normal and retarded children's understanding of semantic relations in different verbal contexts. **Journal of Speech and Hearing Research, 19**, 767-776

Edwards, D. (1973). Sensory-motor intelligence and semantic relations in early child grammar. **Cognition, 2**, 395-434

Evans, D. (1977). The development of language abilities in mongols: a correlation study. **Journal of Mental Deficiency Research, 21,** 103-117

Fillmore, C. (1967). The case for case. In Bach, E. and Harms, R. (eds.), **Universals in Linguistic Theory.** Holt, Rinehart, and Winston, New York, 1-88

Frith, U. and Frith, C. (1974). Specific motor disabilities in Down's syndrome. **Journal of Child Psychology and Psychiatry, 15,** 293-301

Glovsky, L. (1970). A comparison of two groups of mentally retarded children on the ITPA. **Training School Bulletin, 67,** 4-14

Gordon, W. and Panagos, J. (1976). Developmental transformational capacity of children with Down's syndrome. **Perceptual and Motor Skills, 43,** 967-973

Greenwald, C.A. and Leonard, L.B. (1979). Communicative and sensorimotor development of Down's syndrome children. **American Journal of Mental Deficiency, 84,** 296-303

Gunn, P., Berry, P. and Andrews, R. (1982). Looking behavior of Down's syndrome infants. **American Journal of Mental Deficiency, 87,** 344-347

Jones, O. (1977). Mother-child communication with pre-linguistic Down's syndrome and normal infants. In Schaffer, H. (ed.), **Studies in Mother-Child Interaction,** Academic Press, New York, 379-401

Keane, V. (1972). The incidence of speech and language problems. **Mental Retardation, 10,** 3-8

Lackner, J. (1968). A developmental study of language behavior in retarded children, **Neuropsychologia, 6,** 301-320

Lambert, J-L., (1978). **Introduction a L'arrieration Mentale.** Mardaga, Bruxelles

Lambert, J-L., Rondal, J.A. and Sohier, C. (1980). Analyse des troubles articulatoires chez des enfants arrieres menteaux mongoliens et non mongoliens. **Bulletin d'Audiophonologie, 10,** 13-20

Layton, T. and Sharifi, H. (1979). Meaning and structure of Down's syndrome and non-retarded children spontaneous speech. **American Journal of Mental Deficiency, 83,** 439-445

Lenneberg, E. (1967). **Biological Foundations of Language,** Wiley, New York

Lenneberg, E., Nichols, I. and Rosenberger, E. (1964). Primitive stages of language development in mongolism. In McRioch, D. and Weinstein, A. (eds.), **Disorders of Communication,** Williams and Wilkins, Baltimore, 119-137

Lozar, B., Wepman, J. and Haas, W. (1972). Lexical use of mentally retarded and non-retarded children. **American Journal of Mental Deficiency, 76,** 534-539

Lyle, J. (1961). Comparison of the language of normal and imbecile children. **Journal of Mental Deficiency Research, 5,** 40-50

McCarthy, J.M. (1965). **Patterns of Psycholinguistic Development of Mongoloid and Non-mongoloid Severely Retarded Children**, Doctoral dissertation, University of Illinois

Mein, R. (1961). A study of the vocabularies of severely subnormal patients. **Journal of Mental Deficiency Research, 5**, 51-59

Mein, R. and O'Connor, N. (1960). A study of the oral vocabularies of severely subnormal patients. **Journal of Mental Deficiency Research, 4**, 130-153

Miranda, S.B. (1976). Visual attention to defective and high-risk infants. **Merrill - Palmer Quarterly, 22**, 201-228

Miranda, S.B. and Fantz, R.L. (1974). Recognition memory in Down's syndrome and normal infants. **Child Development, 45**, 651-660

Mittler, P. (1970). The use of morphological rules by four years old children: an item analysis of the auditory-vocal automatic test of the ITPA. **British Journal of Disorders of Communication, 5**, 99-109

Mittler, P. (1974). Language and communication. In Clarke, A.M. and Clarke, A.D.B. (eds.), **Mental Deficiency, the Changing Outlook**, Methuen, London, 527-591

Mueller, M. and Weaver, S. (1964). Psycholinguistic abilities of institutionalized and non-institutionalized trainable mental retardates. **American Journal of Mental Deficiency, 68**, 775-783

O'Connor, N. and Hermelin, B. (1959). Some effects of word learning in imbeciles. **Language and Speech, 2**, 63-71

O'Connor, N. and Hermelin, B. (1963). **Speech and Thought in Severe Subnormality**, Macmillan, New York

Owings, N.O. and McManus, M.D. (1980). An analysis of communication functions in the speech of a deinstitutionalized adult mentally retarded client. **Mental Retardation, 18**, 309-314

Parmelle, A.H. and Stern, E. (1972). Development of states in infants. In Clements, C., Purpura, P. and Mayer, F. (eds.), **Maturation of Brain Mechanisms Related to Sleep Behavior**, Academic Press, New York

Piaget, J. (1954). **The Construction of Reality in the Child.** Basic Books, New York

Rheingold, H., Hay, D. and West, F. (1976). Sharing in the second year of life. **Child Development, 47**, 1146-1158

Rondal, J.A. (1978a). Maternal speech to normal and Down's syndrome children matched for mean length of utterance. In Myers, E. (ed.), **Quality of Life in Severely and Profoundly Mentally Retarded People: Research Foundations for Improvement**, American Association on Mental Deficiency, Monograph No. 3, Washington, D.C., 193-265

Rondal, J.A. (1978b). Developmental sentence scoring procedure and the delay-difference question in language development of Down's syndrome children. **Mental Retardation, 16**, 169-171

Rondal, J.A. (1978c). Patterns of correlations for various language measures in mother-child interactions for normal and Down's syndrome children. **Language and Speech, 21,** 242-252

Rondal, J.A. and Lambert, J.L. (1980). **The Speech of Mentally Retarded Adults in a Dyadic Communication Situation: Some Formal and Informative Aspects.** Research report, University of Liege, Institute of Psychology

Rondal, J.A. and Lambert, J.L. (1983). **Language et Communication chez les Handicapes Mentaux : Theorie, Evaluation et Intervention**, Delachaux et Niestle, Paris, (in press)

Rondal, J.A., Lambert, J.L. and Chipman, H. (1981a). **Psycholinguistique et Handicap Mental**, Mardaga, Bruxelles

Rondal, J.A., Lambert, J.L. and Sohier, C. (1980). L'imitation verbale et non verbale chez l'enfant retarde mental mongolien et non mongolien. **Enfance, 3**, 107-122

Rondal, J.A., Lambert, J.L. and Sohier, C. (1981b). Elicited verbal and non-verbal imitation in Down's syndrome and other mentally retarded children: A replication and extension of Berry. **Language and Speech, 24**, 245-254

Ryan, J. (1975). Mental subnormality and language development. In Lenneberg, E. and Lenneberg, E. (eds.), **Foundations of Language Development : A Multidisciplinary Approach, Vol. 2**, Wiley, New York, 269-277

Sabsay, S. (1975). Communicative competence among the severely retarded: some evidence from the conversational interaction of Down's syndrome adults. Paper presented at the meeting of the Linguistic Society of America, San Franciso

Salapatek, P. (1975). Pattern perception in early infancy. In Cohen, L.B. and Salapatek, P. (eds.), **Infant Perception: From Sensation to Cognition**, Academic Press, New York

Schlanger, B.B. (1953). Speech examination of a group of institutionalized mentally handicapped children. **Journal of Speech and Hearing Disorders, 18**, 339-349

Semmel, M. and Dolley, D. (1970). Comprehension and imitation of sentences by Down's syndrome children as a function of transformational complexity. **American Journal of Mental Deficiency, 75**, 739-745

Sersen, E., Astrup, E., Floistad, I. and Wortis, J. (1970). Motor conditioned reflexes and word association in retarded children. **American Journal of Mental Deficiency, 74,** 495-501

Smith, B. (1977). Phonological development in Down's syndrome children. Communication presented at the 85th Annual Convention of the American Psychological Association, San Francisco

Smith, B. and Oller, K. (1981). A comparative study of pre-meaningful vocalizations produced by normally developing and Down's syndrome infants. **Journal of Speech and Hearing Disorders, 46**, 46-51

Spradlin, J. (1963). Language and communication of mental defectives. In Ellis, N. (ed.), **Handbook of Mental**

Deficiency: Psychological Theory and Research, McGraw-Hill, New York, 512-565

Veit, S.W., Allen, G.J. and Chinsky, J.M. (1976). Interpersonal interactions between institutionalized retarded children and their attendants. **American Journal of Mental Deficiency, 80**, 535-542

Wheldall, K. (1976). Receptive language in the mentally handicapped. In Berry, P. (ed.), **Language and Communication in the Mentally Handicapped**, University Park Press, Baltimore, 36-55

Willis, B. (1978). **Mentally Retarded Children - Qualitatively Different Speech**. Unpublished manuscript, Luther College, Decorah, Iowa

Zisk, P. and Bialer, J. (1967). Speech and language problems in mongolism: a review of the literature. **Journal of Speech and Hearing Disorders, 32**, 228-241

COMMENTARY

M. C. Beveridge

Rondal's well constructed paper somewhat underplays the role of the extra-linguistic context in the understanding of language. Normal development leads to a decrease in the amount of extra-linguistic information required by a listener to understand a speaker's message. The messages from a babbling baby are constructed by the eye and the ear of the listener, who largely determines the child's meaning. For an 18 month old child, the meaning of the message is determined by the child's combination of a word with a referential situation shared by the child and the listener(s).

The process by which the child comes to rely less on the extra-linguistic context has not been clearly mapped out. Studies of anaphoric reference in normal children have begun (Karmiloff-Smith, 1981) but as yet the problem has not been studied systematically in handicapped children. We know young children are better at talking about the here and now (Shatz, 1978) but they do learn to refer to the past and future. And being able to do this has linguistic correlates which may well throw up more interesting and important differences between normal and handicapped persons than those described by Rondal, although differences due to the structure of language and those associated with the organization of thought become very closely related in this area.

The context of language is also an issue in the study by Jones (1977) discussed by Rondal. One difference between retarded and non-retarded children suggested by Jones' results is that mothers of retarded children are more directive in their interactions with their children. This directive approach could be associated with the necessity for the mothers of handicapped children to be in control. One way of limiting the range of discourse is by controlling the referents in the situation. The mother needs to know what is being talked about and so keeps the topic firmly in her grasp. Although Rondal (1978) reports no clear differences in the maternal linguistic styles of the mothers of Down's syndrome children, there may be differences in their ability and readiness to interpret their children's communications. Mothers of retarded children have had more practice interpreting their children's ambiguous messages since their children are older than MLU matched non-handicapped children. Thus mothers of some handicapped children may be better able to understand an utterance which normally would be regarded as ambiguous because they are more attentive to the context which they (the mothers) have in part controlled.

From our own studies we would suggest that the communicative context in which retarded persons use language is important beyond the development of basic linguistic structures. We have found, for example, that there was a significant tendency for teachers not to continue communicative interchanges initiated by retarded children (Beveridge and Hurrell, 1980), especially those children with a more excitable personality. Perhaps retarded children are not seen by teachers as interesting communicators; if so, ways of changing this attitude should be studied. And the educational consequences of attitudes change should be evaluated.

We have carried out two other studies which link to the work described by Rondal. The use of language by retarded persons as a means of initiating social contact often shows a sharp increase in frequency during adolescence (Beveridge et al., 1978). Rondal notes that language structures continue to improve during this period and research which investigates the connection of this improvement to social behaviour is required. Also, a recent study has suggested that teaching retarded persons how to communicate with each other about tasks which they find difficult will improve performance on those tasks (Beveridge et al., 1982). These communications involved language which Rondal has shown to be well within the linguistic capacity of retarded persons but this research suggests that they are not readily using these linguistic structures for cognitive and communicative purposes. Why this does not happen is one question which we need to take more seriously from a research perspective.

References

Beveridge, M.C. and Hurrell, P. (1980). Teachers' responses to severely mentally handicapped children's initiations in the classroom. **Journal of Child Psychology and Psychiatry, 21**, 175-181

Beveridge, M.C., Newton, S. and Grantley, J. (1982). Referential communication as a technique in the teaching of work skills to severely subnormal adolescents. **British Journal of Disorders of Communication, 2**, 15-21

Beveridge, M.C., Spencer, J. and Mittler, P. (1978). Language and social behaviour in severely subnormal children. **British Journal of Social and Clinical Psychology, 17**, 75-83

Jones, O. (1977). Mother-child communication with pre-linguistic Down's syndrome and normal infants. In Schaffer, H. (ed.), **Studies in Mother-Child Interaction.** New York, Academic Press, 379-401

Karmiloff-Smith, A. (1981). The grammatical marking of thematic structure in the development of language. In Deutsch, W. (ed.), **The Child's Construction of Language.** New York, Academic Press

Rondal, J. (1978). Maternal speech to normal and Down's syndrome children matched for MLU in Meyers, C.E. (ed.). **Behavior in the Profoundly and Severely Retarded: Research Foundations for Enhancing the Quality of Life**, Washington, A.A.M.D.

Shatz, M. (1978). On the development of communicative understanding: an early strategy for interpreting and responding to messages. **Cognitive Psychology, 10**, 271-287

W. I. Fraser

(1) Can I make a plea for more research into the communication of distress by the profoundly handicapped child. Any clinician, in nurseries where there are profoundly handicapped children, is saddened by the grave deficits in intersubjectivity compared with normal infants' spell binding interest in others, and by the caretakers' inability to detect when or why the child is distressed. Does such research not have more service relevance than studies of syntax in unusual children?

(2) A retarded child's pragmatic skill usually exceeds his syntactic skill, but not always - I should like to ask Wood and Cromer how they explain the misleadingly verbal child - perhaps the "cocktail party" hydrocephalic or autistic child who has overprecise syntax and yet poor pragmatic skills, indeed with no anaphoric reference?

R. F. Cromer

Rondal's presentation gives a good clear account of the problems involved in the "delay-difference" issue in the language development of the retarded. Most of his examples, however, are of measurable states of language rather than underlying processes. That is, a distinction can be made between the actual structures of language inferred from observed utterances, and the processes by which the language system is acquired. In this light, I would like to clarify a reference made to my own studies. In Cromer (1975), I speculated that in some cases a delay in language acquisition might lead to a difference in the following sense: If there is a critical period for language acquisition such that during the critical period certain processes or methods are employed in acquiring new linguistic structures which are different from those used after such a critical period, then children who are delayed in acquisition beyond that critical period will in fact be acquiring the more advanced structures of language by a different process than children acquiring them during the critical period - if they acquire those more advanced structures at all. This speculation was based on the observation that mentally retarded adolescents behaved on a learning task to do with a specific linguistic structure in the way that normal adults behaved, and did not approach the language task in the way that younger normal children did.

It should be noted that the notions of a critical period and of differing methods for acquiring language during and after that period are open to some doubt (see Wode, 1979, 1982), and need to be carefully explored. Rondal rightly notes, "We do not know at this time whether there is only one or several alternative ways to language acquisition". He argues for the extensive use of longitudinal data. To this I would like to add that experimental studies on processes of acquisition are also possible. One need not rely solely on longitudinal data. Indeed, longitudinal studies must be supplemented by experimental studies if one is to explore the processes by which children are acquiring language.

Rondal raises an important issue when he contrasts language considered as an entire system with an approach that emphasizes its separate components. In any particular child, it is necessary to specify the precise nature of any deficit - whether it be phonological, syntactic, semantic, pragmatic, or more broadly "cognitive". Rondal's speculation concerning the non-synchronization of development of various systems making the retarded child's language "different" from that of a younger normal child, receives support from the Curtiss *et al.* and the Blank *et al.* studies mentioned in my discussion comments on Kiernan's paper. Again, it can be noted that not only longitudinal but experimental studies can help to clarify the issues by concentrating on specific *processes* being used during language acquisition.

References

Cromer, R.F. (1975). Are subnormals linguistic adults? In O'Connor, N. (ed.), **Language, Cognitive Deficits, and Retardation**. London, Butterworths, 167-187

Wode, H. (1979). Operating principles and "universals" in L1, L2, and FLT. **International Review of Applied Linguistics, 17**, 217-231

Wode, H. (1982). Some theoretical implications of L2 acquisition research. **Arbeitspapiere zum Spracherwerb, 28.** Englisches Seminar der Universitat Kiel

R. J. Robinson

The first section of this paper is concerned with the concept of delay versus difference in mental retardation, and the comments made about the value and the limitations of this concept in the critique of the following paper by Kiernan are equally applicable. The author himself makes some important general points indicating that neither the "delay" concept nor the "difference" concept will fully explain the nature of mental function, or in this particular context language development, in the retarded. He supports the view advanced in the previous critique that the more detailed the study, the more likely it is to reveal difference rather than delay. Rondal's extensive table, summarizing studies on language development in the retarded, is of great value. The studies listed, which only overlap to a small extent with those summarized by Kiernan, are again broadly in support of the "delay" concept.

The second section is concerned with language in mentally retarded adolescents and adults, with the emphasis strongly on those with Down's syndrome. The most intriguing observation is the suggestion that language may continue to grow and develop into adult life in this disorder. Rondal is suitably cautious about the interpretation of this finding but it appears to be true in two separate studies. It is an observation of potentially very great educational significance and supports the view that education in the mentally retarded should be continued beyond normal school leaving age (a policy which has now been officially adopted in the UK).

The third section is concerned with pre-linguistic behaviour. Behaviour in very early infancy is of considerable interest but it is not clear how relevant it is to language development. This perhaps depends, referring to Kiernan's paper, on whether one is more concerned with the symbolic and syntactical aspects of language, or with its communicative function. If we take the view that language is the use of symbols to express ideas, then we cannot really consider the child's behaviour to be linguistic until he is beginning to show some kind of symbolization - for example with miniature toys. If, however, we emphasize the communicative and motivational aspects of language, then any behaviour which promotes communication and interaction with other people can be regarded as relevant, including smiling.

I have found some of the attempts in this section to relate abnormalities of early behaviour to particular neurological abnormalities rather speculative and unconvincing. For example, the delay in smiling and laughing in Down's syndrome seems much more likely to be related to the general delay in cognitive and social development than to the muscular hypotonia.

D. E. Yoder

Initial comment

This paper provides some good ideas in the area of delay-difference, and also a compilation of quite useful data on language acquisition of the mentally retarded. My comments on the paper address what I perceive to be the need to:

(a) align the title and rationale more clearly with the paper content;
(b) consider a possible reorganization of the paper;
(c) define the population and explain the terminology.

Title vs content of the paper

The title of the paper suggests that it covers linguistic and prelinguistic development in the moderately and severely retarded. In reality, however, the paper covers the a) delay-difference controversy surrounding the language of the retarded; b) language of the adult retarded and c) prelinguistic development/behaviour in retarded infants. The title suggests that development in both the moderate and severely retarded will be covered. Much of the data presented, however, derive from the Down's syndrome population who are usually in the range of moderate retardation (AAMD Level II). Additionally, there is no clear reference to the severely retarded.

In considering the language and communication ability of the moderately retarded it is extremely difficult to find any consistent degree of homogeneity. It is even more unwise to consider language behaviour across both moderately and severely retarded without a careful description of each subject group (Miller _et al._, 1981). There was no such description or differentiation in the paper.

Organization of the paper

While reading the chapter there was a feeling of reading three separate papers. The first discussed and summarized the available data for a position statement on the delay-difference issue. (Note: I assume the author considers this issue synonymous with the often discussed quantitative-qualitative argument applied to the language of the retarded, i.e. Yoder and Miller, 1972.)

The second section covered aspects of language in _moderately_ retarded adults, and the third section, prelinguistic development in retarded children. The problem is that there is no clear transition, link, or progression between the three sections. All three sections contain interesting information and provide at least a partial review of existing developmental literature on the moderately retarded. However, the absence of an introductory and continuing argument for the organization of the paper makes the overall rationale for the chapter unclear. Indeed, the first pages, while interesting, say nothing about either the delay-difference issue or adults until the paragraph which suddenly states that the paper is divided into three parts.

Defining the population and explaining the terminology

My third issue of concern is lumping together the language and communication behaviour of both the moderately and severely retarded. The primary data source for this paper appears to be the language behaviour of the moderately retarded not the severely retarded. Care must therefore be taken to specify _exactly_ what is meant by a moderate and/or severely (if it is used) retarded individual. The two are not homogeneous populations in even the best of circumstances and it is important that an adequate description of the population under discussion be provided. This becomes even more critical when data on the retarded are presented from a number of sources as they are in this chapter.

The recapitulation

The paper first appears to be in need of a title that more aptly reflects the content. Next, there is a need for an introduction that in some fashion offers the reader an argument or rationale for organizing the paper as it has been organized. I am not suggesting that part of the paper be cut out or eliminated, but rather suggesting the need to make the chapter a more cohesive unit. In this way it will avoid the appearance that sections of the paper were randomly put together because they cover some aspect of the language of the retarded. A concluding summary on the chapter would also help in this effort.

Allow me to return to the organization issue once more. It seems that the paper would make much more sense if the delay-difference issue were presented as a rationale for, or introduction to, the issue of development of language in moderately retarded children and adults. In this way the first section on delay-difference could remain, followed by a development section that begins with the information on the prelinguistic child and progresses to the information on adults. This is but a suggestion, however as it stands I think it would be difficult to develop a transition that moves logically from the delay-difference/development issue, to adults and finally back to the prelinguistic retarded child.

References

Miller J., Chapman R. and MacKenzie H., (1981), Individual differences in the language acquisition of mentally retarded children. Paper presented at the 2nd International Congress for the Study of Child Language, University of British Columbia, Vancouver, B.C., Canada

Yoder D. and Miller J., (1972), What we may know and what we can do: Input toward a system. In J. McLean, D. Yoder and R. Schiefelbusch, (Eds.), **Language Intervention with the Retarded: Developing Strategies**, Baltimore, University Park Press, 89-107

Chapter 16

The development of communication and cognition

C.C. Kiernan

INTRODUCTION

The two topics indicated in the title of this contribution represent central areas in the study of mental handicap. Difficulties in acquiring and using communication skills and difficulties in acquiring and handling information are at the core of a definition of mental handicap.

Despite their centrality the two areas have not attracted large amounts of research. In fact, as we will see, research in these fields is largely derived from theories and work with normal children and adults. To the extent that such research and theorizing is well ahead of application to mental handicap the fields represent a rich source of future research.

Theory and research in these areas do not lend themselves to neat exposition. In this contribution we will be selective in coverage and will concentrate more on work on communication than on cognition.

FROM SPEECH TO COMMUNICATION

Two trends in the study of normal child language are of considerable importance to this paper. The first is a switch of emphasis in explaining language development. The Chomskyite view sees language primarily in terms of syntax, and development as involving the unfolding of what are essentially innate linguistic structures (Chomsky, 1965). During the early 1970s research on early language development recognized that Chomsky had underplayed the role of the child's motives in acquiring language. Many early utterances could not be understood in simple syntactic terms. The child's intended meaning had to be taken into account before utterances could be interpreted (cf. Bloom, 1970), and rather than being seen as an unfolding of innate structures, language development began to be seen as motivated by the child's need to communicate, by the desire to affect the behaviour of other people. For example Bruner (1975, p 2) argued that "language is acquired as an instrument for regulating joint activity and joint attention".

The approach to the analysis of language from the viewpoint of communicative functions is termed "pragmatics". Analyses of this type lead to a very different classification of utterances than those given by analyses in terms of syntax or for that matter semantic classifications. For example Halliday's scheme (1973, 1975) involves the following categories (from Yoder and Calculator, 1981):

Instrumental, the use of language as a way of getting things done through requesting goods and services.

Regulatory, the use of language to regulate the behaviour of others, for example through asking someone to do something or establishing a rule.

Interactional, the use of language to establish and maintain relationships, from greeting or calling to persuading others.

Personal, language used to express feelings or attitudes.

Heuristic, the use of language as a way of learning about things.

Imaginative, language use as "let's pretend".

Informative, the use of language as a means of communicating information to other people.

Two crucial points need to be made about this and parallel pragmatic analyses. Firstly, the functions which are described can be achieved through non-verbal as well as through verbal communication. For example, a non-verbal child can lead an adult to a desired object (instrumental function), or draw attention to something which interests him (regulatory), greet others (interactional), express likes and dislikes (personal), or call attention to a novel event (informative).

Secondly, each of the functions described can be realized in more and more complex syntactical structures. For example, an instrumental utterance requesting a ball may be expressed as "ball", or at any level of complexity to "I would be grateful if you could give me that blue and white striped ball". The categories represent an alternative to other analyses.

As we have already noted, theorists within this tradition see the child's reason for acquiring language, from first words to mature grammar, as resting in his desire to regulate joint attention and joint activity. The credibility of this approach is illustrated in a study by Moerk (1978). Moerk classified the verbal interactions of 20 mother-child pairs where the children ranged in age from one year nine months to five years. All the children were of normal intelligence. Seven of Moerk's categories related to functional aspects of language, including the child requesting information or tangible benefits and the mother giving directions or clarifying what the child had said. The data showed that, on average, children spontaneously employed language as a tool to obtain information or tangible advantages around 17 times per hour. Mothers used techniques to elicit and regulate speech and other acts around 40 times per hour on average, and experienced positive practical consequences in around 26 instances per hour. Moerk argues that "such a high frequency of motivating phenomena may help to explain the intense involvement of both partners in verbal behaviour, the frequent instructional activity of the mother, as well as the relatively rapid acquisition of basic language skills by the child" (Moerk, 1978, p 541).

The potential value of pragmatic analyses to work in mental handicap is clear. The approach offers new ways in which we can analyse the behaviour of the severely or profoundly mentally handicapped people. Kiernan et al. (1982) found that around a third of the population of schools for the severely mentally handicapped were said to be unable to use more than three words to express needs or requests. Secondly, the theory proposes that language is acquired through communication and that the types of category mentioned above represent psychologically distinct functions which have to be acquired. As such the analyses suggest ways in which remedial activities can be organized, i.e. through the establishment and development of activities which encourage the development of communication of the types described. Development of programmes of this type is in its infancy (cf. Yoder and Calculator, 1981) but shows much promise.

LINKS TO COGNITIVE DEVELOPMENT

In order to communicate the individual needs to have something to say, a reason for saying it, and a way of saying it (Miller and Yoder, 1972). In other words he needs to be able to formulate his needs and experiences, to want to communicate them and to be able to express himself in terms of the rules of a conventionalized language system.

The basic logic of this formulation is simple. An individual will only be able to communicate about needs, things or experiences which he knows about. During the 1970s a further view linking cognition and communication gained strength. Piaget (1954) argued that the first two years of life, the sensorimotor period, is marked by the development of general skills in representing the world. The theory suggests that the child progresses through six stages of development across six "domains". These domains reflect the development of the object concept, the idea that objects have independent existence, means-ends skills, reflecting understanding of causal relations, imitative skills and others. Within the theory developments within the domains are linked so that there are, for example, typical stage V behaviours in all domains. So if the child is achieving at a stage V level on object concept we would predict that he would be functioning at the same level in all other domains (cf. Uzgiris and Hunt, 1975). Piaget's view was that language was evolved as an aspect of general cognitive development. If this is the case, skills in handling objects and communication skills would represent two manifestations of general cognitive development (Cromer, 1974, 1976; Morehead and Morehead, 1974).

The most explicit attempts to link the development of communication skills to sensorimotor development have been made by Bates and her colleagues (Bates, 1976; Bates *et al*., 1977). Their first phase of development, the perlocutionary stage, lasts from birth to eight or nine months in normal children. During this phase the child does things which, from his point of view, do not signal specific intentions, but adults nonetheless interpret and respond to these responses consistently. This phase pre-dates awareness of means-ends relationships or ability to represent objects. During the second phase of development, from 9 to 13 months, motor and vocal gestures come under intentional control. It is during this stage, the illocutionary period, that the child begins to use adults to obtain objects. This type of behaviour is termed an imperative performative and parallels Halliday's instrumental function. It is also during this period that the child begins to use objects in order to gain adult attention, declarative performances, paralleling Halliday's regulatory function.

Bates links the illocutionary stage with Piaget's "stage V" a period of cognitive development during which the child uses novel means to gain familiar ends. These performatives are initially expressed non-verbally but lead to verbalizations at around the age of 12 to 13 months. The responses reflect the child's developing capacity to conceptualize means-ends relationships, albeit initially in fairly primitive forms.

The third phase of development, between 12 and 16 months, is one in which the child learns to separate spoken words from the specific context of experience, i.e. begins to use words referentially. In achieving this development the child initially inserts words into non-verbal performatives but gradually replaces these cues with words. Bates argues that this phase coincides with the achievement of Piaget's sensorimotor stage VI, during which the child begins to use symbols.

Bates' tie-up with Piagetian theory instances a common phenomenon. It is probably fair to say that Piagetian theory has been more influential in child development than any other contemporary theory. It has stimulated a very large amount of work designed to test the theory on various populations. Work on sensorimotor development has been particularly aided by the availability of standardized scales based on Piaget's writings (Corman and Escalona, 1969; Uzgiris and Hunt, 1975). We will return to the question of the application to communication in a moment but it will be useful firstly to examine the general applicability of the theory to the mentally handicapped.

DEVELOPMENTAL AND DIFFERENCE THEORIES

Much of this research has been conducted within the general framework of the question of the relative value of developmental or difference theories. Developmental theories of mental handicap suggest that the handicapped individual passes through the same stages of development as the normal individual but at a slower rate, and with a lower ultimate ceiling of achievement (e.g. Zigler, 1969). Difference theories argue that the handicapped individual's development is qualitatively different (e.g. Milgram, 1973).

Research on the developmental versus the difference hypotheses has, in general, supported the developmental viewpoint. For example Wilton and Boersma (1974) concluded that the performance of the mentally handicapped in Piagetian conservation tasks paralleled normal development. Weisz and Zigler (1979) review 28 cross-sectional studies and three longitudinal studies which all relate Piagetian theory to mental handicap. They conclude that the overwhelming majority of studies support the developmental rather than the difference viewpoint. Of the exceptions one study is of particular significance. Wohlheuter and Sindberg (1975) assessed institutionalized mentally handicapped children of various levels of handicap from profound to moderate on the development of object permanence. They found that 39 of their 49 subjects followed the pattern predicted by Piagetian theory. The remaining ten subjects showed a variable pattern which appeared to rise and fall over as many as three or four stages. The distinguishing feature of this group was that they had "EEG abnormalities, especially dysrhythmias or a history of seizures" (p 516).

Studies on the development of communication skills informed by the developmental-difference position can be found at several levels. At a descriptive level Owens and MacDonald (1982) developed a taxonomy for classifying communication between mothers and children including categories such as question, answer, reply, declaration, practice (part or whole imitation of himself/herself or others) and suggestion. Owens showed that inter-judge and intra-judge agreement on classification of responses was high (usually well over 80 per cent) and that the proportion of unclassifiable responses was satisfactorily low (on average less than one per cent).

Applying the taxonomy to samples from six Down's syndrome and six non-delayed children gave data which suggested few differences between the groups when level of linguistic competence was equated. The authors recognize that their samples are small but nonetheless they demonstrate the basic applicability of the methodology. Several other workers have explored the use of pragmatically based scales with similar conclusions (e.g. Bochner _et al._, 1982; McLean and Snyder-McLean, 1982).

Studies testing the developmental-difference hypothesis during the sensorimotor period tend to favour the difference hypothesis once the research focuses at a detailed level. In general, normal and handicapped children seem to pass through the various steps on each of the sub-scales but correlation of performance across domains is less well established. In other words Piaget's stage theory is not supported. For example Rogers (1977) assessed performance by 40 mentally handicapped children on object permanence, spatiality, causality and imitation. Rogers found that items in three of the four areas formed usable scales, the exception being spatiality. However, she also found that there was very little agreement across domains in the stage attained by the child. Quite typically a child would be classed as at one stage on the one scale and a quite different one on another.

The conclusions suggested by findings such as these are that the various domains are in fact relatively independent of each other. Rogers found that stage placement on the imitation scale correlated least well with other scales. This finding has also emerged in other studies of the structure of abilities of handicapped children (e.g. Dunst _et al._, 1981; Mahoney _et al._, 1981), and of normal children (Uzgiris, 1976).

Do the skills shown on particular scales relate to emergence of communicative skills of mentally handicapped children? There are several relevant studies. Kahn (1975) using the Uzgiris-Hunt scales, found that seven of eight retarded children with speech were functioning at stage VI whilst only three of eight non-verbal children were functioning at that level. Snyder (1978), working with language-disabled children (not mentally handicapped), related sensorimotor performance to the emergence of non-verbal declaratives and imperatives. She found a relationship to the development of means-end skills in her group but no relation of other sensorimotor skills to either declaratives or imperatives. With autistic retarded children Curcio (1978) concluded that stage V performance on means-end and causality and stage III performance on imitation were pre-requisites for intentional communication. In comparing Down's syndrome with normal children Mahoney _et al._ (1981) concluded that Down's syndrome children were more delayed in their language functioning than might be predicted from their general level of functioning during the sensorimotor phase and concluded that they may suffer from a specific deficit in vocal imitation.

Greenwald and Leonard (1979) compared non-delayed and Down's syndrome children in their use of imperatives and declaratives. Their data showed associations between three scales of sensorimotor development, including means-ends, and communication skills but suggested that the Down's syndrome child relied more heavily on gesture than the normal child. In addition they found that older Down's syndrome children tended to perform linguistically beyond the level predicted by their assessed cognitive skills. This finding echoes other people's work and suggests that time for learning, or treatment programmes, may affect performance independent of cognitive level.

One final consistent finding emerges. In several studies handicapped children show a significant delay in the development of declaratives as opposed to imperatives (Curcio, 1978; Snyder, 1978; Greenwald and Leonard, 1979). As we saw earlier, declaratives represent the first elements in the set of communicative behaviours regulating joint attention. As such, further examination of how these behaviours are acquired may be of considerable value.

Where do these and related studies leave us? First of all they suggest the value of a comparative approach within a Piagetian framework. Even though the Piagetian theory is not consistently supported it provides an important framework for investigation. The studies illustrate a gradual process of breakdown from stage concepts to specific sequences and specific types of behaviour as closely correlated with the emergence of communication skills. They offer fairly specific hypotheses about how intervention might be mounted in order to facilitate development. As such they could be centrally important in remediation.

OTHER APPROACHES TO COMMUNICATION

The work so far described represents an important but very restricted example of contemporary thinking. In this section we will sample other work concerned with the development of communication skills. As we will see the studies have a developmental-difference theory basis and direct implications for training or education.

Our first example is a study by Blacher (1982). Blacher examined the social cognition of handicapped children, i.e. their ability to understand what other people were saying, hearing, seeing and thinking. The purpose of the study was to investigate these skills in relation to those of non-handicapped children, to relate them to social age, and to see whether the skills could be placed in scales. Handicapped children ranged in chronological age from two years to seven years eight months and in ability from mildly to severely handicapped. A group of non-delayed children were also used (chronological age 18 months to four years six months). Three types of task were used; (a) in which the child was asked to show things to another person; (b) where s/he had to hide an object; and (c) where s/he had to comprehend or respond to another person's behaviour through either following the other person's finger or eye pointing. The battery of 16 tasks was again broadly related to notions of perspective taking in Piagetian theory, skills seen as leading on to the ability to take another person's role.

The results of the study suggested that the mentally handicapped children showed development in much the same way as normal children, confirming a developmental approach. However the handicapped group was more likely to produce partial solutions; they would usually adopt a strategy for solving the task but this was often an inappropriate strategy. Analysis in scale terms suggested that, overall, the three groups of items could be scaled, but the "showing" scale was the least strong.

These findings suggest the need for further study of the reasons for slower rates of development. The fact that inappropriate strategies were adopted for solution of tasks may suggest that the children's understanding of the "point of view" of the other person is defective or evolves slowly. On the other hand it may be that the child has not learned the appropriate strategies, but could learn them, or that he has the strategies but does not identify the conditions under which he should use them. Again the research leads in two directions, towards further analysis of underlying phenomena, and towards application. However, as in other cases, application is a form of theory testing. Teaching the child which cues to respond to or how to respond will, if succesful, say a good deal about the fundamental nature of the problem. Lack of success will suggest the need to formulate other hypotheses.

Our final example concerns the application of socio-linguistics in the field of handicap. Sociolinguistic analysis is concerned to explore interaction as it reflects or creates social status or, more generally, social meaning. Bedrosian and Prutting (1978) analysed interactions between four mentally handicapped adults and a speech therapist, their parents, their peers, and with a young normal child. The particular feature of conversations selected by Bedrosian and Prutting was the dominance and submission shown by the participants, as reflected in the types of "bids" offered in interaction. Dominant bids included requests for action or attention, for information or opinion, and commands that the speaker assumes implicitly that he has the power to make such demands. Submissive bids included requests for permission, information or opinion, and were classified on the rationale that requests reflect an admission of lack of power in the interaction and acceptance of the authority of the other.

The results of the study showed that three of the four subjects did not hold a dominant position in any of the conversational settings as assessed through the rate of dominant to submissive bids. The other subject was dominant with her peers and with the normal child but not with parents or the speech pathologist. An individual can be submissive in his or her bids but nonetheless control the flow of a conversation in terms of all of his bids being accepted, whether dominant or submissive. In addition other methods may be used to maintain control.

All the subjects in the study showed control in at least one setting but the types of control expressed varied across subjects and those with whom they interacted. For example one subject had the majority of his bids accepted by his parents and the child but the speech pathologist rejected all of his bids. Three of the subjects used a technique called "arching" in which the individual controls an interchange by responding to a question with a question. However, of the three subjects, one used the technique only once, with his clinician, a second subject used arching only with his parents and the child and the third with her peers and the child.

The Bedrosian and Prutting study has been quoted at length for several reasons. It seems clear that this type of analysis has potentially broad significance in our field. The mentally handicapped have low social status within our society. Current philosophies of care seek to enhance their status. Studies of the type described can link style of interaction to perceived status in a way which leads to a richer picture of mechanisms. Such studies can also suggest ways in which performance may be modified, a possibility successfully followed up in Bedrosian's work (Bedrosian, 1981).

CONCLUDING COMMENTS

In this paper we have briefly reviewed several lines of development of research on communication, with some reference to work on cognitive development. We have not tried to cover either area comprehensively. In particular, coverage of cognitive development is thin but should be completed by other contributions to this volume.

We have seen that the topic of communication has become a central focus, arguably in terms of language development and social adjustment, that research to date is relatively sparse but is leading to a more precise specification of the mechanisms involved in development. Data also suggest ways in which remedial measures may test correlation data through direct intervention.

We have seen that the developmental model, as opposed to the difference model, has gained support, although this conclusion needs to be qualified in several ways. Firstly, as more detailed studies are completed, the weight of evidence swings towards difference theory. This is not surprising since we would anticipate that increasingly precise methods would reveal potentially important differences. Secondly, the proponents of developmental theory have typically excluded individuals with gross brain damage from their propositions (Zigler, 1969). Clearly the idea of simple slowed-down development is unlikely to be tenable if the child has gross damage to the CNS. Recent practice and research in the use of sign languages and symbol systems with individuals suffering severe communication deficits have shown that they are often capable of learning to communicate effectively through use of these alternative or augmentative systems. This often occurs after sustained effort to teach the use of speech has failed (Kiernan, 1983; Kiernan _et al_., 1982). One way in which to "explain" this type of finding is to suggest that the individuals can develop or have retained aspects of brain functioning which allow them to deal with a visuo-spatially based linguistic system but have lost aspects of functioning allowing them to deal with an oral-aural based system (cf. Prior, 1979). One exciting possibility for future multi-disciplinary research may be to tie up the performance of handicapped individuals with neurophysiological findings in ways which have already been attempted with the deaf. Whatever explanation is offered, a difference theory is supported.

Our overall question concerning the developmental model is to what degree can we meaningfully stretch it in explanation of behaviour? Here we need to recall that development is an interactive process involving the organism in the environment. Given the essentially social nature of the development of communication, and in a less clear way cognition, we need to analyse the features of environments which occasion development. Secondly, development is a historical concept. In deciding on remedial procedures we cannot sensibly treat the physically mature 30 year old mentally handicapped man as if he has no history. We may teach strategies for communicating which we identify in children but our methods and goals must reflect the individual's history as embodied in his current behaviour. Thirdly, development as we observe it in normal children and young people is an evolutionary phenomenon. The patterns of development which we observe have allowed the species to survive and flourish. But they are not immutable. As the example of the use of sign language suggests, human beings may retain the potential for adjustment to many different contingencies (Kiernan, 1981). Experience in practical settings suggests that, in that field, we may need to consider how existing capacities can be exploited to meet the goals which would allow the handicapped person to achieve successful adjustments in our society.

REFERENCES

Bates, E. (1976). **Language and Context.** Academic Press, New York

Bates, E., Benigni, L., Bretherton, I., Camaioni, L. and Volterra, V. (1977). From gestures to the first word: On cognitive and social prerequisites. In Lewis, M. and Rosenblum L. (eds.), **Interaction, Conversation and Communication in Infancy.** John Wiley, New York

Bedrosian, J.L. (1981). A sociolinguistic approach to communication skills: Assessment and treatment methodology for mentally retarded adults. Unpublished doctoral thesis, University of Wisconsin

Bedrosian, J. and Prutting, C. (1978). Communicative performance of mentally retarded adults in four conversation settings. **Journal of Speech and Hearing Research, 21**, 79-95

Blacher, J. (1982). Assessing social cognition in young mentally retarded and nonretarded children. **American Journal of Mental Deficiency, 86**, 473-484

Bloom, L. (1970). **Language Development; Form and Function in Emerging Grammars.** M.I.T. Press, Cambridge, Mass.

Bochner, S., Ward, J., Price, P. and Linfoot, K. (1982). Protolinguistic behaviour in institutionalised infants. Paper to the IASSMD Conference, Toronto, August

Bruner, J.S. (1975). Ontogenesis of speech acts. **Journal of Child Language, 2**, 1-19

Chomsky, N. (1965). **Aspects of the Theory of Syntax.** M.I.T. Press, Cambridge, Mass.

Corman, H.H. and Escalona, S.K. (1969). Stage of sensorimotor development: A replication study. **Merrill-Palmer Quarterly, 15**, 351-361

Cromer, R.F. (1974). The development of language and cognition: The cognition hypothesis. In Foss B.M. (ed.), **New**

Perspectives in Child Development, Penguin Books, Harmondsworth, 184-252

Cromer, R.F. (1976). The cognitive hypothesis of language acquisition and its implications for child learning deficiency. In Morehead, D.M. and Morehead, A.E. (eds.). **Normal and Deficient Child Language**, University Park Press, Baltimore, Md., 283-334

Curcio, F. (1978). Sensorimotor functioning and communication in mute autistic children. **Journal of Autism and Childhood Schizophrenia, 8**, 282-292

Dunst, C.J., Brassell, W.R. and Rheingrover, R.M. (1981). Structural and organisational features of sensorimotor intelligence among retarded infants and toddlers. **British Journal of Educational Psychology, 51**, 133-143

Greenwald, C.A. and Leonard, L.B. (1979). Communicative and sensorimotor development of Down's syndrome children. **American Journal of Mental Deficiency, 84**, 296-303

Halliday, M.A.K. (1973). **Explorations in the Function of Language**, Arnold, London

Halliday, M.A.K. (1975). Learning how to mean. In Lenneberg, E.H. and Lenneberg, E. (eds.), **Foundations of Language Development** Vol 1, Academic Press, New York, 239-303

Kahn, J.V. (1975). Relationship of Piaget's sensorimotor period to language acquisition of profoundly retarded children. **American Journal of Mental Deficiency, 79**, 640-643

Kiernan, C.C. (1981). Behavior modification and the development of communication. In Mittler, P. (ed.), **Frontiers of Knowledge in Mental Retardation**, Vol 1. **Social, Educational and Behavioural Aspects**, University Park Press, Baltimore, Md., 171-79

Kiernan, C.C. (1983). The use of nonvocal communication techniques with autistic individuals. **Journal of Child Psychology and Psychiatry**, (In press)

Kiernan, C.C., Reid, B.D. and Jones, L.M. (1982) **Signs and Symbols: A review of literature and survey of use of nonvocal communication systems.** University of London Institute of Education Studies in Education, No. 11, London

McLean, J. and Snyder-McLean, L. (1982). Application of normal first-language learning data to the mentally retarded. Paper to the IASSMD Conference, Toronto, August

Mahoney, G., Glover, A. and Finger, I. (1981). Relationship between language and sensorimotor development of Down's syndrome and retarded children. **American Journal of Mental Deficiency, 86**, 21-27

Milgram, N.A. (1973). Cognition and language in mental retardation: Distinctions and implications. In Routh, D.K. (ed.), **The Experimental Psychology of Mental Retardation.** Aldine, Chicago, 157-230

Miller, J.F. and Yoder, D.E. (1972). A syntax teaching program. In McLean, J.E., Yoder, D. and Shiefelbusch, R. (eds), **Language Intervention With the Retarded.** University Park Press, Baltimore, 191-211

Moerk, E.L. (1978). Determiners and consequences of verbal behaviors of young children and their mothers. **Developmental Psychology, 14**, 537-545

Morehead, D.M. and Morehead, A. (1974). From signal to sign: A Piagetian view of thought and language during the first two years. In Schiefelbusch, R.L. and Lloyd L.L. (eds.), **Language Perspectives - Acquisition, Retardation and Intervention.** University Park Press, Baltimore, 153-190

Owens, R.E. and MacDonald, J.D. (1982). Communicative uses of early speech of nondelayed and Down syndrome children. **American Journal of Mental Deficiency, 86**, 503-510

Piaget, J. (1954). **The Construction of Reality in the Child.** Basic Books, New York

Prior, M.R. (1979). Cognitive abilities and disabilities in infantile autism: A review. **Journal of Abnormal Child Psychology, 7**, 357-380

Rogers, S.J. (1977). Characteristics of the cognitive development of profoundly retarded children. **Child Development, 48**, 837-843

Snyder, L.S. (1978). Communication and cognitive abilities and disabilities in the sensorimotor period. **Merrill-Palmer Quarterly, 24**, 163-180

Uzgiris, I. (1976). Organisation of sensorimotor intelligence. In Lewis, M. (ed.), **Origins of Intelligence.** Plenum Press, New York

Uzgiris, I.C. and Hunt, J. McV. (1975). **Assessment in Infancy.** University of Illinois Press, Urbana, 123-163

Weisz, J.R. and Zigler, E. (1979). Cognitive development in retarded and nonretarded persons: Piagetian tests of the similar sequence hypothesis. **Psychological Bulletin, 86**, 831-851

Wilton, K.M. and Boersma, F.J. (1974). Conversation research with the mentally handicapped. In Ellis, N.R. (ed.), **International Review of Research in Mental Retardation.** Academic Press, London, Vol. 7, 114-144

Wohlheuter, M.J. and Sindberg, R.M. (1975). Longitudinal development of object permanence in mentally retarded children: An explotatory study. **American Journal of Mental Deficiency, 79**, 323-328

Yoder, D.E. and Calculator, S. (1981). Some perspectives on intervention strategies for persons with developmental disorders. **Journal of Autism and Developmental Disabilities, 11**, 107-123

Zigler, E. (1969). Developmental versus different theories of mental retardation and the problem of motivation. **American Journal of Mental Deficiency, 73**, 536-566

COMMENTARY

M. C. Beveridge

Kiernan has discussed the development of language, communication and cognition by reference to theories which look at ways in which each of these psychological systems influences the others' development. However, while it has been a fruitful exercise to research these systems separately, they are actively integrated in the continuous process of understanding the world.

Thinking and using language are often the same psychological event. We can develop and refine ideas through conversations with others. Linguistic formats representing ideas are tested and modified during social exchanges. Thinking does not only take place privately and quietly but can also be a public communicative exchange process involving language. This process involves fast accessing and storage procedures, as well as judgement of other persons' responses.

Russell (1978) describes these socio-cognitive experiences as the way in which children co-ordinate their rule-bound concepts, e.g. conversation, into a system with meaning to other persons of the same culture. This socially supported thinking process results not only in the "Piagetian" logical structure of thought but also real world knowledge. And as Wason and Johnson-Laird (1972) conclude "..... any general theory of human reasoning must include an important semantic component". As well as the many important issues raised by Kiernan we need to know more about how handicapped persons use language to extract knowledge from, and deal with the problems of, the real world. This is difficult research and does not easily lead to generalizable laws of behaviour. We will require a taxonomy of the situations experienced by the handicapped and a detailed study of their ecology.

Recent work with handicapped persons suggests that formal measures of IQ, verbal and reasoning ability and social maturity are not clearly predictive of their ability to solve real problems (Newton, 1981; Beveridge, 1983). And that both the absolute performance of retarded persons and the difference between them and the normal population are related to the type of problem situation presented (Floor and Rosen, 1975; Ryba and Brown, 1979). Furthermore, while teachers who know children well are good at predicting whether they would solve a problem, the same teachers are less successful at predicting the methods children would use to effect solutions. And in general teachers tend to underestimate the children's abilities (Newton, 1981).

Kiernan has rightly stressed role-taking skills as an important aspect of a handicapped person's development. He also cites evidence that retarded adults are likely to take up a submissive role in interactions. Light (1979) has suggested that poor role-taking skills in children are likely to arise from interactions in which adults use their superior status as the mode of control. Research into the effects of control procedures on handicapped children's social sensitivity would be an interesting and probably fruitful line of enquiry.

Kiernan has introduced a number of other issues which I have not touched on, as they seem central to the interests of other critique writers. The only other comment I feel bound to make is that, in my view, the delay-difference question has used up far too much valuable research effort. I am inclined to the view that this issue can only be clarified in the context of a clear analysis of contemporary beliefs and values about the handicapped, and that attempts to find the answer by detailed scientific study alone cannot succeed.

References

Beveridge, M.C. (1983). Language and cognitive problems in mentally handicapped children. In D.J. Muller (Ed.) **Remediations Children's Language: Behavioural and naturalistic approaches.** London: Croom Helm, in press

Floor, L. and Rosen, M. (1975). Investigating the phenomenon of helplessness in mentally retarded adults. **American Journal of Mental Deficiency, 79**, 565-572

Light, P. (1979). **The Development of Social Sensitivity.** Cambridge University Press

Newton, S. (1981). Social aspects of communicative competence in mentally handicapped adolescents and non-handicapped children. Unpublished Ph.D. thesis. University of Manchester

Russell, J. (1978). **The Acquisition of Knowledge** London: Macmillan

Ryba, K.A. and Brown, R.J. (1979). An evaluation of personal adjustment training with mentally retarded adults. **British Journal of Mental Subnormality, 25**, 56-66

Wason, P.C. and Johnson-Laird, P.N. (1972). **Psychology of Reasoning.** London: Batsford

R. F. Cromer

In exploring problems in the acquisition of language and the relationship of that acquisition to cognitive processes, it is essential that one be clear about important terms. One of the most crucial distinctions that needs to be made is that between language, defined as a linguistic system, and communication, which is a broader term that encompasses a great deal more than linguistic entities. The relationship between these terms is not merely one of extent. There can be a good deal of communication without language (as, for example in the communication of feelings and ideas in works of art, in facial expressions, in non-verbal body "language", etc.); while language serves a variety of functions of which communication is only one. In its metalinguistic function, language is used to reflect upon its own code. Language also serves a self-regulatory function and can help to determine or direct the thought processes. Language is often used merely to maintain contact with others by usages in which "communication" in its normal meaning is virtually absent. Language also serves magical functions as in spells and curses, and is used in ritualized verbal formulae seen for example in children's language games.

Kiernan's statement that language is acquired through communication is merely an assumption, and one which has not proven to have been terribly useful at least as far as explaining the syntactic or semantic components of language are concerned. There is even some evidence against the notion that children acquire language structures through communication or that communication plays the major motivating force for linguistic change with age (see early work by Weir, 1962, and recent research by Karmiloff-Smith, 1979). It appears instead that children "work on" the language system as a conceptual puzzle space that must be mastered as an interrelated system (see also, Maratsos and Chalkley, 1980).

The functions that Kiernan lists, based on Halliday, appear to be mainly communicative ones. As Kiernan rightly points out, the functions he describes can be conveyed by non-verbal as well as verbal means. He goes on to note that "each of the functions described can be realized in more and more complex syntactical structures". This is, in fact, the important point and shows the necessity of differentiating clearly language as a linguistic system from the functions that language can serve. What remains unexplained in a functional analysis are the processes by which a child moves to "more and more complex syntactical structures". Describing a list of functions, while informative and important, in no way explains the encoding of these functions in a linguistic system nor the methods by which a child comes to construct those encodings. The work Kiernan cites on caretaker-infant regulation of joint attention and joint activity suffers from the same problem. It does not explain how the child comes to encode information in a linguistic system. As Rondal, in his presentation, states: "If a child is able to interact meaningfully before knowing a language, it does not necessarily follow that the structure of language is derived from or homologous to the structure of prelinguistic communication". Furthermore evidence from child language studies demonstrates that the child is not somehow merely acquiring the forms and structures that he is exposed to; instead, he is actively constructing an integrated linguistic system that follows its own rules and does not closely match the language input to which he is exposed.

Rondal, in his presentation, also cites evidence that mentally retarded adults use similar communicative functions and with similar frequency as non-retarded subjects. He points to the necessity to specify the separate components of language. It is clear that only by differentiating language from the functions it serves can one even begin to talk about "language of the mentally retarded" if the functions for which communication is employed are similar for retarded and non-retarded subjects.

Similar problems are involved when one attempts to explain language acquisition in children in terms of cognitive development. "Having something to say" and "having a reason for saying it" does not explain the acquisition of "a way of saying it". Kiernan cites Piaget's claims that language is a manifestation of general cognitive development. There is, however, some recent evidence against this view. Curtiss _et al._ (1978) and Curtiss (1981) in a study of six mentally retarded children, found no correlation between measures of expressive syntax in language and a variety of Piagetian cognitive tasks. The divergence between syntax and most cognitive abilities was seen most strikingly in one subject with a high expressive syntax score who used complex syntactic and morphological structures, but whose scores on the non-language tests were very low - at about the 2-year-old level. Blank _et al._ (1979) have reported a case demonstrating a similar lack of correspondence betwen syntax and pragmatic skills. This child's language was conceptually appropriate and was described as being structurally and semantically adequate, but his pragmatic communication skills were almost non-existent: when analysed from an interpersonal perspective, his language was inappropriate, detached, and unlike normal human communication. Likewise Kiernan cites a study by Kahn in which seven of eight retarded children with speech were functioning at sensorimotor stage VI, implying that at least one child had speech without having attained that substage. He also cites results from a study by Greenwald and Leonard in which "older Down's syndrome children tended to perform linguistically beyond the level predicted by their assessed cognitive skills". Exceptions of these types are evidence against cognitive and pragmatic theories that claim specific developments to be _necessary_ in order for particular advances in language acquisition to occur. Even rare exceptions are proof against the explanatory adequacy of cognitive and of pragmatic theories of language acquisition. The studies Kiernan cites can be interpreted as showing that specific types of behaviour are _not_ closely causally related to the emergence and development of language.

References

Blank, M., Gessner, M. and Esposito, A. (1979). Language without communication: a case study. **Journal of Child Language, 6,** 329-352

Curtiss, S. (1981). Dissociations between language and cognition: Cases and implications. **Journal of Autism and Developmental Disorders, 11,** 15-30

Curtiss, S., Fromkin, V. and Yamada, J.E. (1978). The independence of language as a cognitive system. Paper presented at the First International Congress for the Study of Child Language, Tokyo, August 7-12

Karmiloff-Smith, A. (1979). **A Functional Approach to Child Language: A study of determiners and reference.** Cambridge: Cambridge University Press

Maratsos, M.P. and Chalkley, M.A. (1980). The internal language of children's syntax: The ontogenesis and representation of syntactic categories. In K.E. Nelson (Ed.), **Children's Language, 2,** pp. 127-214. New York: Gardner Press

Weir, R. (1962). **Language in the Crib.** The Hague: Mouton.

W. I. Fraser

The term communication skill should sometimes to replaced by communication style as this has some practical aspects. What Kiernan calls communication skills are often communication acts carried out in a skilful way. The frequency and type of certain communication acts is the handicapped person's communication style - certain styles, limiting, maladaptive and stigmatizing, are characteristic of the retarded person, and are due to the beliefs, attitudes and communicative styles of the normal caretakers. Such styles, as the very word implies, are susceptible to positive change.

R. O. Robinson

This paper, with its very wide ranging title, quotes a large number of studies on language and mental processes in the mentally retarded. Many of these studies will be unfamiliar to those working with the mentally retarded who come from disciplines other than psychology, and the paper does a valuable service in drawing their attention to this research.

The emphasis of the paper is on concepts and theories, and three particular concepts are discussed at length:

1. The theory of language acquisition which emphasizes motivation, and the practical value to the child of communication, rather than Chomsky's view of language developing from an innate syntactical structure.

2. Piaget's theory of development with its sensorimotor stages.

3. The concept of delay versus difference. Does the mentally retarded individual go through the same processes and stages of development as the normal person, though at a slower rate, or is his development following different pathways?

Concepts are useful if they lead the clinician or other professional working with the mentally retarded to a more enquiring approach to the patient, if they lead to a better understanding of the problems and functioning of the mentally retarded, or if they pose useful questions for research. The danger of concepts and theories is that they may become ends in themselves, and that the real question being asked is whether, for example, observations support or refute the difference or delay theory rather than what they tell us about mental or language processes in the mentally handicapped.

We can ask how useful the three particular conceptual ideas in Kiernan's paper are in practice, and I will take them in a slightly different order from that in which they appear in his paper.

1. The concept of the importance of motivation in the development of language seems a very useful insight. The fascinating ideas of Chomsky, and the linguistic research which has arisen from them, may have led to over-emphasis on syntax and grammar in the development of language, and under-emphasized the motivation on the part of the child to communicate, as well as the motivation of the mother and other adults to communicate with the child and to get him to communicate. The study by Moerk showing the very high frequency with which the mother and the child get tangible results from the communication is very illuminating.

2. The delay versus difference idea will be much more familiar to most workers with the mentally handicapped, and the issue raised is an important practical one. The "delay" idea is deeply embedded into the way mentally retarded children are assessed, the way they are discussed, and the explanations that are given to their parents and those who teach them. The terms "mental age", "development quotient" and "IQ" are all based on the idea that the function of a mentally retarded child can be equated with that of a younger normal child. The fact that these terms have proved so useful corresponds with the fact that most studies broadly support the "delay" concept. However, it is important in practice to remember that function in the mentally retarded is not necessarily a slowed-down version of normal development and that there may be qualitative differences. Very detailed studies are much more likely to reveal small differences, just as detailed studies on the development of normal children would certainly also show a good deal of difference between individuals. Kiernan emphasizes that the differences from the normal sequence of development are also likely to be greater if there is some severe or specific kind of brain abnormality, though the paper by Wohlheuter and Sindberg, which is cited in support of this view, provides such limited clinical and EEG data that the conclusion must be regarded as questionable from that particular evidence. Nevertheless, the idea sounds reasonable, and it is also likely that differences from the normal pattern of development will be greater in the severely than in the mildly retarded. Such a view is somewhat reminiscent of the hypothesis of E.O. Lewis (1933) - now generally forgotten or regarded as obsolete. He believed that the mentally handicapped could be divided into a milder "subcultural"

group who represented the lower end of the normal distribution curve of intelligence, and a more severe "pathological" group with definite structural or other brain abnormalities. For "subcultural" and "pathological" are we now writing "delayed" and "different"?

3. The Piagetian theory of development with its sensorimotor stages seems to have much less to offer to the practical worker with the mentally retarded. A blanket of obscurity descends on this otherwise lucid paper when Piaget is first mentioned, and it is only lifted when the writer moves on to a different concept. Reference to the original papers which Kiernan reviews in this connection shows them to be even more arcane. I do not undervalue the contributions of Piaget to psychological theory, but as set out here the Piagetian school appear to be obscuring straightforward observations on child development by wrapping them up in a complex theory accompanied by an obscure and unnecessary vocabulary (what on earth do "perlocutionary" and "illocutionary" actually mean?). Is it really true that "Piagetian theory has been more influential in child development than any other contemporary theory"? Perhaps it has been more influential in academic psychology than in clinical, therapeutic and educational practice. It has certainly been possible to work in a child development centre for twelve years without ever hearing Piaget mentioned in relation to an individual child.

The final comment on Kiernan's paper concerns the dangers and difficulties of generalizing about mental retardation, or, to put it more accurately, about mentally retarded people. The study by Blacher dealt with children ranging in age from two years to seven years, and in ability from mildly to severely handicapped. Even if we accept the delay rather than the difference theory, is it really possible to put a severely retarded two year old and a mildly retarded seven year old in the same category? Then several studies of children or adults with Down's syndrome are quoted and such studies have the attraction that they are dealing with a large and clinically well defined group of mentally retarded people with the same aetiology. However, such studies often show no awareness of the other problems apart from mental handicap which may exist in patients with Down's syndrome. For example, a high proportion of young children with Down's syndrome have conductive deafness due to glue ears, and this must considerably affect their speech and language. Yet of three studies quoted on speech and language in Down's syndrome, one makes no mention of the children's hearing, one merely states that "no subject had been identified as having a hearing loss" (without saying how many had been tested for one), and the third states that hearing was normal, but does not indicate what tests were done. To ensure that some degree of conductive deafness is not confusing the findings, such studies should certainly include accurate and expert clinical tests of hearing, together with middle ear impedance measurements.

Other medical factors which may confuse psychological findings in Down's syndrome are hypothyroidism and heart disease.

Reference

Lewis, E.O. (1933). Types of mental deficiency and their social significance. **Journal of Mental Science, 79**, 298

J. A. Rondal

Kiernan's chapter should in my opinion be more properly entitled "The development of communication with reference to cognition" unless a more systematic and detailed treatment of cognitive functioning in the retarded is offered and "cognition" in the retarded is analysed per se and not only in reference to language and communicative development.

There are more specific points that I would like to raise in relation to Kiernan's paper. First, functional analysis of communication and language is only one aspect of "pragmatics" and not the whole "viewpoint" of pragmatics as indicated by Kiernan at the beginning of his paper in a too simplified way. Also I would like very much to see addressed the question of the practical value and applicability of Halliday's classificatory scheme for the communicative functions of language. It is the case that Halliday's categories are not mutually exclusive and cannot be easily translated into behavioural terms without considerable overlapping from one category to the others.

Secondly I am much in favour of trying to link the development of communicative skills to cognitive development in the normal as well as in the retarded child. However, I am not at all convinced that researches that emphasize "cognitive products", such as those referred to by Kiernan (e.g., Kahn, 1975; Moerk, 1976), are relevant to language development, rather than to processes and mechanisms leading to transitions in cognitive development.

The specific developmental relationships holding between such cognitive outcomes as, for example, the attainment of sensory-motor stage V or VI, and language acquisition, have never been clearly spelled out in my view. Furthermore, the data with the greatest potential for explaining language acquisition gathered so far are only correlational in nature. It seems to me, in accordance with Moerk (1976) that it is much more plausible that certain general cognitive processes need to have reached a specific level before the child can advance to language mastery. In this respect, the suggestion made by Mahoney et al. (1981) that there may be a specific deficit in vocal imitation in Down's syndrome children is of particular interest. I personally have come to the same conclusion at the end of a study on spontaneous verbal imitation in Down's syndrome and younger normal children in the course of mother-child interactions (cf. Rondal, 1980). In my study, verbal imitations were found to be similar in grammatical structure for the two groups of children at comparable levels of language development. The Down's syndrome children, however, were not producing frequency levels of verbal imitations comparable to those of normally developing 22-month old children before 4, 5 or even 6 years.

It should perhaps be recalled that Piaget (1954) has conceptualized imitation as intermediate between accommodation and assimilation, the two basic components of equilibration, i.e. the true causal factor of cognitive development according to the late Swiss theorist. In this perspective as well as in the light of more recent theorizing along the learning side, for example Bandura's observational social learning theory (Bandura, 1976), it seems clear that vocal imitation should be the object of more attention and more research efforts by the researchers in the field of language development with reference to mental handicap.

Kiernan also addresses the theoretical question of the developmental versus the difference theories of mental handicap. He cites data supporting mostly the developmental viewpoint and seems to conclude that this theoretical viewpoint is the one that should prevail. I basically agree with Kiernan's global assessment of the available literature on this question. It should perhaps be added, however, that the way the delay-difference question is usually raised in the literature is ambiguous and only poorly suited to experimental treatment because the two points of view lack a clear and systematic operational definition (see also my contribution to this volume on this question).

References

Bandura, A. (1976). **Social Learning Theory.** Englewood Cliffs, N.J., Prentice-Hall

Kahn, J. (1975). Relationship of Piaget's sensorimotor period to language acquisition of profoundly retarded children. **American Journal of Mental Deficiency, 79**, 640-643

Mahoney, G., Glover, A. and Finger, I. (1981). Relationship between language and sensorimotor development of Down's syndrome and retarded children. **American Journal of Mental Deficiency, 86**, 21-27

Moerk, E. (1976). A Piagetian functional approach to early language development. Communication presented to the Sixth International Interdisciplinary Seminar on Piagetian Theory and its implications for the helping profession, Los Angeles, January

Rondal, J.A. (1980). Verbal imitation by Down syndrome and nonretarded children. **American Journal of Mental Deficiency, 85**, 318-321

Chapter 17

Acquisition of non-vocal communication and discrimination learning in severely handicapped children

P.M. Smeets and G.E. Lancioni

INTRODUCTION

Communication deficiencies have long been recognized as among the most conspicuous and debilitating limitations in severely developmentally delayed and multiply handicapped children. Nearly all autistic children with an IQ below 50 fail to acquire speech and language (Howlin, 1981; Rutter, 1966). Likewise, about 75 per cent of all retarded children with IQs below 50 show severe limitations in acquiring functional communication skills (Jordan, 1967; Reich, 1978).

The need to develop means of communication for the non-verbal and severely handicapped people has resulted in a plethora of experimental studies, language intervention programmes, curricula, technical aids and communication systems. During the 1960s the emphasis was on evaluating a technology for developing verbal language. Now, 16 years after Lovaas' initial work (Lovaas et al., 1966), a sizeable body of experimental work and carefully designed programmes on developing oral communication in autistic and retarded children is available (e.g., Baer et al., 1972; Bricker and Bricker, 1970; Hewett, 1965; Guess et al., 1976a, b, 1977, 1978; Kent, 1974; Lovaas, 1977; Miller and Yoder, 1974; Striefel et al., 1978). However, despite these encouraging reports, many non-verbal children fail to acquire functional communication skills with these methods. Thus it is understandable that, encouraged by the reports on primates (Gardner and Gardner, 1969; Linden, 1974; Premack and Premack, 1972), the advent of non-vocal communication means such as sign language (Kiernan, 1977; Lloyd, 1980; Poulton and Algozzine, 1980), Bliss symbolics (Vanderheyden et al., 1975), and the Carrier symbols (Carrier, 1973; Carrier and Peak, 1975) were welcomed with considerable enthusiasm. Although the sign languages and the Bliss symbolics were not designed for the severely mentally handicapped, it was assumed that they would be more adequate than oral communication. It was argued that the visual modality of the representational cues not only facilitated the acquisition of stimulus control (Carr, 1979; Hintgen and Coulter, 1967), but also allowed a more rapid shaping of the expressive mode (e.g., Bonvillian and Nelson, 1976; Kirschner et al., 1979). With regard to the Carrier symbols, it was assumed that since chimpanzees (Premack and Premack, 1972) are capable of discriminating symbolic shapes, associative learning, and simple motor responses, low functioning retarded people should also be able to do so (Deich and Hodges, 1982). Yet, in spite of their widespread application, there have been many studies indicating that, particularly for handicapped persons with a mental age of two years or less, the efficacy and efficiency of these methods are limited. Thousands of trials (e.g., Carr et al., 1978) and/or months of training (e.g., Kahn, 1977; Kohl et al., 1978; Munsch and Reichert, 1976; Salvin et al., 1977; Song, 1979; Vanderheyden et al., 1975) were frequently needed to establish a few (i.e. sometimes no more than five or six) signs or symbols in low functioning children.

Now that the initial optimism for these methods has waned, new efforts have been made to develop communication means explicitly designed for persons of low mental age, that is, systems of which the representational cues are permanent and highly transparent. Recent studies (e.g., House et al., 1980; Hurlbut et al., 1982; Lancioni, 1983; Lancioni et al., 1982; Reid and Hurlbut, 1977; Roodenburg and Smeets, 1980) indicate that profoundly handicapped persons can readily learn to respond to instructions conveyed through pictures and small size objects.

Thus, over the past 20 years, there has been a shift towards the use of visual, permanent, and highly iconic stimuli for establishing communication with severely handicapped people. Much time and effort has been invested in the argumentation for and the selection of the physical dimensions of the representational stimuli. By contrast, very few in-depth attempts have been made (Carr, 1979; Carr et al., 1978) to relate the reported acquisition problems with the existing literature on the specific learning deficits of low functioning persons, or with the adequacy of the operant procedures which have been frequently used as part of the instructional paradigm.

Since the inception of the non-vocal communication systems, the study on discrimination learning has become a domain which offers great promise to the understanding and remediation of the problems of severely developmentally delayed children. The results of these studies may be highly relevant with regard to the establishment of stimulus control of non-vocal communication systems. In what follows, we will address three issues which arose when reviewing our own work as well as that of others in this area. These issues concern (a) the discrimination learning of iconic cues, (b) discrimination learning and stimulus overselectivity, and (c) discrimination learning of complex cues.

DISCRIMINATION LEARNING OF ICONIC CUES

Studies on non-vocal communication systems such as sign language, pictures, logographics, and to a certain extent also Bliss symbols, generally imply that, among other factors, the discrimination learning of the selected cues may be facilitated by their iconicity. That is, in contrast to spoken or written words or other highly symbolic stimuli, iconic stimuli have an observable or guessable relationship with their referents (Bonvillian and Nelson, 1976; House et al., 1980; Kahn, 1977; Kirschner et al., 1979; Luftig and Lloyd, 1981; Murphy et al., 1977). Research findings on primates (Gardner and Gardner, 1969), young normal children (Daehler et al., 1976; Gibson, 1969; Stokoe, 1975), cross-cultural differences (Makita, 1968; Rozin et al., 1971), and on severely handicapped children (Griffith and Robinson, 1980; Hurlbut et al., 1982; Murphy et al., 1977; Welch and Pear, 1980) strongly suggest that iconic stimuli are rapidly acquired, maintained and generalized across settings.

Recent evidence, however, suggests that, in contrast to what has been frequently assumed (e.g., Kohl, 1981), iconicity does not represent a unidimensional scale, and that two forms of iconicity should be distinguished, i.e. linguistic and psycholinguistic iconicity. Linguistic iconicity has been defined as the structured, physical or universal characteristic that makes the representational cue evident to most naive observers (Griffith and Robinson, 1980; Westcott, 1971). In essence, linguistic iconicity refers to the visual correspondence between the representational cue and its referent. By contrast, psycholinguistic cues, like abstract cues, do not match the shape of their referents; instead, the referents are implied by other time-, culture-, and experience-bound associations (Brown, 1977; Griffith and Robinson, 1980; Luftig and Lloyd, 1981). This distinction may be of considerable practical and theoretical import particularly with regard to the validity of the results of studies on sign language training. The studies by Baron and Isensee (1977) and Kohl (1981) have shown that signs thought to be iconic by teachers may not be perceived as such by retarded learners. For many hospitalized children and adults, who have been deprived of a wide diversity of experiences such as the turning of keys, milking of cows, steering cars, or airplanes taking off, the topography of the corresponding psycholinguistic signs (which represent a distinctive feature of the action rather than of the object), may be highly abstract. Consequently, the practice of assessing the (degree of) iconicity of the representational stimuli (i.e., signs) on the judgement of normal adults, e.g., the experimenter or college students (Kirschner et al., 1979), may raise serious questions with regard to their validity, particularly for those who have been living in a restricted environment for many years. Moreover, it may also account for some of the conflicting evidence reported in several studies on sign language training. For example, in both studies by Kahn (1977, 1981), the learning rate of profoundly and severely retarded children receiving training on highly iconic signs was not faster than that of other children receiving speech training. Likewise, Kohl (1981) did not observe differential effects on the acquisition rate of iconic *versus* symbolic signs in severely retarded children. It is possible that these findings resulted from the author's definition of iconicity, i.e., signs of which the physical movements approximate the shape *or* the action of their referents. In other words, it cannot be excluded that, depending on their experiences with the object referents, for some of these children the signs were abstract rather than iconic. Additional support for the functional implications of this distinction may be found in the study by Carr *et al.* (1978). In this study a group of hospitalized autistic children were trained to demonstrate a sign in the presence of an object and its corresponding verbal label. The data revealed that the acquisition of two psycholinguistic signs (i.e., milk and banana) was not faster than that of two abstract signs (i.e., apple and candy). The sign most readily acquired by all subjects was the one (i.e., cookie) of which the shape (i.e., round) was similar to that of its referent.

There is, however, also some evidence indicating that the acquisition of difficult to learn abstract cues can be facilitated by allowing them to serve as linguistic iconics. This can be accomplished by stimulus shaping (LeBlanc *et al.*, 1978; Smeets *et al.*, 1982) and by extra-stimulus prompt fading (Lancioni *et al.*, 1981). In the aforementioned studies, the two procedures were used to establish the reading of letters and word recognition in severely retarded and other difficult to teach children. Stimulus shaping consisted of presenting first a picture of an object. Then, over trials, the picture was gradually changed into a letter (or a combination of letters) until it had disappeared. The shape of the letter or of one of the letters of the word was identical to a distinctive feature of the originally portrayed object. In other words, the children continued to respond to the abstract stimulus as if it were highly iconic, which in a way it now was. Likewise, in the study by Lancioni *et al.* (1981), children were trained to say "a", the initial vowel of the Italian word "*ape*" (meaning: bee), when shown a picture of the capital letter A with wings and other attributes of the insect attached to it. Then, over steps, the extraneous cues were faded out so that during the final step they continued to label the letter correctly. Different, though essentially similar procedures were used by Arick and Krug (1978) for teaching autistic children to respond to the abstract symbols of the Non-Slip Program (Carrier and Peak, 1975). In essence, the above studies suggest that it is technically possible to facilitate the acquisition of abstract cues by utilizing refined transfer of stimulus control procedures. Although these procedures have not been widely used (probably because they require elaborate programming and careful preparation of the stimulus materials), they may prove to be very valuable when the flexibility and further extensions of a communication system are restricted by the iconicity of its stimuli.

DISCRIMINATION LEARNING AND STIMULUS OVERSELECTIVITY

To date there is an extensive body of reports on discrimination learning which suggests that handicapped children of low mental age have a strong disposition to respond to only a restricted number of the available cues. This phenomenon, usually referred to as "stimulus overselectivity" (for an extensive review, see Lovaas et al., 1979) has been associated with their reduced level of incidental learning (Bandura, 1969; Ross, 1976). Since most communication systems consist of strings of complex (i.e., multicomponent) stimuli, and non-vocal communication is frequently trained in a multisensory fashion, the literature on stimulus overselectivity may be highly relevant for a better understanding of the language acquisition problems of retarded learners. Yet, as will be discussed below, the results of some of these studies may have been less straightforward than has generally been assumed.

In their initial study, Lovaas et al. (1971) trained autistic children to press a bar in response to a complex stimulus consisting of the simultaneous presentation of three cues, i.e., an auditory, a visual, and a tactile cue. After the subjects had learned to respond to the complex stimulus, the cues were presented individually to assess which one had acquired control over the children's responding. The results revealed that the autistic children used in that study had a strong tendency to respond to only one cue, i.e., usually the auditory or visual cue. Similar observations were made in a subsequent study (Lovaas and Schreibman, 1971). In other words, the data showed not only that the children's discriminations were controlled by a single component, but also that the direction of their overselective responding (i.e., auditory or visual) was unpredictable. Although the unpredictability has not been given much weight in the subsequent studies on stimulus overselectivity, it certainly adds an extra dimension to the problems concerning the discrimination learning of complex cues. Whereas a child's responding to only one or a few components of a complex cue will prevent him from discriminating it from other cues containing similar components, the uncertainty as to which specific component will control his discrimination may make it very difficult to predict which other complex cues he will probably acquire. This problem has been extensively reported on in a recent study by Smeets et al. (1982). In this study, trainable retarded children were trained to identify printed three- and four-letter words through different prompt-fading procedures. For two of these procedures, the prompts (i.e., pictures) were faded out in such a way that the reduced prompts were positioned very near to or became part of one of the letters of the trained word. Subsequent test trials revealed, however, that for children whose discriminations were controlled by only one letter of a word, this was frequently one other than the prompted letter.

The issue of stimulus overselectivity may also be highly relevant to the discrimination of multiple stimuli that are used for establishing stimulus control of complex cues. For example, a common procedure for teaching signs is the simultaneous communication method in which the adult signs to the child while speaking to him (e.g., Smith, 1975). From the early studies of Lovaas cited above, it would be expected that low functioning children respond to only one of these cues, in an unpredictable fashion, i.e., either to the auditory cue (spoken word) or to the visual cue (object or sign). Yet, in his review study Carr (1979) cites some of his own findings (Carr et al., 1978; Dores and Carr, 1979) and those obtained by others (Lovaas et al., 1971; Pronovost et al., 1966; Rincover and Koegel, 1975; Webster et al., 1973) to indicate that when speech stimuli are paired with gestures or other visual stimuli, low functioning (i.e., autistic) children behave as being functionally deaf, i.e., they respond to the visual and not to the speech stimuli. In other words, he suggests that under these conditions, the direction of the overselective attention is highly predictable.

A critical examination of the training procedures may indicate that the reported findings of some of these studies cannot be accepted as evidence to support such a conclusion. First, the case analysis reported by Lovaas et al. (1971) may allow a much different interpretation. This case concerned an autistic boy (Johan) who was first trained to imitate two sounds in front of his teacher. After he had acquired these discriminations, it appeared that he did not imitate the sounds when the visual cues were removed (i.e., when the teacher covered her mouth or face, or turned away from the child). Although this case has become one of the classic examples of stimulus overselectivity, it is highly improbable that the boy could have learned to match the sounds by attending only to the visual component (i.e., the mouth movements). Instead, it is more likely that, in this particular case, the screening of the teacher's mouth or face served as an S- for his imitations. Similar findings have been reported by Rincover and Koegel (1975). These authors observed that when an autistic boy (Cliff) had learned to respond to a verbal instruction, he failed to do so in other settings, unless the chairs and table of the training room were present.

Furthermore, the findings obtained by Rincover and Koegel (1975) on other subjects, and by Webster et al. (1973) may lead to conclusions much different from those drawn by the authors themselves or by Carr (1979). In the study by Rincover and Koegel (1975), an autistic boy (John) was trained to respond to a verbal instruction always or frequently preceded by a gestural prompt. Subsequent analyses revealed that the boy was responding to the visual cue (i.e., a hand movement of the trainer) rather than to the verbal cue (instruction). The findings reported by Webster et al. (1973) closely paralleled those of Rincover and Koegel (1975). In that study, it was reported that a child was trained to blow when given a verbal instruction ("blow") after a small loop of tissue paper was held to his mouth. Subsequent tests revealed that the child would always blow whenever the adult held the paper in front of him, but not when given the instruction alone. For Rincover and Koegel (1975) these and other similar observations provided additional support for the unpredictability of the overselective responding. For Carr (1979), they were representative of the highly predictable control of visual stimuli when presented together with auditory stimuli. Another, more plausible conclusion would be that the discriminative control of the visual stimuli was predictable, not because of their sensory modality, but because of their sequential arrangement. In three of the four case analyses described by Rincover and Koegel (1975), and the one by Webster et al. (1973), the children responded consistently to the first and not to the second cue, regardless of their sensory modalities (i.e., visual - auditory, tactile - auditory, tactile - visual). Although the other studies cited by Carr (1979) do not allow such a detailed analysis of the training procedures, it is possible that also in these studies the complex stimuli consisted of sequential rather than simultaneous arrays of multiple cues. In other words, it is implied here that, in as far as both multisensory cues were new, the training procedures resulted in the children being exclusively controlled by the initial component of the stimulus chain. This form of (over)selective responding would certainly be expected if the initial cue of the sequence was already learned, i.e., served as a prompt (as indeed was the case in some of these case studies). Many studies have shown that, when full prompts are used to facilitate discrimination learning, transfer of stimulus control does not occur unless the sequential order of the two stimuli (i.e., the training stimulus and the prompt) is reversed (Smeets, 1978; Smeets and Striefel, 1976a, b, 1980; Stremel-Campbell et al., 1977).

DISCRIMINATION LEARNING OF COMPLEX CUES

Most studies imply that for children of low IQ levels, stimulus overselectivity is a permanent condition which prevents their acquisition of many adaptive skills through traditional teaching procedures. There are, however, also some studies which indicate that stimulus overselectivity is a modifiable condition and that low functioning children can be trained to respond to all relevant components of complex cues. Such an approach would be very valuable, particularly since more complex (vocal and non-vocal) instructions consist of arrays of multicomponent stimuli.

One way to broaden their breadth of learning may be to overexpose them to the complex stimuli and/or to the components thereof. The studies by Lovaas et al. (1971) and Lovaas and Schreibman (1971) showed that (autistic) children who were overselective initially, responded to more components as a function of their exposure to series of test (i.e., unreinforced probes on single components) and training (i.e., complex) stimuli. In another study, Schover and Newsom (1976) trained non-verbal and verbal autistic children to discriminate figures consisting of three redundant and relevant cues. The results indicated that over-training on a complex stimulus resulted in a statistically significant though modest increase in the number of cues they responded to. But, since the subjects were tested twice, i.e., before and after overtraining, it cannot be excluded that their improved performance could have resulted from continued testing alone. Another study in this direction was carried out by Schreibman et al. (1977). In this study, autistic children were trained in a discrimination task with a stimulus composed of two visual cues. They found that for 13 of the 16 children who were overselective initially, overtraining on the complex cue did not help them to respond to both cues, whereas prolonged testing (i.e., unreinforced probes interspersed with reinforced training trials) eliminated their overselective responding. Although the mechanisms underlying the changed response patterns remain unclear, it is possible that the continued exposure to the test and training stimuli caused the children to sample previously non-functional cues (Trabasso and Bower, 1968).

Another approach to facilitate the responding to multiple cue components may be to establish the previously demonstrated non-functional components as functional. For example, in the study by Lovaas and Schreibman (1971), a boy (Michael) continued to respond to only the visual component of a previously trained auditory-visual cue. After he was retrained on the auditory component alone, he responded to each of both components during subsequent test sessions. Similar observations were made for other autistic and retarded children (Kurt, Marty, Cathleen, and Robert) in another study by Lovaas et al. (1971). However, the results of a subsequent study (Schreibman and Lovaas, 1973) indicate that this procedure may not be adequate for all children. It was observed that, after being trained on a single non-functional component of a complex stimulus (e.g., the head of a "Barbie" doll), the autistic children usually reverted to their previous mode of behaviour, i.e., responded to another stimulus component (e.g., the body) during subsequent test trials. The major weakness of this procedure is not difficult to identify. That is, rather than teaching the children to attend to the combination of stimulus components, the benefits of this procedure depend on the spontaneous transfer of stimulus control from a setting in which the component is presented alone to another setting in which it is presented with other cue components.

A more direct attempt to reduce overselective responding was made by Koegel and Schreibman (1977). In that study, five autistic children were first trained to respond to each of two (i.e., auditory and visual) cues alone. Then, in a conditional learning paradigm, they were required to respond only when the two cues were presented simultaneously and not to respond if their component was presented alone. The results showed that all four subjects acquired the discrimination albeit after many (i.e., between 240 and 990) trials (mean = 645 trials). The extinction curves revealed that for three subjects, the slow learning was associated with sustained responding to the auditory cue. In a subsequent experiment of the same study, a child (autistic) was trained on a series of nine successive discriminations. For each discrimination, the child was first pretrained on a complex stimulus with two visual components. Then she was tested on a conditional discrimination paradigm to determine if she would require training to do so. It was reported that by the third test, the girl had learned to approach all subsequent (i.e., seven) discriminations on both cues available during pretraining. While the results of this study certainly are promising, they also show that the procedure is still far from an efficient one. The data on the extinction of single cue responding and those on the pretraining of the complex stimuli (the training of the first complex stimulus required 4500 trials) imply that the error rate was high.

Perhaps the most effective technique for teaching children to respond to multiple stimulus components is by preventing stimulus overselectivity from occurring. This can be accomplished by a procedure that we refer to as S-delta training. Essentially, this procedure consists of two phases in each of which different though highly related skills are trained. During the first phase, the child is trained to attend to all relevant components of the complex stimulus in a stepwise fashion. This is accomplished by introducing the new stimulus as a very different (i.e., unshaped) and easy to discriminate S-. When the child has learned to discriminate the S- from a previously trained S+, the dimensions of the S- are gradually changed, like the stimulus shaping procedure used by Sidman and Stoddard (1966), into those of the new S+. After the child has learned to discriminate the shaped S- from the previously trained stimulus (S+), the second phase, in which the function of the S- is changed into that of an S+, is introduced. In other words, the child is now reinforced for responding to the training stimulus rather than for not responding to it. At first, the child is trained to perform the response associated with the new S+. For this purpose, presentations of the S+ are interspersed with S- intervals (in which no stimuli are presented). When this has been learned, the S- intervals are substituted for presentations of previously trained (S+) stimuli. This training sequence fits very well with the work of Sutherland and Macintosh (1971), Trabasso and Bower (1968), and Zeaman and House (1963), in which it has been proposed that learning to respond in discrimination learning is a two-stage process. During the first stage, the subject learns which cues are relevant to the discrimination. During the second stage the appropriate responses are associated to these cues.

The S-delta training procedure has been used successfully for teaching sighted and visually impaired (i.e., blind) severely retarded children to respond to large numbers of highly iconic cues, i.e., pictures (Lancioni, 1983), and three-dimensional objects (Lancioni *et al.*, 1982). These discriminations formed the basic ingredients of more elaborate programmes for teaching instructions conveyed through large strings of multicomponent stimuli. In both studies this procedure resulted in a near errorless acquisition of all target discriminations. Moreover, it appeared that after being trained on a sufficient number of exemplars, the subjects were capable of learning new discriminations through more traditional procedures which, in turn, led to their acquisition of additional discriminations without training.

The following account of a part of a programme designed to establish pictorial communication with low functioning children (Lancioni, 1983) illustrates how the S-delta training procedure was used for teaching them to respond to multicomponent stimuli. The goal of this subprogramme was to teach the subjects to assume body positions, i.e., arm and leg positions portrayed by pictures of human figures. The training consisted of two phases, i.e., matching the arm positions (first phase), and of arm-leg positions (second phase). During the first phase 10 arm positions were trained. The training of the first item started with a series of successive presentations of a card showing the upper part of a person (i.e., no legs) with both arms upward. When they had learned to match this arm position, an S- card was introduced. This card showed a face attached to an irregularly shaped torso (with no arms). Initially, this card was presented successively until they no longer responded to it (usually requiring no more than a few trials). Then the S- card was interspersed with the previously trained S+ card (arms up). After having learned this discrimination the shape of the S- card was gradually changed into that of a body (no legs) holding both arms forward. Once they had learned to refrain from responding to the shaped S- card (while continuing to respond to the S+ card), the S- card was treated as an S+. That is, first they were trained to hold both arms forward whenever the new S+ was presented for a number of successive trials. Following criterial performance, presentations of that card were interspersed with those of the first S+ (arms upward). The same procedure was used for the following five arm positions. At that point, the subjects appeared to be capable of learning the remaining three arm positions through a differential reinforcement procedure in which each new arm position was directly presented as an S+. That is, after matching the arm position of each new card for a number of successive trials, the presentations of that card were interspersed with those of previously trained cards.

During the second phase, subjects were taught a total of 62 arm-leg positions, i.e., to match leg positions in combination with the 10 (previously trained) arm positions. This phase started with the random presentation of two cards showing complete human figures, i.e., one on knees with arms upward, and another one on knees with arms forward. When they had learned to discriminate (i.e., to match) these positions, two S- cards, one of a person with arms upward and unshaped legs (the lower part of the body was portrayed as a trapezoid), and another one (also with unshaped legs) with arms forward, the subjects were trained to respond to the S- cards by matching the arm position while standing with one foot on a box. Subsequently, the presentations on these cards were interspersed with those of the two S+ cards, until the subjects met the criterion again. At this point, the procedure was repeated with four new cards, i.e., two S+ cards with human figures on knees, but with different arm positions, and two S- cards showing figures with the same arm positions, but with unshaped legs. Having learned these discriminations, the eight cards were presented in a random sequence in which the shape of the trapezoid (S- cards) was gradually changed into a configuration of two legs standing widely apart. This training continued until consistent differential responding was evident. The leg position of the S- cards was then treated as an S+. That is, the subjects were now trained to match the arms and leg positions (legs widely apart) of the previous four S- cards. Finally, the presentations on the new S+ cards were interspersed with those on the previously trained S+ cards (persons on knees with different arm positions). After they had learned to match the arm-leg positions of all eight cards, the S-delta training of body positions was discontinued. The remaining arm positions (*N* = 6) in combination with the two leg positions (i.e., on knees and legs standing widely apart), were trained through a differential reinforcement procedure identical to that used in the first phase. The same sequence (i.e., S- delta training followed by a differential reinforcement procedure) was repeated for three other leg positions in combination with two or more arm positions. The final 12 arm-leg positions were trained by the differential reinforcement procedure alone. For all subjects the error rate under both training conditions (i.e. S-delta training and differential reinforcement training) was very low, i.e. below three per cent in each phase.

SUMMARY AND CONCLUSION

In this review we have made an attempt to discuss some of the problems of training non-vocal communication skills to low functioning and multiply handicapped children within the framework of the research literature on discrimination learning. Evidently, teaching children to acquire a non-vocal communication system implies a process of discrimination learning.

In the first section we tried to make it clear that iconicity is a learned and functional property of the stimulus configuration rather than a psycho-physical phenomenon. While it is recognized that linguistic and psycholinguistic iconicity is transmitted through the composition of stimulus components, we learned from our studies that most (very) low functioning children did not observe the iconic properties until having learned first to attend to all relevant components.

In the second section we discussed some of the learning problems of these children in light of the literature on stimulus overselectivity. The reviewed studies indicate that when multiple cues or stimulus components are presented simultaneously, children with a mental age of about two years or less have a strong disposition to respond to only a limited number of relevant or irrelevant components of the total stimulus array. Furthermore, these studies also show that the direction of the overselectivity is unpredictable. The reviewed studies suggest that, in contrast to what has been frequently assumed, autistic children do not have a preference for visual stimuli over auditory stimuli, when presented together. However, the analyses of some studies also revealed that the direction of the (over) selective responding can be made predictable by presenting the multiple components sequentially rather than simultaneously. The implications of these findings with regard to the acquisition of non-vocal communication systems are clear. First, as most representational stimuli consist of multiple components, the overselective responding to unpredictable or irrelevant components will prevent these children from learning to discriminate other stimuli incorporating one or more of the same components. This may account for the slow progress reported in several studies. Second, they also indicate that, when the stimulus cues are presented sequentially (as probably will be the case in most clinical settings) rather than simultaneously, low functioning children will respond to only the initial component of the stimulus chain. The reviewed examples illustrate just how critical the moment of the stimulus presentation may be, and that descriptive terms such as "stimulus pairing" may be inadequate to allow a correct interpretation of the obtained findings.

In the third and final section, we gave an overview of the procedures which have been used to establish discriminative control of complex cues. These findings show that overselective responding may be prevented by teaching low functioning children to respond to all relevant components in a stepwise fashion. This we accomplished through the S-delta training procedure. During the course of this process, subjects are first trained to refrain from responding, while learning to attend to larger strings of relevant cue components. It is not until they have mastered this that they are required to make the appropriate responses in the presence of these stimuli. This procedure which is highly consistent with the two-stage attention process as proposed by Sutherland and Macintosh (1971), Trabasso and Bower (1968), and Zeaman and House (1963), proved to be very effective and efficient for teaching low functioning and multiply handicapped children to respond to complex cues. Moreover, it appeared that after this procedure had been used on a limited number of exemplars, the children were capable of benefiting from other, more traditional teaching techniques.

REFERENCES

Arick, J.R. and Krug, D.A. (1978). Autistic children: A study of learning characteristics and programming needs, **American Journal of Mental Deficiency, 83**, 200-203

Baer, D.M., Guess, D. and Sherman, J. (1972). Adventures in simplistic grammar. In: Schiefelbusch R.L. (ed.), **Language of the Mentally Retarded**, University Park Press, Baltimore, 93-105

Bandura, A., (1969). **Principles of Behaviour Modification**, Holt, Rinehart, and Winston, New York

Baron, N., and Isensee, L.M. (1977). Iconicity and learnability. Paper presented at the Second Annual Boston University Conference on Language

Bonvillian, J. and Nelson, K., (1976). Sign language acquisition in a mute autistic boy, **Journal of Speech and Hearing Disorders, 41**, 339-347

Bricker, W.A. and Bricker, D.D. (1970). Development of receptive vocabulary in severely retarded children, **American Journal of Mental Deficiency, 74**, 599-607

Brown, R. (1977). Why are signed languages easier to learn than spoken languages? Keynote address, National Symposium on Sign Language Research and Teaching, Chicago

Carr, E.G. (1979). Teaching autistic children to use sign language: some research issues, **Journal of Autism and Developmental Disorders, 9**, 345-359

Carr, E.G., Binkhoff, J.A., Kologinsky, E. and Eddy, M. (1978). Acquisition of sign language by autistic children. I: expressive labelling, **Journal of Applied Behavior Analysis, 11**, 489-501

Carrier, J.K. (1973). **Application of functional analysis and a nonspeech response mode to teaching language**, Parsons Research Center, Report No. 7, Parsons State Hospital and Training Center

Carrier, J.K. and Peak, T. (1975). **Program Manual for Non-Slip (Non-Speech Language Initiation Program)**, H & H Enterprises, Lawrence, KS

Daehler, M.W., Perlmutter, M. and Myers, N.A. (1976). Equivalence of pictures and objects for very young children, **Child Development, 47**, 96-102

Deich, R.F. and Hodges, P.M. (1982). Teaching nonvocal communications to nonverbal retarded children, **Behavior Modification, 6**, 200-228

Dores, P. and Carr, E.G. (1979). Teaching signlanguage to psychotic children: Assessing simultaneous communication. Paper presented at the Meeting of the American Psychological Association, New York, September

Gardner, R.A. and Gardner, B. (1969). Teaching sign language to a chimpanzee, **Science, 165**, 664-672

Gibson, E.J. (1969). **Principles of Perceptual Learning and Development**, Prentice Hall, Englewood Cliffs, NJ

Griffith, P.L. and Robinson, J.H. (1980). Influence of iconicity and phonological similarity on sign learning by mentally retarded children, **American Journal of Mental Deficiency, 85**, 291-298

Guess, D., Sailor, W. and Baer, D.M. (1976a). **Functional Speech and Language Training for the Severely Handicapped**, Part 1, H & H Enterprises, Lawrence, KS

Guess, D., Sailor, W. and Baer, D.M. (1976b). **Functional Speech and Language Training for the Severely Handicapped**, Part 2, H & H Enterprises, Lawrence, KS

Guess, D., Sailor, W. and Baer, D.M. (1977). **Functional Speech and Language Training for the Severely Handicapped**, Part 3, H & H Enterprises, Lawrence, KS

Guess, D., Sailor, W. and Baer, D.M. (1978). **Functional Speech and Language Training for the Severely Handicapped**, Part 4, H & H Enterprises, Lawrence, KS

Hewett, F. (1965). Teaching speech to an autistic child through operant conditioning, **American Journal of Orthopsychiatry, 35**, 927-936

Hintgen, J.N. and Coulter, S.K. (1967). Auditory control of operant behavior in mute autistic children, **Perceptual Motor Skills, 25**, 561-565

House, B.J., Hanley, M.J. and Magid, D.F. (1980). Logographic reading by TMR adults, **American Journal of Mental Deficiency, 85**, 161-170

Howlin, P.A. (1981). The effectiveness of operant language training with autistic children, **Journal of Autism and Developmental Disorders, 11**, 89-105

Hurlbut, B.I., Iwata, B.A. and Green, J.D. (1982). Nonvocal language acquisition in adolescents with severe physical disabilities: Blissymbols versus iconic stimulus formats, **Journal of Applied Behavior Analysis, 15**, 241-258

Jordan, T.E. (1967). Language and mental retardation. In Schiefelbusch, R.L., Copeland, R.H. and Smith, J.O. (eds.), **Language and Mental Retardation: Empirical Considerations**, Holt, Rinehart, and Winston, New York, 20-38

Kahn, J.V. (1977). A comparison of manual and oral language training with mute retarded children. **Mental Retardation, 15**, 21-23

Kahn, J.V. (1981). A comparison of sign and verbal language training with nonverbal retarded children, **Journal of Speech and Hearing Research, 46**, 113-119

Kent, L.F. (1974). **Language Acquisition Program for the Severely Handicapped**, Research Press, Champaign, IL

Kiernan, C.C. (1977). Alternatives to speech: A review of research and alternative forms of communication with the mentally handicapped, **British Journal of Mental Subnormality, 23**, 6-28

Kirschner, A., Algozzine, B. and Abbott, T.B. (1979). Manual communication systems: A comparison and its applications, **Education and Training of the Mentally Retarded, 14**, 5-10

Koegel, R.L., and Schreibman, L. (1977). Teaching autistic children to respond to simultaneous multiple cues, **Journal of Experimental Child Psychology, 24**, 299-311

Kohl, F.L. (1981). Effects of motoric requirements on the acquisition of manual sign responses by severely handicapped students, **American Journal of Mental Deficiency, 85**, 396-403

Kohl, F.L., Wilcox, B.L. and Karlan, G.R. (1978). Effects of training conditions on the generalization of manual signs with moderately handicapped children, **Education and Training of the Mentally Retarded, 13**, 327-334

Lancioni, G.E. (1983). Using pictorial representations as communication means with low functioning children, **Journal of Autism and Developmental Disorders**

Lancioni, G.E., Ceccarani, P. and Oliva, D. (1981). Aviamento alla lettura tramite insignamento programmato, **Psicologia e Scuola, 7**, 16-27

Lancioni, G.E., Smeets, P.M. and Oliva, D.S. (1982). Teaching severely handicapped adolescents instruction following behaviors by means of three-dimensional stimulus configurations, **Applied Research in Mental Retardation** (in press)

LeBlanc, J.M., Etzel, B.C. and Domash, M.A. (1978). A functional curriculum for early intervention. In Allen, K.E., Holm V.A. and Schiefelbusch R. (eds.), **Early Intervention: A Team Approach**, University Park Press, Baltimore, 331-381

Linden, E. (1974). **Apes, Men and Language**, Penguin Books, New York

Lloyd, L. (1980). Unaided nonspeech communication for severely handicapped individuals: An extensive bibliography, **Education and Training of the Mentally Retarded, 15**, 15-34

Lovaas, O.I. (1977). **The Autistic Child: Language Development Through Behavior Modification**, Irvington, New York

Lovaas, O.I., Berberich, J.P., Perloff, B.F. and Schaeffer, B. (1966). Acquisition of imitative speech by schizophrenic children, **Science, 151**, 705-707

Lovaas, O.I., Koegel, R.L. and Schreibman, L. (1979). Stimulus overselectivity in autism: A review of research, **Psychological Bulletin, 86**, 1236-1254

Lovaas, O.I. and Schreibman, L. (1971). Stimulus overselectivity of autistic children in a two stimulus situation, **Behavior Research and Therapy, 9**, 305-310

Lovaas, O.I., Schreibman, L., Koegel, R. and Rehm, R. (1971). Selective responding by autistic children to multiple sensory input, **Journal of Abnormal Psychology, 77**, 211-222

Luftig, R.I. and Lloyd, L.L. (1981). Manual sign translucency and referential concreteness in the learning of signs, **Sign Language Studies, 30**, 49-60

Makita, K. (1968). Rarity of reading disability in Japanese children, **American Journal of Orthopsychiatry, 38**, 599-614

Miller, J. and Yoder, D. (1974). An ontogenetic language teaching strategy for retarded children, In Schiefelbusch R.L. and Lloyd L.L. (eds.), **Language Perspectives: Acquisition Retardation and Intervention**, University Park Press, Baltimore, 505-528

Munsch, K.M., and Reichert, D. (1976). Symbol communication training with autistic and autistic like children. Unpublished manuscript

Murphy, G.H., Steele, K., Gilligan, T., Yeow, J. and Spare, D. (1977). Teaching a picture language to a nonspeaking retarded boy, **Behavior Research and Therapy, 15**, 198-201

Poulton, K.T. and Algozzine, B. (1980). Manual communication and mental retardation: A review of research and implications, **American Journal of Mental Deficiency, 85**, 145-152

Premack, A.J. and Premack, D. (1972). Teaching language to an ape, **Scientific American, 272**, 92-99

Pronovost, W., Wakstein, M.P. and Wakstein, D.J. (1966). A longitudinal study of the speech behavior and language comprehension of fourteen diagnostic atypical children, **Exceptional Children, 33**, 19-26

Reich, G. (1978). Gestural facilitation of expressive language in moderately and severely retarded preschoolers, **Mental Retardation, 16**, 113-117

Reid, D.H. and Hurlbut, B. (1977). Teaching nonvocal communication skills to multihandicapped retarded adults, **Journal of Applied Behavior Analysis, 10**, 591-603

Rincover, A. and Koegel, R.L. (1975). Setting generality and stimulus control in autistic children, **Journal of Applied Behavior Analysis, 8**, 235-246

Roodenburg, W.F. and Smeets, P.M. (1980). Establishing respondent nonspeech communication in a retarded quadriplegic woman, **Behavioral Engineering, 6**, 91-100

Ross, A.O. (1976). **Psychological Aspects of Learning Disabilities and Reading Disorders**, McGraw-Hill, New York

Rozin, P., Poritsky, S. and Sotsky, R. (1971). American children with reading problems can easily learn English presented by Chinese characters, **Science, 171**, 1264-1267

Rutter, M. (1966). Prognosis: Psychotic children in adolescence and early adult life, In Wing J.K. (ed.), **Early Childhood Autism: Clinical, educational and social aspects**, Pergamon Press, Oxford, 83-99

Salvin, A., Routh, D.K., Foster, R.E. and Lovejoy, K.M. (1977). Acquisition of modified American Sign Language by a mute autistic child, **Journal of Autism and Childhood Schizophrenia, 7**, 359-371

Schover, L.R. and Newsom, C.D. (1976). Overselectivity, developmental level, and overtraining in autistic and normal children, **Journal of Abnormal Child Psychology, 4**, 289-298

Schreibman, L., Koegel, R.L. and Craig, M.S. (1977). Reducing stimulus over-selectivity in autistic children, **Journal of Abnormal Child Psychology, 5**, 425-436

Schreibman, L. and Lovaas, O.I. (1973). Overselective response to social stimuli by autistic children, **Journal of Abnormal Child Psychology, 1**, 152-168

Sidman, M. and Stoddard, L.T. (1966). Programming perception and learning for retarded children, In Ellis N.R. (ed.), **International Review of Research in Mental Retardation, 2**, Academic Press, New York, 151-208

Smeets, P.M. (1978). Establishing generative performance and cross modal generalization of the manual plural sign in a severely retarded deaf girl, **British Journal of Disorders of Communication, 13**, 49-57

Smeets, P.M., Lancioni, G.E. and Hoogeveen, F.R. (1982). Effects of different stimulus manipulations on the acquisition of word recognition in TMR children, **Journal of Mental Deficiency Research** (in press)

Smeets, P.M. and Striefel, S. (1976a). Acquisition of sign reading by transfer of stimulus control in a retarded deaf girl, **Journal of Mental Deficiency Research, 20**, 197-205

Smeets, P.M. and Striefel, S. (1976b). Acquisition and cross modal generalization of receptive and expressive signing skills in a retarded deaf girl, **Journal of Mental Deficiency Research, 20**, 251-260

Smeets, P.M. and Striefel, S. (1980). Transfer of stimulus control from loud tone to normal tone in profoundly retarded adolescents, **Behavior Research of Severe Developmental Disabilities, 1**, 105-121

Smith, C.H. (1975). Total communication utilizing the simultaneous method, In Creedon M.P. (ed.), **Appropriate Behavior Through Communication**, Michael Reese Medical Center, Dysfunctioning Child Center Publications, Chicago, 45-74

Song, A. (1979). Acquisition and use of Blissymbols by severely mentally retarded adolescents, **Mental Retardation, 17**, 253-255

Stokoe, W.C. (1975). The shape of soundless language, In Kavanaugh J.F. and Cutting J.E. (eds.), **The Role of Speech in Language**, MIT Press, Cambridge, MA, 207-228

Stremel-Campbell, K., Contrell, D. and Halle, J. (1977). Manual signing as a language system and as a speech initiator for the nonverbal severely handicapped student, In Sontag, E. (ed.), **Educational Programming for the Severely and Profoundly Handicapped**, Council for Exceptional Children, Reston, VA, 335-347

Striefel, S., Wetherby, B. and Karlan, G. (1978). Developing generalized instruction following behavior in severely retarded people, **American Journal of Mental Deficiency** Monograph No. 3, 267-325

Sutherland, N.L. and Macintosh, N.J. (1971). **Mechanisms of Animal Discrimination Learning**, Academic Press, London

Trabasso, T. and Bower, G.H. (1968). **Attention in Learning**, Wiley, New York

Vanderheyden, D.H., Brown, P.W., MacKenzie, P., Reinen, S. and Scheibel, C. (1975). Symbol communication for the mentally handicapped, **Mental Retardation, 13**, 34-36

Webster, C.D., McPherson, H., Sloman, L., Evans, M.A. and Kuchar, E. (1973). Communicating with an autistic boy by gestures, **Journal of Autism and Childhood Schizophrenia, 3**, 337-346

Welch, S.J. and Pear, J.J. (1980). Generalization of learning responses to objects in the natural environment as a function of training stimulus modality with retarded children, **Journal of Applied Behavior Analysis, 13**, 629-643

Westcott, R. (1971). Linguistic iconism, **Language, 47**, 416-428

Zeaman, D., and House, B.J., (1963), The role of attention in retardate discrimination learning, In Ellis, N.R. (ed.), **Handbook of Mental Deficiency: Psychological Theory and Research**, McGraw-Hill, London, 159-223

COMMENTARY

C. C. Kiernan

The paper by Smeets and Lancioni represents an interesting and valuable analysis of trends in the use of non-vocal communication techniques and ways in which methods of teaching could be improved in order to enhance acquisition.

This critique will address itself primarily to research which complements that described by Smeets and Lancioni.

Survey research on the use of sign languages and symbol systems in special schools in the United Kingdom shows that British Sign Language, within the framework of a scheme called the Makaton Vocabulary (Walker, 1978), has been adopted by 92.3 per cent of all schools for the severely mentally handicapped (ESN(S)) in England, Wales and Scotland (Reid et al., 1983). Symbol systems, in particular Blissymbols (Bailey and Jenkinson, 1982), have been favoured by schools for physically handicapped children but, along with modifications of Rebus symbols (van Oosterum and Devereux, 1982), are being increasingly adopted by ESN(S) schools.

In our opinion two general conclusions emerge from the literature on the use of signs and symbols with the severely mentally handicapped. Firstly, there is ample evidence to suggest that the use of non-vocal systems can allow mentally handicapped children and adults, including students who are also autistic, to communicate effectively (Kiernan, 1983; Kiernan et al., 1983). Secondly, there is no evidence to suggest that learning to use non-vocal systems hinders or prevents the development of speech, in fact just the contrary, improvement in vocalization and speech is commonly reported.

However, the research literature tends to be very inadequate in casting light on correlates of successful performance on critical mechanisms. In particular we can find no clear support for the argument that mental age is important. In general, group and individual case studies have failed to provide documentation of mental age, and variance in results of studies created by substantial differences and by different methods makes generalization even more difficult (Kiernan, 1983; Kiernan et al., 1983). We would argue that the use of mental age as a concept is substantially unhelpful in understanding because it does not indicate the skills which may underly successful sign or symbol use.

As Smeets and Lancioni point out, some of the variables affecting acquisition may relate to teaching method. At a very simple level it is easy to use physical guidance to prompt symbol use and relatively easy to prompt sign formation. On the other hand, speech is very difficult to prompt; a fact which gives non-vocal symbols a head-start. Because the stimuli are permanent, symbols have an inherent advantage over signs and speech. In using them the individual has only to recognize the symbol he wants to use rather than recalling a sign or word.

At a cognitive level there seems to be a clear need to investigate the link between acquisition of sign or symbol use and the acquisition of speech. Schaeffer (1978) and his colleagues have suggested a sort of bridging theory. There is little relevant evidence but Carr and Dores (1981), in a study with mentally handicapped autistic children, have shown a positive relationship between the acquisition of understanding of verbal cues and ability to imitative vocalization. This type of study carries us further in the understanding of possible processes.

Because of their approach Smeets and Lancioni ignore evidence which suggests that the reason for poor progress in non-vocal programmes is related to the type of social situation used in teaching. Very often teaching programmes require the student to learn how to answer questions, "What's this?", "Ball", often with material rewards which sustain motivation. In developmental terms this is a relatively sophisticated form of communication. One would certainly expect that other forms, such as an action request form, "What do you want?", "Drink", where the "reward" is being given the drink to consume, would be acquired more readily. We would suggest that there is a need to pay much more attention to contemporary psycholinguistic research in developing and evaluating sign and symbol programmes (McLean and Snyder-McLean, 1978).

The finding that a significant number of mentally handicapped individuals can learn to use sign or symbol systems where they have had difficulty in learning to use speech, and that a number of these people then can develop speech, raises tantalizing questions concerning the possible neuropsychological correlates of sign learning. It may be that detailed study of such cases may lead to a greater understanding of sign and symbol use and a fuller understanding of the neuropsychology of normal speech development.

References

Bailey, P. and Jenkinson, J. (1982). The application of Blissymbolics. In Peter, M. and Barnes, R. (eds.), **Signs, Symbols and Schools. An Introduction to the use of non-vocal communication systems and sign language in schools.** Stratford: National Council for Special Education, 18-21

Carr, E.G. and Dores, P.A. (1981). Patterns of language acquisition following simultaneous communication with autistic children. **Analysis and Intervention in Developmental Disabilities, 1**, 1-15

Kiernan, C.C. (1983). The use of nonvocal communication techniques with autistic individuals. **Journal of Child Psychology and Psychiatry**, (in press)

Kiernan, C.C., Reid, B.D. and Jones, L.M. (1983). **Signs and Symbols. A Review of Literature and Survey of the Use of Nonvocal Communication Systems.** London: University of London Institute of Education and Heinemann

McLean, J. and Snyder-McLean, L.K. (1978). **A Transactional Approach to Early Language Training.** Ohio: C.E. Merrill
Reid, B.D., Jones, L.M. and Kiernan, C.C. (1983). Signs and symbols: the 1982 survey of use. **Special Education: Forward Trends,** (in press)
Schaeffer, B. (1978). Teaching spontaneous sign language to nonverbal children: theory and method. **Sign Language Studies, 21,** 317-352
Van Oosterum, J. and Devereux, K. (1982). REBUS at Rees Thomas School, **Special Education - Forward Trends, 9,** 31-33. Also in Peter, M. and Barnes, R. (eds.), **Signs, Symbols and Schools. An Introduction to the use of non-vocal communication systems and sign language in schools,** Stratford: National Council for Special Education, 22-24
Walker, M. (1978). The Makaton Vocabulary. In Tebbs, T. (ed.). **Ways and Means.** Basingstoke: Globe Education. 174-184

N. O'Connor

I should first say that as I have never carried out any operant conditioning or behaviour therapy there are aspects of Smeets and Lancioni's chapter which I am hardly competent to review. On this part of the text my defence must be the 16th century Chinese proverb that the outsider's view is clearest. The second observation I wish to make is that this seems to me to be an important paper from a theoretical viewpoint for a number of reasons. Firstly, because it faces up to the problem of discrimination learning which was first raised in the study of subnormality of Zeaman and House (1963), basing their approach on a mathematical model proposed by Wyckoff (1952) concerning selective attending on the part of subjects. In their proposal it is assumed that at any one time only one dimension of a situation can be attended to and considered. For example, if a red circle and a green triangle have to be discriminated, shape and colour are involved as dimensions in the decision process. The subject can consider one or the other as the critical desideratum. In brief, this early research was based on animal studies in which the two items to be discriminated could be shown simultaneously or successively. The latter method may have suggested the techniques discussed by the present authors.

There is no doubt in my mind that selective attention plays an important role in discrimination learning which is almost certainly a two-stage process as suggested by Zeaman and House, involving attentional perception followed by appropriate action. Clearly, if a non-verbal signing system were to be taught, such issues would be relevant in teaching children to discriminate between the signs taught. This part of the problem is dealt with last by Smeets and Lancioni in their extensive study of successive presentation and discrimination of parts of a complex stimulus learning task.

Prior to this they are concerned with the overselectivity of cues and what is called iconicity. Looking first at iconicity, this means what many of us know as Rebus, i.e. the use of signs which resemble their substantives as, of course, words do not. Some primitive written languages were iconic in this sense. (This observation, of course, applies to early Egyptian hieroglyphics and Sumerian.) Rebus as a system of teaching reading is of course used in some schools for the backward. The problem with such languages always arises when one gets as far as abstractions, past tenses, adjectives and adverbs. Iconic representation has obvious limitations and I notice that Smeets and Lancioni do not try to develop any solution of this problem. It might none the less be crucial. Capacity to handle abstraction and generalization are important concomitants of language use. In fact Pavlov considered them to be essential aspects of the secondary signalling system or speech - making conditioning unnecessary. He did not say whether he thought the capacity to generalize arose from speech - or made it possible. If the former were true iconic communication would be on an entirely different level from speech. If the latter held true, generalization might be possible in the absence of speech. Pavlov, it could be argued, supported the former view. Clearly our decision concerning this issue is of great importance in evaluating the suggestions made by Smeets and Lancioni.

On the question of overselectivity, I am prepared to agree that this is commonly found as a phenomenon in the subnormal. It was observed long before Lovaas by Strauss and Lehtinen (1951) and is a probable consequence of limited cognitive capacity. I feel that this point is well established and that the authors' pedagogic use of this finding is an interesting and valuable contribution.

If I were to question anything in the exposition, I would turn discussion towards the general problem of the adequacy of iconic coding to express any but the simplest ideas.

References

Strauss, A.A. and Lehtinen, L.E. (1951). **Psychopathology and Education of the Brain-Injured Child**. Grune and Stratton, New York

Wyckoff, L.B. (1952). The role of observing responses in discrimination learning. **Psychological Review, 59**, 431-442

Zeaman, D. and House, B.J. (1963). The role of attention in retardate discrimination learning. In Ellis N.R. (ed.), **Handbook of Mental Deficiency: Psychological Theory and Research**, McGraw-Hill, London, 159-223

Chapter 18
Selective attention and perception

N. O'Connor

INTRODUCTION

This title draws attention to the fact that we do not see everything that passes before our eyes or disturbs our ears and that between us and what passes for the outside world lies, or rather shimmers, a complex mesh which actively interferes with Watson's (1919) blooming, buzzing confusion, i.e. with perception. So I began to see what could be done with such a heading. Attention and perception interact and select what we see and know; sometimes, for example in handicap, they rearrange our knowledge. How then does one deal with the subject matter of the title?

Firstly, it seemed to me that it had to be analysed, amplified and explained. Secondly, as "attention" has been critically reviewed among students of cognitive psychology very thoroughly and extensively in recent years (Underwood, 1976), this work had to be at least acknowledged. The same is true (Gibson, 1966; Gibson and Gibson, 1955) of perception. It seemed sensible therefore to present a comment on the background of cognitive psychology before presenting some of the clinical findings relating to handicap. This statement will for this reason give a brief history of psychological studies of attention and perception and their selective interrelations and then show how clinical studies have implemented the findings in this area.

Before providing this brief review, I must address the title analytically. Like most statements we make, it is not a simple statement but is logically complex. It conceals several other statements. It assumes that attention and perception are in some sense separate entities although some theories might demonstrate that they are each aimed at the identification and discrimination of objects, persons or events or actions from or against an undifferentiated background. Do the terms therefore in many instances refer to the same operation? Secondly, is "selective" the correct word? Selection requires a selector and the growing child is thought by some psychologists such as Piaget (1970) not to be a self-conscious person at first and perhaps not until he has mastered a number of cognitive operations depending on experience (decentring, for example, i.e. the capacity to imagine the world from a viewpoint other than one's own). Perhaps, therefore, "elective" might be a more comprehensive term than selective. As I will try to show now, models of information processing or analysis through the development of notions of "feedback" make attention and perception so closely interrelated that it becomes almost impossible to separate them.

REVIEW OF RESEARCH RELEVANT TO ATTENTION AND PERCEPTION

It seems reasonable to divide the study of the psychology of attention and perception into three parts, psychophysiology and arousal, information processing and finally specific and general sensory encoding.

Sensory Physiology and Arousal

Firstly, one needs to be aware that in the last century physiological psychologists perfected the study of sensory input defining the effect of intensity of stimulus in creating greater awareness in the subject and noting the effect of stimulus intensity on speed of response. This was the work of the German physiological psychologists Wundt (1903) and Ebbinghaus (1902). At the same time, they defined the detectable quality differences in stimuli as judged by human sense organs. So, for example, pitch differences in sound or differences in intensity of a certain size were noted as minimal detectable differences or just noticeable differences (JNDs) by Titchener (1905), quoted by Woodworth (1938). Luminance differences were similarly observed and currently capacity to discriminate degrees of grey and black displays are studied in infants and children of different ages, and Fantz (1961) for example drew attention to the greater fixation time accorded by infants to patterned as distinct from unpatterned surfaces. These studies all emphasized the qualities of stimuli which were attended to by humans of different ages given normal sensory development. Just discriminable differences in temporal duration for both vision and audition were also observed by Exner (1881) in the last century. Binet and Simon (1916) used the idea of a two point tactile threshold on the skin as a measure of IQ. Such studies ultimately led to other observations concerning deficiencies of discrimination of temporally occurring events in aphasics.

This work mainly from the 19th century and largely German, influenced the work of the great Russian physiologists Sechenov and Pavlov. Pavlov (1927) particularly pointed to the attention-getting qualities of some stimuli, noting two circumstances which influenced stimulus detection, namely the state of the organism and the nature of the stimulus in relation to the environment, especially its relative frequency in that environment. Pavlov (1927) and later Teplov (1964) observed that in certain pathological states of the organism, strong stimuli abnormally gave rise to weak responses and vice versa, his so-called paradoxical and ultra-paradoxical phases. He also noted that under certain conditions of conjunction between stimulus and reward, signal associations could take place resulting in the modification of biological patterns of response and leading to the conditional stimulus, or learned response. This capturing of attention redirected the association of perception and response and led through Watson (1919) and many American psychologists to the systematic establishment of an associationist theory of learning. Additionally, however, Pavlov drew attention to the orienting reflex, i.e. the capacity of the organism to detect novelty in the environment, an example of the complexity of _relational_ attention and perception as distinct from such _absolute_ qualities as the intensity of the stimulus. Subsequent clinical work in Germany and the USA was to make use of this type of attentional skill in noting the effect of brain injury on figure-ground perception in mentally retarded individuals.

However, Pavlov's biggest contribution to our understanding of perceptual and attentional patterns in humans was his later-life observations about the secondary signalling system and its capacity to promote new perceptual combinations and generalizations, i.e. the capacity of a speaker to reorganize the perceptual field of a listener by verbal instruction. Luria's colleagues made use of this capacity in aiding children's perception of complex patterns by simply verbally identifying patterns within the complex visual display presented (Nepomnyashchaya, 1956). Weaknesses within the secondary signalling system would thus be a disadvantage for children's perceptual and attentional instruction.

Historically speaking, the next most relevant topics have been studied much more recently than Pavlov's observations at the turn of the century and its first two decades. These are studies begun in the immediate post-war years into arousal on the one hand and information processing on the other. The developments in this area have given rise notably to measures of evoked potential and contingent negative variation which have demonstrated essentially that subjects may sometimes be reacting neurologically to stimuli whilst not necessarily being aware of these stimuli at a conscious level. The research has also emphasized the need for certain basic levels of arousal to be maintained before adequate functioning of the CNS is possible, a point known to students of the EEG. Whether measured by evoked potential, EEG, or skin potential, the consequences of this concept of arousal for performance among handicapped individuals have been extensively studied by Clausen (1978) and Karrer _et al_. (1979) whose work will be evaluated later when the interaction of arousal level and handicap is discussed.

Information Processing

Studies of information processing began with the work of Broadbent (1958) and consisted at first of recognition of the already well understood successive pattern of the ingestion of percepts, their storage, categorization by concepts, selection and re-presentation or output. Broadbent (1958) had initially drawn attention to the fact that input selection was probably unitary because in binaural listening studies there was a tendency to recall all verbal items from one ear, usually the right, when conflicting inputs were available to each ear. Sometimes input to both ears could be recalled but successively, indicating the unitary nature of input and perhaps therefore the presence of attentional selection. Two aspects of attention are notable: events are recorded in a short-term memory or memories, and then they are attended to selectively. This is well illustrated by an experiment by Sperling (1960) where a set of 12 items arranged in 3 x 4 matrix were displayed tachistoscopically for a very brief period (50 ms). This visual display was followed by signals indicating which row in the display should be recalled. Providing this was done within a very brief period, any row in the total matrix could be recovered showing essentially two things: that the attention of the subject could be directed to any material, even material of which he was consciously unaware; and secondly, that he was attending not to events but to iconically represented items already encoded in short-term memory. The duration of this store was of the order of 300 ms after which the information ceased to be available.

The selection which occurs in this instance is clear but it can be conjectured in addition that word selection may be occurring at all phases of the information processing chain. It is well attested that frequency and recency are factors affecting recall in memory and the role of novelty in attention was mentioned above in connection with the orienting reflex. It is also the case that frequency and recency, as indicated by word counts, affect speed of access to the lexicon or word store.

However, in this discussion our interest must naturally be in individual differences and in the effect of handicap on performance. In this respect we have to consider aspects of limitation of performance in one or other of the operations associated with information processing or learning which we have mentioned, i.e. attentional selection, short-term memory, categorization in long-term memory, access to these categories and verbal or motor output processing. Each of these can of course be affected by growth, and in many cases a particular system is affected as in hemiplegia, developmental dysphasia, blindness, deafness and dyslexia. However, in the case of mental retardation, no particular system is necessarily affected more than the others, but an overall developmental lag may be discerned. Apparently, even in a normally developing nervous system, compensation for injury, whether occurring contralaterally or by normal growth, may compensate for specific functional deficits or for presumedly specific attentional and perceptual defects. This question will be discussed more fully in the next section.

Specific and General Sensory Encoding

Other aspects of normal psychological development may also affect selective attention and perception. A good deal of work, for example, that of Gibson and Gibson (1955) and Deutsch (1955), has suggested that different features in perception may be salient at different times in normal child development. Schema theory, involving the idea of a set of rules governing the nature of a "prototype" or typical object or event, expands this notion of salience. It arose from the work of Bartlett (1932) and has been developed by Attneave (1957) and Rosch (1973). In this kind of theory, perception and attention turn out to be in part governed by long-term categorized memory, or what we could call experience. However, these selectional factors, affecting perception, apply generally rather than differentially according to handicap. The same observation can reasonably be made about the development of short-term memory span which increases with mental age from 3 or 4 digits at mental age 5, to 7 or 8 digits at mental age 16.

Another aspect of development which is of considerable importance is the acquisition of "useful" speech. As already mentioned above, the importance of the term "useful" here is meant to emphasize the fact that although some people acquire some speech, not all those who acquire adequate speech to be able to understand and communicate, acquire enough speech so that they can encode verbally in memory or think verbally. Vigotsky (1962) and Luria (1961) both emphasized the difference between speech for communication and speech for thought.

Other aspects of development likely to affect selective attention and perception must be listed rather than fully described. These include those stressed in Piaget's research, such as the acquisition of the notion of object constancy, despite change of place; the acquisition of the capacity to conserve either one dimension or more than one dimension, e.g. length and breadth of a piece of plasticine, the rationalization of eye-movements in the perception of objects (Zinchenko *et al.*, 1963) and the whole troubled problem of sensory integration and cross-modal transfer (Birch and Lefford, 1963). Each of these cognitive operations is known to be age-related and some are interdependent one on another. Many of these questions are so complex and so far from resolution that it would serve little purpose to describe them in any detail. It is sufficient to say that so far as sensory integration is concerned, it is possible that integration may exist in part at birth but at a crude level and probably many sequences of differentiation and re-integration may have to be gone through or be learned during the first 6 or 7 years of life. This complex problem - for example, when can infants adequately coordinate touch and vision and, are the two systems mutually correlated in adults? - can be in part illuminated by the study of handicap (O'Connor and Hermelin, 1978).

Although one could extend the list of topics directly affecting the way in which attention and perception function, it might be more sensible at this point to turn to the question of cognitive psychopathology or handicap. In the next section therefore a review of the way in which handicap operates on these factors is presented.

THE EFFECTS OF HANDICAP ON ATTENTION AND PERCEPTION

In this section factors referred to in the previous section will be considered in so far as they are affected by specific or more general cognitive handicap. Perhaps more topics than those to be mentioned could be considered relevant, but taking account of the space available and the research findings, it seems reasonable to consider three main areas. Some studies have been directed to the study of attention. These will be considered first. Secondly some early and more recent approaches to brain injury will be considered. These have a direct relevance to perception and through perception to basic elements of cognition. Thirdly the issue of cross-modal transfer and modality specificity will be presented to indicate the effects of both specific and general deficits on sensory encoding.

Attention Problems in Discrimination Learning

The selective nature of attention indicated by Broadbent's (1958) early work left unexamined the developmental aspect of dimensions or features characteristically extracted from visual or auditory experience during childhood. Even Gibson and Gibson's (1955) approach and alternative and opposed theories left these matters unspecified although the work of Vurpillot (1976) and more recent studies of children's perception of faces (Fagan, 1972) have been interesting in indicating that perceptual skills are not uniform across the board. Perhaps one of the most significant contributions to this kind of study among the handicapped was first made by Zeaman and House (1963). Basing their studies on work by Wyckoff (1952), they pointed out that slower learning in mentally retarded individuals was less likely to be a matter of poverty of association between stimulus and response, but more likely to be a failure on the part of the handicapped to identify correctly the critical features of any dimension in a task, which would then be rewarded. Although the ingenuity of this work based on a technique of backward learning curves developed by Hayes (1953) undermined the whole concept of gradual learning originally developed by Hull (1943), the specific scheme of the development of saliency of preferred dimensions at different mental or chronological ages is still a matter of some speculation. In other words, we still have a very inadequate idea of how the direction of attention is accomplished. Some quite interesting work which was carried out with autistic children by Hermelin and O'Connor (1970) showed that visual stimuli dominate in a competition between vision and audition in normals and autistic children, but that touch seems to be more salient with autistic than with control children. This early and relatively crude work with modalities was only a beginning and more contributions to the natural history of salience in children especially in relation to features or dimensions in percepts is urgently needed. However, with the question of the selection of a critical feature of a signal stimulus, it is clear that many severely subnormal children have great difficulty in isolating this feature as the correct - or rewarded - one. In consequence, they may have to make many trials before recognizing the critical feature in any display.

This aspect of attentional focus deserves a more thorough study. So far it has received no study at all although Reed (1973) has proposed a model of a matching to sample task and some of Vurpillot's (1976) studies of what children notice are relevant. Whilst such models are more formally than practically satisfying, they do at least specify the operations involved so that future research can examine each. In my opinion, it is high time such an examination was begun and perhaps one of the best techniques available would be through the study of eye-movement by techniques such as those used by Zinchenko et al. (1963) and recently re-examined by Abravanel (1981). A study by O'Connor and Berkson (1963) showed how this technique can be used to differentiate eye movement in normal, Down's syndrome and the undifferentiated handicapped.

This is one central issue where attentional research is vital to the appreciation of backwardness in learning and which has received scant study in the last two decades.

Brain Injury and the Electrophysiology of Handicap

Another area closely linking attention and perception is that of the study of the effects of brain injury or minimal brain damage on perception and attention. These terms of course derive from neurology and are not strictly applicable in the field of mental handicap. There seem to have been three separate approaches to selective attention and perception in this field. The first originated with the work of Goldstein (1927) in the first world war. The original observation was that certain kinds of localized injuries led to the misperception of figures or to their rotation when reproduced. This work was used by Strauss and Lehtinen (1951) and earlier by Werner and Strauss (1941) to attempt to detect minimal brain damage in children. Weakness of figure perception against a complex background was first used as a test and it was hoped that clinical neurology would correspondingly confirm the diagnosis. Unfortunately, there has been little satisfactory support from this direction and it is time that co-operative research was stimulated. The findings of Strauss and Lehtinen (1951) nevertheless showed satisfactorily that some retarded individuals were deficient in the perception of Gestalts and saw complex figures in terms of isolated parts of their total constitution. Whereas undamaged subjects saw such figures as patterned designs, brain damaged subjects might see them as a collection of separate parts which they could only envisage separately.

This work has not been pursued to my knowledge and instead an extensive attempt has been made to develop studies based on neurological test batteries (Reitan, 1966) or electrophysiological investigations which may place less precise emphasis on localization (Karrer et al., 1979). Reitan's (1966) exploitation of Halstead's neurological tests are in a sense unobjectionable but inapplicable in the area of retardation largely because of the rather obvious inappropriateness in severe retardation of any reasonably close structure-function correspondence.

Karrer et al. (1979) have carried out an extremely extensive and thorough review of the literature on electrophysiological responses in retarded individuals, but generally are not able to present a picture of any clear-cut effects of retardation. Luria's (1963) prediction that the orienting reflex is defective in retarded subjects is not supported and although attentional deficits ought to be associated with unusual EEG records, they note that among Down's syndrome cases an unusual amount of regular EEG is found compared with other aetiological groups despite the gross neuropathology characteristically found in Down's syndrome.

The one finding of interest in this much explored area which has also been carefully covered by Clausen (1978) is the recent discovery by Richlin et al. (1971) that visual evoked potential in retarded subjects is contralaterally dominant compared with controls. Such a finding, if confirmed, might indicate that retarded individuals follow abnormal cognitive strategies as suggested by the activation of different cortical regions. However, the extensive studies carried out by electrophysiologists have made only limited progress and a more promising approach to the study of attentional and perceptual defects might be in one of two directions. Das (1976) has shown that uninstructed orientation is poorer in retarded than in normal subjects, a finding which would in part confirm Luria's (1963) prediction and indicate also the weaknesses which Luria, following Pavlov, would have expected to find in the secondary signalling system in the retarded individuals.

Another aspect of research into the effects of brain injury on attention and perception is part of the renewed study of clumsiness and motor deficiency in children. Such studies are obviously more clinical and in the area of neuropsychology. Hulme et al. (1982a, b) compared judgements of length by vision and kinaesthesis. Clumsy children showed poor visual and kinaesthetic and cross-modal judgements and were poor on spatial tasks of the Wechsler Intelligence Scale. Hulme and his colleagues found that variations in motor skill were correlated with performance on visual perceptual measures. They suggested that clumsiness may be caused by an impairment in visual perception. This promising research indicates a useful approach to perceptual anomalies which might well affect the motor performance of many mentally handicapped individuals. In any case the research deserves to be extended. Other aspects of the work were concerned not so much with a perceptual as with a mnemonic defect. Currently experimental results contra-indicate such a connection.

Another interesting worker in this general area of motor disability and its association with perception is Anwar (1981a, b). Her interest has been in the difficulties of perceptual adaptation shown by Down's syndrome children and the extent to which artificially induced distortions of visual perception lead to "incorrect" pointing or motor movements. Early work took up the question discussed in the past by Hermelin and O'Connor (1961) of the extent to which Down's syndrome children were less motorically or kinaesthetically able than normal children or matched mentally handicapped controls of different aetiology. Current work (Anwar, 1981b) suggests that a more likely explanation of motor incompetence in Down's syndrome is the incapacity of these patients to integrate two or more sensory inputs at the same time. The work of Hogg (1982) is also highly pertinent but is dealt with elsewhere in this volume.

Overall, these clinical-type studies concerned with motor and perceptual deficits and the possible connections between them are of great interest in reflecting both early observations of Binet et al. (1907) concerned with the reproduction of squares and diamonds and the relatively recent work of Bryant (1974) which has pursued this oddity of perceptual motor ability in the development of perception. They reflect also the work of Birch and Lefford (1963) which was concerned with the growth of cross-modal transfer, a problem which we also studied (Hermelin and O'Connor, 1960; O'Connor and Hermelin, 1961). Luria (1961) laid much emphasis on this question and its association with intra-sensory development is still in dispute (Bryant, 1974) although the problem of its dependence on or independence of speech has now largely been resolved in favour of independence.

Specific and General Modality Encoding

The final topic which concerns perception and attention where handicap is relevant has been of special concern to Hermelin and to me. Our recent work (O'Connor and Hermelin, 1978) reports research relevant to this issue and a very brief summary of some of these studies would seem appropriate here.

The experiments which we reported were aimed at comparing specific handicaps such as deafness and blindness with those associated with mental retardation. The reasons why this was done have been discussed elsewhere and are not strictly relevant here. The results show that short-term memory encoding strategies are very much influenced by blindness and deafness, but also by central handicap, or retardation, especially where this prevents the operation of speech as an encoding or "thinking" or mnemonic device. The best summary of our findings based on a score or more experiments reported in the book referred to would be to say that attention and consequent perceptual encoding was strongly influenced by the presence or absence of an appropriate sense organ. Additionally, the absence of a basic form of encoding central to auditory input, i.e. verbal encoding, can have an identical consequence. We found no similar central functional equivalent to verbal encoding in vision, but it is possible to imagine that prosopagnosia might be such an instance, combined as it sometimes is with a deficit of spatial orientation.

Another inference which could be made from our experiments is that transfer of experience from one modality to another by no means always occurs and cannot be presumed. Thus sighted subjects are no better than blind subjects on certain tactile tasks, when blindfold, despite a life-time of visual experience. These two findings combined suggest the vital importance, for regular normal thought or categorization, of intact channels, both peripheral and central. It is also clear that input channels in part determine the precise character of perception, despite the possibility of what we normally call abstraction.

This brief reference to our own work could of course be specified in more detail in any discussion to which this statement might give rise. In conclusion however it is to be hoped that the three areas with which this chapter deals in its section on handicap may have illustrated clearly three important ways in which handicap, whether peripheral or central, may affect selectivity in perception and attention.

REFERENCES

Abravanel, E. (1981). Integrating the information from eyes and hands: A developmental account. In Walk, R.D. and Pick, H.L. (eds.), **Intersensory Perception and Sensory Integration,** New York, Plenum Press, 71-108

Anwar, F. (1981a). Visual motor localization in normal and subnormal development. **British Journal of Psychology, 72**, 43-57

Anwar, F. (1981b). Motor functions in Down's syndrome. In Ellis N.R. (ed.), **International Review of Research in Mental Retardation, 10,** Academic Press, London, 107-138

Attneave, F. (1957). Transfer of experience with a class schema to identification learning of patterns and shapes. **Journal of Experimental Psychology, 54**, 81-88

Bartlett, F.C. (1932). **Remembering: A Study in Experimental and Social Psychology**, Cambridge University Press, London

Binet, A., and Simon, Th. (1916). **The Intelligence of the Feeble-minded**, Translated by E.S. Kite, Training School Vineland Publication, New Jersey

Binet, A., Simon, Th., and Vaney, F.A. (1907). Pedagogie scientifique. **L'Annee Psychologique, 12**, 233-274

Birch, H.G. and Lefford, A. (1963). **Intersensory Development in Children.** Monograph of the Society for Research in Child Development, **28**(5), Serial No. 89

Broadbent, D.E. (1958). **Perception and Communication**, Pergamon Press, New York

Bryant, P.E. (1974). **Perception and Understanding in Young Children.** Methuen, London

Clausen, J. (1978). Psychophysiology of mental retardation. In Ellis N.R. (ed.), **International Review of Research in Mental Retardation, 9**, Academic Press, New York, 85-125

Das, J. P. (1976). Orienting responses of normal and retarded children to verbal stimuli. In Karrer R. (ed.), **Developmental Psychophysiology of Mental Retardation**, Thomas, Springfield, Illinois

Deutsch, J.A. (1955). A theory of shape recognition. **British Journal of Psychology, 46**, 30-37

Ebbinghaus, H. (1902). **Grundzuge der Psychologie**, Quoted in Woodworth, R.S. (1938). **Experimental Psychology**, London, Methuen

Exner, S. (1881). Untersuchungen uber die Lokalisation der Funktionen. In **In der Grosshirnrinde des Menschen**, W. Baumuller, Wien

Fagan, J.F. (1972). Infant's recognition memory for faces. **Journal of Experimental Child Psychology, 14**, 453-472

Fantz, R.L. (1961). The origin of form perception. **Scientific American, 204**, 66-72

Gibson, J.J. (1966). **The Senses Considered as Perceptual Systems**, Houghton Mifflin, Boston

Gibson, J.J. and Gibson, E.J. (1955). Perceptual learning: differentiation or enrichment. **Psychological Review, 62**, 32-41

Goldstein, K. (1927). Die Lokalisation in der Grosshirnrinde. In **Handbuch der Normalen und Pathologischen Physiologie**, Vol. 10. Springer, Berlin, p. 600

Hayes, K.J. (1953). The backward curve: A method for the study of learning. **Psychological Review, 60**, 269-275

Hermelin, B. and O'Connor, N. (1960). Like and cross-modality responses in normal and subnormal children. **Quarterly Journal of Experimental Psychology, 12**, 48-53

Hermelin, B. and O'Connor, N. (1961). Shape perception and reproduction in normal children and mongol and non-mongol imbeciles. **Journal of Mental Deficiency Research, 5**, 67-71

Hermelin, B. and O'Connor, N. (1970). **Psychological Experiments with Autistic Children.** Pergamon Press, Oxford

Hogg, J. (1982). Motor development and performance in severely mentally handicapped people. **Developmental Medicine and Child Neurology, 24**, 188-193

Hull, C.L. (1943). **Principles of Behavior**, Appleton-Century-Crofts, New York

Hulme, C., Biggerstaff A., Moran, G., and McKinlay, I. (1982a). Visual, kinesthetic and cross-modal judgments of length in normal and clumsy children. **Developmental Medicine and Child Neurology. 24**, 461-471

Hulme, C., Smart, A., and Moran, G. (1982b). Visual perceptual deficits in clumsy children, **Neuropsychologia 20**, 475-481

Karrer, R., Nelson, M.N. and Galbraith, G.C. (1979). Psychophysiological research with the mentally retarded. In Ellis N.R. (ed.), **Handbook of Mental Deficiency. Psychological Theory and Research**, Second Edition, Lawrence Erlbaum, Hillside, New Jersey, 231-288

Luria, A.R. (1961). **The Role of Speech in the Regulation of Normal and Abnormal Behaviour**, Pergamon Press, Oxford

Luria, A.R. (1963). **The Mentally Retarded Child**, Pergamon Press, Oxford

Nepomnyashchaya, N.I. (1956). Some conditions of the derangement of the regulating role of speech in oligophrenic children (in Russian). In Luria A.R. (ed.), **Problems of Higher Nervous Activity of Normal and Abnormal Children**, Academy of Pedagogical Sciences, Moscow, 317-333

O'Connor, N. and Berkson, G. (1963). Eye movements in normals and defectives, **American Journal of Mental Deficiency, 68**, 85-90

O'Connor, N. and Hermelin, B. (1961). Like and cross modality recognition in subnormal children, **Quarterly Journal of Experimental Psychology, 13**, 48-52

O'Connor, N. and Hermelin, B. (1978). **Seeing and Hearing and Space and Time.** Academic Press, London

Pavlov, I.P. (1927). **Conditioned Reflexes.** Translated and edited by G.V. Anrep, Oxford University Press, Oxford

Piaget, J. (1970). **Genetic Epistemology.** Columbia University Press, New York

Reed, S.K. (1973). **Psychological Processes in Pattern Recognition.** Academic Press, New York

Reitan, R.M. (1966). A research program on the psychological efects of brain lesions in human beings. In Ellis N.R. (ed.), **International Review of Research in Mental Retardation, 1**, Academic Press, London, 153-218

Richlin, M., Weisinger, M., Weinstein, S., Giannini, M. and Morganstern, M. (1971). Interhemispheric asymmetries of evoked cortical responses in retarded and normal children, **Cortex, 7**, 98-105

Rosch, E.H. (1973). On the internal structure of perceptual and semantic categories. In Moore T.M. (ed.), **Cognitive Development and the Acquisition of Language.** Academic Press, New York, 111-144

Sperling, G. (1960). The information available in brief visual presentations, **Psychological Monographs, 74**(11)

Strauss, A.A. and Lehtinen, L.E. (1951). **Psychopathology and Education of the Brain-Injured Child.** Grune and Stratton, New York

Teplov, B.M. (1964). **Pavlov's Typology.** Compiled, edited and translated by J.A. Gray, Pergamon Press, Oxford

Titchener, (1905). Quoted by Woodworth, R.S. (1938). **Experimental Psychology**, Methuen, London

Underwood, G. (1976). **Attention and Memory.** Pergamon Press, Oxford

Vigotsky, L.S. (1962). **Thought and Language.** Translated by E. Hanfmann and G. Vakar, MIT and John Wiley, New York

Vurpillot, E. (1976). **The Visual World of the Child.** International University Press, New York

Watson, J.B. (1919). **Psychology from the Standpoint of a Behaviorist.** J.B. Lippincott, Philadelphia

Werner, H. and Strauss, A.A. (1941). Pathology of figure-background relation in the child. **Journal of Abnormal Social Psychology, 36,** 236-248

Woodworth, R.S. (1938). **Experimental Psychology.** New York, Holt

Wundt, W. (1903). **Grundzuge der Physiologischen Psychologie,** (5th Edition), Wilhelm Engelman, Leipzig

Wyckoff, L.B. (1952). The role of observing responses in discrimination learning. **Psychological Review, 59,** 431-442

Zeaman, D. and House, B.J. (1963). The role of attention in retardate discrimination learning. In Ellis N.R. (ed.), **Handbook of Mental Deficiency: Psychological Theory and Research,** McGraw-Hill, London, 159-223

Zinchenko, V.P., Von Chzhi-tsun, B. and Tarakanov, V.V. (1963). The formation and development of perceptual activity. **Soviet Psychology and Psychiatry, 2,** 3-12

COMMENTARY

P. E. Bryant

My comments will be very brief. O'Connor's paper was a masterly survey and it is difficult to conceive of any way of adding to it. My purpose will be to point out some possible connections between different parts of O'Connor's statements.

In particular I want to concentrate on two of the questions which were raised in his paper. One is the question about cross modal transfer, the other about object permanence. What is the link between them?

In my view the link is that attention involves not just isolating a critical feature in the environment and attending to it, but also distributing one's behaviour so that more than one input can be dealt with at any one time. It is perhaps easier to make the case that cross modal abilities are something to do with this kind of distribution.

By and large it seems to me that cross modal research has taken the form of a solution in search of a problem. By that I mean that it has never really been very clear why people work on the topic. It is obviously interesting to know how children link, say, visual with tactual information, but what part those links actually play in their behaviour has never been at all clear and often hardly referred to in work on this topic. I should like to suggest the idea that its primary function is to make it possible to cope with more than one input of one kind.

Suppose that one has an object in one's hand and wants for one reason or another to know about its visual appearance, but suppose too that one's vision is occupied with something else, surely it could be a help to be able to link the tactual experience or shape with the visual experience or shape here? Surely the fact that those two experiences can be connected makes it possible to look at one thing, feel another and take in information about both, information which is equivalent? So feeling the shape and being able to relate it to vision actually may release vision for something else and thus make behaviour both more economical and more effective.

It is interesting in this context that O'Connor quotes Anwar's suggestion that the primary difficulty of Down's syndrome children is with linking two sensory inputs. Down's syndrome children, we already know, also have very striking difficulties in tactual perception and that means of course that they are, in cross modal tasks which involve touch, at a disadvantage. There is evidence now that this cross modal and tactual disadvantage is present in infancy (Lewis and Bryant, 1983). It may be for the reasons I have just given that this difficulty leads to severe attentional problems among these children, and that these problems in turn deprive them of the opportunity to learn about their environment. So here is one example of how cross modal perception can be linked not just to attention but also to the question of attentional problems.

But how can the same be said of object permanence? After all this seems par excellence to be a cognitive problem and very much post-attention. However there are very good grounds for thinking that there is a great deal more to the problem of object permanence than this. One thing about it is that it involves the stimulating Piagetian notion of egocentrism. Whatever else object permanence is, it plainly involves notable spatial blunders on the part of very young children. Piaget's original observations that at around the age of six, seven, eight and nine months babies who see an object being hidden in one position retrieve it perfectly well, but when they see it put in a second position instead of looking there, they turn back to the first position and search in that place. Piaget's own interpretation of this curious pattern is rather complicated. It can in fact be divided quite neatly into two parts. In one part he maintains that even though the child is searching for it he does not really understand if it is still there, and it is this part that I should like to ignore.

The second part seems to me to be very much more important. It is that the baby makes the error because he codes space egocentrically. He remembers where things were hidden in terms of past actions. He goes back to the first place because his most powerful memory is of the actions he has made in the past to retrieve the object in question there. He associates the place where the object is hidden with the particular action that he has made to retrieve that object.

In fact there is strong evidence that this part of Piaget's hypothesis is to some extent at least right (Bremner and Bryant, 1977). We tested this hypothesis by taking the baby around to the opposite side of the table at the time that we hid the object in the second place, and by doing that we were able to separate out whether children tended to go back to the same place or to repeat an action as Piaget claimed. Our experiments showed quite clearly that that claim of Piaget's is the right one. Babies disseminate responses, they do not perseverate places.

But what is the explanation for this form of spatial coding? It certainly does not seem to be a very good way of coding space. But on further reflection one can be much more certain that that is more true of an adult than of a baby. To code space egocentrically and in terms of responses would be a very bad thing for an adult to do because an adult is moving around all the time, so that if he wants to retrieve something on his desk and has moved since he last responded to that particular object, then his position vis a vis the object would have changed and simply to repeat the response he made on the last occasion would not work. He would be reaching for thin air. But a baby is rather different. A baby up to the age of six months is pretty static. When he moves it is not under his own steam. For long periods of his life he is lying on his back, static himself and surrounded by static objects. When he sits up it is much the same story. A static person, surrounded by static objects, is quite a different story. Suppose we take a baby lying in a cot with rattles hanging above him; he can presumably see where the rattles are and at a certain age use that information to reach for one. But subsequently if he does not move and the object does not move he only has to repeat the same action in order to get back to it. So at that age egocentric responses could actually work well for the baby. To that extent they are adaptive. But they could be adaptive in another way too, for if a child only has to repeat a response in order to retrieve an object, he does not have to spend a lot of time looking for it and his visual perception therefore is free for other things. Once again we come to the same point as we reached with cross modal perception. The child for whom egocentric codes are adaptive is in principle able to locate objects by movements at the same time and he can in principle distribute his attention.

All this of course is conjecture, but at the very least it provides a reason for finding out a great deal more about handicapped children and the kind of perseverative error which was so skilfully pointed out such a long time ago by Piaget. It is a great shame that so little is known about the possibility of egocentrism in handicapped children. It is especially a pity when one considers Luria's later work on acceleration. He actually showed that it is possible to use very much the same sort of perseverative error as Piaget had but in much older children when language is substituted for visual information about hiding. Surely given the obvious language difficulties of so many handicapped children, this is a topic which should be pursued with a handicapped population.

All that I have said is based on the assumption that it is a distinct possibility that it could be that attentional problems may have a causal role in handicap. In other words I am concerned with the likelihood that some of the problems in handicap are a direct result of children not being able to distribute their attention effectively. But of course it needs to be pointed out that there is no evidence whatsoever of such a causal relation. Simply to show that handicapped children have attentional problems is not enough because the attentional problems may be the result of handicap and not its cause. A child may not be able to attend to what is significant because he is incapable of working out its importance. Since there are as far as I know no convincing data on this question we should perhaps spend more time considering how we ought to get such data. One obvious possibility is the training experiment: train children to attend more efficiently and see if it in any way lessens their handicap. Another way is the longitudinal study and that is to take groups like Down's syndrome children whom one can identify early on, and explore the relationships over time between attentional problems and intellectual development. Time is useful because if A causes B, A should precede B. Yet as far as I know there is very little in the way of longitudinal data of this form on attention.

For my money both methods on their own are inadequate. Very briefly training studies can be arbitrary. They can work in the experiment itself and yet have very little to do with what actually goes on in real life. Longitudinal studies are immensely valuable, but on their own do not exclude a practical alternative. Suppose you find that A regularly precedes B and is related to B, this does not mean that A necessarily causes B; it could be that both A and B have been determined by some other unknown first factor. Those are the weaknesses of the two methods and note that they are very different weaknesses. The strengths are also very different. The strength of the properly controlled training experiment is that it really does isolate, albeit within the experiment, the causal factor. The strength of the longitudinal study is that again, if it is properly controlled, it does spot the genuine relationship even if that relationship is not necessarily a causal one. So together the strengths as well as the weaknesses of these two methods are in fact complementary and the ideal design is therefore to combine them.

Surely studies of this sort are needed to trace the relationships between the various issues about attention and handicap which have been raised so clearly and provocatively by O'Connor, and which touch every aspect of the handicapped child's life at home and at school.

References

Bremner, G. and Bryant, P.E. (1977). Place vs. response as the basis of spatial errors made by young infants. **Journal of Experimental Child Psychology**, **23**, 162-171

Lewis, V. and Bryant, P.E. (1983). Touch and vision in normal and Down's syndrome babies. **Perception**, (in press)

C. C. Kiernan

O'Connor has provided a lucid exposition of research on mental handicap occasioned by his title. What seems to emerge from his paper is that, although there has been a substantial amount of time and effort devoted to these topics, the conclusions which can be drawn are at best tentative. In particular the applied cutting edge of the research is to a degree unclear. This lack of clarity may stem from O'Connor following his brief and approaching his topics from the direction of scientific work, or it may reflect a genuine gap between research and practical consequences.

As O'Connor's paper reveals, work on selective attention and perception with handicapped populations usually has its roots in theory and in parallel work with normal individuals. This type of approach is traditional in many sciences but entails certain dangers. In particular it may lead to a focus on variables which are of importance in experimental settings but which cease to make a significant contribution to behaviour in normal living settings. This can lead to what is termed lack of ecological validity.

One way in which ecological validity can be sought is to begin investigations from phenomena which have clear robustness in practical settings. In other words, to observe what happens in everyday situations, to select what seem to be powerful phenomena, and to construct experimental studies to investigate them which deviate as little as possible from normal interaction.

In pursuing this approach in our own research we have been interested in the finding that children and young people taught to use sign language and symbol systems commonly will acquire facility with the visual medium when they have found difficulty in learning to speak. Observation of these students in their teaching and living environment also shows that they commonly develop speech as a "side-effect" of a non-vocal programme (Kiernan et al., 1983).

This is a striking phenomenon and is what suggests a number of theoretical ideas. In particular, notions that the handicapped child is overselective in his response to stimuli, that he focuses on only a part of the stimulus complex (Lovaas, et al., 1979) or that there is a modality selection operating which biases some children to processing visuo-spatial input more efficiently than auditory-sequential input (O'Connor and Hermelin, 1978) seem to offer good starting points.

In a series of studies we have looked at some of these possibilities (Bowler, 1982; Reid, 1982). Although we wanted to remain as close to the original phenomena as possible we had to make a number of significant changes in mounting our studies. The first was to use children who could use both speech and signs, otherwise we could make no investigations of their interrelation. The second was to create a task which was relatively experience free. This meant that the signs and words taught were made rather artificial. They were in fact arbitrary signs and nonsense syllables given as names to novel cartoon-type pictures. The third was to adopt a rather "teaching" form of communication. The children had to learn the sign or word names for the cartoon figures.

The studies investigated various aspects of acquisition and recall of the material. In one set we found that there were stable individual differences in children's ability to recall sign and word names. Some children were consistently better with words, others with signs (Bowler, 1982). The studies also suggested that, across time, the same biases emerged. This finding provides some support for a modality specific theory but it is important to remember that as many children were biased towards word facility as towards sign facility.

These studies also showed substantial task differences. Where a simple short-term recall paradigm - picture presented, delay, request for recall - was used, effects emerged. When a string of signs, words, or words and signs were called for, the effects disappeared.

The same general conclusion emerges from the other set of studies. Here we found quite consistent effects in acquisition.

Signs were easier to learn than words although again there were substantial individual differences. However, once the signs and words had been learned there was no clear effect of modality in recall in a proactive inhibition paradigm which involved, again, a different set of task variables.

Where do these studies take us? They do suggest that simple formulae derived as interpretation of phenomena from theory need to be carefully tested. But do our studies get close to being ecologically valid? The answer is that they probably do not, largely because the constraints of experimentation forced us to adopt experimental groups which were different from the initial target groups and because our control of motivation reflects a special situation. However the studies do carry us forward somewhat in re-focusing attention on the interaction of (possibly) stable individual differences and task variables. They suggest that when theory-based studies do not receive confirmation in practical settings, we should pay attention to the analysis of the particular characteristics of students and tasks which constitute the phenomena in question in learning settings.

References

Bowler, D. (1982). Short-term memory strategies for verbal and manual sign labels used by mentally handicapped children. Paper to the IASSMD Conference, Toronto

Kiernan, C.C., Reid, B.D. and Jones, L.M. (1983). **Signs and Symbols : a review of literature and survey of the use of nonvocal communication systems.** London: University of London Institute of Education with Heinemann

Lovaas, O.I., Koegel, R.L. and Schriebman, L. (1979). Stimulus overselectivity in autism: A review of research. **Psychological Bulletin, 86**, 1236-1256

O'Connor, N. and Hermelin, B. (1978). **Seeing and Hearing and Space and Time.** London : Academic Press

Reid, B.D. (1982). The acquisition and recall of signs and words by mentally handicapped children. Paper to the IASSMD Conference, Toronto

I. A. McKinlay

Hyperactivity and cerebral dysfunction, whether minimal or sufficient to be described as mental handicap, are themes on which everyone has a point of view. The literature is vast on each. Industries have grown up to support points of view, to feed children with special diets, wonder drugs or programmed teaching packages which have cost individuals and public bodies a fortune. The literature on the long-term effectiveness of these programmes is always going to be presented at a future meeting and the circus moves on, changing the acts according to fashion. Effects of management style on the family predicament in the long term would be worth studying.

At the other end it is possible to become so absorbed by counting the number of yellow beads a Down's child puts in the red box that the predicament of the child and family is not noticed. However the scientific observation of behaviour does influence practice in ways which can be beneficial for children. Michael Rutter and colleagues have saved many European children from amphetamine or methylphenidate by publishing data on "hyperactive" children. The observation that adults could not agree which children were hyperactive and that children behave very differently according to circumstance indicates that people may have more to offer than pills.

The extensive overlap in the literature about hyperactive, learning disabled, clumsy, dyslexic, MCD children can be used to attack proponents of single diagnostic categories and treatment methods. However there is a substantial childhood population of people, some considered mentally handicapped, with widely discrepant cognitive abilities who puzzle their parents, infuriate their teachers and frustrate their doctors. It does not help to say that such discrepancies occur in x% of the population - what do they consist of, what do they mean and why is each child like that (his sister isn't)? We know too little about how to manage, teach and occupy these children, especially in inner cities. And there is much to learn about their prognosis in adult life.

The study of children by the techniques of cognitive psychology and psychophysiology can be expected to continue to advance the cause in parallel to neurobiology. There are hopes that there will be implications for teaching methods from two points of view. Firstly it is encouraging for children to receive appropriate teaching in the right setting. Secondly it is still not unreasonable to hope for measurable improvement.

R. J. Robinson

Selective attention is one area of behaviour where the clinician, neurophysiologist and the psychologist can find common ground. In the macaque monkey, neurons with firing characteristics dependent upon the motivational aspects of reaching and visual attention have been described (for review see Mesulam, 1981).

It appears that there are three or possibly four areas involved with selective attention. The best known of these is the parietal lobe which is the only cortical area to receive second-order polymodal inputs from the three modalities of hearing, vision and touch. It is thus best placed not only for cross modal functions but also for an inner representation of contralateral relationships. Unilateral damage in this area diminishes the space thus represented. The monkey with such a lesion on the left, for example, will with either limb misreach for a desired object towards the left. The intact parietal lobe on the right has skewed his representational bias towards the ipsilateral (damaged) side. Analogous situations co-exist in the human and are perhaps most graphically illustrated by the results of anorthoscopic viewing - a useful technique for testing internal representation of space.

The limbic system and the cingulate gyrus in particular assigns a biological value and hence an attraction to, or aversion from, events in extra-personal space. Stimulation of the cingulate gyrus in the cat causes aversive reaching head and eye movements. Cingulate lesions in the monkey cause contralateral neglect. Similar clinical situations have been described but are not well studied.

The reticular interlaminar thalamic nuclei and the adjacent locus coeruleus mediate the sleep/activity cycle. Clearly there are close associations between arousal and the effectiveness of selective attention. In the monkey unilateral lesions in the mesencephalic reticular formation result in unilateral neglect. In the human focal mesencephalic lesions have severe effects on vigilance and arousal.

Finally, the above three areas are connected reciprocally with the frontal eye fields and are crucial for contraversive eye and head movements. Surrounding the frontal eye fields are areas involved with limb movements, lesions of which interfere with complex sequential manual tasks - without affecting tone or power. Frontal neglect also occurs in human and is marked by deficits of active visual scanning.

Reference

Mesulam, M.M. (1981). A cortical network for directed attention and unilateral neglect. **Ann. Neurol. 10**, 309-315

D. J. Wood

One concept central to O'Connor's analysis - that of elective coding strategies - is an extremely useful one in attempts to describe a wide range of performances in hearing-impaired and deaf children. For example, research by this writer and his colleagues has shown that the reading age estimates of deaf and hearing children are differentially constituted, at least on some tests. These can be attributed to distinctive reading strategies shown by the hearing-impaired. Furthermore research into the receptive language abilities of deaf children in natural, classroom settings, show that they are often quite competent in using pragmatic cues to understand syntactic structures which other evidence suggests they are unable to comprehend in isolation. Chomsky makes a similar point in relation to some language-disordered children. Where a deaf child cannot attend to sound and the structural information it carries, he adopts strategies which capitalize on other, visuo-spatial abilities.

The acceptance of O'Connor's views on elective strategies also leads to the identification of fundamental problems with an exclusive reliance on "ecology based" research. If children can achieve a given level of performance by one of several strategies, then such observations alone are often not sufficient to provide a compelling account of their abilities. In more controlled experiments, it is possible to manipulate the information available to a child and to determine what cues he is or is not attending to. Another implication of this argument is that predictions from laboratory situations to behaviour in a given situation may be weak not because the processes identified are trivial but because they are masked by other, situationally based factors.

Chapter 19

Towards a comprehensive account of motor skill in severely retarded people

J. Hogg

BACKGROUND

It is now well documented that even in mentally retarded individuals not exhibiting obvious neurological damage or abnormalities developmental delays in fine and gross motor development and lack of competence in motor skill will typically occur (for review see Bruininks, 1974; Hogg, 1982). In addition, the suggestion that Down's syndrome individuals in particular show a variety of specific motor deficits has received some support (Gibson, 1978; Anwar, 1981a).

As Prechtl (Commentary) notes, however, absence of classical neurological syndromes does not mean that neural functioning in mentally retarded individuals is normal. It cannot be disputed that any truly comprehensive account of motor skill in retarded people will draw upon information on neural functioning. Indeed, Robinson's (Commentary) plea for collaboration between neurologists and psychologists is endorsed, though for the purpose of this paper the emphasis will be essentially psychological and ultimately educational.

It is also well established that given time and appropriate structure, a variety of aspects of motor behaviour can be increased in competence under certain conditions of performance. Goddard (1919) in "Psychology of the Normal and Subnormal" reported on improvements in the execution of a factory-like task by mentally retarded women who were given general practice on the task (pp.301-302). Subsequent studies have refined his observations. Holman (1933) reported on the discrepancy between the initial performance of retarded individuals on motor and mechanical tasks and their eventual effective performance. This position was elaborated and confirmed employing simple motor tasks (Tizard and Loos, 1954), a range of industrial tasks (Clarke and Hermelin, 1955), and was further extended by Clarke and his associates (reviewed by Clarke and Clarke, 1974). During the 1970s, studies have continued on the conditions under which improvements on initial performance can be advanced, with a growing emphasis on the technology of vocational training (Gold, 1973).

In parallel to this stream of work has been a growing concern to elucidate the specific deficits in motor learning and behaviour that underlie delayed and inadequate motor performance. Much of this work has been derived from general theories of motor behaviour, and part of the aim of this paper is to make this wider theoretical context more explicit since such an analysis within its framework points the way to possible developments in the field of mental retardation. More central to the aim, however, is the consideration of the relation between our understanding of motor skill and performance and lack of competence in contexts demanding skilled activity on the one hand, and the educational or training technology through which such skill is trained. It is hoped that it can be shown that the need to inform such intervention through a knowledge of processes as advocated by Connolly (1975) is at this stage a very real possibility.

THE PLANNING OF MOTOR BEHAVIOUR

The study of motor behaviour is the study of action. Though any action may be seen as a unitary piece of behaviour, it is in reality composed of a variety of distinguishable processes ranging from the neurological to the cognitive. This state of affairs is nicely captured by Bernstein (1962, p.171):

> Each significant act is a solution (or an attempted one) of a specific problem of action. But the problem of action, is something which is not yet, but which is due to be brought about. The problem of action, thus, is the reflection or model of future requirements (somehow coded in the brain); and a vitally useful or significant action cannot be either programmed or accomplished if the brain has not created a prerequisite directive in the form of future requirements we have just mentioned.

This central problem of how motor behaviour is planned and executed, and the processes involved in the acquisition of the behaviour and its refinement into smooth, coordinated patterns of action, has constituted one of the main focuses of research and theory in this area. As Summers (1981) indicates, there have historically been two major theoretical positions regarding the development of skilled movement. The first of these proposes a system in which the execution of the movement is dependent upon information received during its execution from sensory receptors. The behaviour is directed by a feedback loop made up of information concerning the intended action and information concerning its actual course. This has been referred to as "closed-loop" theory. In contrast, an alternative view has been proposed in which the plan or programme of action, once organized centrally, is realized by being "read out" without reference to sensory feedback. That sensory feedback occurs during the action is not denied, but it is argued that it is irrelevant to the realization of the programme. In contrast, such theories are referred to as "open loop".

Given the critical role of feedback, or its absence, in these two theories, attempts to resolve this issue have focused on the extent to which feedback is essential to the performance of skilled movements. The role of feedback is critical to both theories, and on studies attempting to analyse the effect of reduced or absent feedback Summers (1981) concludes that "... at least some simple movements can be made in the absence of peripheral feedback. There is more evidence for motor program control of gross limb movements and highly practised sequential skills than for skills involving fine motor control" (p.44). Further support has come from studies of preprogramming (which as we shall see, have been replicated with retarded individuals). Here the time taken to make a response after a given signal is analysed as a function of the nature of the response to be made. As increasing organizational complexity of the programme is called for, so mobilization of the appropriate processes and information will be required and reaction time will increase (Henry and Rogers, 1960; Klapp et al., 1974). Where, however, the response can be executed and monitored through feedback no such differential effect is noted, i.e. reaction time does not vary with task demands. Again Summers (1981) concludes that some notion of the concept of the motor programme is lent support by preprogramming studies. Nevertheless, commonsense would suggest that even if some actions are programmed in this way, feedback has a part to play in several phases of the programme. Keele and Summers (1976) suggest that (1) it provides information on the initial conditions prior to the movement; (2) a programme can be monitored by feedback; (3) fine adjustments required in realizing a programme may be under feedback control (from Summers, 1981, p.49).

MOTOR PROGRAMMES AND MENTAL RETARDATION

Experimental studies of the kind we are about to review should be seen against the background of slower development of motor function in most severely mentally retarded children. This is the case for global assessments of fine and gross motor behaviour as shown in Carr's (1975) classic study of Down's syndrome infants, for specific perceptual-motor abilities such as visually directed reaching (Cunningham, 1979, with Down's syndrome infants) and for neurological mechanisms (Cowie, 1970, in Down's syndrome, and Molnar, 1978, with non-Down's syndrome infants). It is also worth noting that the bases for these delays may subsequently make themselves felt in other areas of function at a later stage in the person's life. Cowie (1970), for example, invokes the relatively small brain stem and cerebellum in Down's syndrome individuals to account for some of the neurological immaturities noted in her subjects. Several writers working with older retarded individuals who we subsequently review also use this fact to account for deficits in more advanced motor abilities (e.g. O'Connor and Hermelin, 1961; Frith and Frith, 1974). Beyond early infancy Down's syndrome preschool children typically lag behind in both acquisition of motor milestones and also in the proficiency with which they execute fine motor skills (Moss and Hogg, 1981), though these will typically be acquired at a later date. When young Down's syndrome children are matched in MA to their non-handicapped peers, their motor abilities may be better, worse or equivalent, depending on the aspect of behaviour observed (Hogg and Moss, 1983).

The starting point for much of the work on programming of action in this field stemmed from a series of studies undertaken by Berkson (1960a, b, c). Berkson emphasized the difficulties encountered by retarded individuals in performing certain simple acts even when the demands have been perceived and analysed. Wade _et al_., (1978) have pursued this question in an attempt to locate more specifically where difficulties in performance lie. These authors confirmed Berkson's findings that difficulties are related to _response_ parameters involved in performance. With respect to the nature of these parameters, we may infer from another study by those authors that difficulties in making the movements reflect problems in coping with central processing demands of the movement, or an underdeveloped response selection process, _or_ a combination of both factors (Wallace _et al_., 1978).

If we move from relatively preprogrammed movements to what Summers (1981) referred to as "... highly practised sequential skills..." we might again anticipate retard/non-retard differences. In this field interest has tended to focus on more specific questions concerning differences between Down's syndrome and non-Down's syndrome peers of equivalent mental age. Frith and Frith (1974), for example, showed relatively poorer performance by Down's syndrome children, relative to their developmentally similar non-Down's and non-retarded peers, in simple sequential skills demanding anticipation (open-loop performance) and in which sensory feedback (closed-loop performance) was unavailable. Similarly, Dodd (1975) has reported experimental findings suggesting that articulatory deficits in Down's syndrome speech are part of a general motor disability resulting from difficulties in preprogramming sequences of movement. Since motor programmes must reflect a variety of aspects of motor behaviour, including spatial and temporal components, it is necessary to consider further whether the hypothesized deficit cannot be isolated more specifically. Summers (1975, 1981), for example, considers the timing of events an integral part of any motor programme representation. Henderson _et al_. (1981) have suggested that Down's syndrome children's motor programme difficulty resides more specifically in the timing component of the programme than in its spatial component. In more general terms, Henderson et al. (1981) suggest that it is the difficulty in timing that underlies the generally slower movements observed in retarded children and particularly those with Down's syndrome.

Though a relatively limited number of studies have been undertaken on motor programming and mental retardation, the concept has been an influential one. This influence has been reinforced by the fact that one of the few available theories on the development of motor skills in young children has drawn extensively on the concept of the motor programme, extending it to an account of longer sequences of planned movement. Connolly (1970) has proposed a direct analogy between computer programs and motor programmes, the latter being evolved from increasingly more organized subroutines underlying individual component skills. Elliott and Connolly (1973) have related this view specifically to prehension and handicap: "An approach which attempts to analyse manual skills into their constituent subroutines would be of value in the evaluation and treatment of handicap" (p.143).

Despite the value of the concept of the motor programme to retardation studies, some reappraisal is called for in the light of wider developments in the field.

THE SCHEMA CONCEPT AND ITS RELEVANCE TO MENTAL RETARDATION

Schmidt (1976) has drawn attention to a variety of problems inherent in both open- and closed-loop accounts of motor behaviour. Of central concern is the amount of memory storage in the central nervous system that would be called for. For open-loop control every movement would require its own motor programme while for closed-loop control all feedback information from past movements would need to be stored to provide references for current movements. A second major concern relates to the flexibility and novelty exhibited in skilled action. The norm is not repetition of movements in achieving a particular end, but a high degree of variability with respect to the timing and form of movements. Evidence suggests that even when environmental demands and conditions remain unaltered, variation will be observed. As Summers (1981) comments, "It is apparent that skilled individuals could not achieve the tremendous number of different movements required in a complex game just through the use of a finite store of fixed motor programs or references of correctness" (p.53).

The necessity to account for these facts has led to the development of theories of motor behaviour that suggest that the basis for action is through the representation of motor programmes in a schema-like form. Schmidt's (1976) response to these shortcomings has been to draw on both open- and closed-loop theories to evolve the schema theory of motor behaviour. Here we can only briefly indicate the main features of this theory, and more importantly for present purposes, consider some implications for motor behaviour in young children and retarded individuals.

Schema theory involves three major components:

(i) A generalized motor programme which is seen as an abstract memory structure governing a given class of movements.

(ii) The recall schema is the set of relations built up through experience between initial conditions (e.g. position of the limbs), response specifications and actual outcomes. The recognition schema reflects the relation of initial conditions, actual outcomes, and sensory consequences (i.e. exteroceptive and proprioceptive). Of the recall schema Schmidt (1976) notes: "After a great deal of experience the schema becomes well established. When the subject tends to produce a novel movement he enters the schema with the desired outcome and the initial conditions, and the schema rule produces the response specifications for that movement. When the response specifications have been determined, the movement can be carried out by running the motor program" (p.47). A similar set of operations occur for the recognition schema.

(iii) The recognition schema is composed of initial conditions, past actual outcomes and past sensory consequences. It is formulated in the same way as the recall schema. The stronger the recognition schema, the better able the performer is to predict the expected sensory consequences of a novel response. Evaluation of feedback can occur during or after a movement, and this will depend in part on speed of the movement.

Thus, the schema stores only information on the relations between the various operations, and new requirements are interpolated to specify a given realization of a general motor programme. This generalized schema is not dependent on storing a variety of programmes for specific movements (hence dealing with the storage problem) and can also provide the basis for novel movements never previously realized. Though it goes beyond the specific predictions of schema theory, it is possible that higher-order rules might be able to specify a variety of generalized motor programmes as relevant to attaining a given outcome. This state of affairs is certainly consistent with recent observations on motor development in young children. Moss and Hogg (1983) found that with young non-retarded children (12 to 40 months), contrary to Connolly's prediction, manipulative behaviour in dealing with the same task became more variable in the pattern of solution as proficiency increased. Similarly, the more proficient a child, the more he/she would employ differing manipulative strategies to attain the same end. The concept of higher-order schematic direction of motor behaviour explains such results more adequately than the idea of an invariant programme linked to a specific outcome, and would certainly have adaptive advantages should a task demand change.

Schema theory also offers an explanation for the immense variability required in the production of the component phonemes of speech, and suggests an alternative to accounts that require storage of individual programmes for each phoneme.

In terms of training motor skills, two major predictions follow from Schmidt's theory (we will not here draw further distinction between recall and recognition schemata). First, the schema is strengthened by increasing pairings between the various operations noted above. Second, the greater the variability of the behaviour engaged in, i.e. the more variety in values of the pairings, the stronger the resulting schema.

Direct prediction from schema theory concerning variable versus constant practices have also been tested with young children. In a recent review of schema theory Shapiro and Schmidt (1982) note that while these predictions have received only limited support with adults with respect to the recall schema, consistent support has emerged in studies of young children. They suggest that: "One conclusion that emerges from these experiments is that children's motor skills are apparently more easily affected by variability in practice than are those of adults. From the point of view of schema theory, such results are interpreted to mean that the recall schemata are easily developed in children; adults, on the other hand, may have already developed schemata for the relatively simple tasks employed in the experiments reported ...." (p.121). Shapiro and Schmidt (1982) also note that studies of the recognition schema with children have not as yet been undertaken. Further supplementary predictions concerning the recall schema also receive support with children. The developmental level of some of the children in the studies reviewed is relatively low, in that of Kelso and Norman (1978) 35-40 months. This suggests that the extension of such experiments to severely mentally handicapped individuals is feasible, and indeed, in a small-scale replication of Kelso and Norman (1978) with the author, Quigley (1982) has shown that young Down's syndrome children also improved performance in novel movements following variable over constant training.

Kelso and Norman (1978) relate their own findings to Bruner's (1973) suggestion that motor skill is essentially generative rather than repetitive, a view directly in line with Moss and Hogg's (1983) finding of a relation between proficiency and variability.

It should be noted at this stage in our discussion that not only is this particular formulation of schema theory comparatively recent, but its main proponents are actively engaged in its evaluation. While noting the success of the theory in consistently predicting a number of factors of motor learning, Shapiro and Schmidt (1982) note a number of problems that it encounters. Among these are (a) recent evidence that certain simple positioning movements can be made accurately without reference to initial conditions or recognition of feedback; (b) that the distinction between, and operation of, recall and recognition schemata may not be accurate when it suggests their complete independence. While the authors offer specific replies on these points, they conclude that "It is clear that some modifications are in order, but we are not sure as to what direction they will take with the state of the evidence as it is" (p.140). Nor do they regard the state of the evidence regarding motor learning in short-term experiments fully satisfactory.

Nevertheless, acceptance of a theoretical position as a framework for evolving a psychological account of motor skill does not imply a belief that the theory has reached its final form and that it is not susceptible to criticism and development. For reasons that will become clearer later with respect to other findings from psychological studies and training a provisional theory of this sort has considerable heuristic value in the field of mental retardation.

Though the emphasis in this paper has been on the programming of action, it is important to comment on the fact that the use of motor schema theory opens up the possibility of integrating several other streams of work in this area into a comprehensive framework. These are concerned directly with Schmidt's "initial task conditions" and with the use of sensory feedback information. Thus, Nettlebeck and Brewer (1976) and Brewer and Nettlebeck (1977) have shown that mentally retarded adults need more time to inspect a display to which they have to respond than to their peers. This will clearly influence both development of recall and recognition schema as under conditions of time pressure information on initial conditions will fall short of what is required to effect pairings between these conditions, response specifications, and outcomes, on the one hand (recall), and sensory consequences and outcome on the other (recognition). In like vein poor sensory discrimination will affect schema formation through its impact on analysis of initial conditions and with respect to sensory feedback. Both Gordon (1944) and O'Connor and Hermelin (1961) have suggested poor tactile discrimination by Down's syndrome individuals relative to their visual discriminative abilities.

In a complex series of studies, Anwar and Hermelin (Anwar, 1981b, 1983; Anwar and Hermelin, 1979, 1982) have demonstrated both specific problems with respect to proprioceptive feedback in Down's syndrome children, and more general difficulties with regard to certain aspects of cross-modal integration of sensory feedback in mentally retarded children and young people generally. While these studies indicate the specific impact of these factors on motor behaviour, it would be anticipated that in the light of Schmidt's theory they would have direct consequences for the build-up of motor schemata that would have a wider impairing influence.

MOTOR BEHAVIOUR AND INTERVENTION

The consideration I have given to the development of motor programmes and the way in which various processes studied in mentally retarded people might contribute to this development point to two ways in which we might consider the modifiability of motor skill in retarded people. We need to consider first how the various aspects of motor function might in themselves be modified, and second, to look at developments in training technology that are consistent with the wider framework of motor behaviour theory.

Recently, writers concerned with the implications for intervention of studies of motor processes have turned to a theoretical framework that has been explored essentially with respect to memory in retarded people (Anwar, 1983; Wade et al., 1983). The starting point has been Atkinson and Shiffrin's (1968) account of human memory. At the centre of their theoretical framework is the distinction between permanent structural features of the memory system and control processes that can be modified or reprogrammed. The implication of this distinction for those studying memory in retarded individuals has been to explore the means by which memory can be enhanced through the learning of appropriate mnemonic strategies, rather than settling for a structurally fixed constraint on memory implying limited capacity (Borkowski and Cavanaugh, 1979). Brown (1974) suggested that Atkinson and Shiffrin's position becomes of particular interest if we substitute "reprogrammed" by "remediable".

Wade et al. (1983) have suggested that the distinction between structure and control processes explored in the memory field should be extended to the study of motor behaviour. They adopt, however, a relativistic position with respect to the firmness of the distinction, suggesting that if our available training technology does not effect a change in motor behaviour in a given area, then we should regard that task component as "functionally structural". Brown (1974) goes one stage further stating that while a successful training programme indicates that the initial limitation was due to process factors, it is logically impossible to make a final decision on whether a deficit is structural without exhausting every possible training procedure.

From the point of view of those concerned to relate information on processes to remediation, the pursuit of such a distinction is less relevant than the attempt to test the strength of our training technology in modifying performance on specific task components. This requires that we relate our analysis of a given task to the possible components (which may theoretically be structural or control) in order to ensure our training methods are appropriately directed. For example, employing a simple task analysis of the experimental situations in which they have previously investigated reaction time and movement time, Hoover et al. (1981) showed that both these components could be shortened by employing the full range of behavioural teaching techniques (i.e. reinforcement, feedback, prompting, etc.) with moderately and severely retarded young adults. Impressively, the improvement in movement time was found to persist after five months even in the absence of intervening practice. The extension of such studies with respect to other task components reviewed above is called for. Under what conditions can repetitive motor programmes be enhanced, especially with reference to a critical component such as timing? How far are the programmatic aspects of articulation subject to modification leading to an increase in intelligibility?

More generally we can move on to consider the relation between a well documented body of training technology, behaviour modification, and the wider theory of motor behaviour we have described. A central consideration in behaviour modification has been the generalization of trained skills to new materials and situations. Applications of these techniques to motor skills training in a direct fashion often show only limited generalization (Hogg, 1981) and training strategies need to be reconsidered in terms of what Stokes and Baer (1977) refer to as "the training on sufficient exemplars". These authors suggest that the aim of such an approach is to enable the trainee to form an induction that will effect generalization sufficiently to satisfy the problem posed. There is a direct parallel between such training and the variable training employed in the experimental tests of schema theory reviewed, and the incorporation of concepts from schema theory into behavioural teaching technologies is an inviting one. Indeed, Clarke and Clarke (1974) have indicated that the very need for structured teaching of the sort offered by formal training results from the need to "build up schemata" in order to compensate for the lack of spontaneous learning in mentally retarded individuals.

Stokes and Baer's (1977) "training on sufficient exemplars" and Schmidt's (1976) "variable training" have found their clearest realization in general case programming. Colvin and Horner (1983) describe this procedure in the following way: "General case instruction refers to those behaviours performed by a teacher or trainer which increase the probability that behaviours will be successfully performed with different target stimuli, and in different settings, from those used during training". These authors describe the six stages in developing such a programme: "(a) Define the instructional universe; (b) Define the range of relevant stimulus and response variation within the instructional universe; (c) Select examples from the instructional universe for training and probe testing; (d) Sequence the training examples; (e) Teach with the training examples; and (f) Test with non-trained probes examples." Colvin and Horner (1983) describe general case programming through the teaching of a motor skill - screwdriver use - to severely retarded students. Here variations of the screwplane, type, length, thread, head type and size and differing lengths of the screwdriver were cross-tabulated and selected permutations across a range of values taught. Generalization was tested on new untrained combinations and demonstrated to have occurred.

The parallel between the prediction of motor schema theory and the use of training on sufficient exemplars is clear, and the training technology leads to an outcome that is theoretically consistent with the theory. Refinements in the theory with respect to the nature of pairings between initial conditions, outcomes, response specifications and sensory consequences should lead to informed improvements in general case programming, which in turn offers the potential of acting as a testing ground for motor schema theory. Within such a framework difficulties on specific task components may be analysed with respect to the various discrete processes we have considered (e.g. timing, utilization of feedback and so on) and programme revisions effected.

We have, in fact, rejoined the road on which the early pioneers of training motor skills embarked. In sight is the possibility of a genuine rapprochement between basic theory and intervention that offers the potential for a two-way exchange between experiment and training. The more robust experimental demonstrations (e.g. the constant vs variable training outcome) have an obvious entree into training and education, while sensitive intervention designs might not only improve training techniques, but also illuminate theory.

REFERENCES

Anwar, F. (1981a). Motor function in Down's syndrome. In Ellis, N.R. (ed.), **International Review of Research in Mental Retardation, 10**, Academic Press, London, 107-138

Anwar, F. (1981b). Visual-motor localization in normal and subnormal development. **British Journal of Psychology, 72**, 43-57

Anwar, F. (1983). Vision and kinesthesis in motor movements. In Hogg, J. and Mittler, P.J. (eds.), **Aspects of Competence in Mentally Handicapped People: Advances in Mental Handicap Research, 2**, Wiley, Chichester, (in press)

Anwar, F. and Hermelin, B. (1979). Kinaesthetic movement after-effects in children with Down's Syndrome. **Journal of Mental Deficiency Research, 23**, 287-297

Anwar, F. and Hermelin, B. (1982). An analysis of drawing skills in severe subnormality. **Australian Journal of Mental Disability**, (in press)

Atkinson, R.C. and Shiffrin, R.M. (1968). Human memory: A proposed system and its control processes. In Spence, K.W. and Sperce, J.T. (eds.), **The Psychology of Learning and Motivation: Advances in research and theory, 2**, Academic Press, London, 89-195

Berkson, G. (1960a). An analysis of reaction time in normal and mentally deficient young men. I. Duration threshold experiment. **Journal of Mental Deficiency Research, 4**, 51-58

Berkson, G. (1960b). An analysis of reaction time in normal and mentally deficient young men. II. Variation of complexity in reaction time tasks. **Journal of Mental Deficiency Research, 4**, 59-67

Berkson, G. (1960c). An analysis of reaction time in normal and mentally deficient young men. III. Variation of stimulus and of response complexity. **Journal of Mental Deficiency Research, 4**, 69-77

Bernstein, N. (1962). Trends in physiology and their relation to cybernetics. In Bernstein, N. (1967) **The Co-ordination and Regulation of Movements.** Pergamon Press, Oxford, 169-183

Borkowski, J.G. and Cavanaugh, J.C. (1979). Maintenance and generalization of skills and strategies by the retarded. In Ellis, N.R. (ed.), **Handbook of Mental Deficiency: Psychological theory and research.** Second edition, Lawrence Erlbaum, Hillside, New Jersey, 569-617

Brewer, N. and Nettlebeck, T. (1977). Influence of contextual cues on the choice reaction time of mildly retarded adults. **American Journal of Mental Deficiency, 82**, 37-43

Brown, A.L. (1974). The role of strategic behavior in retarded memory. In Ellis N.R. (ed.), **International Review of Research in Mental Retardation, 7**, Academic Press, London, 55-111

Bruininks, R.H. (1974). Physical and motor development of retarded persons. In Ellis, N.R. (ed.), **International Review of Research in Mental Retardation, 7**, Academic Press, London, 209-261

Bruner, J.S. (1973). Organisation of early skilled action. **Child Development, 44**, 1-11

Carr, J. (1975). **Young Children with Down's Syndrome: Their development, upbringing, and effect on their families**, Butterworths, London

Clarke, A.D.B. and Hermelin, B.F. (1955). Adult imbeciles, their abilities and trainability. **Lancet, 2**, 337-339

Clarke, A.M. and Clarke, A.D.B. (1974). Experimental studies: An overview. In A.M. Clarke and A.D.B. Clarke (eds.), **Mental Deficiency: The changing outlook.** Third Edition, Methuen, London, 259-329

Colvin, G.T. and Horner, R.H. (1983). Experimental analysis of generalization: An evaluation of a general case program for teaching motor skills to severely handicapped learners. In Hogg, J. and Mittler, P.J. (eds.), **Aspects of Competence in Mentally Handicapped People. Advances in Mental Handicap Research, 2**, Wiley, Chichester, (in press)

Connolly, K. (1970). Skill development: Problems and plans. In Connolly, K. (ed.), **Mechanisms of Motor Skill Development**, Academic Press, London, 3-21

Connolly, K. (1975). Behaviour modification and motor control. In Kiernan, C.C. and Woodford, F.P. (eds.), **Behaviour Modification with the Severely Retarded**, Associated Scientific Publishers, Amsterdam, 25-33

Cowie, V.A. (1970). **A Study of the Early Development of Mongols:** Institute for Research into Mental Retardation. Monograph 1. Pergamon Press, Oxford

Cunningham, C.C. (1979). Aspects of early development in Down's syndrome infants, Unpublished Ph.D. Thesis, University of Manchester

Dodd, B. (1975). Recognition and reproduction of words by Down's syndrome retarded children. **American Journal of Mental Deficiency, 80**, 306-311

Elliott, J.M. and Connolly, K.J. (1973). Hierarchical structure in skill development. In Connolly, K. and Bruner, J. (eds.), **The Growth of Competence**, Academic Press, London, 135-168

Frith, U. and Frith, C.D. (1974). Specific motor disabilities in Down's syndrome. **Journal of Child Psychology and Psychiatry, 15**, 293-301

Gibson, D. (1978). **Down's Syndrome: The Psychology of Mongolism**, Cambridge University Press, Cambridge

Goddard, H.H. (1919). **Psychology of the Normal and Subnormal.** Kegan Paul, Trench, Trubner, London

Gold, M.W. (1973). Research on the vocational habilitation of the retarded: The present, the future. In Ellis, N.R. (ed.), **International Review of Research in Mental Retardation 6**, Academic Press, London, 97-147

Gordon, A.M. (1944). Some aspects of sensory discrimination in mongolism. **American Journal of Mental Deficiency, 49**, 55-63

Henderson, S.E., Morris, J. and Frith, U. (1981). The motor deficit in Down's syndrome children: A problem of timing? **Journal of Child Psychology and Psychiatry, 22**, 233-245

Henry, F.M. and Rogers, E.E. (1960). Increased response latency for complicated movements and a "memory drum" theory of neuromotor reaction, **Research Quarterly, 31**, 448-458

Hogg, J. (1981). Learning, using and generalising manipulative skills in a preschool classrom by non-handicapped and Down's syndrome children. **Educational Psychology, 1**, 319-340

Hogg, J. (1982). Motor development and performance in severely mentally handicapped people. **Developmental Medicine and Child Neurology, 24**, 188-193

Hogg, J. and Moss, S.C. (1983). Prehensile development in Down's syndrome and non-handicapped preschool children. **British Journal of Developmental Psychology, 1**, (in press)

Holman, P. (1933). The relationship between general mental development and manual dexterity. **British Journal of Psychology, 23**, 279-283

Hoover, J.H., Wade, M.G., and Newell, K.M. (1981). Training moderately and severely retarded adults to improve reaction and movement times. **American Journal of Mental Deficiency, 85**, 389-395

Keele, S.W. and Summers, J.J. (1976). The structure of motor programs. In Stelmach, G.E. (ed.), **Motor Control: Issues and trends**, Academic Press, London, 109-142

Kelso, J.A. and Norman, P.E. (1978). Motor schema formation in children. **Developmental Psychology, 14**, 153-156

Klapp, S.T., Wyatt, E.P. and MacLingo, W. (1974). Response programming in simple and choice reactions. **Journal of Motor Behavior, 6**, 262-271

Molnar, G.E. (1978). Analysis of motor disorder in retarded infants and young children. **American Journal of Mental Deficiency, 83**, 213-222

Moss, S. and Hogg, J. (1981). The development of hand-function in mentally handicapped and non-handicapped preschool children. In Mittler, P. (ed.), **Frontiers of Knowledge in Mental Retardation**, University Park Press, Baltimore, 34-44

Moss, S. and Hogg J. (1983). The development and integration of fine motor sequences in 12-18 month old children: A test of the modular theory of motor skill acquisition. **Genetic Psychology Monographs, 107**, 145-187

Nettlebeck, T. and Brewer, N. (1976). Effects of stimulus-response variables on the choice reaction time of mildly retarded adults. **Americal Journal of Mental Deficiency, 81**, 85-92

O'Connor, N. and Hermelin, B. (1961). Visual and stereognostic shape recognition in normal children and mongol and non-mongol imbeciles. **Journal of Mental Deficiency Research, 5**, 63-66

Quigley, N. (1982). An experiment to investigate motor schemas in Down's syndrome children, Third year Psychology Dissertation, University of Manchester

Schmidt, R.A. (1976). The schema as a solution to some persistent problems in motor learning theory. In Stelmach, G.E. (ed.), **Motor Control: Issues and trends.** Academic Press, New York, 41-65

Shapiro, D.C. and Schmidt, R.A. (1982). The schema theory: Recent evidence and developmental implications. In Kelso, J.A.S. and Clark, J. E. (eds.) **The Development of Movement Control and Co-ordination**, Wiley, Chichester, 113-150

Stokes, T.F. and Baer, D.M. (1977). An implicit technology of generalization. **Journal of Applied Behavior Analysis, 10**, 349-367

Summers, J.J. (1975). The role of timing in motor program representation. **Journal of Motor Behavior, 7**, 299-241

Summers, J.J. (1981). Motor programs. In Holding, D.H. (ed.), **Human Skills**, Wiley, Chichester, 41-64

Tizard, J. and Loos, F.M. (1954). The learning of a spatial relations test by adult imbeciles. **American Journal of Mental Deficiency, 59**, 85-90

Wade, M.G., Hoover, J.H. and Newell, K.M. (1983). Training and trainability in motor skills performance of mentally retarded persons. In Hogg, J. and Mittler, P.J. (eds.), **Aspects of Competence in Mentally Handicapped People: Advances in Mental Handicap Research, 2**, Wiley, Chichester, (in press)

Wade, M.G., Newell, K.M. and Wallace, S.A. (1978). Decision time and movement time as a function of response complexity in retarded persons. **American Journal of Mental Deficiency, 83**, 135-144

Wallace, S.A., Newell, K.M. and Wade, M.G. (1978). Decision and response times as a function of movement difficulty in preschool children. **Child Development, 49**, 509-512

COMMENTARY

I. Janota

There are several types of Down's syndrome. Down's syndrome cases perhaps ought not to be equated with mentally retarded cases in general. This is not only because of the distinct morphological features of the brain; because of the "functional" implications of such features they may respond to the various strategies that aim at a modification of various functions (motor, behavioural, and so on) in a way different from at least some other mentally retarded subjects. I think of Down's cases without any complicating lesions, for example such that arise as a result of vascular disturbances (infarcts), premature ageing (Alzheimer's tangles and plaques and reasonable amyloidosis), or epilepsy (hippocampal and cerebellar scarring).

So, in Down's syndrome there is usually, inside a smaller than normal head, a smaller than normal brain with smaller than normal frontal and temporal regions and a cerebellum smaller out of proportion to the total bulk of the brain. It is not my purpose here to go into details of the differences between the brain in Down's syndrome and the normal brain. The anatomical differences could well be studied afresh because more sense may emerge nowadays than in the past in relating them to function. The implications extend beyond the modern strategies of treatment in Down's to treatment of some of the other mentally retarded subjects.

N. O'Connor

Hogg has given a good comprehensive survey of a difficult field. He has drawn attention to the two basic initial theories of motor co-ordination, feedback monitored movements and motor programming. Further, he has drawn attention to the association of lack of motor skills and cerebellar deficiency in Down's syndrome and indicated the influence of earlier findings such as those of Berkson, Clarke, Cowie, O'Connor and Hermelin, and Tizard and Loos. Quite importantly, he has described R.A. Schmidt's schema theory and offered it as an explanation of the way in which motor control is acquired. I think his suggestion from his own work that movements become more varied with age in developing children is a convincing confirmation of this approach (Moss and Hogg). It has been a repeated finding in the literature that varied training is more efficient than stereotyped and narrowed learning of skills.

I think also that Hogg has referred to two useful studies from recent English work, namely those of Anwar and of Frith and Frith. All these points seem to me to be good. However, I have the task of finding fault as well as offering praise and I should also make some suggestions about new directions for research. Let me begin with critical observations. I can start by pointing out that Anwar, who works with me, had something rather interesting to say in addition to what Hogg reports. One of the key points she makes concerns intersensory integration. Essentially she points out that if subnormal subjects, especially Down's syndrome subjects, are presented with one set of stimuli to direct their motor output, they can achieve a fair degree of accuracy. When, however, additional cues from another modality are added their accuracy declines. Thus being able to feel a target when they point at it helps accuracy, seeing it in addition can reduce precision. A possible reason for this state of affairs is that subnormal people cannot always cope with the co-ordination of the additional load. Their capacity to analyse complex relationships is limited.

This material might suggest a counter-argument to the schema theory, or at least indicate that programmes or schemata are not encapsulated and unalterable motor patterns as they would be in the frog for example. Some of our behaviours are indeed automatic like the frog's tongue striking at the short horizontal yellow strip, or worm, but many of them can be modified while in progress, like drinking a cup of coffee on the Oxford train. It is the latter kind that suffer in the subnormal if multisensory input is involved.

I am led to make one general observation about Hogg's paper. It said some important things. It also, it seems to me, avoided saying at least one important thing. If, as the chapter says, programmes or schemata are vital for motor skills, should we not be speculating about the basis for the poor development of skills in the subnormal and if we do this, might we not reasonably draw on some hints from neuropsychology. I have frequently denied the possibility of demonstrating a structure-function association in subnormality because cortical pathology is so extensive in the severely subnormal and on the other hand often absent in the mildly subnormal. However, where gross deficiencies of motor skill are detectable, may we not reasonably look not only to the cerebellum, which Hogg discusses, but perhaps also as schemata are implicated, to the frontal lobes.

I would like to leave this comment, provocatively, at this point.

H. F. R. Prechtl

Hogg refers in his esssay to "mentally retarded individuals not exhibiting obvious neurological damage or abnormalities". This calls for some comments. Apparently what is meant here is the absence of classical neurological syndromes such as spastic paresis, ataxia or other kinds of cerebral palsy. By no means are neurological functions in severely mentally retarded individuals normal nor is their handicap restricted to "developmental delays in fine and gross motor development and lack of competence in motor skill". As soon as attention is diverted away from the pass or fail of particular milestones in motor development and more to the quality of performances and their neural correlates, a different picture appears. Posture and postural control seem frequently to be deficient in mentally handicapped persons. That motor performances such as the attempt to stand on one leg have a clumsy appearance may be due to a deficiency of anticipatory postural preparations. Examples of such preparations are a lateral shift of the pelvis and a stabilization of the vertebral column by the long spinal muscles, well before the flexor muscles of the leg to be elevated are contracting. Such deficiencies will have far reaching consequences in voluntary motor behaviour and in many kinds of skilled movements. Although these may not be recognized as neurological abnormalities by traditional examiners, they are nevertheless dysfunctions of the central nervous system.

The second point which I would like to mention is the schema concept of Schmidt which plays a central role in Hogg's theorizing. In a recent publication by Shapiro and Schmidt (1982) queries are summarized concerning the schema theory, and some aspects of the theory were refuted.

I will limit myself to two problems with regard to this theory. Neurophysiological studies on trained monkeys have shown that the initial conditions, sensed by proprioception, are not essential for the performance of a simple skilled movement. The conclusion of the above mentioned authors is: "The schema theory relies heavily on the idea of generalized motor programs and impulse-timing mechanisms, and evidence that such ideas might be incorrect will probably require some modifications in the theory" (p. 139). The other point is the distinction of recall schema and recognition schema on which it is concluded that "There seems to be a serious lack of evidence on the question of motor recall versus recognition memory... We can only conclude that more thinking and research on this issue should be done before any definitive conclusions can be made" (p. 132).

In summary, it would be useful if Hogg's paper could include some reference to neural dysfunctions in the mentally handicapped and to more recent re-evaluations of Schmidt's theory.

Reference

Shapiro, D.C. and Schmidt, R.A. (1982). The schema theory: Recent evidence and developmental implications. In: **The Development of Movement Control and Co-ordination**, Kelso, J.A.S. and Clark, J.E. (eds), John Wiley, Chichester, 113-150

D. M. Ricks

I would like in congratulating Hogg on his paper to report my clinical experiences in eliciting simple motor acts in profoundly retarded children and wondered to what extent his interpretations applied. The team with whom I work have had referred to us a succession of children aged 3-5 years, motor intact, apathetic, low-toned, but so profoundly retarded that they do not stand up. Our aim was to elicit weight bearing, assuming this would become progressively difficult, compelling parents to carry them, as they grew older and heavier. All the children had been energetically stimulated to stand by the parents and various staff involved with them. Eventually we found that a simple sequence of movements equipped their children to stand with minimal prompting: a sequence which emerged as a result of much trial and error in our handling - it was not self-evident. Briefly this consisted of securing in the sitting child a plantigrade stance with feet shoulder-width apart, then flexing the knees, moving the hips forward, and lifting, then leading to the child promptly extending hips and knees to stand up. Neither the child's hands nor trunk were held. The simple sequence led to a postural adjustment which resulted in standing. The problem then was that the child stood with locked knees, relaxed thigh extensions and hence could not sit down. Sitting could be elicited by flexing his neck. Thus, facilitating a simple set of motor acts enabled the children to succeed in acquiring a simple motor skill. The point of interest is that the skill was effective and reliable, though "unnatural", and seemed independent of experience or stimulation and was presumably organized at a simple, possibly spinal, level. It gives the impression of a sequence of muscle recruitment programmes at subcortical level available to the child and usually set in motion by "intent", but in these children simply elicited and established with little practice.

J. Hogg

Comment on Ricks' discussion point

Schmidt's motor schema theory is essentially concerned with the refinement of general motor programme rather than their initial acquisition and Ricks' interesting observation really requires some alternative explanation. Importantly, however, he does draw attention to the role of prompting in the acquisition of trained motor skills. From a theoretical point of view the way in which prompting is effective in training has received little attention. Some studies undertaken within the framework of schema theory have shown that when subjects have experienced passive movement, i.e. been prompted through an action, this generalized to their active execution of the action. Since experience of passive movement must be regarded as providing a recognition memory benefit, and active performance of the rapid movement involved is thought to involve recall memory, this finding argues against the independence of the recognition and recall schemata. It does suggest, however, that prompting may lead to the refinement of motor skills by developing the recognition schema. If it could be assumed that Ricks' children had the basic repertoire of individual movements he describes, then perhaps his procedure simply refined existing general motor programmes through prompting and chained them in an adaptive organized sequence.

R. O. Robinson

This is an interesting account of the development of theories concerning the organization of motor behaviour. It is spiced with illustrative empirical results. That a relatively young subject appears to be strong on theory and short on facts is perhaps inevitable, but the clinician cannot help wondering if the latter deficiency cannot in part be redressed by recourse to the clinical neurophysiologist's understanding of the organization of movement. Certain aspects of this bear particularly on points raised in this paper.

1. The role of sensory feedback in the control of movement

Sacchadic eye movements appear to be ballistic. The direction and extent of movement are gauged and the force necessary to move the eye through that distance is applied in the way a bullet is fired from a gun. The eye comes to rest in its new orientation slowed by the mechanical resistance offered by the intraorbital structures in which it rests - not because of feedback received during the eye movement. With this singular exception, the evidence for importance of sensory feedback is overwhelming. Learnt movements in the monkey can be carried through if a limb is deafferented, but slowly and clumsily. I am not aware that any attempt has been made to teach new skills in the deafferented limb. The adequacy of sensory feedback in Down's syndrome has been questioned. Has the effect of augmentation of feedback by the use of, for example, devices employing visco-static dampers or biofeedback techniques been studied? The timing of sensory feedback may be crucial for ordered sequential movements. This can be studied using somato-sensory evoked potentials. The whole loop including reception of sensory stimuli and correction by further motor adjustment can be quantified using cutaneous reflex responses (Jenner and Stevens, 1979). Application of these relatively new techniques, which provide some access to central processing, to the mentally handicapped with motor dysfunction would be of considerable interest.

The role of sensory motor integration is crucial for another reason. Messages descending the motor pathways pass not only to the muscles involved but also to the cerebellum. This allows a correct interpretation of the sensory information caused by the movement. Thus, if the eye is pushed by a finger external objects appear to move in space. The sensory integration which occurs when the eye is moved by the extra-ocular muscles permits an allowance to be made for this so the external world and the subject's relation to it remains stable.

2. The role of abnormal tone and postural settings

Many of the empirical results quoted appear to involve hand function. This, however, relies on successful integration of several other deeper layers of basic motor organization. Thus an axial base must be secured, probably originating in the cerebellar vermis descending vestibulo-spinal tracts which subserve postural reflexes provide a platform for the probably cortico-spinal tract mediated closely specified hand function. A generalized hypotonia is a distinctive feature of Down's syndrome and may well contribute to the disproportionately poor motor performance in these individuals. It would be interesting to know for example whether secure postural provision and fixation of proximal joints improved hand function either previously learnt or in the process of acquisition.

3. The effect of cross modal sensory integration

Again much of the work given appears to study tasks involving eye-hand coordination. Certain individuals with cerebral palsy appear to be confused by incoming visual information and point more accurately or walk across an uneven surface more stably with the eyes closed. Cross modal integration is accomplished in the parietal lobe. This may be of particular interest as it is thought that motor engrams are stored in the area of the left supramarginal gyrus being then projected to the premotor cortex. Disorganization of parietal structures may thus affect accomplished movements in a variety of ways and would bear close examination.

4. The role of learning processes in general

Certain motor skills are innate and do not depend on experience. This applies even to such complicated accomplishments as independent walking. Infants in Albania used to be swaddled tightly until they were a year old. They acquired walking at the same time as children who had gone through the usual sequence of sitting up and crawling. Innate skills presumably depend upon the timing of relevant structural developments - possibly myelination, possibly dendritic arborization. In order therefore to separate the effects of delayed maturation of the nervous system from defects in the end point of its organization, it may be useful to compare innate skills with those acquired through learning.

Although much has been learnt from the intensive study of primate motor function in the past few years, we know as yet too little about the learning and practice of sequenced voluntary movement. I would suggest that a closer collaboration between the neurologist, clinical neurophysiologist and experimental psychologist would be the best way to improve our understanding in this area.

Reference

Jenner, J.R. and Stevens, J.A. (1979). Evidence for transcortical reflex response in man. **Journal of Physiology, 293**, 39-40

J. B. P. Stephenson

The relationship of the cerebellum to the motor or mental functions of severely handicapped people is not well understood. To the neurologist, the motor difficulties of Down's children do not resemble those experienced by those with congenital cerebellar hypoplasia, despite the small size of the Down's cerebellum. I am more impressed by the common observation of cognitive impairment in those non-Down's patients with cerebellar hypoplasia, as those in the disequilibrum syndrome (Hagberg *et al*., 1972).

Further, in the "dancing eyes syndrome" or acute cerebellar encephalopathy of infants or young children, whether or not secondary to extra-cerebral occult neuroblastoma, cognitive impairment is common in follow-up (Stephenson, 1979). Such findings suggest a role of the cerebellum in cognitive development (Stephenson, 1979), despite isolated reports of normality in cerebellar aplasia.

References

Hagberg, B., Sanner, G.M. and Steen, M. (1972). The disequilibrium syndrome in cerebral palsy. **Acta Paediatrica Scandinavica**, Suppl. 226

Stephenson, J.B.P. (1979). Cerebellar disorders. In Rose, F.C. (ed), **Paediatric Neurology**, Blackwell Scientific, Oxford, pp. 206-224

SECTION IV

RESEARCH INTO PSYCHOSOCIAL AND SERVICE ASPECTS

Chapter 20

Family processes and parent involvement

Janet Carr

During the mid-1900s interest in the families of the mentally handicapped increased from "a trickle of armchair papers (to) almost a flood" (Wolfensberger, 1967) with most of the discussion on parent dynamics. By the 1970s the major studies focused on the handicapped child's effect on the family while the first studies demonstrating parents' capacities for helping their own children had begun to appear (Carr, 1974). In the ensuing decade the emphasis has shifted firmly towards these self-help programmes while studies of family functioning and of the effects of changing services have also been prominent.

THE EFFECT ON THE FAMILY

Telling the Parents

Recent reports of how parents were told of their child's handicap reiterate the major findings from previous studies - parents want to be told early, honestly and sympathetically (Carr, 1970). Most studies have been done on parents of children with Down's syndrome and the trend for more parents to be told early has continued: 52% (Reynolds, 1979), 70% (Springer and Steele, 1980) and 84% (Berry et al., 1981) were told within the first two weeks compared with figures from earlier studies of 28% (Drillien and Wilkinson, 1964) and 41% (Carr, 1970). About half the parents in three studies (Gath, 1978; Pueschel and Murphy, 1976; Reynolds, 1979) were dissatisfied with the way they were told, the most common complaint being that they should have been told sooner. Other complaints were that the news was broken by a complete stranger (a paediatrician); that they were given an unnecessarily gloomy prognosis (of a Down's syndrome child) "she will not walk until 3, may not talk until 5, if at all" (Berry et al., 1981); and that they were not told the truth (Lonsdale, 1978). These concerns again are similar to those voiced in earlier studies.

Family Stress

While recognizing that there are undoubtedly families who suffer from the strain of caring for a handicapped child, current research suggests that most are not seriously impaired and cope well with the problems they meet (Cleveland and Miller, 1977; Dunlap and Hollinsworth, 1977; Gath, 1978). Reynolds (1979) points out that "This impression is perhaps contrary to that which is gained by clinicians working in the field" and feels this may be due to the tendency for these workers to see those families who cannot manage well while "the coping family generally does not attract attention" - a point made previously (Carr, 1976). Dupont (1980) however studied a population sample of 39 severely mentally retarded children and found that the families spend an average of over seven hours a day in the care and training of the children (though no control data are available). Several studies have investigated the child's effect on the marital relationship. Nihira _et al_. (1980) found families more likely to report feeling affected by the mentally handicapped child where there was marital disharmony, but it is not possible to determine which was cause and which effect. Where parents volunteered their views just over half indicated adverse effects on the marriage (Dunlap and Hollinsworth, 1977; Lloyd-Bostock, 1976; Lonsdale, 1978). Other workers have studied groups of parents with or without a handicapped child and have found indices of marital satisfaction to be lower where the child is handicapped (Friedrich and Friedrich, 1981) or have found no significant differences (Waisbren, 1980). Children in the latter study were all under 18 months and it may be that more harmful effects are seen with an older child. Gath (1978) found in families of two-and-a-half year olds that the marriage was more likely to be rated as poor where there was a Down's syndrome than a normal baby but equal numbers of marriages were rated as good. Holroyd and McArthur (1976) found that mothers of Down's syndrome children reported fewer problems than did those of autistic children (which will surprise no one familiar with these two groups) and were no more stressed than were mothers of "controls" - children attending a psychiatric clinic. In a study by Ferguson and Watt (1980) mothers of handicapped children reported more family problems than did those of normal children but mothers' scores on the Malaise Inventory (Rutter _et al_., 1970) showed no significant differences. Further, neither problems nor Malaise scores were related "in any straightforward way" to the degree of the child's handicap. This finding, which overthrows common-sense expectations that greater stress will be experienced by mothers of more severely handicapped children, reflects those from studies of mothers of physically handicapped children (Bradshaw, 1980; Carr _et al_., 1983; Dorner, 1975).

Fathers, a hitherto somewhat neglected group, have received attention recently. Waisbren (1980) found that fathers who felt their own parents supportive did more with the child and had more positive feelings about him although they also listed more symptoms of stress. Studies of the effect of the child on the father's career found only a minority of fathers - 6% to 9% - who felt their careers had been affected (Dunlap and Hollinsworth, 1977; Lloyd-Bostock, 1976). Such restrictions as were reported came mainly from middle class parents and as a result of a wish to stay near a particular school. These findings, of a minimal effect on the father's career, are again supported by evidence from families of physically handicapped children, upward social mobility being seen as frequently in families of spina bifida children as in the general population (Carr et al., 1983).

The Effect on Brothers and Sisters

Several workers have looked at the effect of a mentally handicapped child on his siblings. Gath (1973) found a small (10%) increase in deviance reported by parents and teachers of siblings of Down's syndrome children compared with those of controls, but in a later study found no evidence of any significant difference between siblings of Down's syndrome and control babies (Gath, 1978). Parents have reported little effect on their other children (Dunlap and Hollinsworth, 1977; Lloyd-Bostock, 1976; Lonsdale, 1978) who in the main were said to love and accept the handicapped child. Similarly in an interview study of the siblings themselves the majority said they felt unembarrassed and not unduly restricted by, and accepting and affectionate towards, the handicapped child (Hart and Walters, 1979a).

Other studies have revealed evidence of effects on the siblings, much of it conflicting and suggesting complex relationships between factors such as age and gender of child and sibling, social class, birth order and family size. Studies which have found more adverse effects on younger siblings are discussed by Simeonsson and McHale (1981) with the explanation that these children are supplanted in their role by the slower-developing handicapped child. However other studies have found older siblings, especially older and eldest sisters, to be more adversely affected (Cleveland and Miller, 1977; Gath, 1974) and it is suggested that this may be due to demands put on them to care for the child, especially in large and lower class families.

Counselling groups, which anecdotally seem to have been successful, have been run for siblings (Chinitz, 1981; Ellington, 1982; Hart and Walters, 1979b). Participants in these groups were eager to help and teach the handicapped child and a number of projects have set out to enable siblings to do so more effectively (Miller and Cantwell, 1976; Weinrott, 1974). Siblings proved adept at learning and applying behavioural principles but one major benefit seen was improvement in the sibling's own behaviour, especially where there was some concordance between problems in the retarded and non-retarded siblings (an effect also seen with normal siblings: Lavigeur, 1976). It may be that problem behaviours in mildly or moderately retarded children might be tackled by asking them to modify similar (possibly enacted) behaviours in siblings.

SUPPORT FOR FAMILIES

Counselling and Family Therapy

The volume of literature on parent counselling has declined over the years although the topic is still seen as important by professionals (Drotar et al., 1975) and by parents (Marks, 1980). A relatively recent development is that of family therapy for families of mentally handicapped children, which aims to increase acceptance of the child, identify family roles, give practice to the family in relating to the child's problems, etc. (Turner, 1980). Typically the whole family, including the deviant member, is involved in therapy sessions and it is suggested that the mentally handicapped child should participate through the use of drawing, music, clay modelling and so on in place of verbal communication (Gomersall, 1981). It remains difficult to imagine how the profoundly handicapped could be expected genuinely to participate except as a focus for discussion. Black (1982) advocates family therapy at times of crisis and gives examples of successful interventions, some of which combine family therapy with behavioural methods, resulting in a highly appropriate model of help for parents who wish for this type of approach.

Experience of Services

Studies of the services parents require have found parents dissatisfied with the facilities available (Lloyd-Bostock, 1976; Upshur, 1982), especially older parents (Suelzle and Keenan, 1981) or unaware that services they needed did in fact exist (Goddard and Rubissow, 1977). Dunlap and Hollinsworth (1977) found a low level of services (though a remarkably low level also of family stress) in a poor, rural area of Alabama. Families in ethnic minority groups showed a higher percentage of families who had had no help from or knowledge of state resources than did white American families (Justice et al., 1971).

Two studies have investigated the effectiveness of services in easing the parents' burden, with unexpectedly negative results. Wing (1971) reviewing the expanded provision of services in Camberwell, found no corresponding reduction in the demand for residential places. Waisbren (1980) studied families with a retarded or a normal infant living in California and similar families living in Denmark. Despite the markedly higher level of services in Denmark (Schou, 1977) the strain on families of the retarded children appeared similar in the two countries, as was their use of services which in any case did not figure prominently in parents' reports. It is suggested that parents do not always know of services available, and that they accept and tend to take for granted those that exist.

On the other hand a service designed especially to meet the needs of parents, which offers a continuously available emergency service plus short- or long-term care as required and home or hospital based treatment and advice, together with other "well developed educational and social service facilities", has resulted in a very much reduced demand for institutional care for mentally handicapped children - 2.3 per thousand, compared with 9 per thousand for England and Wales (Brimblecombe, 1979). This form of service based on a searching exploration of parents' unmet needs and inviting the parents themselves to choose the help they want, and when they want it, seems to offer a near-ideal source of support.

Alternative Care

Whereas the earlier literature was often concerned with reasons for and effects of admission to an institution, more attention is paid now to questions surrounding alternatives to institutionalization. In a thoughtful review of the literature on community living Landesman-Dwyer (1981) concludes that no one pattern of care has been shown to be appropriate for all mentally handicapped people; that the belief that "smaller is better" is not invariably correct; and that higher staffing ratios do not necessarily result in a higher quality of care. In earlier studies breakdown in community placement was often attributed to client characteristics such as aggressiveness, but more recently factors relating to the community environment and the need to match persons and placements individually have been emphasized.

Willer *et al*. (1981) interviewed families whose retarded relative had been discharged two years previously. Almost half had experienced guilt or anxiety which were more likely to have been resolved if the person had returned home rather than to other community placements. Anxiety was related to the retarded person's future, which had been seen as secure while she/he was in the institution but less so in the community. Meyer (1980) found that over 80% of families questioned felt that, whatever alternative living arrangements were possible, they would prefer their retarded relative to remain in the institution where she/he now was, mainly because of the kind and amount of care they felt the institution afforded. However attitudes may change as a result of experience. Two-thirds of families whose adult child was moved from an institution to a community placement were unhappy about it whereas a year later only 8% responded in a similar way (Landesman-Dwyer, 1981); while hostility expressed by local residents before the opening of a hostel for mentally handicapped adults had virtually disappeared three years later (Locker *et al*., 1981). It seems that more favourable attitudes came about in each case because the dire consequences envisaged as a result of the proposed changes had not materialized.

Family foster care, both on a permanent basis and for short-term relief, has become increasingly important (Bromley and Lister, 1980; Macaskill, 1981) and has led to attempts to identify the factors which predict successful (i.e., non-terminated) fostering. Some foster-parent characteristics, such as sex, education and marital status, have been shown to be poor discriminators (Sternlicht, 1978) but older foster parents have been found to be more successful than younger (Sanderson and Crawley, 1982). Fostering, like other forms of alternative care, has potential drawbacks and foster parents must be carefully selected, trained and supported if placements are to be successful and to the advantage of the mentally handicapped person (Gilbert, 1980).

PARENTAL INVOLVEMENT

One of the major developments in mental handicap has concerned the inclusion of parents in the teaching and training of their children. Some workers have aimed at increasing the rate of developmental progress of the children through the teaching of their mothers. In a number of studies mothers attended a centre for training (Connolly *et al.*; 1980, Ludlow and Allen, 1979; Piper and Pless, 1980), in others they were visited and trained at home (Brassell, 1977; Cunningham *et al.*, 1982; Hanson and Schwarz, 1978; Sandow *et al.*, 1981) while in one study parents received group training (Bidder *et al.*, 1975). In each case mothers worked daily with their children on developmental objectives, putting into practice the methods they had learnt, while progress was assessed at intervals and, usually, compared with that of a similar, non-trained group of children. The methodological problems of these studies have been reviewed elsewhere (Carr, 1982), the most important being those concerned with outcome measures, comparison groups, experimenter bias and lack of long-term follow-up. Nevertheless all but one (Piper and Pless, 1980) showed at least short-term advantages for the experimental children; the accumulation of this evidence, methodological problems notwithstanding, carries weight. The question remains as to whether the effects of this early training are perceptible in later life, and, if not, whether it is still worth while for the benefits conferred in childhood.

In other studies the aim was to enable mothers to teach a variety of skills (self-care, play, language, etc.) and to manage or eliminate behaviour problems in their children. Mothers were visited individually at home, therapists discussed objectives and demonstrated methods, and the mothers were asked to carry out training sessions with their children and to keep records of progress until the therapist's next visit (Burden, 1978; Howlin *et al.*, 1973). In a review of the effectiveness of a home-visiting service the parents' success was found not to be affected by social class; behavioural problems were better dealt with where marital relationships were satisfactory and the family a small one; learning skills were more successfully taught to brighter children (IQ 36 to 51) but IQ did not affect success with behaviour problems; parents receiving more home visits were more successful than those visited less (Callias and Carr, 1975).

A subgroup of studies deals with the implementation of the Portage model (Shearer and Shearer, 1972), a highly structured and systematized approach to parent teaching making use of developmental check lists, curriculum cards and activity charts on which parents record the results of their teaching. This approach has been successfully used with nurses (Revill and Blunden, 1979), health visitors (Holland, 1981) and a variety of workers (Cameron, 1979) functioning as the home advisers. The reservation is sometimes expressed that the teaching of the minimal self-help and educational skills contained in the check lists may not always fulfill the parents' most pressing needs. In some cases home advisers have also offered advice on behaviour difficulties and on other family and service problems (Cameron, 1979) and this dual approach seems to have considerable potential for helping on an individual basis.

Following the pioneering work of Cunningham and Jeffree (1971) others have worked with groups of parents who met regularly for talks and discussion on general topics and also on the needs and problems of their own children (Holland and Hattersley, 1980; Jeffree _et al._, 1977; McCall and Thacker, 1977). Typically, the parents were helped to assess their children and taught principles and/or techniques of behaviour modification and between meetings worked on specific objectives with their children and reported progress at the next meeting. Some groups had sessions also given over to talks by other professionals (Attwood, 1977) while contact between the parents themselves has been seen as an advantage of the group approach (Harris, 1978).

An important question concerns the extent to which parents can maintain and extend the changes they have brought about in their children once training sessions are ended. Doleys _et al._ (1976) at 30-week follow-up found parents' teaching skills significantly above baseline though somewhat lower than immediate post-training levels. Baker _et al._ (1980) report a follow-up of four groups of mothers trained by different methods, all of whom had done significantly better than a control group. Fourteen months later initial gains, in both mothers and children, were maintained and 86% of mothers reported the continuation of "some scorable teaching efforts", but most of this was incidental teaching rather than carried out in regular sessions. Less than a quarter of the parents had embarked on teaching a new skill (16%) or had tackled new behaviour problems (22%). The authors conclude that parent trainers might encourage formal teaching at first but then shift to incidental teaching as this was more likely to endure.

The Stress of Parental Involvement

It has become apparent that some services intended to help have themselves brought stress to families. This may come about because of the number of interventionists involved - "There are frequently five or more professionals in daily contact" (Lacoste,

1978) involving the mother as "therapist, teacher, trainer or, at the least, transporter" (Doernberg, 1978), so that she has her work cut out to keep up with the child's treatment, let alone function as wife, mother to her other children or as a human being in her own right. "If she even considers some time for herself she suffers such guilt that it is not worth it to her" (Doernberg, 1978). The result may be to damage the whole family (Zigler, 1981) and Doernberg questions "whether a small improvement in the child is worthwhile in terms of its cost to the family".

These alarms by professionals are echoed by parents' comments that they felt looked down on by professionals (Berry et al., 1981) who undervalued parents' achievements - "They always tell us how well we are doing but then go on to say, but if you do this it will be more helpful" (Black, 1978) - and rushed them on: "No sooner is one skill mastered than another skill is presented (clouding) the simple sweetness of success" (Fulwood, 1981). A report from a conference describes a family who moved from a well served area to one where little help was available: "Their first reaction was one of relief at being free of all the professionals who had been overwhelming them" (Health and Social Services Journal, 1982).

These complaints seem to be voiced by a minority of parents and the majority welcome the help which enables them to help their own children (Baker et al., 1980; Holland, 1981). Interventionists however should keep alert to the potentially stressful effects of their efforts and aim, always, at the benefit of the whole family as the ultimate goal.

CONCLUSIONS

Respect for parents has increased over the last decade. No longer are they seen as anxious, guilt-ridden, rejecting and over-protective of their handicapped children but as resilient people who have real problems. The view that when they learn of their child's condition they displace their distress in the form of anger against the teller has been challenged, pointing out that at least some angry parents may have had something to be angry about. It must be questioned now whether any further studies are needed to show that parents are shocked to learn that their child is handicapped, suffer sadness, and later adjust. Following welcome evidence of a shift to earlier telling, more useful research could aim at showing in what other ways parents could best be helped at this time. For example reassurance might be given regarding parents' fears that the child may harm their other children, although parents may also need to be aware of the need not to overburden older children, especially girls. No research yet has looked at whether having these older children reduces the burden for the parents; it may be that here there is a real conflict of needs.

The pattern of services for parents has been changing, with a move away from custodial to educational efforts and from institutional to community care. Cynics point out that the latter coincides with the worsening of the economic climate and ask why, if it was so much better, was this not noticed before financial stringency made it attractive. The need now is to examine yet more closely the kind of provision that best serves widely differing handicapped people, at different times in their lives, and their parents. Parallel is the need to make sure that parents know about and are offered the services they need, and this will require close liaison between the various disciplines. Professionals too may need to be more out-going in approaching parents, who too often feel that the effort is all on their side and that the help available, rather than being offered, has to be battled for.

Parents have now in many instances become partners with professionals, working along the same lines and towards the same objectives. As Mittler (1979) says, "Professionals have all become a little intoxicated" by this, and refer to parents as "the only true experts" and "the best resource we have". In some cases this has gone too far and some parents have felt pressured. To quote Mittler again: "We must allow them to choose not to be involved at the level of detailed collaboration that some professionals are now demanding."

With that caution in mind we may yet acknowledge that many parents welcome the opportunity to help their children and the teaching that enables them to do so. Much progress has been made over the last decade; in the next we should look still more urgently for methods by which parents can be more effectively helped to help their children in whatever way they wish.

REFERENCES

Attwood, T. (1977). The Priory parents' workshop. **Child: Care, Health and Development, 3**, 81-91

Baker, B.L., Heifetz, L.J. and Murphy, D.M. (1980). Behavioral training for parents of mentally retarded children: one-year follow-up. **American Journal of Mental Deficiency, 85**, 31-38

Berry, P., Gunn, P., Andrews, R. and Price, C. (1981). Characteristics of Down syndrome infants and their families. **Australian Paediatric Journal, 17**, 40-43

Bidder, R.T., Bryant, G. and Gray, O.P. (1975). Benefits to Down's Syndrome children through training their mothers. **Archives of Disease in Childhood, 50**, 383-386

Black, D. (1982). Handicap and family therapy. In: Bentovim, A., Gorell Barnes, G. and Cooklin, A. (eds.). **Family Therapy. Complementary Framework of Theory and Practice**. London. Academic Press.

Black, J.M.M., (1978). Families with handicapped children - who helps whom and how? **Child: Care, Health and Development, 4**, 239-245

Bradshaw, J. (1980). **The Family Fund**. Routledge and Kegan Paul, London

Brassell, W.R. (1977). Intervention with handicapped infants: correlates of progress. **Mental Retardation, 15,** 18-22

Brimblecombe, F.S.W. (1979). A new approach to the care of handicapped children. **Journal of the Royal College of Physicians of London, 13,** 231-236

Bromley, D. and Lister, P. (1980). Relief families. **Adoption and Fostering, 4,** 43-5

Burden, R.L. (1978). An approach to the evaluation of early intervention projects with mothers of severely handicapped children; the attitude dimension. **Child: Care, Health and Development, 4,** 171-181

Callias, M. and Carr, J. (1975). Behaviour modification programmes in a community setting. In Kiernan, C.C. and Woodford, F.P. (Eds.) **Behaviour Modification with the Severely Retarded.** Associated Scientific Publishers, Amsterdam. 147-171

Cameron, R.J. (1979). A lot can happen at home too. **Remedial Education. 14,** (4), 173-178

Carr, J. (1970). Mongolism: telling the parents. **Developmental Medicine and Child Neurology, 12,** 213-221

Carr, J. (1974). The effect of the severely subnormal on their families. In Clarke, A.M. and Clarke, A.D.B. (eds.), **Mental Deficiency - the Changing Outlook.** Methuen, London. 807-839

Carr, J. (1976). Effect on the family of a child with Down's syndrome. **Physiotherapy, 62,** 20-24

Carr, J. (1982). The methodology of early intervention studies in severe mental handicap. Paper given at the 13th International Study Group on Child Neurology and Cerebral Palsy. Oxford

Carr, J., Pearson, A.M. and Halliwell, M.D. (1983). **The GLC Spina Bifida Survey: 11 and 12 years follow-up.** Final report. DES.

Chinitz, S.P. (1981). A sibling group for brothers and sisters of handicapped children. **Children Today,** Nov-Dec, 21-23

Cleveland, D.W. and Miller, N. (1977). Attitudes and life commitments of older sibs of mentally retarded adults: an exploratory study. **Mental Retardation, 15**(3), 38-41

Connolly, B., Morgan, S., Russell, F.F. and Richardson, B. (1980). Early intervention with Down's Syndrome children. Follow-up report. **Physical Therapy, 60,** 1405-8

Cunningham, C.C., Aumonier, M.E. and Sloper, P. (1982). Health visitor support for families with Down's Syndrome infants. **Child: Care, Health and Development, 8,** 1-9

Cunningham, C. and Jeffree, D.M. (1971). **Working with Parents: Developing a Workshop Course for Parents of Young Mentally Handicapped Children.** Manchester: National Society for Mentally Handicapped Children, NW Region

Doernberg, N.L. (1978). Some negative effects on family integration of health and education services. **Rehabilitation Literature, 39,** 107-110

Doleys, D.M., Doster, J. and Cartelli, L.M. (1976). Parent training techniques: effects of lecture-role playing followed by feedback and self-recording. **Behaviour Therapy and Experimental Psychiatry, 7**, 359-362

Dorner, S. (1975). The relationship of physical handicap to stress in families with an adolescent with Spina Bifida. **Developmental Medicine and Child Neurology, 17**, 765-776

Drillien, C.M. and Wilkinson, E.M. (1964). Mongolism: When should parents be told. **British Medical Journal, 2**, 1306-7

Drotar, D., Baskiewicz, A., Irvin, N., Kennell, J. and Klaus, M. (1975). The adaptation of parents to the birth of an infant with a congenital malformation: a hypothetical model. **Pediatrics, 56**, 710-717

Dunlap, W.R. and Hollinsworth, J.S. (1977). How does a handicapped child affect the family? Implications for practitioners. **The Family Co-ordinator, 26**, 286-293

Dupont, A. (1980). A study concerning the time-related and other burdens when severely handicapped children are reared at home. **Acta Psychiatrica Scandinavia**, Supplement 285, **62**, 249-257

Ellington, S. (1982). Children in the shadows. Working with siblings of handicapped children. Paper presented to the 13th International Study Group on Child Neurology and Cerebral Palsy, St Edmund Hall, Oxford

Ferguson, N. and Watt, J. (1980). The mothers of children with special educational needs. **Scottish Educational Review, 12**, 21-31

Friedrich, W.N. and Friedrich, W.L. (1981). Psychosocial assets of parents of handicapped and non-handicapped children. **American Journal of Mental Deficiency, 85**, 551-553

Fulwood, D. (1981). Mum or Supermum? **Australian Citizen Limited**, Aug. 24, 1-7

Gath, A. (1973). The school age siblings of mongol children. **British Journal of Psychiatry, 123**, 161

Gath, A. (1974). Sibling reactions to mental handicap: a comparison of the brothers and sisters of mongol children. **Journal of Child Psychology and Psychiatry, 15**, 187-198

Gath, A. (1978). **Down's Syndrome and the Family: The early years.** Academic Press, London

Gilbert, P. (1980). Fostering and mental handicap. **Adoption and Fostering, 4**, 3-6

Goddard, J. and Rubissow, J. (1977). Meeting the needs of handicapped children and their families. The evolution of Honeylands: a family support unit, Exeter. **Child: Care, Health and Development. 3**, 261-273

Gomersall, J.D. (1981). Family psychotherapy and mental handicap. Paper presented at pre-conference workshop: Combined Asian and Regional Commonwealth Congress on the Scientific Study of Mental Deficiency, Bromley

Hanson, M.J. and Schwarz, H. (1978). Longitudinal intervention program for Down's Syndrome infants. **Education and Training of the Mentally Retarded, 13**, 403-407

Harris, J. (1978). Working with parents of mentally handicapped children on a long-term basis. **Child: Care, Health and Development, 4**, 121-128

Hart, D. and Walters, J. (1979a). Brothers and sisters of mentally handicapped children. Unpublished manuscript

Hart, D. and Walters, J. (1979b). A group work project with siblings of mentally handicapped children. Unpublished manuscript

Health and Social Services Journal (1982). Reports and Papers, Jan. 7th, 35

Holland, J. (1981). The Lancaster Portage project. **Health Visitor, 54**, 486-488

Holland, J.M. and Hattersley, J. (1980). Parent support groups for the families of mentally handicapped children. **Child: Care, Health and Development, 6**, 165-173

Holroyd, J. and McArthur, D. (1976). Mental retardation and stress on parents; a contrast between Down's syndrome and childhood autism. **American Journal of Mental Deficiency, 80**, 431-436

Howlin, P., Marchant, R., Rutter, M., Berger, M., Hersov, L. and Yule, W. (1973). A home based approach to the treatment of autistic children. **Journal of Autism and Childhood Schizophrenia. 3**, 308-336

Jeffree, D.M., McConkey, R. and Hewson, S. (1977). A parental involvement project. In Mittler, P. (ed.), **Research to Practice in Mental Retardation. Vol 1: Care and Intervention**. IASSMD. University Park Press, Baltimore. 229-236

Justice, R.S., O'Connor, G. and Warren, N. (1971). Problems reported by parents of mentally retarded children - who helps? **American Journal of Mental Deficiency, 75**, 685-691

Lacoste, R.J. (1978). Early intervention: can it hurt? **Mental Retardation, 16**, 266-268

Landesman-Dwyer, S. (1981). Living in the community. **American Journal of Mental Deficiency, 86**, 223-234

Lavigeur, H. (1976). The use of siblings as an adjunct to the behavioural treatment of children in the home with parents as therapists. **Behaviour Therapy, 7**, 602-613

Lloyd-Bostock, S. (1976). Parents' experiences of official help and guidance in caring for a mentally handicapped child. **Child: Care, Health and Development, 2**, 325-338

Locker, D., Rao, B. and Weddell, J.M. (1981). The impact of community care on the public response to the mentally handicapped. **Community Medicine, 3**, 98-107

Lonsdale, G. (1978). Family life with a handicapped child: the parents speak. **Child: Care, Health and Development, 4**, 99-120

Ludlow, J.R. and Allen, L.M. (1979). The effect of early intervention and pre-school stimulus on the development of the Down's Syndrome child. **Journal of Mental Deficiency Research, 23**, 29-43

Macaskill, C. (1981). Placing the mentally handicapped. **Adoption and Fostering, 5**, 46-49

McCall, C. and Thacker, J. (1977). A parent workshop in the school. **Special Education, 4**, 20-21

Marks, L. (1980). Parents' needs and how to meet them. In Simon, G.B. (ed.), **Modern Management of Mental Handicap**, MTP Press, Lancaster. 203-227

Meyer, R.J. (1980). Attitudes of parents of institutionalised mentally retarded individuals towards deinstitutionalization. **American Journal of Mental Deficiency, 85**, 184-187

Miller, N.B. and Cantwell, D.P. (1976). Siblings as therapists: a behavioral approach. **American Journal of Psychiatry, 133**(4), 447-450

Mittler, P. (1979). Patterns of partnership between parents and professionals, **Teaching and Training, 17**, 111-116

Nihira, K., Meyers, C.E. and Mink, I.T. (1980). Home environment, family adjustment and the development of mentally retarded children. **Applied Research in Mental Retardation, 1**, 5-24

Piper, M.C. and Pless, I.B. (1980). Early intervention for infants with Down Syndrome: a controlled trial. **Pediatrics, 65**, 463-468

Pueschel, S.M. and Murphy, A. (1976). Assessment of counselling practices at the birth of a child with Down's Syndrome. **American Journal of Mental Deficiency, 81**, 325-330

Revill, S. and Blunden, R. (1979). A home training service for pre-school developmentally handicapped children. **Behaviour Research and Therapy, 17**, 207-214

Reynolds, A.R. (1979). Some social effects of the mentally retarded child on the family: a third survey. **Australian Journal of Mental Retardation, 5**, 214-218

Rutter, M., Tizard, J. and Whitmore, K. (eds.) (1970). **Education, Health and Behaviour**. Longman, London

Sanderson, H.W. and Crawley, M. (1982). Characteristics of successful family care patterns. **American Journal of Mental Deficiency, 86**, 519-525

Sandow, S.A., Clarke, A.D.B., Cox, M.V. and Stewart, F.L. (1981). Home intervention with parents of severely subnormal pre-school children: a final report, **Child: Care, Health and Development. 7**, 135-144

Schou, A. (1977). Parents support parents. **Research Exchange and Practice in Mental Retardation, 3**, 233-243

Shearer, M. and Shearer, D.E. (1972). The Portage project: a model for early childhood education. **Exceptional Children, 36**, 210-217

Simeonsson, R.J. and McHale, S.M. (1981). Review: Research on handicapped children: sibling relationships. **Child: Care, Health and Development, 7**, 153-171

Springer, A. and Steele, M.W. (1980). Effects of physicians' early parental counselling on rearing of Down's syndrome children. **American Journal of Mental Deficiency, 85**, 1-5

Sternlicht, M. (1978). Variables affecting foster care placement of institutionalized retarded residents. **Mental Retardation, 16**, 25-27

Suelzle, M. and Keenan, V. (1981). Changes in family support networks over the life cycle of mentally retarded persons. **American Journal of Mental Deficiency, 86**, 267-274

Turner, A.L. (1980). Therapy with families of a mentally retarded child. **Journal of Marital and Family Therapy, 6**, 167-170.

Upshur, C.C. (1982). Respite care for mentally retarded and other disabled populations: program models and family needs. **Mental Retardation, 20**, 2-6

Waisbren, S.E. (1980). Parents' reactions after the birth of a developmentally disabled child. **American Journal of Mental Deficiency, 84**, 345-351

Weinrott, M.R. (1974). A training program in behavior modification for siblings of the retarded. **American Journal of Orthopsychiatry, 44**, 362-375

Willer, B.S., Intagliata, J.C. and Atkinson, A.C. (1981). Deinstitutionalization as a crisis event for families of mentally retarded persons. **Mental Retardation, 19**, 28-29

Wing, L. (1971). Severely retarded children in a London area: prevalence and provision of services. **Psychological Medicine, 1**, 405-415

Wolfensberger, W. (1967). Counselling parents of the retarded. In Baumeister, A. (ed.) **Mental Retardation**. Univ. of London Press, London. 329-400

Zigler, E. (1981). A plea to end the use of the patterning treatment for retarded children. **American Journal of Orthopsychiatry, 51**, 388-390

COMMENTARY

F. S. W. Brimblecombe

Family stress

I found this section unclear: first because the author does not define what she means by "family stress" at the start of the section. One definition of stress in the Concise Oxford Dictionary is "Effort, demand upon physical and mental energy". In this sense "stress" can occur in individuals of any age and may be related to their family life or their occupation, whatever this may be. It is something which most of us encounter either continually or from time to time; we vary enormously in our ability and our endurance and a whole set of other variables in our capability to withstand stress with equanimity. It is no surprise to learn that parents with handicapped children are, in this respect, little different from the rest of the population.

With respect, I suggest that the author's observations in this section of her paper are misdirected. I suggest that a more important question would have been "What are the particular causes of stress which affect families with handicapped children?", leading on from a description of these causes to potential ways and means to minimize the particular stress among such families.

An alternative approach to the same problems can be achieved by asking parents "What are their unmet needs?" Frequently the causes of stress are related to unmet (but in some instances potentially meetable) needs. In our Exeter studies we identified three primary areas of unmet need among parents of young handicapped childen.

1. Inadequate information. Parents are still inadequately informed by professionals about the cause and nature of their child's handicap. They are inadequately counselled in regard to their own feelings of guilt, rejection and their need for social readjustment. They are inadequately informed about the long-term future expectations and alternative choices of care for their handicapped child. The potential for parents to learn about these things not only from professionals but from other parents of handicapped children are not always utilized.

2. Inadequate transmission by professionals of the potentially teachable special skills which parents of young handicapped children need (and can) be taught to carry out themselves in order both to give more help to their handicapped child at home and in so doing often reduce their own "stress".

3. Parent relief. In his book "The Anatomy of Courage", Lord Moran, who had been a regimental medical officer in World War I, describes the experience of seeing his battalion being ordered each dawn to leave their trenches and advance against lines of fixed machine guns firing at them. He describes the quality of courage as being analogous to the amount of money in

one's bank account. Some have more than others. If a bank balance has no input, expenditure will empty the account more quickly or slowly depending upon the initial amount available. He emphasized the need for his soldiers to recharge their reserves of courage by periods of rest and recreation. We, in Exeter, suggest that the analogy between this experience and that of constantly caring for a very dependent or hyperactive child is justifiable. Hence the need for periods of parent relief, through contact with a resources centre to which the handicapped child can go at any time when the parents need it; the timing to be determined <u>not by professionals</u> but by parents themselves. No request <u>for parent relief</u> must ever be refused if the confidence and trust between the family and the resource centre is to be sustained.

To be fair to the author, her paper does then describe alternative methods of service, but does not purport to be more than a review of the descriptive literature of the last decade. I am reminded of the words of the late Professor Jack Tizard: "In practice the variance in treatments is usually much greater than the variance in services; in general it would be nearer the truth to say that any model of service can be made to work and that what is of crucial importance is not the service model but the manner in which it is operated."

A. Kushlick

There is growing evidence of the usefulness of describing "family problems", whether or not arising from the presence of a handicapped member, in the form of "outcomes" (or behavioural targets) desired by individual family members under specified conditions compared with their current behaviour under these conditions (Schwartz and Goldiamond, 1975; Goldiamond, 1974). The approach respects important ethical values in making explicit the "rights" of people to attain targets. It also allows public description and participation in identifying targets and choosing interventions to attain them. Scientifically, it allows precise determination of whether or not targets (i.e. precise levels of dependent variables - DVs) are attained, as well as a detailed description of the conditions under which differing levels of the DVs are obtained (the independent variables - IV), (Sidman, 1960). Aspects of this approach are well demonstrated in two studies not quoted in the paper.

In the first, targets (DVs) of increases in family interactions, and of positive statements among family members occurred between parents and their five-year-old child at home. The parents had received a specific training (IV) in ways of communicating opinions when resolving marital differences in child management, increasing support given to the spouse, and in interacting with one another and the child as a triad. The levels of the DVs had been lower under "natural" conditions before the parents had learned how to attend positively to each other in front of the child, to avoid giving instructions incompatible with an instruction given previously by the other spouse, etc. (Kelley et al., 1979).

In the second study, the targets (DVs) of the parents implementing teaching procedures for a six-year-old severely retarded child at home, and of the child's attending to the parents and independently dressing, eating and using simple toys, were attained under the conditions (IVs) of clinic staff training the mother, and the mother training the father on the dressing task at the clinic and at home. The skills generalized without training to teaching the child eating and use of toys (Adubato et al., 1981). Within this model, the target of generalizing parent teaching skills to other teaching objectives and other children under laboratory conditions has been attained on the addition of a very limited amount of theoretical training (IV_2) to training under conditions of imitation or modelling on a trained teacher (IV_1) (Koegel et al., 1978). These demonstrations are relevant to service professionals, managers and planners to the extent that it is possible to replicate them in a wide range of settings and to maintain them over long periods with decreasing service inputs.

The rapidly growing literature on cognitive behaviour modification shows the relevance of this approach to "emotional" problems. States described as depression and anxiety can be impressively relieved, and target behaviours of undertaking activities previously avoided can be attained when the client learns to implement procedures (IVs) like disputing their own inaccurate or imprecise beliefs about events, by increasing the accuracy with which the events and beliefs are described, and by acting on the accurate descriptions (Beck, 1976; Ellis, 1962; Meichenbaum, 1974).

Carr's review of the state of the art of both research and intervention in relation to families with a retarded person is impressively wide-ranging and presents some new ways of intervening in families with a handicapped member. She has made a major contribution towards precision intervention with families and there is no need for modesty in presenting results of effective interventions. There is, however, a great need for presenting detailed descriptions of dependent and independent variables when reporting the outstanding work if it is to become a powerful resource to the people caring for the handicapped and for the handicapped people themselves.

In some instances, and perhaps because of the review's breadth, she presents uncritically overgeneralized and therefore fuzzy results. This makes it difficult for the reader to respond without going to the original papers. In addition, some fallible readers already believe that the new therapeutic and educational technologies are imprecise, ineffective or even harassing to parents. If they go no further, they may quote the review to justify such incorrect beliefs.

The results she presents are clear and lend themselves to optimistic service development and replication where they arise from detailed experimental studies related to attaining specific outcomes for individual family members; they are obscure and lend themselves to inaction and confusion where they are from descriptive-statistical studies with ill-defined or undefined independent variables and with ill-defined rating scale scores as dependent variables.

Thus, it is not possible to respond effectively to the pairs of descriptions of independent and dependent variables (Table C1) or to relationships between them.

Professionals, researchers or parents respond irrationally and emotionally to their interpretation of many events including research results. I predict that these descriptions will do little to help them control their wilder speculations and demands that others agree with their interpretations.

Clear dependent variables are presented:

- mothers working daily on developmental objectives and children who show more developmental changes or progress than a control group of subjects
- mothers teaching a variety of skills: self-care, play, language
- mothers managing and eliminating behaviour problems.

The independent variables in one of the studies are more clearly described:

- home visitors - visit mothers at home
  - discuss the mother's objectives
  - demonstrate methods
  - ask the mothers to carry out teaching sessions
  - keep records.

Data have not been provided on whether or not the independent variable has been sufficiently well described to be replicated by others, or to be implemented and maintained in an ongoing source.

The dependent variables are also more clearly described elsewhere. Reference is made to the clearly described IV package of the Portage Home-Teaching System which has expanded rapidly throughout the UK because of its replicability and acceptability.

In the same context there are some ill-defined IVs and DVs. Thus she quotes uncritically the association of independent variable large "numbers of interventions" with high levels of a dependent variable called "stress" not measured but implied by describing the parent performances inaccurately and exaggeratedly as therapist, teacher, trainer, transporter, keeping up with treatment, functioning as a wife, mothering her other children, and being a human being in her own right. She describes "alarums echoed by parents' comments" and illustrates this by the dependent variable "parent relief at being free of (the independent variable) all the professionals who had been overwhelming them".

Table C1

Independent variables	Dependent variables
Telling the parents (no information on content) "early, honestly and sympathetically".	None.
Presence of a handicapped child in the family.	Family - "not seriously impaired". - "cope well". - "not manage well".
Presence of a handicapped child in the family and "marital disharmony".	Parents report "feeling affected (presumably negatively) by the mentally handicapped child". Parents "indicate adverse effects on the marriage". Parents have "lower indices of marital satisfaction". or Parents show "no significant differences".
Presence of a two-and-a-half year old Down's syndrome child in one group of families and a normal child in a second group.	Parents with a Down's syndrome child rate more marriages as poor and equal numbers as good.
Presence of Down's syndrome child in one group of families and autistic in another.	Down's syndrome parents report fewer problems and no more stress than normal controls.
Presence of a handicapped child and father who "feels his parents were supportive".	Father "did more with the child" and "had more positive feeling" and "listed more symptoms of stress".
Presence of a handicapped child.	Parents report "adverse effect on...siblings". Writer explains adverse effects on: Younger sibling - "handicapped child supplants the role". Older sibling - "demands put on them to care for the child".

This illustrates two common ways in which people defeat themselves:

- saying what they do not mean and meaning what they do not say;
- assuming that as other people make the same error there is no need to change.

Helpful parent-professional collaboration will be seen to take place to the extent that both follow the same guidelines of identifying specific targets (DVs) which they want to attain, and effective methods (IVs) which they choose to follow to attain these. In this collaboration only the parents (or the retarded person him- or herself) are competent to identify the targets they wish to work for, and the methods they wish to follow. Professionals will be helpful to the extent that they guide them in defining the targets clearly enough to know whether or not they are attained, and offer a range of methods likely to be effective in attaining the chosen target.

Carr expresses surprise that increasing service provision does not automatically lead to a decrease in requests from parents for residential care of their children. This seems to arise from the unfounded expectation that complex targets will "automatically" be attained without intervening directly to attain them. It is predictable that parents and professionals transfer more people to these settings in order to attain their objectives. If the target dependent variables of skill acquisition and skill practice by the handicapped person under a wide range of "normal" conditions can best be attained in the residential care setting it is also in the child's interest. Only if this is best attained at home, and only if the service has interventions which clearly value this parental contribution, and demonstrate this with financial and other sorts of technical and mechanical support, would one expect (and consider it ethically correct) that requests for transfer of clients would decline when new services were being developed. Similarly, if services are specifically targeted on relieving whatever is included in the score of "family strain" and "using services", one would expect successful services to attain such targets. Indeed, increases in transfer of people to residential care could be a successful service outcome if the aim of providing the handicapped person with a richer and more varied environment is attained. It would also be a successful outcome if the target had been to arrange an environment where parents and siblings would attain more of their objectives independently of the handicapped person.

The same error arises in interpreting the effectiveness of alternative forms of residential care. Given that effective care includes, at a minimum, individualized education programmes and a wide range of normalized opportunities to practise them, it is not surprising that these do not occur in every setting merely because it is "small" or has a high staff ratio. Incompetence in these tasks and lack of motivation of staff and managers clearly limit this likelihood. However very large institution practises include low staff ratios of 1 to 10 or more people at any time of day, and other features (Felce et al., 1977) which constitute serious obstacles to even the most competent of care staff and managers.

I agree with Carr's recommendation of caution when intervening with families. However I suggest that a precise description of targets and interventions will be found to be a key component of interventions regarded by families and others as constituting high quality care.

References

Adubato A., Adams D. and Budd K.S., (1981), Teaching a parent to train a spouse in child management techniques, **Journal of Applied Behaviour Analysis, 14**, 193-205

Beck A.T., (1976), **Cognitive Therapy and the Emotional Disorders**, International University Press, New York

Ellis A., (1962), **Reason and Emotion in Psychotherapy**, Lyle Stuart, New York

Felce D., Kushlick A., Lunt B. and Powell L., (1977), **Evaluation of locally-based hospital units in Wessex: Detailed rules for setting-up and maintenance of the units**, Report No 124, Health Care Evaluation Research Team, Winchester

Goldiamond I., (1974), Toward a constructional approach to social problems, **Behaviorism, 2**, 1-84

Kelly M.L., Embry L.N. and Baer D.M., (1979), Skills for child management and family support: training parents for maintenance, **Behaviour Modification, 3**, 373-396

Koegel R.L., Glahn T.J. and Nieminen G.W., (1978), Generalization of parent-training results, **Journal of Applied Behavior Analysis, 11**, 95-109

Meichenbaum D.H., (1974), **Cognitive Behavior Modification**, General Learning Press, New Jersey

Schwartz A. and Goldiamond I., (1975), **Social Casework, A Behavioral Approach**, Columbia University Press

Sidman M., (1960), **Tactics for Scientific Research**, Basic Books, New York

P. Mittler

This review highlights some of the more important issues concerned with families of mentally handicapped people. Although it reviews a considerable volume of recent literature, space restrictions make it impossible to discuss any of the areas in depth. A reader who is relatively new to this field may gain the impression that the literature in this field is in important respects inconclusive and methodologically limited.

A number of issues can be identified for discussion:

Families of mentally handicapped children and adults are as heterogeneous as any random segment of the population. Producing and looking after a mentally handicapped child in no way reduces this heterogeneity. Searching for generalizations on the characteristics of families is therefore a scientifically limited enterprise. What is needed is more information and better understanding of the range of individual differences between families.

If each family is different from every other, one task of service providers is to assess and meet the unique needs of each family. This parallels the process of individual programme planning which is now regarded as good practice where the individual mentally handicapped person is concerned.

If this is accepted, what kind of information could research studies provide for this purpose? A few pointers can be identified.

Studies of day-to-day living of families looking after a mentally handicapped person. One of the most illuminating of these, which contradicts some of the conclusions of research reported in the review, can be found in the book "Caring for the Mentally Handicapped Child" (Wilkins, 1979). These and similar observational studies of families are in contrast to studies which simply describe the structural characteristics of families. Furthermore, there is now an impressive and serious literature of books written by parents themselves, including some who are both parents and professionals in the field of mental handicap (e.g. Turnbull and Turnbull, 1978).

We need a more searching analysis of the implications of differences between and within families for the training of professionals and a thorough evaluation of the effectiveness of a range of approaches to training of staff to meet parents' needs - e.g. through stimulation training techniques such as role play.

More systematic studies are needed not only of parents' knowledge of services but also of ways of helping parents to acquire such information: e.g. evaluations of the effectiveness of information leaflets.

The 1981 Education Act legitimizes much more parental involvement in assessment and decision making, alongside professionals. Prospective studies of this process are needed in representative samples of families.

Although, as the review documents, there are numerous studies describing structured parental involvement programmes (e.g. workshops, Portage schemes), few studies have provided rigorous evaluations of outcome and maintenance over a longer period, or explored the extent to which parents' needs and priorities are effectively identified by professions.

Nearly all the studies reviewed concern parents of children; we know little or nothing about parents of adults, particularly older adults (Mittler _et al_., 1981). For example, the finding that parents generally object to moves to deinstitutionalize hospital residents and to make appropriate community provision has important ethical implications (e.g. do we still do it regardless of parents' wishes?) but it would be important to know whether these reservations are sustained.

Above all, we need better studies of parents' needs, based on detailed interviews and knowledge of parents' circumstances and problems, followed by evaluated interventions which aim to meet their needs.

References

Mittler, P., Cheseldine, S. and McConachie, H. (1981). **Roles and Needs of Parents of Handicapped Adolescents.** CERI, OECD, Paris

Turnbull, M.A. and Turnbull, H. (eds.) (1978). **The Other Side of the Two Way Mirror. Parents Speak Out.** Merrill, Columbus, Ohio

Wilkin, D. (1979). **Caring for the Mentally Handicapped Child.** Croom Helm, London

D. Morris

It is encouraging that so much research has been done on this topic and collected in this paper.

There is a sense of unreality when discussing "telling the parents". "To be told early" is followed by "within the first two weeks". This ignores the terrible problem professionals have who recognize a baby born with say microcephaly or Down's syndrome, and how to handle the immediacy of the situation.

In view of the influence of class social factors so clearly identified by the Clarkes, is it not a sad omission and somewhat vague to talk of "mainly middle class parents" when discussing fathers and to talk of "especially in large and lower class families"?

"Counselling" is not an entity but many different things. The nature of the work done, by whom, the advantages and disadvantages of "the named person" and ongoing intervention compared with crisis intervention are challenging topics. Services, their effect on the parents' burdens and home or institutional care is, I think unbalanced, omitting as it does such experiences as Honeylands where as a result placement was reduced to a minimum.

It is heartening to know that "the effectiveness of a home visiting service" was not affected by social class and a confirmation of clinical experience that marital harmony and small family size are advantages. The topic of parental involvement and its advantages and disadvantages are well illustrated and strike a healthy note of caution that the need of professionals to help parents may be out of harmony with the family situation at the time.

The question put by the author of whether further studies are needed about the shock, sadness and eventual adjustment of parents learning they have a handicapped child must surely be in the affirmative, if only to know more of where the success lies in adjustment and even more important the nature of failure. The final note of professional and parent mutuality and how it does or does not work gives a strong lead for future activity.

T. L. Pilkington

Not infrequently there is evidence of family stress, e.g. parental disharmony, that existed prior to the birth of a handicapped child. It can then happen that the mentally handicapped person is manipulated within this situation - for example, by the one insisting that the child must sleep in the parental bed, thus excusing sexual relations with the partner. There are many other ways in which the mentally handicapped can be exploited within pre-existing, often chronic, family conflict. When the child becomes an adult and stays within the family this poses the question as to who is more competent to judge the situation - the parents, the retarded person, or outside professionals? There appears to be a paucity of literature on these aspects.

D. C. Taylor

I read Janet Carr's paper with a good deal of interest. Since it is a review of the literature with which she is extremely well acquainted, I would not take issue with her. In a parallel field authors writing about the psychological effects of severe chronic illness in early childhood have, in the last decade, also become a great deal more cautious in presuming that widespread deleterious effects ensue. These were at one time thought common-place (Taylor, 1983/84). We need to remember most carefully that the changes involved are changes in approach and attitude and in the responses made by human beings at given points in history, rather than imagine that we are dealing with a science of fixed structures.

At a meeting entitled "Scientific Studies in Mental Retardation" it is worth considering the rearing of mentally handicapped children from a broader biological framework. What pressures would encourage human organisms (people) to nurture and raise with such care problematic progeny who cannot contribute to future reproductive success; young who are therefore themselves tangible and persistent reminders of reproductive failure? (It is intriguing that one of the more persistent myths about the mentally handicapped is their propensity for female promiscuity and male sexual aggressiveness which is actually the diametric opposite of biological fact.) There are two obvious possibilities. First is that there is some paragenetic advantage of deviants; and second evolutionary advantages might accrue if very deep consideration is given to the maintenance of all reproductive deviations. Furthermore dealing altruistically with the disadvantaged may provide us with a very general sort of insurance against culling. Of course an interaction between these effects may improve the quality of parenting generally.

There are broadly two main strategies for sexual reproduction labelled r and K (MacArthur, 1962; see Daly and Wilson, 1978). r strategists produce innumerable young who are largely abandoned by their parents to their fate at Nature's hands. K strategists produce very few young but tend to see them through to reproductive age. Such parents tend more towards enduring monogamous relationships. People are the extreme K strategists. Ounsted _et al_. (1966) introducing hyperpaedophilia (the most misunderstood concept ever in development medicine) quoted Lord Brougham and Vaux's interesting observation that defencelessness of the young (of K strategists only of course) continues to provoke parental solicitude after the time when it is usually withdrawn. People are also the extreme neotenous paedomorph so their helpless young persist in an immature state relatively longer than any other animal.

For people to be prepared to show extreme parental solicitude at the price of considerable self-sacrifice, over many years, in order to raise a single developmentally retarded child, represents therefore the summation of these several extreme but intensely human reproductive characteristics. The input of extreme postnatal effort might be seen as a desperate attempt to produce a worthwhile return from a costly K strategy investment. For human beings of course this can also come in the form of "satisfaction".

At one time the majority of these problems were solved by infant mortality, relative mortality, and interference and non-interference at the time of birth. In the last century there was an epoch of social intervention in the form of "hospitals" for the mentally retarded which was paralleled by other forms of social intervention in the lives of children such as precluding them from dangerous jobs of work whilst they were still under 10, a movement which was extended recently as far as attempting to prevent them being emotionally abused. This movement has been closely associated with the reduction of childbearing made possible by reduced infant mortality. It makes people's K strategy even more extreme as it increases the value accorded to any given conceptus. Now responsibility and obligation are being given back to parents and a very large investment in personnel is envisaged to develop and maintain a non-reproducing segment of society. Our apparent willingness to make this heavy wastage (in biological terms) of reproductive effort is (in so far as it is not more apparent than real) in sympathy with our general need to find, at a time of population and resources crisis, unproductive and non-aggressive ways of utilizing human effort. Part of the cost of mental handicap used to include their productivity failure. Now this is becoming less of a distinction perhaps retarded people can be afforded relatively more resources since chronically unemployed retarded individuals might be not much more of a financial burden than chronically unemployed non-retarded people.

A politician might of course be able to deduce from all this a solution, but this is beyond the remit of mental retardation scientists.

References

Daly, M. and Wilson, M. (1978). **Sex, Evolution and Behaviour.** Duxbury Press, North Seituate, Massachusetts

MacArthur, R.H. (1962). Some generalised theorems of natural selection. **Proceedings of the National Academy of Sciences, 48**, 1893-1897

Ounsted, C., Lindsay, J.M. and Norman, R.M. (1966). **Biological Factor in Temporal Lobe Epilepsy.** Heineman, London

Taylor, D.C. (1983/4). The psychological effects of chronic illness in childhood. In Rutter, M. and Hersov, L. (eds.), **Child Psychiatry**, Blackwell, Oxford

Chapter 21

Environment and individuals with severe mental disability

F.S.W. Brimblecombe

INTRODUCTION

This chapter, since it is concerned with severe mental retardation, is concentrated more upon individuals with congenital cerebral malformation or acquired disease than upon the left hand side of the Gaussian distribution of intelligence among a total population of persons who have no organic disease. Severe mental retardation is frequently associated with other severe handicaps which may be motor, sensory or psychiatric in nature. This chapter reviews the extent to which the environment and the physical factors within it can be modified to improve the lives of those affected and the lives of their families. It is concerned therefore with secondary rather than primary prevention.

DIAGNOSIS

Penrose (1938) foresaw the possibility of accurate medical diagnosis in the majority of those affected by severe mental handicap. Crome and Stern (1973) reported that an exact diagnosis was possible in 65 per cent of those affected. Gustavson et al. (1977) in a population based study in Sweden achieved accurate diagnosis in 86 per cent. Mackay (1982) in his Salford study states that in his population of 396 severely mentally handicapped children a clear aetiology could be identified in all but 12 per cent. Of those children who survived infancy, he found that in 55 per cent the cause of their retardation was prenatal in origin, perinatal in 20 per cent and acquired in subsequent childhood in 10 per cent. The significance of X-linked mental retardation as one of the commonest genetic causes has been suspected for many years. This view has been confirmed following the work of Sutherland (1977) who identified a constriction or fragile site on the X-chromosome which could be most consistently identified if lymphocytes were cultured in a folate-deficient medium. Using Sutherland's technique, the marker chromosome is now being found in increasing numbers of families with X-linked but otherwise non-specific mental retardation. Large testes are sometimes seen as a component of the phenotype but, since they are not invariably present in affected males, the view of Herbst and Miller (1980) is that a number (estimated by them to involve 7-19 different genes) of variants of X-linked genes are associated with non-specific mental retardation. These authors, drawing upon the British Columbia Health Surveillance Registry, estimate that X-linked retardation is at least as common in males as is Down's syndrome. The exact prevalence is still to be determined since the fragile X syndrome of mental retardation does not invariably achieve penetrance in males; the chance of demonstrating it in a female carrier appears to diminish with increasing age. It is to be emphasized that the degree of mental retardation in males associated with the fragile X chromosomes varies; some individuals are less severely affected than others.

It is clear that severe mental retardation in any population is not a single diagnostic entity but a summation of a wide variety of disorders. Some, like those associated with chromosomal abnormalities such as Down's syndrome, severe congenital malformations in which the brain is involved as well as other systems (as may occur with neural tube defects in which hydrocephalus is already present at birth), severe microcephaly, and congenital infections as seen in children severely affected by the rubella syndrome, are recognizable at birth or in some instances by antenatal diagnosis. It appears likely that the increasing use of ultra sound and computerized tomography will further increase the numbers that can be recognized at least by the end of the perinatal period.

Other disorders (although of congenital, prenatal or perinatal origin) which cause severe mental retardation may not be identified until severely retarded development becomes obvious during the first and second years of life. Acquired disorders such as the sequelae that can follow infections like meningitis, encephalitis, other genetically determined diseases such as tuberose sclerosis, the effects of trauma or cerebral neoplasm develop at varying stages throughout childhood and adulthood.

In order to assess the effect of any methods of primary or secondary prevention, sophisticated and precise medical diagnosis and a knowledge of the natural history and prognosis of the underlying condition are of considerable importance. For example hyperactivity in young severely mentally disabled children may have a natural tendency to spontaneous remission; the value of programmes of behaviour modification or the use of drugs can only be evaluated against a background of knowledge of the untreated course of the disorder. Similar knowledge about disorders which involve progressive cerebral degeneration is essential if the effects of environmental modification are to be accurately assessed.

SECONDARY PREVENTION

Optimal secondary prevention (minimizing the effects of mental retardation both for those affected and for their families) depends upon interactions between the individual, the family, all agencies concerned with the care of the handicapped, as well as with a wide variety of social and other environmental factors.

IMPAIRMENT -----------------> DISABILITY -------> SOCIAL HANDICAP

MODIFIED BY - CHANGES WITHIN THE FAMILY
- CHANGES IN THE BEHAVIOUR OF OTHER PEOPLE

If the implications of this concept are accepted, then the major outcome upon which attention should be concentrated is the extent of social handicap that results, and efforts to minimize it for each individual and his family emerge as the main priority. Appropriate health care, although integral within this concept, is only one component of secondary prevention in this broad sense.

The meaning of care has become confused partly because it has sometimes been considered perhaps too extensively as the decision making prerogative of those who provide it and insufficiently from the viewpoint of those who require it. This applies to three vital aspects of the lives of the severely mentally handicapped, namely their:

health, social and educational help,
housing,
occupation.

Statutory and voluntary service providers have tended to regard themselves as the decision makers and the planners of necessary services. When these ideas are turned round them the mentally handicapped and their families have rightly said:

What type of health, social and educational help do we need (or not need)?

Where does the handicapped member of our family want to live? (With the family? In local accommodation adjacent to the family home? In a more distant community or institution?)

What type of life style and occupation do we as a family wish our handicapped member (with particular reference to the individuality of the mentally handicapped person himself) to lead?

Traditionally, the severely mentally handicapped and their families have been told or persuaded that from time to time it is best for the handicapped individual to be moved from one place of care to another. But is this ideal? Or should service providers who ideologically may have become committed to a particular system of service provision (and have become rigidly committed to it) remain unaware of the possibility that the help they can provide should be very much more flexibly and geographically available in the context of the wishes and decisions of the handicapped person and his family? In this sense, the meaning of the word care (help) is only one component of the total environmental needs of each individual and his family.

It is clear that this concept, if carried to the extreme, can be dismissed as impracticable and unrealistic particularly at a time of limited resource provision.

THE ESSENTIAL PREREQUISITE NEEDS

Health and educational (learning) needs are among the many integral components required to minimize the effects of severe mental handicap.

Among the essential prerequisites both for their families and for the handicapped themselves are:

(a) Information

From the time that a handicap is identified and through each subsequent stage of life, there is a need for an improved system for the provision of information to the family regarding:

the nature of the child's handicap and its cause,

the future expectations.

All members of the family need to be given every opportunity to come to terms with their own reactions to the fact that a member of their family is mentally handicapped and to make the essential adjustments that will inevitably be needed between each member of the family. This information can be gained from a variety of professional sources and from other families who have a mentally handicapped member.

(b) Skills

Re-establishment of parental control of the situation occurs through the transfer of the special skills required to minimize the effects of the handicap from those who have been professionally trained to the family themselves.

(c) Family Support

The families of a severely mentally handicapped person have tended to become isolated from the rest of society. Family support is needed if first the family and then the mentally handicapped individual are to be restored to a normal place in society. The responsibility of caring constantly for a mentally handicapped person is physically and emotionally exhausting. Each family needs a refuge - a family support unit - to which they can turn, for information, for training in special skills and just for relief. This refuge should be available to them not at the decree of a professional agency but whenever and for whatever length of time they find they need it. The Warnock concepts of a named person for each family is an integral component for the fulfilment of this need.

(d) **Involvement in Decision Making**

The true concept of parents and professionals as partners is difficult to achieve. It is true to say that from time to time the opinions including expectations of each may often seem unrealistic to the other member of the partnership. The transition from childhood to adulthood of the mentally handicapped is not the least of the critical periods which such a partnership has to consider in terms of housing and occupation for the handicapped individual.

THE VARIANCE THAT DERIVES FROM DIFFERING PARENTAL INFLUENCES

Articulate and well informed parents know how to find the services that will best help them. Their critical faculties often help to assist them in ensuring that the handicapped individual finds an environment that will help to enhance his social potential. Inarticulate, less well informed parents may "accept" what is offered without overt criticism, e.g. an environment for the individual which militates against the maximization of social potential. Alternatively they may develop rejecting, hostile and negative attitudes.

THE PAST, THE PRESENT, AND THE FUTURE

Societies in their attitudes to the handicapped have tended to progress through four evolutionary stages, starting with extermination, followed by segregation, then leading to the accordance of second class citizenship status and finally it is to be hoped to the granting of equal rights as citizens.

Most industrialized societies are presently passing through the third of these four stages. The mentally handicapped still encounter from society as a whole the following reactions in their daily encounters with non-handicapped people:

"stranger",
failure of interaction,
ignorance,
power.

Mentally handicapped people appear to the rest of society as different or foreign; they represent something unknown from which they turn aside, partly through fear and largely from ignorance. This leads to a failure to interact and to the isolation of the handicapped from many social activities. The responses of the mentally handicapped to an approach may appear inappropriate and often masks their desire for involvement.

The mentally disabled, even more than other minority groups, are powerless in comparison with the rest of society. This extends not only to the use of financial resources but also at the personal level to the exercise of domination in their personal lives, in their choice of occupation and leisure activities, where they live and the details of their daily routine by the "service providers" who control their destiny.

It is the challenge of today, in our time of resource limitation, to work to modify this situation by sensitive readjustment of what resources are available. We need to look carefully at the word "occupation" (both for the handicapped as well as the non-handicapped) at a time of widespread unemployment. It is the sincere hope of the writer that this symposium will be both creative and stimulate action.

REFERENCES

Crome, L. and Stern, J. (1973). **The Pathology of Mental Retardation**, 2nd Edn., Churchill, London

Gustavson, K.H., Hagberg, B., Hagberg, G. and Sars, K. (1977). Severe mental retardation in a Swedish county II: Etiology and pathogenic aspects of children born 1959-1970, **Neuropadiatrie, 8,** 293

Herbst, D.S. and Miller, J.R. (1980). Non-specific X-linked mental retardation II. The frequency in British Columbia, **American Journal of Medical Genetics, 7,** 461

Mackay, R.I. (1982). The causes of severe mental retardation, **Developmental Medicine and Child Neurology, 24**, 386

Penrose, L.S. (1938). **The Biology of Mental Defect** (4th Edn., 1972), Sidgwick and Jackson, London

Sutherland, G.R. (1977). Fragile sites on human chromosomes. Demonstrations of their dependence on the type of tissue culture medium, **Science, 197**, 265

COMMENTARY

A. D. B. Clarke

The stated aim of this chapter concerns the extent to which the environment and the physical factors within it can be modified for the benefit of the mentally handicapped and their families. There is much here which entirely accords with the experience of this reviewer. It is his task, however, to offer a constructive critique.

The paper opens with a section on "Diagnosis", in which attention is drawn to improved methods. However, the fact that increasingly accurate methods have been developed does not help us very much in handling the severely affected. It was the hope of L.S. Penrose that psychologists might concentrate on relating behaviour to aetiology, but such attempts have not been very fruitful. It seems that where brain damage or malformation is sufficiently grave to produce severe mental retardation, the behavioural outcome does not differ very markedly between different aetiological categories. "Many paths lead to Rome." This first section therefore seems to be only tangentially relevant to the theme.

Under "Secondary Prevention", few would quarrel with the view that efforts to minimize social handicap for the individual and family must be the main priority. Indeed this attitude was current, even if largely unrealized, long before the Swedes produced the "normalization" concept. However, the thesis that decisions about "care" should not merely be the prerogative of those who provide it, is of much more recent origin. Moreover, it is becoming increasingly clear from a number of other fields (e.g. Third World studies) that interventions imposed from above or from outside are far less effective than those where the "consumer" has a vital role to play. Brimblecombe raises some important questions here.

However, the mention of the special skills needed by the parents is given short shrift, and could usefully either be expanded or cross-referenced.

In general, it could be added that the mentally handicapped and their families share some of the problems of other "second class citizens". Although the parents' groups are highly articulate and successful, they are largely led by middle class persons, and for a number of less articulate or otherwise disadvantaged parents, the "inverse care law" operates: those most in need are least likely to obtain appropriate help. This, then, is a widespread problem for society which extends beyond the bounds of mental retardation.

P. Meazzini

The paper by Brimblecombe is both very clear and well documented, although there are some very relevant issues that might have to be dealt with more thoroughly, namely:

1. Prosthetic environment

In his paper, it is not clearly stated what kind of modifications are to be made in order to change the environment and make it more manageable on the part of the handicapped person. In my opinion, any part of the environment should be planned so that it can have prosthetic value for the handicapped person. An environment which is changed according to this philosophy is the best indicator of the actual sensitization of society towards this problem.

2. Educational role of parents

As a matter of fact, a very vast and sophisticated literature is available showing how effective parents can be in managing their children's day-to-day problems, provided they are properly trained (Kozloff, 1974, 1979; Nisi, in press).

In addition well trained parents not only are skilful in managing both educational and psychological problems of their children but also can better control their anxiety, as they play an active role in treating their children.

3. Can genetic factors of handicap be counterbalanced by educational treatment, at least to some extent?

Taking for example a Down's syndrome child, data show that a very early educational intervention can be very effective in favouring his cognitive growth and counteracting the effect of his genetic endowment, at least to a certain extent.

There is also complementary evidence showing that the more postponed the educational intervention, the more difficult is normalization (Lambert and Rondal, 1979; Mastroiacovo *et al*., 1981).

References

Kozloff, M.A. (1974). **Educating Children with Learning and Behaviour Problems**, Wiley, New York

Kozloff, M.A. (1979). A program for families of children with learning and behaviour problems

Lambert, J.L. and Rondal, J.A. (1979). **Le Mongolisme**, Mardaga, Bruxelles

Mastroiacovo, P., Rynders, J.E. and Albertini, G. (1981). **La Sindrome Down**, Il Pensiero Scientifico, Roma

Nisi, A. (in press). L'aformazione dei genitori. In Meazzini, P. (ed.), **Handicappato: Passi Verso L'autonomia**, Giunti e Barbera, Firenze

D. Morris

Since this paper is "concerned with secondary prevention" I find it difficult to rationalize the inclusion of the causes of severe retardation and the implication of their possible prevention.

The principles behind minimizing the effects on the individual and his family are laudable and acceptable, but has not the time come for us to produce some evidence to demonstrate where faults and omissions lie so that they can be corrected, e.g. the paragraph on the meaning of care: "it has sometimes ... too extensively ... the viewpoint of those who require it"? How often is "sometimes" and how extensive is "too" and what ways and means are there of obtaining the viewpoint of the severely retarded consumer.

Decision-making is correctly criticized for not including the views of the retarded and their families. What is needed is evidence to show how this can be done and how the gains can be achieved.

None can disagree with "better forms of information", but what is the nature of successful communication in this area? What are the hurdles and the reasons for failure, such as the need for time, the desired setting in which to communicate with privacy and without interruption? The author would have been more effective if he had quoted from his own experience at Honeylands the ways in which his family support unit has provided a "refuge". We are going to need much more information about the proposed "named person" - who and how he is chosen, who wants to be and who is eligible for being chosen; what mitigates against continuing the role such as change of post or unforeseen absences. Likewise we must consider models of parent-professional partnership, the pitfalls to be avoided and the mechanisms of goals achieved.

S. A. Richardson

In this paper and other papers which deal with the environment of the handicapped persons there has been little attention paid to social environment other than the family setting and the school. Yet for some, especially the severely retarded, their environment is almost entirely circumscribed by the residential institutions in which some are placed. The nature of the experiences provided for mentally retarded persons in institutions has a profound effect on their lives and level of functioning. A pioneer demonstration of institutional environments was carried out by Jack Tizard in the Brooklands experiment. He was appalled at the social conditions for children in the mental retardation hospitals and opened a small residential facility for severely retarded children organized along principles of child development. He demonstrated that the shift in environment caused a reduction in behaviour problems, better physical health and an increase in cognitive functioning. Since then there have been numerous studies of various forms of residential care and increased recognition of the importance of living environments for the development of handicapped persons (Haywood and Newbrough, 1981).

Reference

Haywood, H.C. and Newbrough, J.R. (1981). **Living Environments for Developmentally Retarded Persons.** University Park Press, Baltimore

J. B. P. Stephenson

Brimblecombe in his paper stressed the importance of precise diagnosis as a basis for appropriate help. In addition to the point that explanation aids acceptance, it is likely that the different aetiological types of mental handicap need different methods of management. As a particular example I draw attention to the recently re-discovered entity (Hagberg *et al.*, 1983) known as Rett's syndrome, originally reported in 1966 (Rett, 1966, 1979). These individuals are all female, and their parents report normal development including the acquisition of hand competence, but regression rapidly between the second half of the first year and about two and a half to a state of anxious isolation (which has been described as autistic-like) and apparent profound mental handicap. These girls lose all purposeful hand function, but instead show stereotypy, in particular a tense clasping or squeezing together of the fingers, frequently accompanied by a burst of hyperventilation. Walking is wide based and jerky. Microcephaly develops, and neuromotor signs very slowly evolve over the years, with epilepsy in addition. The "autistic" features appear to become *pari passu* with neurological deterioration. This relatively common syndrome (no longer believed to be associated with hyperammonaemia) must require a particular form of management, and research into this should be as important as investigation into the underlying cause.

References

Hagberg, B., Aicardi, J., Dias, K., Ramos, O. (1983). A progressive syndrome of autism, dementia and loss of purposeful hand use in girls: Rett's syndrome. **Annals of Neurology**, in press

Rett, A. (1966). **Uber ein Cerbal-atrophisches Syndrome bei Hyperammonaemia**, Bruder Hollinek, Wein

Rett, A. (1979). Cerebral atrophy associated with hyperammonaemia. **Handbook of Clinical Neurology**. Ed. Vinken, P.J. and Bruyn, G.W. Vol. 29, pp. 305-329. North-Holland, Amsterdam

Chapter 22

Psychiatry and mental retardation

J.A. Corbett

INTRODUCTION

Historically, definitions of mental deficiency have largely centred around notions of social competence. Implicit in this concept is the idea that the adjustment of people with similar intellectual deficits will depend largely on factors loosely termed adaptive capacity, behaviour, temperament, personality, or superadded psychiatric disorder.

There is much less certainty about the definition, classification, prevalence, management and predictive value of such aspects of individual functioning. This has led to widely differing views about their nature and theoretical basis.

This is reflected in the very discrepant prevalence rates for psychiatric disorder quoted in various studies.

This is not a problem peculiar to mental retardation. Studies of the prevalence of psychiatric illness in the general population have in the past given widely varying estimates (Clare, 1978). There is growing evidence to suggest that once methods of recording and classification of psychiatric disorders can be standardized, closer agreement on prevalence can be obtained even among psychiatrists in different countries.

PREVALENCE STUDIES

For example, general practice studies have shown that over a twelve month period approximately 14% of patients consult their general practitioner at least once for a condition diagnosed as largely psychiatric in nature.

The bulk of these patients would be identified, according to the International Classification of Diseases, as suffering from neurotic or personality disorders, which, therefore, take their place among the commoner conditions in practice. In spite of this only one in twenty are referred to mental health facilities, although these problems are often chronic in nature (Shepherd, 1974). Psychosis accounts for only 4% of total psychiatric morbidity in these studies compared with 25% in psychiatric hospital out-patients and 72% of first admissions to mental hospitals in England and Wales (Marks, 1973). There have been very few studies, of an equivalent nature, in mentally retarded populations and those reported have been largely of hospitalized subjects. Williams (1971) estimated that 59% of 725 patients in a group of mental handicap hospitals were psychiatrically disordered, while Forrest and Ogunremi (1974) gave a prevalence rate of only 10% for severe psychiatric disorder. A census of mentally handicapped patients in hospital (DHSS, 1972) showed 16% of in-patients as having a severe behaviour difficulty, while 16% had less severe behaviour problems. The problem is initially one of definition and various methods of rating have been used. Kushlick _et al._ (1973) described a social and physical incapacity scale and self-help and literacy measures which included items covering disruptive behaviour. This used only four items to assess severe behaviour disorder which occurred in 14% of their sample. Ballinger and Reid (1977) using the standard, clinical interview schedule of Goldberg _et al._ (1970), applied to a population of mental handicap hospital patients and a population attending an adult training centre in the community, estimated a prevalence rate of significant psychiatric disorder of 31% in the hospital group and 13% in the training centre.

Several recent studies have reported on the prevalence of psychotic illness in adults with mental retardation (Reid, 1972; Forrest and Ogunremi, 1974; Heaton Ward, 1977) and it seems clear that a small group of patients in hospital, of around 5-10%, suffer from schizophrenia or manic depressive psychosis. It is important to identify and clearly classify this group, as specific forms of treatment are available for these conditions.

Such patients do not fit easily into community care facilities, particularly during the acute phases of their illness, and yet tend to be rejected by hospital services for the mentally retarded on account of their cognitive and social deficits. Very few total population studies have been carried out. Corbett (1979) estimated that 6.2% of those in hospital or at home had a current or past history of schizophrenic illness while 2.2% had suffered from manic depressive psychosis. Many studies have reported a much larger number of people with behaviour disorders in hospitals for the mentally handicapped, the ratio varying from 10 to 60% (Penrose, 1938; Pollock, 1944). There is much less certainty about the diagnosis and treatment of these conditions, although they are often the main additional handicap causing admission to hospital and outweigh physical handicap, epilepsy and lack of social skills causing severe dependency as the primary reason for hospitalization. Penrose (1938) reported that 10% of the subjects in his Colchester study suffered from psychoneurosis while Craft (1959) reported 33% of the hospital population he studied as having personality disorders.

More recently Forrest and Ogunremi (1974) suggested that the mass of psychiatric pathology in hospitals for the mentally handicapped is made up of adults with persistence of symptoms of childhood psychosis. The terms temperamental or behaviour disorder have been used to define these problems in other studies. Attempts have been made to draw up completely new schemes of classification to describe this group. For example, Menolascino (1970) used terms such as primitive or atypical disorders of behaviour. Other writers have cast doubt on the usefulness of any attempt at classification, suggesting that behavioural abnormalities are so common among the retarded that, taking into account the mental age of the subjects, the behavioural abnormalities may be considered as merely age appropriate.

A final viewpoint suggests that any behavioural symptoms which occur are merely the result of long-term institutional care and are thus a form of institutional neurosis. It must be conceded that any attempt at classification would only be of real value if it were found that symptoms cluster together consistently and that such groupings have predictive value and give some guide as to response to treatment.

CLASSIFICATION

Kendell (1975) points out that every human being has characteristics which he shares with all mankind, those which he shares with some other men, but not all, and lastly those which are unique to him. He goes on to point out that the value of any system of classification depends on the size of the second, relative to the other two. When we come to the management of illness however, we are concerned with its uniqueness (Copeland, 1978). It is the combination of characteristics peculiar to the patient and his illness, which determine those fine adjustments necessary for the administration of treatment and the prediction of outcome. For this we turn not to the diagnosis alone, but to the formulation in which the diagnosis has been interpreted in the light of individual differences.

Psychiatric classification is, therefore, required by research workers seeking groups of patients to study, by workers who hope it will give a broad indication of treatment and prognosis, by health service planners who need to provide different types of care, and by all those who wish to communicate accurately about illness, without having to preface their remarks by long descriptions to identify their subjects.

The various terms used to describe social adaptation and psychiatric illness in the mentally retarded each have their own advantages and disadvantages. Behavioural disorder implies a careful description of the problem, but tends to view the target symptoms in isolation from their developmental background, from other aetiological or historical factors, and the patient's total life situation.

This difficulty arises in behavioural therapies, particularly aimed at the reduction in decelleration target behaviour or undesirable behaviours which may be impairing the subject's functioning, as opposed to the enhancement of skills.

In the absence of any precise account of subjective experience, the presence of emotional disorder may only be deduced with difficulty.

Coffman and Harris (1980) in a recent discussion of the adjustment of people with mental retardation to changes in their environment, noted that concepts of depression, sadness, despair, loneliness, helplessness and hopelessness, unworthiness, and disorientation are largely absent from the literature on mental retardation. There is a tendency instead to use global descriptions of behaviour disorder, psychopathy or psychosis. Yet it is precisely the former cluster of emotional symptons which figure most prominently in the adaptation of non-retarded people to acute stress, for example, resulting from a sudden change from one culture to another, bereavement, divorce or release from prison, etc. They highlight in a very useful way the adaptation experiences of mentally handicapped people. Anna Freud pointed out that most children brought for psychiatric treatment do not complain of emotional symptoms themselves, it is others who complain about them. This does not prevent us from attempting to empathize with the emotional needs of non-retarded children, but we have more difficulty in doing this when the person is handicapped and the behaviour bizarre and unusual so that we have difficulty in entering into his inner world and sharing emotional experiences.

Further difficulty arises from the fact that most studies of psychiatric disorder, and for that matter social adjustment, are of a cross-sectional nature and there are very few examples in the literature of long-term studies of emotional or behavioural disorders in severely retarded people. Recently Koller *et al.* (1983) in an epidemiological study reported that nearly 60% of severely mentally retarded children showed significant behaviour disorders persisting into early adult life. Others that have been reported tend to be of children attending special clinics and the samples have thus been highly selected (Chess, 1977; Reid, 1980).

Finally, the presence of psychiatric illness implies a particular constellation of behavioural symptoms and historical and other features and suggests the problem is amenable to a particular form of treatment.

The introduction and evaluation of a multiaxial classification for child psychiatric disorders for the 9th Revision of the International Classification of Diseases (Rutter *et al.*, 1975) has been linked with a renewed interest in the possible use of a similar scheme of classification for the mentally retarded (Tarjan *et al.*, 1972).

In this scheme the first axis describes the presence of specific psychiatric disorders; the second associated developmental disabilities; the third relates to the level of intellectual functioning; the fourth, associated biological conditions; and the fifth, abnormal psychosocial situations.

The application of this scheme, to an epidemiological study of severely retarded children, has been described by Corbett (1977), and a similar attempt to use a multiaxial approach to the description of psychiatric disorders in adults, in which psychiatric illness and personality are described on separate axes, has also been attempted (Corbett, 1979).

In this latter study an attempt was made to use the ICD glossary for personality disorder to describe the pattern of disorders seen in individual subjects as an additional axis. Symptoms were included only if they were persistent over a period of time and could be traced back into the subject's earlier history, so that the final categories could meet the WHO, criteria for personality disorder of "deeply engrained maladaptive patterns of behaviour, generally recognised by the time of adolescence and continuing through most of adult life" (WHO, 1971).

Although a number of patterns of disorder which were seen did fit the glossary definitions in the ICD, by far the larger number could not easily be described using these criteria.

Additional categories of, what might be termed, impulsive and immature behaviour were defined. In the impulsive group, the subjects' actions were usually unpredictable and ill directed, without regard to their consequences, often with irritability, rapid mood changes and violent behaviour. This group was not dissimilar to that with immature behaviour, where impulsiveness was also a feature, but here there was particular sensitivity to frustration with less adequate interpersonal relationships and marked tension and agitation. The latter group showed many of the characteristics of adolescent behaviour disturbance persisting into adult life, but could not be said to be a normal variation, merely related to mental age. As with other personality categories, there was no marked relationship with either degree of retardation or with age. In this study, there was a tendency for personality disorder to be more common in those subjects with epilepsy, but there was no consistent pattern of behavioural symptoms which could be said to comprise an epileptic personality, fitting in with other recent reviews of the subject (Corbett and Pond, 1979).

There was much greater difficulty in distinguishing personality disorders in adults with mental retardation from the late effects of childhood psychosis, than in distinguishing childhood from adult psychosis.

It must be concluded that the use of existing categories to describe personality disorders in the mentally retarded is inadequate and considerably more research is required, preferably on a longitudinal basis, to achieve greater precision and to ascertain their predictive value.

NATURE OF THE ASSOCIATION BETWEEN BEHAVIOUR DISORDERS AND MENTAL RETARDATION

In looking at the nature of the association between mental retardation and behavioural disturbance, the very heterogeneity of psychiatric disorders makes it most unlikely that a single mechanism will be found in an individual case. It is nevertheless necessary to consider the relative importance of interaction of the possible mechanisms involved, as treatment plans will need to take these into account.

Firstly, it is necessary to get the direction of the association right. Although emotional disturbance may occasionally impair intelligence, for example in hyperkinetic behaviour disorders where poor attention and distractibility may mean that a child does not concentrate sufficiently to learn from experience, it is much more often the case that intellectual retardation antedates the behaviour disturbance. Thus the backwardness or factors associated with it must be implicated in the causation of the psychiatric disorder rather than the other way round and this has been confirmed in a number of longitudinal studies of child development (Douglas *et al*., 1968).

Nearly all severely retarded children have demonstrable organic brain disease (Crome, 1960), and this is also true of a substantial minority of the mildly retarded (Rutter *et al*., 1970a). This is reflected, for example, in the increased frequency of epilepsy as the degree of intellectual retardation increases. There is good evidence that organic brain dysfunction increases the susceptibility to psychiatric disorder in normal children and it may be safely presumed that this implies to intellectually retarded children. This is strikingly seen in the behavioural improvement which may follow hemispherectomy in some subjects with infantile hemiplegia associated with behavioural disorder and epilepsy (Wilson, 1970) or following temporal lobectomy for psychomotor epilepsy (Falconer, 1974). In this case, the behaviourally disruptive effects stem less from the brain lesion itself than from its effect on the remaining intact nervous system.

With a few notable exceptions, such as Lesch Nyhan syndrome, where severe self-injurious behaviour is associated with a specific biochemical abnormality, there is generally speaking a lack of clear cut relationships between localized brain damage, dysfunction or specific biological causes of mental retardation and particular psychiatric or behavioural syndromes.

Thus children with infantile spasms or West's syndrome are likely to suffer intellectual deterioration with a behavioural picture which at times is similar to that seen in childhood psychosis. Infantile spasms may be idiopathic or symptomatic of a wide variety of pathological conditions such as phenylketonuria. In this case, the likelihood of a consistent pattern of impairments or behaviour is related more to the severity and persistence of the cerebral insult, the stage of development at which it occurred and the degree of intellectual retardation than to any direct effect.

Although important, brain damage and dysfunction cannot be the only factors. The rate of psychiatric disorder is higher in intellectually retarded children who have no evidence of brain damage, and in severely retarded children, active brain dysfunction, as evidenced by seizures, is less commonly associated with psychiatric disturbance than in children of normal intelligence (Corbett et al., 1975).

Social factors such as rejection by adults and peers play an important part in causing emotional disturbance and the relationship is again complex. While rejection may affect the child's emotional development, children may equally be rejected because of their undesirable behavioural characteristics (Jacobs and Pierce, 1968).

Temperament has also been shown to affect the adaptability of mentally retarded children. Chess and Korn (1970) concluded that temperament affects the child's adaptive capability.

The child with the highest risk of developing a disturbance was one who had three or more of the following temperamental characteristics; irregularity of biological functioning; withdrawal responses; failure in adaptability; predominantly negative mood and high intensity of emotional response. Chess and her colleagues have shown that these temperamental characteristics can be identified early in infancy, tend to be persistent and are related to the risk of subsequent behavioural disorder, particularly in mentally retarded children.

Intellectually retarded children may be adversely affected by the same kinds of family and social pathology which are associated with disorder in children of average ability, although they are likely to be more vulnerable to these. Parental instability, unsatisfactory discipline and family discord may all lead to behavioural disturbance. Conversely, the presence of the handicapped child may lead to disturbance in other family members, although it does look as though the rate of broken homes in families of retarded children does not differ greatly from that in the general population.

Similarly, there is little evidence of a marked increase in the rate of parental neurosis or in the rates of behaviour disturbance among the siblings of retarded children (Rutter et al., 1970b; Carr, 1974). Where differences have been found there is a strong suggestion that they are related to other stress factors in the family, for example, increased maternal age, larger family size and lower social class (Gath, 1973).

Social deprivation as a causative factor, leading to emotional disturbance, is highlighted by studies of the effect of institutionalization. While emotional disturbance may arise from the ill-effects of poor quality institutional care, these effects are not invariable and depend to a large extent on the quality of care provided (Rutter, 1972). A child may spend long periods in residential care in childhood and develop normally, providing the environment is sufficiently stimulating and there is an opportunity to develop lasting relationships with other people. Nowadays, when fewer children with less severe handicaps are admitted to institutional care, it seems likely that the disturbance is more frequently a cause rather than a result of institutionalization (Saenger, 1960).

Specific Impairments

Of particular importance in understanding the mechanisms underlying failures of social adaptation in the retarded have been recent studies examining specific impairments and skills and relating these to overall behaviour. Wing (1981) using structured interviews with parents and caretakers, together with careful psychological assessment of an epidemiological sample of children, was able to establish a profile of impairments for each child.

Although there was an overlap between groups of children showing particular patterns, Wing and her co-workers concluded that these groupings were more important in determining overt behaviour than the overall level of cognitive functioning of the child, although this also contributed to the clinical picture.

Wing and her colleagues describe patterns of impairment of social interaction, verbal and non-verbal communication and imaginative activities which occurred together so consistently that they could be referred to as "a triad of social and language impairment". They extended their epidemiological sample of children to include those who showed severe language disorder, but functioned above the severely retarded level. They found that 90 out of 163 children showed major impairments in social interaction, that is in the capacity to initiate or respond to social contacts with others, which is seen in normal infants from the second month of life, and was seen in sociable children irrespective of mental age.

This group of children could be further subdivided according to whether they were aloof, passive or active in their social interactions. The passive, socially impaired children showed fewer behavioural problems as long as they could follow their normal routine; while the active children tended to show odd one-sided social approaches. The aloof, socially unaware group of children, with little or no comprehension of speech or imitation or the use of non-verbal communication, showed the most severe behaviour problems, with over-activity and repetitive, aggressive, impulsive behaviour.

Wing points out that Kanner (1946), in defining early infantile autism, selected those children who were socially aloof, but had elaborate repetitive routines, needing good fitting and assembly skills and that they mostly had enough speech to show characteristic pronominal reversal and idiosyncratic use of speech. In her study, Wing found that this was one of the least common profiles and aloofness was more often combined with little or no speech, few skills and simple, repetitive routines.

In the sociable group of children, although there might be specific impairments in motor or visuo-spatial skills which were distressing to the child, and anxiety provoking when they led to failure in the school environment, the patterns of behaviour were understandable to others and predictable from the child's mental age. They accounted for the majority of children who showed emotional or conduct disorders and adaptation reactions.

The child with the triad of language and social impairment is, in contrast, strange and puzzling to other people because whatever his level of speech and practical abilities, he lacks the whole complex of action and response which are necessary for social relationships. Wing suggests that children with social or language impairment are born with or develop, as a result of specific brain damage in early infancy, limitations in their capacity to monitor normal species specific sounds or non-verbal communication. They therefore lack the ability to form complex concepts concerning their environment and recognize that other people are especially interesting and potential partners in social exchanges.

This failure in development of self-awareness in infancy underlies the strange and bizarre behaviour which is later seen in this group of socially impaired children. It does not mean that mentally retarded people with these impairments in social interaction do not become distressed and anxious over their inability to communicate with others and adapt to change in their environment. Wright (1982) has recently pointed out that they may in fact be more prone to affective illness which needs to be understood and treated.

THE DEVELOPMENT OF SELF-CONCEPT

There is now a considerable literature on the development of self-concept which although mainly derived from research with mildly retarded subjects is helpful in understanding the effect of these impairments on individual personality development (Sternlicht, 1976).

Cobb (1961) proposed that the mentally retarded child forms his self-concept through a series of five processes. The first of these is primitive differentiation and integration. The organization of experience into self or non-self is related to drive strength, the amount of sensory stimulation, maturation of the central nervous system, and the quality and quantity of parental nurturance.

The second process, that of naming and identifying and generalizing, is related to the emergence of language. The mentally retarded child who has specific difficulties in this area is particularly handicapped in attaining a sense of personal identity. During the third process of forming self-concept, the child acquires and evaluates his attributes and possessions. Here the mentally retarded child who has a reduced ability to make perceptual and conceptual discriminations will be more tolerant to those inconsistencies and ambiguities of his self-image which might be a source of anxiety to his non-retarded peers.

During the fourth process, he defines aspirations in terms of expectancies of success or failure. It is likely that, during this period, the child who experiences extreme failure or is over-protected will develop an unrealistic estimate of what he is capable of doing or not doing. In the final process, the adolescent revision of self-concept, the mentally retarded young person will be at a particular disadvantage in achieving physical maturity before the slowed down process of self-concept development is stabilized.

We know very little systematically of personality development in the people with mental retardation and much of our understanding must be based on studies of normal development.

It does, however, seem that while emotional immaturity, language disorder and educational failure are particularly important, in the severely retarded organic brain damage and temperamental deviance play an important part in accounting for the increased frequency of behavioural disorders and psychiatric disturbance which are seen.

REFERENCES

Ballinger, B.R. and Reid A.H. (1977). Psychiatric disorder in an adult training centre and a hospital for the mentally handicapped. **Psychol. Med., 7**, 525-8

Carr, J. (1974). The effect of the severely subnormal on their families. In **Mental Deficiency, the Changing Outlook.** Eds A.M. Clarke and A.D.B. Clarke. London: Methuen

Chess, S. (1977). Evolution of behaviour disorders in a group of mentally retarded children. **Journ. Amer. Acad. Child Psych. 16**, 5-18

Chess, S., and Korn, S. (1970). Temperament and behaviour disorders in mentally retarded children. **Arch. Gen. Psychiat. 23**, 122-130

Clare, A. (1978). Psychiatric morbidity in general practice: identification and treatment. In **Current Themes in Psychiatry.** Eds. R.N. Gaind and B.L. Hudson. London: Macmillan Press. pp 165-179

Cobb, H.V. (1961). Self-concept of the mentally retarded. **Rehabilitation Rec. 2**, 21-25

Coffman, T.L. and Harris, M.C. (1980). Transition shock and adjustment of the mentally retarded persons. **Mental Retardn. 18**, 3-8

Copeland, J. (1978). Psychiatric diagnosis and classification. In **Current Themes in Psychiatry.** Eds. R.N. Gaind and B.L. Hudson. London: Macmillan Press

Corbett, J.A. (1977). Population studies in mental retardation. In **Epidemiological Approaches in Child Psychiatry.** Ed. P. Graham. London: Academic Press

Corbett, J.A. (1979). Psychiatric morbidity and mental retardation. In **Psychiatric Illness and Mental Handicap.** Eds. F.E. James and R.P. Snaith. London: Gaskell Press

Corbett, J.A., Harris, R. and Robinson, R. (1975). Epilepsy. In **Mental Retardation and Developmental Disabilities**, Ed. J. Wortis, Vol. **VII**. New York: Brunner Mazel

Corbett, J.A. and Pond, D.A. (1979). Epilepsy and behaviour disorders in the mentally handicapped. In **Psychiatric Illness and Mental Handicap**. Eds. F.E. James and R.P. Snaith. London: Gaskell Press

Craft, M. (1959). Mental disorder in the defective: a psychiatric study among in-patients. **Amer. Journ. Ment. Defic. 63**, 829-34

Crome, L. (1960). The brain and mental retardation. **Brit. Med. Journ. i**, 897-904

DHSS (1972). **Census of Mentally Handicapped Patients in Hospital in England and Wales at the End of 1970**. London: HMSO

Douglas, J.W.B., Ross, J.M. and Simpson, H.R. (1968). **All Our Future**. London: Peter Davies

Falconer, M. (1974). Mesial temporal (Ammon's Horn) sclerosis as a common cause of epilepsy. **Lancet 2**, 767-70

Forrest, A.D. and Ogunremi, O.O. (1974). The prevalence of psychiatric illness in a hospital for the mentally handicapped. **Health Bulletin 32**, 1-4

Gath, A. (1973). School age siblings of mongol children. **Brit. Journ. Psychiat.**, **123**, 161-167

Goldberg, D.P., Cooper, B. and Eastwood, M.R. (1970). A standardised psychiatric interview for use in community surveys. **Brit. Journ. Prevent. and Social Med. 24**, 18-23

Heaton Ward, A. (1977). Psychosis in mental handicap. **Brit. J. Psychiat. 130**, 525-33

Jacobs, J.F. and Pierce, M.L. (1968). The social position of retardates with brain damage and associated characteristics. **Exceptional Child 34**, 677-81

Kanner, L. (1946). Irrelevant and metaphorical language in early infantile autism. **Amer. Journ. Psychiat. 103**, 242-246

Kendell, R.E. (1975). **The Role of Diagnosis in Psychiatry**. Oxford: Blackwell Scientific Publications

Koller, H., Richardson, S.A., and Katz, M. (1983). Behaviour disturbance since childhood among a 5-year birth cohort of all mentally retarded young adults in a city. **Amer. Journ. Ment. Defic. 87**, 386-395

Kushlick, A., Blunden, R. and Cox, G. (1973). A method of rating behaviour characteristics for use in large scale surveys of mental handicap. **Psychol. Med. 3**, 466-78

Marks, I.M. (1973). Research in neurosis: a selective review. 1 Causes and courses. **Psychol. Med.**, **3**, 4, 436-454

Menolascino, F. (1970). **Psychiatric Approaches to Mental Retardation**. New York: Basic Books

Penrose, L.S. (1938). **A Clinical and Genetic Study of 1,280 Cases of Mental Defect**. Medical Research Council Special Report No. 229, London

Pollock, H.M. (1944). Mental illness among mental defectives. **Amer. Journ. Psychiat. 101**, 361-3

Reid, A.H. (1972). Psychosis in adult mental defectives. I Manic depressive psychosis; II Schizophrenic and paranoid psychosis. **Brit. Journ. Psychiat. 120**, 205-218

Reid, A.H. (1980). Psychiatric disorders in mentally handicapped children: a clinical and follow up study. **Journ. Ment. Defic. Res. 24**, 287-98

Rutter, M. (1972). **Maternal Deprivation Reassessed.** Harmondsworth: Penguin

Rutter, M., Graham, P. and Yule, W. (1970a). A neuropsychiatric study in childhood. **Clinics in Dev. Med.** Nos. 35/36. London: S.I.M.P., Heinemann

Rutter, M., Schaffer, D. and Shepherd, M. (1975). **A Multiaxial Classification of Child Psychiatric Disorders.** Geneva: World Health Organisation

Rutter, M., Tizard, J. and Whitmore, K. (1970b). **Education Health and Behaviour.** London: Longman

Saenger, G. (1960). **Factors Influencing the Institutionalisation of Mentally Retarded Individuals in New York City.** A Report to the New York State Interdepartmental Health Resources Board

Shepherd, M. (1974). General practice, mental illness and the British National Health Service. **Amer. Journ. Public Hlth. 64**, 3 230-232

Sternlicht, M. (1976). Personality: One view. In **Mental Retardation and Developmental Disabilities. VIII** Ed. J. Wortis

Tarjan, G., Tizard, J., Rutter, M., Begag, M., Brooke, E.M., De la Cruz, F., Lin, T.Y, Montenegro, H., Stotza, A.H. and Sartorius, N. (1972). Classification and mental retardation. **Amer. Journ. Psychiat. 128**, 34-45 Supp.

WHO (1971). **Draft Glossary of Psychiatric Disorders.** Geneva: World Health Organisation

Williams, C.E. (1971). A study of the patients in a group of mental subnormality hospitals. **Brit. Journ. Ment. Subnorm. 17**, 29-41

Wilson, P.J.E. (1970). Cerebal hemispherectomy in the treatment of infantile hemiplegia. A report of 50 cases. **Brain 93**, 147-180

Wing, L. (1981). Language, social and cognitive impairments in autism and severe mental retardation. **Journ. Autism and Dev. Disorders. 11**, 31-44

Wright, E.C. (1982). The presentation of mental illness in mentally retarded adults. **Brit. Journ. Psychiat. 141**, 496-502

COMMENTARY

A. Kushlick

Corbett values psychiatric descriptive systems to the extent that people using them are enabled to:

1. note symptoms clustering together consistently,
2. make accurate and useful predictions about and
3. receive useful guidance in treating individuals on the basis of the data clusters.

He names the following categories of people who benefit from effective descriptive systems:

1. research workers studying groups of patients (presumably also predicting outcomes related to treatments given by them or others)
2. workers looking for guidance on whether different treatments are effective
3. health service planners who wish to provide different types of care (presumably because these differences reflect different treatment packages)
4. all people wanting "to communicate accurately about illness, without ... long descriptions".

I agree with these aims. However, his text is critical of methods (e.g. behavioural approaches) which already fulfil important criteria of treatment and communication. He also offers alternative directions which, I believe, miss his targets.

Thus, the paper suggests that behavioural therapies necessarily:

1. describe problem behaviour disorder carefully but fail to include in the description
   - "their developmental background"
   - "other aetiological or historical facts"
   - "the patient's total life situation"
2. aim at deceleration of undesirable behaviour rather than enhancing positive skill development
3. are insensitive to emotional disorder because of "the absence of any precise account of subjective experience"
4. avoid issues described by the "concepts of depression, sadness, despair, loneliness and hopelessness, unworthiness and disorientation..."
5. tend "instead to use global descriptions of behaviour disorder, psychopathy or psychosis".

An examination of the behavioural literature will show that behavioural approaches virtually never use the global descriptions which do, however, characterize non-behavioural approaches. It will also show that key features of this approach include positive behavioural targets (dependent variables - DVs), e.g. skill development (plus avoidance of eliminative approaches), a clear description of important features of the client's environment (social and physical) including people in that environment likely to support or obstruct any intervention (independent variables - IVs) towards the targets, the history of development of the current behavioural repertoire, and past attempts (successful and unsuccessful) to deal with this and similar problems (Goldiamond, 1974; Schwartz and Goldiamond, 1975).

My comments will show that to the extent that Corbett recommends deviating from a behavioural approach, he weakens effective responses which aim to strengthen the rich and valuable current repertoire of people called mentally handicapped and their relatives. On the other hand, he appears to advise approaches of which he is himself critical and which are clearly non-behavioural.

Thus, Corbett is critical of his own use of the 9th revision of ICD (Rutter et al., 1975).

1. He was unable to categorize within the labels of ICD the different "patterns of disorder" (presumably of disruptive behaviour topographies) of the majority of people whose behaviour he was attempting to describe.

2. He noted in people of all ages and wide repertoire ranges, behaviour not categorized on the ICD, and which appeared more appropriately categorized - "impulsive... immature" and with such features as "unpredictable... ill directed... without regard to their consequences... irritability... rapid mood changes and violent behaviour... adolescent behaviour disturbance persisting...".

His suggested intervention is "more research... on a longitudinal basis" as a step towards "greater precision" and "predictive value". His original aim of producing guidance in treatment no longer features.

I agree with Corbett that treatment plans are effective to the extent that they take into account the relationship between identifiable, measurable, manipulable IVs and clearly observable levels of dependent variables (DVs). However, he seems to suggest a value in describing as causal (IV-DV) relationships, statistical co-variations and co-relations between coexisting components of the dependent variables, i.e. of behavioural traits themselves, e.g.:

> "emotional disturbance (DV_1) may occasionally impair intelligence" (DV_2)

> "poor attention (DV_1) and distractibility (DV_2) may mean that a child does not concentrate sufficiently to learn" (DV_3)

> "backwardness (DV_1) antedates the behaviour disturbance" (DV_2)

> "backwardness (DV_1) ... must be implicated in the causation of the psychiatric disorder" (DV_2).

In the first two of these instances the behaviours from which the general constructs (intelligence, concentration) are inferred cannot take place at the same time as the so-called cause of their impairment, i.e. at the same time as the person is performing "emotional disturbance" or "poor attention and distractibility". From the management point of view, a powerful constructional intervention (IV) which successfully attains appropriate attention to and concentration on a task (DV_1), will probably also be observed to have improved "emotional disturbance" (DV_2), "poor attention" (DV_3), and "distractibility" (DV_4). Similarly, a powerful intervention (IV) which succeeds in accelerating learning (DV_1), or increasing the duration of on-task behaviour (DV_2), would probably be seen to reduce "psychiatric disorder" (DV_3) or "behaviour disturbance" (DV_4). It is unlikely that attention to a desired learning task would be seen at the same time as "behaviour disturbance". (An exception to this occurs when a "disturbed" person is with a very competent teacher or therapist who continues teaching procedures in the face of the client's negative emotional responses.) A single package of powerful and manipulable independent variables (e.g. clear instructions given after attention has been gained, and at least 5 s after any disruptive behaviour, relevant materials, an effective prompt, if needed, and powerful reinforcers) may well elicit simultaneously such DVs as attention to task, behaviours labelled intelligent, and behaviours labelled emotionally mature. In addition, changes in any component of the IV (e.g. inconsistent instructions or contingent ignoring of on-task and reinforcement of off-task behaviour) may, in some individuals, set the occasion for very "disturbed" behaviour (see Notes). Although the traits may be observed to co-vary in longitudinal or cross-sectional studies of groups, "backwardness" cannot usefully be described in any individual as a cause of "psychiatric disorder".

Only to the extent that a clearly described CNS intervention can be shown to change the client's behaviour dramatically (e.g. surgical removal of localized brain pathology leads to changes in perfomance and/or convulsions) can damaged brain usefully be treated as an IV to the DV ordinary social behaviour at home. Organic brain disease among children labelled severely retarded may usefully be considered a DV in its own right by pathologists or epidemiologists looking for IVs which may cause it. However, compared with easily manipulable IVs, which are available on a minute-to-minute basis throughout the day or night, and which control observable minute-to-minute behaviour DVs (e.g. the types of antecedent, concurrent and consequent features of the client's environments), organic brain disease is an unhelpful explanation and non-manipulable IV of the following important dependent variables: the current repertoire of the child, or his rate of learning new skills under specified conditions.

Because of the short-hand way in which he describes IV-DV relationships, Corbett treats different phenomena as if they were the same:

i) "rejections by adults (IV) ... causing emotional disturbance ... in the child (DV)" is inappropriately presented as the reverse of

ii) presence of children with undesirable behavioural characteristics (IV) causing adults to reject the child (DV).

Corbett makes the same error elsewhere. The statement is made:

> "Family and social pathology", and "parental instability, unsatisfactory discipline and family discord (the IVs) may all lead to behavioural disturbance" (DV).

This is said to be the converse of:

> "the presence of the handicapped child (IV) may lead to disturbances in other family members" (DV).

Powerful and manipulable (potential treatment) IVs controlling the level of emotional disturbance or on-task behaviour in a child at any time are the antecedents (gaining of attention, instructions, arranging materials); concurrents (prompts); and consequences (reinforcers) delivered to the child (inevitably by the adults). The retarded child's behaviours seldom improve, and indeed often deteriorate, in an environment where adults fail to provide an effective teaching interaction intended to shape up appropriate skills. However, even in the presence of the most severely handicapped and assaultive person, adults can deliver very effective teaching interactions, spend more time effectively in the presence of such a person, and create an environment which increases the "on-task" non-disturbed behaviour of the person (Favell, 1983).

Adults whose teaching interaction lacks clear instructions and prompts, includes contingent reinforcement of inappropriate behaviour (Budd *et al.*, 1976) or who spend little time interacting with handicapped people can easily create an environment which increases the handicapped person's disruptive behaviour (Hart and Risley, 1976). However, compared with the high proportion of the observable IVs controlled in a retarded person's environment by non-retarded adults, the behaviour (of all kinds) of the retarded person is only one of many observable IVs controlling the behaviour of the caring adult. Corbett notes that even descriptive-statistical studies fail to show co-variation in rating scale scores of neurosis among parents and siblings of retarded children.

A similar error occurs elsewhere. The following statements are made as if they clearly related to one another:

> "poor quality institutional care" (IV) may cause "emotional disturbances" in the residents (DV)

> "poor quality institutional care" (IV) *does not always cause* "emotional disturbances" (DV)

"the (presumably poor) quality of care provided" (IV) determines the level of emotional disturbance in residential care

Given residential care which is "sufficiently stimulating and the opportunity to develop lasting relationships ..." (IV) (therefore not poor quality) "a child may spend long periods in (this) residential care in childhood and develop normally ..." (DV).

Corbett continues:

Nowadays, "institutionalization" (presumably the quality of the adult-child interaction in residential care) (IV) less frequently causes child "disturbance" (DV) than does child "disturbance" (IV) cause "institutionalization" (DV), i.e. either: the quality of the adult-child interaction in residential care or the process of transfer of the child from home by the parents or others to a residential care setting.

Nowadays, as at any time in the past, the behaviour of children in residential and day care is powerfully controlled by the quality of IVs which make up the environment which teaches and maintains their appropriate or disruptive and emotional behaviours. Similarly, the independent variables controlling the behaviour of frontline staff, professionals, managers and planners of the residential units as well as of the children's parents are controlled by many IVs other than the behaviour of severely retarded children, or the IVs controlled by these children's behaviour. Although I do not believe he meant it this way, the reader would be correct to infer from Corbett's text that he believes the behaviour of all concerned with providing residential care or deciding on transfers is overwhelmingly determined by the retarded themselves. I only want to demonstrate how attempts to make descriptions simple, and to avoid the relevant details, can have the effect of confusing the reader, preventing effective interventions to solve relatively simple problems, and to attribute to powerless clients the deficits of institutional environments designed and provided for their care by people controlling very powerful IVs.

Corbett discusses the identification of the cluster of behavioural traits (DVs) noted in clinical and epidemiological studies of children categorized "autistic":

Skill Deficits	Skill Excesses
social interactions	over-activity
non-verbal communication	passivity
verbal communication	aloofness
imaginative activities	repetitive routines
attention to task on and without request	aggressive impulsive behaviour
	non-compliance with requests

In relation to his own criteria of effective psychiatric descriptive systems, this discussion is weakened by the following features:

- i) describing the list of skill deficits and excesses as a "triad"
- ii) describing the individual domains of deficits as "impairments", i.e. irremediable objective features of the people concerned
- iii) describing the clusters of skill deficits or the individual domains as independent variables "determining overt behaviour" (an undescribed DV).

Our present state of knowledge is unhelpfully inflated by:

- i) suggesting an IV ("specific brain damage in early infancy") as the main cause of the behavioural deficits and excesses (also described as "impairments"). There is no observable evidence of "specific brain damage", and there is no way (except through direct intervention on the brain) of demonstrating how brain damage affects an individual's minute-to-minute behaviour in any setting
- ii) renaming the observed skill deficits (DVs) as new independent variables (IVs) "limitations in their capacity to monitor normal species specific sounds or non-verbal communication"
- iii) presenting the above newly-named IVs as causes of the DV's "lack the ability to form complex concepts concerning their environment" and "lack the ability to ... recognize that other people are especially interesting and potential partners in social exchanges"
- iv) renaming the observed DVs as yet another IV ("failure in self-awareness in infancy")
- v) suggesting that this new IV is causally related to ("underlies") the newly-named DV "the strange and bizarre behaviour"
- vi) suggesting that the observed skill level (DV) called "inability to communicate with others" and "inability to ... adapt to changes in their environment" are IVs explaining the newly-mentioned DVs "becoming distressed and anxious".

On the other hand, the existing level of helpful knowledge is seriously deflated by:

- i) failing to provide information on the large and growing literature demonstrating, in a wide range of settings (home, school, hospital), the effectiveness of easily observable and replicable interventions (IVs) aimed at building specific skills (DVs) from different domains including verbal and non-verbal communication. Modest successes are being attained, despite the difficulties, among people with very low levels of communication and imitation skills who also have longstanding non-comply and assaultive skills. Attention is being directed towards the difficult targets of attaining generalization across skills, settings and people, and maintenance over time under conditions of less intensive programming (Stokes and Baer, 1977; Koegel et al., 1977, 1978).

ii) failure to provide information from the literature describing successful interventions in "normal" environments to decrease emotional behaviours, e.g. tantruming, assaults, self-injuries, shouting, escape and withdrawal (DVs) emitted under observable conditions of antecedents, concurrents and consequences (IVs) by building alternative and incompatible positive behaviours, or by consequating the negative behaviours more appropriately (Favell, 1983).

Corbett recommends an approach to describing the development of the individual personality and "self-concept". In this, very few IVs are mentioned, and the non-observable DV constructs are all inferred from DVs which can be more simply described (as long as there are data) as observable behaviour occurring under specified conditions. The potentially observable DVs of "personality development", "behavioural disorders" and "psychiatric disturbance" are not illuminated by the other variables described, for example:

Stage	Observable IVs	Non-observable IV constructs	Non-observable DV constructs	Observable DVs
I	sensory stimulation (presumably current)	drive strength maturation	differentiation integration	none
	quantity and quality of parental interaction		organization of experience of the self and non-self	
II	none		emergence of language	naming
			personal identity handicap	identifying and generalizing
III	none		makes discriminations listed across	acquires possessions
				evaluates possessions
			acquires attributes listed across	evaluates attributes
				notes inconsistencies and ambiguities in above descriptions and shows tolerance of them

Stage	Observable IVs	Non-observable IV constructs	Non-observable DV constructs	Observable DVs
example continued:				notes inconsistencies etc. and is intolerant and shows anxiety
			reduced ability to make perceptual and conceptual discriminations	does not note above descriptions
IV	none			defines expectancies of success or failure
				defines "extreme failure" and estimates capacity to do or not to do
		overprotection	experiences extreme failure	unrealistically
V	none		process of self-concept x slow x stable	revises self-concept achieves physical maturity
	educational		language disorder emotional immaturity	personality development
		organic brain damage	temperamental deviance	behavioural disorders
				psychiatric disturbance

Other serious deficits are the failure to refer to the rapidly growing literature on:

i) models of describing methods of setting and attaining behavioural targets with a precision which allows outsiders (including parent or teachers) to monitor whether or not they are being attained in the relevant settings, ways of teaching people without previous teacher training to implement teaching procedures after very short (3 days) training (Shearer and Shearer, 1972), and to replicate in new settings with different client groups systems developed in one setting with one client group (Smith *et al*., 1977; Revill and Blunden, 1979; Pugh, 1981).

ii) skills of evaluating people's accounts of their experiences, and of noting different consequences for the behaviour (verbal, non-verbal and feeling or mood) of the person making the description; some of these consequences appear to arise from the degree of precision of the description itself (Beck, 1976; Ellis, 1962; Meichenbaum, 1974).

Neglect of these advances and those represented by the constructional approach (Goldiamond, 1974) may be reflected in Corbett's observation that "depression, sadness, despair, loneliness, helplessness and hopelessness, unworthiness and disorientation are largely absent from the literature of mental retardation". The wider range of available intervention repertoires suggest that they are valuable resources to those working with retarded people with sufficient verbal repertoires, and to parents and other adults caring for all categories of handicapped person (Ellis, 1962; Wolfe and Brund, 1977).

Even if the DVs in diagnostic clusters could be reliably measured, and shown to be independent of one another, and different to other clusters, and even if there were good evidence that a single powerful IV is associated with the occurrence of the cluster or components, there seem few helpful advances which have followed efforts aimed at examining these. A single stable organic IV (e.g. abnormal chromosomal material in Down's syndrome; gross deformities of the brain shape present in a high proportion of people categorized as severely or profoundly retarded) can very seldom be usefully manipulated to alter the minute-to-minute quality of life of a handicapped person. Only one mentally retarded person having frequent convulsions, out of 338 subjected to up to 15 different tests (including lumbar puncture, EEG, skull X-ray, echoencephalography, pneumo-encephalography, cerebral angiography, and others, and found to have obvious signs of brain pathology) was found to be treatable by neurosurgery; he benefited non-specifically after neurosurgery (Kushlick, 1975, a review of Iivanainen, 1974). I believe that there are some possible reasons for the persistence of these unhelpful "explanations".

It might be useful to identify with a view to preventing it a single powerful environmental agent (IV) causing severe brain damage (DV). In relation to this target, it might be helpful to identify many cases with this organic DV in order to look for a key IV among the many possible environmental IVs shared by individuals with the DV, and not shared by members of the unaffected host population. Snow's successful identification of a shared water supply (IV) among people with cholera (DV) (Snow, 1855) is the model. As brain damage (the DV) is difficult to identify before death without brain biopsy, it would be handy to have an easily observable behavioural indicator of specific brain pathology, i.e. one that reliably identified index cases. It would be interesting to know whether the neuropathologists at the conference find behavioural trait data helpful in identifying living people with specific brain pathology.

A second reason for identifying the cluster of behavioural DVs would be to identify people who:

i) shared a particularly advantageous response to a known rare, expensive treatment (IV), i.e. required priority access to special facilities not effective for people without the DV cluster

ii) shared a particularly disadvantageous response to a widely used treatment (IV) which is being frequently and damagingly applied to all developmentally delayed people by professionals because of their inability to discriminate the special category of person who would not be damaged by this environment.

There has long been a view shared by some professionals and parents that people categorized as autistic, blind, deaf, need to live and receive formal education in "specialist" units. One reason for this has been concern that they deteriorate in facilities - residential and day - designed and provided for people with other diagnoses, e.g. for people called "mentally handicapped". This view is clearly rational as long as respected and powerful professionals, managers and politicians describe as "therapeutic" for the people who live there, environments like facilities for retarded people which lack or veto major features of the contingencies and materials known to support residents practising relevant and appropriate skills. Such places often include special features differentially training people in idleness and inappropriate activities (Felce et al., 1977).

It is rational to aim to identify categories of people who share diagnostic features around which effective support groups can organize to avoid admission of people with particular diagnoses to poor facilities and to set up better alternatives.

Similarly, there has long been a professional and lay view that the so-called global "condition" of emotional disturbance in a child is powerfully "caused" by irremediable global defects in the parents. Parents have therefore compounded the effect of the troublesome activities of their child, with irrational beliefs (other people's and their own) that any problems with their children arise because they (the parents) are "worthless" and "guilty" rather than "fallible", and able, like others, to learn from experience. It has, therefore, been rational to note that the children have anatomical and physiological features which could not possibly have been created by parental management. It may even be seen as rational or kind, or supportive, to assert that these features rather than parental contingency management are the major determinants of the children's minute-to-minute behaviour during the day.

I disagree with such an approach.

I believe that the interests of the handicapped client (no matter how deformed the brain, chromosomes or other features), and the members of the family, are best served by creating environments in which individuals living there have opportunities for learning new and relevant skills to enjoy their lives in this natural environment, without major inconvenience to others, and to practise and elaborate on these skills. I also believe that their best interests are served by:

i) describing with all the precision we have, the DVs we are concerned with, i.e. the current minute-to-minute behaviour of the individuals concerned - the strengths for maintenance and development as well as the excesses for weakening

ii) describing with similar precision the observable environmental variables (IVs) which can be easily changed in the ordinary course of people's lives, and which will lead to the attainment of behavioural targets by both the people being cared for and those caring for them.

The behaviours concerned include those described as: a) cognitive; b) emotional and c) activities other than a) and b). The successes attained for people called schizophrenic by teaching new skills to their families (Falloon et al., 1982), is an important recent additional demonstration for those of us working in the complex field of mental retardation of the effectiveness of clear behavioural interventions in relation to problems long regarded with little hope.

NOTES

The unhelpfulness of explaining one DV by reference to another is illustrated in the following analogies:

Walking around "aimlessly" may be described as an impairment causing lack of sitting "purposefully"; alternatively this type of walking may be seen as incompatible with purposeful sitting.

Lack of joining dots may be seen as an impairment causing lack of writing or of performing neurosurgical operations; alternatively joining dots may be viewed as a prerequisite skill of writing and of neurosurgery.

Lack of talking may be described as an impairment causing lack of describing or evaluating behaviour (one's own or others'); alternatively talking may be viewed as a prerequisite skill of evaluating.

References

Beck, A.T., (1976). **Cognitive Therapy and the Emotional Disorders.** International University Press, New York

Budd, K.S., Green, D.R. and Baer, D.M., (1976). An analysis of multiple misplaced parental social contingencies, **Journal of Applied Behaviour Analysis, 9**, 459-470

Ellis, A., (1962). **Reason and Emotion in Psychotherapy**, Lyle Stuart, New York

Falloon, I.R.H., Boyd, J.L., McGill, C.W., Razani, J., Moss, H.B. and Gilderman, A.M., (1982). Family management in the prevention of exacerbation of schizophrenia. A controlled study. **New England Journal of Medicine, 306**, 1437-40

Favell, J.E., (1983). The management of aggressive behaviour. In Schopler, E. and Mesibov, G. (eds.), **Autism in Adolescents and Adults**, Plenum, London

Felce, D., Kushlick, A., Lunt, B. and Powell, L., (1977). **Evaluation of Locally-based Hospital Units in Wessex: Detailed Rules for Setting-up and Maintenance of the Units**, Report No 124, Health Care Evaluation Research Team, Winchester

Goldiamond, I., (1974). Toward a constructional approach to social problems, **Behaviourism, 2**, 1-84

Hart, B.M. and Risley, T.R., (1976). Environmental programming: implications for the severely handicapped. In Prehm and Dietz (eds.), **Early Intervention for the Severely Handicapped: Programming and Accountability**, Severely Handicapped Learner Program, Monograph No. 2, University of Oregon, Portland, Oregon

Koegel, R.L., Glann, T.J. and Nieminen, G.W., (1978). Generalization of parent-training results, **Journal of Applied Behaviour Analysis, 11**, 95-109

Koegel, R.L., Russo, D.C. and Rincover, A., (1977). Assessing and training teachers in the generalized use of behaviour modification with autistic children, **Journal of Applied Behaviour Analysis, 10**, 197-205

Kushlick, A., (1975). Review of **A Study on the Origins of Mental Retardation** (Clinics in Developmental Medicine, No 51) by M. Iivanainen, 1974, Spastics International Medical Publications, in **Journal of Neurological Science, 26**, 462-465

Meichenbaum, D.H., (1974). **Cognitive Behaviour Modification**, General Learning Press, New Jersey

Pugh, G. (ed.), (1981). **Parents as Partners: Intervention schemes and group work with parents of handicapped children**, National Children's Bureau, London

Revill, S. and Blunden R., (1979). A home training service for pre-school developmentally handicapped children, **Behaviour Research and Therapy, 17**, No 3, 207-214

Rutter, M., Schaffer D. and Shepherd M., (1975). **A Multiaxial Classification of Child Psychiatric Disorders**. World Health Organization, Geneva

Schwartz, A. and Goldiamond I., (1975). **Social Casework, A Behavioral Approach**, Columbia University Press

Shearer, M.S. and Shearer D.E., (1972). The Portage Project: A Model for early childhood education, **Exceptional Children, 38**, 210-17

Smith, J., Kushlick A. and Glossop C., (1977). **The Wessex Portage Project: a home teaching service for families with a pre-school mentally handicapped child**, Research Report No 125, Health Care Evaluation Research Team, Winchester

Snow, J., (1855). **On the Mode of Communication of Cholera**, J. Churchill, London, quoted in Susser, M. (1973), **Causal Thinking in the Health Science's Concepts and Strategies in Epidemiology**, Oxford University Press, New York

Stokes, T.F. and Baer D.M., (1977). An implicit technology of generalization. **Journal of Applied Behaviour Analysis, 10**, 349-368

Wolfe, J.L. and Brund, E. (eds), (1977). Twenty years of rational therapy, **Proceedings of the First National Conference on Rational Psychotherapy**, Institute for Rational Living, New York

W. I. Fraser

I would like to compliment Corbett and Kushlick on their vigorous academic dispute. I see it this way - they both agree on the need for better description of retarded patients' behaviours. Kushlick makes a particular issue of the need for specific behavioural act delineation. Behavioural checklists are not, however, the most economical descriptions of facts for clinical, educational or heuristic purposes. Corbett makes a plea for classifications - so does Rawnsley who says we have to start from scratch. I believe that multivariate methods have provided us already with examples of factor analysis of behaviour and cluster techniques. We know from Rotary scales that clusters are stable, and from parallel work by psychiatrists that symptoms of "neurosis" and "depression" cluster. In contrast, retarded individuals receive, in institutions, neuroleptic drugs without a clear diagnosis being made, unless they can speak. Psychiatrists fail to make diagnosis of neurosis and depression when language skills of retarded people are absent.

P. Mittler

What is the nature of the link between brain dysfunction and behaviour disorder in a severely mentally handicapped person? And even if clear evidence of such an association can be demonstrated, this by no means rules out the possibility of behavioural intervention which aims to reduce the severity of or even eliminate the problematic behaviour.

M. D. Mulcahy

Corbett's paper on psychiatry and mental retardation highlights the problems connected with both definition and prevalence and the difficulty of separating the contribution of organic brain damage from social factors and the question of temperament. Further he pays particular attention to the developmental aspects which are essential to the understanding of any psychiatric disturbance whether appearing early or late in life.

The problems of definition remain and will remain for some time even at a simple descriptive level. Impeding the growth of knowledge in this area is the lack of interest within psychiatry and among psychiatrists for the subject of mental handicap whether complicated by psychiatric illness or not. A review of psychiatric textbooks in the R.S.M. library undertaken for the purpose of this commentary showed that most devoted little space to mental handicap and some none at all. The Harvard Guide to Modern Psychiatry is more blunt. It speaks of psychiatrists tending towards "professional disengagement" from mental retardation. Despite such frequent disengagements mental retardation and its large psychiatric connection stubbornly refuse to vanish. Corbett highlights once again the high prevalence of psychiatric morbidity in what is already a very prevalent condition. On a more hopeful note he refers to the promising approaches to diagnosis that have been made in recent years by such psychiatrists as Reid (1980) and Wright (1982). However, we badly need more whole population studies to put into perspective the very high prevalence rates for mental illness reported from the admittedly selected populations of mentally retarded persons in hospital.

Whether or not organic brain damage is present, Corbett emphasizes the importance of and devotes much of his paper to social and developmental factors. The last few years have seen the introduction of early intervention programmes in many countries. These are directed both at remedying a child's specific deficits and perhaps more importantly optimizing the parents' capacity to accept and manage what is otherwise a potentially pathological situation. We must await the outcome of longitudinal studies to see to what extent the problem of the "disturbed" mentally handicapped will resolve itself under the twin influences of early intervention programmes and better environments for the handicapped child. Presumably and hopefully much of the so-called "disturbance" will disappear. There will remain a hard core of patients whose mental illness exists despite rather than because of their mental retardation. The greatest difficulty such patients now face and will continue to experience is the gaining of access to skilled psychiatric care under conditions at least as good as those available to the non-retarded mentally ill.

References

Harvard Guide to Modern Psychiatry (1978). Belknap Press, Harvard

Reid A.H. (1980). Psychiatric disorders in mentally handicapped children: A clinical follow-up study. **J. Ment. Defic. Research, 24**, 287-98

Wright E.C. (1982). The presentation of mental illness in mentally retarded adults. **Brit. J. Psychiat., 141**, 496-502

D. A. Pond

This is a valuable, if selective survey of the literature illuminated by the author's own important studies. It shows up the two usual epidemiological difficulties of case finding and definition of diagnostic categories. Medical and psychiatric research largely and rightly concentrate now on the problems of the severely subnormal, leaving the less severely handicapped to the educational field. There is no difficulty in case finding as regards severe mental retardation; the problem lies with the associated psychiatric disorders, though the latter is more easily done with the formal mental illnesses corresponding to schizophrenia and manic-depression than with behaviour disorders and personality problems - as is of course the case with epidemiological surveys of those of normal intelligence.

The author makes a laudable effort to link the personality problems with normal personality development, but the data so far available do not really enable this suggestion to be carried out in any detail. This is partly because, although he refers to social and family influences affecting personality development even in the retarded, I do not think he gives this adequate weight. I am surprised, for instance, that he does not refer to the studies of Anne Gath.

The second useful concept of which he does not make adequate use is the idea of critical periods. I know that the older formulations of this concept have been rightly almost discredited, but in terms of nature/nurture interaction affecting brain development as is known experimentally, the concept of certain vital environmental experiences at the right time of brain development is crucial. It is of interest that many of the disorders that seem particularly predisposed to communication difficulties (e.g. encephalopathies and infantile spasms) tend to occur at times when language development is going through very critical phases.

K. Rawnsley

The Mental Deficiency Section of the Royal College of Psychiatrists has recently balloted to change its title to the Psychiatry of Mental Handicap. This is welcome but having read Corbett's paper the feeling prevails that the Section must be starting almost from scratch in some fundamental areas. Epidemiological studies have yielded widely different estimates of the frequency of various categories of mental illness in the mentally handicapped. The point has been made that the ordinary diagnostic categories familiar in psychiatry of the non mentally handicapped may not be particularly relevant.

For the newly named Section to fulfil its title and to develop with sure-footed step a research programme involving both epidemiological and clinical approaches is demanded. Problems will abound - the definition of an appropriate population of the mentally handicapped to study; the identification of mental illness in such a population; the categorization of varieties of personality disorder which may be "special" to the mentally handicapped. Longitudinal studies could provide data on the natural history of these disorders with important lessons for prognosis and implication for management.

Bearing in mind the assertions of Forrest and Ogunremi (1974) mentioned in the paper that much mental illness in the handicapped is the residue of childhood psychosis, a lengthy time scale might be necessary for longitudinal studies and the close co-operation of child psychiatrists would be imperative.

The serious limitation of the phenomenological approach in the handicapped makes for real difficulties both in devising suitable diagnostic categories and in placing any particular case. Some alleviation may be expected from the use of multiaxial classification where diagnosis is but one of several dimensions.

Apart from the problem of assessing and labelling symptoms a further difficulty arises in the description and quantification of personality traits. These cannot be ignored as is evident from the comment covering the association between risk of developing "behavioural disorder" and childhood personality.

The newcomer might well recoil in dismay from the complexities of aetiology in this field. The presence of an organic brain lesion may not only generate specific mental consequences, e.g. language impairment, but may produce complicated "knock-on" effects in the field of emotion or of social adjustment. However, the nettle must be firmly grasped because not only will the results be important in mental handicap, they may well have a resonance in the causation and psychopathology of mental illness generally.

Chapter 23

The psychiatrist and the retarded epileptic child

D.C. Taylor

"PEOPLE, NOT PATIENTS"*

At a time of intense demedicalization of mental handicap care, the situation of the mentally handicapped chronically sick child deserves special consideration. Epilepsy is the most prevalent secondary chronic health problem and it identifies a sub-population with markedly increased risks of being in less privileged accommodation. There is a need for continuing, well informed, medical care of the retarded epileptic child, for medical research into the aetiology of seizure disorders associated with handicap, and for psychiatric care of consequent behavioural problems and social difficulties. This paper considers the role of the child psychiatrist, the relationship between epilepsy and handicap, the epidemiology and prevalence of epilepsy in the handicapped children, the influence of ontogeny on the seizures, and concludes by suggesting the variety of ways in which child psychiatrists could be of service.

PSYCHIATRISTS AND EPILEPSY

The mentally handicapped, the mentally ill, and the neurologically sick were gradually separated from one another and from the poor and the criminal as acts of charity and mercy within the great houses of confinement. The confinement was not a medical act but a social or political one (Foucault, 1971; Rosen, 1968) as was the gross overpopulation of the mental hospitals during the 19th century (Hunter and McAlpine, 1974) and as indeed is the late 20th century urge towards dispersion. The much reviled "medical model" in the sense of well ordered bioscientific practice was, in the care of the mentally handicapped, more evident in the breach than the observance. Even so the mental hospitals were the likely destination of most

---

* From P. Mittler's book of the same title.

survivors of cerebral disorder and psychiatrists made considerable contributions to knowledge. The rise of neurology on the one hand, and the psychoanalytic movement and its consequences on the other, served to prejudice the position of the psychiatrists in mental handicap which, together with a change in social attitude and the prospect of the eventual dispersion, has made their position largely untenable. Consequently many psychiatrists now feel daunted at the prospect of coping with the sick handicapped. There is however still a considerable need to bring specifically psychiatric skills to the benefit of the handicapped. I want to promote the idea that the tactics which the child psychiatrist uses in the diabetic or the leukaemia clinic are valuable adjuncts to the care of the epileptic child; but that policy depends on a corpus of knowledge which will first be reviewed.

EPILEPSY AND HANDICAP

Epilepsy is a recurrent, transient, brain dysfunction, with altered consciousness associated with abnormal electrical discharges which may be detectable by electroencephalography. It is best regarded as one form of brain dysfunction which may betoken the co-existence of other forms of brain abnormality, damage, or dysfunction. Hence, when severe and persistent it is not surprising that epilepsy will often be associated with cognitive and behavioural disorder. This association has been under-emphasized in an effort to reduce prejudice about epilepsy (Taylor, 1973). A wide variety of semantic and statistical contortions, including speculations about the representativeness of the samples concerned and the influence of the "epilepsy *per se*", are resorted to in efforts to partition two serious aspects of brain dysfunction; epileptic fits and reduced intelligence. Part of the problem stems from the complexity of their potential interactions.

Some children, who are apparently normal, develop epilepsy and then deteriorate mentally, but other normal children seem able to suffer seizures without coincident or subsequent deterioration. Other children show some evidence of mental handicap before seizures supervene. The epilepsy may seem to worsen their condition. Yet other children, normal or handicapped, develop seizures, deteriorate, and die. There have been great difficulties in coming to terms with these problems. For example, an obscure but long and bitter argument in medicine, which started in 1826, surrounds the origin of the sclerosis of mesial temporal structures seen in so many of the brains of people with epilepsy. To accept the solution, by no means universally accepted, that it is caused by prolonged seizures in early childhood as a result of cell deaths occurring in an exquisitely predictable fashion, and giving rise to a focus of chronic epilepsy, means tolerating a very complex form of causality. I do accept this argument and my view is that it is only one aspect of a general reciprocal enabling between the liability to seizures and the pre-existence of any form of cerebral imperfection. The general liability to seizure which is inherent in the organization of any complex central nervous system is severely tested during each of the brain's major growths/transformations but especially in its first postnatal epoch. One clue to the cerebral developmental component of seizure risk is the omnipresent sex difference in attack rate and outcome of the epilepsies (Ounsted and Taylor, 1972). Another is the changing patterns of seizure disorder, electrocerebral activity, and treatment needs in a developing child with a static cerebral lesion.

The problem about the relationship between "brain damage" and "epilepsy *per se*" is nicely typified in certain hydranencephalics. These children's primitive brain stem functions may do service to seeming normality for a while postnatally (Warkany and Dignan, 1975). They may produce the most primitive levels of seizuring, twitches, or even infantile spasms (Neville, 1972). Similarly other children with major but lesser impairments to proper cerebral functioning will not necessarily declare them until the appropriate challenge arises in their ontogeny. If fits supervene to draw attention to this impairment the seizure process may be falsely attributed a causal role. The mystery of the infantile spasms in hydranencephalus only exists in a logic which insists that one must be "causal" of the other. As we shall see, the earlier the onset of epilepsy, that is to say the earlier the brain declares its inability otherwise to contain its dysfunctional condition, the worse the eventual outlook. But the earlier the onset of epilepsy the less the child needs to have achieved to pass as relatively normal. This is partly the problem of the so-called pertussis encephalopathy. A toxic-febrile state is induced in a large number of babies at one fixed point very early in development. The normal random toxic-febrile events would of course be more scattered in time. Drawn together to one fixed point in time this toxic-febrile reaction tests the integrity of the central nervous system to a degree where the occasional child confesses, before it otherwise would, its parlous nature. Thus, tried out over the fulcrum of this one test, there appears the spurious effect of a causal relationship between "encephalopathy" and "vaccine". And hence the apparent origins of other epileptic encephalopathies. This does not preclude the onset of encephalopathic disorders in otherwise normal children but is an alternative explanation which suits some cases better.

Parents, and indeed doctors, looking into this for meaning (why is this happening to me?) see epilepsy in a variety of guises; as a transient severe fright, as a wrecker of lives, or as a killer. There are true sources of the prejudice at the core of the stereotype. Epilepsy is socially aversive (Ounsted, 1971). The only valid way in which the rubric "epilepsy" is meaningful is its social meaning.

INCIDENCE AND PREVALENCE

Despite the caveats that are placed on the figures, it is almost universally found, in most populations, that about one third of mentally retarded people (below IQ 50) suffer epilepsy. Eyman et al. (1970) quote a (1969) report that 31% of 23 000 retardates in Western USA have a history of seizures and 26% are currently taking anticonvulsant drugs. Their own study based on 6 029 patients shows similar proportions. Similarly, in "a city in the UK" Richardson et al. (1979) report that seizures had occurred in 26% of their retardates and were a current impairment in 17%. Figures from a recent survey at Calderstones Hospital kindly provided by Dr Saroj Soni, show that on census day 283 of the 1260 residents or 22.4% suffered from epilepsy. The relatively low figure is accounted for by the immediate proximity of the Langho Epileptic Colony and in part by an active policy of enabling epileptic retardates to live in the community and a hospital policy of not admitting young people. In a careful epidemiological study in Camberwell Corbett et al. (1975) found that 32% of 155 children with IQ<50 had a history of seizures, 39% of boys and 26% of girls. The problem in estimating the frequency of a behaviour such as epilepsy is that any seizure may be the first, or the last, and all sorts of figures can be derived from life time experience or any part thereof (Taylor and Marsh, 1977). In Corbett's study for example, only 19% had one or more fits in the last year. In some handicapping conditions seizure frequency declines due to deaths, and in others, such as Down's syndrome it increases with age along with the Alzheimer process. Damage to the cortex, and to deep structures in the temporal lobe in particular, relate to an increased risk of epilepsy. Since epilepsy and mental handicap are not diseases (Taylor, 1982) but rather administratively convenient labels, we learn less from epidemiological studies than we think (unless the studies are for administrative convenience) and the epidemiology produced at the intersection of two administrative groups produces rather sparse scientific insights. Thus increases or decreases in the totals could only be explained by case by case analysis at the disease level, unless again it was an administrative effect.

Administratively convenient figures about childhood epilepsy have been produced, by Ross et al. (1980) from a national cohort suggesting a rate for febrile convulsions of about 2.1% and of non-febrile epilepsy at age 11 of 4.1/1000, and by Graham and Rutter (1968) from a sub-sample, the Isle of Wight, aged 5-14 at 4.3/1000, or 7.2/1000 if children on anticonvulsants were added in (but taking the children off anticonvulsants might increase or decrease the total suffering epilepsy (Taylor and McKinlay, 1982)). Ross et al. (1980) estimated that 0.9/1000 or 650 young people per year would require sheltered accommodation after school leaving age. A Health Authority catering for 250 000 with say 70 000 young people will need to cope with 63 such youngsters, about one third of whom will be severely handicapped and another third require strenuous treatment and have problem behaviours. For the time being, in a climate of financial stringency, these young people are being kept increasingly within their local areas. We do not yet know at what cost to their families and themselves. Hitherto, Ross et al. (1980) show, about one third have been in special schools and two thirds of these as opposed to one in five of those at normal school suffered a seizure in their 16th year. The experience of the Oxford group (Lindsay et al., 1979a, b, c, 1980; Harrison and Taylor, 1976) suggests that these epilepsies are likely to remain chronic and be associated with cognitive or psychiatric handicaps.

EPILEPSY AND ONTOGENY

The classification of epilepsy is very unsatisfactory but, since it is a behaviour, one effective method is to describe its objective and subjective concomitants. Viewed in this way the epilepsies are age related and developmental age related (Glaser, 1982), but in addition some types of epilepsy, in particular generalized major convulsive seizures, appear sporadically throughout development under certain types of provocation. Usually, the age-typical epilepsies of early childhood betoken serious, age related brain problems or prior damage, but some are merely age related responses to ephemeral states. Thus the outcome of the epilepsies of early childhood is usually, but not necessarily, poor.

Neonatal Seizures

Dennis (1979) in a meticulous long term survey of neonatal seizures has illustrated the above argument. The seizures may be the immediate declaration of serious developmental problems, the reaction to age specific illness (neonatal meningitis for example) or a transitory metabolic disturbance. Future work on the precise morphology of the seizures is necessary to determine whether the seriously impaired central nervous system can produce the age appropriate seizure actions as well as can the child reacting to hazard with a normal central nervous system.

Infantile spasms have, since West's description, been the classic age related seizure disorder. Jeavons and Bower (1961, 1964) and Jeavons et al., (1973) have illustrated its original very poor prognosis and shown in more recent studies that it is also the age related response to ephemeral brain disorder. Their series was dominated by boys (104:46) of whom 33 had died in the 1973 study but of whom 16% were eventually normal. The natural history of the spasms once started is less relevant to outcome than their age at onset. The better outcome is enjoyed by the group of unknown cause and the group attributed to immunization (perhaps thus illustrating that they are much the same group), whereas those whose disorder was attributed to a recognizable disorder fared worse.

Within a few years of the development of the EEG for clinical use Gibbs _et al._ (1939) had identified a "variant" on classical petit mal. Lennox (1945) later showed that these patients responded poorly to diones and were intellectually retarded. (Lennox made every effort to reduce this prejudicial association which had developed so strongly at the hands of Pierce Clark and the American Epilepsy Colonists.) Gastaut _et al._ (1966) remarked that little had been done to develop the concept, except by Sorel (1964), though such children were abundantly evident in the mental handicap hospitals. Of the children in his series 80% were imbecile or severe imbeciles though there were "a few normal children whose IQ seldom exceeded 90". Half the 100 cases showed atrophy on EEG. The EEG trace, showing slow waves and multiple spikes at between 1.5 and 2.5 Hz variably through most leads, proved to be age related, to onset between 1 and 6 years and very rarely after 10 but in some handicapped people up to 18, and would "emerge" from hypsarrhythmic backgrounds occasionally. This ontogenetic characteristic is made clear by Chevrie and Aicardi (1972) in one of their distinguished studies. Their 80 patients were identified by the EEG trace. They showed startling deviations. Eighteen were microcephalic (more than 2 standard deviations below the mean), 30% were retarded at the onset of the epilepsy, 6 suffered prenatal damage and 10 postnatal. More important to the ontogenetic argument 70% had experienced various fits _before_ the appearance of the "classic" "Lennox-Gastaut" EEG trace. Ninety three per cent were below "normal" intelligence.

Throughout these studies (and seen again in the study of childhood temporal lobe epilepsy by Lindsay _et al._) the curious paradox persistently recurs; the prognosis of the known is always worse than the unknown. The more apparent disorders are likely to be more damaging, the more damaging disorder more likely to be pursued with diagnostic vigour. But there is scope to consider the ephemeral disorder producing the age related response.

Throughout these studies the early onset cases _within_ each age related disorder carries the poorer prognosis. Just as the outcome of early infantile autism (the retardation syndrome which has enjoyed the best follow up study) is related to intelligence, so the outcome of epilepsies is related to intelligence and each to the evidentness of brain damage. Thus in Chevrie and Aicardi (1972) the mean age at first seizure was 17.6 months for the severely retarded, 30.6 months for the moderately retarded, and not different for the mildly retarded and normal at around 46.0 months. Age interacted with whether or not a diagnosis could be made. Chevrie and Aicardi (1979) considered 437 patients with seizures starting in the first year of life. One hundred and three were followed for less than one year, but by then 21 had died and a further 20 died during the study. Originally 137 were regarded as "cryptogenic" and 156 symptomatic. By the end of the study 228 of the 293 were classed as handicapped and 73% of the handicapped and 18% of the non-handicapped still suffered seizures. In this study age at onset was a better predictor of outcome than the type of epilepsy. Of 166 boys and 127 girls in the sample each left 81 boys and 81 girls with chronic epilepsy, a situation which Ounsted and Taylor (1972) remarked upon as of general biological interest.

THE USE OF PSYCHIATRIC SKILLS

The epilepsy of young mental retardates has many of the characteristics which are attractive to child psychiatrists in their liaison work. The disorders are common, intractable, and of uncertain or poor prognosis though not without hope; several complex therapies need to be tried, all of which have troublesome unwanted effects; they are very disturbing to parents and other care givers. Seizure disorders in retardates limit the chances of optimal placements as exemplified in the DHSS document, "Mental Handicap: Progress, Problems and Priorities": 10 000 hospital residents are compared with the best developed community services in Sheffield and Wessex. Forty four per cent of children in hospital as opposed to 18% in children's homes suffered epilepsy including controlled epilepsy. It is necessary for these children to enjoy better medicine and have a medical advocate. Child psychiatrists could play a useful role; in keeping assessment current; in keeping therapy simple; in keeping hope alive. Psychiatrists will usually come into contact for the first time at a time of situational or behavioural crisis. The dangers of being tested in this way deserve some discussion at the outset of a psychiatric intervention. This may allow future involvements to be on a less pressured "hiding to nothing" basis. The psychiatrist should deploy routine skills.

1. Psychiatrists have particular expertise in taking long and detailed histories. It may be years since a proper detailed review was undertaken. It affords the possibility of understanding the original onset of the disorder, the fears to which it gave rise, the additional impairments it created, the effects on the family, their styles of coping. It may reveal previous treatment policies which were more effective. The content of the current crisis may reveal it to be other than was supposed, a purely medical deterioration, but a situation caused by quite other issues; the anxiety or the metabolic changes associated with puberty; a less understanding teacher.

> Listening to a mother presenting the problems of her mentally handicapped boy's seizures, the extent of her morbid attachment became apparent. The mother's life was dominated by the terrors associated with a lethal familial disorder which had killed most of her relatives and her mother in middle life. This disorder had not previously been diagnosed. Attention given to her afforded her the chance to separate from her son to enable them both to receive appropriate investigation instead of continually harassing local government officials and despairing local medical practitioners.

2. Psychiatrists should be skilled at negotiating, with parents, with ward staff, with attendants, to alter their point of view, their anxieties, their attitudes to therapy, their willingness to try strategies and manoeuvres which they had previously blocked.

> An 8 year old boy presented with mental handicap, visual handicap and epilepsy. He was referred because of difficult behaviour. One of the reasons which made parenting very tentative was his "seizures". Despite an abnormal EEG in the past these seemed somewhat unlikely to be real epileptic attacks. Investigation showed this to be the case and his behaviour was improved by psychological help and by removal of unwanted effects of an unnecessary drug. Parental self-esteem improved and the boy did better at school.

3. Psychiatrists should be skilled in the understanding of threatening events and empathy with suffering. All too often in the routine of outpatient visits aimed at securing seizure control, the essentially intractable nature of the illness, and the fact that a chronic disorder has to be <u>coped with</u> is lost sight of. Desperation leads to polypharmacy, a difficult treatment schedule, and further failure. A reorientation to the "best compromise strategy" allows recovery of limited success rather than constant failure to achieve an unrealistic aim.

> Another small severely handicapped boy was first seen at an epilepsy centre at the age of five, for the management of a most severe and intractable seizure state. His parents were in deep and desperate symbiosis with him and at the time they could hardly bear to leave him in the hospital. Their constant revisiting and their repeated complaints about treatment led them finally to remove the child from care. He was subsequently taken to a treatment centre abroad where spirited physical manoeuvres were tried on him, and most of his drugs were stopped. For several years this produced some benefit though he required constant vigilance because of his drop attacks. When the drop attacks came back his parents again sought help from the psychiatrists. It was clear that it was their syndrome of chronic grief rather than the epilepsy which was likely to be modifiable. Mistakenly they were encouraged to seek more vigorous antiepilepsy therapy. This proved a disastrous episode and the parents are now back in supportive psychotherapy where at least some help can be offered to them as they manage this severe intractable epilepsy.

4. Psychiatrists have a special awareness of the variety and subtlety of losses of intellectual skills and faculties. Apparent sudden deterioration in social functioning might prove

to be due to alterable organic psychosyndromes produced by status of minor epilepsy, drug intolerance, intoxication or intercurrent illness. While conscious of the possibility of deterioration of the underlying disease they need not glibly accept that explanation.

5. Psychiatrists should be particularly tolerant of limited therapeutic success and oriented towards a long term view of therapy. Busy paediatricians beset with patients in acute crises may at times lose sight of the very long term nature of managing epilepsy in retarded children.

6. Child psychiatrists have a traditional concern with maximizing children's opportunities of growth and the development of their skills. At times, with epileptic children, parental management will have become unduly restrictive, and this in turn may keep a child in unstimulating situations where he is prone to the very seizures they so much fear. An empathic psychiatrist may help liberate them, or at least allow them to come to terms with the restrictions they themselves have imposed. This skill is especially necessary when the question of placing a child in a school or residential home comes into question.

7. Psychiatrists often control therapeutic areas which may allow parents and child to be admitted for lengthy periods not usually possible in acute children's wards. By offering a place under joint supervision a longer term trial of treatment or a fuller review of behaviour can be undertaken.

> A 14 year old handicapped girl was referred to a psychiatrist by the local Social Services Department and the Education Welfare Officer supported by the local child psychiatrist and a local paediatrician. She was accused of impossible behaviour in out-patients and returning with unfailing regularity to the emergency department having complained of having had a seizure where her subsequent behaviour would produce chaos in the department. Although she had been for years an epileptic child under the care (as far as it was possible) of the local paediatrician, her life and that of her family was so chaotic that she had never been able to be admitted for review. She was finally admitted to an adolescent unit where her histrionic acting out was separated from her relatively infrequent seizures which were thoroughly investigated and for which an appropriate therapy was instituted. After some weeks in the unit an appropriate place was found for her in a school for epileptic children where she has settled satisfactorily. Her behaviour was transformed and she was able to grow within her personality into a charming and modestly able girl.

8. Psychiatrists are used to providing support for other team members who are feeling frustrations or anger or impotence. Extension of this support in liaison psychiatry to the attending physician may enable the physician to reorient to the task of

continuing to cope with a difficult child with intractable untreatable problems.

> A very severely mentally affected child with a disfiguring condition spent his entire life in seizures which sporadically increased so as to embarrass respiration. He responded to no treatment. A psychiatrist well versed in using neurosedative drugs also tried everything he knew and equally failed. Whereupon the paediatrician rallied and was able to cope with the child.

9. Psychiatrists are well versed in using powerful neurosedative and psychoactive drugs which are sometimes required and which can make intolerable situations bearable.

CONCLUSION

The way in which society deals with the mentally handicapped is through social and political rather than through medical acts. At a time of intense demedicalization we should be aware that the dispersion of the handicapped to "routine" medical care may prove disadvantageous to the management of epilepsy which is evident in about one third of the seriously retarded. The "medical model", which is regarded as having failed the handicapped, failed more in the sense of never achieving anything like an appropriate standard of medical practice than through the overweaning (hubris) which characterizes some other areas of medicine. The political forces at work threaten to undermine even those medical practices which are of benefit to the handicapped.

Epilepsy relates to development in complex ways but the resultant developmental disorders and their consequences are susceptible to help from well trained child psychiatrists.

REFERENCES

Chevrie, J.J. and Aicardi, J., (1972), Childhood epileptic encephalopathy with slow spike-wave. A statistical study of 80 cases, **Epilepsia, 13**, 259-271

Chevrie, J.J. and Aicardi, J., (1979), Convulsive disorders in the first year of life. Persistence of epileptic seizures, **Epilepsia, 20**, 643-649

Corbett, J.A., Harris, R. and Robinson, R.G., (1975), Epilepsy. In: Wortis J. (ed). **Mental Retardation and Developmental Disabilities**, vol VII, Bruner Mazel, New York

Dennis, J., (1979), The implications of neonatal seizures. In: Korobkin R. and Guilleninault C. (eds). **Advances in Perinatal Neurology**, Spectrum Publishers, New York

Department of Health and Social Security, (1980), **Mental Handicap: Progress, Problems and Priorities**

Eyman, R.K., Capes, L., Moore, B.C. and Zachofsky, T., (1970), Maladaptive behaviour of institutionalized retardates with seizures, **Am. J. Ment. Defic, 74**, 651-9

Foucault, M., (1971), **Madness and Civilization**, Tavistock, London

Gastaut, H., Roger J., Soulayrol, R., Tassinari, H., Regis, H., and Dravet, C., (1966), Childhood epileptic encephalopathy with diffuse slow spike-waves (otherwise known as "Petit Mal Variant") or Lennox Syndrome, **Epilepsia, 7**, 139-179

Gibbs, F.A., Gibbs, E.L., and Lennox, W.G., (1939), The influence of the blood sugar level on the wave and spike formation in petit mal epilepsy, **Arch. Neurol. Psychiatr., 41**, 1111-1116

Glaser, G., (1982), Critical periods in brain development related to behaviour: The developing neurophysiology of the self, In: Apley J. & Ounsted C. (eds) **One Child**, Spastics International Medical Publications, London

Graham, P., and Rutter, M., (1968), Organic brain dysfunction and child psychiatric disorder, **British Medical Journal**, Sept, 695-700

Harrison, R.M., and Taylor, D.C., (1976), Childhood seizures: A 25 year follow-up, **Lancet, i**, 948

Hunter, R., and McAlpine, I., (1974), **Psychiatry for the Poor**, Dawsons of Pall Mall, London

Jeavons, P.M., and Bower, B.D., (1961), The natural history of infantile spasms, **Archives of Diseases in Childhood, 36, 185**, 17-22

Jeavons, P.M., and Bower, B.D., (1964), **Infantile Spasms**, Spastic Society and Heinemann, London

Jeavons, P.M., Bower, B.D., and Dimitrikoudi, M.C., (1973), Long-term prognosis of 150 cases of West Syndrome, **Epilepsia, 14**, 153-164

Lennox, W.G., (1945), The Petit Mal Epilepsies; their treatment with Tridione, **J. Amer. Med. Ass., 129**, 1069-1974

Lindsay, J., Ounsted, C. and Richards, P., (1979a), Long-term outcome in children with temporal lobe seizures 1. Social outcome and childhood factors, **Developmental Medicine and Child Neurology, 21**, 285-298

Lindsay, J., Ounsted, C. and Richards, P., (1979b) idem, 2. Marriage, parenthood and sexual indifference, **Developmental Medicine and Child Neurology, 21**, 400-433

Lindsay, J., Ounsted, C. and Richards, P., (1979c) idem, 3. Psychiatric aspects in childhood and adult life, **Developmental Medicine and Child Neurology, 21**, 630-636

Lindsay, J., Ounsted, C. and Richards, P., (1980) idem, 4. Genetic factors, febrile convulsions and the remission of seizures, **Developmental Medicine and Child Neurology, 22**, 429-440

Neville, B.G.R., (1972), The origin of infantile spasms; evidence from a case of hydranencephaly, **Devel. Med. Child. Neurol., 14**, 644-647

Ounsted, C., (1971), Some aspects of seizure disorders, In: Gairdner D. and Hull, D. (eds) **Recent Advances in Paediatrics**, 4th edn. J & A Churchill, London, pp 363-400

Ounsted, C. and Taylor, D.C., (1972), **Gender Differences: Their**

Ontogeny and Significance, Churchill Livingstone, Edinburgh

Richardson, S.A., Katz, M., Koller, H., McLaren, J. and Rubinstein, B., (1979), Some characteristics of a population of mentally retarded young adults in a British city. A basis for estimating some service needs, **J. Ment. Defic. Res.**, **23**, 275-285

Rosen, G. (1968), **Madness in Society**, Routledge & Kegan Paul, London

Ross, E.M., Peckham, C.S., West, P.B., and Butler, N.R., (1980), Epilepsy in childhood: findings from the National Child Development Study, **British Medical Journal**, Jan., 207-210

Sorel, L., (1964), L'epilepsie myokinetique grace de la premiere enfance avec pointe-onde lente et son traitement (petit mal variant), **Rev. Neurol.**, **110**, 215-225

Taylor, D.C., (1973), Aspects of seizure disorders: II. On prejudice, **Develop. Med. Child. Neurol.**, **15**, 91-94

Taylor, D.C., (1982), The components of sickness: diseases, illnesses and predicaments, In: Apley, J. and Ounsted, C. (eds) **One Child**, Spastics International Medical Publication, London

Taylor, D.C. and McKinlay, I.A., (1982), When not to treat epilepsy with drugs, **Symposium of Paediatric Neurology**, Royal College of Physicians, in press

Taylor, D.C. and Marsh, S.M., (1977), The strategy and implications of long term follow-up studies with a note of the cause of death, In: Penry J.K. (ed) **Epilepsy, the Eighth International Symposium**, Raven Press, New York

Warkany, J., and Dignan, P., (1975), Congenital malformations: hydranencephaly, In: Wortis, J. (ed) **Mental Retardation and Developmental Disabilities**, VII, Bruner Mazel, New York

COMMENTARY

A. E. Baert

The WHO Regional Office for Europe has published reports on the role of the psychologist, of the nurse and of the social worker in community mental health care. It became quite clear that one could not discuss the role of one member of the team without due consideration of the tasks and functions of the other members. It also became clear that a staff member is required who can integrate, appreciate and discriminate the somatic psychological and social aspects especially during the problem solving process. Society has up to now seen the psychiatrist as the person best suited for this role.

In Finland, at Tampere, Antinen together with a team of economists has recently undertaken a cost-effectiveness study on the contributions of various professionals in community mental health care. This study indicated that the consultant psychiatrist, although he had the highest payment calculated per hour, from the cost-effectiveness point of view was by far the most effective member of the team, particularly when the impact on the treatment process was considered.

I. A. McKinlay

The medicine of mental handicap has been poorly articulated in recent years and has come to be associated with institutional management. Medicine for handicapped people has thereby fallen into disrepute. Recruitment has been very poor and the level of specific expertise within the medical services of the mentally handicapped has declined. Fortunately at the same time there has been a developing expertise within paediatrics, paediatric neurology and child psychiatry which is available to mentally handicapped children through child development centres and other facilities. It is of the greatest importance to the planners of health care for handicapped people that the types of ideas so clearly expressed by Taylor are understood.

There has been a predominance of interest in the arrangements for the care of handicapped children with a view to closing large institutions but not enough serious thought about planning for mentally handicapped people's health.

P. Mittler

In a recent survey of over 3200 children attending schools for severely mentally handicapped children in NW England, teachers reported 80% of children in day school as free of seizures; 16% had a history of seizures and less than 2% had fits daily (Mittler and Preddy, 1981). These figures may well underestimate frequency but do indicate the possibility that seizures have been brought under control in many cases.

Reference

Mittler, P. and Preddy, D. (1981). Mentally handicapped pupils and school leavers : a survey in NW England. In Cooper, B. (ed.) **Assessing the Handicaps and Needs of Retarded Children.** Academic Press, London

B. G. R. Neville

The main concern with this paper is the psychiatrists' contribution to improving the understanding and care of retarded epileptic children. The training and service implications are enormous and include the following:

1. Psychiatrists with an interest in childhood epilepsy can easily become experienced at the investigation and drug management and are then in a better position to manage the rest of the child and family than the average paediatrician/paediatric neurologist. The track record of a select group of such doctors in the UK is excellent, but in the main they have kept a strong commitment to neurology whatever their nominal appointment. I doubt that the majority of child psychiatrists would, on their own, be in such a position to be a safe primary referral destination for the symptom of epilepsy in childhood.
2. The aims of a child development centre to produce an accurate problem list for a handicapped child, and to advise on management are known to be deficient in the field of child psychiatry. Psychiatrists are rarely part of the core assessment team, and once a unit has been going for a period of ten years, the number of children referred to psychiatrists with maladjustment of various sorts is a continuing reproach upon the incomplete nature of the original definition of problems.
3. In view of the development of intervention programmes, for example Portage, in which the system is closely defined, it is now essential that the skills of psychiatry and psychology are included at an early stage, presumably by a child psychiatrist being a regular member of the team: that is to say, part of the group who work together for at least five sessions a week.
4. A psychiatrist has some responsibility to ensure that the "team approach" does not result in the loss of the single identifiable person who knows all the problems of a particular family.
5. A psychiatrist is important in guiding research projects.

6. Population statistics are essential to discover the way in which a referral system, particularly the referral of children with epilepsy, to a consultant psychiatrist may distort the perception of the problem of epilepsy to the psychiatrists themselves.

7. In many children's departments, psychologists have been increasingly involved in the problems of social adjustment of young children with epilepsy, and the use of the word "psychiatrist" in this paper needs clarification. A similar question can be asked about social workers who are not prominently advertised in this paper!

8. The degree to which current social attitudes, particularly educational, influence the outcome for people with epilepsy needs further discussion, more now that a new education act will be aiming to eliminate this effect without a very clear idea of how this is to be best achieved.

9. A much greater sharing of training between psychiatry/neurology/development is an essential consequence of this approach.

C. Ounsted

Every English newborn baby is given a unique number in our great Health Service. He keeps that number until he dies. We are all life-long patients and doctors are freely available to us at all times.

Taylor spells out the especial medical needs of those handicapped patients who suffer seizures. These are many, subtle and usually denied. Some years ago, I described how children with epilepsy and mental handicap transform their families: how they induce false beliefs and strange behaviours in their parents. The parental change often leads to conflict with doctors, teachers and the law. I called this parental sickness "hyperpaedophilia". No one accepted the concept. I did not see why, until Taylor showed me that each sickness has three components: disease, illness and predicament. Then I understood: theirs was a cruel predicament and it drove them out of their minds. The child in the parents' head was quite other from the one that the doctor saw.

This is a meeting for "Scientific Studies in Mental Retardation". Studies, that is to say, of the real world of living children and not of those ideal beings who exist in our heads. Taylor surveys the field with honest clarity and discerns at least nine roles an interested physician can play in caring for the seizure-prone handicapped. One of these is making a reconciliation between the real and the ideal child. Doctors who can bring this about need to know more than biochemistry and multiple regressions. "It is desirable that physicians are as systematically acquainted with predicaments (that is, know something about the world) as they are with diseases" (Taylor, 1982).

He put it better than I can.

Reference

Taylor, D.C. (1982). The components of sickness: diseases, illnesses and predicaments. In: One Child. Apley, J. and Ounsted, C. (eds). Spastics International Medical Publications, London, pp 1-14

D. A. Pond

The first part of Taylor's paper critically reviews the epidemiological data on the prevalence of epilepsy and psychiatric disorders in the severely subnormal. I agree with his assessment that crude figures are administratively useful in showing the size of the problem, but because both epilepsy and psychiatric disorders cover a multitude of different conditions, less light is thrown on scientific problems such as aetiology, patho-physiology, prognosis and especially treatment. Each and every affected person is almost unique, differing in one way or another from others superficially similar. It follows therefore that the anecdotal single case history approach is a more fruitful method of study of many of the scientific clinical problems. Taylor continues to make a good deal of his own interesting studies on the effect of age and maturation on the manifestations of epilepsy however seemingly "caused". It is disappointing that systematic experiments on the effect of age on epilepsy in experimental animals have not been carried out. They would be worthwhile even though the species differences in susceptibility to epilepsy are very great.

The second section of Taylor's paper sets out the various different ways in which child psychiatrists can and should contribute to the understanding of management of the psychiatric disorders often found in the handicapped, especially if they have epilepsy as well. Unfortunately few psychiatrists have the knowledge and skill attributed to them in this article, mainly because outside a few special centres most of them will see so few such cases a year and they will be bewilderingly different. More practicable would be for the expert psychiatrists to teach those caring for the handicapped most of the skills of history-taking, special empathy and the broad family view of problems that Taylor singles out as among abilities sadly often missing in other physicians.

Paediatricians are the chief assessors of the handicapped when it is first suspected and then diagnosed - hopefully in an assessment centre with a multi-disciplinary team. Later, and especially when the patient is no longer a child, other medical carers are involved, of whom probably neurologists and GPs are the most important. All of these need to acquire at least some of the skills of the psychiatrist. As Taylor points out in this era of demedicalization of the long-time care of the handicapped, whether residential or not, the necessary expert medical supervision may be the baby thrown out with the bath-water. There is a case, well made out by Taylor, for properly informed psychiatrists especially child psychiatrists to be involved. However, in my view, direct case management is less important than the teaching of skills to those with direct responsibility for the handicapped, including non-medical staff (nurses, psychologists, social workers) as well as doctors, since many of the skills mentioned by Taylor can be perfectly well acquired and practised by the former.

S. A. Richardson

It is important to recognize the purposes for which a classification has been developed. The classification of epilepsy has been based on the medical model of working backwards from the manifestation of the disease to its pathology and aetiology. This has been useful in arriving at decisions on medication and considering aetiology. The medical form of classification gives scant if any information about the consequences of the disease for the patient. No classification has been available for this aspect of epilepsy. We have recently developed such a classification and used it to describe epilepsy in a mentally retarded population over the first 22 years of life (Richardson _et al._, 1980, 1981). The variables used in the classification include the proportion of time when there were symptoms, or during which anticonvulsant medication was given; the frequency of seizure episodes during the period of symptoms or during the period of medication; the degree of severity of the seizures; the amount of time medication was given; and any side-effects of medication.

In the overall population of young people with mental retardation, they experienced one or more seizures seven times more frequently than young people from similar backgrounds who were not mentally retarded. The more severely retarded more often had seizures, had them earlier and over a longer time span than the mildly retarded.

References

Richardson, S.A., Koller, H., Katz, M. and McLaren, J. (1980). Seizures and epilepsy in a mentally retarded population over the first 22 years of life. **J. Appl. Res. Ment. Retard.**, **1**, 123-138

Richardson, S.A., Koller, H., Katz, M. and McLaren, J. (1981). A functional classification of seizures and its distribution in a mentally retarded population. **Am. J. Ment. Defic.**, **85** (5), 457-466

J. B. P. Stephenson

I am delighted that Taylor altered the title of his paper from the original "Seizures in mentally retarded patients". His compelling arguments for the contribution of the child psychiatrist and the major medical component of the care of the mentally handicapped leave little room for adverse criticism. This being so, I will concentrate my remarks on the way in which the appearance of seizures may be associated with the genesis of mental retardation (or other cognitive and higher cerebral functional impairments), and how this may be so. Taylor points to the adverse prognosis of age dependency, early onset, and of known aetiology. It is important to separate these independent factors. One of the best known (nowadays) age-dependent epilepsies is the "benign focal epilepsy of childhood" whose prognosis is implicit in its title. Even very early onset, as in the dominantly inherited benign familial neonatal convulsions (Quattlebaum, 1979) need have no serious consequences. However, in tuberose sclerosis, whether mental handicap supervenes depends entirely on the age of onset of seizures. Without seizures, mental handicap (due to tuberose sclerosis) does not occur. How can one get meaning out of these observations? Let us work backwards from the seizure to the "fundamental" abnormality. Beneath the seizure is the electrical storm, the spikes in the electroencephalogram. At times, behind this is a general chaos or slowing of the background rhythms. We can go on to presume an underlying neurotransmitter fault without necessary overt EEG change, as a matter of speculation. I would like to consider the available evidence very briefly. The seizures of infancy which lead to severe or profound mental handicap tend to be associated with disruptive EEG chaos, typically hypsarrhythmia with infantile spasms. The chaos rather than the seizures seem to halt development. One can call this infantile minor epileptic status analogously to the better known minor epileptic status of the Lennox Gastaut syndrome in older pre-school childen. In this condition also the spike-wave trains rather than the seizures themselves disrupt cognition. I have evidence (unpublished) that this disturbance (electrical and behavioural) can be "switched off" by a brief course of ketogenic diet or steroid (betamethasone), but what is being switched off is unknown. If the technique of betamethasone "switch-off" is employed, there may be a lag of several days between the abolition of EEG spikes and the disappearance of the abnormal neurological signs (drooling, etc.) (unpublished data). It may be inferred that although EEG spikes (or EEG chaos) may be easily observed, an underlying neurotransmitter disturbance or such-like which outlasts the EEG spiking is of more fundamental importance. As a further inference, it may be presumed that intellectual decline can antedate not only the appearance of seizures, but even the EEG disruption, if the chemical (?) circuitry first goes awry. Research strategies to look at ways of defining and modifying this substratum of minor epileptic status are urgently needed.

Reference

Quattlebaum, T.C. (1979). Benign familial convulsions in the neonatal period and early infancy. J. Pediatr., **95**, 257

Chapter 24

Mainstreaming handicapped students

P. Meazzini

INTRODUCTION

The prevailing Zeitgeist concerning the handicapped person differs from the past for the following reasons (Mercer and Payne, 1975b; Bricker, 1978; Snell, 1978; etc.):

1) there is growing scepticism in relation to the educational and rehabilitative results obtained by special institutions (Kanner, 1964; Love, 1973; Dunn, 1973; Cancrini, 1977; etc.);

2) the belief that the disabled and the handicapped should be integrated within the normal school setting is becoming more and more widespread;

3) the focus is gradually moving from the medical model to the educational one. This shift appears to be particularly advantageous in that it may limit the medicalization of the field which has brought about detrimental consequences in the normalization process of the handicapped student.

WHY SPECIAL INSTITUTIONS MAY FAIL AND OFTEN DO

There is quite a long history of outcome oriented research which has attempted to measure the efficacy of special institutions. In fact Goldfarb (1943) was one of the first to evaluate the extent to which special institutions were able to achieve their goals, i.e. to increase the cognitive and social skills of their handicapped students.

At that time his conclusion was striking in that it showed that special institutions very rarely were able to achieve their formal goals, but rather that the common practice was to shift to the easier and more comfortable custodial goals.

It is a well established sociological fact (Etzioni, 1964, 1971) that many an organizational system, irrespective of the type of output (industrial, educational, etc.), does in fact tend gradually to change its goals. Usually this change favours those that hold power within the institution.

Taking this shift for granted, the problem was therefore to pin-point the various factors which permitted such institutions to move from educational and rehabilitative goals to these custodial ones.

The major factors seemed to be:

1) the absence of a sound methodology backing the educational and rehabilitative programmes. As a result, the quality of staff performance lowered as their expectations dropped (Kanner, 1964; Thompson and Grabowski, 1977);

2) inadequate training programmes that failed to supply the staff with effective professional skills (Love, 1973);

3) unsuitable ratio between staff and handicapped subjects which was mainly the result of limited community supplied resources;

4) uses and abuses of psychometric testing, which opened the way to a self-fulfilling prophecy. As many writers have pointed out, there is very little hope of educating a child, if one believes that nothing or very little can be done to improve his intelligence;

5) a physical and social environment which was usually deprived and dull, with the result that the learning of the cognitive prerequisites and skills was seriously hindered (Meazzini and Galeazzi, 1977);

6) modelling, by means of which inadequate behaviours shown by the peers were added to the already low functioning skill repertoires of the handicapped student;

7) the absence of effective counter-control procedures that might have been very useful in correcting the drawbacks of institutions by allowing the reaching of more effective goals (Skinner, 1972).

Data which showed how institutions were affected by all these factors were used as an empirical groundwork in the fight against any form of segregation that was a major factor of the social philosophy of the 1970s.

These data, however, in spite of their validity and intrinsic interest would not have resulted in any conspicuous change, had not social attitudes and policy towards the disabled and the handicapped changed at the same time.

The new key word became "mainstreaming" or integration of handicapped and non-handicapped people, that was to be extended to the largest possible number of handicapped persons.

This shift, however, did not necessitate the disappearance of special institutions (Italy is an exception to the rule!), its main purposes being:

1) to underline the fact that the basic goal of any organization dealing with the handicapped is to provide those skills which permit a smoother integration process within the community;

2) to make use as little as possible of those institutions where this goal appears to be unfeasible;

3) to sensitize and organize the various social subsystems in such a way that each of these in their turn could develop integrating skills.

MAINSTREAMING THE HANDICAPPED STUDENTS: THE RATIONALE

There are various factors at the basis of mainstreaming that can be thus summarized (Cancrini, 1977; Turnboll and Schultz, 1979; Bricker, 1978; Meazzini, in press):

Sociological Factors

These are mainly connected with:

1) Goffman's analysis of asylums (1961) which emphasized the psychical and social deterioration of patients living in asylums. This empirically backed analysis served as an additional tool against special institutions;

2) a growing awareness that deviance and the labelling of such is the result of a matching process between the values held by the establishment and the behaviours (social, cognitive, etc.) of the persons examined (Basaglia, 1968, 1971; Guskin et al., 1975; etc.);

As a result, any form of classification and the ensuing labelling lost at least part of its credibility, in that it proved to be value biased. Although evaluation is unavoidable, the tendency was and still is to limit as much as possible the classification and labelling of the deviant, including the handicapped person (Dunn, 1973; Snell, 1978; etc.).

In addition, it was shown that most classification systems:

- lack the necessary requirements (Rutter and Shaffer, 1980; Yule, 1980);
- favour negative labelling that may produce undesirable side effects (Edgerton, 1967).

Psychological Factors

The rapid growth of behaviour analysis and modification with its strong environmental bias was to favour a shift from institution to community and from a medical model to a psycho-ecological one.

In brief, behaviour analysis and modification stresses that:

1) the causes of many psychical and educational problems lie within the eco-systems in which people live and not within the people themselves;

2) eco-systems can be altered in order to eliminate pathogenetic factors and to favour the normalization and integration of handicapped students;

3) there is no need to resort to a particularly sophisticated system of classification. Behaviours must be observed and measured in terms of quantitative parameters such as frequency, duration and intensity. In this way labelling tends to be avoided;

4) educational curricula and behavioural management procedures have been worked out and constantly refined, which

show that a reasonable amount of success can be reliably achieved even with very severely handicapped students (Thompson and Grabowski, 1977; Snell, 1978; etc.);

5) educational agencies such as school and family must be actively involved in any educational and rehabilitative process.

Therefore behaviour analysis and modification appears to be the most suitable psychological approach to favour integration in that it:

- eschews labelling;
- actively modifies the various eco-systems, in which the handicapped persons live and operate;
- supplies psychologists, teachers and paraprofessionals with efficient and sound methodology.

Legal Aspects

In both the USA and some European countries, laws have been passed and legislative decisions taken which give all handicapped children the right to free public education.

As a result strategies must be implemented which allow handicapped children to be placed in the least restrictive yet productive educational and working setting.

Apart from these common features, however, legislative philosophy shows marked differences from one country to another as regards the extent to which integration is to be planned and carried out.

Should all handicapped persons be integrated, irrespective of the severity of their handicap? If not, where is the dividing line? These are only some of the questions which receive different answers according to the values and attitudes dominant in a specific country.

Despite these differences, all over the world the trend is definitely towards mainstreaming. This is, however, easier said than done, as correct integration requires a very close collaboration among professionals such as architects, engineers, sociologists, psychologists, teachers, etc., and a deep change in many social and teaching routines.

MAINSTREAMING HANDICAPPED STUDENTS: FROM THEORY TO PRACTICE

According to the latest eco-behavioural trends (Wahler, 1972; Gallagher, 1980; Salzinger et al., 1980) which are to a certain extent but a refinement and extension of more traditional behaviour analysis, mainstreaming can be successfully implemented, provided that both social environment and handicapped students are supplied with integrating skills.

In fact it is no longer the case of focusing one's attention on the student who is isolated from his eco-systems, as in this case mainstreaming would be far from successful (Cantrell and Cantrell, 1976, 1980).

The time is ripe again for repolishing the concept of "prosthetic environment" (Lindsley, 1970) and extending it to all eco-systems where the handicapped person lives and operates. In addition different environmental layers can be analysed within each eco-system. The main ones are:

1) physical environment, by which one implies physical components as broad as architectural variables (Danford, 1976) or more restricted ones such as lighting (Painter, 1976);

2) social environment, which refers to social events as various as rules prevailing within eco-systems, scheduling, i.e. the sequence in which classroom or other eco-systems are arranged, attitudes held towards the handicapped child, etc.;

3) interpersonal environment, which refers to the extremely intricate and ever changing pattern of interpersonal relationships in which the handicapped child plays either a passive or an active role.

It is necessary to operate upon each of these different layers within each eco-system in order to make them more and more integrating, while at the same time building in the handicapped student those skills which are demanded by the eco-system.

The role of the professional (psychologist, social worker, etc.) becomes that of a mediator trying to lower or change environmental demands while at the same time increasing the skill repertoires of the handicapped child.

As a matter of fact, however, a professional such as a behavioural psychologist has as a rule always worked only on the environment, in particular the social and interpersonal one, his interactions with the handicapped being very limited (Meazzini, 1978, in press).

In other terms the traditional behavioural approach to the handicapped has always implied the behavioural modification to those people who are in close contact with the handicapped person, be they parents, teachers, peers, managers, etc. (Kozloff, 1974, 1979; Fredericksen *et al*., 1972).

From this perspective, the normalization of the handicapped student is always the result of the improved professional skills of their educational agents.

It can be said that little attention has been paid so far to the physical components of environment (Gallagher, 1980). The result is a poor understanding of how these components affect people's behaviour and how they should be modified to make them more and more in line with the philosophy of mainstreaming.

Prosthetic School Physical Environment

"Prosthetic environments are much more common than most of us realize. Stimulus substitution techniques which are in common use include Braille books and magazines for the blind, bells which ring for the blind when the 'walk' light is on a traffic intersection and standardized light position and intensity for the colour blind. Common effector substitutes are ramps, elevators, and handrails for those with walking disability and specially designed homes and automobiles for paraplegics" (Lindsley, 1970, p.184).

The analysis of school physical environment should be the very first task to be accomplished as its inadequacy may bring about secondary handicaps such as dependency on someone to carry out chores and tasks that the handicapped student would otherwise have been able to manage, had the school building been planned in a more suitable way.

Some of the main questions to be answered are:

- are there ramps, elevators, etc., that enable all students and particularly the handicapped one to move freely around the school building?
- are there toilets and other services suitable to meet the needs of motor and mental handicapped students?
- are physical components such as lighting, classroom acoustics, etc., suitable both to normal and handicapped students?
- are there open space environments, resource classrooms, etc., which may be effectively used in the teaching of the handicapped child?

Whereas the answers to the first two questions are clearcut, data are scanty and less clear for the other two. "There is very little research measuring the effects of architectural variables on young handicapped children" (Rogers-Warren and Wedel, 1980).

Prosthetic Social Environment

Any organization implies a set of rules and agreements which allow it to work and effectively reach its goals. To a certain extent, these rules are but a formalized expression of social and organizational attitudes held by those in a position of authority.

In the case of a school setting, teachers' and parents' values and attitudes are dominant over those of the student and may either hinder or help any process of mainstreaming.

At this point the problem is how to modify the attitudes and behaviours of teachers and parents so that mainstreaming can take place:

This implies:

1) ascertaining what features of the handicapped student make him more likely to be rejected by the social school system;

2) sensitizing all who operate within the school setting so that more flexible rules and more suitable attitudes towards mainstreaming can be generated;

3) training teachers and paraprofessionals to manage the various behavioural problems that are likely to be shown by the handicapped students.

The literature relevant to these three items show that:

1) the main factors which may influence acceptance are the visibility of the handicap (Adams and Cohen, 1974; Richardson _et al._, 1974), practical communication difficulties, social and cognitive skill repertoires and contact (Thomas, 1978);

2) social psychology may offer effective procedures to change people's attitudes, including those towards the handicapped students. These procedures include conference, panel discussion, small group interactions, role-playing, etc. (Shakespeare, 1974; Orio and Rossi, 1978);

3) untrained teachers and paraprofessionals may feel very anxious about their handicapped students. As a result they tend either to reject them or to leave them by themselves. Obviously this problem can be solved by planning and implementing training packages, which supply them with the necessary behavioural and teaching skills. This may well prove to be the best way of treating their anxiety.

Prosthetic Classroom Organization

Unfortunately there is little empirical evidence to measure the effect of all those variables which are part of the classroom organization. We do not know as yet what is the optimal teacher-child ratio, 1:1; 1:2; 1:3 (Frankel and Graham, 1976). No significant difference has been found in child attention and on-task behaviour when this ratio was varied accordingly.

There is no clear answer either to the question regarding the size of the group in which the handicapped student can be placed, although it seems plausible that small classrooms and groups of children would be advisable (Baker and Gump, 1964).

The effect of density and physical placement is at last somewhat clearer. It has been proved that aggression is increased and social interaction decreased when the group size is increased but the total amount of space remains constant (Hutt and Vaizey, 1966) and that on-task behaviour is higher when children are spaced equidistantly (on chairs, or sitting in assigned spaces) than when they are allowed to crowd together.

Scheduling seems to be another powerful variable. Once again, however, data are lacking as regards the effects of scheduling on handicapped students, apart from one study in which Fredericksen and Fredericksen (1977) compared fixed schedules with random schedules. During fixed schedules, twelve tasks were presented in the same order each day and during random scheduling the first ten activities were presented in a different pre-determined random schedule each day. On the whole academic behaviours were lowered and disruptive ones increased during random schedules.

Finally the use of restricted environments is another factor worth investigating. The available results show that "... cubicles or other restricted settings may be of some help in the initial steps of teaching children particularly when attending behaviour is being shaped" (Rogers-Warren and Wedel, 1980, p.7).

As one can see, the effects brought about by classroom organization have not been thoroughly investigated.

A few recommendations, however, appear to be relevant to prosthetic classroom organization:

1) teacher-child ratio should be the lower, the more seriously handicapped the child is (Meazzini, in press);

2) group size and density should be kept as low as possible when moderately and seriously handicapped students are placed in the classroom;

3) scheduling should remain fixed whenever possible;

4) restricted environments may be useful in teaching basic learning prerequisites such as attention.

Educational Design

Although it is one of the most relevant variables in classroom organization, educational design deserves a place by itself, so large is the literature available.

Apart from their theoretical groundwork, most educational designs share these common features:

1) entry evaluation is carried out in order to find out the assets and liabilities of each handicapped student;

2) operational objectives are formulated that are tailored to the student's needs;

3) teaching material and sequence of steps are then decided upon;

4) implementation takes place either in the usual classrooms or elsewhere in the school setting;

5) ongoing monitoring is provided in order to check whether any progress is being made towards the previously established objectives;

6) troubleshooting and corrective procedures are scheduled, should the objectives not be reached.

On the whole, an effective educational design should have the following features (Mercer and Payne, 1975a; Snell, 1978):

1) focus should be on teaching first the learning prerequisites and cognitive skills. Emphasis should be laid particularly on language training;

2) curricular programmes should be directive and tightly organized, the more so, the more seriously handicapped the child is;

3) motor, memory and verbal skills should be specifically taught in kindergarten, where very early mainstreaming can and should take place;

4) behavioural consistency is required on the part of both teachers and parents, if handicapped students are to generalize their skills from school to home setting.

Finally the content of any curriculum should include any information that is relevant to manage the demands coming from the various eco-systems where the handicapped students live (Bender *et al.*, 1978). In other words, any curriculum should have ecological validity, i.e. supply the handicapped students with those skills that can facilitate the integration process and are demanded by his particular eco-systems (Janes, in press).

Teacher and Parent Training

The actual implementation of the curriculum is a specific task of teachers who necessarily have to be trained in order to fulfil it.

Despite minor differences, the usual syllabus for teachers' training aims at supplying them with cognitive and behavioural skills.

Cognitive skills (Meazzini, 1978; Ricci, in press) enable teachers to view any behavioural event within a specific theoretical framework. These skills are basic, as they draw teachers' attention to particular variables and push them to search for specific causal factors, that many a time change according to the theoretical framework adhered to by the teacher.

On the contrary, behavioural skills refer to the teachers' capacity in managing behavioural problems and implementing the educational design. These skills are as various as observing and recording behaviours, establishing cognitive and behavioural objectives, implementing intervention strategies, constructing instructional steps, evaluating the educational and behavioural outcome, etc.

Training procedures should include practical workshops, role-playing, modelling, case-work, video-tape observations and in-service training which appears to be a very effective strategy in that it enables teachers to generalize their skills from the training to the school setting (Ricci, in press).

Training, however, should not be limited to teachers and other professionals. Parents also must be trained so that they eventually acquire the basic skills necessary to manage their children's behavioural problems and to teach them self-independent skills (Kozloff, 1974; Nisi, in press). In addition, they should be able to understand the educational aims and strategies implemented by the teacher and other professionals and actively collaborate with them.

As Kaufman (1978) pointed out, teachers and parents both trained within the same theoretical framework bring about the best educational results, in that behavioural consistency is assured.

There is no doubt that parent training can be a very effective tool in favouring mainstreaming, although research is still necessary to pinpoint the various factors that affect the outcome of parent training (Nisi, in press).

EFFECTIVENESS OF MAINSTREAMING

Unfortunately mainstreaming has not been thoroughly investigated as yet. Data are particularly lacking as regards relevant factors of mainstreaming such as (1) ratio of handicapped and non-handicapped students within the same classroom; (2) type of curriculum most suited to meet the needs of the handicapped student; (3) teachers' training; (4) ecological engineering; (5) level of severity of handicap below which mainstreaming is not advisable; (6) age at which mainstreaming should start, although there is a widespread belief that the earlier, the better (Bricker, 1978; Bricker _et al_., 1980; Turnboll and Blacher-Dixon, 1980; etc.).

In addition most experimental programmes designed to evaluate the outcome of mainstreaming lack the necessary methodological sophistication so that at present it is difficult to formulate precise mainstreaming programmes (Turnboll and Blacher-Dixon, 1980).

However, data are available that document some positive outcomes of mainstreaming. It has been empirically proved that mainstreamed handicapped students learn socially appropriate behaviours through modelling (Cooke et al., 1977; Peterson et al., 1977); tend to normalize their play behaviour (Guralnick, 1976); enhance a positive self-concept (Kennedy, 1976); are effectively prepared for integration in later years and in different social settings (Wynne, 1975).

In addition, mainstreaming seems to affect the attitudes of people who are in contact with them. Thus sensitivity to the needs of handicapped children is developed on the part of their non-handicapped peers and teachers (Hobbs, 1975; Karnes and Zehrbach, 1977) and more positive attitudes are found in the parents of the normal child (Bricker, 1978).

Therefore it may be concluded that the literature available to date on mainstreaming shows very promising paths, although many problems are still to be solved and many dangers lie ahead, the greatest of which seems to be the overruling power of ideology that risks nullifying any empirical effort at measuring all relevant variables of mainstreaming.

In this respect Italy is a paradigmatic and to a certain extent an inconsistent case. In fact laws were passed which abolished all special institutions and enforced mainstreaming of all handicapped students, irrespective of the type and severity of the handicap. On the other hand neither school setting nor school personnel were prepared to meet these new demands.

Basically the thrust towards mainstreaming was thus ideological and emotional with few rational guidelines being provided that could make mainstreaming possible. In addition no experimental programme was set up to find out how to plan and implement mainstreaming.

The result of this typically Italian approach could easily be imagined and has in fact come about: chaos as regards services and frustration on the part of the teaching staff, which may well lead to legislative steps that may dramatically limit mainstreaming and restore segregation once again.

Finally the lesson that comes from Italy can be easily summarized: good laws and social sensitization are but pre-requisites to mainstreaming which can become reality provided that the skills of professionals dealing with the handicapped students be greatly improved.

In conclusion, top marks to Italian legislative bills and social sensitization but very low marks to the Italian way of planning and implementing mainstreaming. Unfortunately imagination is not sufficient to solve such a complicated social and educational problem as mainstreaming.

REFERENCES

Adams, G.R., and Cohen, A.S., (1974). Children's physical and interpersonal characteristics that affect student-teacher interactions, **Journal of Exceptional Children, 43**, 1-5

Baker, R.G. and Gump, P.V. (1964). **Big School, Small School**, University Press, Stanford, Cal.

Basaglia, F. (1968). **L'Istituzione Negata**, Einaudi, Torino

Basaglia, F. (1971). **La Maggioranza Deviante**, Einaudi, Torino

Bender, M., Valletutti, P.J., and Bender, R. (1978). **Teaching the Moderately and Severely Handicapped, 1,2 and 3**, University Park Press, Baltimore

Bricker, D.D. (1978). A rationale for the integration of handicapped and non-handicapped pre-school children. In Guralnik M.J. (ed.), **Early Intervention and Integration of Handicapped and Non-handicapped Children**, University Park Press, Baltimore

Bricker, D.D., Seibert, J.M. and Casuso, V. (1980). Early intervention. In Hogg, J. and Mittler, P.J. (eds.), **Advances in Mental Handicap Research, 1**, Wiley, New York

Cancrini, L. (1977). **Bambini Diversi a Scuola**, Boringhieri, Torino

Cantrell, R.P. and Cantrell, M.L. (1976). Preventive mainstreaming: impact of a supportive service program on pupils, **Exceptional Children, 42**, 381-386

Cantrell, R.P. and Cantrell, M.L. (1980). Ecological problem solving. A decision making heuristics for prevention-intervention education strategies. In Hogg, J. and Mittler, P.J. (eds.), **Advances in Mental Handicap Research, 1**, Wiley, New York

Cooke, T.P., Apolloni, T. and Cooke, S. (1977). Normal pre-school children as behavior models for retarded peers, **Exceptional Children, 43**, 531-532

Danford, S. (1976). Behavioral ecology: toward a technology of performance and effectiveness. Paper presented at the American Psychological Association Annual Meeting, Washington D.C. September

Dunn, L.M. (ed.) (1973). **Exceptional Children in the School: Special Education in Transition**, New York, Holt, Rinehart and Winston

Edgerton, R.B. (1967). **The Cloak of Competence: Stigma in the Lives of the Mentally Retarded**, University of California Press, Berkeley

Etzioni, A. (1964). **Modern Organization**, Prentice-Hall, Englewood Cliffs, New Jersey

Etzioni, A. (1971). **A Comparative Analysis of Complex Organizations**, The Free Press, London

Frankel, F. and Graham, V. (1976). Systematic observation of classroom behavior of retarded and autistic pre-school children, **American Journal of Mental Deficiency, 81**, 7384

Fredericksen, L.W. and Frederickson, C.B. (1977). Experienced evaluation of classroom environments: scheduling planned activities, **American Journal of Mental Deficiency, 81,** 421-427

Fredericksen, N., Jensen, O. and Beaton, A. (1972). **Prediction of Organizational Behavior**, Pergamon Press, New York

Gallagher, J.J. (ed.) (1980). **Ecology of Exceptional Children, New Directions for Exceptional Children, 1**

Goffman, E. (1961). **Asylums**, Doubleday, New York

Goldfarb, W. (1943). The effects of early institutional care on adolescent personality, **Journal of Experimental Education, 12**, 106-129

Guralnick, M.J., (1976). The value of integrating handicapped and non-handicapped pre-school children, **American Journal of Orthopsychiatry, 46**, 236-245

Guskin, S.L., Bartel, N.R. and MacMillan, D.L. (1975).Perspective of the labeled child. In Hobbs, N. (ed.), **Issues in the Classification of Children**, Jossey-Bass, San Francisco

Hobbs, N. (1975). **The Future of Children**, Jossey-Bass, San Francisco

Hutt, C. and Vaizey, M. (1966). Differential effects of group density on social behavior, **Nature, 209**, 1371-1372

Janes, D. (in press), Le abilita integranti. In Meazzini, P., (ed.) **Handicappato: Passi Verso L'autonomia**, Giunti-Barbera, Firenze

Kanner, L.A. (1964). **A History of the Care and Study of the Mentally Retarded**, Charles C. Thomas, Springfield. Ill.

Karnes, M.B. and Zehrbach, R.P. (1977). Alternative models for delivering services to young handicapped children. In Jordan, J.B. (ed.), **Early Childhood Education for Exceptional Children**, Council for Exceptional Children, Reston, Va.

Kaufman, K.F. (1978). Teaching parents to teach their children: the behavior modification approach. In Feingold, B. and Bank, C. (eds.), **Developmental Disabilities of Early Childhood**, Charles C. Thomas, Springfield, Ill.

Kennedy, P.K. (1976). Longitudinal sociometric and cross-sectional data on mainstreaming hearing impaired children, **Volta Review, 78**, 71-81

Kozloff, M.A. (1974). **Educating Children with Learning and Behavior Problems**, Wiley, New York.

Kozloff, M.A. (1979). **A Program for Families of Children with Learning and Behavior Problems**, Wiley, New York

Lindsley, O.R. (1970). Children are not retarded. In Fargo, G.A., Behrns, C. and Nolen, P. (eds.), **Behavior Modification in the Classroom**, Wadsworth, Belmont, Cal.

Love, H.D., (1973). **The Mentally Retarded Child and his Family**, Charles C. Thomas, Springfield, Ill.

Meazzini, P. (1978). **La Conduzione della Classe**, Giunti-Barbera, Firenze

Meazzini, P. (ed.) (in press). **Handicappato: Passi Verso L'autonomia**, Giunti-Barbera, Firenze

Meazzini, P. and Galeazzi, A. (1977). L'integrazione del minore handicappato nella scuola pubblica, **Formazione e Cambiamento, 2**, 103-116

Mercer, C.D. and Payne, J.S. (1975a). Programs and services. In Kaufman, J.M. and Payne, J.S. (eds.), **Mental Retardation: Introduction and Personal Perspectives**, Charles E. Merrill, Columbus

Mercer, C.D. and Payne, J.S. (1975b). Biological and environmental causes. In Kaufman, J.M. and Payne, J.S., (eds.), **Mental Retardation: Introduction and Personal Perspectives**, Charles E. Merrill, Columbus

Nisi, A. (in press). La formazione dei genitori. In Meazzini, P. (ed.), **Handicappato: Passi Verso L'autonomia**, Giunti-Barbera, Firenze

Orio, S. and Rossi, G. (1978). **Diversi: Perche**, Emme Edizioni, Milano

Painter, M. (1976). Fluorescent lights and hyperactivity in children: an experiment, **Academic Therapy, 12**, 181-184

Peterson, C., Peterson, J. and Scriven, G. (1977). Peer imitation by non-handicapped pre-schoolers, **Exceptional Children, 43**, 223-225

Ricci, C. (in press). La formazione dell'insegnante. In Meazzini, P. (ed.), **Handicappato: Passi Verso L'autonomia**, Giunti-Barbera, Firenze

Richardson, S.A., Ronald, L. and Kleck, R.E. (1974). The social status of handicapped and non-handicapped boys in a camp setting, **Journal of Special Education, 8**, 143-152

Rogers-Warren, A. and Wedel, J.W. (1980). The ecology of pre-school classrooms for the handicapped. In Gallagher J. (ed.), **Ecology of Exceptional Children, New Directions for Exceptional Children, 1**, 1-24

Rutter, M. and Shaffer, D. (1980). DSM III. A step forward or back in terms of the classification of child psychiatric disorders?, **Journal of the American Academy of Child Psychiatry, 19**, 371-394

Salzinger, S., Antrobus, J. and Glick, J. (1980). **The Eco-system of the "Sick" Child**, Academic Press, New York

Shakespeare, R. (1974). **The Psychology of Handicap**, Methuen, London

Skinner, B.F. (1972). **Cumulative Record**, Appleton-Century-Crofts, New York

Snell, M.E. (ed.) (1978). **Systematic Instruction of the Moderately and Severely Handicapped**, Charles E. Merrill, Columbus

Thomas, D. (1978). **The Social Psychology of Childhood Disability**, Methuen, London

Thompson, T. and Grabowski, J. (eds.) (1977). **Behavior Modification of the Mentally Retarded**, Oxford University Press, New York

Turnboll, A.P. and Blacher-Dixon, J. (1980). Pre-school mainstreaming: impact on parents. In Gallagher, J.J. (ed.), **Ecology of Exceptional Children, New Directions for Exceptional Children, 1**, 25-46

Turnboll, A.P., and Schultz, J.B. (1979). **Mainstreaming Handicapped Students**, Allyn and Bacon, Boston

Wahler, R.G. (1972). Some ecological problems in child modification. In Bijou, S.W. and Ribes-Inesta, E. (eds.), **Behavior Modification: Issues and Extensions**, Academic Press, New York

Wynne, S. (1975). **Mainstreaming and Early Childhood Education for Handicapped Children: A Guide for Teachers and Parents**, Final Report, Bureau of Education for the Handicapped, Washington D.C.

Yule, W. (1980). The epidemiology of child psychopathology. In Lahey, B.B. and Kazdin, A.E. (eds.), **Advances in Clinical Child Psychology**, **4**, 1-51

COMMENTARY

J. Carr

The integration of handicapped children within the normal school system has been increasingly accepted over recent years, and in Britain the concept has been embodied in the Warnock Report.

The major tenet of those who argue for integration is that the handicapped should live among the non-handicapped and make use of the same medical, social and educational facilities as are used by the non-handicapped. It is worth remembering that special facilities were brought into being because in the past it was seen that the handicapped were not benefiting from - in some cases had very little access to - the normal facilities. Special schools ensured that at least some teaching came the handicapped child's way. The aim of the present movement is to allow the handicapped the special provision that they need within the framework of normal life; but where the normal and the handicapped co-exist it is a common enough occurrence for more attention to be given to the more stimulating, more responsive, more rewarding children. In our philanthropic urge towards desegregation, we need to ensure that we do not simply return the handicapped to the bottom of the heap.

Mention is made of the need for not only teachers and other professionals but also parents to be "trained so that they eventually acquire the basic skills necessary to manage their children's behavioural problems and to teach self-independent skills". Parents vary in how far they wish to learn these skills, and their right <u>not</u> to learn them if they do not wish to must be recognized. Parents vary too in their enthusiasm for educational integration.

Some fear that the special facilities which they see as essential to the handicapped child's education will not be available in integrated education; many fear that their handicapped children will suffer from the jibes and unkindness of the non-handicapped; others again feel that integration will take place in theory rather than in practice and that the two groups will effectively remain far apart. These are real fears, and parents must be assured that facilities at least as good as those they have become accustomed to will be available, and that active steps will be taken to help the handicapped and non-handicapped to get to know and to appreciate each other (by, for example, "peer tutoring" programmes (Rose, 1981)). Parents who feel confident that the integrated system is genuinely in the interests of their own children, and is not simply an ideological goal, will have added incentive for participating in training programmes.

How far integration should go, and whether it should apply to handicapped people regardless of the severity of their handicap, is touched on. Anderson (1976) saw the possibility of "a continuous provision", from children in ordinary classes with extra helpers, to those based in ordinary classes but withdrawn for certain activities; then those based in special classes but either joining ordinary classes for certain activities, or joining in only for social activities such as meals and playtime; and finally the separate day school with formal links with the ordinary school. Anderson was writing mainly about the physically handicapped child but the model is a feasible one for the mentally handicapped, even if in practice the last two levels are the only ones commonly found in this country, at least for the severely mentally handicapped.

For social and humanitarian reasons the onus is on the special schools to show that they offer clear advantages to the handicapped child. This they have not been able to do; without such advantages they have little to recommend them. Segregation should now be the last, not the first, resort.

References

Anderson, A.M. (1976). Special schools or special schooling for the handicapped child? **Journal of Child Psychology and Psychiatry, 17**, 151-155

Rose, C.D. (1981). Social integration of school-age ESN(s) children in a regular school. **Special Education: Forward Trends, 8**, (4), 17-22, Research Supplement

J. M. A. Hermanns

Meazzini makes a strong plea for mainstreaming handicapped students, or more in general, for integrating handicapped persons as much as possible in society. He points out that institutions for special care for the handicapped persons have the tendency to become worlds in themselves, with their own rules and goals. The handicapped become citizens of this small world and in a way lose their position in the society outside.

In this way the special institutions have an important contribution to the process of labelling and isolation of these persons, who in one way or the other are "different". Integration in society thus has become harder and harder. Finding a balance between making the handicapped person a slave of special provisions and to putting him or her at the mercy of an unprepared environment will take a long time.

Meazzini gives a number of suggestions about how to facilitate the process of mainstreaming. The core of these is to change the child's eco-system by behaviour analysis and modification. No one could in principle have objections against this. On the other hand one must realize that the basic mechanisms of society to deal with deviations from what is considered to be normal are of a more fundamental nature. These mechanisms are embedded in the socio-political, cultural and economic characteristics of a given society. An analysis of societal processes along with designing practical solutions should be undertaken.

W. I. Fraser

I should like to consider what happens to "mainstreamed" handicapped children when they grow up and the stresses accumulate. I would believe that the reason parents wish private institutions with their inbuilt permanence, is their guess that their offspring will not cope well with changes, and they wish to protect, by specialized provision, their children from stress.

There are ex cathedra statements, such as Taylor's, that the retarded person has a greater susceptibility to stress. Do we know? Are mainstreaming experiences more stressful than institutions? Will the problems of coping - and neurosis - be the same in mainstreamed adults? Will our psychiatric services be sensitive and relevant?

S. A. Richardson

Different combinations of impairments and positive individual characteristics will influence the form and manner by which a person is accepted by others. Visible disabilities and/or an unattractive appearance create a social barrier in initial encounters. An attractive appearance may offset a visible disability. A highly atypical appearance, which is outside the range of appearance people are accustomed to seeing, results in a violation of expectation. This violation of expectation causes anxiety and fear which interferes with the usual initial stages of social intercourse. The person whose expectations are violated gives major attention to the source of the violation, i.e. the impairment, and disregards the other characteristics of the person that he or she would normally attend to. He or she also becomes more formal in behaviour, and will break off the social contact if possible. This is a brief summary of the concept of violation of expectation which is described with supporting research evidence in Richardson, (1976).

Impairments which are not visible may not cause an obstacle in the initial stages of a social encounter but become apparent later, e.g. forms of behaviour disturbances, intellectual impairment and sensory impairments. These affect social relationships over time and continued social relationships with the people may be a source of repeated aggravation and negative experience.

Clearly the person most disadvantaged in social relationships is someone who combines visible and non-visible characteristics which violate expectation and cause continued unpleasant experience for others.

The issue raised is to whether a mentally impaired child may benefit from being in a special class and being sheltered from the stresses of being in an ordinary class where there is likelihood of being socially isolated, failing in school tasks and being possibly teased and bullied by peers. It is necessary to look ahead to the years after the child leaves school and is attempting to cope with adult life including seeking and holding a job in open employment. Although there may be stresses attendant to being in a regular school, the experiences may also provide valuable preparation and socialization for post-school life. By keeping a mentally impaired child in a less stressful and sheltered environment of a special school the child may be ill prepared for functioning in the adult world, be unable to make the transition to adult life and be in need of continued sheltering in some form of adult service setting. It should not be assumed that the stresses of a disabled child being in an ordinary classroom are necessarily negative and destructive.

Reference

Richardson, S.A., (1976). Attitudes and behaviour toward the physically handicapped. In: **Developmental Disabilities: Psychologic and Social Implications**, D. Bergsma and A.E. Pulver (eds.) National Foundation, March of Dimes, Birth Defects, Original Article Series, XII (4), 15-34

W. Yule

Meazzini rightly stresses that dissatisfaction with suggested special education is one of the factors in the development of pressure towards "mainstreaming", or fuller integration of handicapped individuals within society. I happen to share his belief that broadly based systems of behaviour modification based on social learning theory can make a significant contribution both in analysing the objectives of an education system and in providing necessary skills to meet these objectives. However, I feel that the paper has mirrored the US concerns with normalization and mainstreaming to the exclusion of European concerns with integration.

Few people would nowadays question the humanitarian goal of helping all children to live as fully and as fulfilled as possible in adult society. But different societies have different values and these are reflected in their specific arrangements for educating handicapped children. As in other fields of comparative education, there is a need for detailed research studies to compare the differing ways of approaching the goal of integration. And I do mean good research studies, not just occasional visits which result in graphic journalistic essays extolling other solutions without also seeing the problems.

The Warnock Report (DES, 1978) usefully distinguished three main different types of integration:

1. LOCATIONAL INTEGRATION which exists when special education classes or units share the same site as ordinary schools. This, in itself, does not guarantee any mixing of handicapped and non-handicapped pupils. A great deal depends on the formal and informal social structures of the organizations, as well as on their physical layout.

2. SOCIAL INTEGRATION occurs when children with special educational needs mix with other children for most social activities at school but remain segregated for teaching sessions.

3. FUNCTIONAL INTEGRATION is achieved when children with special needs join regular classes either full-time or part-time.

With these distinctions in mind, one can begin to ask more detailed questions about what form of integration to aim for, for which group of children and what resources are required to achieve these goals. Evidence to date suggests that the more mentally handicapped the child, the more the disability involves neurological deficits, the more likely that child will be rejected by his normal peers. In considering the pros and cons of different forms of integration, it is necessary to consider the needs and wishes of the children, of their parents, of other pupils, the nature of any disability and its severity - to list but a few. The aim is to prevent defects and disabilities becoming handicaps. As yet, there are insufficient data to achieve that aim since few experimental evaluations of alternative provisions have been undertaken.

By focusing on potential specific solutions for particular groups of severely and multiply handicapped children, one very real danger of poor integration schemes is made obvious. Most specific disabilities are thankfully rare. Affected children will be widely scattered. There is a danger that hard-won experience and skills may no longer be readily available in specific locations unless, as the Warnock Committee recommended (8:14) "... a number of special schools should be designated as specialist centres for relatively rare or particularly complex disabilities ...". Integration of children should not lead to dissipation of special teaching skills.

In Britain, as in the USA, recent legislation has recognized parental rights over their children's education. I agree with Meazzini that parents must have access to effective help at various points, most of them predictable, during their child's school career (Yule and Gorrell-Barnes, 1978; Mittler and Mittler, 1982). I also agree with him that "prosthetic environments" are not necessarily destructive. All of us function better in some situations than in others. If disabled individuals can function at higher levels (and therefore be less handicapped) by the judicious structuring of the environment, this option must be seriously considered. Indeed, and paradoxically, it is my distinct impression that more and more groups of parents are setting up private schools, such as those run by the Autistic Society or at Ravenswood, especially to create a sheltered ("prosthetic"?) environment in which their children can continue to develop through adolescence and into adulthood. At a time when received opinion is favouring integration, the reasons for this apparently contrary movement should be carefully considered.

References

Department of Education and Science (1978). **Special Educational Needs: Report of the Committee of Enquiry into the Education of Handicapped Children and Young People**, Mrs. H.M. Warnock, HMSO, London

Mittler, P. and Mittler H. (1982). **Partnership with Parents.** National Council for Special Education, Stratford-upon-Avon

Yule, W. and Gorrell-Barnes, G. (1978). The child with handicap. In **Good Enough Parenting : Report of a Group on Work with Children and Young People and the Implications for Social Work Education**, Central Council for Education and Training in Social Work, London

Chapter 25

Evaluation of services and staff training

P. Mittler

INTRODUCTION

The Gap Between Knowledge and Application

According to the United Nations' estimates, more than 40 million of the world's population suffer from significant mental handicap. The numbers will rise to 60 million by the end of the century (WHO, 1976). Most of them live in rural areas and are virtually unreached by services. Many impairments in the Third World are the result of acquired disorders such as severe malnutrition, or brain infections following a period of normal development. Many could be prevented or treated if we applied existing knowledge in the form of simple low-cost measures (WHO, 1983).

Obstacles to implementation of existing knowledge in the Third World and in our own European countries should not be simplistically attributed to shortage of money or to governments setting other priorities. The problems are also related to the way in which knowledge is communicated, disseminated and applied, the organizational and service structures which have been developed, the structure of our professional hierarchies and the ways in which they communicate with one another. Evaluation strategies must in future concern themselves with organizational structures and processes to a greater extent than they do now. Behavioural technologies have helped us to evaluate change at a micro level; but we have to develop even more powerful techniques at the macro level; of systems and organizations if we are to arrive at a better understanding of achieving social change through the application of knowledge.

Indeed, the gap between knowledge and application could itself be the subject of formal evaluation. There are gaps enough in our own countries, many perhaps unnecessarily large - for example, the access of the more socially disadvantaged sections of our population to health care, including measures concerned with primary prevention of handicapping conditions. The disproportionate numbers of such families who suffer multiple disadvantage are reflected in morbidity and mortality statistics (Townsend and Davidson, 1982), as well as in a variety of other indices, including referral to special schools for children with learning difficulties (Tomlinson, 1981).

Changing Pattern of Services in the UK

We have inherited a pattern of services for mentally handicapped people from an earlier age when social and professional attitudes to the mentally handicapped reflected different values and assumptions from those which are current today. At the beginning of the century, society thought fit to segregate mentally handicapped people from the mainstream of society and established large residential colonies - the word was well chosen. Mentally handicapped people were thought to be incapable of contributing to the economy and were by definition incapable of responding to training. Steps to prevent them intermarrying with one another or with non-handicapped people were also thought to be necessary by a society which was concerned about the risks of declining national intelligence and inferior genetic stock.

As a direct consequence of previous policies and attitudes, we are now faced with the task of reflecting current social and political priorities with buildings and services which originated 100 years ago.

In England and Wales, there are some 45 000 adults in the former colonies that we now call hospitals; it is official government policy to discharge at least one third of them to appropriate community services and to transfer the necessary funds from health authorities to local government to enable this to be done within a short period of time. The shift of emphasis from hospital to community services was recommended by a Royal Commission in 1957 but in practice the considerable expansion of community services since then has been for the benefit of people already in the community; it has not resulted in the discharge of many people from hospital, so that numbers in hospitals are far higher than envisaged in national planning targets.

There is now considerable uncertainty about the nature of community services that will be needed in the future. Until recently, it was assumed that community services for mentally handicapped people would take the form of Adult Training Centres, which now provide for about 45 000 people daily, residential hostels which now cater for about 14 000 adults and special schools with a further 32 000 pupils. Although these institutions will be needed for many years to come - indeed, they will have to provide for many of the people coming out of hospital - there is concern that ATCs, hostels and special schools represent environments that are too segregated from everyday living, and cannot by their nature promote the full integration of mentally handicapped people into the community; they are in the community, but not of it. In particular, there is now a strong emphasis on the use of ordinary housing dispersed amongst other houses in the community, with the residents of each house having access to as much help and support as their individual needs require: some would be fully staffed, others might merely need to be visited once a week. A number of reports of such schemes are now becoming available both for children (Shearer, 1981) and adults (King's Fund Centre, 1980; DHSS, 1983; Baker *et al*., 1977).

Less progress has been made in decentralizing special schools and Adult Training Centres; less than one per cent of mentally handicapped children of school age are attending special classes in ordinary schools in the UK (DES, 1981); no recent figures are available on the extent to which adults have access to ordinary facilities such as Further Education Colleges, vocational training schemes or sheltered or open employment, though there is descriptive evidence that they are beginning to do so (e.g. Bradley and Hegarty, 1981).

In addition to access to ordinary services, more emphasis is now being placed on services being brought to mentally handicapped people and their families in their own homes; the model here is of a home visitor who helps the family to teach their child basic self-care and communication skills and to provide any other possible service to help the family to keep their relative at home, rather than admit to residential care. This may include physical adaptations to the home, as well as financial help in many cases. The best known example of a published programme of domiciliary help is the Portage model (Bluma *et al*., 1976), but many other approaches are now being developed, with an emphasis on parental involvement in partnership with professionals (Mittler and Mittler, 1983).

An increasing number of nurses who have previously worked in mental handicap hospitals are now being retrained to work in the community, helping to relocate hospital residents and providing specialist support for them in ordinary houses, working with families to prevent admission to hospital. They are frequently working in a small community team, alongside a specialist social worker or teacher, with back up from a psychiatrist, psychologist or therapist. Community teams work with families, and sometimes also fulfil advisory functions for staff with less experience of severely handicapped people. Each team should cover a total population unit of around 50 000 people (Independent Development Council, 1982).

Expressing Accountability

Since services for mentally handicapped people are increasingly becoming absorbed into services for the rest of the population, it follows that they will become subject to the same political, financial and social pressures as any other service. One consequence of developing local community based services must inevitably be that decision on priorities and direction of services for the mentally handicapped will be made by laymen - that is by elected representatives of the local community for whom mental handicap is only one of the many competing responsibilities and who cannot be expected to be either knowledgeable about or sympathetic to the needs of a group of people who have until recently been segregated from society.

On the other hand, mentally handicapped people may benefit from the growing insistence on accountability which is now being demanded of service providers. This can take a variety of forms. In the case of children, accountability to the child is reflected in the individual educational programme which is now embodied within legislation in the 1981 Education Act and US Public Law 94-142. An individual programme for each adult is also regarded as desirable by an increasing number of professionals and service providers, though resources of time and the skills of staff to draw up such programmes will set limits on the realization of this goal for some time to come. Nevertheless, the growing use of the principles of goal planning for the individual or management by objectives for service planning is a step in the right direction (Houts and Scott, 1975; Revill and Blunden, 1980).

Monitoring

The principle of accountability can also be expressed through continuous monitoring of the quality and quantity of services. It can be argued that every service should have a statement both of its general aims and of the specific objectives which express those aims; these objectives should be formulated in such a way that there can be no doubt about whether or not they have been attained. As Kushlick (1975) has shown in an analysis of government policy documents, there has to be a clear statement of who will do what, under what conditions, to what criteria and with what consequences.

The 1971 White Paper *Better Services for the Mentally Handicapped* represented a significant step in the right direction. Not only did it identify general aims in the form of a philosophy of community orientated services but it also suggested some approximate guidelines in the form of targets of the numbers of individuals for whom places should be found in a range of different services. For example, it suggested that by 1991 each population unit of 100 000 people should provide a total of 150 places in Adult Training Centres, residential local authority places for 60 adults and ten children, and special schools for 70. It also suggested that adult numbers in hospital should be reduced from 52 000 in 1969 to 26 500 in 1991 - a reduction from 113 to 55 per 100 000 population.

In the event, the targets proved accurate in some respects but were wildly unrealistic in others. But whatever their short-comings, they did provide useful local guidelines in respect of the numbers of people for whom services were needed. From a national viewpoint, local authorities succeeded during the 1970s in providing about 2000 new Adult Training Centre places a year and also came fairly close to their targets for schools and residential places for adults. But they remained virtually at a standstill in providing residential places for children.

The figures for children reflect the most extreme failure of forecasting; the White Paper predicted that the number of children in hospital would remain between 6000 and 7000; in fact, there will be virtually no children at all in hospital for long term care by the end of the decade, if present trends continue. Admissions to hospital for long term care have virtually ceased, partly because better support services are being provided in the community and partly because hospitals refuse to admit children. At the same time, the children that remain in hospital are rapidly reaching the age of 16 and now count only in the adult statistics. Very few have been discharged to community services.

Setting targets for number of places to be provided makes it possible to monitor implementation of service objectives and for public authorities to express accountability to the public and to clients and consumers. But numbers of places planned and provided is only the first step in monitoring. It merely provides a starting point for many other approaches which aim to compare service aims with achievements.

One example of a self-monitoring tool is the checklist of standards on quality of services published by the National Development Group for the Mentally Handicapped (NDG, 1980). These are based on a set of goals and principles of service delivery concerned with meeting the assessed and agreed needs of individuals, the use of ordinary services and interdisciplinary collaboration based on joint planning. The 224 standards are in the form of specific questions covering the whole spectrum of services, whether administered by health or local authorities or voluntary organizations; they are set out in such a way as to enable staff to write in answers and proposed action, as well as target dates for review.

APPROACHES TO EVALUATION

I have been using the concept of monitoring to describe procedures which service providers themselves could use to assess the quality of their service. But it will be apparent that some of these procedures are not very different from those used by professional research workers described as independent evaluators. Monitoring of a service requires that the aims and philosophies of the service be written down, that clear criteria are identified which permit comparison between aims and achievements not only in terms of quantitative data such as number of places provided, but also more qualitative indices such as measure of satisfaction of consumers and clients and procedures whereby their view can be fed back to improve the system of service delivery. There must also be records of service activity, and above all clients' records must be kept in such a way as to make it clear whether or not they are making progress and whether individual programme plans are being implemented, and with what result.

In contrast to monitoring, the concepts and methods of evaluation tend to be used for studies carried out by an independent research team of the effectiveness of a service, possibly in the form of controlled comparisons between one form of service provision and another.

Evaluation is particularly demanded when new treatment or innovative services are being introduced; evidence for their effectiveness or for their superiority over traditional approaches is demanded. It is curious that such a demand is rarely made of traditional services themselves. We assume that traditional methods of providing services have proved their worth and need not be questioned, at least not till alternatives are being considered. Even then, it is the innovation that is on trial and must prove itself superior to other methods. If established methods are subjected to continuous monitoring and review, their limitations can be readily identified and possibly rectified.

The Anti-Evaluation Position

Before looking at some examples of service evaluation, we should note that traditional concepts of evaluation are being questioned in some quarters, primarily for ideological reasons. Before dismissing this position as unscientific and iconoclastic, we can briefly examine some of the underlying arguments, using first "community care" and then integrated education as benchmarks.

Deinstitutionalization

The question at issue can be put very simply: Must we prove that mentally handicapped people "do better" in community services than those living in long stay hospitals?

There are those who would argue that the current ideology of community based services represents a fundamental human right for mentally handicapped individuals and therefore an inescapable public commitment. On this argument, society need not wait for research workers to provide comparative studies on the effects of community vs hospitals based services, even if such studies were technically feasible. On this view, the move to community services represents both a moral and a policy imperative. Policy makers make the decision, evaluators assess the consequences.

A parallel has even been drawn with child abuse: since our society regards child abuse as inherently undesirable, we do not think of delaying intervention and action until we have clear data indicating that the development of abused children compares unfavourably with non-abused controls. I rather doubt whether this analogy can be sustained but it does illustrate the thesis that research workers do not live in an ethical or policy vacuum, and that many decisions and changes in service systems cannot wait for carefully conducted evaluations.

The debates concerning institutional care have changed considerably. Few would now argue for the retention and development of large mental handicap hospitals on the grounds that they provide a superior form of service; too many research reports and committees of inquiry have documented the difficulty hospitals experience in maintaining even a minimal standard. The case has been made: very few people are now opposed to the principle or the goal of deinstitutionalization though many remain sceptical whether the needs of the most severely handicapped can be adequately met by community services, even if the money did materialize. Doubts are also expressed about the tolerance of the community, and whether community based staff have the skills or the motivation to provide the necessary services, particularly for people with the most severe disabilities and behaviour problems.

Some Cautions From the Literature

Research that is already available should caution us about assuming that merely moving mentally handicapped to smaller living units outside hospitals necessarily has any measurable effect on their behaviour or on their learning of skills.

For example, studies of Landesman-Dwyer (1983) in Washington State indicate that transfer of selected long stay residents from large institutions to small duplex type staffed houses did not necessarily have any beneficial effects on their social interactions with others, or on their community living skills. Such changes only occurred if staff roles were systematically changed, so that staff were strongly encouraged to make specific demands on residents to take part in activities and programmes appropriate to their new surroundings. Furthermore, levels of activity of those who remained in the hospital were shown to be affected by the extent and nature of the demands being placed on them - people were much more active in day programmes that made strong demands for participation than when simply left on wards with little more than custodial care.

Studies such as those by Landesman-Dwyer provide a timely warning that simply relocating people from environments that we regard as unacceptable or normative does not in itself result in measurable gains. It is only the first step in the development of a programme of teaching in the natural environment rather than in an artificial setting divorced from the context in which the skills are to be used - hence the vital importance of staff training and retraining.

We can sound a similar cautionary note concerning the effects of increases of staff. It is tempting to assume that improvements will automatically follow an increase in direct care staff. In fact, there is evidence both from normal child care and from residential institutions for mentally handicapped people that this is not necessarily the case (King _et al._, 1971; Raynes _et al._, 1979). The number of staff on a ward can be doubled without any effect on the number and nature of interactions between staff and residents, the implementation of programmes or the skills of residents.

Here again, we return to the vital importance of the staff learning to teach and work with residents, but also of the need for matching skills at the level of organization and management which will ensure that staff can be helped to put their skills into practice, to share tasks and roles so that, for example, one concentrates on group activities while another works with individuals on a one to one basis (McBrien and Weightman, 1980). Similarly, the work of Tizard and Raynes provides measures of delegation to direct care staff, the extent of block treatment, rigidity, depersonalization, informative speech and community involvement. All these can be used to assess the day to day quality of care.

Integrated Education

If the case for the development of community based services is relatively uncontroversial, the same can by no means be said about removing children from special schools and placing them in ordinary schools. Although the current ideology strongly favours integrated education, there is also much support for the quality of teaching found in many special schools for mentally handicapped children, and a corresponding reluctance to dismember special schools and lose or disperse the expertise of the staff. Special schools are under attack not so much because of what they do but because of what they represent - education segregated from non-handicapped children, a system which is itself handicapped in preparing children to live successfully in an integrated society. Advocates of integration do not necessarily live under the illusion that ordinary schools can meet the needs of severely handicapped children now, nor are they in doubt that teachers will need training and support from more experienced colleagues. The case for integration is based on the social as well as the educational needs of both handicapped and non-handicapped children.

Given the much more finely balanced arguments surrounding the integration debate, can parents and policy makers look to research for any clear guidelines which might help them to weigh the arguments and evidence on both educational, social and societal grounds?

At this point we have to face our inadequacies and admit that the voluminous literature does not offer conclusive evidence one way or the other. This is not to deny the validity of many well conducted studies, nor of those trends which do appear to emerge from the research. It is merely that the way in which the question is posed admits of no definite answer so far.

We are dealing here with what has been called the agricultural model of evaluation; in essence, the question is of the type "does fertilizer A have a better effect on crop yield than fertilizer B?"

It is no coincidence that the statistical techniques on which most of us were brought up were directly transmitted from agricultural research. They still have their uses but we are struggling to develop evaluation tools which, while no less rigorous, are more appropriate to the kinds of questions which need to be tackled in evaluation of complex interactive, multivariate and excessively noisy systems. Inevitably, policy makers often ask their questions in the agricultural mode and are disappointed that research workers are either unable to answer or hedge their conclusions with impossible qualifications and statistical complexities.

We cannot tackle the question by simply comparing children taught in special schools with others taught in ordinary schools. The main obstacle is selection artefact: we shall not be comparing like with like because the characteristics of children who happen to have been selected for special schools are likely to be different from those selected to remain in ordinary schools. Even if we try to control for IQ, sex, social class and other classical variables, many other variables will slip through the net, not all of which lend themselves to accurate measurement. Two children may have the same IQ, sex, social class, come from the same street and school but the one who is referred to a special school is more likely to show behaviour problems, to come from ethnic minority families, and to show additional evidence of social disadvantage (Wedge and Prosser, 1973; Tomlinson, 1981).

Once in special schools, it is almost impossible for research workers to disentangle effects of special schooling *per se* from the complex network of associated variables, such as self-concept, social esteem and friendship patterns, family and peer attitudes. Most comparative studies have tried to distinguish educational attainments from social variables, such as popularity and friendship patterns, but the conclusion of most reviews of the literature is equivocal and uncertain. This conclusion was first reached by Kirk (1964) but has not been significantly modified by a great deal of later research (e.g. Cave and Madison, 1978; Corman and Gottlieb, 1978). Finally, very few of the studies reviewed have been concerned with severely mentally handicapped children; so few of them are receiving integrated education that comparison between those who are in ordinary and special schools is virtually impossible at present.

Furthermore, most of the American studies compare children in special classes with those taught in ordinary classes; in this country, only one per cent of mentally handicapped children are in special classes and probably even fewer in ordinary classes.

Similar selection artefacts can be seen when we try to compare the progress of mentally handicapped children in day special schools with that of the small number of children left in hospital schools. Children who are admitted to hospital are in general more severely and multiply handicapped than those in day schools; furthermore, they tend to be much older (Preddy and Mittler, 1981). For these reasons, it is difficult to conclude from such studies that hospitals have an adverse effect on children's development; more carefully designed longitudinal studies would be needed, comparing the growth of a comparable group of children in both hospital and home environments; alternatively, studies which assess the effects of removing children from one environment to another, as did Tizard's classic Brooklands studies (Tizard, 1964). Even here, we have no evidence concerning long term maintenance of the original gains in social and verbal development; some of Kushlick's data suggest that skills may sometimes be lost, even in "good" environments.

The only moderately satisfactory way of comparing outcomes in special and ordinary schools would be to study a large group of children being considered for special education, allocate them quite randomly to special and ordinary schools and continue to monitor the outcome on a wide range of variables for the whole of their childhood and for as long as possible in their adulthood. Even if such a programme were ethically defensible, I have never met a research worker who would wish to tackle it, or a research agency that would even consider funding it.

The movement to provide more integrated education for mentally handicapped children cannot therefore be founded on a firm body of research data which confidently point to the benefits of such programmes for children or to the satisfactions of their parents, compared to provision in special schools. Nevertheless, the ideology and the commitment to integrate are increasing, with the support of a growing number of parents, professionals and policy makers. Legislation has been passed in several countries mandating integrating education; in many parts of Italy, special schools and residential institutions have been closed by Act of Parliament, and their clients placed in ordinary schools or ordinary forms of provision. In the USA, Public Law 94-142 mandated legislation in "the least restrictive environment" on the basis of an individual educational programme; in this country the new 1981 Education Act recommends education in ordinary schools "as far as is practicable, in line with the views of the parents, the ability of the school to meet the child's needs, the provision of efficient education for other children and the efficient use of resources of the local education authority" (DES, 1981).

Although this is hardly the language of commitment, research already available does have something to offer to education authorities in search of guidelines on ways of promoting a more integrated educational service. There are innumerable studies which describe particular examples of integration, which give detailed accounts of the processes involved in its development, which interview protagonists and participants and which examine both the social and educational outcomes on the children. Although few of these studies involve severely mentally retarded children, the overall conclusion that can be drawn from them is broadly positive. In this country, the early work of Anderson (1973) and the more recent studies at NFER by Hegarty et al. (1981) certainly indicate that integration can work, as well as emphasizing that a great deal of careful planning is needed to ensure that integration is not merely locational but social and educational as well. Detailed descriptive studies are also available on integration in action in several European countries, as part of the OECD study on the handicapped adolescent (OECD, 1981).

EXAMPLES OF EVALUATION METHODS

A number of studies in the United Kingdom have concerned themselves with the evaluation of services. Rather than attempt a summary of their findings, it may be useful to give some indication of the kind of methods and approaches that have been used, the difficulties encountered and the ways in which the data have been interpreted. I propose to concentrate on the evaluation of the Sheffield services, partly because it constitutes an attempt at evaluating a comprehensive service comprising both health and local authority services, partly because it illustrates a wide range of research methods and partly because it is conveniently finished. But those who wish to study other equally wide ranging and significant examples of service evaluation can examine the many studies of the Wessex programme of decentralizing residential care from large hospitals into smaller locally based hospitals published by Kushlick and his colleagues in the Health Care Evaluation Research Team. A major evaluation is also under way of a development which aims to provide comprehensive services for all mentally handicapped people living in Cardiff, carried out by Blunden and the Mental Handicap in Wales Research Unit. It is of interest that all three research teams have themselves played a major part in policy development.

Perhaps the most thoroughgoing evaluation of a service is that carried out by Heron and his colleagues in Sheffield (Heron and Myers, 1983). The evaluation has special significance because the Department of Health and Social Security made a genuine attempt to use Sheffield as a demonstration project for a model service for all mentally handicapped people in the city, a service in which joint planning between health and local authorities would ensure coordination and a rational sharing of responsibilities. It is no coincidence that the Sheffield Feasibility Study Report was published in 1971, the same year as the national plan embodied in the White Paper _Better Services for the Mentally Handicapped_ (DHSS, 1971).

The story of the evaluation is itself a chapter in the history of evaluation research, not only in relation to the well nigh impossible mission of evaluating a new service four years after it began but also because the lessons of the evaluation were immediately used by planners in order to plan a new service, more in line with modern thinking, and drawing directly on the lessons of the evaluation itself (Sheffield AHA, 1981). A further evaluation study will be needed to judge the quality of the phoenix being born from the ashes of the old blueprint.

It may be of interest to summarize the range of research tools developed by the research team, bearing in mind that "before and after" studies were ruled out from the start. Despite this unavoidable limitation, the research team was able to conduct an impressive range of evaluation techniques. These included the following:

i) Studies were done comparing aspects of services in Sheffield with those in Leeds, a city of comparable size and social structure about 40 miles away. Comparisons were carried out of services available to families of mentally handicapped children in both cities, and parents were interviewed about their satisfaction with the services available to them and their children. Comparisons were also made in respect of case-finding, and an intensive study of assessment and early intervention services for the under fives. Interviews with parents in both cities clearly highlighted their need for detailed information, their wish to take a full part in the process of assessment and decision making and to have access to professionals in one place. The study also identified a major challenge for the future: while parents were in general reasonably satisfied with the specialist services (90% in Sheffield and 68% in Leeds), they were critical of the lack of knowledge of handicap in generic services - family doctors, midwives, health visitors, social workers, and psychologists; they also found it hard to gain access to the home help service and to information about aids and allowances.

Detailed interviews were held with some 400 staff and 200 parents in both cities, resulting in the sobering finding that far fewer differences existed between the cities than had been expected (Heron and Myers, 1983). The perceptions of parents and staff of the availability of services were similar in both cities, but the Sheffield service was distinguished by the availability of specialist social workers attached to area social work teams. A major problem of dissemination and communication in Sheffield is reflected in the finding that only half the staff interviewed were held to be adequately informed about the Sheffield project, and one in six had no knowledge of the project at all.

ii) An intensive study of the Ryegate Assessment Centre for children was also carried out, using time-sampling observations, interviews with parents and staff, and systematic analysis of records over a two-year period.

iii) In order to provide a data base for a particularly close examination of services for school leavers and young people, four consecutive annual cohorts of school leavers were each followed up after three years. This provided an invaluable source of information on the characteristics and needs of school leavers and their families. Interviews were held with the young people themselves, their parents, the supervisors of the services with whom they came into contact and, where appropriate, their employers. The cohort studies showed that the young people were not moving through the training system in the way outlined in the original service plans.

iv) The Sheffield plan provided for an innovative feature in the form of an assessment unit for school leavers. The research team were able to compare the stated aims of this service with outcomes. For example, one of the aims of this service was to provide intensive on the job training for staff of other ATCs in the city. This was assessed in part by a study of the attitudes, priorities and activities of staff of the ATCs, replicated with a two year interval. At the time of the second study, there had been a marked increase in the number and quality of individual programme plans, greater specificity of aims, a more optimistic outlook about the potential of ATC students to benefit from training, more time spent in direct interaction with students. But staff reported considerable difficulties in carrying out annual reviews of individual programme plans, partly due to lack of support and leadership from middle management outside the Centres; similarly, it was difficult to initiate programmes designed to involve parents in the activities of the Centres. Questionnaires and staff interviews also reflected the difficulties experienced in securing support from outside professionals.

Although many substantive improvements took place in the period of study, it was difficult for research workers to isolate the contribution of any one group of variables to the outcomes. The work of the Adolescent Assessment Unit undoubtedly exercised a marked effect but other developments may also have had effects which are difficult to measure. This was a period of change, when both national and local policies for day services were under review (National Development Group, 1977), and staff were quite properly exposed to a range of influences on their attitudes and activities.

v) In addition to these studies of day and community services, the research team conducted a series of studies of residential care. Some of these compared the original plans for the division of responsibility for residential care between health and local authority services, finding that they bore little relation to the final outcome. Despite the development of reasonably clear guidelines, the actual allocation of clients to different forms of provision was largely random.

vi) The team's studies of residential short term care are of particular interest, since hardly any research is available on this subject. Detailed interviews were held with a stratified random sample of all parents. These reflected an alarming disparity between the perceptions of planners and parents concerning the type of short term care arrangements which met the needs of families and clients.

I have concentrated on the Sheffield studies because they provide an example of an evaluation of a comprehensive city wide service in which attempts were made to develop a partnership between health and local authorities, a model which is now generally being adopted by policy makers at national and local level.

Who Should Evaluate?

Now that the Sheffield studies are complete, it is interesting to speculate about the extent to which the evaluation could have been carried out by the service providers themselves.

It is true that Sheffield was a "special case" for independent evaluation; on the other hand, the lesson of Sheffield may well be that evaluation of services should be the responsibility of the service providers themselves. Most Social Services Departments have their own research staff, and access to advice and consultancy from professional research workers can often be arranged.

If service providers are going to take more responsibility for carrying out their own monitoring and evaluation procedures, much more attention will need to be given to record systems, particularly of client progress in relation to objectives developed during the course of individual programme planning. If client progress is to be the final yardstick of the success of a service, then clear records of learning and skill acquisition will need to be perceived as at least as important as drug sheets and laundry lists.

Evaluation research uses a broad range of techniques. While some undoubtedly require considerable research training and experience, it is possible that others might be carried out by authorities themselves, using their own research and administrative staff and whatever help they can obtain from universities and research departments. In suggesting that evaluation skills should be shared with and disseminated to service providers, I am only following the example of other scarce professionals who see themselves as "giving their skills away" - educational psychologists and speech therapists are two examples that spring to mind of professions that increasingly work through others in a consultancy rather than a clinical role, in this case with teachers and parents. It has already been suggested that teachers have more in common with research workers than is apparent at first sight - both need to define their objectives, to collect accurate data, to convince themselves and others that change has taken place (Mittler, 1975).

In summarizing some of the main evaluation methods that have been used in the Sheffield, Wessex, Welsh and other studies, it may be useful to bear in mind the extent to which these methods could be used by service providers themselves.

Examples of Evaluation Methods

1. Simple quantitative monitoring studies of number of places provided, number of clients served, staffing ratios, compared with plans, measuring of progress on an annual basis towards stated goals.

2. Descriptive, qualitative studies of the operation of specific services. This can be done by observation and straight impressionistic description; for example, a hospital in process of run-down, the process of relocating residents in community service, attitudes and practices of staff in both settings; effects on an ordinary school of the arrival of a group of handicapped children; effects of introducing new operational policies on a unit.

3. Attitudes and attitude change to mentally handicapped people particularly in relation to previous knowledge, increasing contact, exposure to media programmes, personal contacts.

4. Evaluation of specific components of a service by staff, by parents and by mentally handicapped people themselves. Care has to be taken to avoid a "halo effect", since recipients of a service are more inclined to be positive than negative. Such studies can be repeated after an interval in an effort to assess changing perceptions of the service.

5. Detailed interviews with key informants, such as staff, parents and clients themselves using open-ended ethnographic interviewing techniques, as well as semi-structured interviews and questionnaires. These can test attitudes, knowledge of available services, priorities for mentally handicapped people.

6. Quantitative observational studies - e.g. of the number and nature of interactions between staff and clients.

7. Studies which experimentally manipulate features of the environment - number of staff, nature of staff demands, size and homogeneity of client groupings, physical changes in environment such as room size, use of different furniture arrangement.

8. Studies of the effects of organizational and managerial change - for example, the effect of decentralizing staff decision making to ward level, as in the studies carried out by King *et al*. (1971) and more recently by Raynes *et al*. (1979). Such studies can be carried out not only in traditional hospitals, but also in smaller units whether run by health or local authorities.

9. We need to pay closer attention to the effects of change on particular groups of individuals, rather than concentrating exclusively on attempts to examine global group differences. For example, the studies by Landesman-Dwyer (1983) which examined effects on mentally handicapped people of moving from institutions into ordinary homes, strongly suggested that effects were much more marked on some groups than others. "Those who had previously been passive recipients of staff attention or who oriented to objects, but who were not extreme on any behavioural dimension, seemed to benefit from the smaller living units, when successful adaptation is defined in terms of interacting with objects and people in the environment." But those who before transfer were most sociable and most verbal failed to show gains, while people who were showing high rates of stereotyped behaviour got worse over time, regardless of where they lived.

We therefore need a more refined typology of environments which will enable us to assess the effects of different environments on different groups of individuals. An interesting parallel has been drawn with Rutter's studies of the effects of different kinds of comprehensive schools; attempts were made to identify specific features of school organization and functioning which could be shown to influence outcome measures such as pupil performance. The study revealed strong interactions between attitudes of teaching staff and environmental features of the school in affecting learning outcomes for pupils (Rutter *et al*., 1979).

STAFF TRAINING

The voluminous research literature on human services joins forces with common sense in suggesting that the behaviour of staff manning the services is the key element in affecting the quality of the service and the range of outcomes for clients.

If this is correct, then the training of staff must be seen as the priority of priorities in the coming decades. Assuming that some resources for staff training are available, what can we learn from work that has been done so far?

1. The most urgent need is to provide on the job training for those in direct daily contact with mentally handicapped people - parents, direct care staff and volunteers.

2. The nature of the training should be concerned with the day to day skills needed to help mentally handicapped people to learn basic skills for everyday living - self-care, communication and social independence, interaction with other people, use of leisure, the whole range of personal and community living skills.

3. There needs to be a strategic plan for staff training at local and national level, in place of the somewhat random and *ad hoc* way in which staff are chosen to attend courses at the present time. One way to achieve this is by means of pyramid or cascade training - a system in which those who are chosen for training assume a contractual commitment to train others in their turn. One example of such an approach is the training in behavioural methods of teaching developed by Foxen and McBrien in Manchester (McBrien, 1981). About 100 educational psychologists were trained in 20 workshops held in a school and lasting five days on condition that they agreed to set up similar courses on returning to their own areas. The workshop involved working with teachers and children. More than 1500 school staff have satisfied the criteria for course completion. The materials are now available in self-instructional form.

4. Staff training, however well planned and executed, is only a starting point. There has to be managerial commitment and organizational change to enable staff to put their training into practice.

5. There is no necessary relationship between knowledge and application. Staff can be given information through books and lectures, but direct application to their day to day work does not necessarily follow.

6. Consequently, staff training must provide practical experience of application on the job. In preparation for this, repeated practice first in simulated and then in real situations is essential.

7. There is ample evidence that even well trained and apparently well motivated staff do not maintain their behaviour, and that effects soon wash out. Good managerial support, relevant record keeping and continuous monitoring may help to maintain staff behaviour but are by no means guaranteed to do so.

8. Improvement in the behaviour of clients does help to maintain staff motivation and behaviour. If staff feel that their

clients are not making progress, despite their efforts, they are likely to give up quite quickly, no matter what incentives are provided by management. On the other hand, the quality of record keeping is often so poor that staff are not aware of the progress that has taken place - hence the importance of clear objectives and records which demonstrate step by step learning.

9. Failure of staff to use their learning in a wide range of settings and with all clients with whom they work is one of the most depressing and significant conclusions of the extensive literature. Since the "Train and Hope" approach has failed, we must now develop methods of direct training for generalization. One way to do this is to train in the real environment in the first place.

10. The ultimate and most rigorous test of a service lies in its effects on the recipients of the service themselves. No matter how well plans are being implemented, or how favourable the attitudes and practices of staff and the support of management, the clients to whom the service is directed must be shown to benefit. Many evaluation studies have either not concerned themselves with client outcomes or have assumed that improvements in staff or management practice must be in the interests of the consumer.

How, then, do we devise measures which are sufficiently sensitive to measure change? In the past, evaluations tended to be made by repeated measurements of IQ, often with disappointing results. But unless IQ changes are due to errors of measurement in the first place, there is no strong reason why IQs should rise; indeed, the construction of the tests assumes a measure of constancy; furthermore, IQ is largely a measure of previous rate of development, and is at least to some extent genetically determined.

Of much greater functional importance are criterion-referenced assessments which determine whether or not a particular behaviour is or is not present. For example, we can assess the extent to which a group of hospital residents acquire specific new social or communication skills when they move to a group home or when they are exposed to a different method of teaching or care. This requires the collection of reliable baseline measures, the identification of unambiguous and specific dependent variables to serve as criteria for outcome and equally clear definition of the independent variables being studied or manipulated. It is also important to assess the extent to which newly acquired skills are generalized to a range of situations; in other words, it is not enough to show that a client has learned to use a spoon as a result of a feeding programme if he only does so in the presence of one specific trainer, a particular room or even a particular type of spoon. This may well be only the first goal of teaching; later steps may involve a formal teaching programme in which he is systematically taught to generalize his learning to other settings, other tasks and in the presence of other adults (Baer and Stokes, 1977).

The evaluation of behavioural change has until recently been carried out by means of comparisons between experimental and control groups and with the help of experimental designs and statistical treatments deriving from the agricultural or the drug trial model, involving double-blind trials. While there are some forms of evaluation in which these techniques are both appropriate and essential, their limitations are now generally recognized in evaluation of human services. The reasons for this have been elaborated by many writers. Fortunately, sensitive but equally rigorous methods of evaluation are being increasingly used. These often take the form of time-series designs, including multiple baselines and phased interventions. To take just one example, the Mental Handicap in Wales Research Team is evaluating new community based services by introducing them into different areas at different times and comparing baseline measurements with those taken during and after intervention.

CONCLUDING COMMENTS

This symposium, like many others, has shown yet again that although there is much that we do not know and more about which we are uncertain, there is nevertheless a substantial body of knowledge concerning the nature of mental handicap, its causes and prevention, and its effects on mentally handicapped people, their families, neighbourhoods and communities. We have also learned a good deal about methods of helping mentally handicapped people to learn and to develop their skills and abilities.

Mentally handicapped people need more than advocates and pressure groups to insist on a fair share of resources. There is a need to develop mechanisms to ensure that the services which are provided for them are informed by a working knowledge of what is possible and that staff employed in the service have the necessary skills and support to put knowledge into practice.

Now that there is a reasonable consensus of the kinds of services which are required to cater for the very wide range of needs found in any group of mentally handicapped people, it is all the more necessary to ensure that services are continuously reviewed so that gaps between aims and achievement can be narrowed. One way to do this is through the medium of the individual programme plan - the commitment expressed by the community through its employees to help the individual reach clearly stated goals. Another approach is through the monitoring of service goals in the light of their success in meeting the agreed needs of the clients.

It is customary to distinguish between continuous monitoring of service provision and formal evaluation of a service, usually by an independent research team. In practice, there do not appear to be many examples of service providers monitoring either the quantity or quality of their own service, although the means to do so are availabe. Furthermore, when we come to examine the tools used by professional research workers called in to conduct formal evaluations, we find that at least some of the tools are not so specialized that they could not be used by less highly trained staff. This leads me to the conclusion that evaluators should be training others to use evaluation techniques, and that evaluation is too important to be left to evaluators.

Services for mentally handicapped people inevitably reflect the extent to which they are valued by society. Although the statements of politicians and other social leaders may suggest a more liberal and tolerant attitude, the actual quality of provision and the expressed attitudes of members of the public may fall far short of the prevailing rhetoric.

The current ideological commitment is to help mentally handicapped people to live, learn and work in their own communities and to avoid all unnecessary segregation, particularly if it involves admission to large residential institutions. But those who are responsible for planning and providing services are not necessarily in sympathy with the general aims of integration, nor can they be expected to be knowledgeable either about the needs of mentally handicapped people or how they can be met. In most democracies, decisions on priorities and on the allocation of scarce resources are made by elected members of the public both at local and at national levels; their task is to serve all sections of the community, and this may sometimes be at the expense of minority groups. If we wish to influence policy, it is the elected representative that we must reach. They are the real decision makers.

ACKNOWLEDGEMENTS

I am grateful to Professor Alastair Heron for his helpful comments on an earlier draft of this paper.

REFERENCES

Anderson, E. (1973). **The Disabled Schoolchild: A study of Integration in Primary Schools.** London: Methuen

Baer, D.M. and Stokes, T. (1977). Discriminating a generalisation technology. In Mittler, P. (ed.) **Research to Practice in Mental Retardation, II,** Baltimore, Md.: University Park Press

Baker, B.L., Seltzer, G.B. and Seltzer, M.M. (1977). **As Close as Possible: Community Residences for Retarded Adults,** Boston: Little, Brown

Bluma, S., Shearer, J., Frohman, A. and Hilliard, J. (1976). **Portage Guide to Early Education,** London: NFER Nelson

Bradley, J. and Hegarty, S. (1981). **Students with Special Needs in FE: A Review of Current and Completed Research relating to young people in the 14-19 age range with special educational needs.** London: Further Education Unit, Department of Education and Science

Cave, C. and Madison, P. (1978). **A Survey of Recent Research in Special Education.** London: National Foundation for Educational Research

Corman, L. and Gottlieb, J. (1978). Mainstreaming mentally retarded children: A review of research. In Ellis, N.R. (eds.) **International Review of Research in Mental Retardation, 9,** New York: Academic Press

Department of Education and Science, (1981). **The Education Act, 1981.** Circular 8/81

Department of Education and Science, (1983). **Statistics of Education, 1, Schools.** London: HMSO

Department of Health and Social Security, (1971). **Better Services for the Mentally Handicapped.** London: HMSO

Hegarty, S., Pocklington, K. and Lucas, D. (1981). **Educating Pupils with Ordinary Needs in the Special School.** London: NFER Nelson

Heron, A. and Myers, M. (1983). **Intellectual Impairment: the Battle against Handicap.** New York and London: Academic Press

Houts, P.S. and Scott, R. (1975). **Goal Planning with Developmentally Disabled Persons.** Hershey Medical Centre, Pennsylvania State University

Independent Development Council for People with Mental Handicap (1982). **Elements of a Comprehensive Local Service for People with Mental Handicap.** London: IDC, King's Fund Centre

King, R., Raynes, N. and Tizard, J. (1971). **Patterns of Residential Care: Sociological Studies in Institutions for Handicapped Children.** London: Routledge and Kegan Paul

King's Fund Centre (1980). **An Ordinary Life: comprehensive locally based services for mentally handicapped people.** London: King's Fund Project Paper No. 24

Kirk, S. (1964). Education. In Stevens, H. and Heber, R. (eds.) **Mental Retardation.** Chicago: Chicago University Press

Kushlick, A. (1975). Improving the services for the mentally handicapped. In Kiernan, C.C. and Woodford, P. (eds.), **Behaviour Modification with the Severely Retarded.** Amsterdam: Associated Scientific Publishers

Landesman-Dwyer, S. (1983). The changing structure and function of institutions: A search for optimal group care environments. In Landesman-Dwyer, S. and Vietze, P. (eds.). **The Social Ecology of Residential Environments: Person x Setting Transactions in Mental Retardation.** Baltimore, Md: University Park Press (in press)

McBrien, J. (1981). Introducing the EDY project, **Special Education: Forward Trends, 8,** 29-30

McBrien, J. and Weightman, J. (1980). The effect of room management procedures on the engagement of profoundly retarded children. **British Journal of Mental Subnormality, 26,** 38-46

Mittler, P. (1975). **Research to Practice in the Field of Handicap.** London: Institute for Research in Mental and Multiple Handicap

Mittler, P. and Mittler, H. (1983). Partnership with parents: An overview. In Mittler, P. and McConachie, H. (eds.) **Parents,**

Professionals and Mentally Handicapped People: Approaches to Partnership. London: Croom Helm

National Development Group for the Mentally Handicapped (1977). **Day Services for Mentally Handicapped Adults,** Pamphlet 5. London: DHSS

National Development Group for the Mentally Handicapped (1980). **Improving the Quality of Services for Mentally Handicapped People: A Checklist of Standards.** London: DHSS

Organisation for Economic Cooperation and Development (1981). **The Education of the Handicapped Adolescent: Integration in School.** Paris: Centre for Educational Innovation and Research, OECD

Preddy, D. and Mittler, P. (1981). **Children with Severe Learning Difficulties: A Survey in North West England.** Report to Department of Education and Science. University of Manchester, Hester Adrian Research Centre

Raynes, N., Pratt, M. and Roses, S. (1979). **Organisational Structure and the Care of the Mentally Retarded.** London: Croom Helm

Revill, S. and Blunden, R. (1980). **A Manual for Implementing A Portage Home Training Service for Developmentally Handicapped Pre-School Children.** Windsor: NFER Nelson

Rutter, M., Maughan, B., Mortimore, P. and Ouston, J. (1979). **Fifteen Thousand Hours: Secondary Schools and their Effects on Children.** London: Open Books

Shearer, A. (1981). **Bringing Mentally Handicapped Children out of Hospital.** London, King's Fund Project Paper No. 30

Sheffield Area Health Authority and Metropolitan District Borough (1981). **Strategic Planning of Services for the Mentally Handicapped.** Sheffield Health Authority

Tizard, J. (1964). **Community Services for the Mentally Handicapped.** London: Oxford University Press

Tomlinson, S. (1981). **Educational Subnormality: a study in decision making.** London: Routledge and Kegan Paul

Townsend, P. and Davidson, N. (1982). **Inequalities in Health: The Black Report.** Harmondsworth: Penguin

Wedge, P. and Prosser, H. (1973). **Born to Fail?** London: National Childrens Bureau

World Health Organisation (1976). **Disability Prevention and Rehabilitation.** A/29 Inf. Document 1. Geneva: WHO

World Health Organisation (1983). **Mental Handicap.** Report prepared by Joint Commission on International Aspects of Mental Retardation. Geneva: WHO (in press)

COMMENTARY

A. Heron

In a symposium concerned mainly with the "aetiology, early diagnosis, treatment and prevention" of intellectual impairment present at birth, it would have been all too easy to overlook the wider connotations of the term "treatment" in this context. For those children and adults who have mistakenly been perceived as "chronically ill", the object of "treatment" must be to minimize the extent of disability with which the young child enters adolescence, and to ensure that the residual disability does not prove more of a handicap than it should. An impairment at birth will be less of a disability by the end of the first few years of life if early detection and appropiate intervention have resulted in adequate and suitable guidance and support for the parents or other carers. How far the resulting disability proves to be a handicap will largely depend on the attitudes, behaviour and degree of supportive acceptance elicited from the society (and its health, educational and social services) of which the disabled person is a member.

Wisely, those responsible for the symposium programme recognized the need for an overview of such a wider connotation of "treatment", with the result that Mittler has in his paper taken a long hard look at the key questions relating to "service provision". At the very outset, he has emphasized the growing need for scientific study of the structural models and functional processes involved. In an international setting the service delivery models can and do vary widely (Heron and Myers, 1983, pp 48-64) and Mittler rightly stresses the relative absence of, and the need for, both effective systems of internal self-monitoring and of independent evaluation. Although one can readily agree that the former could with profit employ the research tools evolved by the latter, I think the present distinction between the two should be preserved.

As I observed recently in a different context (Heron, 1982), "any and every service to any section of the community should be 'self-monitoring'. I mean by this that part of the organisation and operation of the service should include a process of regularly examining how they are doing their job. That applies to the service as a whole, to sections of the service and, ultimately, to individuals." This principle has been fully accepted as an integral part of the strategic plan (Sheffield JCC, 1981) for the new joint Local Authority/Health Authority mental handicap service in Sheffield, to which Mittler referred when noting the unusual event that "the lessons of the evaluation were immediately used by the planners in order to plan a new service more in line with modern thinking". This however turns our attention to the role of independent evaluation, as distinct from self-monitoring.

In the light of my own experience and that of others, I have become convinced that the main need for independent evaluation lies with innovation: if the service is of a new kind from which lessons may be learned, it should be evaluated. But although this view was already accepted in 1970 by those who designed the 8-million pound Sheffield Development Project - and so made possible our later work, which Mittler has summarized - it is essential to learn from that experience. Planners, administrators and service providers should not wait years for the findings of a "summative" evaluation of the Sheffield type. The future utility of programme evaluation lies with a "formative" approach, in which the independent evaluators work from the outset with the planners, administrators and service providers. For such an approach to meet acceptable standards of rigour and objectivity, however, there would not only be need for an explicit statement of the basic philosophy underlying the service to be evaluated. It would also be essential to combine a high degree of specificity for both "goal" and "critical factor" identification with equally specific measures of outcome, such as "change of behaviour", for individual clients in the real-life situation. "The simpler the criteria, the easier would it be to demonstrate to what extent they have been met, and therefore how well the programme aims have been achieved. Weakness in approach, in methods, and in practice can be identified, so that fresh discussion by the providers can lead to modifications agreed by all to be necessary" (Heron, 1982).

The "cautionary examples from the literature" provided by Mittler would seem to reinforce the argument for independent formative evaluation of service innovations. The key determinant of anticipated outcome represented by the positive action of staff in their new roles indicates the limitations of internal monitoring in such circumstances (though it does not of course remove the necessity for it, as emphasized already). This illuminating treatment of methodological problems facing those involved in the "integrated education" debate provides, among much else of value, an opportunity to consider the random allocation requirement of the fully experimental model in the evaluation field.

There is general recognition in the specialist literature on service programme evaluation methodology that this is an ideal rarely to be achieved, for the practical and ethical reasons cited by Mittler in relation to "special" and "ordinary" schools. But in the context of the widespread policy of movement from institutional towards genuine "life in the community", there may be new possibilities for the classical approach. I have in mind that the locus of the ethical decision may be seen as shifting from the acceptability of random allocations to the desirability of it. There is a very proper concern, to some extent based on experience gained in the earlier movement to deinstitutionalize residents in long-stay psychiatric hospitals, that inadequate support - both professional and social - can make life in the open community a change for the worse, not for the better. The only way to avoid this is to ensure in advance that community-based services and associated voluntary support are mobilized and properly organized, in relation to the flow towards them. Given the necessity for providing appropriate pre-discharge training, this will almost always mean waiting lists. In such circumstances random allocation of equally "suitable" candidates becomes ethically desirable, given that there is no sound basis for deciding that one particular "ordinary life" opportunity in the local community is "better" or "more suitable" than another.

Lest there be those whose confidence in clinical judgement is strong enough to make them deny the possibility that the candidates for a community placement could be "equally suitable", we must note in Mittler's summary of the Sheffield results that, unintentionally, "the actual allocation to different forms of (residential) provision was largely random". If some of the "criterion-referenced" assessments to which he draws attention were to be further developed and more widely used, it might prove possible and ethically preferable to substitute, in suitable circumstances, a deliberate random allocation, to scarce new opportunities, for such an unintentional one.

Most of the time, however, the practicalities of different situations will make necessary the use of less-than-ideal methods, as was the case in Sheffield. Mittler has referred to these - and to others - so I need not dwell on this topic. Rather I would emphasize the fact that the cumulative effect of the thirteen project reports of the Evaluation Research Group in Sheffield was in the end what mattered. In one of the best and most thoughtful reviews of evaluation of service programmes that I have encountered, Windle and Bates (1974, p.425) observe that "it may be wise to aim for convergent validation of a result rather than a single crucial test. Data from independent sources which corroborate each other may be more convincing and less liable to error than even very carefully collected data from a single source".

To conclude these brief observations which have arisen from an appreciative study of Mittler's paper, let me say that I agree wholeheartedly that those of us with first-hand experience of attempting the evaluation of service delivery programmes should be "giving our skills away" by training others, including those without a professional research background. I also think I understand what he means when he says that "evaluation is too important to be left to evaluators". My advocacy of the "formative" approach demands mutual understanding and real teamwork, between the evaluators and those responsible for planning, administering and providing the new service they all hope will better the chances of disability being less handicapping for those who entered life intellectually impaired.

References

Heron, A. (1982). The place of evaluation in the planning of new integrated health, nutrition and education services in early childhood day-care settings. Resource paper to WHO/UNICEF Seminar "Alternative approaches to day-care", Nairobi, 6-11 December

Heron, A. and Myers, M. (1983). **Intellectual Impairment: The Battle Against Handicap.** London and New York, Academic Press

Sheffield Joint Consultative Committee (1981). **Strategic Planning of Services for the Mentally Handicapped.** Sheffield, Health Authority and Metropolitan District Council

Windle, C. and Bates, P. (1974). Evaluating program evaluation: a suggested approach. In **Evaluation of Behavioural Programs in Community, Residential and School Settings**, Davidson, P.O., Clark, F.W. and Hamerlynck, L.A. (eds.). Champaign, Illinois, Research Press

Chapter 26

Mental retardation – a world view

N. Sartorius

The most recent development in WHO's programme on mental retardation is the forthcoming publication of a white paper on the subject prepared in collaboration with the joint commission of members of the International Association of Scientific Study on Mental Deficiency (IASSMD) and the International League of Societies for Persons with Mental Handicap (ILSPMH). Other recent developments also include a major collaborative study on services for the mentally ill, including those retarded, which has just been completed in four developing countries, and case studies on mental health and psychosocial development of children in a further set of eight countries. There has also been a major effort within the framework of a WHO programme on prevention of disability and rehabilitation in the community, mainly for those with multiple handicaps.

The most recent policy-making decision, however, was made some six years ago. On 18 May 1977, the thirtieth session of the World Health Assembly adopted a resolution urging member states to accord adequate priority in their health policies and in their development plans to actions that would prevent mental retardation and provide necessary care and support for mentally retarded individuals and their families. This resolution also set out the Organization's policy on mental retardation. Action within existing services was to be given priority, emphasis was to be put on interventions concerning children, simple methods for detection and care were to be developed, all of this with broad intersectoral involvement. National commitment was urged and seen as a key to programme development.

These 1977 discussions of the Assembly were a further important chapter in the long history of WHO's involvement in the field of mental retardation.

Already in 1953 - only a few years after the creation of the Organization - a Joint Expert Committee convened by WHO with the participation and involvement of the United Nations, the International Labour Organization (ILO) and the United Nations Educational, Scientific and Cultural Organization (UNESCO) formulated general principles on which action was to be based and which proved to be as difficult to implement as they were wise. I will just mention three of the policy recommendations made at the time because they illustrate the spiral development of thinking about the problem, returning to the same position every so often, although on a higher level and perhaps with a less striking statement.

These three recommendations were first, that the family should be the unit receiving care; secondly, that regardless of the type of service proposed, the parents should not be penalized economically and socially for keeping their child at home; and thirdly, that it is the social costs of mental retardation which should form the basis of planning on how to deal with the problem and not other considerations. These and several other principles enunciated in the early 1950s disappeared in subsequent years; more recently they seem to have been rediscovered in many circles.

In the years which followed, a number of expert committees, consultations, workshops and seminars brought together specialists in different disciplines from a variety of countries. These meetings were convened by WHO, by a variety of non-governmental organizations, by governments and by professional associations. Some of these groups were incisive, and brilliantly creative; others focused on a single aspect of the problem; others still seemed uninspiring but pragmatic.

They reviewed problems, commented on policies, proposed measures, indicated solutions and lamented governmental and professional inactivity in spite of the seriousness and public health importance of the problem and the availability of effective measures to combat it. This lament has been echoed by others, and even today it unfortunately reflects the truth in many settings. In too many countries nothing is being done about the mentally retarded. In some, a token school for the mentally retarded in the capital city survives on charitable donations and is usually shown to visitors who are amazed by the standards of care provided and cannot understand how a developing country can afford a service of that quality for its mentally retarded. The fact that no more than 30 people out of a million have access to such facilities is somehow too often overlooked. In other countries plans for action are discussed and announced, but for one or another reason no action gets off the ground. This is not to say that there are no examples of effective programmes and no serious government effort to help the mentally ill and retarded; but by and large, in the majority of countries in the world, the programmes for the mentally impaired receive little priority and even feebler support.

This is so almost regardless of evidence on the prevalence of mental retardation in the community which seems to be similar in most of the countries in which studies have been done; and in spite of the occasional exhortations of well-meaning visiting experts, the desperation of parents and the efforts of many in the teaching profession. Occasionally, and usually for a short while, a specific aspect of mental impairment catches the public's eye, a few articles appear in the newspapers, and a question is raised in parliament. Then again the flicker of attention dies away, and the problem slides back into a veritable sea of passivity.

A multitude of reasons are usually offered to explain why this is so. They include the scarcity of resources for health programmes in general, the small numbers of trained staff, the simultaneous existence of many other, often lethal, problems, and the stigma traditionally attached to those whose minds are affected. Lack of relevant data, sometimes giving rise to research (the results of which, regardless of their value, are unlikely to be used except accidentally), is also invoked as a constraint on programme development, and so is the reluctance of personnel to deal with the matter.

Other explanations are offered too, with varying degrees of conviction. But, although they sound so logical, these explanations are not sufficient. Programmes for other conditions, too, have to overcome a stigma, compete for scarce resources, and rely on untrained staff. Therefore, there must be another reason or set of reasons for the disparity between the size, severity and public health significance of the problem on the one hand and the absence of vigour in the answers of society on the other.

In my opinion the central reason for the lack of strong positive action is the lack of agreement on a number of conceptual, strategic and technical issues concerning mental retardation. Because there is no consensus, demands for action lack thrust, and are deprived of the force that would come from unanimity, even if such unanimity were no more than a truce between warring parties, schools of thought and professions - a truce that should be called because all of them have the fate of the mentally impaired at heart.

I will list a few of those issues. Although some of them may be banal and seem to you to be completely clarified, they are still a major blocking uncertainty in many countries of the world, both developed and developing.

The first of these unresolved issues which needs an agreed answer is the relationship between mental impairment, disability and mental illness. Arguments about the correct answer rage and involve a number of professional groups, government agencies and non-governmental organizations, parents and human rights activists. There is no unanimity, no agreement, no consensus about the answer: and yet the answer to this question is of immediate importance. It would help to define who has to carry the principal responsibility in the multidisciplinary and multisectoral programmes for the mentally retarded. It would help to define the direction of our search for solutions. It would also play a decisive role in the choice of professions which would be given primary responsibility for programmes, influence the training of health and other social service professionals, and contribute to decision-making about the allocation of funds.

The division of opinion is present at international, national and subnational levels. The protagonists of opposing views seem to have equally powerful arguments. They are no doubt all right in what they say; but if the field is to advance, consensus rather than balanced opposition is needed to unify effort. This issue is handled as if the acceptance of one of the viewpoints were a victory in a sporting event or a debating society; but it is not. It is a key to action and the effective growth of programmes that may make the life of the mentally impaired more tolerable. There are subaspects of this issue - concerning, for example, the names and numbers of categories for retardation and their place in the national and international classification and so forth: these and similar issues, however, are secondary to the disorder/disease/impairment/disability conundrum.

International governmental and non-governmental organizations are not immune to these debates either, as the unclear and sometimes frustrating territorial pacts among them amply illustrate.

Nor is the terminology used in different languages and by different disciplines very helpful. In a number of languages the word "impairment" has no direct equivalent; words such as subnormality, backwardness, slowness, deficiency, under-endowment, exceptionality, are all used - sometimes as euphemisms, sometimes to introduce new ideas, sometimes to express a theoretical viewpoint. Their translation from the language of the inventor to others further distorts images and confuses the issue. All of this makes the production of incisive statements, understood by all concerned, almost impossible. The current WHO effort to introduce new definitions of terms of impairment, disability and handicap in this area is promising but it will take time before it is well known, understood and - above all - generally accepted.

Another question which is of similar, though perhaps less immediately visible, importance concerns the strategies for health-education on mental impairment. By and large, general and health education have as their central message, either that mentally retarded people are people equal to all others although they have certain impairments; or that mental retardation is a serious affection of the very function which makes people human - of the life of the mind and all its expressions.

The first type of message may help to achieve a better acceptance of the mentally retarded, but the cost of achieving this may be a reinforcement of the attitude already held by many that optimal level of mental functioning is a relatively low value and therefore its absence is not of crucial importance. This in turn can result in a number of setbacks in the difficult task of increasing the priority of actions that will promote mental health and maintain and protect mental life. The measles immunization programmes in some countries have found significant strength in the argument that measles encephalitis affects mental functioning, which is a most precious capacity of man. Perhaps they would not have been introduced if it had been said that an impairment of the mental functions matters little and that those impaired are to be considered equal to everyone else.

If, on the other hand, in order to enhance priority of mental health programmes, the essential value of a sane mind and normal mental functioning is stressed, the acceptance of the mentally retarded becomes significantly endangered. The complex answer that both should be stressed, that is, that health education should promote the importance of mental life and stress the capacity of individuals of impaired mental function to adjust and function well, is perhaps true but lacks penetrance and immediacy: it cannot be used as a slogan for action. It is a story, not a rallying cry. Unfortunately today there is still far too little clear agreement on the need to stress that mentally retarded people have the same rights as any other person, even though they are different from them because of their impairments.

There are a number of other questions that need agreed answers suitable for incorporation into a doctrine and into clear programme proposals, if these proposals are to be as effective as those that have made such an enormous difference in dealing with smallpox and tuberculosis.

One such question concerns the relative priority of interventions in persons with multiple impairments. Of course, ideally, all the problems should be tackled at once. Unfortunately, this is not possible in most cases. If so, what general guidelines can be recommended for the selection of a focus of action? Frequency, severity, cost of intervention, parental concern, and public awareness are all criteria which could be used. Which criterion or combination of criteria is to be recommended? There is no way that this question can be avoided. If a vague answer or an answer overflowing with conditionals and subjunctives is provided it will be ignored and decisions will be made at random or according to the first clear, even if totally incorrect, recommendation. In some of the programmes of WHO, it was necessary to produce simple schemes with decision trees for interventions which were then used in training and in programme development. The process of producing such dichotomous decision trees was difficult and accompanied by much conviction that this cannot be done at all without impoverishing psychiatry and care. Yet, when they were produced and applied, the schemes did not in fact make work any less human or rich in possibilities to interact. They provided a framework, facilitated decisions and made it possible to teach and act better even in conditions of almost total absence of trained personnel and resources.

An agreed recommendation about ways to tackle multiple handicap, a set of criteria to decide which should be tackled first if such a decision has to be made, may also be difficult to develop. It is however very necessary, and very probably eminently feasible. The experience with WHO's manual on disability prevention (DPR/80 1 version II, _Training the_

Disabled in the Community, An Experimental Manual on Rehabilitation and Disability Prevention for Developing Countries, Hellander, Mendis, Nelson) confirms both the feasibility and the need for such information and recommendations.

No doubt social and cultural factors will have to play a major role in such a set of criteria. So, for example, if stigma attached to mental retardation is particularly pronounced it may be difficult to develop a programme if its strategy is first to identify all mentally retarded persons and then aim to correct, say, their visual deficit. In such circumstances it may be better to start a campaign which will identify all those with visual deficits, since in most communities eyesight is recognized as important. If a vision of, say, less than 5/10 is associated fairly frequently with mental retardation, the process will result not only in correcting the vision of most of those with impaired sight but it will also identify mentally retarded individuals who can be helped.

Another question requiring agreed guidelines is the choice of severe versus milder mental retardation as a target for public health action. There still seems to be much doubt and no apparent consensus even about the answer to the question whether those two groups in fact are two different groups by aetiology, pathogenesis, nature of impairment or form of disability, or one group, in which there are no sharp borderlines between the different forms of retardation. Both preventive and rehabilitative action will, to a degree, be different depending on that choice. So, also, will health education campaigns, parent education, the sources of funds and support for the effort.

There are some 100 million mildly retarded and perhaps 15 million severely retarded people in the developing world. Helping the mildly retarded may help economic development incomparably more than the humanitarian effort for the severely retarded. Which should be selected? True, the choice is never based on humanitarian or economic grounds alone. Other factors will have to be considered. A consensus, however, on the nature of the difference and cost-efficiency of intervention in each of the two groups - if they are indeed two groups - would be immensely helpful.

This question has become urgent now that many developing countries are introducing general education which is likely to reveal that millions of children are slightly or significantly less capable than their peers in school. What advice could be given to teachers now, to government authorities, to parents? A simultaneous question that arises concerns the relative importance and cost of impairment in settings of different levels of socioeconomic development. While, in general, agricultural or less-developed countries may have more possibilities for absorbing a mentally impaired person into a niche in society, an industrialized country can usually afford more funds and resources to enable the impaired to adjust. The total cost, however, and in particular the social cost of looking after different types of mental retardation, is rarely properly assessed and consequently administrative decision-making proceeds on overgeneralizations and prejudice rather than on realistic estimates. In this perspective, the central issue is undoubtedly a sensible estimate based on agreed interpretation of all available data, and on the size of the need for service. In the United Kingdom about half of those retarded are in touch with services. What should be a target figure for the UK, and for other parts of the world? Who should pay for it and to whom should the money be given?

More data, consensus, or both may also help to assess epidemiological trends in mental retardation. Several ingredients for the estimation of trends are already available and include greater life expectancy for many of the retarded, a decrease in numbers of those whose mental impairment will be due to easily preventable infectious disease of the brain if immunization programmes become as successful as we hope they will, and an increase in numbers of those at high risk of becoming disabled in an increasingly sophisticated and industrialized society.

Knowledge about other factors which could affect trends in different cultures is less firm. The nature and impact of the diminution of family size on child upbringing in conditions of multiple risk of malnutrition and infectious disease is still insufficiently researched and documented in many countries of the world. The provision of information for parents could make a major difference in patterns of child rearing. The example of the effects of swaddling a child in conditions of nutritional poverty illustrates this point. Although it is simple to say over the radio that unbinding the child will make its movements freer such a message may affect rates of mental impairment if one omits to say that the difference between the bound and free child's energy expenditure per day is some 500 kilocalories and that therefore the nutritional intake should be increased once the child is unbound. Severe health hazards from any source such as pollution, excessive effort, new diseases, do not have to affect the brain directly. They can do so by adding another influence to an unfavourable combination of factors each of which singly would not have made any difference.

Finally, there is another major issue that lacks an agreed answer. How do we answer a government which is willing to commit a limited amount of money or other resources to activities concerned with mental retardation, its prevention, and control? To invest this it will turn to the scientific community or to WHO asking for costed options. For example, what can be done most usefully if it were to become possible for government to spend say 20 American cents per year per mentally retarded person in the country? Should this be spent on immunization programmes against measles? On the education of mothers of healthy children? On the building of a sheltered workshop? On research?

If no consensus about the answer can be obtained, perhaps here again agreement on criteria for the selection of options could be achieved, and a casebook produced of options, their human, material and social cost as well as benefits which were obtained so as to start an exchange of views on the matter.

At present there are masses of recommendations but little clarity in their order of precedence. This would not matter if a country made a commitment to attack the problem seriously, with a perspective of many years ahead, with a willingness to build up coordinating mechanisms and national plans based on locally obtained evidence and manpower. But such commitment at present does not exist in many countries and does not usually come out of the blue. It is likely that it will have to be preceded by useful, low-cost, convincing interventions, the outcome of which can be shown to all concerned as a guarantee that the activity will result in useful programmes.

This list of questions could be further extended. Many scientifically answerable and, as yet, unanswerable questions were in fact raised during this workshop. For action on problems of mental retardation and for governmental and individual commitment to such action we need a simple and streamlined set of messages. For some of these there is enough scientific evidence to formulate a demand for action, a recommendation, or a guideline. For others, where such evidence is lacking, a consensus on what is best should be reached and preached by all concerned. This in no way prevents further search for evidence and further scientific effort. It only means that while searching for the true answers the scientists and all others concerned with the mentally retarded should agree on the best direction and most promising line of action. Action will take place anyway, and if not based on an agreement between the experts it may be marginally less effective and useful than when such advice is available.

Index